Frommer's

Walt Disney World® & Orlando with Kids

1st Edition

by Jim & Cynthia Tunstall

WILEY

Wiley Publishing, Inc.

Published by:

Wiley Publishing, Inc.

111 River St.
Hoboken, NJ 07030-5774

ISBN 0-7645-4499-3

Editor: Naomi P. Kraus
Production Editor: Heather Wilcox
Cartographer: John Decamillis
Photo Editor: Richard Fox
Production by Wiley Indianapolis Composition Services

For information on our other products and services or to obtain technical support,
please contact our Customer Care Department within the U.S. at 800/762-2974,
outside the U.S. at 317/572-3993 or fax 317/572-4002.

Wiley also publishes its books in a variety of electronic formats. Some content that
appears in print may not be available in electronic formats.

Manufactured in the United States of America

5 4 3 2 1

Contents

List of Maps

Acknowledgments

Angie Ranck and Katie Wilmeth of the Orlando/Orange County Convention & Visitors Bureau; Sandra Robert, Gary Buchanan, and Karen Haynes of the Walt Disney World staff; Camille Dudley at Universal Orlando; and Kjerstin Dillon with SeaWorld are perennial troopers who make sure we survive our time in the trenches.

Our grandsons, Jake and Andy Tourigny, give us a youthful perspective and the energy to attack the theme parks time after time.

The editorial staff at Frommer's would also like to thank David Brady, Kevin Rafferty, and Dave Smith at Disney, and Katie Elliott at Universal, for their invaluable insights and assistance.

An Invitation to the Reader

In researching this book, we discovered many wonderful places—hotels, restaurants, shops, and more. We're sure you'll find others. Please tell us about them, so we can share the information with your fellow travelers in upcoming editions. If you were disappointed with a recommendation, we'd love to know that, too. Please write to:

Frommer's Walt Disney World & Orlando with Kids, 1st Edition
Wiley Publishing, Inc. • 111 River St. • Hoboken, NJ 07030-5774

About the Authors

Jim and Cynthia Tunstall have racked up plenty of time waiting in Walt Disney World lines. They were there when the Magic Kingdom opened in 1971, and in the more than 3 decades since that watershed moment they've sampled virtually everything that's part of an Orlando vacation with their kids and grandkids. Their many insider experiences allow them to separate the good from the bad and the ugly, and they give you the best ways to cut through the lines, the crowds, and the theme park PR in order to find the things that are right for you.

Based 90 minutes from WDW, they've written six other Orlando and Florida books, including *Walt Disney World & Orlando For Dummies* and *Florida For Dummies.* They have also contributed to *Frommer's Florida* and *Frommer's Florida from $70 a Day.*

An Additional Note

Please be advised that travel information is subject to change at any time—and this is especially true of prices. We therefore suggest that you write or call ahead for confirmation when making your travel plans. The authors, editors, and publisher cannot be held responsible for the experiences of readers while traveling. Your safety is important to us, however, so we encourage you to stay alert and be aware of your surroundings. Keep a close eye on cameras, purses, and wallets, all favorite targets of thieves and pickpockets.

Other Great Guides for Your Trip:

Frommer's Florida

Frommer's Walt Disney World & Orlando

Frommer's Portable Tampa & St. Petersburg

Frommer's Best-Loved Florida's Driving Tours

Frommer's Irreverent Guide to Walt Disney World

The Unofficial Guide to Walt Disney World

The Unofficial Disney Companion

Beyond Disney: The Unofficial Guide

Frommer's Star Ratings, Icons & Abbreviations

Every hotel, restaurant, and attraction listing in this guide has been ranked for quality, value, service, amenities, and special features using a **star-rating system.** Hotels and restaurants are rated on a scale of zero (recommended) to three stars (exceptional). Attractions, shopping, nightlife, towns, and regions are rated according to the following scale: zero stars (recommended), one star (highly recommended), two stars (very highly recommended), and three stars (must-see).

In addition to the star-rating system, we also use **six feature icons** that point you to the great deals, in-the-know advice and unique experiences that separate travelers from tourists. Throughout the book, look for:

Finds	Special finds—those places only insiders know about
Fun Fact	Fun facts—details that make travelers more informed and their trips more fun
Moments	Special moments–those experiences that memories are made of
Overrated	Places or experiences not worth your time or money
Tips	Insider tips—great ways to save time and money
Value	Great values—where to get the best deals

The following **abbreviations** are used for credit cards:

AE	American Express	DISC	Discover	V	Visa
DC	Diners Club	MC	MasterCard		

Frommers.com

Now that you have the guidebook to a great trip, visit our website at **www.frommers.com** for travel information on more than 3,000 destinations. With features updated regularly, we give you instant access to the most current trip-planning information available. At Frommers.com, you'll also find the best prices on airfares, accommodations, and car rentals—and you can even book travel online through our travel booking partners. At Frommers.com, you'll also find the following:

- Online updates to our most popular guidebooks
- Vacation sweepstakes and contest giveaways
- Newsletter highlighting the hottest travel trends
- Online travel message boards with featured travel discussions

How to Feel Like an Orlando Family

If we're ever in doubt, and we confess that at times we are, we only need to look into the eyes and smiles of our grandsons, and the tens of thousands of other kids we see on a visit to Orlando, to come to one conclusion: This is a magical place where children and families are the real VIPs.

For every business that caters to adult travelers, there are three or four others that roll out the red carpet to children of all ages and their families. They tempt you with special check-in desks, kid-friendly menus, character meet-and-greets, and slightly lower admission prices for those 3 to 9 years old. Some hotels and motels have special programs for youngsters—and, in a few cases, teenagers—giving them their own space to hang around with their peers. A handful of landing zones offer rooms themed on cartoon characters or action heroes. And almost every one of them lets kids ages 17 and under stay free with paying adults.

Thank Walter Elias Disney and his wannabes for that.

Uncle Walt laid the foundation for what, in the past 3 decades, has become America's *No. 1 vacation destination* for the young and young at heart.

Until his heirs opened the Magic Kingdom in 1971, water-skiing and alligator wrestling shows were the only attractions, and central Florida's motels and restaurants had to make most of their living off business travelers or those who came to visit relatives at a high-and-dry naval training center.

Nowadays, The Kingdom That Walt Built tries to make you a POD—Prisoner of Disney—by tempting you with four theme parks, a dozen smaller attractions, two nightclub districts for when mom and dad need a rest, tens of thousands of hotel rooms including timeshare holdings, scores of restaurants, and two cruise ships. Universal Orlando and SeaWorld add four theme parks, while the smaller fry ante up 80 lesser attractions, an avalanche of restaurants, and enough hotel rooms to boost central Florida's total to more than 110,000.

Of course, all of that comes with a price and you're the one paying.

Amusement Business, a trade journal that charts theme-park attendance, says a typical family of four spends about $250 a day for admission, parking, a fast-food lunch, and two small souvenirs. That's without a room, other meals, transportation to and from Orlando, and other expenses.

There's also an intangible price to pay: anxiety. There are so many things to see and do that a 2-week stay and deep pockets won't allow you the time to hit all of the parks and attractions. That unravels some travelers and can leave the unwary family feeling slightly frazzled.

But here comes the cavalry. Us. Over the years, we have explored the parks with our kids and grandkids, dined with many a child at Orlando's restaurants, and snooped around and inside area resorts and hotel so that we can give you an inside track. With this book, you'll have the tools to plan ahead and make sure

Orlando Area Theme Parks

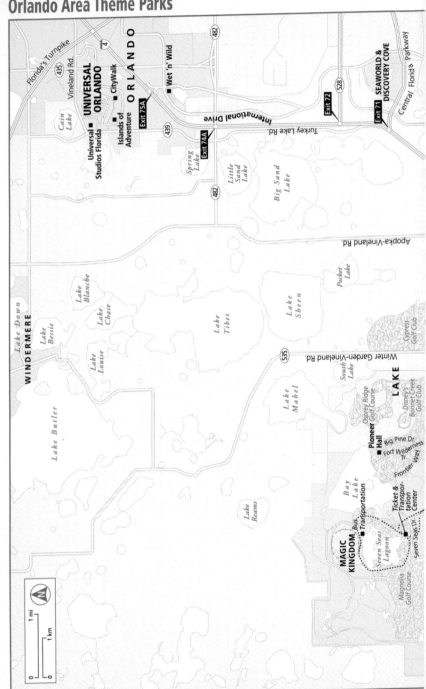

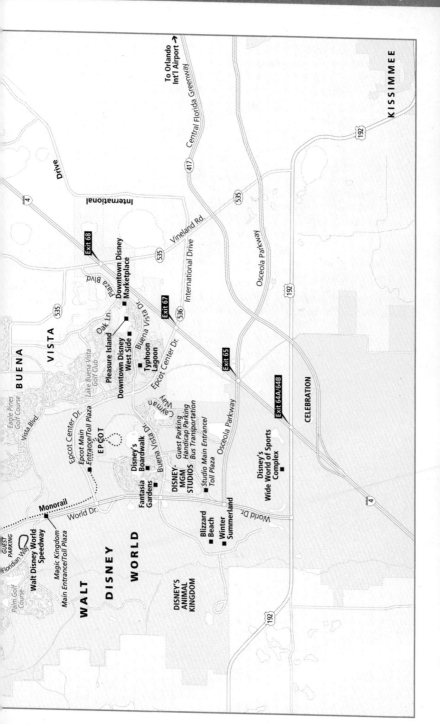

Fun Fact **By the Numbers**

While the post September 11, 2001, economy has cut into tourism, Central Florida still handles a staggering number of tourists. The individual parks don't release figures, but *Amusement Business* estimates theme-park attendance. Its figures show the four Disney parks handle about 40 million visitors annually, Universal's two have about 14½ million, and Sea-World of Florida chips in another 5½ million.

all members of your family have a good time. There's more than enough information here to make you a savvy shopper. Our job: to make your family vacation easy to arrange and as enjoyable as possible so you'll be able to relax while you're here and feel like you're kids again (and your kids will feel like they've hit the theme-park jackpot). At the same time, we're going to give you options to make your vacation affordable. We noted some of the best deals in this corner of the planet and ways to keep expenses to a minimum while having maximum fun. And Orlando tourism gurus will make sure your family has a steady stream of new things to see.

1 Frommer's Favorite Orlando Family Experiences

From Cinderella Castle to Space Mountain, everybody loves the Magic Kingdom, but here are some other things to try at Disney and Universal, and in the greater Orlando area (see chapters 6 and 7 for details):

- **Spend a day at Epcot.** This is a great stop if your kids are old enough to have inquiring minds. You can travel around the world at the World Showcase pavilions, get your thrills riding Mission: Space and Test Track, then have a different look into the future at Innoventions, where space-age products and interactive games await you. And, what better way to cap your day than watching the **IllumiNations** fireworks show! For more details, see "Epcot," in chapter 6.

- **Star Gaze at the Orlando Science Center.** But the planetarium is only part of the fun. Your heirs can dabble in Weird Science, 123 Math Avenue, KidsTown, and lots more at this popular downtown attraction. See p. 263.

- **Visit Disney–MGM Studios.** This park has lots of great things for kids and movie buffs. If you have kids over 8, don't miss Tower of Terror and Rock 'n' Roller Coaster. The whole family should see Fantasmic!—the after-dark fireworks, live action, and laser lights show.

- **Check Out Gatorland.** Located between Orlando and Kissimmee, this throwback park is a great way to spend a half day at less than half the price of the major theme parks. Make sure to see Gator Jumparoo, which has been the signature show since the park opened in 1949. If you have deep pockets and your kids are over 12, they (or you) can be a Trainer for a Day. And don't forget a visit to the gift shop if the boys (and some girls) in your party want an offbeat gator gift. See p. 260.

- **Experience Universal Orlando.** Universal Studios Florida and its sister, Islands of Adventure, combine cutting-edge, high-tech special effects with great creativity,

Moments   Chills & Thrills

For parents and older children (who meet the mandatory height requirements) looking for the ups and downs of a good ride, here are the top stomach churners and G-force generators in Orlando (see chapters 6, "What Kids Like to See & Do in Walt Disney World," and 7, "What Kids Like to See & Do Beyond Disney," for more information):

- **Incredible Hulk Coaster** (Islands of Adventure). You'll blast from 0 to 40 mph in 2 seconds, spin upside down, and endure seven rollovers and two plummets on this glow-in-the-dark roller coaster. See p. 242.
- **Rock 'n' Roller Coaster** (Disney–MGM Studios). You'll launch from 0 to 60 mph in 2.8 seconds and go into the first inversion as 120 speakers in your "stretch limo" mainline Aerosmith at (yeeeow!) 32,000 watts. See p. 200.
- **Dueling Dragons** (Islands of Adventure). Your legs dangle as you ride through five inversions at 55 to 60 mph and—get this—three times come within 12 inches of the other roller coaster. See p. 245.
- **Summit Plummet** (Disney's Blizzard Beach). This one starts from a 120-foot-high perch and turns into the world's fastest body slide, a test of your courage and swimsuit as it has you moving sans vehicle at 60 mph. See p. 217.
- **Twilight Zone Tower of Terror** (Disney–MGM Studios). The free-fall experiences (there are several scenarios) are more than thrilling—they're scary (one of the ride's designers is too scared to get on it). Once your legs stop shaking, *some of you* will want to ride again. See p. 202.
- **The Amazing Adventures of Spider-Man** (Islands of Adventure). 3D doesn't get any better than this ride that has you twisting, spinning, and soaring before a simulated 400-foot drop that feels awful real. See p. 241.
- **Mission: Space** (Epcot). If you're claustrophobic or prone to motion sickness, stay clear of this ride that simulates liftoff and G-force, and gets the seal of approval from the NASA astronauts who helped design it. See p. 185.
- **Kraken** (SeaWorld). This floorless, open-sided coaster uses speed (up to 65 mph), steep climbs, deep drops, and seven loops to create a stomach-churning ride that lasts far too long for some folks. See p. 254.

though the latter is more appealing to preteens, teens, and adults. Not-to-be-missed attractions: Back to the Future . . . The Ride, Terminator 2: 3-D Battle Across Time, Men in Black Alien Attack, Jimmy Neutron's Nicktoon Blast, Dueling Dragons, the Incredible Hulk Coaster, The Amazing Adventures of Spider-Man, and Dudley Do-Right's Ripsaw Falls.

- **Explore Eco-Entertainment at SeaWorld and Discovery Cove.** Journey to Atlantis and Kraken give SeaWorld a little zip, but it's still better to come here looking for what this place best offers—hands-on encounters with critters and up-close views of animals ranging from polar bears to killer whales (kids of all ages will be entranced). Its newer sister, Discovery Cove, gives you a chance to swim with dolphins (alas, at press time it cost $229) as part of its package.

- **Become a Monorail Co-Pilot.** If there's no one but the pilot aboard, ask to sit up front and you and your kids can pretend to drive Disney's monorail. This won't work at peak times such as the opening or closing times of the theme parks, and your best chance is if you can board at the Grand Floridian, Contemporary, or Polynesian resorts. See p. 158.

2 The Best Hotel Bets

Get all of the information you'll need on these and other area hotels and motels in chapter 4, "Family-Friendly Accommodations." But here are the high points:

- **Most Family-Friendly Hotels:** All Disney properties cater to families, with special menus for kids, video-game arcades, free transportation to the parks, many recreational facilities, and, in some cases, character meals. Camping at woodsy **Fort Wilderness** (© 407/ 934-7639) makes for a special family experience. If bunk beds and a geyser going off in the lobby sound good, check into the **Wilderness Lodge** (© 407/934-7639). On the No-Mickey Front, **Holiday Inn Family Suites** (© 877/387-5437 or 407/387-5437), **Holiday Inn Nikki Bird Resort** (© 800/206-2747 or 407/396-7300), and **Holiday Inn Sunspree Resort Lake Buena Vista** (© 800/366-6299 or 407/239-4500) offer Kid Suites, kids' clubs, and more. See chapter 4 for more family-friendly accommodations.

- **Best Moderately Priced Hotels:** Disney's **Port Orleans Resort** (© 407/934-7639) has Southern charm in its French Quarter and Riverside areas, and the pool in the French Quarter has a water slide that curves out of a dragon's mouth. See p. 80. In the free world, **Hawthorn Suites Lake Buena Vista** (© 800/936-9417 or 407/597-5000) is near to but sheltered from Disney, and has large rooms, free American breakfasts, and weekday social hours. See p. 90.

- **Best Value/Deal:** That's easy: Disney's **All-Star Movies Resort** (© 407/934-7639; p. 81), **All-Star Music Resort** (© 407/934-7639; p. 81), **All-Star Sports Resort** (© 407/934-7639; p. 82), and **Pop Century Resort** (© 407/ 934-7639; p. 82). If you're going to stay on WDW property, you can't beat them, though they would be significantly overpriced outside of the realm. The **Hampton Inn Maingate West** (© 800/ 936-9417 or 407/396-6300; p. 95) is one of the nicest, most modern of the inexpensive properties in the Kissimmee area, and it's only 1½ miles west of Disney.

- **Best Budget Motel:** The **Ramada Inn Resort Eastgate** (© 800/ 272-6232 or 407/396-1111) has clean rooms, is located close to Disney, and there's a restaurant next door. All these things make it a good budget choice. See p. 96. But if price is your lone consideration, it's hard to beat the nearby **Econo Lodge Maingate Resort** (© 800/356-6935 or 407/390-9063), where rates are as low as $39 double. See p. 95.

- **Best Spa for Kids:** That's not a typo. The **Holiday Inn Family Suites** (© 877/387-5437 or 407/387-5437) started something good with its **Sugar & Spice Kids Spa,** with services from $10 to $99. (It has services for grownups, too.) The resort also has a lounge, fitness center, and whirlpool so that parents can spend a little time on their own. See p. 91.

- **Best Kids' Programs:** The Wizard of Diz has dandy kids' centers at some resorts, but there also are great ones outside Disney. Our top five outside Mickey's World are Camp Hyatt at the **Hyatt Regency Grand Cypress** (© 800/233-1234 or 407/239-1234), Ritz Kids at the **Ritz-Carlton** (© 800/241-3333 or 407/206-2400), Camp Nikki at **Holiday Inn Nikki Bird** (© 800/206-2747 or 407/396-7300), La Petite Academy at **Gaylord Palms** (© 877/677-9352 or 407/586-0000), and Camp Holiday at **Holiday Inn Sunspree** (© 800/366-6299 or 407/239-4500). You can find more details in chapter 4, "Family-Friendly Accommodations."

- **Tops for Toddlers:** Watch their faces light up when larger-than-life raccoon mascots Max and Maxine show up to tuck them in at **Holiday Inn Sunspree Resort Lake Buena Vista** (© 800/366-6299). See p. 91.

- **Tops for Teens:** We've yet to find a mainstream hotel that comes close to the activities offered in Common Grounds, the teen clubs aboard the **Disney Cruise Line**'s *Wonder* and *Magic* (© 800/951-3532). Activities for 13 to 17 year olds include karaoke, a Hawaiian pool party, and improv. See p. 45.

- **Best Location: Disney's Grand Floridian Resort & Spa** (© 407/934-7639; p. 72), **Polynesian Resort** (© 407/934-7639; p. 74), and **Contemporary Resort** (© 407/934-7639; p. 72) are on Seven Seas Lagoon or Bay Lake. They're also on the WDW monorail route, providing quick and easy access to the parks. The **Portofino Bay Hotel** (© 888/322-5541 or 407/503-1000; p. 97), **Hard Rock Hotel** (© 800/232-7827 or 407/503-7625; p. 98), and **Royal Pacific** (© 800/232-7827 or 407/503-3000; p. 100) are within walking distance of Universal's parks and CityWalk, and there's also boat service available.

- **Best Views:** The whole family can watch the Magic Kingdom's new Wishes fireworks display from the comfort of your room if you book one on an upper floor on the west side of the **Contemporary Resort** (© 407/934-7639; p. 72). And you have a front-row seat for the action at SeaWorld from the upper east-side floors at the **Renaissance Orlando Resort at SeaWorld** (© 800/327-6677; p. 100).

- **Best Family Pools:** Arguably, the best pool in O-Town is at the **Hyatt Regency Grand Cypress Resort** (© 800/233-1234 or 407/239-1234). It's a half-acre

---

(Fun Fact **From All Sides**

In order to produce the 13-minute IllumiNations spectacular each night at Epcot, Disney uses 68 fireworks firing positions and more than 1,100 shells.

lagoon-like pool that flows through rock grottoes, is spanned by a rope bridge, and has 12 waterfalls and two steep water slides. See p. 88. The **JW Marriott's Lazy River** (© **800/241-3333** or 407/206-2300) finishes a close second. It's a 24,000-square-foot winding stream through small waterfalls and rock formations. See p. 89. Most of the Walt Disney World resorts have terrific pools, too.

3 The Best Dining Bets

While Orlando can't compete with U.S. destinations such as New York or San Francisco, it has everything on the restaurant front from fast-food joints that will satisfy your kids to 5-Diamond winners for a more adult palate. Look for more details on these and other eateries in chapter 5, "Family-Friendly Dining."

- **Best Character Meal:** Hands down, it doesn't get any better than **Chef Mickey's** (© **407/939-3463**) breakfasts and dinners at Disney's Contemporary Resort. These "events" feature their respective namesake and other characters, but a word of warning: They draw *up to 1,600 guests* each morning. See p. 145.

- **Best Kids' Menu Range:** When it comes to the deepest menu for young taste buds, **Pastamore Ristorante** at Universal CityWalk (© **407/363-8000**) gives kids a choice of nine entrees. See p. 134.

- **Best Offbeat Kids' Menu:** With a menu that offers beef or chicken teriyaki, shrimp tempura, pork dumplings, and sushi, it's hard to beat **Ran-Getsu of Tokyo** (© **407/345-0044**) in this category. See p. 136.

- **Best Burgers:** From Cheeseburgers in Paradise to Cuban Meatloaf Survival Sandwiches, **Jimmy Buffett's Margaritaville** at Universal CityWalk (© **407/224-2155**) has some of the juiciest and most unusual burgers in town. See p. 134.

- **Best Outdoor Eating:** Kids can get into the festive jungle atmosphere while digging into their own wild menu at the **Rainforest Cafe** in Downtown Disney West Side, which offers indoor as well as patio dining (© **407/827-8500**). See p. 121. The terrace at **Artist Point** (© **407/939-3463**), the premier restaurant at Disney's Wilderness Lodge, overlooks a lake, waterfall, and scenery evocative of America's national parks. See p. 124. And the **Rose & Crown** at Epcot (© **407/939-3463**) delivers a front-row seat for the IllumiNations fireworks display. See p. 114.

- **Best Value:** At **Romano's Macaroni Grill** (© **407/239-6676**), the ambience and northern Italian cuisine score very high, and prices are low, low, low. See p. 130.

- **Best Spot for a Parent's Night Out:** Dinners don't get much more romantic than those at the Victorian-style **Victoria & Albert's** (© **407/939-3463**). The meal is comprised of six courses served by a maid and butler. See p. 122.

- **Best Ice Cream:** Go for the splurge (and maybe a larger waist size) at **Ghirardelli Soda Fountain and Chocolate Shop** (© **407/934-8855**) in Downtown Disney West Side. See p. 281.

- **Best Barbecue:** Hands down, follow your nose to **Bubbalou's Bodacious BBQ** (© **407/628-1212**) after catching a whiff of the

Tips · Orlando's Best Online Sites

Given Orlando's enormous popularity, it should come as no surprise that hundreds of websites are devoted to it. They have a lot of information about everything from Walt Disney World history to getting around town.

There are several sites written by Disney fans, employees, and self-proclaimed experts. Our favorite (www.hiddenmickeys.org) is about **Hidden Mickeys,** a park tradition (see chapter 6, "What Kids Like to See & Do in Walt Disney World"). These subtle Disney images can be found scattered throughout the realm, though they sometimes are in the eye, or imagination, of the beholder. **Deb's Unofficial Walt Disney World Information Guide (http://allearsnet.com)** is another pleaser for Disney fans, which has tons of family info on hotels, restaurants, attractions, and more. And you should definitely take a look at Disney's official site, **www.disneyworld.com,** if you're planning a pilgrimage to the Land of the Mouse.

If a trip to one of Universal Orlando's theme parks or CityWalk is on your dance card, then stop at **www.universalorlando.com.** You can order tickets, make reservations, and find out about special events, among other things on the site. And fish fans can get in the know about SeaWorld at **www.seaworld.com** and Discovery Cove at **www.discoverycove.com.**

If you're seeking general information about the city, accommodations, dining, nightlife, or special events, head over to the Orlando/Orange County Convention & Visitors Bureau site at **www.orlandoinfo.com.** *Orlando Weekly* (**www.orlandoweekly.com**) offers cutting-edge reviews and recommendations for arts, movies, music, restaurants, and much more from Orlando's premier alternative weekly. Links at the site include dining, arts and culture, shopping, and news.

tangy hickory smoke. It tastes as good as it smells. See p. 144.

- **Best Italian Cuisine:** We have to give the nod to **Pacino's Italian Ristorante** in Kissimmee (☎ 407/396-8022). It has great food and a moderately priced menu. See p. 143.

- **Most Entertaining Restaurant:** It's hard to contain yourself when the corny jokes and lively music kick into gear at the **Hoop-Dee-Doo Musical Revue** at Disney's Fort Wilderness Resort and Campground (☎ 407/939-3463). See p. 283.

- **Best Steak House:** At the **Yachtsman Steakhouse** at Disney's Yacht Club Resort (☎ 407/939-3463), the aged steaks, chops, and seafood are grilled over a wood fire. See p. 124.

- **Best Breakfast:** Disney character breakfasts certainly get the nod if you have children under 10 in tow. But in terms of volume, it's hard to beat the Sunday brunch at **Atlantis** in the Renaissance Orlando Resort at SeaWorld (☎ 407/351-5555). See p. 135.

- **Most Kid-Friendly Service:** The entire family eats free at the fun, all-you-can-stuff breakfast buffet at **Holiday Inn Family Suites Resort** (© 877/387-5437), and kids 12 and under (the real VIPs at this hotel) eat lunch and dinner free, too, when accompanied by paying adults. See p. 91.

- **Best Late-Night Dining:** The trendy **B-Line Diner** (© 407/345-4460) at the Peabody Orlando is open around the clock for eclectic fare ranging from steaks to falafel sandwiches to grits and eggs. You and your kids won't be able to resist the desserts. See p. 136.

- **Best Spot to Celebrate Food:** **Emeril's** at Universal's CityWalk (© 407/224-2424) is a great choice for a high-end special occasion. See p. 131. For the pure party

factor, you can't beat **Jimmy Buffett's Margaritaville** (© 407/224-2155) at CityWalk. See p. 134.

- **Best Special Sunday Brunch:** The **House of Blues** (© 407/934-2583), at Disney's West Side, has a down-home gospel brunch featuring live foot-stomping music and an array of Southern/Creole vittles that includes greens, red beans and rice, jambalaya, catfish, shrimp, and beef. The food is so-so—the same quality of a dinner show, which this is, morning-style. But the entertainment makes it a certifiable winner. Reservations aren't accepted for parties under six, so arrive early for the 10:30am or 1pm show. See p. 129.

2

Planning a Family Trip to Walt Disney World & Orlando

Talk about overload! Central Florida has so many hotels, restaurants, attractions, and package plans that you might have an anxiety attack if you don't do a little advance planning. That's why we've filled this chapter with things travelers with kids need to know before arriving. In addition to the information contained in the following pages, you'll find more tips in chapters 4 through 6—those covering the area's best hotels, restaurants, theme parks, and smaller attractions.

1 Visitor Information

As soon as you decide to go to Orlando, contact the **Orlando/ Orange County Convention & Visitors Bureau** and its visitor center, 8723 International Dr., Suite 101, Orlando, FL 32819 (© **407/363-5872;** www.orlandoinfo.com). Staffers can answer questions, assist you with reservations, help you find discounts, and send maps and brochures, such as the *Official Visitors Guide, African-American Visitors Guide, Area Guide to Restaurants, Unexpected Orlando,* and *Official Accommodations Guide.* A free packet should arrive within 3 weeks and include a "Magicard," which is good for $500 in discounts on rooms, car rentals, attractions, and more. If you don't require a human voice, you can get all of the above by calling © **800/643-9492** or 800/551-0181.

The bureau's website also offers information on special vacation packages specifically designed for families, and has a list of over 200 things to see and do in Orlando.

For general information about **Walt Disney World,** including brochures and videos (there's even one tailored to preschoolers that's a great way to introduce your child to the theme parks), write to Walt Disney World, Box 10000, Lake Buena Vista, FL 32830-1000; call © **407/934-7639** or 407/824-4321; or, on the Internet, go to www.disneyworld.com.

For information about **Universal Studios Florida, CityWalk,** and **Islands of Adventure,** call © **800/ 837-2273** or 407/363-8000, or write to **Universal Orlando,** 1000 Universal Studios Plaza, Orlando, FL 32819. On the Internet, visit **www.universal orlando.com.**

You can also ask the **Kissimmee– St. Cloud Convention & Visitors Bureau,** P.O. Box 422007, Kissimmee, FL 34742-2007 (© **800/333-5477** or 407/847-5000; www.florida kiss.com), for maps, brochures, coupon books, and a vacation planning kit, which details accommodations and attractions.

For information on Orlando's **International Drive** area, call © **866/ 243-7483** or on the Internet go to **www.InternationalDriveOrlando. com.** The staff has information about rooms, restaurants, attractions, shops, and the I-Ride Trolley. The website features 50 fun things to do in the

Walt Disney World & Orlando—Red Alert Checklist

- From the *literally red*-alert news desk: Once you arrive, you'll see a lot of folks sporting a boiled-lobster complexion. They ignored the No. 1 survival rule for an Orlando vacation: **Use sunscreen!** From early spring through late fall, Florida's sun can deliver a dangerous burn (especially to kids), including sun poisoning, if you're not protected with a 25- or higher-rated sunscreen. (We've even seen it happen on winter days.) Also, don't forget to reapply sunscreen throughout the day—one application when you're sweating in the parks will not protect you and your kids for very long. You can also protect yourself by wearing wide-brimmed hats, airy clothes, and sunglasses. If your child's in a stroller, make sure he or she is properly shaded. Also, to avoid dehydration, remember to drink plenty of fluids. Don't forget to pack a pair of comfortable walking shoes for those days spent pounding the theme-park pavement. And remember—*children need protection* as much or more than you, and they may not recognize the symptoms of a burn until it's too late.
- Don't get shut out at dinnertime. You can make same-day or day-before reservations in most Orlando restaurants, but there are some exceptions to the rule, especially for restaurants serving Disney's character meals, which can have a waiting list a mile long. So use Walt Disney World's version of a reservation, **Priority Seating** (© 407/ 939-3463), which lets you stake a claim to a table 30 or more days in advance. If your children want to dine with characters, you can get Priority Seating 90 days in advance—and in many cases, you'll need the lead time (we kid you not).
- Many families come with their hearts set on (and days planned around) specific attractions, hotels, or restaurants. But some dreams don't come true. Disney *has reduced park hours,* limited the days certain shows are staged, and continues to temporarily close some hotel

area, many of them suitable for families with kids of all ages.

ONLINE INFORMATION

The websites we listed above are good for a ton of other information. Disney's **www.disneyworld.com** has theme park maps, current ticket prices, directions, park hours on specific days, ride and show information, thumbnails about WDW restaurants, resort prices, information about special events, indoor and outdoor recreation options, the Disney Cruise Line, an online booking service, and more.

Deb's Unofficial Walt Disney World Information Guide (http://allearsnet.com/index.html) is an excellent source of family fun, and arguably the best unofficial Disney guide on the Internet, though it's one that at times isn't entirely objective. Disney doesn't own it, but it's run and written mainly by Disney fans, so you have to factor out (or in, if you prefer) their exuberance while digesting the many tips this site offers. The no-nonsense, text-driven site includes comprehensive insider information on tickets, detailed restaurant menus, the scoop on the Disney Cruise Line, and other rooms, restaurants and attractions to cut expenses in response to the weakened economy. Universal Orlando, SeaWorld, and smaller players have taken similar steps. Before you promise your kids or yourself anything, make sure your dreams can come true by calling or checking the websites provided in this book. Also note that in the best of times, theme park rides break down or have to be shut down for routine maintenance (though you don't get a break on ticket prices when your favorite rides or shows are dark). Some of the websites listed earlier in this chapter , have **"rehab"** schedules and update them almost daily.

- If you purchased traveler's checks, have you recorded the check numbers and stored the documentation separately from the checks?
- Did you pack your camera and an extra set of camera batteries, and purchase enough film or E-cards? If you packed film in your checked baggage, did you invest in protective pouches to shield film from airport X-rays? It may be better to buy your film in a local discount store such as Wal-Mart or a drugstore such as Walgreens after you arrive.
- Do you have a safe, accessible place to store cash?
- Did you bring ID cards that could entitle you to discounts such as AAA and AARP cards, student IDs, and so forth?
- Speaking of identification, did the adults in your family bring a photo ID? That's very important since September 11, 2001. Some parks may make you produce one.
- Did you bring emergency drug prescriptions and extra glasses and/or contact lenses?
- Do you have your credit-card PINs?
- If you have an E-ticket, do you have documentation?
- Did you leave a copy of your itinerary with someone at home?

valuable tips. There are pages specifically aimed at parents of infants and toddlers, 5 to 11 year olds, expectant moms, and families bringing one or more of their children's friends.

The sites built by Universal Orlando, **www.universalorlando. com**, and SeaWorld, **www.seaworld. com**, offer ride descriptions, ticket prices, and information beyond the theme parks. But both lack the thoroughness of Deb's and the Disney sites.

The city's newspaper, the *Orlando Sentinel,* produces an online site at **www.orlandosentinel.com**. It has a variety of entertainment information. And if you go to **www.go2orlando. com**, you'll find the focus on attractions, accommodations, restaurants, discounts, and more.

2 Money

ATMS

The easiest and best way to get cash away from home is from an ATM (automated teller machine). The

Cirrus (© 800/424-7787; www. mastercard.com) and **PLUS** (© 800/ 843-7587; www.visa.com) networks span the globe; see the back of your card to learn which network you're on, then call or check online for ATM locations in Orlando. Be sure you know your personal identification number (PIN) and your daily withdrawal limit before departing.

ATMs inside the Disney theme parks are on Main Street in the Magic Kingdom and at the entrances to Epcot, Disney–MGM Studios, and Animal Kingdom. They're also at Pleasure Island; in Downtown Disney Marketplace; Disney resorts; and the Crossroads Shopping Center.

There also are ATMs near Guest Services at Universal Studios Florida, Islands of Adventure, and SeaWorld.

Inside the entrance of most of the parks, you'll find maps listing all ATMs. If this isn't the case when you visit, look for them at Guest Relations or Guest Services near the entrances, or at most shops.

Outside the parks, most malls have at least one ATM and they're in some convenience stores, such as 7-Elevens and Circle Ks, as well as in grocery or drugstores. But there often is an extra charge for using non-bank ATMs. Depending on your institution, those charges can range from $1 to $3.50 per transaction—the average is $2.75 across Florida—when you're using an ATM not affiliated with your bank.

Be *very* careful when using ATMs— the land of Mickey can lull you into a false sense of security. Goofy and Pluto won't mug you, but some of their estranged neighbors might. This is a big city, and its crime rate is the same as others. Even in seemingly safe places, when entering your ATM PIN,

make sure you shield the keyboard from others in line. And if you're using a drive-thru, keep your doors locked.

CREDIT CARDS

Credit cards are a safe way to carry money, they provide a convenient record of all your expenses, and they generally offer good exchange rates. You can also withdraw cash advances (though you'll start paying hefty interest on the advance the moment you receive the cash) from your credit cards at banks or ATMs, provided you know your PIN. If you've forgotten yours, or didn't even know you had one, call the number on the back of your credit card and ask the bank to send it to you. It usually takes 5 to 7 business days, though some banks will provide the number over the phone if you provide personal information, such as your mother's maiden name.

Disney parks, resorts, shops, and restaurants (but not most fast-food outlets) accept American Express, Diners Club, Discover, MasterCard, Visa, and the Disney Visa Card. Some WDW resorts offer a debit card that can be used in park shops and restaurants if you give them a credit card imprint. All charges on the card are immediately billed to your credit card. If you decide to use this debit card, opt for express checkout (available at all Disney resorts), so you won't end up on yet another nauseating wait in line. Your bill, with all of your charges detailed on it will get delivered to your room the night before you leave, and you can skip the checkout line the

---

(*Tips*   **Online Ticketing**

The Big Three offer online booking of tickets, hotel rooms, vacation packages, and more. Disney's site is **www.disneyworld.com**. Universal Orlando's is **www.universalorlando.com**. SeaWorld's site is **www.seaworld.com**. All offer online discounts. In SeaWorld's case, you may find discounted 1-day tickets.

What Things Cost in Orlando	U.S.$
Taxi from airport to Walt Disney World (up to four people)	51
Double room at Disney's Grand Floridian Resort & Spa (very expensive)	339–840
Double room at Disney's Coronado Springs Resort (moderate)	133–209
Double room at Disney's All-Star Music Resort (inexpensive)	77–124
All-you-can-eat dinner buffet at Akershus in Epcot	
Adult	18.99
Child	7.99
Child's pizza at Epcot's Coral Reef Restaurant	4.99
Chef Mickey's character breakfast at Disney's Contemporary Resort	
Adults	16.99
Child	8.99
Huggies Pull-Ups, 21 count, at Walgreen's	10.99
2.5-ounce jar of baby food entree at Publix	0.75
Tube of sun block in the theme parks	8.99
Evening movie tickets at AMC, Pleasure Island	
Adult	8.50
Child	5.50
4-Day Park Hopper admission to Walt Disney World	
Adult	208
Child	167
1-day, 1-park admission to Walt Disney World	
Adult	52
Child	42
1-day, 1-park admission to Universal Orlando or SeaWorld	
Adult	51.95
Child	42.95
Admission to Orlando Science Center	
Adult	15
Child	10

next day unless something's wrong with the total.

You can also buy **Disney dollars** (currency with cute images of Mickey, Minnie, and so on) in $1, $5, and $10 denominations. They're good at WDW shops, restaurants, and resorts, as well as Disney stores everywhere. But we don't recommend buying them either because you'll have to cash in leftover bills for real currency upon leaving WDW, which means still another line, or keep them as a souvenir (a rather expensive souvenir, at that). Also, watch out if you have a refund coming. Some things, such as strollers, wheelchairs, and lockers, require a security deposit, and, as a marketing ploy, Disney staffers frequently try to slip you a Mickey instead of the real thing.

You can cash traveler's or personal checks of $25 or less (drawn on U.S. banks, if you have a driver's license and major credit card), and exchange foreign currency at **SunTrust** Bank, 1675 Buena Vista Dr., across from Downtown Disney Marketplace. The bank also has an ATM. It's open weekdays from 9am to 4pm, and until 6pm on Thursday (© **407/828-6106**).

TRAVELER'S CHECKS

Traveler's checks are something of an anachronism from the days before the ATM made cash accessible 24/7. But remember that you will likely be charged an ATM withdrawal fee if the bank is not your own, so if you're withdrawing money every day, you might be better off with traveler's checks—provided that you don't mind showing identification every time you want to cash one. (Keep in mind that some places won't take traveler's checks at all, though that's rare in tourist-friendly Orlando.)

You can get traveler's checks at almost any bank. **American Express** offers denominations of $20, $50, $100, $500, and (for cardholders only) $1,000. You'll pay a service charge ranging from 1% to 4%. You can also get American Express traveler's checks over the phone by calling ✆ **800/221-7282;** Amex gold and platinum cardholders who use this number are exempt from the 1% fee. AAA members can obtain checks without a fee at most AAA offices.

Visa offers traveler's checks at Citibank locations nationwide, as well as at several other banks. The service charge ranges between 1.5% and 2%; checks come in denominations of $20, $50, $100, $500, and $1,000. Call ✆ **800/732-1322** for information. **MasterCard** also offers traveler's checks. Call ✆ **800/223-9920** for a location near you.

IF YOUR WALLET GETS LOST OR STOLEN

Be sure to tell all of your credit card companies the minute you discover your wallet has been lost or stolen and file a report at the nearest police precinct. Your credit card company or insurer may require a police report number or record of the loss. Most credit card companies have an emergency toll-free number to call if your card is lost or stolen; they may be able to wire you a cash advance immediately or deliver an emergency credit card in a day or 2. Visa's U.S. emergency number is ✆ **800/847-2911** or 410/581-9994. American Express cardholders and traveler's check holders should call ✆ **800/221-7282.** MasterCard holders should call ✆ **800/307-7309** or 636/722-7111. For other credit cards, call the toll-free number directory at ✆ **800/555-1212.**

Identity theft or fraud are potential complications of losing your wallet, especially if you've lost your driver's license along with your cash and credit cards. Notify the major credit-reporting bureaus immediately; placing a fraud alert on your records may protect you against liability for criminal activity. The three major U.S. credit-reporting agencies are **Equifax** (✆ **800/766-0008;** www.equifax.com), **Experian** (✆ **888/397-3742;** www.experian.com), and **TransUnion** (✆ **800/680-7289;** www.transunion.com). Finally, if you've lost all forms of photo ID call your airline and explain the situation; they might allow you to board the plane if you have a copy of your passport or birth certificate and a copy of the police report you've filed.

3 When to Go

This is theme-park central, and its busiest seasons are whenever kids are out of school, including late May to just past Labor Day, long holiday weekends, the winter holidays (mid-Dec to early Jan), and spring break (late Mar into Apr). And don't forget that kids in other hemispheres have different holiday periods. Obviously, the experience is best when the crowds are thinnest and

(Tips) Weather Wise

Florida has winter and summer rainy spells. They don't necessarily ruin a vacation, but you can save a bit by bringing lightweight ponchos from home. The theme parks love to see you get soaked and will in turn soak you for $5 or $6 for a throwaway that's about as sturdy as plastic wrap (and sells for $1.95 in discount stores). Speaking of rainy days, crowds are smaller and there are plenty of indoor things to do. The flip side: Many of the major outdoor thrill rides at Disney, Universal, and SeaWorld are closed during rain and lightning storms.

the weather is the most temperate. Hotel rooms are also priced lower during the off-season, but that season doesn't follow the traditional winter/summer patterns of most areas.

Peak-season rates can go into effect during conventions and special events. Even something as remote as Bike Week in Daytona Beach (about an hour by car northeast) can raise prices, including during the off season. These kinds of events especially impact moderate-priced properties outside Walt Disney World. **Best times:** The week after Labor Day until the week before Thanksgiving, the week after Thanksgiving until mid-December, and the 6 weeks before and 4 weeks after school spring vacations. **Worst times:** During the December holidays and summer, when out-of-state visitors take advantage of school breaks and some locals haul their families to the parks (smart locals take advantage of discounts in Florida residents' months, usually May and Nov). Packed parking lots are the norm during the week before and after Christmas, and summer brings a double whammy: Crowds are very large and the weather is oppressively hot and humid.

You may have noticed that the best times to avoid crowds happen to coincide with the times your kids will likely be in class. *We strongly advise you to think about pulling your kids out of school* for a few days around an off-season weekend to avoid long lines. (You probably can keep them in their schools' good graces by asking teachers to let them write a report on an educational element of the vacation. Epcot, for example, has a ton of science and technology exhibits.) Even during these periods, though, the number of international visitors guarantees you won't be alone.

Note: If you're taking advantage of a land/cruise package (see "Disney Cruise Packages," later in this chapter), make sure you take into account hurricane season, which runs June 1 to November 30. Inland, the worst may be a ton of rain and enough wind to wipe the smile off your face. But at sea, these storms can be very dangerous and will put a major damper on your family's vacation.

Also, don't take tornadoes and lightning—two particularly active summer curses—too lightly. Central Florida is the lightning capital of the United States, and short but intense electrical storms aren't uncommon in summer (young kids may be frightened, but we've seen teens absolutely enthralled by the natural electric show). Just make sure all observing is done from a safe place.

Central Florida Average Temperatures

	Jan	Feb	Mar	Apr	May	June	July	Aug	Sept	Oct	Nov	Dec
High °F	71.7	72.9	78.3	83.6	88.3	90.6	91.7	91.6	89.7	84.4	78.2	73.1
°C	22.0	22.7	25.7	28.7	31.3	32.5	33.2	33.1	32.0	29.1	25.7	22.8
Low °F	49.3	50.0	55.3	60.3	66.2	71.2	73.0	73.4	72.5	65.4	56.8	50.9
°C	9.6	10.0	12.5	15.7	19.0	21.8	22.7	23.0	22.5	18.6	13.8	10.5

KIDS' FAVORITE ORLANDO EVENTS

January

Capital One Florida Citrus Bowl. New Year's Day kicks off with this football game in downtown Orlando. It pits the second-ranked teams from the Southeastern and Big Ten conferences against each other. If your family's sports crazy, this is a good place to go. Tickets start at $65. Call ℂ **800/297-2695** or 407/423-2476 for information or **Ticketmaster** at ℂ **877/803-7073** or 407/839-3900 for tickets (on the Internet, visit **www.fc sports.com**). A free downtown parade is held a few days before the game and features marching bands and some floats. Most kids will find it entertaining. January 1.

Walt Disney World Marathon. About 16,000 runners enter this 26.2-mile race through the resort area. It's open to all, including runners with disabilities. Some Disney packages include the $90 entry fee. The registration deadline is in early November, and preregistration is required. There's also a 13.1-mile mini-marathon ($50) and *100-yard through 5K runs ($5–$30) for families and kids.* Call ℂ **407/939-7810** or go to **www.disneysports. com**. Races are the second week in January.

February

Silver Spurs Rodeo. Real yippee-I-O cowboys compete in calf roping, bull riding, barrel racing, and more. The rodeo is a celebration of the area's rural roots and a nice escape from tourist central. If your child's ever played cowboy (or girl), it's a real treat for the family. It's held at the Silver Spurs Arena, 1875 E. Irlo Bronson Memorial Hwy. (U.S. 192), Kissimmee. Call ℂ **407/847-4052** or visit **www.silverspurs rodeo.com** for details. Tickets are $18 for adults, $8 for kids 12 and younger. Third weekend in February.

March

Atlanta Braves. The Braves have been holding spring training at Disney's Wide World of Sports Complex since 1998. There are 15 games during the 1-month season, and they usually offer a much more up-close experience than your young fans will get at a major league ballpark. Tickets are $12 to $20. For information call ℂ **407/828-3267** or check out **www.disneysports. com**. To purchase tickets, call Ticketmaster ℂ **877/803-7073** or 407/839-3900. The team arrives in mid-February; games begin in early March.

Houston Astros. Here's another event for the sports-minded family. The Astros train at Osceola County Stadium, 1000 Bill Beck Blvd., Kissimmee. Tickets are $8 to $15. Get them through Ticketmaster at ℂ **877/803-7073** or 407/839-3900. For information, check the Astros' website at **www.astros.com**.

Florida Film Festival. The Enzian Theater has been showcasing American independent and foreign films for more than a decade. This 10-day festival sponsored in part by

Universal Orlando usually features a selection of family-friendly films that you and your kids might not otherwise get a chance to see, and some of the films presented are made by teenage students. If your child is a budding director, it's worth attending. In 2001, this was named 1 of the top 10 such events in the world by *The Ultimate Film Festival Survival Guide*. Call **407/629-8587**, or look up **www.floridafilmfestival.com**.

April

Orlando Rays Baseball Season. This Tampa Bay Devil Rays farm team plays its Southern League (Class AA) games at the Disney Wide World of Sports complex from April to early September. Admission is $5 to $8. There are often family-related promotions staged at the games. For general information, call © **407/939-4263** or check online at **www.orlandorays.com**. You also can buy tickets through Ticketmaster (© **877/803-7073** or 407/839-3900).

May

Disney's All-Star Kids Classic Inline Marathon. Everyone's a winner when children ages 3 to 12 race on in-line skates in several age-limited races at Walt Disney World's Wide World of Sports. All children get an award and goodie bag for participating. Proper skating safety equipment is required. It costs $5 to enter your child. For more information, call © **407/828-3267** or surf the Web to **www.disneysports.com**.

Orlando International Fringe Festival. Over 100 diverse acts from around the world participate in this eclectic event, held for 10 days in May at various venues in downtown Orlando. Everything performed on outdoor stages, from sword swallowing to *Hamlet*, is available free to Fringe attendees after they purchase a festival button for about $10. There's also a special **Kids Fringe** during the festival's two weekends. Events include storytelling, theater performances, and a live cartoon band. Tickets for indoor events vary, but most are under $10. Call © **407/648-0077** or visit **www.orlandofringe.com**.

Epcot International Flower and Garden Festival. This 6-week-long event showcases gardens, topiary characters, floral displays, speakers, and seminars. Children will likely be entertained by the topiaries in the Kids Garden, a family-friendly hedge-style maze, and animal and insect demonstrations (where ladybugs and butterflies get released). The festival is free with regular park admission ($52 adults, $42 kids 3–9). For more information, call © **407/824-4321** or visit **www.disneyworld.com**. The festival kicks off in late April and goes through early June.

July

Independence Day. There's a free fireworks display in downtown Orlando at Lake Eola Park. For information, call © **407/246-2827**. Disney and Universal both put on fireworks extravaganzas at their theme parks. Other fireworks events are listed in the local newspaper, the *Orlando Sentinel*. July 4.

September

Night of Joy. The first weekend in September, the Magic Kingdom hosts a festival of contemporary Christian music featuring top artists. This is a very popular family event, so obtain tickets early. Performers also make an appearance at Long's Christian Book & Music Store (p. 279) in College Park, about 20 minutes north of Disney. Admission to the concert is $35.95 per night (8pm–1am) or $57.95 for

2 nights. Use of Magic Kingdom attractions is included. Call ☏ **407/824-4321** for concert details; for information about the free appearance at Long's, call ☏ **407/422-6934.** Universal has gone head-to-head with Disney on this one, scheduling its **Rock the Universe** (☏ **800/837-2273**) concert of Christian rock music the same weekend. Speakers and numerous top bands are featured, and Universal Studios Florida usually stays open late. The event skews a bit more towards adults and older kids. Tickets are $34.95 for 1 night (4pm–1am) or $53.95 for both.

October

Orlando Magic Basketball. The local NBA team plays half of its 82-game regular season between October and April at the TD Waterhouse Centre, 600 W. Amelia St. Ticket prices range from $16 to $150. Single-game tickets can be hard to come by the day of the game. Call ☏ **407/896-2442** for details, **877/803-7073** or 407/839-3900 for tickets. Online go to **www.nba.com/magic.**

Halloween Horror Nights. Universal Orlando's Islands of Adventure (☏ **800/837-2273** or 407/363-8000; www.universalorlando.com) transforms its grounds for 20 or more nights into haunted attractions with live bands, a psychopath's maze, special shows, and hundreds of ghouls and goblins roaming the streets. (**Note:** This event is too intense for most children but will probably appeal to some older teens.) The studio essentially closes at dusk, reopening in a new macabre form from 7pm to midnight or later. Adult admission ($51.95) is charged for this event, where liquor flows freely. Guests can't wear costumes so Universal employees can spot their peers.

Mickey's Not-So-Scary Halloween Party. The Magic Kingdom (☏ 407/934-7639; www.disneyworld.com) invites you to join Mickey and his pals for a far-from-frightening time. In this one, you can come in costume and trick-or-treat through the Magic Kingdom from 7pm to midnight on any of 10 or so nights in October (you'll get bags and can collect candy from characters in set areas in the park). The alcohol-free party includes parades, live music, and storytelling. The climax is a bewitching fireworks spectacular. This is your best Halloween bet if you have young kids. A separate admission fee is charged ($32.95 adults, $27.95 kids 3–9); tickets go on sale at the end of April and nearly always sell out.

Epcot International Food & Wine Festival. Here's your chance to sip and savor the food and beverages of 25 cultures. More than 60 wineries from across the United States participate. Events include wine tastings for adults, seminars, food, dinners, concerts, and celebrity-chef cooking demonstrations. Tickets for the dinner-and-concert series or wine tastings are $79 to $125 including gratuity. The party's not just for adults; kids get their own activities as well. In 2003, kid-friendly options at the festival included an interactive salute to fruits by the Kitchen Kabaret Players, the chance for children ages 4 to 10 to bake their own Toll House cookies at The Land, and a pumpkin patch celebration. The event also features 25 food-and-wine marketplaces where appetizer-size portions of dishes ranging from pizza to octopus on purple potato salad sell for under $5 each (it's a fun way to introduce older kids to exotic cuisines). Entrance to the festival is included in park admission. Call ℂ **407/ 824-4321** for details or check out **www.disneyworld.com**. October 1 to mid-November.

November

ABC Super Soap Weekend. Thirty-something daytime soap celebs are on hand for parades, parties, Q&As, music, and more in a wild weekend catering to fans and fanatics. If you and your older kids are soap-happy, you'll be in heaven. The events are included with Disney–MGM Studios admission ($51.95 adults, $41.95 kids 3–9). Call ℂ **407/397-6808** or surf over to **www.disneyworld.com** for details. First week in November.

Walt Disney World Festival of the Masters. One of the largest art shows in the South takes place at Downtown Disney Marketplace. The exhibition features top artists, photographers, and craftspeople, all winners of juried shows throughout the country. Most kids find the chalk art displays very entertaining. Special child-oriented art activities are also offered throughout venues in Downtown Disney. Free admission. Call ℂ **407/824-4321** or visit **www.disneyworld.com**. 3 days during the second weekend in November.

December

Christmas at Walt Disney World. During the Mickster's holiday festivities, Main Street in the Magic Kingdom is lavishly decked out with lights and holly, and carolers greet visitors. An 80-foot tree is illuminated by thousands of colored lights. Epcot, Disney–MGM Studios, and Animal Kingdom also offer special embellishments and entertainment throughout the holiday season, as do all of the Disney resorts.

Some holiday highlights include **Mickey's Very Merry Christmas Party,** an after-dark (7pm–midnight) ticketed event ($41.95 adults, $31.95 kids 3–9). This takes place on select nights at the Magic Kingdom and offers a parade, fireworks, special shows, and admission to certain rides. You also get cookies, cocoa, and a souvenir photo. The best part? Shorter lines for the rides. The not-so-best part? Fewer rides are open.

Holidays Around the World and the **Candlelight Procession** at Epcot feature hundreds of carolers, storytellers from a host of international countries, celebrity narrators telling the Christmas story, a 450-voice choir, and a 50-piece orchestra in a very moving display. Fireworks are included. One other cool item that kids love: the world's largest gingerbread house, which is appropriately decorated with cookies and frosting. Admission to the event is included in your park

---

(Fun Fact Return Engagement . . . Maybe

The Osborne family of Arkansas built a collection of three-million-plus Christmas lights. It was so bright that neighbors complained and eventually went to court in what became a nationally known battle. Disney came to the rescue, and, in 1995, moved the entire thing to Orlando, adding two million or so bulbs. The show was canceled for the 2003 holiday season while Disney–MGM Studios built a new stunt show, but the family is optimistic that the December extravaganza will return at a new location for the 2004 season. If it does, put this awesome family-favorite on your must-see list; there are few displays (if any) on the planet like it.

admission fee. Call ✆ **407/824-4321** for details on all of the above or go to **www.disneyworld.com**. The holiday fun lasts from mid-December to early January.

Macy's Holiday Parade at Universal Studios Florida. *That's not a typo!* Universal and Macy's teamed up for the first time in December 2002 to offer a smaller version of **Macy's Thanksgiving Day Parade.** The Universal version runs from mid-December to early January, featuring 16 floats and giant balloons used in the New York City parade (✆ **800/837-2273** or 407/363-8000; www.universalorlando.com). It's a sure kid-pleaser. Park admission ($51.95 for adults, $42.95 for kids 3–9) is required. Mid-December to early January.

Grinchmas at Islands of Adventure. The famous Seussian Scrooge, The Grinch, spreads his own brand of grumpy holiday cheer at Islands from late November through early January. Families can explore his lair, see a holiday-themed show and attend a tree-lighting ceremony. All of the fun is included in your park admission fee.

Walt Disney World New Year's Eve Celebration. For 1 night a year, the Magic Kingdom is open until the wee hours for a massive fireworks explosion and child-focused dance parties take place at several locations in the park. Other New Year's festivities at WDW include a big bash at Pleasure Island featuring music headliners (not for kids, and a very pricey ticket), a special Hoop-Dee-Doo Musical Revue at Fort Wilderness, and guest performances by well-known musical groups at Disney–MGM Studios and Epcot. Call ✆ **407/824-4321** for details or visit **www.disneyworld.com**. December 31.

4 What to Pack

You're going to be spending a lot of time on your feet and possibly in the heat, so it's important to pack comfortable clothes and footwear. You won't need anything dressy unless you are going to an upscale restaurant or attending an event that requires it (and this is theme-park-ville, so most won't). Assume the weather will be warm to hot, so make shorts and lightweight clothing a priority but remember layering if you're coming December through February, when it can get downright cold at night.

Don't forget to bring sunglasses, a hat, a bathing suit and cover-up if you're coming in summer, plenty of socks (the humidity and miles of walking makes a change of socks every now and then good practice), and your camera.

Pack a small tote bag filled with toys, puzzles, and activities to keep your kids busy on the plane, or in the car. If you're flying, be sure to pack a supply of sucking candies or chewing gum to help your children adjust to the cabin pressure.

If you're traveling with a toddler or baby, a lightweight and inexpensive stroller with an attached umbrella is a good way to keep the little one dry and out of the sun. You can rent them at the parks if you don't want to schlep yours from home. Nearly every hotel will have cribs (of varying quality) on hand. Most restaurants can supply a highchair, but we used to tote a nearly weightless portable chair that attached to tabletops—you can find these online at **www.babycenter.com** and **www.amazon.com** if they aren't available at your local baby store. You won't need to cart lots of diapers or formula; there are Walgreen's drug stores that carry familiar brands. Just remember

Tips Leave That Baby Gear at Home

There's no reason to schlep like a Sherpa when you can rent nearly any-thing you'll need on vacation. All brands of baby and toddler gear are available by the day or week through a company called **Littleluggage** (© **877/FLYBABY**; www.littleluggage.com) and they'll deliver to your hotel.

to bring enough to tide you over until you can get to a store. If your child has sensitive skin, bring along your own baby wipes. And don't forget sun-screen suitable for infants and a hat!

As for older kids, keep them to one bag apiece and invest in suitcases or duffle bags with wheels—you do not want to be lugging their luggage as well as your own. Kids are usually

happy with one or two pair of shoes (sneakers or hiking boots and sandals), jeans, and T-shirts or whatever's fash-ionable. They should also pack a sweatshirt or sweater and a jacket for cooler months. Backpacks for all kids over 5 are another good idea to stow discarded jackets, books, pens, paper, souvenirs, suntan lotion, baseball cap, water bottle, map, and sunglasses.

5 Insurance, Health & Safety

TRAVEL INSURANCE AT A GLANCE

Check your existing insurance policies and credit card coverage before you buy travel insurance. You may already be covered for lost luggage, cancelled tickets, or medical expenses. The cost of travel insurance varies widely, depending on the cost and length of your trip, your age, health, and the type of trip you're taking.

TRIP-CANCELLATION INSURANCE

Trip-cancellation insurance helps you get your money back if you have to back out of a trip, if you have to go home early, or if your travel supplier goes bankrupt. Allowed reasons for cancellation can range from sickness to natural disasters to the State Depart-ment declaring your destination unsafe for travel, which isn't likely to happen in Orlando. (Insurers usually won't cover vague fears, though, as many travelers discovered who tried to cancel their trips in Oct 2001 because they were wary of flying.) In this unstable world, trip-cancellation insurance is a good buy if you're getting tickets well

in advance—who knows what the state of the world, or of your airline, will be in 9 months? Insurance policy details vary, so read the fine print—and espe-cially make sure that your airline or cruise line is on the list of carriers cov-ered in case of bankruptcy. For infor-mation, contact one of the following insurers: **Access America** (© **866/807-3982**; www.accessamerica.com); **Travel Guard International** (© **800/826-4919**; www.travelguard.com); **Travel Insured International** (© **800/243-3174**; www.travelinsured.com); and **Travelex Insurance Services** (© **888/457-4602**; www.travelex-insurance.com).

MEDICAL INSURANCE

Most health insurance policies cover you if you get sick away from home—but check, particularly if an HMO insures you. If you require additional medical insurance, try **MEDEX International** (© **800/527-0218** or 410/453-6300; www.medexassist.com) or **Travel Assistance Interna-tional** (© **800/821-2828**; www.travelassistance.com; for general informa-tion on services, call the company's

Worldwide Assistance Services, Inc., at © **800/777-8710**).

LOST-LUGGAGE INSURANCE

On domestic flights, checked baggage is covered up to $2,500 per ticketed passenger. On international flights (including U.S. portions of international trips), baggage is limited to approximately $9.07 per pound, up to approximately $635 per checked bag. If you plan to check items more valuable than the standard liability, see if your valuables are covered by your homeowner's policy, get baggage insurance as part of your travel-insurance package, or buy Travel Guard's "Bag-Trak" product. Don't buy insurance at the airport; it's usually overpriced. Be sure to take any valuables or irreplaceable items with you in your carry-on luggage, as many valuables (including books, money, and electronics) aren't covered by airline policies.

If your luggage is lost, immediately file a lost-luggage claim at the airport, detailing the luggage contents. For most airlines, you must report delayed, damaged, or lost baggage within 4 hours of arrival. The airlines are required to deliver luggage, once found, directly to your house or destination free of charge.

CAR-RENTAL INSURANCE

Car-rental insurance costs about $20 a day. If you hold a private auto insurance policy, you probably are covered in the U.S., but not abroad, for loss or damage to the car, and liability in case a passenger is injured. The credit card you used to rent the car also may provide some coverage.

Car-rental insurance probably does not cover liability if you caused the accident. Check your own auto insurance policy, the rental company policy, and your credit card coverage for the extent of coverage: Is your destination covered? Are other drivers covered? How much liability is covered if a passenger is injured? (If you rely on your credit card for coverage, you may want to bring a second credit card with you, as damages may be charged to your card, and you may find yourself stranded with no money.)

For more on car-rental insurance, see "Getting Around," in chapter 3.

THE HEALTHY TRAVELER

Limit your family's exposure to the sun, especially during the first few days of your trip and, thereafter, from 11am to 2pm. Use a sunscreen with a high protection factor and apply it liberally. Remember that children need more protection than adults.

You should also bring along moleskin and check your kids' feet and your own for blisters at the end of each day. High humidity and lots of sustained walking for those unaccustomed to it can lead to unhappy feet.

WHAT TO DO IF YOU GET SICK AWAY FROM HOME

If you worry about getting sick away from home, consider purchasing **medical travel insurance** and carry your ID card in your purse or wallet. In most cases, your existing health plan will provide the coverage you need. See "Travel Insurance at a Glance," above, for more information.

If you suffer from a chronic illness, consult your doctor before your

---

⌐Tips   Quick ID

Tie a colorful ribbon or piece of yarn on your luggage handle, or slap a distinctive sticker on the side of your bag. This makes it less likely that someone will mistakenly grab it. And if your luggage gets lost, it will be easier to find.

departure. For conditions like epilepsy, diabetes, or heart problems, wear a **Medic Alert Identification Tag** (℡ 800/825-3785; www.medic alert.org), which will immediately alert doctors to your condition and give them access to your records through Medic Alert's 24-hour hot line.

Pack **prescription medications** in your carry-on luggage, and carry prescription medications in their original containers, with pharmacy labels—otherwise, they won't make it through airport security. Also bring along copies of your prescriptions in case you lose your pills or run out. Don't forget an extra pair of contact lenses or prescription glasses.

TRAVELING SAFELY WITH YOUR CHILD

There is one major safety issue when traveling with kids that usually comes up a lot more frequently in Orlando than it does in other destinations (though it's thankfully not common): The Lost Child.

Theme parks are hives of activity and it's easy for you or your child to get distracted or confused, and the next thing you know, Junior is missing. The good news is that the theme parks know this, and if it has to happen, better it happen here than in a lot of other places. So do not panic, no matter how inclined you may be to do so.

If a child turns up missing, report it immediately to a park employee. They are all trained to deal with lost kids—and to spot little lambs who've apparently gone astray from their flock. After reporting your missing child, ask the employee where lost children are brought (there are usually one or two central locations in each park) and head there. The odds are Johnny or Jenny is either already there or will arrive there shortly.

The best way to prevent any of this from happening is to take a few preventive steps:

- Dress your young children in something that's easily identifiable so you don't lose them in a crowd.
- Always set up a central, specific, and easily located spot for your kids to meet you should you all get separated. Saying "I'll meet you at Cinderella Castle," rather than "I'll meet you at the entrance to Cinderella's Royal Table," is a recipe for disaster.
- Hold on tight to young kids when exiting the park at closing time, at parades, and when exiting shows. It's very easy to get separated when you're smack in the middle of a massive wave of people.
- Either sew or affix a name tag to your child's clothing (though not in a place it can casually be read) with your child's first and last name; your hometown; your cell-phone number, if you are carrying one; and the name of the hotel you are staying at. The minute you get into the park, show your kids the distinctive name-tags that Disney employees wear and tell them to report to one of them if they get lost.
- Don't assume rides or restrooms have a single exit, so always give a specific place for your child to meet you. Otherwise, you may end up in two different spots . . . and at least one of you will panic.

6 Words of Wisdom & Helpful Resources

SPECIAL FAMILY ADVICE

If you have enough trouble getting your kids out of the house in the morning, dragging them thousands of miles away may seem like an insurmountable challenge. But family travel can be immensely rewarding,

Moments   Kid-Friendly Tours

SeaWorld earns its reputation as an education-friendly park with a variety of small-group tours. One of the most interesting is the **Polar Expedition Guided Tour.** This hour-long trek gives kids a chance to come face-to-face with a penguin and get a behind-the-scenes look at polar bears and beluga whales. **Animal Rescue,** another hour-long tour, lets guests see some of the park's rescue and rehabilitation work with several species, including manatees and sea turtles. Both cost $10 per person, plus park admission (© **800/406-2244**; www.seaworld. com). Both tours are kid-friendly, though the latter may appeal more to the older ones. Both are on a first-come, first-served basis, so reserve your place at the Guided Tour Information Desk when you enter the park. In June, July, and August, **Camp SeaWorld** has 200 classes including sleepover programs and family courses (© **800/406-2244**; www. seaworld.com).

At Walt Disney World, the kid-friendliest tour is the **Family Magic Tour,** an interactive scavenger hunt that costs $25 per person, plus admission (© **407/939-8687**; www.disneyworld.com).

giving you new ways of seeing the world through smaller pairs of eyes.

No city in the world is geared more to family travel than Orlando. In addition to theme parks, its recreational facilities provide loads of opportunities for family fun. Most restaurants have low-priced ($4–$7) children's menus plus fun distractions such as place mats to color while younger diners wait for their vittles. Many hotels have children's activity centers (see chapter 4, "Family-Friendly Accommodations," for details).

Keep an eye out for coupons discounting meals and attractions. The Calendar section in Friday's *Orlando Sentinel* newspaper often contains coupons and good deals. Many restaurants, especially those in tourist areas, offer great discounts that are yours for the clipping. Check the information you receive from the Orlando/Orange County Convention & Visitors Bureau (see "Visitor Information," earlier in this chapter), including free or cheap things to do. Also, many hotel lobbies have free coupon books available.

Some theme parks offer parent-swap programs in which one parent can ride without the children, then switch off and let the other parent ride without returning to the end of the line. Inquire at Guest Services or Guest Relations, near the park entrances.

Here are more suggestions for making traveling with children easier:

- **Are Your Kids Old Enough?** Do you really want to bring an infant or toddler to an overcrowded, usually overheated world that he or she may be too young to appreciate? Our younger grandson, Andy, is 6 and enjoys some of the kids' attractions, but many thrill rides frighten him. Younger children may need a nap when you want to see Festival of the Lion King at Disney's Animal Kingdom. They're dead weight if you have to carry them from Jaws to Catastrophe Canyon at Universal Studios Florida. And when it comes to thrill-ride central—Islands of Adventure—the young have slim pickings. When all is said and done, it comes down to one question: Will the whole family enjoy a trip that's going to cost you the GNP of a developing nation?

- **Planning Ahead** Make reservations for "character breakfasts" at Disney (see chapter 5, "Family-Friendly Dining") when you make hotel reservations. Also, in any park, check the daily schedule for character appearances (all of the major ones post them on maps or boards near the entrances) and make sure the kids know when they're going to get to meet their heroes. It's often the highlight of their day. (Be wary, however, of promising specific characters as schedules and character line-ups can change.) Advance planning will help you avoid running after every character you see. The "in" thing is getting character autographs. Take our advice: Buy an autograph book at home instead of paying theme-park prices.

- **Packing** Although your home may be toddler-proof, hotel accommodations aren't. Bring blank plugs to cover outlets and whatever else is necessary to prevent an accident from occurring in your room. Locals can spot tourists by their bright red, just-toasted sunburn; both parents and children should heed this reminder: *Don't forget to use sunscreen.* If you forget to bring it, it's available at convenience stores and drugstores. Some theme-park shops also carry it; *buy a 25 SPF rating* or higher. Young children should be slathered, even if they're

in a stroller, and be sure to pack a wide-brim hat for infants and toddlers. Adults and children should also drink plenty of water to avoid dehydration.

- **Accommodations** In most cases, kids under 18 stay free with paying adults, but to be certain, ask when you book your room. Most places have pools and other recreational facilities to give you a little no-extra-cost downtime. If you want to skip a rental car and aren't staying at Disney, Universal/International Drive and Lake Buena Vista are the places to be. Hotels often offer family discounts, and some provide free or moderate-cost shuttle service to the homes of the Mouse, the Shrek, and Whale. I-Drive also has a self-serving trolley.

- **Ground Rules** Set up firm rules before leaving home on things like bedtime and souvenirs. Your kids are going to be on an adrenaline high here—you may be, too—so don't let giddiness seize your senses.

- **At the Parks** Getting lost is as easy as remembering your name. For adults and older kids, arrange a lost-and-found meeting place as soon as you land, and if you become separated, head there immediately. Attach a name-tag to younger kids and find a park employee if they become lost.

- **Read the Signs** Most rides (as well as *this book*) explain **height restrictions,** if any, or identify those that may unsettle youngsters or expectant moms. Save yourself some grief before you get in line and are disappointed. Make these

---

Tips **Kids & Flying**

Delta, Walt Disney World's official airline, has stopped allowing families with children to board first on its Orlando flights. It's fairer to the other passengers and better for the kids, who won't be cooped up as long.

rules firm—a trip down a darkened tunnel or scary loop-de-loop can make your child cranky all day and maybe scared of rides for a long while after. (The ride listings in chapter 6 note any minimum heights; so do the guide maps you can get in the parks.)

- **Take a Break** The Disney parks, Universal Orlando, and SeaWorld have stylized play areas offering parents and kids a break. Schedule time to use them. Many of these kid zones include water toys, and some parks have major water-related attractions, so you'd be smart to pack a change of clothes. Rent a locker (about $7) and store spare duds until you need them. During summer, the Florida humidity can keep you feeling soggy all day, so you'll appreciate the fresh clothing even if you don't go near the water.
- **Show Time** Schedule an inside air-conditioned show two or three times a day, especially mid-afternoons in the summer. You may even get your littlest tykes to nap in the darkened theater. For all shows, arrive about 20 minutes early to avoid the bad seats, but not so early that the kids go nuts waiting (most waits are outside).
- **Snack Times** When dreaming of your vacation, you probably don't envision hours spent standing in lines, waiting and waiting. It helps to store some lightweight snacks in a fanny pack or backpack, especially when traveling with small children. This may save you some headaches and will certainly save you some money over park prices.
- **Bring Your Own?** Unless you have an infant, are particularly attached to your stroller, or it's specially designed for triplets, it's usually better to use one provided by the parks (about $8 for a single,

$15 for a double). That way you avoid hauling yours to and from the car or on and off the trams, trains, or monorails. Strollers at all the theme parks have canopies to provide shade for your kids. Note, however, that Disney strollers are designed for toddlers and kids up to around age 5, not infants. For infants, we advise bringing a snugly sling or backpack-type carrier, which will make life a lot easier on you while you're in line for attractions (strollers are almost never permitted on ride lines or inside attractions). If you do bring your own stroller for your infant or toddler, make sure it's collapsible or you won't be able to take it on the Disney transport system.

You can find good family-oriented vacation advice on the Internet from sites like the **Family Travel Network** (www.familytravelnetwork.com); **Traveling Internationally with Your Kids** (www.travelwithyourkids.com), a comprehensive site offering sound advice for long-distance and international travel with children; and **Family Travel Files** (www.thefamilytravelfiles.com), which offers an online magazine and a directory of off-the-beaten-path tours and tour operators for families.

We've listed some additional tips for tackling the theme parks in chapter 6, "What Kids Like to See & Do in Walt Disney World."

FOR TRAVELERS WITH SPECIAL NEEDS

There's no reason for anyone with disabilities to miss most of the fun that Orlando and the theme parks have to offer—as long as you engage in a little advance planning. Autistic children, wheelchair-bound adults, and hearing-impaired teens all come to Orlando, and all of them are accommodated to the best of each park's ability.

ACCOMMODATIONS

Every hotel and motel in Florida is required by law to have a special room or rooms equipped for wheelchairs. A few have wheel-in showers. Walt Disney World's **Coronado Springs Resort** (℗ **407/934-7639** or 407/939-1000; www.disneyworld.com), which opened in 1997, has 99 rooms designed to accommodate guests with disabilities. Make your special needs known when making reservations. For other information about special Disney rooms, call ℗ **407/939-7807.**

If you don't mind staying 15 minutes from Disney, **Yvonne's Property Management** (℗ **877/714-1144** or 863/424-0795; www.villasinorlando.com) is a rental agent for, among other things, some handicapped-accessible homes that have multiple-bedrooms, multiple-baths including accessible showers, full kitchens, and pools outfitted with lifts. Most cost less than $200 a night and are located in Davenport.

Medical Travel Inc. (℗ **800/778-7953;** www.medicaltravel.org) is another source of rentals, scooters and vans, and medical equipment, and can satisfy other needs of disabled travelers, including those with terminal illnesses, and their families.

Some hotels also have special "hypo allergenic" rooms for those with severe allergies or asthma. These rooms usually offer special ventilation systems, pillows, toiletries, etc. Ask about this when booking your hotel if this is an issue for you or your child.

TRANSPORTATION

Public buses in Orlando have hydraulic lifts and restraining belts for wheelchairs. They serve Universal Orlando, SeaWorld, the shopping areas, and downtown Orlando. If staying at Disney, most shuttle buses on the Disney transportation system can accommodate wheelchairs.

If you need to rent a wheelchair or electric scooter for your visit, **Walker Medical & Mobility Products** offers delivery to your room, and there's a model for guests who weigh up to 375 pounds. These products fit into Disney's transports and monorails as well as rental cars. Get more information by calling ℗ **888/726-6837** or 407/518-6000, or on the Internet go to **www.walkermobility.com.** **CARE Medical Equipment** (℗ **800/741-2282** or 407/856-2273; www.caremedicalequipment.com) offers similar services.

Amtrak (℗ **800/872-7245;** www.amtrak.com) provides redcap service, wheelchair assistance, and special seats if you give 72 hours notice. Travelers with disabilities are entitled to a 15% discount off the lowest available adult coach fare. Documentation from a doctor or an ID card proving your disability is required. Amtrak also provides wheelchair-accessible sleeping accommodations on long-distance trains. Service dogs are permitted aboard and travel free. TDD/TTY service is also available at ℗ **800/523-6590,** or you can write to P.O. Box 7717, Itasca, IL 60143.

INSIDE THE THEME PARKS

Many attractions at the parks, especially the newer ones, are designed to be accessible to a wide variety of guests. People with wheelchairs and their parties are often given preferential treatment so they can avoid lines.

The available assistance is outlined in the guide maps you get as you enter the parks. All of the theme parks offer parking close to the entrances for those with disabilities. Let the parking booth attendant know your needs, and you'll be directed to the appropriate spot. Wheelchair and electric cart rentals are available at most major attractions. If you bring your own, keep in mind that wheelchairs wider than 24½ inches may be difficult to navigate through some attractions. And crowds may make it tough for any guest.

AT WALT DISNEY WORLD Disney's many services are detailed in each theme park's *Guidebook for Guests with Disabilities*. Although the resort will no longer mail them to you prior to your visit, you can pick one up at Guest Relations near the front entrances to the parks. You can call ℂ **407/824-4321** or 407/824-2222 for answers to any questions regarding special needs. If you want to see one in advance and have a computer, go to the main WDW website, **www.disney world.com**, then click "Parks & More," on the top menu, then click "FAQ" on the left of the page. When that loads, click "Guests with Disabilities FAQ" on the left side, then scroll down and click your desired park. *Note:* If the page loads in a type size that requires bionic eyes, there's a box at the bottom right of that page that lets you increase the type-size percent.

Examples of services are as follows:

- Almost all Disney resorts have rooms for those with disabilities.
- Braille guidebooks are available at City Hall in the Magic Kingdom and Guest Relations in the other parks (a $25 refundable deposit is required).
- Service animals are allowed in all parks and on some rides.
- All parks have special parking lots near the entrances.
- Assisted listening devices are available to amplify the audio at selected attractions at WDW parks. Also, at some attractions, hearing-impaired guests can use hand-held wireless receivers that let them read captions about the

attractions. Both are free but require a $25 refundable deposit.

- Wheelchairs and electric carts can be rented at all of the parks.
- Downtown Disney West Side, with crowded shops and bars, may be hard to navigate in a wheelchair. The movie theater is, however, wheelchair accessible.
- For information about Telecommunications Devices for the Deaf (TDDs) or sign-language interpreters at Disney World live shows, call ℂ **407/827-5141.** You can usually get an ASL interpreter at several events and attractions if you call no later than 7 days in advance.
- If your child is autistic or has a similar disability, Disney offers a special Guest Assistance Card that will enable you and your child access to a special holding area while waiting to get into an attraction. Bring a signed note from your physician detailing your child's condition to the Guest Services desk at any of the theme parks.

On a final note, if you or your child has a life-threatening food allergy (or just a bad one), Disney will try and accommodate you so that your family can have a meal at the park. Your best bet is to do this at a sit-down restaurant. When making your Priority Seating reservations (see p. 105 for more on Priority Seating), inform the reservations clerk that the allergy is an issue. When you get to the restaurant, ask to speak to a chef about your particular concerns. You may end up having to

---

Tips **Phone Warning!!!**

Orlando is too big for its britches. **Even local calls** require extra digits. Callers in the city's 407 area code—and other parts of Orange County—have to dial 10 digits, even when calling across the street: **407** plus the seven-digit local number.

pay a full adult price for your child if the dish they require doesn't appear on the kid's menu, but you won't pay extra to have it specially prepared. *Warning:* If your child has a peanut allergy, forget about eating any Asian food in the parks—it's made with peanut oil. If you have doubts about what's in a dish, just ask—most restaurants carry an ingredient list.

AT UNIVERSAL ORLANDO Guests with disabilities should go to Guest Services, located just inside the main entrances, for a *Disabled Guest Guidebook,* a Telecommunications Device for the Deaf (TDD), or other special assistance. Wheelchair and electric cart rentals are available in the concourse area of the parking garage. Universal also provides audio descriptions on cassette for visually impaired guests and has sign-language guides and scripts for its shows (1–2 weeks' notice is required; ✆ **800/837-2273** or 407/363-8000 for details).

Guests in wheelchairs or electric carts, who can't transfer out of the them, may not be able to ride some of Universal's thrill rides, which can't accommodate those devices. Note also that children or adults in casts or with leg braces may also be prohibited from boarding a few rides. Call in advance or ask at Guest Services upon entering the park. You can also learn more about restrictions and the services offered at the parks on the Internet at **www.universalorlando.com**. From the main page, click either on Islands of Adventure or Universal Studios Florida, then scroll down on the left side to "ADA page."

Note: All Universal Orlando resorts offer rooms designed for those with mobility impairments. Note, however, that if you or your child has severe pet allergies, that pets are accepted at all of the Universal resorts.

AT SEAWORLD The park has a guide for guests with disabilities, although most of its attractions are easily accessible to those in wheelchairs. SeaWorld also provides a Braille guide for the visually impaired and a very brief synopsis of its shows for the hearing impaired. For information, call ✆ **407/351-3600** or check out the park's website at **www.seaworld. com** (click "Park Information" on the left side of the Orlando page, then hit "Accessibility Guide;" the guide in question is very detailed and offers individual medical recommendations for most of the attractions at Sea-World).

OTHER RESOURCES You also can get information online at the **Orlando/Orange County Convention & Visitors Bureau**'s website, **www.orlandoinfo.com**. In the "Visitor Information" menu at the top of the page, click "special needs."

Many travel agencies offer tours and itineraries for travelers with disabilities. **Accessible Journeys** (✆ **800/846-4537** or 610/521-0339; www.disability travel.com) caters to slow walkers and wheelchair travelers and their families and friends.

Organizations that offer assistance to disabled travelers include the **Moss-Rehab Hospital** (www.mossresource net.org), which provides a library of accessible-travel resources online; the **Society for Accessible Travel and Hospitality** (✆ **212/447-7284;** www. sath.org; annual membership fees: $45 adults, $30 seniors and students), which offers a wealth of travel resources for all types of disabilities and informed recommendations on destinations, access guides, travel agents, tour operators, vehicle rentals, and companion services; and the **American Foundation for the Blind** (✆ **800/232-5463;** www.afb.org), which provides information on traveling with Seeing Eye dogs.

FOR GRANDPARENTS

Many family vacations now include several generations, and traveling with the grandkids to Orlando will provide a host of memorable experiences on both ends of the age spectrum.

Mention you're a senior when you make reservations. Although all of the major U.S. airlines except America West have cancelled senior discount and coupon book programs, many hotels offer discounts for seniors (Loews Hotels, which runs Universal Orlando's resorts even offers a special package to grandparents traveling with their grandkids). In most cities, people over 60 qualify for reduced admission to theaters, museums, and other attractions, as well as discount fares on public buses.

You can order a copy of the **Mature Traveler Guide,** which contains local discounts mainly on rooms but also on attractions and activities, from the **Orlando/Orange County Convention & Visitors Bureau,** 8723 International Dr., Suite 101 (southeast corner of I-Dr. and Austrian Row), Orlando, FL 32819 (© **800/643-9492** or 800/551-0181; www.orlando info.com).

Members of **AARP** (formerly known as the American Association of Retired Persons), 601 E St. NW, Washington, DC 20049 (© **800/424-3410** or 202/434-2277 weekdays; www.aarp.org), get discounts on hotels, airfares, and car rentals. AARP offers members a wide range of benefits, including *Modern Maturity* magazine and a monthly newsletter. Anyone over 50 can join.

Amtrak (© **800/872-7245;** www. amtrak.com) offers a 15% discount on the lowest available coach fare (with certain travel restrictions) to people 62 and over.

FOR SINGLE PARENTS

Single parents face special, unique challenges when they travel with their children. **Parents Without Partners** (© **561/391-8833;** www.parents withoutpartners.org) provides links to numerous single-parent resources.

Single mom Brenda Elwell's website (**www.singleparenttravel.net**) is full of advice garnered from traveling around the world with her two children.

FOR GAY & LESBIAN FAMILIES

The popularity of Orlando with gay and lesbian travelers, including families, parallels the growing number of same-sex households in the area. **Gay, Lesbian & Bisexual Community Services of Central Florida,** 934 N. Mills Ave., Orlando, FL 32803 (© **407/228-8272;** www.glbcc.org), is a great source of information on central Florida. Welcome packets usually include the latest issue of the *Triangle,* a quarterly newsletter dedicated to gay and lesbian issues, and a calendar of events pertaining to the gay and lesbian community. Though not a tourist-specific packet, it includes information and ads for local gay and lesbian clubs. **In the Company of Women** (© **407/331-3466;** www. companyofwomen.com) and **Gay Orlando Network** (www.gayorlando. com) are two other planning resources for travelers.

TRAVELING WITH PETS

Many of us wouldn't dream of going on a family vacation without our pets. And more and more lodgings and restaurants are pet-friendly. Policies vary, however, so call ahead to find out the rules.

None of the Disney resorts except Fort Wilderness allow animals to stay on-premises (service dogs are the exception) or have their own kennels, but resort guests are welcome to board their animals overnight in kennel facilities at the Ticket & Transportation Center. Universal Orlando & SeaWorld will board small animals during the day only.

An excellent resource for those lugging Fluffy and Fido is **www.pets welcome.com**, which dispenses medical tips, names of animal-friendly

Tips The Peripatetic Pet

It is illegal in Florida to leave your pet inside a parked car, windows rolled down or not. The sweltering heat can easily kill an animal in only a few minutes. All of the major theme parks have kennel facilities—use them.

Make sure your pet is wearing a name-tag with the name and phone number of a contact person who can take the call if your pet gets lost while you're away from home. Better yet, the American Kennel Club has an affiliated nonprofit **Companion Animal Recovery** service, where a veterinarian embeds a microchip into your pet, so that it can be identified—collar or not—should it get lost and end up in a shelter or veterinary office. The service is open to all pets, not just dogs and has an excellent track record. For more information, check out the organization's website at **www.akccar.org**.

lodgings and campgrounds, and lists of kennels and veterinarians. Also check out *The Portable Petswelcome. com: The Complete Guide to Traveling with Your Pet* (Howell Book House), which features the best selection of pet travel information anywhere. Another resource is *Pets-R-Permitted Hotel, Motel & Kennel Directory: The Travel Resource for Pet Owners Who Travel* (Annenberg Communications).

Another valuable source is **www. dogfriendly.com**, which has Orlando and Orlando area links that include accommodations, eateries, attractions, and parks that welcome our canine companions.

If you plan to fly with your pet, the FAA has compiled a list of all requirements for transporting live animals at **http://airconsumer.ost.dot.gov**. Click the "Travel Tips & Publications" link

on the home page, then select "Traveling with Animals." You may be able to carry your pet on board a plane if it's small enough to put inside a carrier that can slip under the seat. Pets usually count as one piece of carry-on luggage. Note that summer may not be the best time to fly with your pet: Many airlines will not check pets as baggage in the hot summer months. The ASPCA discourages travelers from checking pets as luggage at any time, as storage conditions on planes are loosely monitored, and fatal accidents are not unprecedented. Your other option is to ship your pet with a professional carrier, which can be expensive. Ask your veterinarian whether you should sedate your pet on a plane ride or give it anti-nausea medication. Never give your pet sedatives used by humans.

7 Planning Your Trip Online

SURFING FOR AIRFARES

The "big three" online travel agencies, **Expedia.com, Travelocity.com,** and **Orbitz.com,** sell most of the air tickets bought on the Internet. (Canadian travelers should try expedia.ca and Travelocity.ca; U.K. residents can go for expedia.co.uk and opodo.co.uk.) Each has different business deals with the airlines, and may offer different

fares on the same flights, so it's wise to shop around. Expedia and Travelocity will also send you **e-mail notification** when a cheap fare to your favorite destination is available. Of the smaller travel agency websites, **SideStep** (www. sidestep.com) has the best reviews from Frommer's authors. It's a browser add-on that purports to "search 140 sites at

Frommers.com: The Complete Travel Resource

For an excellent travel-planning resource, we highly recommend **Frommers.com** (www.frommers.com). We're a little biased, of course, but we guarantee that you'll find the travel tips, reviews, monthly vacation giveaways, and online-booking capabilities thoroughly indispensable. Among the special features are our popular **Message Boards,** where Frommer's readers post queries and share advice (sometimes even our authors show up to answer questions); **Frommers.com Newsletter,** for the latest travel bargains and insider travel secrets; and **Frommer's Destinations Section,** where you'll get expert travel tips, hotel and dining recommendations, and advice on the sights to see for more than 3,000 destinations around the globe. When your research is done, the **Online Reservations System** (www.frommers.com/book_a_trip) takes you to Frommer's preferred online partners for booking your vacation at affordable prices.

once," but in reality only beats competitors' fares as often as other sites do.

Also remember to check **airline websites,** especially those for low-fare carriers such as Southwest, JetBlue, AirTran, WestJet, or Ryanair, whose fares are often misreported or simply missing from travel agency websites. Even with major airlines, you can often shave a few bucks from a fare by booking directly through the airline and avoiding a travel agency's transaction fee. But you'll get these discounts only by **booking online:** Most airlines now offer online-only fares that even their phone agents know nothing about. For the websites of airlines that fly to and from your destination, go to "Getting There," later in this chapter.

Great **last-minute deals** are available through free weekly e-mail services provided directly by the airlines. Most of these are announced on Tuesday or Wednesday and must be purchased online. Most are only valid for travel that weekend, but some (such as Southwest's) can be booked weeks or months in advance. Sign up for weekly e-mail alerts at airline websites or check mega-sites that compile comprehensive lists of last-minute specials,

such as **Smarter Living** (www.smarterliving.com). For last-minute trips, **site59.com** in the U.S. and **last minute.com** in Europe often have better deals than the major sites.

If you're willing to give up some control over your flight details, use an **opaque fare service** like **Priceline** (www.priceline.com; www.priceline.co.uk for Europeans) or **Hotwire** (www.hotwire.com). Both offer rock-bottom prices in exchange for travel on a "mystery airline" at a mysterious time of day, often with a mysterious change of planes en route. The mystery airlines are all major, well-known carriers—and the possibility of being sent from Philadelphia to Chicago via Tampa is remote; the airlines' routing computers have gotten a lot better than they used to be. But your chances of getting a 6am or 11pm flight are pretty high. Hotwire tells you flight prices before you buy; Priceline usually has better deals than Hotwire, but you have to play their "name our price" game. If you're new at this, the helpful folks at **BiddingForTravel** (www.biddingfortravel.com) do a good job of demystifying Priceline's prices. Priceline and Hotwire are great for flights within North America and between the U.S. and Europe. But for flights to other parts of the world, consolidators will almost always beat their fares.

For much more about airfares and savvy air-travel tips and advice, pick up a copy of *Frommer's Fly Safe, Fly Smart* (Wiley Publishing, Inc.).

SURFING FOR HOTELS

Shopping online for hotels is much easier in the U.S., Canada, and certain parts of Europe than it is in the rest of the world. If you try to book a Chinese hotel online, for instance, you'll probably overpay. Also, many smaller hotels and B&Bs—especially outside the U.S.—don't show up on websites at all. Of the "big three" sites, **Expedia** may be the best choice, thanks to its long list of special deals. **Travelocity** runs a close second. Hotel specialist sites **hotels.com** and **hoteldiscounts. com** are also reliable. An excellent free program, **TravelAxe** (www.travelaxe. net), can help you search multiple hotel sites at once, even ones you haven't heard of. It has an immense number of Orlando hotels in its database, and best of all, it almost always shows you the price you'll pay for your room, including the hotel taxes! (It doesn't include resort fees, however,

and it doesn't monitor Disney Resort hotels either.)

Priceline and Hotwire are even better for hotels than for airfares; with both, you're allowed to pick the neighborhood and quality level of your hotel before offering up your money. That said, *we don't recommend you use them unless you have older kids and are willing to opt for a second room.* Here's why: The sites only guarantee double occupancy and won't guarantee bed types, crib space, rollaways, or even that the hotel you get will have lots of child-friendly amenities. They also won't book a Disney resort. So unless you're willing to get two rooms (you can request adjoining ones once your bid is accepted, though that's not guaranteed either), you could end up in a small room that won't fit all of you very comfortably.

For information on the hotel rooms Priceline uses in Orlando, check out **BiddingForTravel** (www.biddingfor travel.com). This must-see site should always be your first stop before bidding on a room through Priceline. The site not only lists the hotels the service uses, but can also tell you the amount of recent winning bids. One recent winning bid got a rate of $70 a night at the Wyndham Palace Resort & Spa

---

Online Traveler's Toolbox

- **Visa ATM Locator** (www.visa.com), for locations of PLUS ATMs worldwide, or **MasterCard ATM Locator** (www.mastercard.com), for locations of Cirrus ATMs worldwide.
- **Intellicast** (www.intellicast.com) and **Weather.com** (www.weather. com). Gives weather forecasts for all 50 states and for cities around the world.
- **Mapquest** (www.mapquest.com). This best of the mapping sites lets you choose a specific address or destination, and in seconds, it will return a map and detailed directions.
- **Universal Currency Converter** (www.xe.com/ucc). See what your dollar or pound is worth in more than 100 other countries.

(p. 84)—more than $100 off the rack rate.

Note that Priceline is much better at getting five-star lodging for three-star prices than at finding anything at the bottom of the scale. *Note:* Hotwire overrates its hotels by one star—what Hotwire calls a four-star is a three-star anywhere else.

SURFING FOR RENTAL CARS
For booking cars online, good deals can usually be found at rental-car company websites (see appendix B, "Useful Toll-Free Numbers & Websites"),

although the major online travel agencies also offer rental-car reservations services. We prefer **Travelocity,** because it's rental page actually shows you what your car will cost you after including taxes and surcharges (though not including any rental fees for car seats).

One other excellent rental-car site is **Breezenet Rental Cars** (www.bnm. com), which allows you to compare the rental rates offered by various national and local agencies at various airports, including Orlando's.

8 Getting There

BY PLANE
THE MAJOR AIRLINES
There are 35 scheduled airlines and nearly as many charter companies serving the more than 30 million passengers who land in Orlando in a normal year. **Delta** (© 800/221-1212; www.delta.com) runs nearly 25% of the flights into Orlando International Airport. It offers service from about 150 cities.

Others include **Air Canada** (© 888/247-2262; www.aircanada. ca); **America West** (© 800/235-9292; www.americawest.com); **American** (© 800/433-7300; www. americanair.com); **British Airways** (© 800/247-9297; www.british-airways.com); **Continental** (© 800/525-0280; www.continental.com); **Northwest** (© 800/225-2525; www. nwa.com); and **US Airways** (© 800/428-4322; www.usairways.com).

Several so-called no-frills airlines—low fares but few niceties—fly to Florida. The biggest is **Southwest Airlines** (© 800/435-9792; www.south west.com), which has flights from many U.S. cities to Orlando and Tampa. **Spirit Air** (© 800/772-7117; www.spiritair.com) is another no-frills choice. **JetBlue Airways** (© 800/538-2583; www.jetblue.com) is a low-cost carrier that operates out of a

number of U.S. cities, and offers direct flights to Orlando out of New York City. The latter has child-pleasing video screens that offer 24 TV channels and is a huge favorite with Frommer's editors.

The newest no-frills airline is really the stepsister of Delta: **Song Airlines** (© 800/359-7664; www.flysong. com). By early 2004, the airline expects to have personal video monitors—for child-distracting satellite TV and video games—installed on all of its jets.

ORLANDO'S AIRPORT
Orlando International Airport (© 407/825-2001; www.state.fl.us/ goaa) offers direct or nonstop service from 60 U.S. cities and two dozen international destinations, serving more than 30 million passengers most years. It's a thoroughly modern and user-friendly facility with restaurants, shops, a 446-room on-premises Hyatt Regency, and centrally located information kiosks.

All major car-rental companies are located at or near the airport; see "Getting Around," in chapter 3, and appendix B for more information about car rentals.

AIRPORT TRANSPORTATION
Orlando International is 25 miles east

Tips Stuck on You

Your preteen or teen just got his or her first set of contact lenses and is probably very attached to them. But if your kids wear those lenses on a plane, they could possibly become too attached. The air in an airplane cabin is especially dry and sucks moisture out of the eyes. If your kids aren't careful, their contact lenses (or yours, for that matter) could get vacuum-sealed onto their eyes. And we doubt you want your first sight-seeing experience in Orlando to be an emergency room. Your best bet is for everyone to ditch the lenses for the plane ride, but if that isn't possible, make sure all lens-wearers put in lots of re-wetting drops over the course of the plane ride.

of Walt Disney World and 20 miles south of downtown. At rush hour (7–9am and 4–6pm), the drive can be a torturous hour or more; at other times, it's about 30 to 40 minutes. **Mears Transportation Group** (© 407/423-5566; www.mears transportation.com) has vans that shuttle passengers from the airport (you catch them at ground level) to Disney resorts and official hotels, as well as most other Orlando properties. Their air-conditioned vehicles operate around the clock, departing every 15 to 25 minutes in either direction. Rates vary by destination. Round-trip fare for adults is $25 ($18 for kids) between the airport and downtown Orlando or International Drive; $29 ($21 for kids) for Walt Disney World/ Lake Buena Vista or West U.S. 192.

QuickTransportation/Orlando (© 888/784-2522 or 407/354-2456; www.quicktransportation.com) is more personal. Their folks greet you at baggage claim with a sign bearing your name. They're more expensive than Mears, but they're coming for you. And they're only going to *your* resort. This is a good option for four or more people. Rates run from $80 (up to seven, round-trip) to I-Drive/Universal and $130 for the Disney realm.

Tiffany Towncar (© 888/838-2161 or 407/370-2196; www.tiffany towncar.com) offers a $95 round-trip rate for up to five people in a van from

Orlando International to Disney ($70 to International Dr. or Universal).

DRIVING TO WALT DISNEY WORLD   To get from the airport to the attractions, take the **North** exit out of the airport to **Highway 528 West.** Follow signs to I-4; it takes about 30 to 40 minutes to get to Walt Disney World if the traffic isn't too heavy (double or worse in rush hour or when there's an accident). When you get to I-4, follow the signs **west** toward the attractions.

Note: It's always a good idea when you make reservations to ask about transportation options between the airport and your hotel. Also be sure to ask how far you have to travel to pick up and drop off a rental car. Some lots are miles from the airport, adding to the time you'll spend waiting in line and catching shuttles.

GETTING THROUGH THE AIRPORT

With the federalization of airport security, security procedures at U.S. airports are more stable and consistent than ever. Generally, you'll be fine if you arrive at the airport **1 hour** before a domestic flight and **2 hours** before an international flight; if you show up late, tell an airline employee, and you may be taken to the front of the line.

Bring a **current, government-issued photo ID** such as a driver's license or passport, and if you've got an E-ticket, print out the **official confirmation page;** you'll need to show your confirmation at the security checkpoint, and your ID at the ticket counter or gate. (Children under 18 do not need photo IDs for domestic flights, but adults with them do.)

Security lines are getting shorter than they were during 2001 and 2002, but some doozies remain. If you have trouble standing for long periods of time, tell an airline employee; the airline will provide a wheelchair. Speed up security by **not wearing metal objects** such as big belt buckles or clanky earrings. If you've got metallic body parts, a note from your doctor can prevent a long chat with the security screeners. Keep in mind that only **ticketed passengers** are allowed past security, except for folks escorting disabled passengers or children.

Federalization has stabilized **what you can carry on** and **what you can't.** The general rule is that sharp things are out, nail clippers are okay, and food and beverages must be passed through the X-ray machine—but that security screeners can't make you drink from your coffee cup. Bring food in your carry-on rather than checking it, as explosive-detection machines used on checked luggage have been known to mistake food (especially chocolate, for some reason)

for bombs. Travelers in the U.S. are allowed one carry-on bag, plus a "personal item" such as a purse, briefcase, or laptop bag. Carry-on hoarders can stuff all sorts of things into a laptop bag; as long as it has a laptop in it, it's still considered a personal item. **The Transportation Security Administration (TSA)** has issued a list of restricted items; check its website (www.tsa.gov/public/index.jsp) for details.

In 2003, the TSA will be phasing out **gate check-in** at all U.S. airports. Passengers with E-tickets and without checked bags can still beat the ticket-counter lines by using **electronic kiosks** or even **online check-in.** Ask your airline which alternatives are available, and if you're using a kiosk, bring the credit card you used to book the ticket. If you're checking bags, you will still be able to use most airlines' kiosks; again, call your airline for up-to-date information. **Curbside check-in** is also a good way to avoid lines, although a few airlines still prohibit it; call before you go.

At press time, the TSA is also recommending that you **not lock your checked luggage** so screeners can search it by hand if necessary. The agency says to use plastic "zip ties" instead, which can be bought at hardware stores and easily cut off.

Travel in the Age of Bankruptcy

At press time, two major U.S. airlines were struggling in bankruptcy court, and most of the rest weren't doing very well either. To protect yourself, **buy your tickets with a credit card,** as the Fair Credit Billing Act guarantees that you can get your money back from the credit card company if a travel supplier goes under (and if you request the refund within 60 days of the bankruptcy). **Travel insurance** can also help, but make sure it covers against "carrier default" for your specific travel provider. And be aware that if a U.S. airline goes bust mid-trip, a 2001 federal law requires other carriers to take you to your destination (albeit on a space-available basis) for a fee of no more than $25, provided you rebook within 60 days of the cancellation.

Tips Flying with a Cold

It's even more difficult for kids to make their ears pop during takeoff and landing. The eustachian tube is especially narrow in children; the passage is even tighter when mucous membranes are swollen. This can make ascent and descent especially painful—even dangerous—for a child with congested sinuses. If your little one is suffering from a cold or the flu, it's best to keep him grounded until he recuperates, if that's an option. If you simply must travel with your child as scheduled, give him an oral child's decongestant an hour before ascent and descent or administer a spray decongestant before and during takeoff and landing. Nursing and/or sucking on a bottle or pacifier will help alleviate pressure in your infant or toddler; a cough drop or sucking candy should work for older kids (don't give these to younger ones who might choke on them if there's turbulence).

FLYING FOR LESS: TIPS FOR GETTING THE BEST AIRFARE

There's no shortage of discounted and promotional fares to Florida. November, December, and January (excluding holidays) often bring fare wars that can result in savings of 50% or more, but, in a sagging economy, specials may be available more often. Watch for ads in your local newspaper and on TV, call the airlines, or check out their websites. Here are some ways to keep your airfare costs down:

- Passengers who can book their tickets **long in advance,** who can **stay over Saturday night,** or who **fly midweek** or **at less-trafficked hours** will pay a fraction of the full fare. If your schedule is flexible, say so, and ask if you can secure a cheaper fare by changing your flight plans.
- No-frills airlines have reduced their price advantage, but some **charter** flights still go to Florida, especially during the winter season and particularly from Canada. They often cost less than regularly scheduled flights, but they're very complicated. It's best to go to a good travel agent and ask him or her to find one for you.
- Search **the Internet** for cheap fares (see "Planning Your Trip Online," earlier in this chapter).
- Join **frequent-flier clubs.** Accrue enough miles, and you'll be rewarded with free flights. It's free, and you'll get the best choice of seats, faster response to phone inquiries, and prompter service if your luggage is stolen, your flight is canceled or delayed, or if you want to change seats. You don't need to fly to build frequent-flier miles—**frequent-flier credit cards** provide thousands of miles for doing your everyday shopping.
- For more tips about air travel, including a rundown of the major frequent-flier credit cards, pick up a copy of *Frommer's Fly Safe, Fly Smart* (Wiley Publishing, Inc.).

9 Tips on Flying with Children

SAFE SEATS FOR KIDS

Note: Most airlines require that an infant be 2 weeks old to travel—bring a birth certificate. American and Continental only require that the child be 7 days old. Alaska lets babies fly as soon as they're born.

The practice of allowing children younger than 2 to ride for free on a parent's lap may be prohibited by the

Tips Don't Stow It—Ship It

If ease of travel is your main concern and money is no object, you can ship your luggage with one of the growing number of luggage-service companies that pick up, track, and deliver your luggage (often through couriers such as Federal Express) with minimum hassle for you. Traveling luggage-free may be ultra-convenient, but it's not cheap: One-way overnight shipping can cost from $100 to $200, depending on what you're sending. Still, for some people, it's a sensible solution to lugging heavy baggage. Specialists in door-to-door luggage delivery are **Virtual Bellhop** (www.virtual bellhop.com), **SkyCap International** (wwww.skycapinternational.com), and **Luggage Express** (www.usxpluggageexpress.com).

time you read this. At press time, the FAA was writing a rule that would require all children under 40 pounds to be have their own tickets and be secured in a child safety seat.

Most major American airlines offer discounted infant tickets for children 2 years of age or younger, to make it more affordable for you to reserve a separate adjacent seat for your baby and a restraining device.

For now, if a seat adjacent to yours is available, your lap child can sit there free of charge. When you check in, ask if the flight is crowded. If it isn't, explain your situation to the agent and ask if you can reserve two seats—or simply move to two empty adjacent seats once the plane is boarded. You might want to shop around before you buy your ticket and deliberately book a flight that's not very busy. Ask the reservationist which flights tend to be most full and avoid those. Only one extra child is allowed in each row, however, due to the limited number of oxygen masks.

On international journeys, children can't ride free on parents' laps. On flights overseas, a lap fare usually costs 10% of the parent's ticket. Children who meet the airline's age limit (which ranges from 11–15 years old) can purchase international fares at 50% to 75% of the lowest coach fare in certain markets. Some of the foreign carriers make even greater allowances for children.

Note: Children riding for free will usually not be granted any baggage allowance.

Airlines offer child meals, if requested in advance. Ticketed babies can get "infant meals" on America West, Delta, and US Airways, and all major airlines except Alaska and Southwest will warm bottles on request.

CHILD SEATS: THEY'RE A MUST

According to *Consumer Reports Travel Letter,* the National Transportation Safety Board says that, since 1991, the deaths of five children and injury to four could have been prevented had the children been sitting in restraint systems during their flights. Even in the event of moderate turbulence, children sitting on a parent's lap can be thrust forward and injured. When you consider that a commercial aircraft hits a significant amount of turbulence at least once a day on average, you'd do well to think about investing a few hundred dollars for a safety seat.

The FAA recommends that children under 20 pounds ride in a rear-facing child-restraint system, and says children that weigh 20 to 40 pounds should sit in a forward-facing child-restraint system. Children over 40 pounds should sit in a regular seat and wear a seat belt.

All child seats manufactured after 1985 are certified for airline use, but make sure your chair will fit in an airline seat—it must be less than 16 inches wide. You may not use booster seats or seatless vests or harness systems. Safety seats must be placed in window seats—except in exit rows, where they are prohibited, so as not to block the passage of other travelers in the case of an emergency.

The airlines themselves should carry child safety seats on board. Unfortunately, most don't. To make matters worse, overzealous flight attendants have been known to try to keep safety seats off planes. One traveler recounts in the November 2001 issue of *Consumer Reports Travel Letter* how a Southwest attendant attempted to block use of a seat because the red label certifying it as safe for airline use had flaked off. That traveler won her case by bringing the owner's manual and appealing to the pilot—you should do the same.

Until the new FAA rule comes into effect, if you can't afford the expense of a separate ticket, book a ticket toward the back of the plane at a time when air travel is likely to be slowest—and the seat next to you is most likely to be empty. The reservationist should also be able to recommend the best (meaning the least busy) time for you to fly.

EASING TRAVEL WITH THE TOTS IN TOW
Several books on the market offer tips to help you travel with kids. Most concentrate on the U.S., but two,

---

In-Flight Fun for Kids

With one of these children's game books on board, even the longest plane ride will go faster.

Great Games for Kids on the Go: Over 240 Travel Games to Play on Trains, Planes, and Automobiles
by Penny Warner
Retail price: $12.95
Ages 4 to 8
This book is full of entertaining educational games to help your kids while away the miles. Each game is highly engaging and entertaining and requires few materials and very little space.

Brain Quest for the Car: 1100 Questions and Answers All About America
by Sharon Gold
Retail price: $10.95
Ages 7 to 12
This book features cards with questions about American geography, culture, and customs.

Vacation Fun Mad Libs: World's Greatest Party Game
by Roger Price
Retail price: $3.99
Ages 8 and up
As suggested by the title, this book is chock-full of Mad Libs. Your kids will want to keep playing even after you've touched down.

Family Travel & Resorts: The Complete Guide (Lanier Publishing International; $19.95) and *How to Take Great Trips with Your Kids* (The Harvard Common Press; $9.95), are full of good general advice that can apply to travel anywhere. Another reliable tome, with a worldwide focus, is *Adventuring with Children* (Foghorn Press; $14.95).

If you plan carefully, you can actually make it fun to travel with kids.

- If you're traveling with children, you'll save yourself a good bit of aggravation by **reserving a seat in the bulkhead** row. You'll have more legroom, and your children will be able to spread out and play on the floor underfoot. You're also more likely to find sympathetic company in the bulkhead area, as families with children tend to be seated there.
- **Check your luggage** and limit family members to one backpack or bag for which they are responsible. This will make life much simpler.
- Have **a long talk with your children** before you depart for your trip. If they've never flown before, explain to them what to expect. If they're old enough, you may even want to describe how flight works and how air travel is even safer than riding in a car. Explain to your kids the importance of good behavior in the air—how their own safety can depend upon their being quiet and staying in their seats during the trip.
- Ask the flight attendant **if the plane has any special safety equipment for children.** Make a member of the crew aware of any medical problems your children have that could manifest during flight.
- **Be sure you've slept sufficiently** for your trip. If you fall asleep in the air and your child manages to

break away, there are all sorts of sharp objects that could cause injury. Especially during mealtimes, it's dangerous for a child to be crawling or walking around the cabin unaccompanied by an adult.

- **Be sure your child's seat belt remains fastened properly,** and try to reserve the seat closest to the aisle for yourself. This will make it harder for your children to wander off—in case, for instance, you're taking the red-eye or a long flight overseas and you do happen to nod off. You will also protect your child from jostling passersby and falling objects—in the rare but entirely possible instance that an overhead bin pops open.
- **Try to sit near the lavatory,** though not so close that your children are jostled by the crowds that tend to gather there. Consolidate trips there as much as possible.
- Each child's bag should contain **clean, self-containing compact toys.** Leave electronic games at home. They can interfere with the aircraft navigational system, and their noisiness, however lulling to children's ears, will surely not win the favor of your adult neighbors. Magnetic checker sets, on the other hand, are a perfect distraction, and small coloring books and crayons also work well, as do card games like Go Fish.

  By all means, don't leave home without a favorite blanket or stuffed animal—especially if it's your kid's best friend at bedtime. It might also come in handy if the going gets rough and kids need something comforting to cuddle.

- The responsible adult (you, for example) will need a bag as well, filled with **age-appropriate extras** such as a deck of cards, postcards, pens, an address book, extra bottles, pacifiers, diapers, and chewing gum to help relieve ear pressure buildup during ascent and descent. A package of wipes is also handy. If baby is on board, you'll definitely need a change of clothes for him/her and possibly for you.

- You'll certainly be grateful to yourself for **packing tidy snacks** like rolled dried fruit, which are much less sticky and wet and more compact and packable than actual fruit. Blueberry or raisin bagels also make for a neat, healthy sweet and yield fewer crumbs than cookies or cakes. Ginger snaps, crisp and not as crumbly as softer cookies, will also help curb mild cases of motion sickness. And don't forget to stash a few resealable plastic bags in your bag. They'll prove invaluable for storing everything from half-eaten crackers and fruit to checker pieces and matchbox cars.

- **Juice or cookies** will not only keep them distracted during ascent and descent—often the scariest parts of flight for a child—they will also help their little ears pop as cabin air pressure shifts rapidly. Juice (paper cartons travel best) will also keep them swallowing and help them to stay properly hydrated.

- If your children are very young, don't forget to pack bottles and extra milk or formula, as these are unavailable on most aircraft. Many airlines prohibit flight attendants from preparing formula, so it's best to pack your baby's food premixed.

BY CAR

Orlando is 436 miles from Atlanta; 1,312 miles from Boston; 1,120 miles from Chicago; 1,009 miles from Cleveland; 1,170 miles from Dallas; 1,114 miles from Detroit; 1,088 miles from New York City; and 1,282 miles from Toronto.

- From Atlanta, take I-75 south to the Florida Turnpike to I-4 west.

- From points northeast, take I-95 south to Daytona Beach and I-4 west.

- From Chicago, take I-65 south to Nashville, then I-24 south to I-75, then south on the Florida Turnpike to I-4 west.

- From Cleveland, take I-77 south to Columbia, South Carolina, and then I-26 east to I-95 south to I-4 west.

- From Dallas, take I-20 east to I-49, south to I-10, east to I-75, then south on the Florida Turnpike to I-4 west.

- From Detroit, take I-75 south to the Florida Turnpike, then exit on I-4 west.

- From Toronto, take Canadian Route 401 south to Queen Elizabeth Way, then south to I-90 (New York State Thruway), east to I-87 (New York State Thruway), south to I-95 over the George Washington Bridge, then south on I-95 to I-4 west.

AAA (© 800/222-1134; www.aaa.com) and some other auto club members should call their local offices for maps and optimum driving directions.

BY TRAIN

Amtrak trains (© 800/872-7245; www.amtrak.com) pull into stations at 1400 Sligh Blvd. in downtown Orlando (23 miles from Walt Disney World), and 111 Dakin Ave. in Kissimmee (15 miles from WDW). There are also stops in Winter Park, 10 miles north of downtown Orlando, at 150 W. Morse Blvd.; and in Sanford, 23 miles northeast of Orlando, 800 Persimmon Ave., which is also the end terminal for the Auto Train (see below).

FARES As with airline fares, you sometimes can get discounts if you book far in advance. There may be some restrictions on travel dates for discounted fares, mostly around very busy holiday times. Amtrak also offers money-saving packages—including accommodations (some at WDW resorts), car rentals, tours, and train fare (𝒞 **800/321-8684**).

The good news for families is that up to two children ages 2 to 15 can ride for half-fare with a paying adult; one child under 2 rides for free with an accompanying adult. The discounts apply year-round and on all trains, except Amtrak's Acela train.

AMTRAK'S AUTO TRAIN This option offers the convenience of bringing your car to Florida without having to drive it all the way. It begins in Lorton, Virginia—about a 4-hour drive from New York, 2 hours from Philadelphia—and ends at Sanford, 23 miles northeast of Orlando. (There are no stops in between.) Reserve early for the lowest prices. Fares average $530 ($1,100 with a berth) for two passengers and an auto. Call 𝒞 **800/872-7245** for details.

10 Package Deals for Families

The number and diversity of package tours to Orlando is staggering. But you can save money if you're willing to do the research. Start by looking in the travel section of your local Sunday newspaper and checking the ads in the back of travel magazines such as *Travel & Leisure* and *Condé Nast Traveler.* Also, stop at a sizable travel agency and pick up brochures from several companies. Go over them at home and compare offerings to find the optimum package for your trip.

You should also obtain the *Walt Disney World Vacations* brochure from Disney (see contact details at the beginning of this chapter), which lists WDW packages. Disney's array of choices can include airfare, accommodations on or off Disney property, theme-park passes, a rental car, meals, a Disney cruise, and/or a stay at Disney's beach resorts in Vero Beach or Hilton Head, South Carolina. And unlike the main Disney number, the number to call for a Disney vacation package is *free:* 𝒞 **800/828-0228** (the alternate number, 407/828-8101, is a toll call). Some packages are tied to a season, while others are for special-interest vacationers, including golfers, honeymooners, or spa aficionados.

Since opening in 1971, Disney hasn't offered a lot in the way of discounts. It filled parks, resorts, and restaurants without them. But depressed tourism after September 11, 2001, has humbled WDW and made Mickey a bit more willing to offer deals. Make sure to press Disney reservation clerks or your travel agent for the best deal they can find.

Although not on the same scale as Disney's options, Universal Orlando packages have improved greatly with the addition of the new Islands of Adventure theme park, the CityWalk grub-and-club district, and the Portofino Bay, Hard Rock, and Royal Pacific hotels. The options include lodging, VIP access to Universal's theme parks, and discounts to other non-Disney attractions. Some include round-trip air. Contact **Universal Studios Vacations** at 𝒞 **888/322-5537** or 407/224-7000, or online go to **www.universalstudiosvacations.com**.

SeaWorld also offers 2- and 3-night packages that include rooms at a handful of hotels, car rental, and tickets to SeaWorld. Call 𝒞 **407/351-3600,** or, online, go to **www.seaworld.com**.

The airlines are another good source of package deals. **Delta** has them in several price ranges. They may include round-trip air, accommodations, rental car or round-trip airport transfers, unlimited admission to Disney parks, and other features. In packages utilizing WDW resorts, you get all of the advantages given to guests at these properties (see chapter

Tips **A Magical Gathering**

If you have a large family or are traveling together with others, then Disney launched a new program in 2003 that might work for you. The **Magical Gatherings** program caters to groups traveling together to Walt Disney World and offers online trip-planning tools to help you put together a vacation for the extended family.

Large groups of eight or more people (ages 3 or above) traveling together to Walt Disney World—**Grand Gatherings,** as Disney calls them—also get free assistance from a Disney trip-planner, who will help you get hotel rooms, make dining reservations, recreation, schedule golf tee times, and put together special event and attractions options (these extras will cost you) that appeal to all age groups and that are not available to individuals and smaller families. Options (which can be reserved up to 90 days in advance) include special character breakfast options, safari outings at Animal Kingdom, and a fireworks cruise on the Seven Seas Lagoon.

If you're interested in this option, call Disney at ✆ **407/934-7639** or go to **www.disneyworld.com/magicalgatherings** and request a Magical Gathering Vacation Planning Kit or an interactive DVD. When you make the request, ask for specialized planning brochures for groups that include preschoolers, including information about favorite attractions for younger children, child-care options, and tips for a well-planned vacation with preschool-aged children.

4 for details). There are three price options: standard, ultimate, and preferred. Prices vary widely depending on the resort you choose, your departure point, and the time of year. Delta also has Orlando packages that don't include tickets to Disney parks. You can learn more by calling ✆ **800/872-7786** or heading over to **www.deltavacations.com**.

Other major airlines offering air/land packages include **American Airlines Vacations** (✆ 800/321-2121; www.aavacations.com) and **Continental Airlines Vacations** (✆ 800/301-3800; www.coolvacations.com).

Several big **online travel agencies**—Expedia, Travelocity, Orbitz, Site59,

and Lastminute.com—also do a brisk business in packages. If you're unsure about the pedigree of a smaller packager, check with the Better Business Bureau in the city where the company is based, or go online at **www.bbb.org**. If a packager won't tell you where it's based, don't fly with them.

Before you invest in a package tour, get some answers. Ask about the **accommodations choices** and prices for each. Then look up the hotels' reviews in a Frommer's guide and check their rates for your specific dates of travel online.

Finally, look for **hidden expenses.** Ask if airport departure fees and taxes, for example, are included in the cost.

11 Disney Cruise Packages

There's hardly a Florida tourist market that WDW hasn't tried to tap. Ocean-going vacations are no exception. The

Disney Cruise Line launched the *Magic* and *Wonder* in 1998 and 1999, respectively.

Tips As the Stomach Turns

Nothing spoils a cruise like a storm—or worse. In the first case, consider avoiding hurricane season (June 1–Nov 30, though the peak is July to mid-Oct). These fickle storms can spoil your fun and upset your tummy. Even if you avoid the season, pack anti-motion sickness pills or patches.

Speaking of spoiling a cruise, several cruise ships including the Disney *Magic* had outbreaks of a virus that causes stomach flu-like symptoms in the fall of 2002. That's no ill reflection on one line: Cruise ships are closed environments, and sometimes a passenger brings the illness on . . . and it's hard to keep something from spreading in close quarters, especially if the ship isn't scrubbed down enough. For an Internet rating by the **Centers for Disease Control,** go to **www2.cdc.gov/nceh/vsp/vspmain.asp**. Note, however, that the site is often weeks out of date.

The *Magic* is Art Deco in style, with Mickey in the three-level lobby and a *Beauty and the Beast* mural in its top restaurant, Lumiere's. The *Wonder*'s decor is Art Nouveau. Ariel commands its lobby, and its featured eatery, Triton's, sports a mural from *The Little Mermaid.*

Subtle differences aside, these are nearly identical twins. Both are 83,000 tons with 12 decks, 877 cabins, and room for 2,400 guests. Cabins are large and can easily accommodate a family of three or four; and many have bunk beds and can sleep five. Most have one and a half bathrooms—something you won't find on any other cruise ship and a boon for families.

There are some adults-only areas on the ships, but no casinos. Both ships have extensive kids' and teens' programs—they're broken into four age groups—and state-of-the-art computer equipment. These are exceptionally well executed and the best in the cruise business. There are also nurseries for 3-month-old to 3-year-old passengers.

Restaurants, shows, and other onboard activities are very family oriented. One of the unique features is a dine-around option that lets you move among main restaurants (each ship has four) from night to night while keeping the same servers. You can buy a soft-drink package for your kids ($15–$35, depending on the duration of your cruise) that nets them free and unlimited soda refills.

The 3- and 4-day voyages visit Nassau and Castaway Cay, a WDW island. There also are 7-day eastern Caribbean (St. Thomas, St. Maarten, and Castaway Cay) and 7-day western Caribbean (Key West, Grand Cayman, Cozumel, and Castaway Cay) itineraries.

Seven-day land-sea packages include 3 or 4 days afloat, with the rest of the week at a WDW resort. Prices at press time ranged from $829 to $4,999 per adult, $399 to $1,199 for kids 3 to 12, and $139 for kids under 3, depending on your choice of stateroom and resort. Packages are available that add round-trip air and unlimited admission to WDW parks, Pleasure Island, and other attractions. Cruise-only options for 3 nights are $439 to $2,749 for adults, $229 to $799 for kids 3 to 12, and $99 for those under 3; 4-night cruises are $539 to $3,149 for adults, $329 to $899 for kids 3 to 12, and $99 for kids under 3. Disney's 7-night cruises sell for $829 to $4,999 for adults, $399 to $1,199 for kids 3 to 12, and $139 for kids under 3.

Cruises depart from Port Canaveral, about an hour east of Orlando by car. If you buy the package, transportation to and from Orlando is included. You can get discounted fares if you book well in advance and go during non-peak periods. For information, call ✆ **800/951-3532** or go to **www.disneycruise.com**.

12 Show & Tell: Getting the Kids Interested In Orlando

In most cases, you really won't have to do all that much to get your child interested in Orlando. It will be more a case of trying to restrain the obvious enthusiasm your youngsters will display at the idea of meeting Mickey and the gang, or riding the Hulk Coaster. That said, involving your kids in the planning of the vacations will certainly help avoid any disappointments and will make them feel as if they're contributing to the experience.

Before you leave (we recommend at least 3–4 weeks), ask the folks at Disney to send you one of their vacation videos, which should be of interest to most of the family. You can get it by writing to Walt Disney World, Box 10000, Lake Buena Vista, FL 32830-1000, calling ✆ **407/934-7639** or 407/824-4321, or, on the Internet, go to **www.disneyworld.com** and choose the "Order a Free Vacation Planning Kit" option from the bottom menu. If you request it, you can also get a **"Preschooler Vacation Kit"** prepared just for your younger children. Your little ones will no doubt enjoy watching the video and you can gauge their reactions to certain rides and attractions. This is also a good time to explain to young kids about height and weight restrictions that may keep them from riding a few attractions so you can avoid disappointment later on.

You might want to buy your younger children an autograph book before leaving, so they can get character autographs in the parks. This is a wildly popular activity and a good souvenir for your children to bring back from Orlando.

Also, the folks at Go2Orlando.com have created a site just for kids at http://travel.go2orlando.com/top/1,1419,G-Go2Orlando-Go2Kids-X!Front,00.htm (click "Kids" on the left menu). The website has trip-planning links on the area's coolest pools, advice on getting character autographs, kid-written reviews of the parks, and ideas about souvenirs. There's also a **Fun & Games** link for before the trip and once you're on the road.

Break out some Disney classic films before you go to get your kids in the mood. No matter what your child's age, you'll find something that Disney put out appropriate for them, be it the 2003 hit film *Pirates of the Caribbean* for your teens or the enchanting *Cinderella* for your little ones.

Videos and documentaries on animals, as well as age-appropriate books, will prepare your kids for the sights and sounds they'll experience at Animal Kingdom and SeaWorld. Similarly, books and videos on the different cultures represented in the World Showcase will give your kids a rudimentary introduction to the countries that they'll walk though at Epcot.

If you're visiting Universal's parks, you can watch Nickelodeon with your young kids and tell them they'll get to visit the studios where some of the shows are staged. Or read them the *Cat in the Hat* and they'll be charmed when they actually get to ride through the story at Islands of Adventure. Older kids and teens might appreciate a selection of classic Marvel comic books, or could be induced to watch some of the films that many of Universal's rides are based on, including *Shrek*, *Back to the Future*, *Men in Black*, *Twister*, and *Jurassic Park*.

3

Getting to Know Walt Disney World & Orlando

Orlando wasn't much of a family town before Disney opened its Magic Kingdom theme park in 1971.

But Uncle Walt and Mickey changed that. They blazed a pioneering trail that, over the last 33 years, has spawned a crush of over-development. Disney may not be the exact center of the Orlando universe, but it's a close call. Walt Disney World has grown into four major theme parks, two nighttime entertainment districts, 21 resorts and timeshare properties, nine partner hotels, two full-fledged water parks, and loads more. Those are Disney's ways of trying to keep you, your kids, and your tourist dollars from straying to Universal Orlando, SeaWorld, or its other competitors. They are good at it, for although WDW is pretty easy to navigate, once you get your bearings, it's sprawled enough that you might hesitate to leave.

But all of that unrelenting cheerfulness, days of $2.50 sodas, and the solar-fried musk of sweaty patrons make it a small world, after all. Besides, you're cheating yourself if you don't spend some time away from Walt Disney's world, especially if you have teenagers, for whom Universal Orlando (and its thrill rides) is a major mecca; or aquarium lovers of any age, who will find SeaWorld a wonderfully relaxed place to visit. And don't overlook some of the less frazzled things to do in O-Town with your kids, including the Orlando Science Center. We'll let you know all about the area's layout and what's where in the first section of this chapter.

The good news is that getting around the major tourist areas of Orlando is relatively easy if you have a car, you're a decent navigator, and if traffic is cooperating. If you plan on staying only in Walt Disney World, you can even make do without the car (we'll give you the pros and cons of using Disney's own transportation network later on). The major attractions are all centered around large interstates or highways, and the city has done its utmost best to make sure your family (and its tourist dollars) won't get lost on the way to your chosen destination. That said, if you do get lost, you'll find a ton of roadside billboards on most major thoroughfares that will lead you to the city's biggest attractions.

1 Orientation

VISITOR INFORMATION

Once you're in town, you can stop at the **Orlando/Orange County Visitors Center,** 8723 International Dr., Suite 101, Orlando (© **407/363-5872;** www.orlandoinfo.com). Folks working at the bureau will answer questions and give you maps, brochures, and coupons good for discounts or freebies. It's worth a

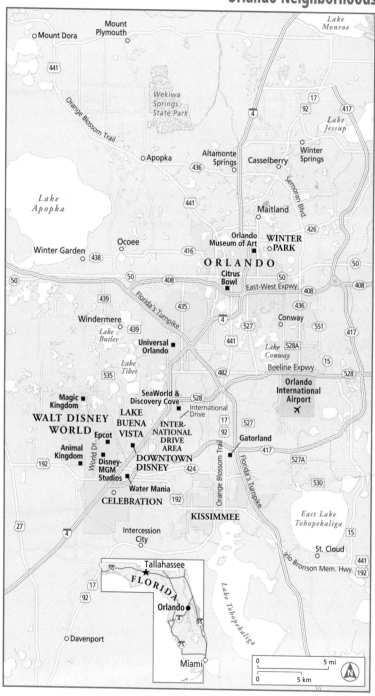

visit even if you take our advice in chapter 2 and send for them before arriving. The bureau sells discount tickets to several attractions (savings on single-day passes to Universal and SeaWorld are $3 or less; only Disney's 4-day or longer passes are discounted). Its multilingual staff will also make dinner reservations and hotel referrals for you. The bureau is open daily, 8am to 6 or 7pm, except Christmas. From I-4, take Exit 74A east 2 blocks, turn south on International Drive and go 1 mile. The center is on the left, at I-Drive and Austrian Row.

The **Kissimmee–St. Cloud Convention & Visitors Bureau** is located at 1925 E. Irlo Bronson Memorial Hwy./U.S. 192, Kissimmee (© **800/333-5477** or 407/847-5000; www.floridakiss.com). It's open Monday to Friday, 8am to 5pm and offers maps, brochures, and coupons, too. From I-4 take Exit 64A/ U.S. 192 east about 12 miles to Bill Beck Boulevard, then go left into the bureau's parking lot.

If you're driving into town from the north on I-75, you can stop at the **Disney Welcome Center** in Ocala, Florida (exit 350 at Hwy. 200), about 90 miles north of Orlando (© **352/854-0770**). The center sells tickets and Mickey ears, helps plan your park itinerary, and makes hotel reservations. Hours are 9am to 6pm daily. But don't come looking for cut-rate tickets. Disney really doesn't do many discounts, though you can save a few bucks if you buy multiday park-hopper passes (see chapter 6, "What Kids Like to See & Do in Walt Disney World").

Finally, nearly all hotel lobbies and many restaurants, highway rest stops, and attractions have racks containing brochures for various activities. The brochures often include discount coupons.

INFORMATION (& MORE) AT THE AIRPORT

Orlando's theme-park fun starts almost from the minute you get off the plane.

Orlando International Airport has two Disney shops. The **Magic of Disney** (© **407/825-2370**) is in the main terminal, third level, right behind the Northwest Airlines ticket desk. **Disney Earport** (© **407/825-2410**) is in the main terminal, across from the Hyatt Regency. They sell WDW multiday tickets, make dinner show and hotel reservations at Disney resorts, and provide brochures and assistance. They're open daily, usually 7am to 8pm; but don't use these airport stores to buy things unless you're on your way home and forgot to buy that must-have Pooh doll for your favorite niece. Chances are you'll find a better selection and (possibly) cheaper prices elsewhere in town.

The **Universal Studios Stores** (© **407/825-2473**), usually open daily from 7am to 8pm, sell park tickets at two locations: Airside A, main terminal, and Airside B, Delta side before security, both on the third level. **SeaWorld** stores, at Airside A and B, are open from 7am to 8pm (© **407/825-2614**).

CITY LAYOUT

Orlando's major artery is Interstate 4 or **I-4.** This runs across Florida from Tampa to Daytona Beach. Exits from I-4 take you to all of the Disney properties, Universal, SeaWorld, International Drive, U.S. 192, Kissimmee, Lake Buena Vista, and downtown Orlando. Most are well marked, but construction is common and exit numbers can change. For the latest exit numbers, see **www11.myflorida.com/trafficoperations/exitnumb/i_4.htm**. If you get directions by exit number, always ask the name of the road, too, to avoid getting lost. Note that the road in question is often a traffic-laden nightmare loathed by locals. (Cellphone users can dial © **511** to get a report of I-4 delays.)

The **Florida Turnpike,** a toll road, crosses I-4 and links with I-75 to the north and Miami to the south. **U.S. 192/Irlo Bronson Memorial Highway** is

> ## *Tips* Stem the Tide
>
> If you're coming to Orlando with a diaper wearer in tow, **Babies Bottom** delivers Pampers and other brands to your hotel. While prices are higher than discount stores, they're comparable to the theme parks and the selection is greater. This may be a good choice if you don't have a car to go bargain shopping. The company prefers advance orders (© **877/693-1670;** www.babiesbottom.com) of 48 hours or more.

an east–west artery that reaches from Kissimmee to U.S. 27, crossing I-4 near World Drive, the main Disney entrance road. Construction on 192, planned to last into 2004, creates backups as bad as the ones on I-4 during rush hour (7–9am and 4–6pm daily). Farther north, the **BeeLine Expressway** (Hwy. 528), also a toll road, goes east from I-4 past Orlando International Airport to Cape Canaveral and Kennedy Space Center. The **East–West Expressway** (also known as Hwy. 408) is a toll road that can be helpful in bypassing surface traffic in the downtown area.

If you're jockeying between Disney and Universal, one of the lesser traffic evils is **Apopka–Vineland Road.** It tends to be less cluttered than I-4 or International Drive. Follow it north from Lake Buena Vista and the northeast side of WDW to Sand Lake Road, then go right to Turkey Lake Road, then left to Universal.

I-4 and Highway 535 border **Walt Disney World** to the east (the latter is also a northern boundary) and U.S. 192/Irlo Bronson Memorial Highway border it to the south. World Drive is WDW's main north-south artery. Epcot Center Drive (Hwy. 536/the south end of International Dr.) and Buena Vista Drive cut across the complex in a more or less east-west direction; the two roads cross at Bonnet Creek Parkway. Despite a reasonably good highway system and explicit signs, **it's easy to get lost** or miss a turn here. Don't panic or pull across several lanes of traffic to make an exit, especially once you're on Disney property. All roads lead to the parks, and you'll soon find another sign directing you to the same place. It may take a bit longer, but Goofy will still be there.

Note: If you're going to be driving around town, we highly recommend you get a good detailed map of the area. The map the Orlando/Orange County Visitors Bureau sends in their visitor packet (p. 11) is good, and most car-rental agencies offer good maps as well.

ORLANDO NEIGHBORHOODS IN BRIEF

Walt Disney World The empire, its big and little parks, resorts, restaurants, shops, and assorted trimmings, are scattered across 30,500 acres. The surprising thing to some folks: WDW isn't in Orlando. It's southwest of the city, off I-4. Stay here and learn that convenience has its price; rooms run as much as double what they do in nearby Kissimmee. For little kids, however, this is the Promised Land.

Lake Buena Vista This is Disney's next-door neighbor. It's where you'll find "official" (though not Disney-owned) hotels. It's close to Downtown Disney and Pleasure Island, and is a good spot for families who want Disney, but not the heavy Mickey themes and prices. This charming area has manicured lawns, tree-lined thoroughfares, and free transportation throughout the realm.

Celebration Imagine living in a Disney world. This is an attempt to re-create a squeaky-clean Mickey magic town. Located on 4,900 acres, Celebration has thousands of residents living in gingerbread homes and apartments. Celebration's downtown area is, however, designed for tourists. It's architecturally interesting and offers shops, restaurants, theaters, and a hotel. If yours is a yuppie family, particularly one with reasonably deep pockets, this may be your dream world. Think of it as an upscale Main Street, U.S.A.

Downtown Disney This is more Disney dessert than an actual neighborhood, and, simply put, it's what WDW has taken to calling its two nighttime entertainment areas, Pleasure Island and Disney's West Side, as well as its shopping complex, Downtown Disney Marketplace. We consider this area a part of WDW/Lake Buena Vista, and it's best suited for older kids, teens, and parents.

Kissimmee This once-sleepy city is closer to Disney than Orlando. It's just a few miles from Mickey and has some of the least expensive offerings in the area, but it also has a distinctly tacky side with budget motel chains and every fast-food joint known to civilization (which may be a perk if you have a lot of kids in tow). The town centers on U.S. 192/Irlo Bronson Memorial Highway, which, as we mentioned earlier, has traffic problems created by perpetual road construction.

International Drive Area (Hwy. 536) Can you say tourist mecca? Known as **I-Drive,** it extends 7 to 10 miles north of the Disney parks between Highway 535 and the Florida Turnpike. From bungee jumping and ice-skating to dozens of theme restaurants and T-shirt shops, this is *the* tourist strip in central Florida, and it has a ton of options for families. It also has numerous hotels and shopping areas, it's home to the Orange County Convention Center, and it offers easy access to SeaWorld and Universal Orlando. The central and northern sections are already packed, but developers somehow manage to shoehorn more in, year after year. The south end is less cluttered and easier to navigate.

Downtown Orlando To get to downtown, you have to travel on I-4 east (it feels more like north, but the road signs say otherwise). This is where you will find less tourist-focused nightlife and attractions, including the Orlando Science Center, a multimillion-dollar complex. It's not an ideal place to stay with the kids as most of the hotels are aimed at the business set, but you can get a great deal on a top hotel if you come on weekends. Scores of clubs and restaurants (good places for parents to take a night off) are located in the heart of the city, which is one of the fastest growing in the country.

Winter Park Just north of downtown Orlando, Winter Park is the place many of central Florida's old-money families call home. It's home to Park Avenue, a collection of upscale shops and restaurants along a cobblestone street that's frequented by the lunch and dinner crowds. With the main attractions being shopping, dining, and small museums, this part of the 'burbs is not a good place for most kids or thrill-ride junkies.

2 Getting Around

In a city that thrives on its attractions, you won't find it difficult to get around—especially if you have a car. (Don't count on public transportation to get you where you want to go quickly.) If you're traveling outside the tourist areas, avoid the periods from 7 to 9am and 4 to 6pm like the plague, which they are. Rush hours are bad anywhere, but the commuter traffic here is complicated by tourist traffic and, given that this is a 24/7 town, it doesn't get better on weekends. Most of the parks don't open until 9am or so, and they usually stay open at least until dusk, so you won't miss much by leaving a little later. (The exception is Animal Kingdom, where the critters move around early, then hide when the sun comes out; see "Animal Kingdom" in chapter 6, "What Kids Like to See & Do in Walt Disney World.")

International Drive has two alternate means of transportation—pedestrian and trolley power. We don't recommend the former because, though there are plenty of sidewalks, you may be taking your life in your hands if you try to cross this busy road, especially if you've got little kids. The **I-Ride Trolley** (© **407/248-9590;** www.iridetrolley.com) is a safer bet. It makes 78 stops between the Belz Factory Outlets on the north end of the drive and SeaWorld to the south. The trolley runs every 15 minutes, from 8am to 10:30pm, and costs 75¢ for adults and 25¢ for seniors; kids under 12 ride free with a paying adult; *exact change is required.* There's an unlimited 1-day pass available for $2 per person. This is a great way to avoid I-Drive's bumper-to-bumper driving.

The good news if you are driving is that road signs have become more accurate than they were a few years back. But to make sure you're heading the right way, follow the directions we supply for the various attractions and hotels later in this book. Also, call your destination before leaving and ask whether new construction or other temporary roadblocks might be in your way.

Some hotels (usually not the inexpensive ones) offer transportation to and from some theme parks and other tourist destinations; however, some of them charge you for this service. If the hotel does charge for shuttle service, when you add up the cost of transporting your family (and consider that you'll be at the mercy of your shuttle's schedule—not always the ones your kids will adhere to), you're often better off with the car.

BY DISNEY TRANSPORTATION SYSTEM

If you're going to stay at Disney and spend a majority of your time visiting its parks and attractions, then using the thorough and free transportation network that runs throughout Mickey's realm is an option you should consider.

Guests at Disney resorts and "official" hotels get unlimited transportation via bus, monorail, ferry, and water taxi to all of Disney's major parks from 2 hours prior to opening until 2 hours after closing. There also is service to the hotels, Downtown Disney, Typhoon Lagoon, Blizzard Beach, Pleasure Island, and other resort areas. Disney properties offer transportation to other area attractions as well, but you'll have to pay extra.

The system has several advantages. It's free, which may save you on car rental, insurance, and gas (Disney resort guests don't pay for parking, so that's not a savings). You may avoid a wait to enter the parking lots, and, if your kids are old enough to strike out on their own and your party wants to split up, you can board a transport to different areas.

Fun Fact **Crash & Burn**

Talk about culture clash. The Race Rock Café on International Drive, known for parking NASCAR racers in its lobby and having mini-racers streaking across the ceiling, was once the home of an opera-theme restaurant. It lasted until, well, the fat lady sang (ouch).

The disadvantages? There are some serious ones. The system can be slow as molasses, and you're at the mercy of Disney's schedule. Sometimes you have to take a ferry to catch a bus to get on the monorail to reach your hotel. The system makes a complete circuit, but it's not necessarily the most direct path for you. It can take an hour or more to get somewhere that's right across the lagoon from you. This is especially true if you stay at the Disney resorts that lie in the outer reaches, such as Fort Wilderness.

Another problem: If you're staying at Disney's Value and Moderate resorts, and you've got little kids in tow, be advised that you're going to have to hike quite a bit from the theme park exit to the bus stops that will get you back to your hotel. Even exhausted adults won't relish the walk at the end of a tiring day, and it'll be that much worse if you're carrying a days' worth of souvenirs, a diaper bag, camera bag, and so on. Buses to these resorts can also get crowded, and the last thing tired and cranky kids will want to do is stand for what could be a long ride in a sardine can.

And, finally, without a car, you may be stuck spending your entire vacation in pricey Mickeyville.

If you have time before locking in your trip, use the maps in this book to find the attractions you want to visit and their proximity to the various WDW resorts. You also can download them at **www.disneyworld.com** (you'll need Adobe Acrobat Reader). From the home page, click "Reservations & Tickets," then "Transportation" on the left side, and then "View and Download Some Maps."

The best rule when using Disney transportation: Ask the driver or someone at your hotel's front desk to help you take the most direct route or the easiest one for your children. Keep asking questions along the way. Unlike missing a highway exit, missing a bus stop means you may reach your pension and your kids will be old enough to vote before you arrive at your destination.

BY CAR

To rent or not to rent—that's the question. If you're going to stay happily immersed in everything Disney, or if you're going to lock into International Drive or Universal, you might do just as well without your own wheels. **But remember:** You could be a prisoner of those areas unless you rent a car at least a few days during your stay. In Disney's case, the least expensive properties, the All-Star resorts, are among the farthest from the Disney parks. Waits between buses can be considerable—if not unendurable, especially with kids.

During peak hours in the busy seasons, you may have trouble getting a seat on the bus, so keep that in mind. Also, if you're hauling strollers consider the frustration factor of loading and unloading them and other kiddie paraphernalia on and off buses, ferries, and trams. (Renting strollers in the parks will alleviate this problem.)

A car may drastically cut the commute time between the parks and hotels not directly on the monorail routes, so decide how much your time is worth and what the car will cost, adding the $7 per day theme-park parking charge (not if you're a Disney resort guest—parking is free if you stay at a Disney hotel).

In general, if you're going to spend all of your time at Disney and you're laid-back enough to go with the flow of traffic within the transportation network, there's no sense renting a car that will sit in the parking lot. This is especially true if you're staying at one of the Disney resorts on the monorail system.

But if you're staying a week or more, you'll probably want a car for at least a day or 2 to venture beyond the traditional tourist areas. You can discover downtown Orlando, visit museums, or tour the Space Coast. Trust us: You and your kids will need a good dose of sanity after spending a few days in the Mickey madness.

RENTING A CAR

All of the major car-rental companies are represented in Orlando and maintain desks at or near the airport (see appendix B, "Useful Toll-Free Numbers & Websites," in the back of this book for contact information). Many agencies provide discount coupons in publications targeted at tourists. When you're planning your trip and poring over all those brochures, watch for discounts on car rentals. You may also want to ask your travel agent if he or she has a recommendation, or whether a discount is included in packages. Also, it never hurts to ask about specials. Be advised that city and state rental taxes and surcharges (often not included in a quoted rate) can often add almost 25% to your rental bill, so make sure to ask if taxes were included in any rate quotes that you get.

Note: Under Florida law, children 35 pounds and under must ride in car seats in all vehicles. Most rental agencies in Orlando will provide a car seat if you ask for it when you reserve your car, though they will almost always charge you extra for it (usually between $5–$10 per day).

Be sure to ask for a seat that's the correct size for your child—a toddler shouldn't be put in a seat that's too large for them, and so on. Most major car-rental websites provide excellent information on choosing the proper seat restraints for your kids; we like **Avis**'s (**www.avis.com**) and **Hertz**'s (**www.hertz.com**) best.

All children under 12 and above the 35-pound mark must wear seat belts. It's recommended that they sit in the back seat, especially if the car you're driving has airbags. Infants should *never* be placed in a car seat in the front of your vehicle.

GETTING A GOOD DEAL

Car-rental rates vary even more than airline fares. The price you pay will depend on the size of the car, where and when you pick it up and drop it off, the length of the rental period, where and how far you drive it, whether you purchase insurance, and a host of other factors. A few key questions could save you hundreds of dollars:

- Are weekend rates lower than weekday rates? Ask if the rate is the same for pickup Friday morning, for instance, as it is for Thursday night.
- Is a weekly rate cheaper than the daily rate? Even if you need the car for only 4 days, it may be cheaper to keep it for 5.

Tips **Fun While Driving**

Alamo Rent A Car has a **"Fun For Kids"** page on its website (**www.alamo. com**) that features printable quizzes, word games, and more to keep your kids happy while on a car trip. Several of the items on the page are Disney-related, making it even more appropriate for an Orlando-related car trip.

- Does the agency assess a drop-off charge if you don't return the car to the same location where you picked it up? Is it cheaper to pick up the car at the airport compared to a downtown location?
- Are special promotional rates available? If you see an advertised price in your local newspaper, be sure to ask for that specific rate; otherwise, you may be charged the standard cost. Terms change constantly, and reservations agents are notorious for not mentioning available discounts unless you ask.
- Are discounts available for members of AARP, AAA, frequent-flier programs, or trade unions? If you belong to any of these organizations, you may be entitled to discounts of up to 30%.
- How much tax will be added to the rental bill? Local tax? State use tax?
- What is the cost of adding an additional driver's name to the contract?
- How many free miles are included in the price? Free mileage is often negotiable, depending on the length of your rental.
- How much does the rental company charge to refill your gas tank if you return with the tank less than full? Though most rental companies claim these prices are "competitive," fuel is almost always cheaper in town. Try to allow enough time to refuel the car yourself before returning it.

Some companies offer "refueling packages," in which you pay for an entire tank of gas upfront. The price is usually fairly competitive with local gas prices, but you don't get credit for any gas remaining in the tank. If a stop at a gas station on the way to the airport will make you miss your plane, then by all means take advantage of the fuel purchase option. Otherwise, skip it.

Many packages are available that include airfare, accommodations, and a rental car with unlimited mileage. Compare these prices with the cost of booking airline tickets and renting a car separately to see if these offers are good deals. See "Package Deals for Families," in chapter 2, for details on packages and where to find them.

Internet resources can make comparison-shopping easier. See "Planning Your Trip Online," in chapter 2, for tips on the best sites.

CAR-RENTAL INSURANCE

Before you drive off in a rental car, be sure you're insured. Hasty assumptions about your personal auto insurance or a rental agency's additional coverage could end up costing you tens of thousands of dollars—even if you are involved in an accident that was clearly the fault of another driver.

If you already hold a **private auto insurance** policy, you are most likely covered in the United States for loss of or damage to a rental car and liability in case of injury to any other party involved in an accident. Be sure to find out whether you are covered in the area you are visiting, whether your policy extends to all persons who will be driving the rental car, how much liability is covered in case an outside party is injured in an accident, and whether the type of vehicle you are renting is included under your contract. (Rental trucks, sport utility vehicles, and luxury vehicles such as the Jaguar may not be covered.) There is also another area—"loss," as in "loss of income," as in the loss of the income that rental car would have made for the rental-car company. Many insurers don't cover this.

Most **major credit cards** provide some degree of coverage as well—provided they were used to pay for the rental. Terms vary widely, however, so be sure to call your credit-card company directly before you rent.

If you are **uninsured,** your credit card may provide primary coverage as long as you decline the rental agency's insurance. This means that the credit card will cover damage or theft of a rental car for the full cost of the vehicle. If you already have insurance, your credit card may provide secondary coverage—which basically covers your deductible. *Credit cards will not cover liability*, or the cost of injury to an outside party and/or damage to an outside party's vehicle. If you do not hold an insurance policy, you may seriously want to consider purchasing additional liability insurance from your rental company. Be sure to check the terms, however: Some rental agencies cover liability only if the renter is not at fault; even then, the rental company's obligation varies from state to state. Bear in mind that each credit-card company has its own peculiarities; call your own credit-card company for details before relying on a card for coverage.

The basic insurance coverage offered by most car-rental companies, known as the **Loss/Damage Waiver (LDW)** or **Collision Damage Waiver (CDW),** can cost as much as $20 per day. The former should cover everything, including loss: It usually covers the full value of the vehicle with no deductible if an outside party causes an accident or other damage to the rental car. In all states but California, you will probably be covered in case of theft as well. Liability coverage varies according to the company policy and state law, but the minimum is usually at least $15,000. If you are at fault in an accident, however, you will be covered for the full replacement value of the car but not for liability. Most rental companies will require a police report in order to process any claims you file, but your private insurer will not be notified of the accident. Check your own policies and credit cards before you shell out money on this extra insurance, because you may already be covered.

BY BUS

Stops for the **Lynx** bus system (© **407/841-2279;** www.golynx.com) are marked with a "paw" print. It will get you to Disney, Universal, and I-Drive ($1.25 adults, 50¢ kids 8–18), but it's slow and generally not tourist-friendly. We can't recommend using it, especially if you've got toddlers and younger children.

Mears Transportation (© **407/423-5566;** www.mearstransportation.com) runs buses to attractions, including Kennedy Space Center, Universal Orlando, SeaWorld, and Busch Gardens in Tampa, among others. The company also offers a **SuperPass** that might be a good value for families staying in the International Drive and Lake Buena Vista areas who don't want to rent a car. The pass includes round-trip airport transfer to your hotel as well as unlimited transfers to Walt Disney World, SeaWorld, Universal Orlando, and Wet 'n Wild for a number of consecutive days. You have to arrange your attractions transfers at least 3 hours in advance. The price depends on the number of days you're staying in Orlando and runs from $63 for adults, $56 for children 4 to 11 for 3 nights to $107 for adults, $100 for children for 7 nights. Additional nights cost $15 per adult or child. Check the website or call for more information and rates.

BY TAXI

Taxis line up in front of major hotels and a few smaller properties. The front desk will be happy to hail one for you. You can also call **Yellow Cab** (© **407/ 699-9999**) and **Ace Metro** (© **407/855-0564**). Rates run as high as $3.25 for the first mile, $1.75 per mile thereafter, though sometimes you can get a flat rate. In general, cabs are economical only if you have four or five people aboard.

Note: Under Florida law, children 35 pounds and under must ride in car seats in all vehicles, including taxis. For a taxi ride, you'll need to bring your own seat, which naturally makes this mode of travel inconvenient for families whose kids will require a seat.

Tips **Look Both Ways**

We don't recommend foot travel anywhere in Orlando, but occasionally you'll have to walk across a parking lot or street. *Be careful.* Orlando is the most dangerous large city in the country for pedestrians, according to the 2002 Mean Streets study. Wide roads designed to move traffic quickly and a shortage of sidewalks, streetlights, and crosswalks are to blame. So stay close to your kids and keep a wary eye on traffic.

FAST FACTS: Walt Disney World & Orlando

American Express There's an American Express Travel Service Office downtown at 2 W. Church St., SunBank Center, ✆ **407/843-0004.**

Babysitters Some hotels listed in chapter 4 offer supervised evening babysitting services, and some have child-care facilities with counselor-supervised activity programs. Disney's Animal Kingdom Lodge, Beach Club, Boardwalk, Contemporary, Grand Floridian, Polynesian, and Wilderness Lodge resorts offer programs with activities, entertainment, and meals. They're open to kids 4 to 12 (must be toilet trained), run from 4:30 or 5pm to midnight and cost $10 per child per hour, meal included. Reservations are a good idea (✆ **407/939-3463**). Babysitting rates elsewhere usually run $10 to $15 per hour per child; some offer discounts for the second, third, or fourth child. **Kid's Nite Out** (✆ **407/827-5444**) offers in-room babysitting.

Business Hours Most theme parks open at 9am and stay open at least until 6 or 7pm (sometimes as late as 9pm during summer and holidays). Business office hours are generally Monday through Friday from 9am to 5pm.

Camera Repair Colonial Photo, 634 N. Mills Ave. in downtown Orlando (✆ **407/841-1485**) repairs most 35mm and some digital brands.

Doctors & Dentists All theme parks have first-aid centers. There's a 24-hour toll-free number for **Poison Control:** ✆ **800/282-3171.** Disney offers in-room medical service 24 hours a day by calling ✆ **407/238-2000. Doctors on Call Service** (✆ **407/399-3627**) is a group that makes house and room calls in most of the Orlando area. **Centra-Care** has several walk-in clinics listed in the Yellow Pages, including ones on International Drive (✆ **407/370-4881**) and at Lake Buena Vista near Disney (✆ **407/934-2273**).

To find a dentist, contact **Dental Referral Service** (✆ **800/336-8478;** www.dentalreferral.com). Folks there can tell you the nearest dentist who meets your needs. Phones are manned weekdays from 10am to 7pm Eastern. Check the Yellow Pages for local 24-hour emergency services.

Emergencies Dial ✆ **911** for police, firefighters, or an ambulance. For less urgent requests, call ✆ **800/647-9284.** Multilingual operators provide directions and help with lost credit cards, accidents, and much more.

Hospitals **Sand Lake Hospital** is at 9400 Turkey Lake Rd. (✆ **407/351-8550**), near Universal. From I-4 take the Sand Lake Road exit and go left on Turkey Lake. It's 2 miles on your right. **Celebration Health** (✆ **407/764-4000**) is near Disney. From I-4, take the U.S. 192 exit. At the first light, go right on Celebration Avenue. At the first stop sign, take another right.

Internet Access You will find a few local cybercafes listed at **www.cybercafes.com** or **www.netcafeguide.com/mapindex.htm**. Many hotels provide in-room Web access, and Disney has several Internet kiosks set up in its theme parks so that visitors can check e-mail.

Libraries Orange County has 14 libraries (www.ocls.lib.fl.us) including the downtown Orlando Public Library, 101 E. Central Blvd. (© **407/835-7323**), and South Creek Library, 1702 Deerfield Blvd. (© **407/858-4779**).

Lost Children Every theme park has a designated spot for adults to be reunited with lost children (or lost spouses). Ask where it is when you enter (or consult the free park guide maps) and instruct your children to ask park personnel to take them there if they get separated from you. Point out what park personnel look like. Young children should have name-tags that include parents' names, name of the hotel where they're staying, and a contact number back home in the very rare case that parents can't be located.

Maps AAA is an excellent source of free maps if you or someone you know is a member. The local car-rental companies are also good sources of maps. You can also pick maps up for $5 or less at most Orlando convenience and discount stores.

Newspapers & Magazines The *Orlando Sentinel* is the major local newspaper. The Friday edition of the *Sentinel* includes extensive entertainment and dining listings as does the *Sentinel*'s website, **www.orlandosentinel.com**. *Orlando Weekly* is a free, alternative paper with entertainment and art listings focused on events outside tourist areas.

Pharmacies **Walgreens**, 1003 W. Vine St. (Hwy. 192), just east of Bermuda Avenue (© **407/847-4222**), operates a 24-hour pharmacy. There's an **Eckerd Drugs** at 12125 Apopka–Vineland Rd. (© **407/238-9333**) that's open until 7pm (5pm Sun).

Post Office The post office most convenient to Disney and Universal is at 10450 Turkey Lake Rd. (© **800/275-8777**). It's open Monday through Friday from 9am to 5pm, Saturday from 9am to noon.

Radio Local stations include 101.1 FM (rock), 94.5 FM (R&B), 89.9 FM (jazz), 90.7 FM (classical), 92.3 FM (country), 580 AM (news), and 990 AM (Radio Disney).

Safety Don't let the aura of Mickey, Minnie, Donald, and Daisy allow you to relax your guard; Orlando has a crime rate that's comparable to that of other large U.S. cities. Stay alert and remain aware of your surroundings. It's a good idea to keep your valuables in a safe-deposit box (inquire at your hotel's front desk), although many hotels today are equipped with in-room safes. Keep a close eye on your valuables when you're in public places—restaurants, theaters, and airport terminals. Renting a locker is always preferable to leaving your valuables in the trunk of your car, even in the theme-park lots. Be cautious, even when in the parks (we know of at least one mom whose purse was stolen in one of the theme parks while she was busy with one of her kids), and avoid carrying large amounts of cash in a backpack or fanny pack, which could be easily accessed while you're standing in line for a ride or show.

If you're renting a car, carefully read the safety instructions that the rental company provides. Never stop for any reason in a suspicious or an unpopulated area, and remember that children should never ride in the front seat of a car equipped with air bags.

One safety issue that often comes up when families with young kids visit Orlando is that of lost kids (and it happens a lot more than most people think). If you and your family have a safety plan in place ahead of time, you'll save lots of heartache and worry. For more on this topic, see p. 25.

Taxes Florida's 6% sales tax is charged on all goods except most edible grocery items and medicines. Additionally, hotels add another 5% or 6% to your bill for a total of 11% or 12%.

Telephone Because of its growth spurt, Orlando has had to go to 10-digit dialing. If you're making a local call in Orlando's 407 area code region, even across the street, *you must dial the 407 area code followed by the number you wish to call,* for a total of 10 digits.

Weather Look for the "Weather Channel" on Bright House Cable, the local cable provider. Most hotels carry basic cable. The *Orlando Sentinel* also includes a daily forecast. You can also get weather information from the National Weather Service, 8am to 4pm, by calling ✆ **321/255-0212**. (They answer as National Weather Service in Melbourne, Florida, but after that you get an option to punch in 412 from a touch-tone phone, which plugs you into the Orlando forecast.) Also check with the Weather Channel online at **www.weatherchannel.com**.

Family-Friendly Accommodations

Unquestionably, families and kids are the real VIPs in central Florida, which has more than 110,000 rooms including scores of places located in or near the major tourist draws: Walt Disney World, Universal Orlando, SeaWorld, and the rest of International Drive. Many of these places let kids 17 and under stay free with paying adults—and some even offer free meals to preteens or roll out the red carpet in other ways!

Beautifully landscaped grounds are the rule at properties in WDW, neighboring Lake Buena Vista, Universal Orlando, and on the southern portions of I-Drive. But heavier traffic and, at times, higher prices come with those trimmings. No matter what your budget or crowd tolerance, there's something for everyone. If you're looking for an inexpensive or moderately priced motel, for instance, check out the options in Kissimmee and, to a lesser degree, on the northern end of International Drive.

Once you've decided on a date for your Orlando vacation, book your accommodations as soon as possible, especially if you want to stay at Disney or Universal. Advance reservations are a necessity if you're hunting modest or primo rooms in these areas. In addition to the individual listings in this chapter, there are several places to find discounts. **HotelKingdom.com** (© 877/766-6787 or 407/294-9600; www.hotelkingdom.com) is a good source of room or vacation rental bargains. Another good place to look is the **Orlando/Orange County Convention & Visitors Bureau** (© 800/643-9492; www.orlandoinfo.com). You can also use the Kissimmee–St. Cloud website (**www.floridakiss.com**) or call © 800/333-5477.

1 Choosing Your Orlando Hotel

There seemed to be no end to Orlando's hotel boom a few years ago. About 4,000 new rooms were added every year through 2000. Disney alone has 29 (soon to be 30) resorts, timeshares, and "official" hotels with more than 27,000 rooms and 784 campsites at Fort Wilderness. That's about 25% of the area's roster. But America's bruised economy and the September 11, 2001, terrorist attacks dealt the Mouse a major setback that lingers on. Disney's planned Pop Century resort would have added a whopping 5,760 rooms in the spring of 2002, but its opening was delayed until December 2003.

Still, Orlando's tourist-based economy is slowly recovering. Two major properties—a Ritz-Carlton and a neighboring JW Marriott—opened in mid-2003, and others, such as the Omni Orlando Resort, are on the horizon.

In this section, we'll help give you the tools to choose the ideal hotel for your family vacation in Orlando. We discuss options for saving money on room rates, outline common amenities at Orlando hotels that will appeal to families, give details on discount hotel packages, and—most important of all when looking for a hotel in Orlando—the pros and cons of staying at a Walt Disney World resort.

SAVING MONEY ON HOTEL RATES

All of the rates cited in the following pages are "rack rates." That means they're typical prices listed in the hotel brochures or the ones hotel clerks give by rote over the telephone. ***Don't pay them!*** You almost always can negotiate a better price through package deals, by assuring the clerks they can do better, or by mentioning you belong to one of several organizations that get a discount, such as AAA, AARP, or a labor union. Even your credit card might get you a **5% to 10% discount** at larger chains. (Disney and the other lodging players have been a little more willing to cut rates since occupancy fell drastically following the events of Sept 11, 2001, but that bonus may disappear as hotels and motels begin to fill up again.) Any discount you get will help ease the impact of local resort taxes, which aren't included in the quoted rates. *These taxes add 11% to 12% depending on where you're staying.*

The **average, undiscounted hotel rate** for the Orlando area is about $110 per night double, and that rate in good times climbs 5% a year. The lowest rates at WDW are those at the All-Star resorts, which, depending on the season, run from $77 to $124. They're pricier than comparable rooms in the outside world; they're tiny, basic, and tacky, too, but they *are on Disney soil* and your kids will probably love the visual overload (though you may not).

Walt Disney World's value seasons (read: lowest rates) are available from just after New Year's to mid-February, late August through September (except Labor Day weekend), and early November to mid-December (excluding Thanksgiving week). Regular season rates are available from late April to late August and throughout October. Peak rates—the high ones—are around from mid-February to late April and during the December holiday season.

If you're not renting a car or staying at a Walt Disney World or Universal resort, be sure to ask when booking your room if the hotel or motel offers **transportation to the theme parks** and, if so, whether there's a charge. (You'll find this in our listings, but things sometimes change.) Some hotels and motels offer free service with their own shuttles. Others use Mears Transportation (see "Getting Around," in chapter 3). Rates can be $15 or more per person round-trip (some hotels make these arrangements for you; others require you to do it). On the other hand, if you have a car or pickup, expect to pay $7 or $8 a day to park it at Disney, Universal, and SeaWorld.

If you stay at a WDW resort or one of Disney's "official" hotels, transportation is complimentary within WDW. For more information on this and the other advantages (and disadvantages) of staying at Disney properties, see "The Perks & Downsides of Staying with Mickey," below.

In or out of Walt Disney World, if you book your hotel as part of a **package** (see "Package Deals for Families," in chapter 2, for more details), you'll likely enjoy some kind of savings. Call the **Walt Disney Travel Company** at ☎ **800/828-0228** or head online to **www.disneyworld.com** to book resort packages or hotel rooms at WDW.

Outside Disney, you may be quoted a rate better than the rack rates contained in the following listings. Even then, try to bargain, especially with privately owned hotels. When it comes to big chains, discounts are a bit more elusive. When dealing on a national level, you'll find some; on the local level, clerks usually lack incentives to fill rooms, but try anyway. Also, no matter what your

⎛Value⎞ Staying for Less

Although many folks participate in the airlines' frequent-flier programs, not many take advantage of the major hotel chains' frequent-stay clubs. Even if you don't stay in a hotel for more than your yearly vacation, you may be able to realize savings by joining its program.

Like the airlines' scheme, some hotels let you build points for staying at a participating property, dining in its restaurant, or using some other service. Although programs vary, points can be traded for free nights, discounted rates, special perks, or, in some cases, frequent-flier miles. And the price to join is right—it's free. And just joining a hotel club may make you eligible for discounts, give you express check-in and checkout privileges, and provide free breakfasts, local calls, or a morning newspaper.

Here are a few frequent-stay programs that offer perks to travelers:

- **Six Continents Hotels Priority Club** (℅ 800/272-9273; www.priority club.com) covers the Inter-Continental Resorts, Crowne Plaza hotels and resorts, Holiday Inns, and Staybridge Suites. Priority Club members get express check-in, access to discounted rates at select hotels, and other perks. Freebies vary according to hotel but often include breakfast, local phone calls, and/or parking.
- **Choice Hotels International Choice Privileges** program (℅ 888/770-6800; www.guestprivileges.com) covers Sleep, Quality, Comfort, and Clarion properties. Participants receive perks such as express check-in, special rates, room upgrades based on availability, extended checkout times, and free local calls and newspapers.
- **Hyatt Hotel's Gold Passport** program (℅ 800/304-9288; www.gold passport.com) gives members a private reservation phone number and express check-in, complimentary newspapers, and access to the hotel's fitness center. You'll also receive special offers and discounted rates from select Hyatt properties.
- **Hilton HHonors Worldwide** program (℅ 800/548-8690; www.hiltonh honors.com) covers Hilton, Conrad, DoubleTree, Embassy Suites, Hampton Inn, and Homewood Suites properties. It offers expedited check-in, a dedicated reservation line, late checkout, and a free daily newspaper.

Other frequent-stay programs include **Starwood Hotels Preferred Guest** (℅ 888/625-4988; www.starwood.com/preferredguest) and **Marriott Rewards** (℅ 801/468-4000; www.marriottrewards.com).

landing zone, try again when you arrive. But we don't recommend coming without a reservation, and taking chances on your negotiating skills and room availability. This works in some places (and we give you some local options later in this chapter), but Orlando is a year-round destination. It has a heavy convention and business trade, and school lets out during varying times of the year in other countries. If you come without a reservation, you may face leftovers.

Ask about discounts for students, government employees, seniors, military, firefighters, police, AFL-CIO, corporate clients, and, again, AARP or AAA.

Special discounts and packages may also be featured on hotel websites, especially those of the larger chains.

HOTEL RATES IN THIS CHAPTER

The hotels listed in this chapter are categorized by location and price. As you might expect, many of the inexpensive properties are the farthest from the action and/or have the most spartan accommodations.

Keep in mind, however, that this isn't one of the world's best bargain destinations. Unlike other Florida tourist areas, there are few under-$60 motels that meet the standards demanded for listing in this book. That's why we've raised the price bar. The ones in our **inexpensive** category charge an average of less than $90 per night for a double room. Those offering $90 to $180 rooms are in the **moderate** category; $181 to $250 rooms are listed as **expensive;** and anything over $250 is **very expensive.** Any included extras (such as breakfast) are listed for each property. Orlando has peak and off seasons, often with complicated boundaries. Even remote things such as Bike Week in Daytona Beach or the International Sweet Potato Growers convention in Orlando can raise prices. These events especially impact moderately priced properties outside WDW.

Our rack rates are per night double unless otherwise noted, and don't include hotel taxes of 11% to 12%. Also, most Orlando hotels and motels let **kids under 12 (and usually under 18) stay free** with a parent or guardian if you don't exceed maximum room occupancy. But to be safe, verify when booking a room.

RESERVATION SERVICES

Many of the hotels listed under "Places to Stay in the Kissimmee Area," found later in this chapter, can be booked through the **Kissimmee–St. Cloud Convention & Visitors Bureau** (© 800/333-5477; www.floridakiss.com). The same goes for Orlando and the **Orlando/Orange County Convention & Visitors Bureau** (© 800/643-9492; www.orlandoinfo.com).

Florida Hotel Network (© 800/293-2419; www.floridahotels.com), **Central Reservation Service** (© 800/555-7555 or 407/740-6442; www.crshotels.com), and **Hotels.com** (© 800/246-8357; www.hotels.com) are three other services that can help with room reservations and other kinds of reservations in central Florida. You can also book Walt Disney World hotels direct by calling © 800/828-0228 or 407/934-7639, or visiting www.disneyworld.com; Universal Orlando's properties can be booked by calling © 800/837-2273 or 407/363-8000, or surfing over to www.universalorlando.com.

HOTEL AMENITIES FOR FAMILIES

In the "Amenities" section of the accommodations descriptions that follow, we mention **concierge levels** where available. In these hotels within a hotel, guests pay more to enjoy a luxurious private lounge (sometimes with great views), free continental or full breakfasts, hot and cold hors d'oeuvres served at cocktail

---

Tips Tight Squeeze

An average hotel or motel room in Orlando has 325 to 400 square feet and two beds for four people. It's hardly a castle, but most travelers find that adequate for a short stay. We've made a special note in the listings of properties where the rooms are substantially larger or smaller than that average.

hour, and/or late-night cordials and pastries. Rooms are usually on higher floors, and guests are pampered with special services (including private registration and checkout, a personal concierge, and nightly bed turndown) and amenities (upgraded toiletries, bathroom scales, terry robes, hair dryers, and/or more). The free food may make these rooms more economical for families than one might otherwise think (especially if you're staying in a hotel where breakfast isn't included in the rate). Ask for specifics when you reserve a room.

You'll also find counselor-supervised **child-care** or **activity centers** at some hotels. Very popular in Orlando, these can be marvelous, creatively run facilities that might offer movies, video games, arts and crafts, storytelling, puppet shows, indoor and outdoor activities, and more. Some provide meals and/or have beds where a child can sleep while you're out on the town. Check individual hotel listings for these facilities.

THE PERKS & DOWNSIDES OF STAYING WITH MICKEY

The decision on whether to bunk with the Mouse is one of the first you'll have to make when planning an Orlando vacation and you'll probably get a strong pro-WDW argument from any younger kids in your family. In the sections "Places to Stay in Walt Disney World" and "'Official' Hotels in Lake Buena Vista" of this chapter, you'll find information on the hotels, villas, timeshares, and campsites that are owned by Disney or are "official" hotels—those that are privately owned but have earned Disney's seal of approval. All 30, including one that should open in 2004, are in WDW or nearby Lake Buena Vista.

In addition to their proximity to the theme parks, there are other advantages to staying at a Disney property or one of the "official" hotels. The following amenities are included at all Disney resorts, and **some** are offered by the "official" hotels, but make sure to ask when booking:

- Unlimited **free** transportation on the Walt Disney World Transportation System's buses, monorails, ferries, or water taxis to and from the four WDW parks, from 2 hours prior to opening until 2 hours after closing. Free transportation also is provided to and from Downtown Disney West Side and Pleasure Island, Downtown Disney Marketplace, Typhoon Lagoon, Blizzard Beach, and the WDW resorts. Three of them—the Polynesian, Grand Floridian, and Contemporary resorts—are on the Disney monorail system. This included service can save money you might otherwise spend on a rental car, parking (note, however, that parking is free if you stay at a Disney resort), and shuttles. It also means you're guaranteed admission to all of the parks, even during peak times when parking lots sometimes fill up.
- Reduced-price **children's menus** in many restaurants.
- **Character** breakfasts, lunches, and/or dinners at some restaurants.
- TVs equipped with the Disney Channel, **nightly bedtime stories** (Channel 22, 7–10pm, audio only), and WDW information stations.
- The **Extra Magic Hour** (see the box "The Early Bird . . .," below).
- A guest services desk where you can buy tickets to all Disney parks and attractions and get information without standing in long lines at the parks.
- Playing privileges, preferred tee times, and, in some cases, free transportation to Disney golf courses (see "Hitting the Links," in chapter 8).
- WDW has some of the **best swimming pools** in Orlando and recently has built new ones or remodeled old ones as zero-entry or zero-grade pools, meaning there's a gradual slope into the water on at least one side rather than

only a step down. These include pools at the Grand Floridian, Animal Kingdom, and Polynesian resorts.

- Mears shuttle service (see "Getting There," in chapter 2) access for trips to non-Disney parks and attractions (fees vary), including the **Kennedy Space Center** (see chapter 11).
- On-premises National car-rental discounts (also available at the Walt Disney World Swan and Dolphin, but not at the other "official" hotels).
- The ability to purchase reduced-price **Ultimate Parkhopper** passes for the length of your stay. (Available at all "official" hotels as well.) The passes can offer some significant savings. See p. 149 for details on Disney's passes.
- Disney's **refillable mug program** lets you buy—for around $11—a bottomless mug for soda, coffee, tea, and/or cocoa at its resorts. The offer is for the length of your stay, but it isn't transferable to the theme parks and you can only use it at the property at which it is bought.

But there are also **disadvantages** to entering Mickey's boudoir:

- The complimentary **Walt Disney World Transportation System** can be *excruciatingly slow.* Sometimes you have to take a ferry to catch a bus to get on the monorail to reach your hotel. It can take an eternity to get to a place that's right across the lagoon from you. And, to add insult to injury, some resort bus stops are a considerable hike from the park entrances, so your family's aching feet will be subjected to even more torture at the end of the day. Keep this in mind if there are fidgety kids or adults in your party.
- Resort rates are about **20% to 30% higher** than comparable hotels and motels away from the parks.
- Without a car or another means to get off the property, you'll be a POD (Prisoner of Disney) and WDW's stiff prices for meals, trinkets, and more.
- If you don't spend a little time away from the Wizard of Diz, you'll miss the real Florida.
- Mickey, MICKEY, MICKEY . . . eek! The mouse can get old after a few days, unless you take a break. (Admittedly, your kids will have less problem with this issue than you will.)

WALT DISNEY WORLD CENTRAL RESERVATIONS OFFICE & WALT DISNEY TRAVEL COMPANY

To book a room or package at Disney's resorts, campgrounds, and "official" hotels, call the **Walt Disney World Travel Company** at ℂ **800/828-0228.** You also can contact **Central Reservation Operations (CRO)**, P.O. Box 10000, Lake Buena Vista, FL 32830-1000 (ℂ **407/934-7639**).

CRO and the Travel Company can recommend rooms suited to your budget and needs, such as being near a particular park, those with supervised child-care, or a pool large enough to swim laps. They can even recommend rooms on a particular resort that are closer to the pools or food courts. But the folks who answer

⌐Tips The Early Bird . . .

In October 2002, WDW launched its **Extra Magic Hour,** which lets resort guests into the parks an hour before other guests. At press time, the schedule was: Magic Kingdom, Sunday and Thursday; Animal Kingdom, Monday and Friday; Disney–MGM Studios, Tuesday and Saturday; and Epcot, Wednesday.

> ⌒ *Tips* **Web Surfing in Walt Disney World**
>
> WDW has installed phones with large touch screens and Internet capacity at 65 locations in the theme parks, resorts, and elsewhere. For 25¢ a minute (4-min. minimum), you can use them to check e-mail, surf the Web, and make dining reservations from places such as the Magic Kingdom's Pirates of the Caribbean or Splash Mountain.

the phones usually don't volunteer information about a better deal or a special *unless you ask.*

Be sure to inquire about Disney's numerous package plans, which can include meals, tickets, recreation, and other features. The right package can save you money and time; but having a comprehensive game plan first is helpful in computing the cost of your vacation in advance. This is especially true if you're traveling with more than one child and plan to stay in only one room—the cost per person will usually drop quite a bit on a package deal.

CRO and the Travel Company can give you information about various theme-park ticket options, the airlines, and car rentals. They can also make dinner-show reservations for you at the resort of your choice.

OTHER SOURCES FOR HOTEL PACKAGES

In addition to the Disney sources above, there are several other travel companies that offer packages utilizing Disney resorts. These include **Delta Vacations** (© **800/872-7786;** www.deltavacations.com), **American Airlines Vacations** (© **800/321-2121;** www.aavacations.com), and **Continental Airlines Vacations** (© **800/301-3800;** www.coolvacations.com). Give each a call, ask for brochures, and compare offerings to find the best package for you. See "Package Deals for Families," in chapter 2, for more information on available packages.

On a slightly smaller scale than Disney, **Universal Orlando** offers several travel packages that can include resort stays, VIP access to the parks, discounts to other Orlando attractions, and cruises. One major perk that Universal Resort guests get that Disney simply can't provide given the size of its hotels is front-of-the-line access to most major rides in the Universal theme parks. This is a big plus for families with preteens and teens whose patience is zero but willingness to ride stomach-churning coasters is infinite. Airfare and car rentals are also available. You can book a package by calling © **888/322-5537** or 407/224-7000. On the Internet, visit **www.universalstudiosvacations.com**.

2 Places to Stay in Walt Disney World

The resorts in this part are Disney-owned or "official" Disney hotels with some of the same perks. All are on the Disney Transportation System, which means those of you who don't mind being entombed in Mouseville can do without a car.

If you decide Disney is your destination, come up with a short list of preferred places to stay, then call **Walt Disney World Travel Company** (© **800/828-0228**) or WDW **Central Reservations** (© **407/934-7639**) for rates. Web wanderers can get information at **www.disneyworld.com**.

If you come by auto you will see big signs along all of the major roads on Disney property pointing the way to the various resorts. You'll find these hotels listed on the map, "Walt Disney World & Lake Buena Vista Accommodations,"

Walt Disney World & Lake Buena Vista Accommodations

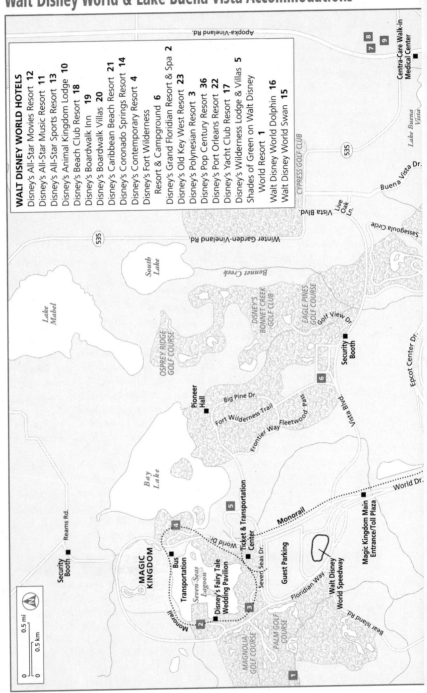

WALT DISNEY WORLD HOTELS

Disney's All-Star Movies Resort **12**
Disney's All-Star Music Resort **11**
Disney's All-Star Sports Resort **13**
Disney's Animal Kingdom Lodge **10**
Disney's Beach Club Resort **18**
Disney's Boardwalk Inn **19**
Disney's Boardwalk Villas **20**
Disney's Caribbean Beach Resort **21**
Disney's Coronado Springs Resort **14**
Disney's Contemporary Resort **4**
Disney's Fort Wilderness
   Resort & Campground **6**
Disney's Grand Floridian Resort & Spa **2**
Disney's Old Key West Resort **23**
Disney's Polynesian Resort **3**
Disney's Pop Century Resort **36**
Disney's Port Orleans Resort **22**
Disney's Yacht Club Resort **17**
Disney's Wilderness Lodge & Villas **5**
Shades of Green on Walt Disney
   World Resort **1**
Walt Disney World Dolphin **16**
Walt Disney World Swan **15**

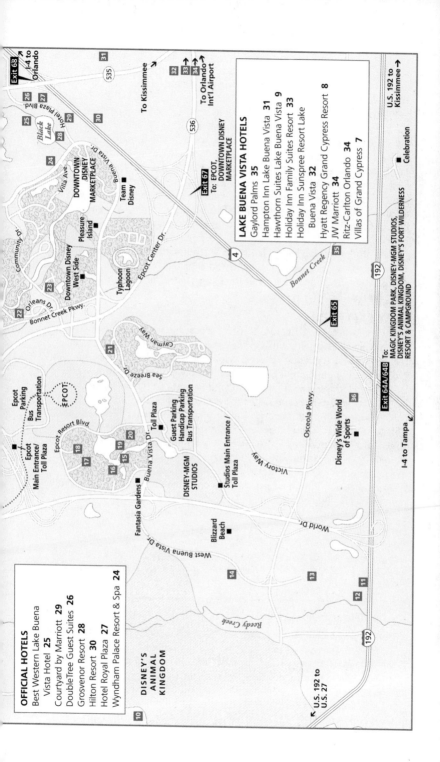

OFFICIAL HOTELS
Best Western Lake Buena Vista Hotel **25**
Courtyard by Marriott **29**
DoubleTree Guest Suites **26**
Grosvenor Resort **28**
Hilton Resort **30**
Hotel Royal Plaza **27**
Wyndham Palace Resort & Spa **24**

LAKE BUENA VISTA HOTELS
Gaylord Palms **35**
Hampton Inn Lake Buena Vista **31**
Hawthorn Suites Lake Buena Vista **9**
Holiday Inn Family Suites Resort **33**
Holiday Inn Sunspree Resort Lake Buena Vista **32**
Hyatt Regency Grand Cypress Resort **8**
JW Marriott **34**
Ritz-Carlton Orlando **34**
Villas of Grand Cypress **7**

DISNEY'S ANIMAL KINGDOM

DISNEY-MGM STUDIOS

DOWNTOWN DISNEY MARKETPLACE

Downtown Disney West Side

Pleasure Island

Team Disney

Typhoon Lagoon

Blizzard Beach

Fantasia Gardens

EPCOT

Epcot Main Entrance/ Toll Plaza

Epcot Parking Bus Transportation

Epcot Resort Blvd

Buena Vista Dr.

West Buena Vista Dr.

Studios Main Entrance / Toll Plaza

Guest Parking Handicap Parking Bus Transportation

Guest Parking

Sea Breeze Dr.

Cayman Way

Bonnet Creek Pkwy.

Orleans Dr.

Community Dr.

Villa Ave.

Buena Vista Dr.

Hotel Plaza Blvd.

Black Lake

Epcot Center Dr.

Bonnet Creek

Osceola Pkwy.

Victory Way

World Dr.

Reedy Creek

Disney's Wide World of Sports

Celebration

Exit 68 ↗ I-4 to Orlando

Exit 67 To: EPCOT, DOWNTOWN DISNEY MARKETPLACE

Exit 65

Exit 64A/64B To: MAGIC KINGDOM PARK, DISNEY-MGM STUDIOS, DISNEY'S ANIMAL KINGDOM, DISNEY'S FORT WILDERNESS RESORT & CAMPGROUND

I-4 to Tampa

U.S. 192 to U.S. 27 ↙

U.S. 192 to Kissimmee →

To Kissimmee ↗

To Orlando→ Int'l Airport →

535

536

4

192

on p. 68. If you couldn't resist bringing along Fido or Fluffy, resort guests can board their pets overnight at the kennels at the Transportation & Ticket Center on Seven Seas Drive, near Disney's Polynesian Resort (pets are not allowed in WDW hotels!).

Prices in the following listings reflect the range available at each resort when this guide was published. Rates vary depending on season and room location, but the numbers should help you determine which places fit your budget.

Kid's Night Out (☎ **407/827-5444**) provides **babysitting** services at all Disney resorts. The **supervised kids' clubs** listed at the Animal Kingdom, Beach Club, Contemporary, Grand Floridian, and Polynesian resorts are open to all guests. Disney advises parents to reserve spots for their kids in the clubs well in advance by calling ☎ **407/WDW-DINE** (reservations can be made up to 60 days in advance). To qualify for entrance into the club, kids must be at least 4 years of age and toilet-trained.

Note: **Rollaway beds** aren't available at WDW resorts; **cribs** are at no charge. If you're carrying medications or other kid stuff that needs to be kept cool, **refrigerators** can be rented at all of the Disney hotels for a charge of $10 per day, plus tax.

VERY EXPENSIVE

Disney's Beach Club Resort ★ This retreat, located near Epcot (a tram from the hotel takes you straight to the park's International Gateway entrance), tries to mimic a luxurious Victorian Cape Cod resort (the decor scheme will probably be lost on the young ones), though the Victorian gem in this world is the Grand Floridian (see below). What your kids will be thrilled about is Stormalong Bay, a huge free-form swimming pool and water park, that sprawls over 3 acres between this resort and its sister, the Yacht Club (later in this chapter). One of the best at Walt Disney World, it features a 150-foot serpentine **water slide and a kids' pool** area, 2- to 3-feet deep, for little ones. Room views range from the pool (more expensive) to the parking lot. Some rooms have balconies.

The **Sandcastle Club** features activities, entertainment, a meal, and a snack for youngsters ($10 per hour per child, 2-hr. minimum, ages 4–12, 4:30pm–midnight). The Beach Club also offers the chance to charter a reproduction of a 1930s mahogany runabout to cruise Crescent Lake or see Epcot's Illumi-Nations fireworks display ($179.24 plus tax for 30 min. for up to seven people). Call ☎ **407/824-2621** or 407/939-7529 for information.

1800 Epcot Resorts Blvd. (off Buena Vista Dr.; P.O. Box 10000), Lake Buena Vista, FL 32830-0100. ☎ 407/934-7639 or 407/934-8000. Fax 407/934-3850. www.disneyworld.com. 583 units. $289–$660 double;

Tips New Arrival

Disney's **Beach Club Villas** (☎ 407/934-7639 or 407/934-2175; fax 407/934-3850; www.disneyworld.com) make up a resort inspired by Cape May seaside homes of the early 20th century. The 208-room resort ($289–$449 studios, $390–$1,010 villas) is a member of the Disney Vacation Club, the timeshare division that rents studios and one- and two-bedroom villas to mainstream guests when their owners are not staying on property. It's a great option for large families who might otherwise have to get two hotel rooms at a regular Disney resort. The villas are close to Epcot's International Gateway.

$495–$2,110 suite. Extra person $25. Children 17 and under stay free in parent's room. Rollaway beds not available, cribs free. AE, DC, DISC, MC, V. Free self-parking, $6 valet. Take I-4 east to Exit 67, Hwy. 536/Epcot Center Dr. Follow signs to WDW, then to the resort. Pets $9 a night. **Amenities:** 2 restaurants; grill; 4 lounges; 2 outdoor heated pools; kids' pool; 2 lighted tennis courts; Jacuzzi; watersports equipment; children's club; arcade; playground; WDW Transportation System, transportation for a fee to non-Disney theme parks; business center; salon; 24-hr. room service; babysitting; guest laundry; nonsmoking rooms. *In room:* A/C, TV, dataport, minibar, fridge ($10 a night), hair dryer, iron, safe.

Disney's Boardwalk Inn ★★★

Romantics usually appreciate staying at (or at least visiting) Disney's plush 1940s-style "seaside" resort, set on 45 acres along Crescent Lake, near Epcot. It's a place to recapture a little bit of yesterday, whether that means kicking back in a rocker overlooking a village green or prowling the shops, restaurants, and clubs that line the resort's ¼-mile boardwalk, which really heats up after the sun goes down. That alone should tell you this is not necessarily the best place for you if you have really young kids (though you'll see plenty of them here anyway). Families with older kids and teens (who will like the posh surroundings and the ESPN club) will do just fine. Rooms are Cape Cod style; some have balconies, and corner units have a bit more space. The priciest rooms overlook the boardwalk (which has **midway-style games** for a fee) or pool; the less expensive ones overlook the parking lot but are sheltered from the boardwalk noise (good if your family is full of light sleepers). Hang on to your swimsuit if you hit the pool's **200-foot "keister coaster"** water slide, which is very popular with kids. (The pool also has spraying fountains.)

Note: There is no kids' club at this hotel, so if you want to hit the Boardwalk's clubs after dark and have kids too young to be left asleep in the room, you'll need to hire a babysitter. During the day, guests can use the facilities at the Yacht and Beach Clubs.

2101 N. Epcot Resorts Blvd. (off Buena Vista Dr.; P.O. Box 10000), Lake Buena Vista, FL 32830-1000. ℂ 407/934-7639 or 407/939-5100. Fax 407/934-5150. www.disneyworld.com. 378 units. $289–$675 double; $545–$2,340 suite. Extra person $25. Children 17 and under stay free in parent's room. Rollaway beds not available, cribs free. AE, DC, DISC, MC, V. Free self-parking, valet $6. Take I-4 east to Exit 67, Hwy. 536/Epcot Center Dr. Follow signs to WDW, then to the resort. Pets $9 a night. **Amenities:** 3 restaurants; groceries; grill; 2 lounges; 3 clubs; 2 outdoor heated pools; kids' pool; 2 lighted tennis courts; croquet; health club; Jacuzzi; children's activity center; 2 arcades; playground; concierge; WDW Transportation System, transportation to non-Disney parks for a fee; business center; shopping arcade; 24-hr. room service; babysitting; guest laundry; valet; nonsmoking rooms; concierge-level rooms. *In room:* A/C, TV, dataport, fridge ($10 a night), hair dryer, iron, safe.

Disney's Boardwalk Villas ★★

Located on the same site as the Boardwalk Inn, the villas are an out-of-the-mainstream option that may make sense for those traveling in larger groups. Sold as timeshares, they're also rented to traditional tourists. Rooms range from standard-size studios to 1-, 2-, and 3-bedroom villas (the latter with 2,100 sq. ft. and beds for 12). Most have a balcony or patio and the same trimmings as the Boardwalk Inn, above. (They also share the same amenities.) Larger rooms have kitchens or kitchenettes, a good feature for those who want to prepare food or formula for kids. The service is great, the location near Epcot is convenient, and the spacious rooms are nice for families traveling together.

2101 N. Epcot Resorts Blvd. (off Buena Vista Dr.; P.O. Box 10000), Lake Buena Vista, FL 32830-1000. ℂ 407/934-7639 or 407/939-5100. Fax 407/934-5150. www.disneyworld.com. 520 units. Studios $289–$434; villas $385-$1,865. Extra person $25. Children 17 and under stay free in parent's room. Rollaway beds not available, cribs free. AE, DC, DISC, MC, V. Free self-parking, $6 valet. Take I-4 east to Exit 67, Hwy. 536/Epcot Center Dr. Follow signs to WDW, then to the resort. Pets $9 a night. **Amenities:** 3 restaurants (steak/seafood, Mediterranean); groceries; grill; 2 lounges; 3 clubs; 2 outdoor heated pools; kids' pool; 2 lighted tennis courts;

Tips **Sink Space**

Disney's resort rooms have notoriously cramped bathrooms (shutting the door with one person standing inside can require the skills of a contortionist). Bathing kids will be something of a challenge as well. The good news: Most rooms sport double sinks, usually set in a small dressing area outside the bathroom. (All-Star resorts have singles.) So while you may bang your shin on the shower, you won't have to wait in line to brush your teeth.

---

croquet; health club; Jacuzzi; children's activity center; 2 arcades; playground; concierge; WDW Transportation System, transportation to non-Disney parks for a fee; business center; shopping arcade; 24-hr. room service; babysitting; guest laundry; valet; nonsmoking rooms; concierge-level rooms. *In room:* A/C, TV, dataport, kitchenette, fridge, coffeemaker, hair dryer, iron, safe, microwave.

Disney's Contemporary Resort 🦆 If location is one of your priorities, it's hard to beat this aging Disney hotel, which is right beside the Magic Kingdom, and one of only three resorts **on the monorail system** (the Grand Floridian and Polynesian are the others). The Contemporary also offers great views of the Magic Kingdom and Seven Seas Lagoon from its west side and Bay Lake on its east. But know that this 15-story A-frame dates to WDW's infancy, and a complete renovation in 1999 didn't fully restore it to the same class as some of the top dogs in this price category. Room decor tends to be a bit dull, and the pool is nothing special (there is, however, a wading pool for toddlers). On the plus side, the rooms can fit up to five people instead of the usual four (though space will be tight). Kids love the **Mouseketeer Clubhouse,** which offers activities, entertainment, a meal, and refreshments ($10 per hour per child, 2-hr. minimum, ages 4–12, 4:30pm–midnight). Other kids facilities include a playground with a sandbox and a pretty decent arcade.

Our verdict: There are lots of child facilities, but it's still wiser to ride the monorail through—yes, it goes straight through the resort (a fact most kids find very cool)—and get better value for your dollars elsewhere. If you do bunk here, avoid the Garden Wing rooms and stick to the upper-floor Tower Rooms, which have nicer views and are a tad quieter than the lower-floor rooms exposed to noisy public areas and the monorail.

4600 N. World Dr. (P.O. Box 10000), Lake Buena Vista, FL 32830-1000. © **407/934-7639** or 407/824-1000. Fax 407/824-3539. www.disneyworld.com. 1,008 units. $239–$545 double; $820–$2,405 suite. Extra person $25. Children 17 and under stay free in parent's room. Rollaway beds not available; cribs free. AE, DC, DISC, MC, V. Free self-parking, $6 valet. Take I-4 east to Exit 67, Hwy. 536/Epcot Center Dr. Follow signs to WDW, then to the resort. Pets $9 a night. **Amenities:** 3 restaurants (steak, New American, buffet); food court; 2 lounges; outdoor heated pool; kids' pool; 6 lighted tennis courts; fitness center; Jacuzzi; watersports equipment; kids' club; arcade; playground; concierge; WDW Transportation System, transportation to non-Disney parks for a fee; business center; salon; 24-hr. room service; babysitting; guest laundry; valet; nonsmoking rooms; concierge-level rooms. *In room:* A/C, TV, dataport, fridge ($10 a night), hair dryer, iron, safe.

Disney's Grand Floridian Resort & Spa 🦆🦆🦆 *Moments* From the moment you step into the opulent five-story domed lobby of this Victorian-themed resort, you'll feel as if you've slipped back to an era that started with the late 19th century and lasted through the Roaring '20s. Close to the Magic Kingdom, the property is one of three on the monorail system. It has become the romantic choice for couples, especially honeymooners, who like luxuriating in the first-class spa and health club—the best in WDW. But fear not if you're toting along children. Though it's admittedly not the most popular place to stay for families with young kids, the Floridian does get its share of them and has a number of special options for kids.

The inviting Victorian-style rooms overlook a garden, pool, courtyard, or the Seven Seas Lagoon. The standard rooms are large enough to fit five; the dormer and Lodge Tower rooms can fit only four. Cribs, highchairs, and playpens are free of charge to guests, though you may have trouble fitting them in your room all at once. If you ask in advance, your kids will even find child-size bathrobes waiting for them in your room.

The pool here is nice enough, though not exceptional. The **Mouseketeer Clubhouse** features activities, entertainment, a meal, and a snack ($10 per hour per child, 2-hr. minimum, ages 4–12, 4:30pm–midnight). Older children might enjoy a chance to partake of a formal afternoon tea, which costs $24.50 per person and is served in the Garden View Lounge from 2 to 6pm (be sure to reserve a spot well in advance by calling (℃ **407/WDW-DINE**).

The hotel also offers a trio of special **Grand Adventure programs** for young children, and smaller special activities are usually offered as well. On Disney's Pirate Cruise Adventure, potty-trained children ages 4 to 10 depart from the Grand Floridian Marina to visit exotic "ports of call" to follow clues and collect "buried treasure." Most kids will have a jolly good time. It's offered Monday, Wednesday, and Thursday from 9:30 to 11:30am and the $28.17 price tag includes lunch. For information on the resort's two culinary-themed Adventure programs, see "Pint-Size Food Experiences" on p. 124.

4401 Floridian Way (P.O. Box 10000), Lake Buena Vista, FL 32830-1000. (℃ **407/934-7639** or 407/824-3000. Fax 407/824-3186. www.disneyworld.com. 867 units. $339–$840 double; $900–$2,450 suite. Extra person $25. Children 17 and under stay free in parent's room. Rollaway beds not available, cribs free. AE, DC, DISC, MC, V. Free self-parking, $6 valet. Take I-4 east to Exit 67, Hwy. 536/Epcot Center Dr. Follow signs to WDW, then to the resort. Pets $9 a night. **Amenities:** 5 restaurants (American, seafood); grill; 3 lounges; outdoor heated pool; kids' pool; 2 lighted tennis courts; health club; spa; watersports equipment; children's center; arcade; playground; concierge; car-rental desk; WDW Transportation System, transportation to non-Disney parks for a fee; business center; shopping arcade; salon; 24-hr. room service; babysitting; guest laundry; valet; nonsmoking rooms; concierge-level rooms. In room: A/C, TV, dataport, minibar, fridge ($10 a night), hair dryer, iron, safe.

Disney's Old Key West Resort ⟨★⟩

An understated theme (at least by Disney standards) makes the Old Key West a good choice for those not into gingerbread overload, though we've heard some complaints about slow Disney transportation to and from this resort (you're better off with a rental car). This resort, located between Epcot and Downtown Disney West Side, offers some of the quietest, homiest rooms on WDW property. Architecturally mirroring Key West at the turn of the 20th century, Old Key West is affiliated with the Disney Vacation Club—a timeshare program—but many units are rented when not being used by owners. The 156-acre complex has tree-lined brick walkways edged by

---

(Moments A Piece of Yesterday, Today

The *Grand 1*, the Grand Floridian's 44-foot yacht, is available for hire for groups of 2 to 12. It cruises Seven Seas Lagoon and Bay Lake, where in the evenings you can see the Magic Kingdom's Wishes fireworks display or arrange a gourmet-dinner cruise. Voyages are $350 per hour including a captain and deck hand ((℃ **407/824-2439**).

white picket fences. Two-bedroom villas have beds for eight; grand villas (2,202 sq. ft.) sleep 12. Villas have whirlpool tubs. All of the accommodations sport balconies or patios, and all have kitchens or kitchenettes. The extra space and the kitchenettes make this a good bet for large families. There's no child-care available on the premises, but you can use the kids' clubs at other Disney resorts. Daily activities for both kids and adults are usually offered, and there's a playground and arcade.

Warning: Old Key West has no lifeguards at any of its pools and parents must accompany their kids to the pool at all times.

1510 N. Cove Rd. (off Community Dr.; P.O. Box 10000), Lake Buena Vista, FL 32830-1000. 🕐 407/934-7639 or 407/827-7700. Fax 407/827-7710. www.disneyworld.com. 761 units. $254–$369 studio; $340–$775 1- and 2-bedroom villas; $1,040–$1,460 grand villa. Call for extra adults. Children 17 and under stay free in parent's room. Rollaway beds not available, cribs free. AE, DC, DISC, MC, V. Free self-parking. Take I-4 east to Exit 67, Hwy. 536/Epcot Center Dr. Follow signs to WDW, then to the resort. Pets $9 a night. **Amenities:** Restaurant (American); groceries; 4 outdoor heated pools; kids' pool with sand playground; 3 tennis courts (2 lighted); Jacuzzi; sauna; watersports equipment; 2 game rooms; WDW Transportation System, transportation to non-Disney parks for a fee; massage; babysitting; guest laundry; nonsmoking rooms. *In room:* A/C, TV, kitchen or kitchenette, fridge, coffeemaker, hair dryer, microwave.

Disney's Polynesian Resort ⭐

Just south of the Magic Kingdom, the 25-acre Polynesian Resort bears some similarity to the South Pacific (tropical foliage, luaus, and waterfalls), but there's no denying this is Disney World thanks to Mickey's minions scurrying hither and yon. (And the monorail, which stops here, is a dead giveaway as well.) The resort's extensive play areas (including a water-themed one) and themed swimming pools make it a good choice for those traveling with kids (who usually find the resort agreeably exotic). The Volcano pool featuring a water slide and underwater jets is a major hit with kids, though it can get crowded. Public areas have canvas cabanas, hammocks, and big swings overlooking a 200-acre lagoon.

Most rooms (spread across three-story "longhouses") accommodate five; the resort will provide highchairs, playpens, and bed rails in your room upon request. Concierge rooms at this resort come with a free fridge. If your kids are young and don't have much stamina, you might want to request a room closest to the Great Ceremonial House, where the resorts' restaurants, shops, and monorail station are located. Some rooms here offer child-pleasing views of Cinderella Castle (for a price, of course), so request your desired view when making your reservation. Families with allergy-sufferers or smoke-sensitive individuals should request a room in one of the resorts smoke-free buildings. The main knock against this resort: The guest rooms aren't much different than when they opened in the 1970s, making them well located but overpriced for what's inside.

Kids who enroll in the **Neverland Club** get activities, entertainment, movies, free video games, a meal, and a snack ($10 per hour per child, 2-hr. minimum, ages 4–12, 4pm–midnight). Advance reservations for the kids' club are an absolute must and can be made by calling 🕐 **407/WDW-DINE.**

See the review of the **family-friendly Spirit of Aloha Dinner Show** on p. 284.

600 Seven Seas Dr. (P.O. Box 10000), Lake Buena Vista, FL 32830-1000. 🕐 407/934-7639 or 407/824-2000. Fax 407/824-3174. www.disneyworld.com. 853 units. $299–$560 double; $390–$675 concierge level; $495–$2,490 suite. Extra person $25. Children 17 and under stay free in parent's room. Rollaway beds not available, cribs free. AE, DC, DISC, MC, V. Free self-parking, $6 valet. Take I-4 east to Exit 67, Hwy. 536/Epcot Center Dr. Follow signs to WDW, then to the resort. Pets $9 a night. **Amenities:** Restaurant (Pacific Rim); cafe; 2 lounges; 2 outdoor heated pools; kids' pool; watersports equipment; children's club; arcade; playground; concierge; WDW Transportation System, transportation to non-Disney parks for a fee; shopping arcade; 24-hr.

Tips **Springing into Existence**

In 2004, Disney will open a turn-of-the-20th-century-style timeshare complex called the **Saratoga Springs Resort Spa.** The new property will have 484 rooms, about one-third of which will be new; the others will be remodeled villas from the now-defunct Disney Institute. The resort's pool area will replicate a spring with bubbles escaping from the rocks. Purchase prices for a 1-week share of the units will start at about $12,000 and reach as much as $150,000, plus maintenance fees.

---

room service; babysitting; guest laundry; valet; nonsmoking rooms; concierge-level rooms. *In room:* A/C, TV, fridge ($10 a night), hair dryer, iron, safe.

Disney's Yacht Club Resort ✹✹   This resort is a cut above its sister, the Beach Club (see above), because the rooms, views, service, and atmosphere are a step better. It's also geared more toward adults and families with older children, although young kids are catered to (this is Disney after all). Epcot is a 10- to 15-minute walk from the front door, but you can save a lot of shoe leather by using the tram to the World Showcase's International Gateway. The theme is a turn-of-the-20th-century New England yacht club, and the atmosphere is posh. The Yacht Club shares **Stormalong Bay,** a huge free-form swimming pool and water park, with the Beach Club. It features a 150-foot serpentine water slide and a special kids' pool area, 2- to 3-feet deep, for little ones.

Rooms have beds for up to five and most have balconies; views run from asphalt to Crescent Lake and the gardens; you would, however, have to be a contortionist to see the lake from some of the "water-view" rooms, so if this is a must, make sure that you request one with a direct view.

There's no kids' club at the hotel, though guests can park their kids at the Sandcastle Club at the Beach Club next door. *Note:* The Yacht Club offers charters of a reproduction of a 1930s mahogany runabout to **cruise Crescent Lake** or see Epcot's IllumiNations fireworks display ($179.24 plus tax for 30 min.; ✆ **407/824-2621**). Older kids will likely enjoy the experience.

1700 Epcot Resorts Blvd. (off Buena Vista Dr.; P.O. Box 10000), Lake Buena Vista, FL 32830-1000. ✆ 407/934-7639 or 407/934-7000. Fax 407/924-3450. www.disneyworld.com. 630 units. $289–$510 double; $425–$660 concierge level; $525–$2,290 suite. Extra person $25. Children 17 and under stay free in parent's room. Rollaway beds not available, cribs free. AE, DC, DISC, MC, V. Free self-parking, $6 valet. Take I-4 east to Exit 67, Hwy. 536/Epcot Center Dr. Follow signs to WDW, then to the resort. Pets $9 per night. **Amenities:** 2 restaurants; grill; lounge; 2 outdoor heated pools; kids' pool; 2 lighted tennis courts; Jacuzzi; watersports equipment; croquet; arcade; playground; concierge; WDW Transportation System, transportation to non-Disney parks for a fee; business center; shopping arcade; salon; 24-hr. room service; babysitting; guest laundry; valet; nonsmoking rooms; concierge-level rooms. *In room:* A/C, TV, dataport, minibar, fridge ($10 a night), coffeemaker, iron, safe.

Walt Disney World Dolphin ✹✹   Most kids love the whimsical touch of architect Michael Graves, who designed this Starwood resort and its sister, the Walt Disney World Swan (below). The Dolphin centers on a 27-story pyramid with two 11-story wings that are crowned by 56-foot twin dolphin sculptures that look more like the whale in *Pinocchio*. It's close to Epcot and right across the street from the Fantasia Gardens mini-golf courses.

On check-in, young guests get a **"Kids Passport"** that entitles them to a free ice cream cone or cup at the Dolphin Fountain or Splash Terrace restaurants after they have collected five stamps from various parts of the hotel, including

> (*Tips* **When a WDW Property Is Not a WDW Property**
>
> There are nine "official" Disney hotels that aren't owned by Mickey's stockholders. But there are a couple of asterisks. Walt Disney World Swan and Walt Disney World Dolphin have Uncle Walt's name and they're on mainstream WDW resort property, but they're not Disney-owned resorts, so we consider them "officials." The good news for you: You can get discounted room rates and other special offers at the Swan and Dolphin that you won't get at a Disney-owned resort.

restaurants, shops, and other facilities. Another nice touch for kids is the **"Straight A" Club;** if your child shows a report card filled with all "A"s, he or she gets a free ice cream.

Rooms offer views of the grounds and parts of the World and they are scheduled for upgrading sometime in late 2003 (ask before you book). Corner rooms have a little more space. Unlike the Disney-owned resorts, you can get a rollaway bed, though space will be somewhat tight. You cannot, however, rent refrigerators, though you can get an empty minibar that really doesn't get all that cold for $25 per day (ouch!). And whether you want to or not, you'll also pay an added resort fee of $10 per day (double ouch!) if you stay here.

The resort's free-form sculpted grotto pool with waterfalls, water slide, rope bridge, and three secluded whirlpools sprawls across 2 acres between the Dolphin and the Swan. It's a major hit with the young set. Kids enrolled in the supervised **Camp Dolphin** enjoy arts and crafts, movies, a video arcade, and dinner ($10 per hour per child, 2-hr. minimum, ages 4–12, 5:30pm–midnight). Be sure to reserve a space for your child well in advance by calling © **407/934-4241.** The Dolphin and Swan also share a beach on Crescent Lake and a Body by Jake health club.

1500 Epcot Resorts Blvd. (off Buena Vista Dr.; P.O. Box 22653), Lake Buena Vista, FL 32830-2653. © **888/828-8850** or 407/934-4000. Fax 407/934-4099. www.swandolphin.com or www.disneyworld.com. 1,509 units. $325–$519 double; $485–$3,150 suite. Resort fee $10. Extra person $25. Children 17 and under stay free in parent's room. Rollaway beds $25/night, cribs free. AE, DC, DISC, MC, V. Free self-parking, valet parking $10. Take I-4 east to Exit 67, Hwy. 536/Epcot Center Dr. Follow signs to WDW, then to the resort. Pets $9 a night. **Amenities:** 4 restaurants (steak, Mexican, American); grill; 2 lounges; 4 outdoor heated pools; 4 lighted tennis courts; health club; watersports equipment; children's center; 2 game rooms; playground; concierge; car-rental desk; WDW Transportation System, transportation to non-Disney parks for a fee; shopping arcade; salon; 24-hr. room service; massage; babysitting; guest laundry; valet; nonsmoking rooms; concierge-level rooms. *In room:* A/C, TV, Nintendo, dataport, minibar, hair dryer, iron, safe.

Walt Disney World Swan 🌟🌟   Not to be outdone by the huge dolphins at its sister property, this high-rise Westin resort is topped with dual 45-foot swan statues and seashell fountains. It offers a good location—close to Epcot, Fantasia Gardens, and the Boardwalk's nightlife—and a chance to be in the WDW mainstream without being quite so bombarded by mouse decor. It shares a beach, 2-acre pool area, health club, a number of restaurants, and other trimmings with the Dolphin (see above). Note that the beach next to the pool offers a great view of Epcot's IllumiNations fireworks.

The hotel underwent a massive renovation in 2003 that included upgrading all of its guest rooms. Rooms now sport Westin's famous "Heavenly Beds," the perfect thing to come home to after a busy day in the parks. Guest rooms here are just a tad smaller than those at the Dolphin. The hotel offers a childproofing room kit with socket covers and a nightlight (ask for it at check-in). Alas, the hotel has the same awful resort fee and "empty minibar" charge (don't use the minibar to store necessary medications—it's not cold enough!) as its sister property.

Kids staying at the Swan can enroll in the supervised Camp Dolphin program next door at the Dolphin and are eligible for the "Kids Passport" and "Straight A" programs as well.

1200 Epcot Resorts Blvd. (off Buena Vista Dr.; P.O. Box 22786), Lake Buena Vista, FL 32830-2786. ✆ 888/828-8850 or 407/934-3000. Fax 407/934-4499. www.swandolphin.com or www.disneyworld.com. 758 units. $325–$519 double; $485–$3,150 suite. Resort fee $10. Extra person $25. Children 17 and under stay free in parent's room. Rollaway beds $25/night, cribs free. AE, DC, DISC, MC, V. Free self-parking, valet parking $10. Take I-4 east to Exit 67, Hwy. 536/Epcot Center Dr. Follow signs to WDW, then to the resort. Pets $9 a night. **Amenities:** 4 restaurants (American, Italian, Pacific Rim); grill; lounge; 4 outdoor heated pools; 4 lighted tennis courts; health club; watersports equipment; children's center; 2 game rooms; playground; concierge; car-rental desk; WDW Transportation System, transportation to non-Disney parks for a fee; shopping arcade; salon; 24-hr. room service; massage; babysitting; guest laundry; valet; nonsmoking rooms; concierge-level rooms. *In room:* A/C, TV, Nintendo, dataport, minibar, hair dryer, iron, safe.

EXPENSIVE

Disney's Animal Kingdom Lodge ★★ This resort has the feel—with a little imagination—of an African game-reserve lodge complete with thatched roofs. Not surprisingly, this is the closest you can stay to Animal Kingdom, but almost everything else on WDW property is quite a distance away. Locations aside, this is a great place for families, who will appreciate the animals and activities (a lot of them quite educational) for kids.

The lodge's comfortable rooms follow a *kraal* (semicircular) design that gives patient guests a view of 130 bird species and 75 giraffes, gazelles, and other grazing animals on a 30-acre savanna. Most kids—and adults, for that matter—will find the notion of waking up to a giraffe outside their window pretty cool. (Not all rooms have savannah views—you have to pay more for that—though you can get the scenery for nothing through large picture windows in the lobby, where information displays will help your kids understand what they are seeing.) All lodge rooms have a balcony, complete with "mosquito netting" curtains, and all come with animal identification checklists your kids can use to keep track of their sightings (you can also get these upon check-in). If you do get a room overlooking the Savannah, be sure that your children understand that dropping food and other items off the balconies to the animals is strictly *verboten.*

The 9,000-square-foot pool is popular with kids and has a water slide, a wading area for young children, and a good view of the savanna. **Simba's Clubhouse,** the kids' program, offers activities, entertainment, a meal, and a snack ($10 per hour per child, 2-hr. minimum, ages 4–12, 4:30pm–midnight). Be sure to reserve a space for your kids well in advance (call ✆ **407/WDW-DINE**). There are also daily **Junior Researcher** (animal familiarization) and **Junior Chef** (cookie decorating) enrichment programs that are free for children staying at the lodge, as is the nightly African storytelling. Both programs are geared to children ages 3 to 9; if you're interested, ask about them at check-in. All in all, this is the best of the Disney properties when it comes to providing both an educational and entertaining environment for kids.

Warning: Because of animal safety issues, the resort doesn't allow balloons of any sort into the rooms. You will be forced to check yours upon entry and won't get it back until departure, so to avoid upsetting little ones, do yourself a favor and don't buy one for them at the theme parks if you're staying here.

2901 Osceola Pkwy., Bay Lake, FL 32830. ✆ **407/934-7639** or 407/938-3000. Fax 407/939-4799. www.disneyworld.com. 1,293 units. $199–$515 double; $425–$610 concierge level; $635–$2,505 suite. Extra person $25. Children 17 and under stay free in parent's room. Rollaway beds not available, cribs free. AE, DC, DISC, MC, V. Free self-parking, valet parking $6. Take I-4 east to Exit 67, Hwy. 536/Epcot Center Dr. Follow signs to WDW, then to the resort. Pets $9 a night. **Amenities:** 2 restaurants (African, American); lounge; outdoor heated pool; kids' pool; health club; children's center; arcade; playground; concierge; WDW Transportation System, transportation to non-Disney parks for a fee; shopping arcade; limited room service; babysitting; guest laundry; nonsmoking rooms; concierge-level rooms. *In room:* A/C, TV, dataport, fridge ($10 a night), hair dryer, iron, safe.

Disney's Wilderness Lodge ★★★   The geyser out back, the mammoth stone hearth in the lobby, and bunk beds for the kids are just a few reasons this resort is a family favorite. The building looks like a rustic national park lodge, in part because it's patterned after the one at Yellowstone. Surrounded by 56 acres of oaks and pines, it offers a remote, woodsy setting that we find a plus but can also be a drawback: It's more difficult to access other areas via the WDW Transportation System.

The comfy rooms offer two queen beds or a queen and a set of bunk beds (which have side rails). The deluxe rooms are an especially good deal for families as they have a seating area with a pullout couch, TV, and refrigerator that's separated from the main bedroom by French doors—perfect if parents want a little privacy after the kids are in bed. If a view is important, ask for a room with a woods view.

The geyser we mentioned "blows" periodically throughout the day and is a hit with kids. The lodge also has an immense serpentine pool with a short water slide. The kids' program, **Cub's Den,** includes activities, entertainment, movies, video games, a meal, and a snack ($10 per hour per child, 2-hr. minimum, ages 4–12, 5pm–midnight). Reserving a place at the club for your kids is strongly suggested (call ✆ **407/WDW-DINE**).

The 181 units at the **Villas at Disney's Wilderness Lodge** were added in 2000. This is another Disney Vacation Club timeshare property (the Boardwalk Villas and Old Key West are others) that rents vacant rooms, usually to larger groups and families. It offers a more upscale experience, although you get less kitchen space here than in Old Key West. The one- and two-bedroom villas have 727 and 1,080 square feet, respectively.

Note: If you have a budding engineer in your party, the lodge offers **"Wonders of the Lodge,"** a free tour touting its architecture, Wednesday through Saturday at 9am. Most kids, however, will probably find it boring. The lodge does offer a special family option that both kids and adults will enjoy: The Flag Family program. If you're selected, the entire family can traipse up to the Wilderness Lodge's roof in the morning (times seem to vary, so ask) and raise the American flag that flies over the resort. You'll get a picture, a certificate, a fabulous view. If you're interested, ask at the front desk upon check-in.

901 W. Timberline Dr. (on the southwest shore of Bay Lake just east of the Magic Kingdom; P.O. Box 10000), Lake Buena Vista, FL 32830-1000. ✆ **407/934-7639** or 407/938-4300. Fax 407/824-3232. www.disney world.com. 909 units. $199–$515 lodge; $350–$475 concierge level; $720–$1,155 suite; $279–$955 villas. Extra person $25. Children 17 and under stay free in parent's room. Rollaway beds not available, cribs free. AE, DC, DISC, MC, V. Free self-parking. Take I-4 east to Exit 67, Hwy. 536/Epcot Center Dr. Follow signs to WDW, then to the resort. Pets $9 a night. **Amenities:** 2 restaurants; 2 lounges; outdoor heated pool; kids' pool; 2 Jacuzzis; watersports equipment; children's center; arcade; playground; WDW Transportation System, transportation to non-Disney parks for a fee; limited room service; babysitting; guest laundry; nonsmoking rooms; concierge-level rooms. *In room:* A/C, TV, fridge ($10 a night), hair dryer, iron, safe.

MODERATE

Note: None of the Moderate resorts have particularly good connections to the WDW transportation network. Worse, the stops for the buses to the resorts outside of the theme parks can be a long, long, long hike away from the main exits. If you opt to stay at one of these resorts and you're lugging around young kids and the usual paraphernalia that goes along with them, we strongly suggest you opt for a rental car.

Disney's Caribbean Beach Resort ★

The Caribbean Beach isn't as bargain basement as the All-Star resorts (a little later in this chapter), but it still offers value for families who don't need a lot of frills or amenities. The units are grouped into five villages, each with a sandy beach, around a lake. (This is one of several WDW resorts that share a general layout with slightly different themes.) When booking, ask for a recently refurbished room; if you're family's too large for one room, there are a number of connecting rooms available. Even then, your party better be into togetherness—the bathrooms are very tight. The main swimming pool, in an area called Old Port Royale (where you'll also find the resort's food court and shops), replicates a Spanish-style fort complete with slide and the **Pirate Cay** play area is nearby. Both are popular with kids.

Note: The resort's restaurants and shops are quite a hike from most rooms; those in the Martinique and Trinidad North areas are closest. The nearest park is Disney–MGM Studios, but it can take 45 minutes to get there if you use the Disney Transportation System.

900 Cayman Way (off Buena Vista Dr.; P.O. Box 10000), Lake Buena Vista, FL 32830-1000. © **407/934-7639** or 407/934-3400. Fax 407/934-3288. www.disneyworld.com. 2,112 units. $133–$209 double. Extra person $15. Children 17 and under stay free in parent's room. Rollaway beds not available, cribs free. AE, DC, DISC, MC, V. Free self-parking. Take I-4 east to Exit 67, Hwy. 536/Epcot Center Dr. Follow signs to WDW, then to the resort. Pets $9 a night. **Amenities:** Restaurant; grill; lounge; large outdoor heated pool; 6 smaller pools in the villages; kids' pool; Jacuzzi; watersports equipment; arcade; 3 playgrounds; WDW Transportation System, transportation to non-Disney parks for a fee; limited room service; babysitting; guest laundry; nonsmoking rooms. *In room:* A/C, TV, fridge ($10 a night), hair dryer, iron, safe.

Disney's Coronado Springs Resort ★

Here's another clone of the Disney moderate class. Were it not for exterior gingerbread and interior decor, it would be hard to tell one from another. The American Southwestern theme carries through four- and five-story hacienda-style buildings with terra-cotta tile roofs and shaded courtyards, all of which surrounds a 15-acre lake. As with most WDW properties, it has an above-par pool, in this case inspired by a 46-foot Mayan pyramid with a water slide, and the children's pool has a spouting fountain. Keeping with the theme (which most kids adore), the playground has a faux archaeological dig site. The rooms are identical in size to those in the Caribbean Beach Resort; don't expect to fit more than one person into the bathroom at a time. If a member of your party has a mobility impairment, keep in mind that there are 99 disabled-access rooms at the resort. The rooms nearest the central public area, pool, and lobby tend to be noisier, but if you avoid them, you'll have a longer hike to the food court (one of the better ones in WDW) and shops. The nearest park is Animal Kingdom, but the Coronado is at the southwest corner of WDW and a good distance from a lot of the other action.

1000 Buena Vista Dr. (near All-Star resorts and Blizzard Beach), Lake Buena Vista, FL 32830. © **407/934-7639** or 407/939-1000. Fax 407/939-1003. www.disneyworld.com. 1,967 units. $133–$209 double; $275–$1,105 suite. Extra person $15. Children 17 and under stay free in parent's room. Rollaway beds not available, cribs free. AE, DC, DISC, MC, V. Free self-parking. Take I-4 east to Exit 67, Hwy. 536/Epcot Center Dr. Follow signs to WDW, then to the resort. Pets $9 a night. **Amenities:** Restaurant; grill/food court; 2 lounges; 4 outdoor heated pools; kids' pool; health club; Jacuzzi; sauna; watersports equipment; 2 arcades; playground; WDW Transportation System, transportation to non-Disney parks for a fee; business center; salon; limited room service; massage; babysitting; guest laundry; nonsmoking rooms. *In room:* A/C, TV, dataport, fridge ($10 a night), hair dryer, iron, safe.

Disney's Port Orleans Resort ★ *Value*   It's one of our favorite resorts based on value, location, and lower-decibel level, and Disney has turned it into two resorts in one: the French Quarter and Riverside, though only one will be open at a time during a 2-year renovation scheduled to end in spring 2005 (Riverside was in operation when we stayed there). Overall, this New Orleans–style resort offers some romantic spots and is relatively quiet, making it popular with couples and less popular with the toddler set (though there are still plenty of them to go around).

Port Orleans has the best location (just east of Epcot and Disney–MGM Studios), landscaping, and, perhaps, the coziest atmosphere of the resorts in this class—but it's still a clone of the others. The rooms and bathrooms won't induce claustrophobia, but they are a tight fit for four people. Make sure to ask for a recently refurbished room. The rooms are spread out across several buildings with different southern themes. If you've got little ones, try to get into Riverside's Magnolia or Oak Manor rooms, which are closest to the food court, shops, and main pool. The **Riverside Mill** food court has a nice selection of items for kids, plus a nice play area tucked in the corner next to the building's water wheel. The **Doubloon Lagoon pool** in the French Quarter is a family favorite, with a water slide that curves out of a dragon's mouth; Riverside's **Ol' Man Island pool** is shaped like an old-fashioned swimming hole and is a little more sedate (though there's an obligatory water slide as well).

2201 Orleans Dr. (off Bonnet Creek Pkwy.; P.O. Box 10000), Lake Buena Vista, FL 32830-1000. © 407/934-7639, 407/934-5000 (French Quarter), or 407/934-6000 (Riverside). Fax 407/934-5353 (French Quarter) or 407/934-5777 (Riverside). www.disneyworld.com. 3,056 units. $133–$209 double. Extra person $15. Children 17 and under stay free in parent's room. Rollaway beds not available, cribs free. AE, DC, DISC, MC, V. Free self-parking. Take I-4 east to Exit 67, Hwy. 536/Epcot Center Dr. Follow signs to WDW, then to the individual resorts. Pets $9 a night. **Amenities:** Restaurant (American); food court; lounge; 2 outdoor heated pools; 2 kids' pools; Jacuzzi; watersports equipment; arcade; playground; WDW Transportation System, transportation to non-Disney parks for a fee; limited room service; babysitting; guest laundry; nonsmoking rooms. *In room:* A/C, TV, fridge ($10 a night), hair dryer, iron, safe.

Shades of Green on Walt Disney World Resort ★ *Value*   While most resorts were suffering under the 2001–2003 economic downturn, demand at this resort was so high the U.S. Army announced a $55 million expansion and renovation that will have doubled its room count by the time you read this. Shades of Green is open only to guests in the military and their spouses, some Department of Defense employees, military retirees and widows, 100% disabled veterans, and Medal of Honor recipients. If you qualify, don't think of staying anywhere else—it's the *best bargain on WDW soil*. Rates here aren't based on category (except the suites) but on military rank and grade. In its past life, this resort was the Disney Inn. It's nestled among three of Disney's golf courses, near the Magic Kingdom. All of the smoke-free rooms have balconies or patios and offer pool or golf-course views. The standard rooms are larger than most at WDW and can accommodate four; the suites, which are a good deal for families, offer kitchenettes (no microwaves though) and can accommodate six to eight people. Note that unlike the other Disney resorts, cribs here will cost you $5 per day. Transportation—though slow—is available to all of the Disney parks and attractions.

1950 W. Magnolia Dr. (across from the Polynesian Resort). © 888/593-2242 or 407/824-3400. Fax 407/824-3665. www.shadesofgreen.org. 587 units. $70–$116 double (based on military rank), 6- to 8-person suites $200–$225 (regardless of rank). Extra person $15. Children 17 and under stay free in parent's room. Rollaway beds not available, cribs $5/night. AE, DC, DISC, MC, V. Take I-4 east to Exit 67, Hwy. 536/Epcot Center Dr. Follow signs to WDW, then to the resort. Pets $9 a night. **Amenities:** 2 restaurants (American, Italian);

2 lounges; 2 heated outdoor pools; kids' pool; 2 lighted tennis courts; arcade; playground; activities desk; WDW Transportation System, transportation to non-Disney parks for a fee; babysitting; guest laundry; non-smoking rooms. *In room:* A/C, TV, fridge ($5 per day), coffeemaker, hair dryer, iron, safe ($1 per day).

INEXPENSIVE

Note: All of Disney's inexpensive resorts are out of the way and offer less than ideal transportation connections. If you and your brood stay at one of them, we recommend you rent a car.

Disney's All-Star Movies Resort   Most kids love the larger-than-life themes at the three All-Star resorts, but most adults need dark glasses and Thorazine to combat the visual overload. Still, the themes—in this case, giant cartoon characters such as Buzz Lightyear and Woody—serve a designed Disney purpose: They mask a 21st-century rendition of a 1950s Holiday Inn. The rooms are spartan and very small at 260 square feet, though Disney tries to make them look larger by using smaller than normal furniture. Speaking of small, wait until you step into the bathroom. Don't think about opening the door while one of your roommates is on the commode, or you might break his or her kneecaps. And the soundproofing leaves something to be desired. Note that 96 of the rooms are equipped for people with limited mobility. Like its two siblings (next), this resort is buried in WDW's southwest corner to avoid frightening the higher-paying guests. Pools are themed after *The Mighty Ducks* and *Fantasia*, and they are usually noisy and crowded.

1991 W. Buena Vista Dr., Lake Buena Vista, FL 32830-1000. © 407/934-7639 or 407/939-7000. Fax 407/939-7111. www.disneyworld.com. 1,900 units. $77–$126 double. Extra person $10. Children 17 and under stay free in parent's room. Rollaway beds not available, cribs free. AE, DC, DISC, MC, V. Free self-parking. Take I-4 east to Exit 67, Hwy. 536/Epcot Center Dr. Follow signs to WDW, then to the resort. Pets $9 a night. **Amenities:** Food court; lounge; 2 outdoor heated pools; kids' pool; arcade; playground; WDW Transportation System, transportation to non-Disney parks for a fee; limited room service; babysitting; guest laundry; nonsmoking rooms. *In room:* A/C, TV, dataport, fridge ($10 a night), safe.

Disney's All-Star Music Resort   Giant trombones and musical themes from jazz and calypso to rock and Broadway can't hide the fact that this is a clone of the All-Star Movies Resort (see above). Tiny rooms and bathrooms, where an opening door can cause injury, are the norm again. But rooms in this class do have perks: They're *more than $50 a night* (and in some cases hundreds of dollars) cheaper than other Disney resorts. As for size, a lot of folks don't come to lounge in a room, so if you're only going to be inside to sleep, the cramped quarters (maximum capacity four, but no more than two adults) may not matter. Note that Disney is home to a ton of cheerleading championships and other kids' events—and all of the participants usually get housed at the All-Stars (a junior cheerleading squad was in town the last time we were here), making for a rather noisy environment. For (relative) quiet, ask for a room on the third floor of a building. The main theme pools revolve around a guitar and grand piano (quieter and better for older kids). The closest park is Animal Kingdom, which you can reach (not necessarily in an expedient manner) by the transportation system.

(*Tips* **Value in the Eyes of the Beholder**

Disney's All-Star resorts added a "preferred room" rate in 2002, but don't expect much for the top rate of $126, $17 more than the previous high. Guests who book it are paying for location: Preferred rooms are closer to the pools, food court, and/or transportation.

> ⌒ **Tips** **Getting Away**
>
> If you want to be on Disney soil but put a lot of miles between you and
> the madness, Mickey's timeshare arm, the Disney Vacation Club, offers the
> option of renting a room 2 hours south at its **Vero Beach Resort** on the
> Atlantic Ocean. Studios, standard motel-style rooms, one- and two-bed-
> room villas, and three-bedroom cottages are available ($165–$1,105 per
> night double), but you'll need to arrange your own transportation
> (✆ **407/939-7775**; www.dvcresorts.com).

1801 W. Buena Vista Dr. (at World Dr. and Osceola Pkwy.; P.O. Box 10000), Lake Buena Vista, FL 32830-1000.
✆ **407/934-7639** or 407/939-6000. Fax 407/939-7222. www.disneyworld.com. 1,920 units. $77–$126 double. Extra person $10. Children 17 and under stay free in parent's room. Rollaway beds not available, cribs
free. AE, DC, DISC, MC, V. Free self-parking. Take I-4 east to Exit 67, Hwy. 536/Epcot Center Dr. Follow signs
to WDW, then the resort. Pets $9 a night. **Amenities:** Food court; lounge; 2 outdoor heated pools; kids' pool;
arcade; playground; WDW Transportation System, transportation to non-Disney parks for a fee; limited room
service; babysitting; guest laundry; nonsmoking rooms. *In room:* A/C, TV, dataport, fridge ($10 a night), safe.

Disney's All-Star Sports Resort   Yogi Berra said it best: "It's *déjà vu* all over
again." It's a different theme, but the same routine: tight quarters like those in
the All-Star Movies and Music resorts, above, but your kids, especially young
ones, probably won't mind (on the contrary—sports-crazed kids love it). Rooms
here are housed in buildings designed around football, baseball, basketball, tennis, and surfing motifs. For instance, the turquoise surf buildings have waves
along the roofs, surfboards mounted on exterior walls, and pink fish swimming
along balcony railings. Again, if your threshold for visual overload is low, you
may need to visit a sanatorium once you've left this La-La Land. Surfboard Bay
and the Grand Slam are the two themed pools—note that unlike the other Disney resorts, the inexpensive ones don't provide towels at the pool, so you'll have
to use the ones in your room.

One last warning: The rates and themes tempt lots of families with little kids
and the noise level can get very high, so if you're looking for a quiet family vacation, steer clear of these resorts.

1701 W. Buena Vista Dr. (at World Dr. and Osceola Pkwy.; P.O. Box 10000), Lake Buena Vista, FL 32830-1000.
✆ **407/934-7639** or 407/939-5000. Fax 407/939-7333. www.disneyworld.com. 1,920 units. $77–$126 double. Extra person $10. Children 17 and under stay free in parent's room. Rollaway beds not available, cribs
free. AE, DC, DISC, MC, V. Free parking. Take I-4 east to Exit 67, Hwy. 536/Epcot Center Dr. Follow signs to
WDW, then to the resort. Pets $9 a night. **Amenities:** Food court; lounge; 2 outdoor heated pools; kids' pool;
arcade; playground; WDW Transportation System, transportation to non-Disney parks for a fee; limited room
service; babysitting; guest laundry; nonsmoking rooms. *In room:* A/C, TV, dataport, fridge ($10 a night), safe.

Disney's Pop Century   The newest of WDW's inexpensive or, as Mickey calls
them, value-class resorts, was to have opened in early 2002 but the post–September
11, 2001, economic slump put it in cold storage until December 2003, when the
massive resort began opening in stages. The themes here are decade-long capsules
of the 20th century, broken into two half-century blocks: the Legendary Years
(1900s–40s) and the Classic Years (1950s–90s), the first area to open. The bottom
line: You and the kids will get a good price and the same postage stamp-size accommodations, in this case with larger-than-life icons such as Play-Doh, a Duncan
yo-yo, and 8-track tapes. Its **six swimming pools** carry shapes ranging from a cross-
word puzzle and soda bottle to a bowling pin and a computer. The resort is across
from Disney's Wide World of Sports (p. 219).

1050 Century Dr. (P.O. Box 10000), Lake Buena Vista, FL 32830-1000. ℂ **407/934-7639** or 407/938-4000. Fax 407/938-4040. www.disneyworld.com. 5,760 units. $77–$126 double. Extra person $10. Children 17 and under stay free in parent's room. Rollaway beds not available, cribs free. AE, DC, DISC, MC, V. Free parking. Take I-4 east to Exit 67, Hwy. 536/Epcot Center Dr. Follow signs to WDW, then to the resort. Pets $9 a night. **Amenities:** Food court; lounge; 6 outdoor heated pools; kids' pool; arcade; playground; WDW Transportation System, transportation to non-Disney parks for a fee; limited room service; babysitting; guest laundry; non-smoking rooms. *In room:* A/C, TV, dataport, fridge ($10 a night), safe.

A DISNEY CAMPGROUND

Disney's Fort Wilderness Resort & Campground ⚐   Why not take the
kids camping? Pine and cypress trees, lakes, and streams surround this woodsy 780-acre resort, which offers a host of recreational opportunities for the whole family. It's close to the Magic Kingdom but quite a distance from everything else, though if you're a true outdoors type, you may want to be sheltered from some of the Mickey make-believe. There are 784 campsites for RVs, pull-behind campers, and tents (110/220-volt outlets, outdoor cooking grills, and comfort areas with showers and restrooms). Some sites are open to **pets**—at an additional cost of $5 per site, not per pet, which is cheaper than using the WDW resort kennel, where you pay $9 per pet. The 408 wilderness cabins (actually mobile homes with an outdoor deck and grill) offer 504 square feet, enough for six people once you pull down the Murphy beds (there's also a set of bunk beds for kids), and they also have full kitchens.

Nearby Pioneer Hall is home to the popular Hoop-Dee-Doo Musical Revue, which we review on p. 283. The resort also has nightly **sing-along and marsh-mallow-roasting** get-togethers (you'll have to buy or bring along your own marshmallows) followed by screenings of family-friendly movies in an outdoor theater. We detail many of the cool outdoor recreational activities available at this resort (including hayrides) in chapter 8.

103520 N. Fort Wilderness Trail (P.O. Box 10000), Lake Buena Vista, FL 32830-1000. ℂ **407/934-7639** or 407/824-2900. Fax 407/824-3508. www.disneyworld.com. 784 campsites, 408 wilderness cabins. $35–$82 campsite double; $229–$329 wilderness cabin double. Extra person $2 campsites, $5 cabins. Children 17 and under stay free with parent. Rollaway beds not available, cribs free. AE, DC, DISC, MC, V. Free self-parking. Take I-4 east to Exit 67, Hwy. 536/Epcot Center Dr. Follow signs to WDW, then to the resort. **Amenities:** 2 restaurants (American); grill; lounge; 2 outdoor heated pools; kids' pool; 2 lighted tennis courts; watersports equipment; outdoor activities (fishing; horseback, pony, and hay rides; campfire programs); 2 game rooms; playground; WDW Transportation System, transportation to non-Disney parks for a fee; babysitting; guest laundry; nonsmoking cabins. *In room:* A/C, TV/VCR, kitchen, fridge, coffeemaker, outdoor grill, hair dryer (all in cabins only).

3 "Official" Hotels in Lake Buena Vista

These resorts, designated "official" Disney hotels, are located on or around Hotel Plaza Boulevard, at the northeast corner of WDW. They're near Downtown Disney Marketplace, Downtown Disney West Side, and Pleasure Island. The boulevard has enough greenery to make it a nominee for Main Street, U.S.A. (if it weren't for autos spewing exhaust at the walkers and joggers on the sidewalks).

Guests at these hotels enjoy some WDW privileges (see "The Perks & Downsides of Staying with Mickey," earlier in this chapter), including free bus service to the parks and the ability to purchase discounted length-of-stay passes, but make sure when booking to ask which privileges you get, as they vary from hotel to hotel and year to year. Their locations spare you from some of the pixie dust, but the boulevard's high-speed traffic causes some of its own irritation. Also note the Walt Disney World Dolphin and Walt Disney World Swan (listed in the previous section) should be considered the eighth and ninth "official" hotels, because they're not Disney-owned. The difference is they're on the mainstream property.

Another perk of the "official" hotels is that they generally have less relentless Disney themes, although some do offer character breakfasts a few days each week (ask the person answering the reservation line for details and schedules). They are also often a lot cheaper than equivalent accommodations at the House of Mouse and are usually a step above the moderate Disney-owned resorts. Almost all of the resorts have kiddie pools, in-room electronic games (for an extra fee), and arcades or other activities for children.

You can make reservations for all of the properties listed below through Central Reservations Operations (☎ **407/934-7639**) or through the hotel numbers included in the listings. However, to ensure you get the best rates, call each hotel or its parent chain (or check their websites) to see if there are specials available.

You'll find all of these hotels located on the map "Walt Disney World & Lake Buena Vista Accommodations," earlier in this chapter.

EXPENSIVE

Wyndham Palace Resort & Spa ★★   This is the most upscale and expensive of the Hotel Plaza Boulevard–area properties and is popular with families, even though it primarily caters to business travelers. For that reason, some of its best rates are offered in July and August (a bonus for families with a liberal budget). Many of the business-standard rooms have balconies or patios; kids will probably prefer the Sony PlayStation access over the views; ask for one above the 5th floor with a "recreation view," which face the Wyndham's pools, Downtown Disney, Pleasure Island (with its brief midnight fireworks), and, in the distance, Disney–MGM Studios' Tower of Terror. If a member of the family has severe allergies, ask for one of the resort's Evergreen rooms, which offer individual air filtration systems and nonallergenic amenities. At press time, the resort had a Disney **character breakfast** on Sundays. The Palace is known for its spacious fitness center and full-service European-style spa (massage, wraps, steam room, saunas, salon, fitness center, and more), which are open to the public. There are also three pools and a host of available recreational options.

1900 Buena Vista Dr. (just north of Hotel Plaza Blvd.; P.O. Box 22206), Lake Buena Vista, FL 32830. ☎ **800/ 996-3426** or 407/827-2727. Fax 407/827-6034. www.wyndham.com. 1,014 units. $179–$398 double; $289–$749 suite. Resort fee $9. Extra person $20. Children 17 and under stay free in parent's room. Rollaway beds $15/night, cribs free. AE, DC, DISC, MC, V. Free self-parking, valet parking $10. From I-4, take Exit 68, Hwy. 535/Apopka–Vineland Rd., north to Hotel Plaza Blvd. and go left. At 3rd stoplight, turn right onto Buena Vista Dr. It's the 1st hotel on the right. **Amenities:** 2 restaurants (Continental, steak); grill; 4 lounges; 3 outdoor heated pools; kids' pool; 3 lighted tennis courts; half basketball court; sand volleyball court; spa; Jacuzzi; sauna; children's center; arcade; playground; concierge; complimentary bus service to WDW parks; transportation for a fee to non-Disney parks; salon; 24-hr. room service; massage; babysitting; guest laundry; valet; nonsmoking rooms; concierge-level rooms. *In room:* A/C, TV w/PlayStation and pay movies, dataport, minibar, coffeemaker, hair dryer, iron.

MODERATE

Best Western Lake Buena Vista Hotel ★ *Value*   This 12-acre lakefront hotel is reasonably modern, with nicer rooms and public areas than you might find in others within the chain. Tropical-themed rooms are located in an 18-story tower, and all have balconies. Accommodations here are definitely a step above and larger than the rooms in Disney's moderate category. The views improve from the eighth floor and up, and those on the west side have a better chance of seeing something Disney. The hotel's 18th-floor lounge, Toppers,

---

(*Tips* **Yet Another Add-On**

Several of the properties in this chapter add resort fees to their daily room rates. That's part of an unfortunate but growing hotel trend of charging for services that used to be included in the rates, such as use of the pool, admission to the health club, or in-room coffee or phones. If it's a concern, ask if your hotel charges such a fee when booking so you don't get blind-sided at checkout.

---

offers an excellent view of the Magic Kingdom's fireworks, but you'll have to do that one without the kids as they aren't allowed in. The tropical pool here is decent and has a separate wading area for little ones.

You can reserve an oversize room with a sleeper sofa (about 20% larger) or a WDW fireworks-view room for $15 more a night. You can also get the same rooms with full American breakfast for up to four people for $20 more per night. (If you're a foursome, it's a reasonably good deal; if not, buy breakfast elsewhere.) *Note:* It definitely pays to surf the corporate website at **www.best western.com** if you plan to stay here. It sometimes offers great deals and special rates for this hotel.

2000 Hotel Plaza Blvd. (between Buena Vista Dr. and Apopka–Vineland Rd./Hwy. 535), Lake Buena Vista, FL 32830. (C) **800/348-3765** or 407/828-2424. Fax 407/828-8933. www.orlandoresorthotel.com. 325 units. $99–$159 standard for 4; $199 suite. Resort fee $5. 5th person $15. Rollaway beds $10/night; cribs free. AE, DC, DISC, MC, V. Free self-parking. From I-4, take Exit 68, Hwy. 535/Apopka–Vineland Rd., north to Hotel Plaza Blvd. and go left. It's the 1st hotel on the right. **Amenities:** Restaurant (American); grill; outdoor heated pool; kids' pool; arcade; playground; guest services desks; complimentary bus service to WDW parks; transportation for a fee to other parks; limited room service; babysitting; guest laundry; nonsmoking rooms. *In room:* A/C, TV w/pay movies, Nintendo, coffeemaker, hair dryer, iron, safe.

Courtyard by Marriott *(Value*   This moderately priced member of the Marriott chain is popular with families. The best things we can say about it: The inner and outer glass elevators provide a free thrill ride, it's in a good location, and the price is pretty—well—decent. That said, we'd stay at some of the other moderate "official" hotels—notably the Best Western Lake Buena Vista Hotel or DoubleTree Guest Suites—first. Furthermore, by this chain's standards, we'd rather be at the Marriott Village at Little Lake Bryan (see "Other Lake Buena Vista Area Hotels," on p. 87). The rooms are bland, and the two pools are just ok. If you come here, ask for a room on floors 8 to 14 on the hotel's west side for a view of the Magic Kingdom and fireworks.

1805 Hotel Plaza Blvd. (between Lake Buena Vista Dr. and Apopka–Vineland Rd./Hwy. 535), Lake Buena Vista, FL 32830. (C) **800/223-9930** or 407/828-8888. Fax 407/827-4623. www.courtyardorlando.com. 323 units. $99–$229 double. Extra person $15. Children 17 and under stay free in parent's room. Rollaway beds $15/night; cribs free. AE, DC, DISC, MC, V. Free self-parking. From I-4, take Exit 68, Hwy. 535/Apopka–Vineland Rd., north to Hotel Plaza Blvd. and go left. It's the 3rd hotel on the left. **Amenities:** Restaurant; 2 lounges; 2 outdoor heated pools; kids' pool; Jacuzzi; arcade; playground; guest services desk; complimentary bus service to WDW parks, transportation for a fee to non-Disney parks; car-rental desks; limited room service; guest laundry; nonsmoking rooms. *In room:* A/C, TV w/pay movies, Nintendo, coffeemaker, hair dryer, iron, safe.

DoubleTree Guest Suites (🏅)   Children have their own check-in desk and theater, and they get a gift upon arrival at this hotel, the best of the "official" hotels for families traveling with little ones. (Don't forget that everyone gets a tasty **chocolate chip cookie** as an added bonus!) Adults may find some of the public areas lacking in personality—this is, after all, Mickeyville. But all of the accommodations in this seven-story hotel are two-room suites that offer 643 square feet—large by most standards—with refrigerators, microwaves, and space for up to six to catch some zzzzs. The large pool offers lush landscaping and a child's wading area. This is the easternmost of the "officials," which means it's farthest from the other Disney action, but closest to the free-world (read: moderately priced) shops in the Crossroads Shopping Center on Apopka–Vineland Road. It's not as good as the Holiday Inn Family Suites and Holiday Inn Sunspree (both listed below) in the child-offerings department, but those two aren't on WDW property.

2305 Hotel Plaza Blvd. (just west of Apopka–Vineland Rd./Hwy. 535), Lake Buena Vista, FL 32830. ✆ 800/ 222-8733 or 407/934-1000. Fax 407/934-1015. www.doubletreeguestsuites.com. 229 units. $119–$249 double. Extra person $20. Children 17 and under stay free in parent's room. Rollaway beds $10/night, cribs free. AE, DC, DISC, MC, V. Free self-parking. From I-4, take Exit 68, Hwy. 535/Apopka–Vineland Rd., north to Hotel Plaza Blvd. and go left. It's the 1st hotel on the left. **Amenities:** Restaurant; 2 lounges; outdoor heated pool; kids' pool; 2 lighted tennis courts; arcade; playground; concierge; car-rental desk; complimentary bus service to WDW parks, transportation for a fee to non-Disney parks; limited room service; guest laundry; nonsmoking rooms. *In room:* A/C, TV, Nintendo, dataport, fridge, coffeemaker, hair dryer, iron, safe, microwave.

Grosvenor Resort *(Overrated)* This lakeside resort has a great location, within walking distance of Downtown Disney Marketplace's shops. The high-rise with low-rise wings has a British Colonial look and public areas that make for wonderful "we-stayed-here" snapshots. Unfortunately, the rooms are a hit-or-miss proposition. We've gotten complaints and have seen a couple of examples of rooms in need of refurbishing. Nevertheless, its frequent package deals make it popular with budget travelers, so if you choose to stay here, our best advice is to complain to the front desk if you get a dud. Ask for a Tower Room on the west side (floors 9–19) for a limited view of Lake Buena Vista. The resort offers **kid's suites** (bunk beds separated from the adults) and **children's suites** (full size bed for adults and three singles for kids). At press time, **Disney character breakfasts** (including a special kids' buffet) were available 3 days a week. The Aquatic Center has a pool shaped like a Dutch windmill that some older kids might find interesting.

1850 Hotel Plaza Blvd. (just east of Buena Vista Dr.), Lake Buena Vista, FL 32830. ✆ 800/624-4109 or 407/ 828-4444. Fax 407/828-8192. www.grosvenorresort.com. 626 units. $119–$199 double. Extra person $15. Children 17 and under stay free in parent's room. Rollaway beds $17/night, cribs free. AE, DC, DISC, MC, V. Free self-parking, valet parking $8. From I-4, take Exit 68, Hwy. 535/Apopka–Vineland Rd., north to Hotel Plaza Blvd. and go left. It's the 2nd hotel on the right. **Amenities:** 2 restaurants (American); 3 lounges; 2 outdoor heated pools; 2 lighted tennis courts; fitness center; Jacuzzi; arcade; playground; concierge; car-rental desk; complimentary bus service to WDW parks, transportation for a fee to non-Disney parks; babysitting; guest laundry; nonsmoking rooms. *In room:* A/C, TV w/pay movies, in-room video games, and VCR, dataport, fridge, coffeemaker, safe.

Hilton Resort ⭐ You can't stay any closer to the shops at Downtown Disney Marketplace than this low-key hotel. Renovations done from 1998 to 2002 modernized this resort's public areas—including the addition of a Disney Store—and many of its rooms. If there is a knock against this spot, it's that you can stay comfortably and for less elsewhere on the Boulevard—but the hotel caters primarily to business travelers, so it can afford to charge the higher rates. The comfortable rooms are pleasantly neutral. The newly renovated junior suites are especially spacious and can sleep up to six—great for families. From the 6th through 10th floors on the north and west sides, you'll find a view of Downtown Disney and, in the distance, the Magic Kingdom fireworks. The pool area is nice enough, with a wading spot for kids; the arcade is state-of-the-art. Guests here are eligible for the **Extra Magic Hour** (see "The Perks & Downsides of Staying with Mickey," earlier in this chapter). At press time, there also was a

Sunday Disney character breakfast. All things considered, including value received and location, the Hilton ranks in the middle of the "official" hotel field.

1751 Hotel Plaza Blvd. (just east of Buena Vista Dr.), Lake Buena Vista, FL 32830. ℂ 800/774-1500 or 407/827-4000. Fax 407/827-3890. www.hilton.com. 814 units. $179–$329 double; $299–$1,500 suite. Resort fee $8. Extra person $20. Children 17 and under stay free in parent's room. Rollaway beds $10/night, cribs free. AE, DC, DISC, MC, V. Free self-parking, valet parking $10. From I-4, take Exit 68, Hwy. 535/Apopka–Vineland Rd., north to Hotel Plaza Blvd. and go left. It's the 4th hotel on the left. **Amenities:** 3 restaurants; deli; 3 lounges; 2 outdoor heated pools; kids' pool; fitness center; Jacuzzi; sauna; children's center; arcade; concierge; car-rental desk; complimentary bus to WDW parks, transportation for a fee to non-Disney parks; business center; shopping arcade; salon; 24-hour room service; babysitting; guest laundry; nonsmoking rooms; concierge-level rooms. *In room:* A/C, TV w/pay movies, Nintendo, dataport, minibar, coffeemaker, hair dryer, iron.

Hotel Royal Plaza ⚐★   The Plaza is one of the boulevard's originals, but renovations over its 25 years (its most recent makeover was 3 years ago) have kept it in relatively good shape. A favorite with budget-minded families, its hallmark is a friendly staff that provides good service. Poolside rooms have balconies and patios; the tower rooms have separate sitting areas, and some offer whirlpool tubs in the bathrooms (which sport Bath & Body Works toiletries that should appeal to mom and older girls). All rooms have sleeper sofas. If you want a view from up high, ask for a room facing west and WDW; the south and east sides keep a watchful eye on I-4's gridlock. *Note:* Though the pool area is attractive, there is no kiddie pool at this hotel, so families with very young children might want to look elsewhere.

1905 Hotel Plaza Blvd. (between Buena Vista Dr. and Apopka–Vineland Rd./Hwy. 535), Lake Buena Vista, FL 32830. ℂ 800/248-7890 or 407/828-2828. Fax 407/827-6338. www.royalplaza.com. 394 units. $119–$235 double; $159–$695 suite. Resort fee $7. Extra person $15. Children 17 and under stay free in parent's room. Rollaway beds not available, cribs free. AE, DC, DISC, MC, V. Free self-parking, valet parking $8. From I-4, take Exit 68, Hwy. 535/Apopka–Vineland Rd., north to Hotel Plaza Blvd. and go left. It's the 2nd hotel on the left. **Amenities:** Restaurant; lounge; outdoor heated pool; 4 lighted tennis courts; fitness center; Jacuzzi; guest services desk; complimentary bus service to WDW parks, transportation for a fee to non-Disney parks; limited room service; guest laundry; nonsmoking rooms. *In room:* A/C, TV w/pay movies, VCR, Nintendo, dataport, minibar, coffeemaker, hair dryer, iron, safe.

4 Other Lake Buena Vista Area Hotels

The hotels in this section are within a few minutes' drive of the Disney parks (and you'll need a rental car if you stay at them). They offer great location, but not Disney-related privileges given to guests in the "official" hotels, such as Disney bus service and character breakfasts. On the flip side, since you're not paying for those privileges, hotels in this category are generally a shade cheaper for comparable rooms and services.

Note: These hotels are also listed on the "Walt Disney World & Lake Buena Vista Accommodations" map in this chapter.

VERY EXPENSIVE

Gaylord Palms ⚐★⚐★   Central Florida's newest star is a convention center, but it appeals to family vacationers, too. Its entertainment, recreation, dining, and other amenities turn some guests into willing prisoners of this property—with the exception of time pledged to the theme parks. The Gaylord's 4½-acre, 140-foot-high atrium has a glass dome and miniature version of the Castillo de San Marcos, the old fort at St. Augustine. (Kids will find it either fascinating or impressive, depending on their ages.)

The resort and its rooms are divided into themes: **Emerald Bay,** a 362-room hotel within the hotel, has an elegant air; **St. Augustine** captures the essence of

---

Tips   **Coolest Pools**

Our favorite hotel splash zone in Orlando is the Hyatt Regency Grand Cypress Resort's half-acre, **800,000-gallon swimming pool,** which has caves, grottoes, waterfalls, and a 45-foot water slide. Our runner-up is the JW Marriott's **Lazy River,** a shallow, slow-current journey around the Grande Lakes property. Other cool pools include **Stormalong Bay,** which is shared by Disney's Beach and Yacht Club resorts, the **Mayan pyramid–themed pool** at WDW's Coronado Springs resort, and the **beach pool** with its fort and water slide at Universal's Portofino Bay Hotel.

America's oldest city; **Key West** delivers the laid-back ambience of Florida's southernmost city; and the **Everglades** uses a misty swamp, snarling faux gator, fiber-optic fireflies, and tin-roofed shanties to muster a wild-and-woolly air. All the guest rooms are business standard—comfortable but bland—except for those in Emerald Bay, which offers doggone nice rooms that fall just short of luxurious. All rooms come with a refrigerator and the daily resort fee you'll be forced to shell out gets you two bottles of mineral water (we've heard complaints about the tap water, so stick to the bottle stuff) and two bottles of orange juice.

At 4,000 square feet, **La Petite Academy** ($10 per child per hour, no minimum, ages 3–14, ✆ **407/586-2505**) offers a ton of LEGO fun, a karaoke stage, an art studio, and Sega, PlayStation, and Nintendo games. The kids' **Marine Activity pool** has an octopus slide and beach play areas, and cabanas at the adult pool have Internet access. And if you need to unwind further, try the 20,000-square-foot branch of the famous **Canyon Ranch Spa.** Our biggest gripe: Room-to-room and room-to-hall soundproofing should be better in this classy resort.

6000 Osceola Pkwy., Kissimmee, FL 34747. ✆ 877/677-9352 or 407/586-0000. Fax 407/586-2259. www.gaylordpalms.com. 1,406 units. $169–$460 double. Resort fee $10. Extra adult $20. Children under 18 stay free in parent's room. Rollaway beds and cribs $25/night. AE, DC, DISC, MC, V. Free self-parking, valet parking $12. Take I-4 Exit 65/Osceloa Pkwy. east to the hotel. **Amenities:** 3 restaurants; 4 lounges; 2 outdoor heated pools; 2 whirlpools; fitness center; spa; children's center; playground; concierge; tour desk; car-rental desk; free transportation to Disney parks, transportation for a fee to others; business center; shopping arcade; salon; room service; massage; babysitting; dry cleaning; nonsmoking rooms; concierge-level rooms. *In room:* A/C, TV w/pay movies and PlayStation, dataport, computer screens and keyboards, coffeemaker, hair dryer, iron, safe.

Hyatt Regency Grand Cypress Resort ★★★ *(Finds)*   This landing zone is a favorite of families seeking an upscale resort experience without Mickey Mouse extras. The lobby has lush foliage and several colorful birds, including a **macaw named Lulu** that waves to passersby and naturally attracts youthful attention. The 18-story atrium has inner and outer glass elevators (take the kids for a ride on the outers for a panoramic rush). The rooms are large and comfortable, and rollaways, cribs, bed rails, highchairs, and refrigerators are all available upon request. The rooms on the west side, from floors seven and up, have a distant view of Cinderella Castle and the Magic Kingdom fireworks.

The Hyatt gets our vote for **Orlando's coolest pool,** a half-acre, 800,000-gallon extravaganza with caves, grottoes, waterfalls, and a 45-foot slide. Adults and kids will love it! The Hyatt shares a golf club and academy, racquet club, and equestrian center (kids' lessons are available) with its sister, the **Villas of Grand Cypress** (✆ **800/835-7377** or 407/239-4700; http://grandcypress.com). The **Camp Hyatt** kids' program offers numerous options, including boating, swimming, arts and crafts, video games, and horse-related activities ($20 for 3 hr., $42 for 7 hr., not including lunch, ages 4–14). There's also a lakeside white-sand beach.

1 N. Jacaranda (off Hwy. 535), Orlando, FL 32836. ℂ **800/233-1234** or 407/239-1234. Fax 407/239-3800. www.hyattgrandcypress.com. 750 units. $239–$585 double; $395–$5,750 suite. Optional $12 resort fee (includes health club, free local calls, daily newspaper, and in-room coffee). Extra person $25. Children 18 and under stay free in parent's room. Rollaway beds and cribs free. AE, DC, DISC, MC, V. Free self-parking, valet parking $15. Take I-4 Exit 68, Hwy. 535/Apopka–Vineland Rd., north, then left at 2nd traffic light after ramp light onto Hwy. 535. It's on the right. **Amenities:** 4 restaurants (American, seafood, steaks); deli/general store; 4 lounges; large outdoor heated pool; 45 holes of golf; 12 tennis courts (5 lighted); 2 racquetball courts; spa; health club; watersports equipment; children's center; arcade; playground; concierge; free Disney shuttle, transportation to non-Disney parks for a fee; car-rental desk; salon; 24-hr. room service; massage (in-room); babysitting; guest laundry; valet; nonsmoking rooms; concierge-level rooms. *In room:* A/C, TV, Nintendo, dataport, minibar, hair dryer, iron, safe.

Ritz-Carlton Orlando, Grande Lakes Orlando's newest destination for deep-pocketed travelers opened in July 2003, the ninth Ritz in Florida and part of a 500-acre complex that also includes a JW Marriott (see below). The posh resort's many kid-friendly options make it an attractive choice for families with cash to burn. The grounds are beautiful and the entrance and lobby area have the feel of an Italian palazzo, and kids get their own separate check-in desk and welcome kit. Expect the usual quality and staff friendliness associated with this brand in a smoke-free environment.

All rooms have a balcony and two sinks, hand-painted Italian furniture, and plenty of room to move around in. (Kids won't mind zoning out in front of the 27-in. flat-screen TV.) The hotel will provide highchairs, cribs, rollaways, and strollers for kids on request (some for an extra fee). If you call in advance, the staff will childproof the electrical outlets in your room and remove alcoholic drinks from the minibar. Rooms on the west side, especially on floors 6 through 14, have a view of SeaWorld and its brief nighttime fireworks, as well as the resort's pool, golf course, waterways, and woodlands. In addition to use of the resort's pools, guests can enjoy those at the JW Marriott, including the **Lazy River.** Additionally, the resort has a 40,000-square-foot full-service spa.

The **Ritz-Kids program** has two options: an hourly one ($10 per hour per child, including snacks and beverages, no minimum, ages 4–13, 9am–10pm) and a full one ($55 per child, dinner included, no minimum, ages 4–13, 2–10pm). Activities include swimming, nature walks, Frisbee games, junior tennis, croquette, and more. There's also a nanny service ($20 per hour for up to three kids). There's also a 75-minute **Golf Fore Kids Etiquette Class** ($25 including drinks, snack, and gift, ages 5–12, Sun and Wed) that teaches youngsters some of the sport's rules.

4012 Central Florida Pkwy. (at intersection with John Young Pkwy.), Orlando, FL 32837. ℂ **800/241-3333,** 800/576-5760, or 407/206-2400. Fax 407/206-2401. www.grandelakes.com. 584 units. $199–$425 double; $329–$890 club-level. Extra person $30. Children 17 and under stay free in parent's room. Rollaway beds $15/night, cribs free. AE, DC, DISC, MC, V. Self-parking $8, valet $15. From I-4, take Exit 72, Hwy. 528/Bee Line Expwy. east to the John Young Pkwy., then south to Central Florida Pkwy. **Amenities:** 3 restaurants; cafe; snack bar; 2 lounges; outdoor heated pool; kids' pool; 18 holes of golf; 3 tennis courts (lighted); spa; health club; children's center; arcade; playground; concierge; free transportation to Universal and SeaWorld, transportation to Disney parks for a fee; business center; car-rental desk; salon; 24-hr. room service; babysitting; valet; nonsmoking rooms, concierge-level rooms. *In room:* A/C, TV, dataport, minibar, iron, safe.

EXPENSIVE

JW Marriott Orlando, Grande Lakes This less expensive sister of the Ritz-Carlton Orlando (see above) is another smoke-free resort with one of the niftiest pools in Orlando, the 24,000-square-foot **Lazy River** pool, which takes you on a slow, winding tropical journey through rock formations and small waterfalls (depth 3–5 ft.). Standard rooms at the Moorish-themed resort are on par with those in Disney's moderate class and are in tiptop condition. Those on the west side, especially on floors 6 through 26, have a view of SeaWorld and its brief nighttime fireworks, as well as the resort's pool, golf course, waterways, and woodlands. The hotel's playground has a sandbox where young kids like to hang out. JW junior guests are eligible for the **Ritz Kids program** and **Golf Fore Kids Etiquette Class** at the Ritz-Carlton Orlando (see above). Additionally, the two properties share pool, spa, golf, and tennis amenities.

4040 Central Florida Pkwy. (at intersection with John Young Pkwy.), Orlando, FL 32837. © 800/241-3333, 800/576-5750, or 407/206-2300. Fax 407/206-2301. www.grandelakes.com. 1,000 units. $179–$329 for 4–6. Extra person $25. Children 17 and under stay free in parent's room. Rollaway beds $15/night, cribs free. AE, DC, DISC, MC, V. Self-parking $8, valet $15. From I-4, take Exit 72, Hwy. 528/Bee Line Expwy. east to the John Young Pkwy., then south to Central Florida Pkwy. **Amenities:** 3 restaurants (Italian, French, American); cafe; lounge; 2 outdoor heated pools; kids' pool; 18 holes of golf; 3 tennis courts (lighted); spa; health club; children's center; arcade; playground; concierge; free transportation to Universal and SeaWorld, transportation to Disney parks for a fee; business center; car-rental desk; salon; 24-hr. room service; babysitting; nonsmoking rooms. *In room:* A/C, TV, dataport, minibar, coffeemaker, hair dryer, iron, safe.

MODERATE

Hawthorn Suites Lake Buena Vista ★ (Value)   One of the things that appeals to us most about this property, which opened in summer 2000, is a floor plan that allows separation of kids and adults, which allows mom and dad some (relative) private time. Its 500-square-foot standard rooms have four areas: a living room with a sleeper sofa, chair, and TV; bedroom with recliner and TV; full kitchen with dining room table for four; and bathroom with vanity. Two-bedroom units are also available. We think the extras here are a big plus for families, too. The Hawthorn offers a free American breakfast buffet daily, a social hour (hors d'oeuvres, beverages, and snacks) Monday through Thursday, and a light meal on Wednesday evenings. The pool is small, but its downright restful compared to the pools at some other hotels. The atmosphere is friendly, the service is

---

Tips Marriott Montage

The December 2000 christening of **Marriott Village at Little Lake Bryan,** 8623 Vineland Ave., Orlando, FL 32821 (© 877/682-8552 or 407/938-9001; fax 407/938-9002; www.marriottvillage.com), brought together three of the flagship's properties in a cluster just east of Lake Buena Vista, 3 miles from WDW. No matter what your budget is, you'll likely find a room here that satisfies your needs. The resort includes a 400-room SpringHill Suites ($129–$179 double), a 388-room Fairfield Inn ($119–$169 double), and a 312-room Courtyard by Marriott ($139–$179 double). Children under 17 stay free in parent's room, and an extra person costs an additional $10.

All rooms have fridges. Each property has adult and kids' pools and activities, fitness centers, whirlpools, and guest services desks. All offer transportation for a fee ($10–$12 per person per day) to Disney parks and non-Disney parks. There are three restaurants within walking distance. To get there, take I-4 Exit 68, Highway 535/Apopka–Vineland Road, then head south to Vineland, and go left ½ mile to the village. There's free self-parking, and valet parking costs $8.

good, and it's just 3 minutes from Hotel Plaza Boulevard. All in all, this is an excellent value choice, especially for those on a budget.

8303 Palm Pkwy., Orlando, FL 32836. ℂ **800/936-9417**, 800/527-1133 (forgive the music before the chain identifies itself), or 407/597-5000. Fax 407/597-6000. www.hawthornsuiteslbv.com. 120 units. $99–$179 for 4–6. Rollaway beds $10/night, cribs free. AE, DC, DISC, MC, V. Free self-parking. From I-4, take Exit 68, Hwy. 535/Apopka–Vineland Rd., east to Palm Pkwy., then right ¼ mile to hotel. **Amenities:** Outdoor heated pool; basketball court; exercise room; Jacuzzi; free shuttle to Disney parks, transportation for a fee to other parks; guest laundry; nonsmoking rooms. *In room:* A/C, TV w/pay movies, dataport, kitchen, fridge, coffeemaker, hair dryer, iron, microwave.

Holiday Inn Family Suites Resort ★★ (Finds)

This all-suite property, conveniently located a mile from Disney, does a fantastic job catering to families with its two-bedroom Kid Suites, which feature a second semiprivate bedroom equipped with bunk beds, game tables, two TVs, and changing themes (from Disney to Coke to the comics). In the Classic Suites, the semiprivate bedroom has a queen-size bed. Several three-bedroom Kid Suites offering an additional private bedroom and bathroom, with space for up to nine people, have recently been installed. The Sweet Heart Suites with a heart-shaped tub and 50-inch surround sound TV caters to couples, but the Cinema Suites, with a 60-inch surround sound TV and DVD players, have a private bedroom and sleeper sofa and an older child will probably think the setup very cool. All suites have kitchenettes. Parents with young kids should ask for East Track rooms, which are closest to the resort's wonderful kiddie pool and playground. Families with older kids might prefer the more sedate West Track rooms, which border an Olympic-size pool and have two whirlpools.

The resort, voted the best Holiday Inn property in North America for 2003, has theme nights (movies, magic, and more). Kids have their own check-in desk, recreation center, and little ones will especially love the resort's mini train, which usually offers rides in the morning. A new addition is the **Sugar & Spice Kids Spa** (ℂ **866/KIDS-SPA**; www.kidsspa.com), which allows your kids to be pampered with special treatments and packages designed for boys and girls (prices range from $10 for a costume photo to $99 for a spa package). The spa is open 9am to 9pm and appointments should be booked in advance as its very popular with families. Another great bonus for families: Room rates include a free breakfast and **kids 12 and under eat** lunch and dinner free with paying adults.

Note: At press time, the hotel announced that it was partnering with Nickelodeon and would embark on a $20 million renovation that would last until 2005. As part of the renovation, the hotel (which will be renamed Nickelodeon Family Suites by Holiday Inn) rooms will be redecorated, and character breakfasts with Nickelodeon characters will be instituted. Call to ask what changes and renovations will have been made by the time you arrive.

14500 Continental Gateway (off Hwy. 536), Lake Buena Vista, FL 32830. ℂ **877/387-5437** or 407/387-5437. Fax 407/387-1489. www.hifamilysuites.com. 800 units. $135–$189 Residential Suite; $146–$199 Kid Suite and Classic Suite; $166–$219 Cinema and Sweet Heart Suite. No rollaway beds, cribs free. AE, DC, DISC, MC, V. Free self-parking. From I-4, take Exit 67, Hwy. 536/International Dr., east 1 mile to the resort. **Amenities:** Restaurant; lounge; general store; several fast-food counters; large lap pool; family swimming pool; fitness center; 2 Jacuzzis; 3 outdoor Ping-Pong tables; 2 shuffleboard courts; game room; playground; mini-golf course; complimentary recreation center for ages 4–12; kids' library; tour desk; free transportation to Disney parks, transportation for a fee to other parks; coin-op washers and dryers. *In room:* A/C, TV w/pay movies and VCR (some with Nintendo), dataport, fridge, coffeemaker, hair dryer, iron, safe, microwave.

Holiday Inn Sunspree Resort Lake Buena Vista ★

Just a mile from the Disney parks, this is another hotel that caters to kids big time. They get their own check-in desk, a welcome from raccoon mascots Max and Maxine (who will tuck them in at night if you make a reservation for a nominal fee), and a fun bag with a video game coupon and lollipop. The hotel's 231 **Kid Suites** have beds for up to six (bunk beds are placed in a separate sleeping area for children, which also has Nintendo video games) and themes (a jail, a fort, a space capsule, and more). All of the suites have kitchenettes. Child safety kits and outlet covers are provided upon request. If you like sleeping in, ask for a room that doesn't face the pool area (a delightful spot that's very popular with the young set).

Camp Holiday offers kids ($6 per child per hour, no minimum, ages 4–12, 11am–10pm) activities such as games, movies, arts and crafts, magic shows, and karaoke. Free movies are also shown daily in the Castle Theater. Note also that kids under 12 eat free when accompanied by adults, though it isn't fine dining.

13351 Apopka–Vineland Rd./Hwy. 535 (between Hwy. 536 and I-4), Lake Buena Vista, FL 32821. ℂ **800/ 366-6299** or 407/239-4500. Fax 407/239-7713. www.kidsuites.com. 507 units. $99–$149 standard for up to 4; $119–$179 Kid Suite. Rollaway beds $10/night, cribs free. Resort fee $2. AE, DISC, MC, V. Free self-parking. Pets under 25 pounds $25 for the duration of your stay. From I-4, take Exit 68, Hwy. 535/Apopka–Vineland Rd., south ¼ mile. **Amenities:** Food court; outdoor heated pool; kids' pool; fitness center; Jacuzzi; kids' club; arcade; playground; guest services desk; free shuttle to Disney parks, transportation to non-Disney parks for a fee; guest laundry; limited room service; nonsmoking rooms. *In room:* A/C, TV/VCR, fridge, coffeemaker, hair dryer, iron, microwave.

INEXPENSIVE

Hampton Inn Lake Buena Vista　　Location rules at this modern property, which is only 1 mile from the entrance to Hotel Plaza Boulevard on the northeast corner of Disney. It's not fancy, but the price is right and there are lots of nearby places to eat, shop, and party. It's also relatively close to Downtown Disney Marketplace. Rooms on the fourth or fifth floors have microwaves and mini-fridges; request one and ask if the rate is higher than for a room on a lower floor. Some connecting rooms (useful for larger families) are available. The amoeba-shaped pool is nothing special, but it'll cool you off when you need it.

8150 Palm Pkwy., Orlando, FL 32836. ℂ **800/370-9259** or 407/465-8150. Fax 407/465-0150. www.hampton innlbv.com. 147 units. $69–$129 for up to 4. 5th person $10. Rates include continental breakfast. Children 17 and under stay free in parent's room. Rollaway beds $10/night, cribs free. AE, DC, DISC, MC, V. Free self-parking. From I-4, take Exit 68, Hwy. 535/Apopka–Vineland Rd., east to Palm Pkwy., then right ¼ mile to hotel. **Amenities:** Outdoor heated pool; Jacuzzi; guest services desk; free shuttle to Disney parks, transportation to non-Disney parks for a fee; nonsmoking rooms. *In room:* A/C, TV w/pay movies, dataport, coffeemaker, hair dryer, iron.

5 Places to Stay in the Kissimmee Area

This tin-glitz highway is dotted with burger barns and T-shirt shops. It's not what you'd call scenic, and the visuals are further dampened by something that tests motorists' patience: seemingly perpetual road construction that slows traffic to turtle speed. But U.S. 192, also known as Irlo Bronson Memorial Highway—and locally as that *bleeping-bleeper*—has a number of inexpensive motels (don't be surprised if the paper is peeling off the walls in some cases) located within 1 to 8 miles of Disney, to which most provide or can arrange transport. There are a few good family options here, especially for those on a budget. Hitching a ride to Universal Orlando and SeaWorld can be trickier, but an always-safe bet is to contact Mears Transportation (see "Getting Around," in chapter 3). The round-trip cost usually runs from $10 to $20 per person per day.

Note: You'll find the hotels and motels described on the map "Kissimmee Area Accommodations" on p. 93.

Kissimmee Area Accommodations

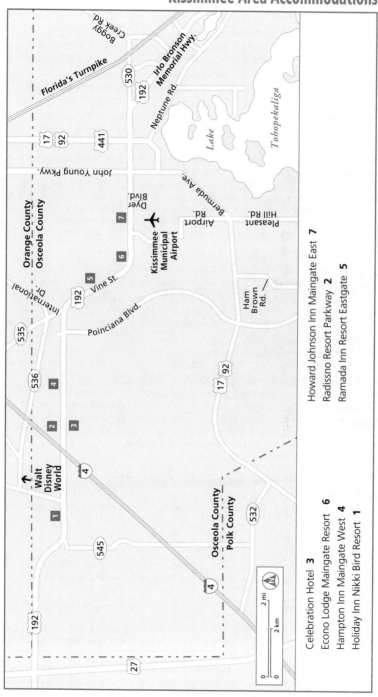

Celebration Hotel **3**
Econo Lodge Maingate Resort **6**
Hampton Inn Maingate West **4**
Holiday Inn Nikki Bird Resort **1**

Howard Johnson Inn Maingate East **7**
Radissno Resort Parkway **2**
Ramada Inn Resort Eastgate **5**

MODERATE

Holiday Inn Nikki Bird Resort ⭐ Here's another family-friendly property with a roaming mascot (Nikki Bird) and a dedication to kids. The hotel renovated its rooms in 1997 and is still in good shape. It features standard rooms as well as **Kid Suites** (themes vary) that have a separate sleeping area for youngsters. Kids 12 and under eat free with a paying adult. **Camp Nikki** ($8 per child per hour, no minimum, ages 4–14, 11am–10pm) offers outdoor activities, such as tennis and sand-castle building, as well as indoor arts and crafts, games, and movies. The hotel has not one but two kids' pools for water-loving youngsters (and three whirlpools for worn-out parents).

7300 W. Irlo Bronson Memorial Hwy. (U.S. 192), Kissimmee, FL 34747. © **800/206-2747** or 407/396-7300. Fax 407/396-7555. www.hicentralflorida.com. 530 units. $89–$149 for up to 4. Rollaway beds $10/night, cribs free. Resort fee $3.75. AE, DC, DISC, MC, V. Free self-parking. Take I-4 Exit 64B/U.S. 192 west. It's 1½ miles past the Disney entrance on the left. **Amenities:** Restaurant (American); grill; lounge; 3 outdoor heated pools; 2 kids' pools; lighted tennis court; exercise room; Jacuzzi; kids' club; playground; concierge; free shuttle to Disney parks, transportation to non-Disney parks for a fee; guest laundry; valet. *In room:* A/C, TV w/pay movies, VCR, and Nintendo, dataport, fridge, coffeemaker, tea maker, hair dryer, iron, microwave.

Radisson Resort Parkway ⭐ Located 1½ miles from Disney, this 20-acre property was last renovated in 2001 and has standard motel-style rooms (two double beds or a king) with views ranging from the pool or courtyard to the parking lot. Aside from the reasonable prices and location, its offerings include a dining program where kids 10 and under eat free with paying adults The main pool, with waterfalls and a water slide (and a wading pool for young kids), will make sure your children won't mind spending cost-cutting time away from the parks. And the hotel is one of the few to offer free shuttle service to all of the major parks.

2900 Parkway Blvd., Kissimmee, FL 34747. © **800/333-3333** or 407/396-7000. Fax 407/396-6792. www. radissonparkway.com. 718 units. $89–$129 for up to 5. Rollaway beds $11.20/night, cribs free. AE, DC, DISC, MC, V. Free self-parking. From I-4, take Exit 64A/U.S. 192 east to 1st light, Parkway Blvd., then left. **Amenities:** 2 outdoor heated pools; kids' pool; 2 lighted tennis courts; exercise room; arcade; playground; free shuttle to Disney, Universal, and SeaWorld parks; limited room service; babysitting; guest laundry; nonsmoking rooms. *In room:* A/C, TV w/movies, dataport, minibar, coffeemaker, hair dryer, iron, safe.

INEXPENSIVE

The accommodations listed here lack a lot of kid-friendly amenities, but they help stretch a family budget. In addition to these, there are scores of other inexpensive but serviceable motels, including chains (see appendix B). Most are within a few miles of Disney, have rooms in the 300-square-foot range, and arrange transportation to the parks. Many sell attractions tickets, *but be careful:* Many deeply discounted ticket offers are too good to be true. Some folks land at the parks with *invalid tickets* or waste a half-day or more listening to a timeshare pitch to get 30% to 40% off the regular price (single-day Disney park

---

⌐ Fun Fact Not So Magical

When Disney built the town of Celebration, it planned 800 hotel rooms as part of the community. Three years later, in 1997, it raised the ante to 1,039. Now the entertainment giant wants to add another 1,000 rooms. Is enough, enough? The Celebration Patriots, a growing group of residents opposed to the plan, holler, YES! Stay tuned to see which side wins.

> ### *Tips* Coming in 2004 & Beyond
>
> The 1,200-acre ChampionsGate development southwest of WDW is build-
> ing a 730-room **Omni Orlando Resort**. Located at I-4 and Highway 532, it
> will have two golf courses, a spa, and six restaurants and bars. Developers
> plan to add 3,400 rooms in coming years. Not to be second best, **Reunion
> Resort & Club** will be a $2 billion, 2,300-acre vacation community. Plans
> call for 3,000 hotel rooms plus 5,000 homes and timeshares. The project
> and its three golf courses will be on both sides of I-4, south of Disney in
> northwest Osceola County. While there isn't a projected opening date yet,
> **Four Seasons Hotels and Resorts** has purchased 400 acres in Celebration
> with plans to build a 425-room hotel with an 18-hole golf course. The site
> also will have single-family homes.

tickets are $52 for adults, $42 for kids 3–9). If a discount is more than $2 to $5
per ticket, it's probably too good to be true.

Stick to buying tickets through the parks or accept the modest discounts
offered by such groups as AAA, AARP, and the visitor information centers listed
in chapter 2.

Econo Lodge Maingate Resort *(Value* Location and price are the perks here.
The inn is 1¼ miles from the WDW entrance, and its rates are a bargain,
though the property lacks any sign of pizzazz. The rooms are clean, and connecting rooms are available, but the price means you're not getting any frills.
Note: This two-story hotel doesn't have elevators.

7514 W. Irlo Bronson Memorial Hwy. (U.S. 192), Kissimmee, FL 34747. © 800/365-6935, 407/390-9063, or
407/396-2000. Fax 407/390-1226. www.enjoyfloridahotels.com. 445 units. $39–$119 double. Resort fee
$2.75. Extra person $10. Children 18 and under stay free in parent's room. Rollaway beds $10/night, cribs
free. AE, DC, DISC, MC, V. Free self-parking. From I-4, take Exit 64B/U.S. 192 west 2¼ miles; hotel is on the
left past Reedy Creek Blvd. **Amenities:** Restaurant; lounge; outdoor heated pool; Jacuzzi; arcade; guest services desk; car-rental desk; free shuttle to Disney parks, transportation to non-Disney parks for a fee; limited
room service; guest laundry; nonsmoking rooms. *In room:* A/C, TV.

Hampton Inn Maingate West Built in late 1997, this inn has a newer, nicer
feel because it hasn't been around long enough to earn all of the battle scars usually found in U.S. 192 accommodations. While it's more expensive on the front
end than the Econo Lodge, it's also much more modern and upbeat. The inn is
located 1½ miles west of the WDW entrance road. Rates include a free continental breakfast and cookies and milk in the lobby at night.

3000 Maingate Lane, Kissimmee, FL 34747. © 800/936-9417 or 407/396-6300. Fax 407/396-8989. www.
hamptoninnmaingatewest.com. 118 units. $69–$119 double. Extra person $10. Children 17 and under stay
free in parent's room. Rollaway beds $10/night, cribs free. AE, DC, DISC, MC, V. Free self-parking. From I-4,
take Exit 64B/U.S. 192 west 3 miles, then right on Maingate Lane (across the street from Celebration). **Amenities:** Outdoor heated pool; guest services desk; free shuttle to Disney parks, transportation to non-Disney
parks for a fee; nonsmoking rooms. *In room:* A/C, TV, dataport, fridge, coffeemaker, iron, microwave.

Howard Johnson Inn Maingate East *(Value* Like most motels fronting U.S.
192, this HoJo—across the street from Celebration—offers traffic congestion
and noise, but it's only 2 miles from Disney. Rooms are typical of the chain—
basic, but a fraction nicer than those in the Econo Lodge, a little earlier in this
section. One kid under 12 eats free with each paying adult. Efficiencies and
suites with full kitchens offer views of the pool and are probably worth the extra
dollars.

Tips   Homes Away from Home

Families who like all the comforts of home—especially larger ones—can bypass motels in favor of rental condos or homes. Rates vary widely depending on quality and location, and many require at least a 2- or 3-night minimum. A lot of these properties are 5 to 15 miles from the theme parks and offer no transportation, so having a car is a necessity.

On the plus side, most have two to six bedrooms and a convertible couch, two or more bathrooms, a full kitchen, multiple TVs and phones, and irons. Some have washers and dryers. Homes often have their own pools, while condos have a common one. They can be a big bargain if your family is large enough that it will require more than one hotel room.

On the minus side, they can be sterile. Most don't have daily maid service, and restaurants are often as far away as the parks. (There's another reason you'll need a car.) Unless they're in a gated community, don't expect onsite security. And some don't even offer dinnerware, utensils, or salt-and-pepper shakers—so make sure to ask. The same goes for child necessities such as cribs.

Rates range from about $75 to $350 per night ($300–$1,800 per week).

Popular players include **Endless Summer Vacation Homes** (© 800/554-4378; www.esvflorida.com); **Holiday Villas** (© 800/344-3959; www.holidayvillas.com); and **Summer Bay Resort** (© 888/742-1100; www.summerbayresort.com).

6051 W. Irlo Bronson Memorial Hwy. (U.S. 192), Kissimmee, FL 34747. © 800/288-4678 or 407/396-1748. Fax 407/649-8642. www.hojomge.com. 567 units. $45–$95 double; efficiencies $10 more; suites $20 more. Resort fee $2. Extra person $10. Children 18 and under stay free in parent's room. Rollaway beds $11/night, cribs free. AE, DC, DISC, MC, V. Free self-parking. From I-4, take Exit 64A/U.S. 192 east 1 mile. Motel is on the left. **Amenities:** Restaurant; 2 outdoor heated pools; kids' pool; Jacuzzi; arcade; guest services desk; free bus to Disney parks, transportation to non-Disney parks for a fee; guest laundry; nonsmoking rooms. *In room:* A/C, TV w/pay movies and Nintendo, dataport, safe.

Ramada Inn Resort Eastgate (Value)   If you're looking for a peer in quality to the HoJo (above), this Ramada—4 miles from Disney—is it. Built in 1983 and remodeled in 1998, it's a cut cleaner than many of the chain's standard motels, but no fancier. Standard rooms sport balconies. The **Kid Suites** aren't sweet, but they do offer a queen-size bed for the adults and bunk beds for their heirs. One **kid eats free** with each paying adult. The property does have recreational facilities—including a lighted tennis court and a miniature putting green—not common to this class of hotel.

5150 W. Irlo Bronson Memorial Hwy. (U.S. 192), Kissimmee, FL 34746. © 800/272-6232 or 407/396-1111. Fax 407/396-1607. www.floridaramada.com. 402 units. $59–$129 double. Resort fee $2.60. Extra person $10. Children 17 and under stay free in parent's room. Rollaway beds $10/night, cribs free. AE, DC, DISC, MC, V. Free self-parking. From I-4, take Exit 64A/U.S. 192 east 2½ miles to the motel. **Amenities:** Restaurant (American); lounge; outdoor heated pool; kids' pool; lighted tennis court; Jacuzzi; arcade; playground; car-rental desk; free shuttle to Disney parks, transportation to non-Disney parks for a fee; limited room service; guest laundry; valet; nonsmoking rooms. *In room:* A/C, TV w/pay movies and Nintendo, dataport, coffeemaker, hair dryer, iron, safe.

6 Places to Stay in the International Drive Area

The hotels and resorts listed here are 7 to 10 miles north of Walt Disney World (via I-4) and 1 to 5 miles from Universal Orlando and SeaWorld. Though you won't fully get away from Toon Town anywhere in central Florida, International Drive hotels tend to have few, if any, fur-wearing critters (which probably won't please the kids looking for Mickey). The advantages of staying on I-Drive: It's a self-supporting place, filled with accommodations, restaurants, and small attractions; it has its own inexpensive trolley service (see "Getting Around," in chapter 3), and it's centrally located for families who want to do Disney, Universal, SeaWorld, *and* the downtown area. The disadvantages: The north end of I-Drive is badly congested. The shops, motels, eateries, and attractions along this stretch can be as tacky as those on U.S. 192, and many of the motels and hotels don't offer free transportation to the parks. The going rate is $6 to $15 round-trip.

You'll find these places located on the map "International Drive Area Accommodations" in this section.

VERY EXPENSIVE

Peabody Orlando ★★ (Moments)   Kids and fun-loving adults flock to this hotel's main lobby, where five mallards march from the elevators into a fountain daily at 11am, accompanied by John Philip Sousa's "King Cotton March" and their own red-coated duck master (see p. 261 for more on the ducks). That's just one of the magnets at a grand hotel that has one of the friendliest staffs in central Florida.

That said, though it's one of our favorites in O-Town, the Peabody is primarily a business and convention hotel and usually only sees lots of kids during school vacation times, when parents coming to town on business tend to bring their offspring along. This isn't the best choice for the mainstream vacationer, but if you want to stay on I-Drive and do end up here, your kids certainly won't suffer. It's classy without being stuffy, and, if your budget allows the splurge, you won't be disappointed. Rooms are large and comfortable and the west-side rooms (6th floor and up) offer a distant view of Disney fireworks. The kids' pool has a mini waterfall, and there are tennis courts for sports-oriented kids.

Tip: Your best chance at getting lower rates is in July and August, when the convention trade falls flat, and occupancy drops to as little as 20%.

9801 International Dr. (between Bee Line Expwy. and Sand Lake Rd.), Orlando, FL 32819. ⓒ 800/732-2639 or 407/352-4000. Fax 407/354-1424. www.peabodyorlando.com. 891 units. $380–$480 standard room for up to 3; $520–$1,600 suite. Extra person $20. Children 17 and under stay free in parent's room. Rollaway beds $15/night, cribs free. AE, DC, DISC, MC, V. Free self-parking usually, but in busy times there is a $5 charge, valet parking $8. From I-4, take Exit 74A, Sand Lake Rd./Hwy. 482, east to International Dr., then south. Hotel is on left across from Convention Center. **Amenities:** 3 restaurants; deli; 3 lounges; outdoor heated pool; kids' pool; 4 lighted tennis courts; fitness center; spa; Jacuzzi; concierge; guest services desk; business center; shopping arcade; transportation to WDW and other parks for a fee; 24-hr. room service; babysitting; massage; valet; nonsmoking rooms; concierge-level rooms. *In room:* A/C, TV, dataport, minibar, hair dryer.

Portofino Bay Hotel ★★★ (Finds)   Universal Orlando's premier hotel is as grand as Disney's Grand Floridian (p. 72). It's a replica of Portofino, Italy, with a harbor and canals on which boats travel to the theme parks. The Old World ambience is carried throughout the public areas, restaurants, and rooms by a staff that tries hard to match the Peabody's friendliness.

The luxurious rooms are large (with sleep space for up to five), and the beds have Egyptian-woven sheets. The pillows are so soft that you'll want to take them home. (Alas, they're too big for your suitcase, so ask the resort how to order one.)

Tips Smaller Homes Away from Home

Several area timeshare resorts rent rooms or apartments to tourists when the owners aren't using them. The **Disney Vacation Club (✆ 407/939-7775;** www.dvcresorts.com) offers studios and one- to two-bedroom apartments at the Villas at Disney's Wilderness Lodge, Disney's Boardwalk Villas, Disney's Beach Club, and Disney's Old Key West (all reviewed earlier in this chapter). Some have small fridges and microwaves; others have full kitchens. Rates start at about $250 per night. Outside the world, per-night rates begin at $200 to $250 per night for one- and two-bedroom apartments with kitchens. As with hotel rooms, you can get major discounts off the rack rates (as low as $70 a night) for these properties if you do your homework. An especially nice choice is the **Sheraton's Vistana Villages,** 12401 International Dr. (✆ **407/238-5000;** www.starwoodvo.com). Another good place to look is the **Marriott's Grande Vista,** 5925 Avenida Vista, off International Drive (✆ **800/845-5279;** www.vacationclub.com), which has a kids' activity center on the premises.

Kids Suites have a private bedroom with a king bed and a separate room with two small beds, a beanbag chair, TV, VCRs, and CD player (your young ones will love their pint-size bathrobes). Hypoallergenic rooms are available.

The Loews hotel chain, which manages the property, is known for its child-friendly programs (including a special program for grandparents traveling with their grandchildren—call the hotel for details). **Campo Portofino** is a supervised children's activity and game center ($10 per child per hour, no minimum, ages 4–14, 5pm–midnight). **Kids Kloset** loans things such as games, books, car seats, potty seats, and other items. The resort also supplies pagers for **teens,** giving them some freedom without being completely out of touch with their parents. Mom and dad can relax while the kids are otherwise occupied at the privately run Greenhouse Spa, which features a state-of-the-art fitness center and full-service spa. Like many of the Disney properties, the Portofino doesn't just have swimming pools; its beach pool has a fort with a water slide (the villa pool offers several cabanas).

One of the biggest pluses: Guests get no-line access to most rides at Universal Studios Florida and Islands of Adventure, as well as seating privileges at shows and restaurants. It's a big advantage if you have fidgety children.

5601 Universal Blvd., Orlando, FL 32819. ✆ **888/322-5541** or 407/503-1000. Fax 407/224-7118. www.loewshotels.com/hotels/orlando. 750 units. $275–$390 double; $459–$2,200 villas and suite. Extra person $25. Children 17 and under stay free in parent's room. Rollaway beds $25/night, cribs free. AE, DC, DISC, MC, V. Self-parking $6, valet parking $12. From I-4, take Exit 75B, Kirkman Rd./Hwy. 435 and follow the signs to Universal. **Amenities:** 3 restaurants (Northern Italian); deli; 3 lounges; 2 outdoor heated pools (1 for concierge and suite guests only); kids' pool; bocce courts (concierge and suite guests only); fitness center; spa; watersports equipment; kids' club; arcade; concierge; tour desk; free water-taxi transportation to Universal Studios, Islands of Adventure, and CityWalk, free shuttle to SeaWorld, transportation for a fee to WDW parks; business center; shopping arcade; 24-hr. room service; babysitting; guest laundry; valet; nonsmoking rooms; concierge-level rooms. *In room:* A/C, TV, hair dryer, iron, safe.

EXPENSIVE

Hard Rock Hotel ★★ When it comes to location, you can't get any closer to CityWalk or Universal Studios Florida, and it's probably the coolest joint in town for teens and preteens. This California mission–style resort with a rock 'n'

International Drive Area Accommodations

DoubleTree Castle **11**
Hard Rock Hotel **4**
Peabody Orlando **12**
Portofino Bay Hotel **2**
Quality Inn Plaza **9**
Radisson
   Barcelo Hotel **8**
Radisson Hotel Universal
   Orlando **1**
Red Horse Inn **6**
Renaissance Orlando
   Resort at SeaWorld **13**
Residence Inn Orlando **7**
Royal Pacific Resort **3**
Sheraton Studio City **5**
Sierra Suites Orlando
   Convention Center **10**

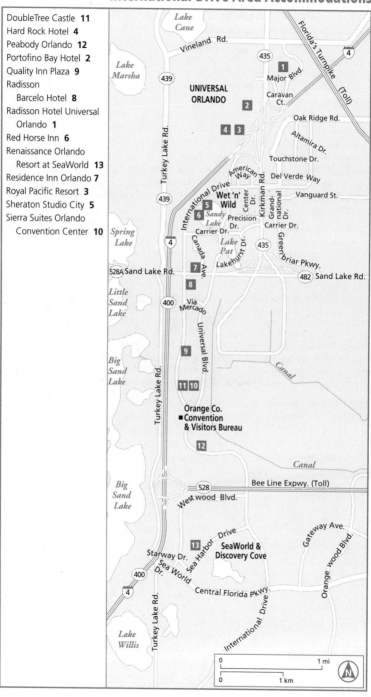

roll theme opened in 2001 with rates a level cheaper than its Universal sister, the Portofino (see above) and a pool outfitted with a **240-foot water slide** and 12 underwater speakers.

The Hard Rock is a notch above some of Disney's comparable properties, including Animal Kingdom Lodge. All rooms here sleep four people, are very comfortable and, though the bathrooms aren't big, there is (like at the Disney resorts) a separate dressing area that has a sink. Like the Portofino, the best views here are on the "bay" side, overlooking the piazza. Unfortunately, though the rooms are pretty soundproof, a few notes seep through some walls, so ask for a room that's situated away from the lobby area if you have light sleepers. **Kids Suites** have a separate room with two small beds, a TV, and separate bathroom. **Camp Lil' Rock** is a supervised children's activity and game center ($10 per child per hour, no minimum, ages 4–14, 5pm–midnight). Kids amenity bags are available on request. The hotel also offers a special package for grandparents traveling with their grandkids.

There is a Hard Rock Cafe several hundred yards from the hotel, but the resort has two of its own restaurants on property. Like at the Portofino, staying here means no-line access to almost every ride at Universal Studios Florida and Islands of Adventure, and seating privileges for shows and restaurants. It's a huge plus if you're here during a busy season.

5000 Universal Blvd., Orlando, FL 32819. © **800/232-7827** or 407/503-7625. Fax 407/224-7118. www. loewshotels.com/hotels/orlando. 654 units. $209–$369 double; $419–$1,675 suite. Extra person $20. Children 17 and under stay free in parent's room. Rollaway beds $25/night, cribs free. AE, DC, DISC, MC, V. Self-parking $6, valet parking $12. From I-4, take Exit 75B, Kirkman Rd./Hwy. 435 and follow the signs to Universal. **Amenities:** 2 restaurants; grill; 2 lounges; outdoor heated pool; kids' pool; fitness center; kids' club; arcade; concierge; free water-taxi transportation to Universal Studios, Islands of Adventure, and City-Walk, free shuttle to SeaWorld, transportation for a fee to WDW parks; shopping arcade; 24-hr. room service; babysitting; guest laundry; valet; nonsmoking rooms. *In room:* A/C, TV, hair dryer, iron, safe.

Renaissance Orlando Resort at SeaWorld ★★

This stylish hotel, the classiest in this I-Drive price category, offers large rooms and, while it doesn't have much in the way of kids' amenities, it's a great location for theme-park nomads: It's across from SeaWorld and about 10 to 15 minutes from Universal Orlando and Walt Disney World. The lobby charms kids and adults alike with a 10-story atrium, koi pond (at up to 25 lb., they're huge!), free-flight aviary, and **six glass elevators** that overlook the atrium. Kids get a **small stuffed dolphin** upon check-in. East-side rooms, especially from the sixth floor up, have a nice view of SeaWorld, which is within walking distance (but watch the traffic). North- and south-side rooms have balconies overlooking the atrium. The pool area is nice enough, and there's a small wading pool for young kids.

6677 Sea Harbour Dr., Orlando, FL 32821. © **800/327-6677** or 407/351-5555. Fax 407/351-9991. www. renaissancehotels.com. 778 units. $149–$269 double. Extra person $20. Children 17 and under stay free in parent's room. Rollaway beds and cribs free. AE, DC, DISC, MC, V. Free self-parking, valet parking $9. From I-4, take Exit 72, Hwy. 528/Beeline Expwy., east to International Dr., then go south to Sea Harbour Dr. and turn right. **Amenities:** 2 restaurants; grill; 3 lounges; outdoor heated pool; kids' pool; 4 lighted tennis courts; health club; spa; 2 Jacuzzis; sauna; arcade; playground; concierge; tour desk; car-rental desk; transportation for a fee to all the parks; business center; shopping arcade; 24-hr. room service; massage; babysitting; guest laundry; valet; nonsmoking rooms. *In room:* A/C, TV w/pay movies and PlayStation, dataport, safe.

Royal Pacific Resort ★★ *Value*

The third of Universal Orlando's three resorts has an open-air courtyard with an exquisite orchid garden, palm trees, waterfalls, and lagoons, including one in which a float plane with a 90-foot wingspan is docked (the scene reminds more than a few people of *Gilligan's Island*). The

(*Tips*) **So You Didn't Book a Room . . .**

As we mentioned earlier, coming to Orlando without a reservation isn't a good idea. But if you do and you're looking for a basic room, try these chain properties (see also appendix B). They're moderate or inexpensive in price and located in the budget motel corridors. All are relatively convenient to the attractions. While we can't vouch for them or their family-friendliness personally, their brand names generally mean reliability:

In Kissimmee:

- **Best Western Eastgate,** 5565 W. Irlo Bronson Memorial Hwy., Kissimmee (© **407/396-0707**).
- **Best Western Kissimmee,** 2261 E. Irlo Bronson Memorial Hwy., Kissimmee (© **407/846-2221**).
- **Comfort Suites Maingate Hotel,** 7888 W. Irlo Bronson Memorial Hwy., Kissimmee (© **407/390-9888**).
- **Comfort Suites Resort Maingate East,** 2775 Florida Plaza Blvd., Kissimmee (© **407/397-7848**).
- **Days Inn Maingate East,** 5840 W. Irlo Bronson Memorial Hwy., Kissimmee (© **407/396-7969**).
- **Days Inn Maingate–West,** 7980 W. Irlo Bronson Memorial Hwy., Kissimmee (© **407/997-1000**).
- **DoubleTree Villas Maingate,** 4787 W. Irlo Bronson Memorial Hwy., Kissimmee (© **407/397-0555**).
- **Howard Johnson Maingate West,** 8660 W. Irlo Bronson Memorial Hwy., Kissimmee (© **407/396-4500**).
- **Quality Suites Maingate East,** 5876 W. Irlo Bronson Memorial Hwy., Kissimmee (© **407/396-8040**).

In the International Drive Area:

- **Days Inn Convention Center/SeaWorld,** 9990 International Dr., Orlando (© **407/352-8700**).
- **Days Inn East of Universal Studios,** 5827 Caravan Court, Orlando (© **407/351-3800**).
- **Days Inn International Drive,** 7200 International Dr., Orlando (© **407/351-1200**).
- **Holiday Inn Express International Drive,** 6323 International Dr., Orlando (© **407/351-4430**).
- **Travelodge International Drive,** 5859 American Way, Orlando (© **407/345-8880**).

You can also try **Discount Hotels of America** (© **877/766-6787** or 407/294-9600; www.discounthotelsamerica.com).

Royal Pacific doesn't quite succeed at creating a Polynesian paradise (you can hear the screams of riders on the Hulk Coaster from the pool area), but it's definitely the best Universal resort in the theme department.

The rooms, though smaller than those at other Universal resorts, are attractively decorated with lovely wood accents and carvings; they are better than some at comparable Disney resorts. The **Mariner's Club** is a children's activity and game center ($10 per child per hour, no minimum, ages 4–14, 5–11pm). And the **lagoon pool** area—the largest in Orlando—has a beach and play zone that's very popular with the young set. Kids will likely enjoy the free water-taxi ride that goes from all of Universal's resorts to its theme parks (though it's admittedly a slow ride). The big plus: Guests get no-line access to almost every ride at Universal Studios Florida and Islands of Adventure, and seating privileges for shows and restaurants. The big minus: The self-parking lot is a very long hike from the hotel, and you have to pay $6 for that privilege.

Note: Loews hotels are pet-friendly and we've heard several complaints in specific reference to this hotel about run-ins with barking dogs.

6300 Hollywood Way, Orlando, FL 32819. © **800/232-7827** or 407/503-3000. Fax 407/503-3202. www.loewshotels.com/hotels/orlando. 1,000 units. $179–$319 double; $279–$1,400 suite. Extra person $20. Children 17 and under stay free in parent's room. Rollaway beds $25/night; cribs free. AE, DC, DISC, MC, V. Self-parking $6, valet parking $12. From I-4, take Exit 75B, Kirkman Rd./Hwy. 435 and follow the signs to Universal. **Amenities:** 2 restaurants (Asian-Polynesian, American); 3 lounges; outdoor heated pool; kids' pool; sauna; Jacuzzi; kids' club; arcade; concierge; free water-taxi transportation to Universal Studios, Islands of Adventure, and CityWalk, free shuttle to SeaWorld, transportation for a fee to WDW parks; babysitting; valet; nonsmoking rooms. *In room:* A/C, TV, dataport, hair dryer, iron, safe.

MODERATE

DoubleTree Castle   Built on a medieval castle theme, this nine-story I-Drive property is entertaining from the moment you enter. Topped with spiraling turrets and two rooftop terraces, the castle is painted in pink, lavender, and gold pastels and adorned in public areas with art, antique dolls, weaponry from around the world, and unusual timepieces. Canned Renaissance music adds to the theme. As if that weren't enough, you get Doubletree's famous chocolate chip cookies upon check-in. Rooms are standard motel-style with two queen-size beds or a king-size bed. The circular pool is equipped with fountains for extra fun. The hotel sometimes shows family films on a poolside screen on weekends.

8629 International Dr., Orlando, FL 32819. © **800/952-2785** or 407/345-1511. Fax 407/248-8181. www.doubletreecastle.com. 216 units. $89–$219 double; $139–$269 suites. Resort fee $2. Extra person $10. Children 17 and under stay free in parent's room. Rollaway beds $15/night; cribs free. AE, DC, DISC, MC, V. Free self-parking. Take I-4 Exit 74A, Sand Lake Rd./Hwy. 482, go east to International Dr., then south to Austrian Row. **Amenities:** Restaurant (tapas); cafe; 2 lounges, outdoor heated pool; exercise room; arcade; guest services desk; free transportation to Disney, Universal, and SeaWorld parks; limited room service; guest laundry; valet; nonsmoking rooms. *In room:* A/C, TV w/PlayStation, dataport, fridge, coffeemaker, hair dryer, iron, safe.

Radisson Barcelo Hotel ⭐   Like many I-Drive properties, the Radisson offers a good location for people whose vacations center on Universal Orlando or SeaWorld, and a central location for travelers who plan to visit Disney and the downtown, too. Rooms are brightly decorated (the Deluxe towers rooms are larger and worth the extra dough) and have refrigerators, but views are basic. The seventh floor (the highest) will give you a look at SeaWorld to the south. Otherwise, you'll be watching traffic on I-4 or I-Drive. Guests get privileges at the adjacent YMCA Aquatic and Fitness Center. As a plus, kids 10 and under eat free with a paying adult at breakfast.

8444 International Dr., Orlando, FL 32819. © **888/380-9696** or 407/345-0505. Fax 407/352-5894. www.radisson-orlando.com. 520 units. $79–$199 double. Extra person $15. Children 17 and under stay free in parent's room. Rollaway beds $10/night; cribs free. AE, DC, DISC, MC, V. Free self-parking. From I-4, take Exit 74A, Sand Lake Rd./Hwy. 482, turn right on International Dr., go ½ mile, and hotel is on the right. **Amenities:** Restaurant; grill; lounge; outdoor heated pool; lighted tennis court; bocce court; playground; guest services desk; free shuttle to Universal Orlando and SeaWorld, transportation for a fee to Disney parks; guest laundry;

valet; nonsmoking rooms. *In room:* A/C, TV w/pay movies and Nintendo, dataport, fridge, coffeemaker, hair dryer, iron, safe.

Radisson Hotel Universal Orlando ☆

Location alone earns this hotel a star, though it doesn't have a huge number of kid-friendly amenities. Built for the convention trade, the former Radisson Twin Towers got a name change in the mid-1990s when people started flocking to Universal Orlando, which is right across the street. The rooms are reasonably nice and fit for a property that is 2 decades old (the last renovation was in 1997). Rooms on the west side, floors 6 through 18, offer views of the Universal parks and CityWalk.

5780 Major Blvd., Orlando, FL 32819. ℂ 800/333-3333, 800/327-2110, or 407/351-1000. Fax 407/363-0106. www.radissonuniversal.com. 742 units. $99–$199 double. Extra person $15. Children 17 and under stay free in parent's room. Rollaway beds $15/night; cribs free. AE, DC, DISC, MC, V. Free self-parking. From I-4, take Exit 75B, Kirkman Rd./Hwy. 435, go north to Major, then right. **Amenities:** Restaurant; food court; 2 lounges; outdoor heated pool; kids' pool; exercise room; Jacuzzi; arcade; free transportation to Universal and SeaWorld, transportation for a fee to Disney; salon; limited room service; nonsmoking rooms. *In room:* A/C, TV, dataport, coffeemaker, hair dryer, iron.

Residence Inn Orlando International Drive ☆

Marriott's Residence Inns were designed to offer home-away-from-home comfort for business travelers, but the concept works just as well for families. The all-suite hotel is well kept and is situated within a mile of many of International Drive's attractions, shops, and restaurants. The attractive one-bedroom suites are a roomy 500 square feet and sleep four. All have full kitchens. Some two-bedroom suites are available. An evening social hour is held Monday through Thursday. A welcome basket that includes popcorn is included in the rates. On the downside, there is neither a kids' pool nor other specific child-friendly amenities.

7975 Canada Ave. (just off Sand Lake Rd., a block east of International Dr.), Orlando, FL 32819. ℂ 800/227-3978 or 407/345-0117. Fax 407/352-2689. www.marriott.com. 176 units. $89–$159 double; $129–$189 studio suite. Extra person $15. Children 17 and under stay free in parent's room. Rollaway beds $10/night; cribs free. Rates include buffet breakfast. AE, DC, DISC, MC, V. Free self-parking. From I-4, take Exit 74A, Sand Lake Rd./Hwy. 482, go east to Canada, then left. Pets welcome for $100 deposit (half nonrefundable) plus $10 per day. **Amenities:** Outdoor heated pool; exercise room; Jacuzzi; free bus service to Disney, transportation for a fee to the other theme parks; guest laundry; valet. *In room:* A/C, TV w/pay movies, dataport, kitchen, fridge, coffeemaker, iron, safe.

Sheraton Studio City

If you and the kids love classic Hollywood (think Bogart, Marilyn, Elvis, James Dean, and the Duke), you'll probably love the décor at this 21-story I-Drive property. Built in 1974, it got its new name and a $15.5-million makeover in 1999. Rooms have an Art Deco flavor and the personality of a high-rise motel. It's very popular with families, there are several facilities for kids, and the security is excellent (you have to show a room key to get to the guest elevators), but the service can be hit or miss.

5905 International Dr. (between Universal Blvd. and Kirkman Rd.), Orlando, FL 32819. ℂ 800/327-1366 or 407/351-2100. Fax 407/352-8028. www.sheratonstudiocity.com. 302 units. $99–$189 for up to 4; $179–$269 suites. Resort fee $3.50. Extra person $20. Children 17 and under stay free in parent's room. Rollaway beds $15/night; cribs free. AE, DC, DISC, MC, V. Free self-parking. From I-4, take Exit 75A, Kirkman Rd., south to International Dr., then right. **Amenities:** 2 restaurants (American); lounge; outdoor heated pool; kids' pool; exercise room; arcade; concierge; rental-car desk; free shuttle to Disney and Universal, transportation for a fee to SeaWorld; salon; limited room service; babysitting; guest laundry; nonsmoking rooms. *In room:* A/C, TV w/PlayStation, dataport, coffeemaker, hair dryer, iron, safe.

Sierra Suites Orlando Convention Center

This respite from I-Drive is on the less-than-congested Universal Boulevard, a few blocks north of where the boulevard spills into International Drive at the Convention Center and Peabody

Orlando (reviewed earlier in this chapter). You can walk to some minor attractions, and if you take the footpath west a few hundred feet, you can catch the I-Ride Trolley (see "Getting Around," in chapter 3). Size-wise, the rooms are standard motel fare (yes, they're rooms despite the kitchens and the name the property calls itself) though they are clean and comfortable. You'll have to do without a kiddie pool, though the regular pool is just fine. There's a complimentary grocery shopping service.

8750 Universal Blvd. © 800/474-3772 or 407/903-1500. Fax 407/903-1555. www.sierra-orlando.com. 137 units. $99–$159 for up to 4. Rates include free continental breakfast. Rollaway beds not available; cribs free. AE, DC, DISC, MC, V. Free self-parking. From I-4, take Exit 74A, Sand Lake Rd./Hwy. 482, go east to the 3rd light (Universal), go right/south, and hotel is ½ mile on the right. **Amenities:** Outdoor heated pool; exercise room; Jacuzzi; arcade; guest services desk; free shuttle to Disney, Universal, and SeaWorld; guest laundry; valet; nonsmoking rooms. *In room:* A/C, TV, dataport, kitchen, coffeemaker, hair dryer, iron, safe.

INEXPENSIVE

Quality Inn Plaza   The rooms at this property—across from the Pointe Orlando shopping plaza and its child-magnet FAO Schwartz—are spread through five-, six-, and seven-story buildings. Ask for a recently renovated room as we've had reports of hit-or-miss quality (no pun intended). The biggest advantage in staying here is proximity to I-Drive nightlife, restaurants, and shops. One kid under 12 eats free with each paying adult. Ask for a quiet room away from I-Drive to avoid the morning traffic noise.

9000 International Dr., Orlando, FL 32819. © 800/999-8585 or 407/996-8585. Fax 407/996-6839. www.qualityinn-orlando.com. 1,020 units. $59–$109 for up to 4. Resort fee $1.50. Rollaway beds $10/night, cribs free. AE, DC, DISC, MC, V. Free self-parking. From I-4, take Exit 74A, Sand Lake Rd./Hwy. 482, turn east at bottom of ramp. Turn right at first intersection, International Dr. The property is 1 mile on the right. Pets $10 a night. **Amenities:** Restaurant (American); deli; lounge; 3 outdoor heated pools; 2 arcades; guest services desk; free transportation to Universal and SeaWorld, transportation for a fee to Disney; limited room service; guest laundry; valet; nonsmoking rooms. *In room:* A/C, TV w/pay movies, fridge, coffeemaker, safe, microwave.

Red Horse Inn   Built in 1972, this old-style Southwestern two-story motel is a clean bargain, but it's also a refurbishment work-in-progress and rooms can be hit or miss (ask for a recently renovated one to prevent disappointment). Ours, for instance, had a poorly working drain. Public areas such as the reception desk boast some of the Western artwork of Jack Pardue and the Cactus Cantina Lobby Bar is decked out with real saddles (if your kids are cowboy fans, they'll love it). The location is near Universal Orlando, Wet 'n Wild, and the north I-Drive outlet malls. Guests can use the fitness center, game room, pool, and other facilities at the Red Horse's Hollywood-themed sister property, Sheraton Studio City (see above).

5825 International Dr. (between Universal Blvd. and Kirkman Rd.), Orlando, FL 32819. © 877/936-4100 or 407/351-4100. Fax 407/996-4599. www.redhorseorlando.com. 159 units. $59–$99 double. Resort fee $3.50. Extra person $10. Rates include continental breakfast. Children 17 and under stay free in parent's room. Rollaway beds $15/night, cribs free. AE, DC, DISC, MC, V. Free self-parking. From I-4, take Exit 75A, Kirkman Rd., south to International Dr., then right. Small pets welcome for $10/night. **Amenities:** Outdoor heated pool; kids' pool; concierge; free transportation to Universal and SeaWorld, transportation for a fee to Disney; babysitting; guest laundry; valet; nonsmoking rooms. *In room:* A/C, TV, dataport, safe.

5

Family-Friendly Dining

If you're a fast-food fan, you'll find hundreds of choices here, thanks to Orlando's 30-something years of growth as a family destination. Theme and theme-park restaurants, only a rung or two higher on the culinary scale, aren't far behind in the numbers. That's why local cuisine is usually regarded as sub par when compared to that of foodie havens such as New York, San Francisco, and Las Vegas, which in recent years has escaped its blue-plate image. In fairness, though, some of Orlando's 4,000 restaurants can go head-to-head with the competition. (Disbelievers should grab a chair at **Emeril's** at CityWalk, **Victoria & Albert's** at Disney's Grand Floridian Resort & Spa, or **Manuel's on the 28th** in downtown Orlando.)

Because most central Florida visitors spend much of their time at Disney or Universal, we're going to focus a lot of our energy there, but we won't leave out worthwhile restaurants beyond the giants. We're going to sample what's cooking along International Drive and visit a fair share of other dining rooms that have benefited from the culinary infusion created by the attractions.

Note to parents: Keep in mind that most moderate to inexpensive restaurants have kids' menus ($4–$6, often including a beverage and fries), and many offer distractions, such as coloring books and mazes, to keep your two-footed critters busy until the chow arrives. We'll make a note of those available at press time, but things change, so **ask** when reserving a table.

You'll also want to pay attention to the places that offer **"character meals"** (see the listings later in this chapter). Also note that the higher the meal costs, the less likely you'll be in the same dining room as a lot of little ones. So, if you hanker an evening to rekindle the romance while the kids crash in an activity center or stay with a babysitter (see chapter 4), try one of the adult restaurants we've included. (They're easy to spot—they're the ones without kids' menus.)

For online information about area restaurants, visit **www.disneyworld.com**, **www.universalorlando.com**, **www.orlandoinfo.com**, or the websites in the listings that follow.

PRIORITY SEATING AT WDW RESTAURANTS

Walt Disney World's Priority Seating is like a reservation but less rigid. It means you get the *next table available after* you arrive, but a table isn't kept empty while the eatery waits for you. Therefore, you probably will wait 15 to 30 minutes, even if you arrive on time. You can arrange Priority Seating 90 days or more in advance at most full-service restaurants in the Magic Kingdom, Epcot, Disney–MGM Studios, Animal Kingdom, the Disney resorts, and Downtown Disney. Priority Seating also can be arranged for character meals (later in this chapter) and dinner shows. To make arrangements, call ✆ **407/939-3463.** You'll get a confirmation number for your Priority Seating reservation—bring it with you. Dinner shows (see chapter 10, "Entertainment for the Whole Family") can be booked 2 months or more in advance. *Note:* Since the Priority Seating phone number was instituted in 1994, it has become much more difficult to obtain a table as a walk-in. So we *strongly* advise you to call ahead.

Note: If you're making a Priority Seating reservation for a meal at select Disney restaurants on major holidays, you may be asked to guarantee your reservation with a credit card. You can cancel this reservation up to 48 hours in advance of your meal. If you cancel after that or don't show, you'll get charged $10 per person on the reservation.

If, however, you don't reserve in advance, you can take your chances by making reservations at the restaurants or:

- **In Epcot** at Guest Relations near the entrance or Universe of Energy.
- **In the Magic Kingdom** via the telephones at several locations including the Walt Disney World Railroad station just inside the entrance.
- **In Disney–MGM Studios** via the telephones just inside the entrance.
- **In Animal Kingdom** at Guest Relations near the entrance. You can get Priority Seating at the Rainforest Cafe at Animal Kingdom. Since this is a *verrry* popular place, the sooner you call the better.

Also, keep these restaurant facts in mind:

- As of July 1, 2003, *all Florida restaurants* and bars that serve food are smoke free.
- The Magic Kingdom (including its restaurants) serves no alcoholic beverages, but liquor is available at Animal Kingdom, Epcot, and Disney–MGM Studios restaurants and elsewhere in the WDW complex.
- All sit-down restaurants in Walt Disney World take American Express, Diners Club, Discover, MasterCard, and Visa.
- Unless otherwise noted, restaurants in the parks **require park admission.**
- Guests at Disney resorts and official properties can make restaurant reservations through guest services or concierge desks.
- Nearly all WDW restaurants with sit-down or counter service offer children's menus with items ranging from $4 to $6, though in a few cases they're $9 to $12. Some include beverages and fries.

A NOTE ABOUT PRICES

The prices for adult meals at Orlando restaurants—except at theme parks and other attractions—are no more exorbitant than you'd find anywhere else. Restaurants in this chapter are listed by location, and prices reflect the cost of an average entree per person. Restaurants in the **Inexpensive** category charge under $10 for an entree; those in the **Moderate** category charge $11 to $20. **Expensive** restaurants will set you back $21 to $30, and **Very Expensive** restaurants will top that, sometimes by a large margin.

Tips How Early Can You Book It?

At the time this book went to press, Priority Seating arrangements could be made up to 90 days in advance for all character meals, and meals at the Disney resorts and theme parks; up to 180 days in advance for a meal at Victoria & Albert; and up to 2 years in advance at Disney's Hoop-Dee-Doo and Spirit of Aloha dinner shows. For arrangements, call (407/939-3463.

One last note: The restaurants we list in this chapter occasionally change menus (and sometimes more than just occasionally). So items we feature here may not be on the menu when you visit. And, as entrees vary, so do prices. That said, it's time to divide and conquer.

1 Restaurants by Cuisine

AFRICAN

Boma (Animal Kingdom Lodge, $$$, p. 125)

Jiko—The Cooking Place ✿ (Animal Kingdom Lodge, $$$, p. 126)

AMERICAN

B-Line Diner (International Drive Area, $$, p. 136)

Cinderella's Royal Table ✿ (Magic Kingdom, $$$, p. 116)

Cosmic Ray's Starlight Café (Magic Kingdom, $, p. 117)

50's Prime Time Café (Disney–MGM Studios, $$, p. 120)

Hard Rock Cafe (Universal Orlando, $$, p. 134)

Hollywood Brown Derby (Disney–MGM Studios, $$$, p. 117)

Liberty Tree Tavern (Magic Kingdom, $$, p. 117)

Panera Bread ✿ (Downtown and elsewhere, $$, p. 143)

Planet Hollywood (Pleasure Island, $$, p. 128)

Plaza Restaurant (Magic Kingdom, $, p. 117)

Sci-Fi Dine-In Theater Restaurant (Disney–MGM Studios, $$, p. 121)

Tusker House (Animal Kingdom, $, p. 122)

BARBECUE

Bubbalou's Bodacious BBQ ✿ (Winter Park, $, p. 144)

Wild Jacks (International Drive, $$, p. 138)

BRITISH

Rose & Crown Pub & Dining Room (Epcot, $$, p. 114)

BRUNCH

Atlantis ✿ (International Drive Area, $$$$, p. 135)

CALIFORNIA

California Grill ✿✿✿ (Disney's Contemporary Resort, $$$, p. 125)

Pebbles ✿✿ (Lake Buena Vista, $$, p. 130)

Rainforest Cafe ✿ (Downtown Disney Marketplace & Animal Kingdom, $$, p. 128 and p. 121)

Wolfgang Puck Grand Café ✿ (Disney's West Side, $$, p. 129)

CANADIAN

Le Cellier Steakhouse (Epcot, $$, p. 114)

CARIBBEAN

Bahama Breeze (International Drive, $$, p. 136)

Jimmy Buffett's Margaritaville (Universal's CityWalk, $$, p. 134)

CHARACTER MEALS

Cape May Café (Disney's Beach Club Resort, $$, p. 145)

Chef Mickey's ✿✿ (Disney's Contemporary Resort, $$, p. 145)

Cinderella's Royal Table ✿ (Magic Kingdom, $$, p. 145)

Crystal Palace Buffet ✿ (Magic Kingdom, $$, p. 145)

Donald's Prehistoric Breakfasto-saurus (Animal Kingdom, $$, p. 145)

Garden Grill ✿ (Epcot, $$, p. 146)

Liberty Tree Tavern ✿ (Magic Kingdom, $$, p. 146)

1900 Park Fare ✿ (Disney's Grand Floridian Resort & Spa, $$, p. 146)

Key to Abbreviations: $$$$ = Very Expensive $$$ = Expensive $$ = Moderate $ = Inexpensive

'Ohana Character Breakfast
(Disney Polynesian Resort, $$,
p. 146)

Princess Storybook Breakfast
(Epcot, $$, p. 146)

CHINESE

Lotus Blossom Café (Epcot, $,
p. 115)

Nine Dragons (Epcot, $$, p. 114)

CUBAN

Bongo's Cuban Cafe (Disney's
West Side, $$, p. 129)

Rolando's ⊛ (Casselberry, $$,
p. 143)

FOOD COURT

Sunshine Season Food Fair (Epcot,
$, p. 115)

FRENCH

Bistro de Paris (Epcot, $$$$,
p. 110)

Chefs de France (Epcot, $$$,
p. 110)

Citricos ⊛ (Disney's Grand Floridian Resort & Spa, $$$$, p. 122)

Le Provence ⊛ (Downtown
Orlando, $$$, p. 141)

Maison & Jardin ⊛ (Altamonte
Springs, $$$, p. 141)

GERMAN

Biergarten (Epcot, $$, p. 113)

Sommerfest (Epcot, $, p. 115)

INTERNATIONAL

The Boheme ⊛ (Downtown
Orlando, $$$$, p. 140)

Cafe Tu Tu Tango ⊛ (International
Drive, $$, p. 138)

Dux ⊛⊛ (International Drive,
$$$$, p. 135)

Manuel's on the 28th ⊛⊛⊛
(Downtown Orlando, $$$$,
p. 140)

Park Plaza Gardens (Winter Park,
$$$, p. 142)

Victoria & Albert's ⊛⊛⊛ (Disney's
Grand Floridian Resort & Spa,
$$$$, p. 122)

ITALIAN

Delfino Riviera ⊛ (Universal's
Portofino Bay Hotel, $$$$,
p. 131)

Enzo's on the Lake ⊛⊛
(Longwood, $$$$, p. 140)

L'Originale Alfredo di Roma
(Epcot, $$$, p. 112)

Mama Della's (Universal's
Portofino Bay Hotel, $$$,
p. 132)

Mama Melrose's Ristorante Italiano
(Disney–MGM Studios, $$,
p. 120)

Pacino's Italian Ristorante ⊛
(Kissimmee, $$, p. 143)

Pastamore Ristorante ⊛ (Universal's
CityWalk, $$, p. 134)

Portobello Yacht Club ⊛ (Pleasure
Island, $$$, p. 128)

Romano's Macaroni Grill ⊛ (Lake
Buena Vista, $, p. 130)

Tony's Town Square Restaurant
(Magic Kingdom, $$$, p. 116)

JAPANESE

Mikado Japanese Steak House ⊛
(Marriott's Orlando World
Center, $$$, p. 142)

Ran-Getsu of Tokyo (International
Drive, $$$, p. 136)

Tempura Kiku (Epcot, $$$, p. 113)

Teppanyaki (Mitsukoshi) Dining
Room (Epcot, $$$, p. 113)

Yakitori House (Epcot, $, p. 116)

MEXICAN

Cantina de San Angel (Epcot, $,
p. 115)

San Angel Inn ⊛ (Epcot, $$,
p. 114)

MISSISSIPPI DELTA

House of Blues (Disney's West
Side, $$, p. 129)

MOROCCAN

Marrakesh ⊛ (Epcot, $$$, p. 112)

NEW ORLEANS

Boatwright's Dining Hall (Disney's
Port Orleans Resort, $$, p. 126)

Emeril's ★★ (Universal's
CityWalk, $$$$, p. 131)

NORWEGIAN

Akershus (Epcot, $$, p. 113)
Kringla Bakeri og Kafe (Epcot, $,
p. 115)

PACIFIC RIM

'Ohana ★ (Disney's Polynesian
Resort, $$, p. 127)
Tchoup Chop ★★ (Universal's
Royal Pacific Hotel, $$$,
p. 133)

PIZZA

Toy Story Pizza Planet
(Disney–MGM Studios, $,
p. 121)

SEAFOOD/STEAKS/CHOPS

Artist Point ★ (Disney's Wilder-
ness Lodge, $$$, p. 124)
Blackfin Seafood Grill & Bar ★
(Winter Park, $$$, p. 141)
Cape May Café (Disney's Beach
Club Resort, $$, p. 126)
Charlie's Lobster House (Interna-
tional Drive, $$$$, p. 135)

Coral Reef ★ (Epcot, $$$, p. 112)
Crabby Bill's ★ (Kissimmee, $$,
p. 142)
Flying Fish Café (Disney's
Boardwalk, $$$, p. 125)
Fulton's Crab House ★ (Pleasure
Island, $$$$, p. 127)
The Palm (Universal's Hard Rock
Hotel, $$$$, p. 132)
Plantation Room (Celebration,
$$$, p. 142)
Wild Jacks (International Drive,
$$, p. 138)
Yachtsman Steakhouse ★ (Disney's
Yacht Club Resort, $$$$,
p. 124)

SOUTHWESTERN

Chili's Grill & Bar (Lake Buena
Vista, $$, p. 130)

TAPAS

Cafe Tu Tu Tango ★ (International
Drive, $$, p. 138)
Spoodles (Disney's Boardwalk,
$$$, p. 126)

2 Places to Dine in Walt Disney World

From hot-dog stands to posh restaurants, there are nearly 350 places to eat in
WDW's theme parks (Epcot, Magic Kingdom, Disney–MGM Studios, and
Animal Kingdom), resorts, and "official" hotels. That doesn't include eateries
located in entertainment and shopping areas (Pleasure Island, Downtown Disney West Side, and Downtown Disney Marketplace), some of which are listed
in the Lake Buena Vista section. Yet, with only a few exceptions, you won't find
them winning accolades from *Bon Appétit*. The food in most Disney restaurants
is on par with Universal Orlando's—filling and palatable, but generally overpriced for the quality received. The exception: **kids' menus.** Many sit-down and
counter-service eateries in the parks (all Disney sit-down restaurants do) offer
kids' meals for $4 to $6, but sometimes as high as $12. While some are strictly
a la carte, many include a beverage, fries or other side dishes (but usually not
dessert or specialty drinks) in the sticker price.

Note: All Disney sit-down restaurants have highchairs and booster seats.

IN EPCOT

An ethnic meal at one of the World Showcase pavilions is a traditional part of the
Epcot experience, but we remind you that many of the following establishments
are overpriced for the quality received. Unless money is no object, you may want
to consider the lower-priced walk-in places located throughout the park. They

> ⌒ **Tips** **Special Tastes**
>
> Looking for kosher food? Worried WDW can't entertain your vegetarian taste buds? Disney usually can handle those diets and other special ones (people who need fat-free or sugar-free meals—folks who have allergies or a lactose intolerance, for instance) as long as guests give Disney advance notice—usually no more than 24 hours. You can do that when you make Priority Seating arrangements (☎ **407/939-3463**) or, if you're staying at a Disney resort, at its Guest Relations desk.

don't require reservations (for details check the Epcot guide map you'll receive upon entering). Or eat at one of the full-service restaurants at lunch, when entree prices are lower. Almost all of those listed here serve lunch and dinner daily *(hours vary with park hours)*, and, unless otherwise noted, they offer **children's meals** (usually for ages 3–11). All but one or two require theme-park admission. These restaurants are located on the "Epcot Dining" map on p. 111.

Note: Because the clientele at even the fanciest Epcot World Showcase restaurant comes directly from the park, you don't have to dress up for dinner. **Priority Seating,** which reserves your place but not a specific table, is available at all WDW sit-down restaurants and is strongly recommended. Otherwise, the chances of getting a table without a wait—often a long wait—are pretty slim. Call ☎ **407/939-3463** for Priority Seating.

VERY EXPENSIVE

Bistro de Paris TRADITIONAL FRENCH   Located above Chefs de France (see below), this pricey bistro offers an occasionally changing menu that might include roasted veal chops with chanterelle mushrooms, rack of lamb or venison with grilled vegetables, and seared scallops with shiitake mushrooms. It's not a good choice for families unless the adults arrange for a sitter and come sans the kiddos. The restaurant has a respectable list of French wines.

France Pavilion, World Showcase. ☎ 407/939-3463. www.disneyworld.com. No kids' menu. Priority Seating. Main courses $29–$35 dinner. AE, DC, DISC, MC, V. Daily 5pm–1 hr. before park closes. Parking $7.

EXPENSIVE

Chefs de France TRADITIONAL FRENCH   Three renowned French chefs—Paul Bocuse, Roger Verge, and Gaston LeNotre—designed the menu, which is respectable by theme-park standards but doesn't threaten better French restaurants in the free world. Dinner entrees include seared grouper, salmon, and shrimp with crab-stuffed tomatoes and spinach ravioli. There's also a tasty vegetarian offering (layers of pasta infiltrated by zucchini, tomato, eggplant). Kids can dig into chicken strips, a burger on a brioche, or fried orange roughy, all with French names most adults can't pronounce. There's a substantial wine list to complement the menu, and the desserts are among the better ones in the World. Dining areas have an intimate, Art Nouveau feel thanks to candelabras and glass-and-brass dividers, but the service, at times lacking, can chill the fun.

France Pavilion, World Showcase. ☎ 407/939-3463. www.disneyworld.com. Kids' menu w/activities, highchairs, boosters. Priority Seating. Main courses $10–$18 lunch, $15–$30 dinner, kids $5.45–$5.85. AE, DC, DISC, MC, V. Daily noon–3:30pm and 5pm–1 hr. before park closes. Parking $7.

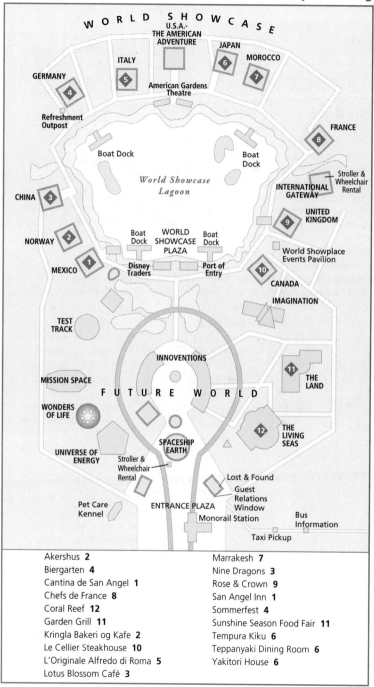

WORLD SHOWCASE

U.S.A.-
THE AMERICAN
ADVENTURE

JAPAN

MOROCCO

ITALY

GERMANY

American Gardens
Theatre

Refreshment
Outpost

FRANCE

Boat Dock

Boat
Dock

Stroller &
Wheelchair
Rental

World Showcase
Lagoon

INTERNATIONAL
GATEWAY

CHINA

UNITED
KINGDOM

NORWAY

Boat
Dock

WORLD
SHOWCASE
PLAZA

Boat
Dock

World Showplace
Events Pavilion

MEXICO

Disney
Traders

Port of
Entry

CANADA

IMAGINATION

TEST
TRACK

INNOVENTIONS

MISSION SPACE

THE
LAND

FUTURE WORLD

WONDERS
OF LIFE

THE
LIVING
SEAS

UNIVERSE OF
ENERGY

Stroller &
Wheelchair
Rental

SPACESHIP
EARTH

Lost & Found

Guest
Relations
Window

Pet Care
Kennel

ENTRANCE PLAZA

Monorail Station

Bus
Information

Taxi Pickup

Akershus **2**	Marrakesh **7**
Biergarten **4**	Nine Dragons **3**
Cantina de San Angel **1**	Rose & Crown **9**
Chefs de France **8**	San Angel Inn **1**
Coral Reef **12**	Sommerfest **4**
Garden Grill **11**	Sunshine Season Food Fair **11**
Kringla Bakeri og Kafe **2**	Tempura Kiku **6**
Le Cellier Steakhouse **10**	Teppanyaki Dining Room **6**
L'Originale Alfredo di Roma **5**	Yakitori House **6**
Lotus Blossom Café **3**	

Coral Reef 𝕗 SEAFOOD   We've seen both kids and adults mesmerized by the Reef's **5.6-million-gallon aquarium.** Mood is half the fun here as Disney denizens swim to "La Mer" and other classical music. Tiered seats, mainly in semicircular booths, give everyone a good view. Diners get fish-identifier sheets with labeled pictures so they can put names on the faces swimming by their tables (let the kids color or otherwise put their "signatures" on them). This is one of the most popular restaurants in all of the parks and it's definitely a winner with kids. Nevertheless, it still suffers the theme-park curse: The food is good but overpriced. Highlights include grilled mahimahi with wasabi-mashed potatoes and collard greens and grilled catfish with pepper-Jack cheese grits. Kids can dine on grilled chicken breast or fish, cheese pizza, or pasta in sauce, the Reef serves wine by the glass.

(Fun Fact   **Fast Food**

Disney guests eat about 10 million burgers, 8 million hot dogs, and 9½ million pounds of fries every year. That's enough fries to circle the planet three times. And it takes nearly two million pounds of ketchup to accompany all that fast food.

Living Seas Pavilion, Future World. 𝕔 **407/939-3463.** www.disneyworld.com. Kids' menu w/activities, highchairs, boosters. Priority Seating recommended. Main courses $12–$22 lunch, $16–$32 dinner, kids $5–$9. AE, DC, DISC, MC, V. Daily 11:30am–3pm and 4:30pm–park closing. Parking $7.

L'Originale Alfredo di Roma *Overrated* SOUTHERN ITALIAN   It's the most popular place in Epcot, but diners sometimes grumble about the prices and servers who can be too carefree (kids like it when they occasionally burst into song, however). L'Originale is actually L'Replica of Alfredo De Lelio's eatery in Rome, and the menu includes his celebrated fettuccine dished out in an exhibition kitchen. On the meatier side, a smallish veal chop is grilled and served with Chianti and truffle sauce, mushrooms, asparagus, and roasted potatoes. Kids can choose from fettuccini, lasagna, or spaghetti, the latter with meatballs. The wine list is reasonably extensive. The dining room noise level can be quite high (it's filled with families, after all), so if you want a quieter meal, ask for a seat on the veranda.

Italy Pavilion World Showcase. 𝕔 **407/939-3463.** www.disneyworld.com. Kids' menu w/activities, highchairs, boosters. Priority Seating. Main courses $11–$25 lunch, $17–$38 (most under $25) dinner, kids $5–$7. AE, DC, DISC, MC, V. Daily noon–park closing. Parking $7.

Marrakesh 𝕗 *Finds* MOROCCAN   This dining spot exemplifies the spirit of Epcot more than any other restaurant, yet a lot of guests ignore it because they're worried the menu is too exotic. Speaking of exotic, belly dancers entertain while your eyes feast on options such as marinated beef shish kabob; braised chicken with green olives, garlic, and lemon; and roast lamb au jus. On the kids' side, the choices are grilled chicken breast, beef on a skewer, or a burger. Older kids will likely find the atmosphere to their taste. The restaurant's hand-set mosaic tiles, latticed shutters, and painted ceiling represent some 12 centuries of Arabic design. Exquisitely carved faux ivory archways frame the dining area. There's a small selection of wine and beer for the adults in the family.

Morocco Pavilion, World Showcase. 𝕔 **407/939-3463.** www.disneyworld.com. Kids' menu w/activities, highchairs, boosters. Priority Seating. Main courses $12–$19 lunch, $17–$26 dinner; $28–$30 prix fixe; kids $4–$6. AE, DC, DISC, MC, V. Daily noon–park closing. Parking $7.

Tempura Kiku *Overrated* JAPANESE   Tempura batter can hide the flaws of almost anything inside—but in this case it can't hide the puny size of the shrimp, chicken, and other morsels within. This counter-service joint usually offers a tasty meal, but one can't help but think of Long John Silver's (which likely means that your kids will be happy enough). Tempura Kiku also serves sushi, sashimi, Kirin beer, plum wine, and sake along with specialty drinks.

Japan Pavilion, World Showcase. © 407/939-3463. www.disneyworld.com. No kids' menu. No Priority Seating. Main courses $9–$14 lunch, $13–$25 dinner. AE, DC, DISC, MC, V. Daily 11am–1 hr. before park closes. Parking $7.

Teppanyaki (Mitsukoshi) Dining Room JAPANESE   If you've been to any of the Japanese steakhouse chains *(teppanyakis),* you know the drill: Diners sit around grill tables while white-hatted chefs rapidly dice, slice, stir-fry, and sometimes launch the food onto your plate with amazing skill. The theatrics should keep your kids' attention riveted, though, unfortunately, the culinary acrobatics here are better than the cuisine. Expect entrees to have chicken, steak, shrimp, scallops, lobster, or a combination. Kids can order grilled chicken, tempura-style shrimp, or chicken, steak, or shrimp stir-fry. Like Tempura Kiku (see above), Kirin beer, plum wine, and sake are served.

Japan Pavilion, World Showcase. © 407/939-3463. www.disneyworld.com. Kids' menu w/activities, highchairs, boosters. Priority Seating. Main courses $12–$22 lunch, kids $5–$7; $14–$32 dinner, kids $5–$9. AE, DC, DISC, MC, V. Daily 11am–1 hr. before park closes. Parking $7.

MODERATE

Akershus NORWEGIAN   Akershus is a re-created 14th-century castle where you can sample a 40-item smorgasbord of hot and cold dishes, making it a bargain for big eaters. Sure it's cheesy. But it's also reasonably good chow, though some diners will find it difficult to adapt to the Scandinavian taste. Entrees change but usually include venison stew, baked and smoked salmon, peel-and-east shrimp, mustard herring, and an array of breads and cheeses. Children will appreciate the setting, but unless your young ones have adventurous tastes, they should definitely stick to the kids' menu, which offers grilled cheese, PBJs, pasta and meatballs, hot dogs and macaroni and cheese. The staff is friendly, and the white-stone interior, leaded-glass windows, and archways add to the atmosphere. Norwegian beer and aquavit are served.

Norway Pavilion, World Showcase. © 407/939-3463. www.disneyworld.com. Kids' menu w/activities, highchairs, boosters. Priority Seating. Lunch buffet $14 adults, $6 kids 3–11; dinner buffet $20 adults, $9 kids. AE, DC, DISC, MC, V. Daily noon–park closing. Parking $7.

Biergarten *Overrated* GERMAN   The Biergarten simulates a Bavarian village at Oktoberfest with a working water wheel and geranium-filled flower boxes adorning Tudor-style houses. Unfortunately, the festive atmosphere hardly makes up for the bland, methane-producing food. Entertainment might be an oompah band or a strolling accordionist, and guests are encouraged to dance and sing along. The all-you-can-gobble buffet is filled with Bavarian fare (assorted sausages, chicken schnitzel, sauerbraten, spaetzle, and sauerkraut) as well as rotisserie chicken. Kids appear to like the merrymaking, and though there's no child-specific menu, the buffet is extensive enough that even a picky eater should find something to their liking. Beck's and Kirschwasser are the featured adult beverages.

Germany Pavilion, World Showcase. © 407/939-3463. www.disneyworld.com. No kids' menu, highchairs, boosters. Priority Seating. Lunch buffet $15 adults, $6 children 3–11; dinner buffet $20 adults, $8 children. AE, DC, DISC, MC, V. Daily noon–3:45pm and 4pm–park closing. Parking $7.

Le Cellier Steakhouse CANADIAN If you're hankering for steak and you're already in Epcot, the convenience of Le Cellier is a plus, but it doesn't compare to the area's better steakhouses (see Yachtsman Steakhouse on p. 124). The restaurant's French Gothic facade and steeply pitched copper roofs lend a castle-like ambience. The dining room resembles a wine cellar, and you'll sit in tapestry-upholstered chairs under vaulted stone arches. Red-meat main events include the usual range of cuts—including filet, veal chop, and prime rib. Other options include cast-iron seared halibut, grilled pork loin, and sautéed shrimp with pasta. The kids' menu ranges from a cheeseburger or chicken nuggets to a child-size 6-ounce steak. Wash down your meal with a Canadian wine or choose from a selection of Canadian beers.

Canadian Pavilion, World Showcase. ✆ 407/939-3463. www.disneyworld.com. Kids' menu w/activities, highchairs, boosters. Priority Seating. Main courses $9–$18 lunch, $16–$26 dinner, kids $5–$9. AE, DC, DISC, MC, V. Daily noon–park closing. Parking $7.

Nine Dragons REGIONAL CHINESE When it comes to decor, Nine Dragons shines with carved rosewood furnishings and a dragon-motif ceiling. Some windows overlook a lagoon. But (is there an echo?) the food doesn't match the surroundings. Main courses feature Mandarin, Shanghai, Cantonese, and Szechuan cuisines, but portions are small. The dishes include spicy beef stir-fried with squash; lightly breaded lemon chicken; and a casserole of lobster, shrimp, and scallops sautéed with ginger and scallions. Kids' choices (finicky eaters beware) are sweet and sour chicken or fried rice with a spring roll. You can order Chinese or California wines with your meal.

China Pavilion, World Showcase. ✆ 407/939-3463. www.disneyworld.com. Kids' menu w/activities, highchairs, boosters. Priority Seating. Main courses $9.50–$19 lunch, $12–$30 dinner, $42.50 sampler for 2, kids $4.75. AE, DC, DISC, MC, V. Daily 11:30am–park closing. Parking $7.

Rose & Crown Pub & Dining Room BRITISH Visitors from the U.K. flock to this spot, where English folk music and the occasionally saucy server entertain you as you feast your eyes and palate on a short but traditional menu. It beckons with fish (cod) and chips wrapped in newspaper (kids love 'em), bangers and mash, prime rib with Yorkshire pudding, and, the best of the bunch, an English pie sampler (pork and cottage, and chicken and leek). Offerings for younger guests include cheese pizza, pasta with marinara sauce, roasted chicken, and fish and chips. Wash it down with a pint of Irish lager, Bass Ale, or Guinness Stout.

   Note: The outdoor tables (weather permitting) offer a fantastic view of IllumiNations (p. 194). You can request one when making Priority Seating arrangements, and if you can, make the request *at least* 30 days in advance.

United Kingdom Pavilion, World Showcase. ✆ 407/939-3463. www.disneyworld.com. Kids' menu w/activities, highchairs, boosters. Priority Seating for dining room, not for pub. Main courses $11–$14 lunch, $14–$20 dinner, kids $5.25–$6.50. AE, DC, DISC, MC, V. Daily 11am–1 hr. before park closes. Parking $7.

San Angel Inn ✮ MEXICAN It's always night at the San Angel, where you can feast on some of the best South-of-the-Border cuisine in all of the theme parks—not that there's a lot of competition. Candlelit tables set the mood, and the menu delivers reasonably authentic food (unless you're from the southwest and used to the real McCoy). The atmosphere is more romantic than family-oriented, and it's probably better for older kids rather than little ones (though you'll see them anyway). *Mole poblano* (chicken brought to life with more than 20 spices, carrots, and a hint of chocolate) is one top seller. Another favorite: *filete*

Tips Flamed Out

If you're a smoker, don't plan on lighting up over dinner. In mid-2003, a state constitutional amendment banned smoking in Florida's restaurants as well as bars that earn 10% or more of their income from food.

---

motuleño (grilled beef tenderloin over black beans, melted cheese, pepper strips, and fried plantains—a sweet, banana-like fruit). Chicken strips, cheeseburgers, and chicken tortillas fill out the kids' menu.

Mexico Pavilion, World Showcase. (© 407/939-3463. www.disneyworld.com. Kids' menu w/activities, highchairs, boosters. Priority Seating. Main courses $9.25–$17.50 lunch, $18–$23.50 dinner, kids $5. AE, DC, DISC, MC, V. Daily 11:30am–park closing. Parking $7.

INEXPENSIVE

Cantina de San Angel MEXICAN Counter-service eateries are the most common places to grab a bite in the parks and probably the best for families with young kids who don't do well sitting still in the confines of a restaurant. This one is a notch above Taco Bell. Come here if you want a palatable burrito, taco, churro, or frozen margarita on the fly. The only kid-specific choice is a $3.50 beef burrito.

Mexico Pavilion, World Showcase. (© 407/939-3463. www.disneyworld.com. No Priority Seating. Meals $6.50–$8. AE, DC, DISC, MC, V. Daily 11:30am–1 hr. before park closes. Parking $7.

Kringla Bakeri og Kafe NORWEGIAN We love this combination cafe-bakery. Grab-and-go options include a plate of smoked salmon and scrambled eggs, smoked ham and Jarlsberg cheese sandwiches, pastries, and waffles with strawberry preserves. Kids must choose from the adult options, and they'll probably do better with the bakery items.

Norway Pavilion, World Showcase. (© 407/939-3463. www.disneyworld.com. No Priority Seating. Sandwiches and salads $4–$6. AE, DC, DISC, MC, V. Daily 11am–park closing. Parking $7.

Lotus Blossom Café CHINESE If you've tried one of those Oriental walk-up joints in mall food courts, you know what to expect. It's an inexpensive self-service outlet that won't make a gourmet's wish list. Expect slightly above fast-food quality stir-fry, hot-and-sour, lo mein, and pork-fried rice. Sweet and sour chicken or an egg roll with fried rice ($3–$4) are the only kiddie options.

China Pavilion, World Showcase. (© 407/939-3463. www.disneyworld.com. No Priority Seating. Meals $4–$6.50. AE, DC, DISC, MC, V. Daily 11am–park closing. Parking $7.

Sommerfest GERMAN The quick-bite menu includes bratwurst and frankfurter sandwiches (one is still a hot dog) with sauerkraut. There is no specific menu for kids and this won't do it for really young children, although preteens and up should be fine.

Germany Pavilion, World Showcase. (© 407/939-3463. No Priority Seating. All items under $7. AE, DC, DISC, MC, V. Daily 11am–park closing. Parking $7.

Sunshine Season Food Fair *Value* FOOD COURT The food isn't gourmet, but of all cafeterias or counter-service stops in the World, Sunshine Season, in The Land, has the most diversity because it has six walk-ups in one and it may be the best option for families, as it has several things to please the kids, including cheese pasta and corn dogs ($3.50–$4.50) as well as some kid-friendly choices on the main menus. There's a sandwich shop (subs and more), a barbecue joint (ribs, chicken, pork), a potato place (with stir-fry, chili, and veggies), and a pasta counter (fettuccine, vegetable lasagna, and chicken Alfredo). There's also a small bakery and ice-cream stand. Colorful umbrella tables under a tent ring a splashing fountain, and hot-air balloons add to the festive décor. Its real value is that family members with different tastes can dine at the same time under one roof.

Land Pavilion, Future World. ✆ 407/939-3463. www.disneyworld.com. No Priority Seating. Meals $5–$8. AE, DC, DISC, MC, V. 11am–park closing. Parking $7.

Yakitori House JAPANESE   While it sounds exotic, the food in this cafeteria is the same quality as that in the Lotus Blossom Café—just above mall caliber. Main events include teriyaki shrimp, chicken, and beef skewers; beef curry; sushi; and shrimp tempura. Fried chicken with rice or chicken and beef teriyaki ($3.25–$4) are the kids' choices.

Japan Pavilion, World Showcase. ✆ 407/939-3463. www.disneyworld.com. No Priority Seating. Meals $5–$7.50. AE, DC, DISC, MC, V. 11am–park closing. Parking $7.

IN THE MAGIC KINGDOM

In addition to the places mentioned here, there are plenty of fast-food outlets throughout the park. You may find, however, that a quiet sit-down meal is an essential but all-too-brief way to get away from the forced-march madness. These restaurants are located on the "Walt Disney World & Lake Buena Vista Dining" map on p. 118 and "The Magic Kingdom" map on p. 160. And remember: Magic Kingdom restaurants *don't serve alcohol.* So the adult members of your party will have to go elsewhere if they like a drink with their meal.

EXPENSIVE

Cinderella's Royal Table ⚓ AMERICAN   Can you pass up the chance to eat in Cinderella Castle, the Magic Kingdom's icon? Those who enter are usually swept off their feet by the Gothic interior, which includes leaded-glass windows and a spiral staircase that overlooks commoners in the lobby. (There's also an elevator to the dining area.) The servers treat you like a lord or lady (we're not kidding, that's how they'll address you—your children will be charmed) and the menu has fetching names, but the fine print reveals traditional entrees. The Earl's Poulet, plainly speaking, is roasted chicken, the Loyal Knight is spice-crusted salmon, and the Grand Duke is a New York strip. The kids' fare: chicken strips, cheeseburgers, or cheese dogs.

Note: The Character Meal here is the hottest ticket in town and Priority Seating reservations are extremely tough to get. Lunch and dinner times offer no characters, but it's far easier to get a seat. So if your kids want to eat in the castle (and most find it a special treat), you'll have a far easier time getting in to later meals than you will at breakfast.

Cinderella Castle, Fantasyland. ✆ 407/939-3463. www.disneyworld.com. Kids' menu w/activities, highchairs, boosters. Priority Seating. Main courses $11–$16 lunch, $20–$26 dinner, kids $5. AE, DC, DISC, MC, V. Daily 11:30am–2:45pm and 4pm–1 hr. before park closing. Parking $7.

Tony's Town Square Restaurant ITALIAN   Inspired by the cafe in *Lady and the Tramp,* Tony's dishes out nondescript (sometimes cardboard-quality) lunches and dinners in a pleasant if somewhat harried dining room. It's also one of the top spots to bring young kids. Evening fare includes a variety of seafood, sautéed veal medallions with wild mushrooms, and breaded eggplant with tomato sauce and mozzarella cheese. With spaghetti, cheese ravioli, and cheese and pepperoni pizzas in the lineup, Tony's has one of the kid-friendliest menus in the kingdom. The original movie cels on the walls may inspire you to reenact the film's famous spaghetti smooch as your kids chow down. There's additional seating in a sunny, plant-filled solarium.

Main Street. ℂ **407/939-3463.** www.disneyworld.com. Kids' menu w/activities, highchairs, boosters. Priority Seating. Main courses $11–$16 lunch, $18.50–$24 dinner, kids $5. AE, DC, DISC, MC, V. Daily 8:30–10:45am, noon–2:45pm, and 4pm–park closing. Parking $7.

MODERATE

Liberty Tree Tavern AMERICAN   Step into a replica of an 18th-century Colonial pub and its historic atmosphere, including oak-plank floors, pewter-ware-stocked hutches, and a big brick fireplace hung with copper pots. The background music suits the period. The (hey, kids!) nightly **character dinner** (p. 146) has an all-you-can-eat array of roast turkey, beef, and pork loin with trimmings that adults may find less than compelling. Food here is served family-style (platters are set on tables and you serve yourself from that point on). The menu at lunch is similarly decent: Kids' fare includes mac and cheese, chicken strips, a cheeseburger, or hot dog.

Liberty Square. ℂ **407/939-3463.** www.disneyworld.com. Kids' menu w/activities, highchairs, boosters. Priority Seating. Main courses $11–$15 lunch, kids $5; character dinner $21, kids $10. AE, DC, DISC, MC, V. Daily 11:30am–3pm and 4pm–park closing. Parking $7.

INEXPENSIVE

Cosmic Ray's Starlight Café AMERICAN   The low-budget menu at this food court includes chicken (whole or half rotisserie, dark meat, white meat, fried, or grilled) and sandwiches (burgers, hot dogs, corned beef, including kosher options). There's also a kids' corn dog ($3.49) and lots of kids seemed to like the brownies (which have no sugar added) for dessert. Ray's is typical theme-park on-the-fly cuisine.

Main Street. ℂ **407/939-3463.** www.disneyworld.com. Priority Seating. All items $6–$8. AE, DC, DISC, MC, V. Daily 11am–park closing. Parking $7.

Plaza Restaurant AMERICAN   The sundaes, banana splits, and other ice-cream creations—arguably the best in WDW—at this 19th-century inspired restaurant draw more folks than anywhere else, especially during the dog days of summer. The atmosphere and the ice cream draw tons of families. The Plaza also has tasty if expensive sandwiches (turkey, Reuben, cheese steak, chicken, and burgers) that come with an order of fries or potato salad. On the kids' side, choices include a grilled cheese, two mini hot dogs, or a mini hot dog and mini burger. You can eat inside in an Art Nouveau dining room or on a veranda over-looking Cinderella Castle.

Main Street. ℂ **407/939-3463.** www.disneyworld.com. Kids' menu w/activities, highchairs, boosters. Priority Seating. Meals $9–$11; ice cream $4–$6; kids $5. AE, DC, DISC, MC, V. Daily 11am–park closing. Parking $7.

AT DISNEY–MGM STUDIOS

There are more than a dozen places to eat in MGM. Some have movie-lot names such as Studio Commissary and Starring Rolls Bakery. Those listed below are the best of the bunch. They're located on two maps, "Walt Disney World & Lake Buena Vista Dining" (p. 118) and "Disney–MGM Studios Theme Park" (p. 195).

EXPENSIVE

Hollywood Brown Derby AMERICAN   Modeled after the famed Los Angeles celebrity haunt where Louella Parsons and Hedda Hopper held court, the

Walt Disney World & Lake Buena Vista Dining

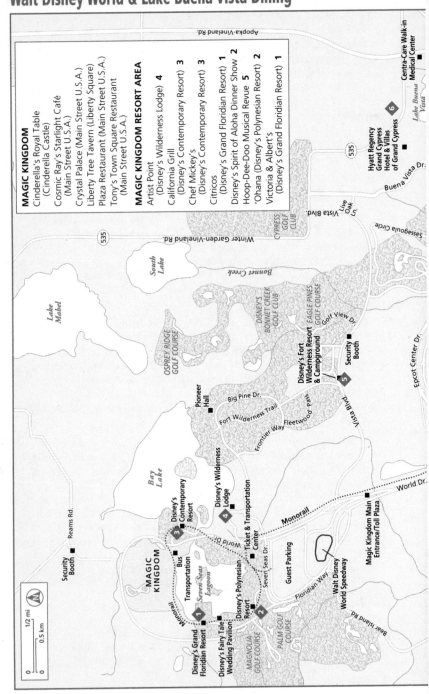

MAGIC KINGDOM

Cinderella's Royal Table
 (Cinderella Castle)
Cosmic Ray's Starlight Café
 (Main Street U.S.A.)
Crystal Palace (Main Street U.S.A.)
Liberty Tree Tavern (Liberty Square)
Plaza Restaurant (Main Street U.S.A.)
Tony's Town Square Restaurant
 (Main Street U.S.A.)

MAGIC KINGDOM RESORT AREA

Artist Point
 (Disney's Wilderness Lodge) **4**
California Grill
 (Disney's Contemporary Resort) **3**
Chef Mickey's
 (Disney's Contemporary Resort) **3**
Citricos
 (Disney's Grand Floridian Resort) **1**
Disney's Spirit of Aloha Dinner Show **2**
Hoop-Dee-Doo Musical Revue **5**
'Ohana (Disney's Polynesian Resort) **2**
Victoria & Albert's
 (Disney's Grand Floridian Resort) **1**

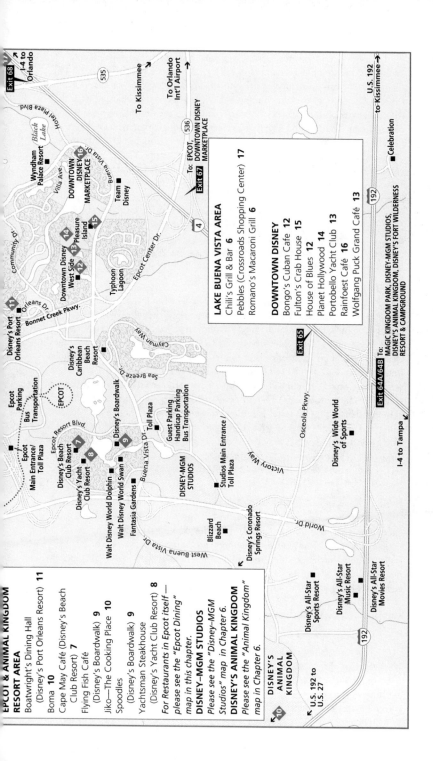

EPCOT & ANIMAL KINGDOM RESORT AREA

Boatwright's Dining Hall (Disney's Port Orleans Resort) **11**
Boma **10**
Cape May Café (Disney's Beach Club Resort) **7**
Flying Fish Café (Disney's Boardwalk) **9**
Jiko—The Cooking Place **10**
Spoodles (Disney's Boardwalk) **9**
Yachtsman Steakhouse (Disney's Yacht Club Resort) **8**
For Restaurants in Epcot itself — please see the "Epcot Dining" map in this chapter.

DISNEY'S-MGM STUDIOS

Please see the "Disney-MGM Studios" map in Chapter 6.

DISNEY'S ANIMAL KINGDOM

Please see the "Animal Kingdom" map in Chapter 6.

LAKE BUENA VISTA AREA

Chili's Grill & Bar **6**
Pebbles (Crossroads Shopping Center) **17**
Romano's Macaroni Grill **6**

DOWNTOWN DISNEY

Bongo's Cuban Cafe **12**
Fulton's Crab House **15**
House of Blues **12**
Planet Hollywood **14**
Portobello Yacht Club **13**
Rainfoest Café **16**
Wolfgang Puck Grand Café **13**

dining room décor features 1,500 caricatures of the stars who patronized the California restaurant—everyone from Bette Davis to Sammy Davis Jr. This Derby offers a fun meal, albeit a pricey one, and is a good spot for older kids, or for families looking for something with a slightly more sophisticated edge that still has kiddie options. Owner Bob Cobb invented the original restaurant's signature Cobb salad in the 1930s. (It's popular enough that this Derby serves 31,000 a year.) Most kids won't be interested in that option, but hot dogs, grilled chicken, fried grouper, or mac and cheese should tempt them. Adult dinner entrees include pan-seared grouper with balsamic roasted asparagus and mustard-crusted rack of lamb with acorn squash and sweet-and-sour cabbage. The Derby's signature dessert, grapefruit cake with cream-cheese icing, is a perfect meal capper (there are smoothies and ice cream options for younger tastes). The Derby has a full bar and a modest selection of California wines.

Hollywood Blvd. ☎ 407/939-3463. www.disneyworld.com. Kids' menu w/activities, highchairs, boosters. Priority Seating. Main courses $13–$22 lunch, $17–$27 dinner, kids $5–$6. AE, DC, DISC, MC, V. Daily 11:30am–park closing. Parking $7.

MODERATE

50's Prime Time Café *Overrated* AMERICAN   The fun factor is far better than the food at this restaurant based on a 1950s time warp/sitcom psychodrama. The atmosphere includes black-and-white TVs showing clips from such classics as *My Little Margie* and *Topper*. The servers add to the fun, greeting diners with lines like, "Hi Sis, I'll go tell Mom you're home," and they may threaten to withhold dessert if you don't eat all your food. Kids can really get into the spirit, and adore seeing their parents admonished for dinner-table infractions, but we won't blame you if you choose to abstain. The entrees—fried chicken, meatloaf, and pot roast, among others—simply don't deliver on the taste front, although the desserts aren't bad. The kids' cuisine (hot dogs, chicken nuggets, mac and cheese, and PBJs) seems safer. Adult beverages include Long Island ice tea and margaritas.

Near the Indiana Jones Stunt Spectacular. ☎ 407/939-3463. www.disneyworld.com. Kids' menu w/activities, highchairs, boosters. Priority Seating. Main courses $12.50–$19 lunch and dinner, kids $5. AE, DC, DISC, MC, V. Daily 11am–park closing. Parking $7.

Mama Melrose's Ristorante Italiano *Overrated* ITALIAN   The best (and safest) adult bets here are the wood-fired flatbreads (grilled pepperoni, four-cheese, portobello mushroom, and others for $11.50–$12.50). The menu is fleshed out with some Italian pretenders, including veal osso buco and oak-grilled salmon with sun-dried tomato pesto. The bambino menu has chicken nuggets, cheese or pepperoni pizza, a burger, and spaghetti with meat sauce. Our advice: Unless you plan to suck down a lot of sangria, find another place to eat.

Tips **Express Lane**

At press time, Disney was offering preferred seating at the end-of-the-day spectacular, Fantasmic! All you need to do is make Priority Seating arrangements (☎ 407/939-3463) and request the Fantasmic! package for the Hollywood Brown Derby ($36.99 adults, $9.99 kids 3–11), Mama Melrose's Ristorante Italiano ($28.99 adults, $9.99 kids), or Hollywood & Vine ($19.99 adults, $9.99 kids). *Note:* Those prices are above the cost of ordering off the menu and finding your own seats at Fantasmic!

Tips Dining Plans

Disney's **Dream Maker Silver** package plan allows you to choose meals from its flex features. The **Dream Maker Gold** plan includes three meals a day. Call ☎ **407/934-7639** or visit www.disneyworld.com (click "Reservations & Tickets") for details.

Near the Backlot Tour. ☎ **407/939-3463**. www.disneyworld.com. Kids' menu w/activities, highchairs, boosters. Priority Seating. Main courses $11.50–$21 lunch, $15–$21 dinner, kids $5. AE, DC, DISC, MC, V. Daily 11:30am–park closing. Parking $7.

Sci-Fi Dine-In Theater Restaurant *Overrated* AMERICAN   Ho-hum. If you read the 50's Prime Time listing above and give it a science fiction spin, you'll know what to expect: family-friendly fun, but subpar food. The Sci-Fi is meant to look like a 1950s Los Angeles drive-in movie emporium. Diners sit in chrome convertibles under a starlit sky and are treated to zany newsreels, cartoons, and B horror-movie clips, such as *Frankenstein Meets the Space Monster*. Fun-loving carhops deliver free popcorn and your meal. Unfortunately, the latter needs CPR. Speaking of fun loving, the **kids' menu** uses names such as Space Mush and Meteor for standards such as macaroni and cheese and grilled chicken. (You'll also find mini burgers, hot dogs, and corn dogs.) On the adult side, adjectives such as slow roasted, sautéed, and pan-seared can't hide your basic, overpriced beef, pork, poultry, fish, and pasta. It takes a few too many specialty drinks to kill the taste.

Note: The dining room here is dark and the clips, though pretty harmless, could scare a young child. Take this into consideration before dining here.

Near Indiana Jones Epic Stunt Spectacular. ☎ **407/939-3463**. www.disneyworld.com. Kids' menu w/activities, highchairs, boosters. Priority Seating. Main courses $11–$17.50 lunch, $13–$17.50 dinner, kids $5. AE, DC, DISC, MC, V. Daily 10:30am–park closing. Parking $7.

INEXPENSIVE

Toy Story Pizza Planet PIZZA   There's no joy or originality here. Come if you want individual pizzas, salads, or a quick snack on the fly. There is no kid-specific menu, but what child doesn't like pizza?

In the Muppet's Courtyard. ☎ **407/939-3463**. www.disneyworld.com. No Priority Seating. All meals $5.50–$9. AE, DC, DISC, MC, V. Daily 10:30am–park closing. Parking $7.

IN THE ANIMAL KINGDOM

There are few worthwhile restaurants in the newest of Disney's parks, and most that exist are counter-service or grab-and-go places. In our opinion only two are worth listing.

MODERATE

Rainforest Cafe ⭐ CALIFORNIA   Kids love the jungle aesthetics at this very family-friendly restaurant. (Adults do, too, after a few tropical concoctions!) Expect a thick cover of faux foliage, more than one kingdom's share of simultaneous animal calls, aquariums, and California cuisine with an island spin at this Rainforest, and its cousin, listed later in this chapter on p. 128. Menu offerings tend to be tasty and sometimes creative. Fun dishes include Rumble in the Jungle Turkey Wrap (with romaine, tomatoes, and bacon), and Maya's Mixed Grill (ribs, chicken breast, and shrimp). The kids-club menu has the

Tips **Beat the Crowds**

Because Animal Kingdom has fewer good places to eat than other Disney parks, lines can be monstrously long at lunch. If you're planning to buy eats in the park, consider dining before 11:30am or after 1:30pm.

usual suspects: pizza, chicken tenders, and burgers. Tables situated among the dining room's vines and generally inanimate animals are usually packed, a barometer of the lack of options at Animal Kingdom as much as the popularity of this restaurant. Beer, wine, and other intoxicants are served.

Just outside Animal Kingdom entrance. *Admission not required.* (There's an entrance inside, too.) ℭ 407/ 938-9100. www.rainforestcafe.com. Kids' menu w/activities, highchairs, boosters. Reservations recommended. Main courses $10–$40 (most under $25) lunch and dinner, kids $6. AE, DC, DISC, MC, V. Daily 8am–7pm. Parking $7.

INEXPENSIVE

Tusker House AMERICAN   Taste is present at this counter-service restaurant, even if quantity and quality aren't. The menu has rotisserie chicken, grilled salmon, a turkey wrap, and a marinated veggie sandwich on focaccia bread. Kids' selections are mac and cheese or a PBJ for $3.49. It's a good place for a grab-and-go meal with the kids. Beer and wine are served.

In Africa, near entrance. ℭ 407/939-3463. www.disneyworld.com. No Priority Seating. Main courses $7–$8. AE, DC, DISC, MC, V. Daily 10:30am–4:30pm. Parking $7.

IN THE WALT DISNEY WORLD RESORTS

Most restaurants listed in this category continue the Disney trend of being above market price. On the flip side, many offer food that's a notch or two better than what you find in the theme parks. These restaurants are located on the "Walt Disney World & Lake Buena Vista Dining" map on p. 118.

VERY EXPENSIVE

Citricos ⚐ MODERN FRENCH   The Grand Floridian's number-two restaurant (Victoria & Albert's is number one) offers a menu featuring what the resort calls French, Alsatian, and Provençal cuisine with California and Florida touches (except when it comes to kiddie cuisine, which ranges from a mac and cheese and chicken tenders to pasta and a costly grilled tenderloin). Adult vittles change regularly, but you might find a yummy basil-crusted rack of lamb, roasted halibut with asparagus and shiitake mushrooms, or sautéed salmon with roasted fennel and potatoes. The Old World decor includes plenty of wrought-iron railings, mosaic-tile floors, flickering lights, a show kitchen, and a view of the Seven Seas Lagoon and Magic Kingdom fireworks. Add a three-course wine pairing for $25.

4401 Floridian Way, in Disney's Grand Floridian Resort & Spa. ℭ 407/939-3463. www.disneyworld.com. Kids' menu w/activities, highchairs, boosters. Priority Seating. Main courses $22–$33, kids $6–$12. AE, DC, DISC, MC, V. Wed–Sun 5:30–10pm.

Victoria & Albert's ⚐⚐⚐ *Finds* INTERNATIONAL   This **adult restaurant** (it's definitely not a place for the kids) is something to consider if you have a healthy budget and a desire for a romantic evening without the young 'uns. It's Disney's most elegant restaurant and truly a dining event. Dinner is next to perfect—if the portions seem small, we dare you to make it through all six courses—and the setting is exceptionally romantic. This luxurious experience begins with a personalized menu and a rose for the lady in your party. The fare

Tips   More Kid Cuisine . . .

Here are a few more places in the Disney resorts and parks to find food that might tickle younger tastes. Many of these are walk-up or casual eateries that don't require Priority Seating arrangements, though you should consider making them at Narcoossee's, Grand Floridian Cafe, Big River Grille & Brewing Works, Kona Cafe, and Cap'n Jacks (© 407/939-3463).

- **Aunt Polly's Dockside Inn,** Magic Kingdom, PBJs ($4).
- **Big River Grille & Brewing Works,** Boardwalk Resort, grilled cheese, burgers, hot dogs, PBJs, and mac and cheese ($4.50–$5).
- **Cap'n Jacks,** Downtown Disney, grilled chicken, penne pasta, hot dogs, and grilled cheese ($5.50).
- **ESPN Club,** Boardwalk Resort, chicken tenders, mac and cheese, PBJs, burgers, and hot dogs ($5.50).
- **Flame Tree Barbecue,** Animal Kingdom, hot dogs and PBJs ($3.50).
- **Grand Floridian Cafe,** Grand Floridian Resort & Spa, pizza, PBJs, mini burgers, chicken strips, and mac and cheese for kids 11 and under ($5.50); grilled chicken, penne pasta, grilled junior steak, and seared fish for those 12 to 16 ($10).
- **Kona Café,** Polynesian Resort, chicken fingers, grilled cheese, PBJs, burgers, and hot dogs ($5.50).
- **Lottawatta Lodge,** Blizzard Beach, chicken strips, fish and chips, grilled cheese, PBJs, burgers, and hot dogs ($4).
- **Narcoossee's,** Grand Floridian Resort & Spa, grilled fish, petite filet, chicken fingers, pasta marinara or with butter, and burgers ($6–$12).
- **Pecos Bill Café,** Magic Kingdom, hot dogs ($3.50).
- **Pinocchio Village Haus,** Magic Kingdom, hot dogs and PBJs ($3.50).
- **Pizzafari,** Animal Kingdom, cheese pizza and PBJs ($5–$6).
- **Plaza Pavilion,** Magic Kingdom, PBJs ($3.50).
- **Sand Trap Bar & Grill,** Bonnet Creek Golf Club, grilled cheese, grilled chicken, cheeseburgers, and hot dogs ($6.75).
- **Toontown Farmer's Market,** Magic Kingdom, PBJs ($3.50).
- **Typhoon Tilly's,** Typhoon Lagoon, chicken strips, fish and chips, grilled cheese, PBJs, burgers, and hot dogs ($4).
- **Whispering Canyon Café,** Wilderness Lodge, chicken drumsticks or fingers, PBJs, burgers, mac and cheese, and grilled cheese ($5.50–$9).

changes nightly, but expect a feast fit for royalty (and costing a royal fortune). You might begin with Kobe beef carpaccio, followed by Monterey abalone with lemon and baby spinach. Then, pheasant consommé might precede an entree such as tamari-glazed blue fin tuna over bok choy stir-fry or veal tenderloin. English Stilton served with a burgundy-poached pear sets up desserts such as vanilla bean crème brûlée and Kona chocolate soufflé. The dining room is crowned by a domed, chapel-style ceiling; Victorian lamps softly light 20 exquisitely appointed tables; and your servers (always named Victoria and Albert) provide service that will have you begging to take them home. We suggest a wine pairing.

> **Fun Fact Pint-Size Food Experiences**
>
> Disney's Grand Floridian Resort & Spa offers two special cooking programs for children. **Grand Adventures in Cooking** invites up to 12 youngsters, 3 to 10 years old, to make dessert in a 2-hour decorating class ($19.95 per child, usually Tues and Fri). The **Wonderland Tea Party** gives kids the same age a 1-hour primer in cupcake decorating—with their fingers! They also feast on heart-shaped PBJs and sip apple juice "tea" while they play with Alice and the Mad Hatter ($22.95 per child, weekdays). Call *C* **407/824-3000** or 407/939-3463 for details on both programs.

4401 Floridian Way, in Disney's Grand Floridian Resort & Spa. *C* **407/939-3463**. www.disneyworld.com. No kids' menu. Priority Seating required. Jackets required for men. Not recommended for children. Prix fixe $95 per person, $145 with wine pairing; $125 Chef's Table, $185 with wine. AE, DC, DISC, MC, V. 2 dinner seatings daily Sept–June 5:45–6:30pm and 9–9:45pm; 1 dinner seating July–Aug 6:45–8pm. Chef's Table 6pm only. Free self- and validated valet parking.

Yachtsman Steakhouse *★* SEAFOOD/STEAKS/CHOPS Even by outside-the-park standards, the Yachtsman earns a B+ among steakhouses and it's a good place to have a special dinner out with the kids. Its grain-fed western beef is aged, cured, and cut here. You can see the cuts in a glass-enclosed aging room, and the exhibition kitchen provides a tantalizing glimpse of steaks, chops, and seafood being grilled over oak and hickory. Adult options range from an 8-ounce filet to a 12-ounce strip to a belly-busting 24-ounce T-bone. A filet and warm-water lobster tail combo tops the price chart. If you're not in the mood for beef, the Yachtsman also serves Chilean sea bass, scallops, and one daily vegetarian special. The junior menu features 6-ounce cuts of steak or prime rib, grilled chicken, chicken strips, burgers, hot dogs, and pasta. The decor includes knotty-pine beams, plank floors, and leather-and-oak chairs. The staff is very cordial. The Yachtsman has an extensive wine list, though it's not in the same league as the other two contestants in this category.

1700 Epcot Resorts Blvd., in Disney's Yacht Club Resort. *C* **407/939-3463**. www.disneyworld.com. Kids' menu w/activities, highchairs, boosters. Priority Seating recommended. Main courses $20–$50 (most over $25), kids $5.50–$10. AE, DC, DISC, MC, V. Daily 5:30–10pm. Free self- and valet parking.

EXPENSIVE

Artist Point *★ (Finds)* SEAFOOD/STEAKS/CHOPS Enjoy a grand view of Disney's Wilderness Lodge while you select from a seasonal menu at this upscale but very family-friendly spot. Kids can dig into grilled chicken, baked salmon, pasta with cheese sauce, a burger, or PBJ, while adults try something a bit more daring. You might discover a mixed grill of venison, a lamb chop, and rabbit sausage with a root vegetable mash; a spicy Asian-style shrimp and noodle bowl; or the house special, cedar-plank roasted salmon with maple-whiskey glaze. The dining room's interior is dotted with western-theme murals (your kids can hunt for Hidden Mickeys; see p. 200), and large windows offer a view of a lake and waterfall. There's terrace seating for fair weather. Expect a reasonably extensive wine list and a wine pairing (three 2½-oz. portions for $14).

901 W. Timberline Dr., in Disney's Wilderness Lodge. *C* **407/939-3463**. www.disneyworld.com. Kids' menu w/activities, highchairs, boosters. Priority Seating recommended. Main courses $23–$34, kids $5.50–$9. AE, DC, DISC, MC, V. Daily 5:30–10pm. Free self- and valet parking.

Boma AFRICAN   One of two main restaurants in Animal Kingdom Lodge, this one is themed after an African marketplace. Its show kitchen and wood-burning grill crank out dinner delicacies even more varied than those at the buffet at Akershus in the Norway pavilion (p. 113). If your family has diverse eating habits (you love to experiment, your kids would shudder at the thought), this is one of the best spots in the World to head for a meal. Adventurous diners can expect such treats as Moroccan seafood salad (mussels, scallops, shrimp, and couscous), curried coconut seafood stew, chicken pepper pot soup, and much more. While there isn't a specific kids' menu, there are some items on the buffet that have their names written all over them, including chicken tenders, spaghetti and meatballs, and mac and cheese. The desserts are pretty good, but be advised that many have alcohol in them. The restaurant is set up in "pods," each with a chef who can answer your questions about the cuisine. There's also a breakfast buffet.

2901 Osceola Pkwy., at Disney's Animal Kingdom Lodge. ✆ 407/939-3463. www.disneyworld.com. Highchairs, boosters. Priority Seating. Breakfast buffet $14.99, $7.99 kids 3–11; dinner buffet $23.99, $9.99 kids. AE, DC, DISC, MC, V. Daily 7–11am and 5–10pm. Free self-parking.

California Grill ★★★ CALIFORNIA   Located on the Contemporary Resort's 15th floor, this stunning restaurant offers views of the Magic Kingdom and lagoon below while your eyes and mouth feast on an eclectic menu. A Wolfgang Puckish interior incorporates Art Deco elements (curved pear-wood walls, vivid splashes of color, polished black granite surfaces), but the central focus is an exhibition kitchen with a wood-burning oven and rotisserie. The adult menu's headliners change to take advantage of fresh market fare but may include seared yellowfin tuna, black grouper with mushroom risotto, and soft-shell crabs with corn salad. The Grill also has a nice sushi and sashimi menu (tuna, crab, and shrimp, among others) ranging from appetizers to large platters. Most kids will wrinkle their noses at those choices, but the Grill has options for youngsters, including cheese pizza, mac and cheese, fish and chips, grilled chicken, and a small steak. Most of these are substantially overpriced, which is one of the reasons this is one of the few spots in WDW that isn't crawling with kids—it's probably best to save this one for a night your children are with a babysitter or at a kids' club. The list of California wines helps complement the meal and views.

Note: It can be tough to get a table at the Grill, especially on weekends and during Disney fireworks hours, so make a reservation as early as possible.

4600 N. World Dr., at Disney's Contemporary Resort. ✆ 407/939-3463. www.disneyworld.com. Kids' menu w/activities, highchairs, boosters. Priority Seating recommended. Main courses $18–$32.50, sushi and sashimi $10–$20, kids $6.75–$9. AE, DC, DISC, MC, V. Daily 5:30–10pm. Free self-parking.

Flying Fish Café SEAFOOD   Chefs at this Coney Island–inspired restaurant take the stage in a show kitchen that turns out adult entrees such as potato-wrapped red snapper, coriander-crusted yellowfin tuna, and oak-grilled salmon or mahimahi. None of these will tempt your offspring, but the grilled chicken or steak, fish and chips, or cheese pasta should. The food is better than what you'll find at the Coral Reef (p. 112) and Cape May Café (p. 126), but not in the same league as Artist Point or some of O-Town's other quality seafood restaurants. The atmosphere here is a bit more upscale than you'd think; kids old enough to appreciate that fact will be impressed, but this might not be the best place for kids too young to sit still. That said, this is a nice escape from the Mickey madness.

2101 N. Epcot Resorts Blvd., at Disney's Boardwalk. ✆ 407/939-3463. www.disneyworld.com. Kids' menu w/activities, highchairs, boosters. Priority Seating. Main courses $20–$34, kids $5.50–$12. AE, DC, DISC, MC, V. Daily 5:30–10pm. Free self-parking.

Jiko—The Cooking Place ☆ AFRICAN The Animal Kingdom Lodge's signature restaurant is a nice diversion from the normal Disney restaurants and a complementary addition to the multicultural dining rooms at Epcot's World Showcase. Jiko's show kitchen, sporting two wood-burning ovens, turns out a unique menu of international cuisine with African overtones that make for interesting dining on the adult end. Dishes, depending on the season, include grilled buttermilk-curry shrimp, pan-roasted monkfish, grilled salmon with heirloom potatoes and spinach in a horseradish vinaigrette, and pomegranate-glazed quail. Kids face some usual (pizza, grilled cheese, chicken strips, PBJs, and mac and cheese) and unusual suspects (salmon fillets or steak). The wine list features a number of South African vintages.

2901 Osceola Pkwy., at Disney's Animal Kingdom Lodge. ☎ 407/939-3463. www.disneyworld.com. Kids' menu w/activities, highchairs, boosters. Priority Seating. Main courses $17.50–$29, kids $5.50–$8.75. AE, DC, DISC, MC, V. Daily 5:30–10pm. Free self-parking.

Spoodles TAPAS This lively family restaurant features an open kitchen and is a good place to take the kids (the noise factor alone should indicate its popularity with the young set). The enterprising tapas menu also encourages food sharing, which increases the fun factor for adults (and is a good intro to some new cuisine for preteens and up). Kids face chicken fingers, cheese or pepperoni pizza, burgers, hot dogs, cheese pasta, PBJs, and fried shrimp. Adult fare includes sautéed chile garlic shrimp, fried calamari, and a sampler platter. Entrees include Moroccan-spiced tuna and a grilled pork porterhouse with goat-cheese polenta. Spoodles has added a respectable wine list, including tableside sangria presentations. *Note:* Although popular, the quality here doesn't rival Cafe Tu Tu Tango, another tapas favorite (p. 138). During the peak summer tourist season, thanks to its location at the Boardwalk, the wait can be long, even with Priority Seating, so this may not be the best option for famished families.

2101 N. Epcot Resorts Blvd., at Disney's Boardwalk. ☎ 407/939-3463. www.disneyworld.com. Kids' menu w/activities, highchairs, boosters. Priority Seating. Main courses $15–$25, tapas $5–$20, kids $6–$7. AE, DC, DISC, MC. V. Daily 7–11am, noon–2pm, and 5–10pm. Free self-parking.

MODERATE

Boatwright's Dining Hall NEW ORLEANS A family atmosphere (noisy), good food (by Disney standards), and reasonable prices (ditto) make Boatwright's a hit with Port Orleans Resort guests, if not outsiders. Most entrees have a Cajun/Creole spin and portions are large. The spicy jambalaya has shrimp, chicken, and sausage. There really isn't anything French about the pot roast, but it is tasty. Boatwright's is modeled after a 19th-century boat factory, complete with the wooden hull of a Louisiana fishing boat suspended from its lofty beamed ceiling. Most kids like the wooden toolboxes on every table; each contains a saltshaker that doubles as a level, a wood-clamp sugar dispenser, a pepper-grinder-cum-ruler, a jar of unmatched utensils, shop rags (read, napkins), and a little metal pail of crayons. On the food side, they can choose from pasta with cheese or sauce, grilled cheese, chicken fingers, fried shrimp, burgers, or hot dogs. (At breakfast they can get Mickey Mouse–shaped pancakes!)

2201 Orleans Dr., in Disney's Port Orleans Resort. ☎ 407/939-3463. www.disneyworld.com. Kids' menu w/activities, highchairs, boosters. Priority Seating recommended. Main courses $7–$11 breakfast, $14–$20 dinner, kids $5–$6. AE, DC, DISC, MC, V. Daily 7–11:30am and 5–10pm. Free self-parking.

Cape May Café *Overrated* SEAFOOD As a rule, all-you-can-eat marine feasts tend to promise more than they deliver, and this is no exception. Yes, there's an honest seafood selection (clams, mussels, and microscopic peel-and-eat shrimp).

But seafood served buffet style—allowed to sit out where it collects all sorts of airborne bacteria—isn't an ideal meal in our book, especially inland. If you're still inclined, the restaurant has a full bar, and it's said that enough alcohol kills any germ (though your kids will be in the lurch). If you're inclined but not willing to take the risk, the buffet also has chicken, ribs, and flank steak. The kids' bar has fried shrimp, chicken fingers, and mac and cheese. The dessert bar is popular with all ages. The Café also offers a character breakfast (p. 145).

1800 Epcot Resorts Blvd., at Disney's Beach Club Resort. ☎ 407/939-3463. www.disneyworld.com. Kids' menu w/activities, highchairs, boosters. Priority Seating. Dinner buffet $24 adults, $10 children 3–11. AE, DC, DISC, MC, V. Daily 5:30–9:30pm. Free self- and valet parking.

'Ohana ⋆ PACIFIC RIM   This restaurant's star is earned on the fun front, but the decibel level at this kid-magnet turns some folks off. Inside, you're welcomed as a "cousin," which fits because 'Ohana means "family" in Hawaiian. As your food is being prepared over an 18-foot fire pit, the staff keeps your eyes and ears filled with all fun, including storytelling and games (there's even a hula hoop contest for the kids). The meal is served from 30-foot skewers (grilled shrimp, marinated steak, barbecued pork loin, and seasoned turkey). There is no kid-specific menu, though you can get alternative options for fussy eaters on request. Tropical alcoholic drinks are available for an added fee. *Note:* Ask for a seat in the main dining room, or you won't get a good view of the entertainment.

1600 Seven Seas Dr., at Disney's Polynesian Resort. ☎ 407/939-3463. www.disneyworld.com. Kids' menu w/activities, highchairs, boosters. Priority Seating strongly encouraged. $24 adults, $10 children 3–11. (See p. 284 for more details on the restaurant's luau.) AE, DC, DISC, MC, V. Daily 7:30–11am and 5–10pm. Free self- and valet parking.

3 Places to Dine in Lake Buena Vista

In this section, we've listed restaurants located in Downtown Disney and the Lake Buena Vista area. Many of these eateries can be found on the "Walt Disney World & Lake Buena Vista Dining" map on p. 118. Downtown Disney is located 2½ miles from Epcot off Buena Vista Drive. It encompasses the Downtown Disney Marketplace, a very pleasant complex of shops and restaurants on a scenic lagoon; the adjoining Pleasure Island, a nighttime entertainment venue; and Downtown Disney West Side, a slightly more upscale collection of shops, restaurants, Cirque du Soleil (p. 292), and a movie theater.

Note: Pleasure Island's restaurants don't require admission.

AT PLEASURE ISLAND
VERY EXPENSIVE

Fulton's Crab House ⋆ SEAFOOD   Lobster (Maine and Australian) and crab (king and Dungeness) dominate the menu in this fun and fashionable eatery, which is housed in a replica of a (permanently moored) 19th-century Mississippi riverboat. It's one of the area's best seafood houses, but you might want to bring your banker along for the ride (one reason this should probably be considered only for a special family splurge, though your kids will like the atmosphere). One popular meal for two combines Alaskan king crab, snow crab, and lobster with potatoes and creamed spinach. The cioppino and Dungeness crab cakes are delicious. And there's a scattering of Florida seafood, including stone crabs (mid-Oct to mid-May). Kids can go for land (filet, grilled chicken breast, chicken tenders, burgers, hot dogs, and spaghetti) or sea (fried shrimp or fish and chips). Fulton's has a good wine list.

> (*Tips* **Coming Soon**
>
> The Earl of Sandwich is bringing his name and famous platters to Downtown Disney. At press time, there wasn't a firm opening date, but it should be up and running no later than the second half of 2004.

1670 Buena Vista Dr., aboard the riverboat docked at Downtown Disney. © 407/934-2628. www.levy restaurants.com. Kids' menu w/activities, highchairs, boosters. Priority Seating. Main courses $9–$45 lunch, $17–$45 dinner, kids $5–$12. AE, DC, DISC, MC, V. Daily 11:30am–4pm and 5–11pm. Free self-parking.

EXPENSIVE

Portobello Yacht Club ✮ SOUTHERN ITALIAN   The pizzas here go beyond the routine to *quattro formaggio* (mozzarella and provolone with sun-dried tomatoes) and *margherita* (Italian sausage, plum tomatoes, and mozzarella). But it's the less casual entrees that pack people into this place. The menu changes from time to time. You may find a nice *costoletta di vitello alla griglia* (a grilled 14-oz. veal chop with garlic whipped potatoes and asparagus) or *spaghettini alla portobello* (pasta with pieces of Alaskan king crab, scallops, shrimp, and clams in light olive oil, wine, and herbs). Steak, penne pasta with chicken, cheese pizza, spaghetti with meat sauce, chicken tenders, burgers, and hot dogs will keep most kids happy (though the service is geared more to adults and wait times between courses can be a bit too much for little ones). Situated in a gabled Bermuda-style house, the Portobello has a small cellar but a nice selection of wine to match the meals.

1650 Buena Vista Dr., in Pleasure Island. © 407/934-8888. www.levyrestaurants.com. Kids' menu w/activities, highchairs, boosters. Priority Seating. Main courses $15–$50, pizzas $9, kids $5–$12. AE, DC, DISC, MC, V. Daily 5–11pm. Free self-parking.

MODERATE

Planet Hollywood (*Overrated* AMERICAN   Some folks come for a first look, but most diners are fans that flock here for the scenery (including a planetarium-like ceiling and Peter O'Toole's *Lawrence of Arabia* duds). The compulsion is much like that of Hard Rock Cafe fans (p. 134), who go for the tunes. The Planet's servers can cop an attitude, and the food is blasé, including the kids' burgers, hot dogs, pizza, and chicken fingers. Adults find wings, pot stickers, sandwiches, burgers, ribs, fajitas, pizzas, pasta, and questionable steaks. Although its unquestionably popular with families and kids like the themed decor, this is not the best food in the World, the noise level may be too much for young children to cope with (as well as their parents), and the lines can get long during special events and in peak season.

1506 Buena Vista Dr., at Pleasure Island (look for the big globe). © 407/827-7827. www.planethollywood. com. Kids' menu w/activities, highchairs, boosters. Limited Priority Seating. Main courses $8–$21 (most under $15), kids $5–$7. AE, DC, DISC, MC, V. Daily 11am–1am. Free self-parking.

AT DOWNTOWN DISNEY MARKETPLACE
MODERATE

Rainforest Cafe ✮ CALIFORNIA   Don't arrive starving (or with restless kids) unless you have Priority Seating reservations. Without them, waits average 2 hours, and the service here tends to be slow. Expect fare with an island spin at this Rainforest and its cousin in Animal Kingdom (p. 121). Fun dishes include Caribbean Coconut Shrimp (with a sweet mango sauce), and Maya's Mixed

Grill (ribs, chicken breast, and shrimp). The name game continues for kids with Rainforest Rascal (mini burgers) and Jurassic Chicken Tidbits (nuggets), plus pizza, hot dogs, and mac and cheese. With the hundreds of kids running around in a jungle-like setting Tarzan would be at home in, this is not the place for a quiet dinner, though your kids will likely have a blast. The beer, wine, and other alcoholic beverages on the menu should steady your nerves.

Downtown Disney Marketplace, near the smoking volcano. ℂ 407/827-8500. www.rainforestcafe.com. Kids' menu w/activities, highchairs, boosters. Priority Seating. Main courses $10–$40 lunch and dinner (most under $25), kids $6. AE, DISC, MC, V. Sun–Thurs 11:30am–11pm; Fri–Sat 11:30am–midnight. Free self-parking.

DISNEY'S WEST SIDE
MODERATE

Bongo's Cuban Cafe *Overrated* CUBAN   Singer Gloria Estefan and her husband, Emilio, created this eatery with high expectations. Alas, the food isn't great, though the prices say it ought to be. The *palomilla* (a thin, tenderized steak) can't match what you find in Rolando's (see later in this chapter) or some other Cuban eateries in Miami, Bongo's home. The *ropa vieja* (shredded beef) is tasty but on the dry (and sometimes cool) side, and the *arroz con pollo* (chicken with yellow rice, something of a national dish) would be a highlight if the portion matched the price. The best bet: The Cuban sandwich—thinly toasted bread with ham, pork, and cheese—is safe and sanely priced. Kid cuisine includes chicken breast or nuggets, a small steak, and burgers, but we wouldn't take children here unless they are over 10 and like Latin music. If you don't mind loud Latin music and groupies, park it inside and enjoy a cold beer or glass of sangria. For quieter times, try the patio or upstairs lounge.

1498 Buena Vista Dr., in Disney's West Side. ℂ 407/828-0999. www.bongoscubancafe.com. Kids' menu w/activities, highchairs, boosters. No Priority Seating. Main courses $7–$28 lunch, $13–$28 (many under $20) dinner, kids $6–$7. AE, DC, DISC, MC, V. Daily 11am–2am. Free self-parking.

House of Blues MISSISSIPPI DELTA   Most folks come for the blues bands and Sunday's Gospel Brunch (very popular with families), a foot-tapping, thigh-slapping music affair worth high marks on the entertainment side. The noise level is high and the atmosphere is informal, so you won't have to worry about any noise your kids might make. The food, however, is so-so. The roast beef is tough, the fish is dry, and the jambalaya is loaded with rice and noticeably absent of the good stuff. (The omelets are good, and there are enough fillers—bacon, salads, dessert, and bread—to do the job. Few leave hungry.) Dinners are a notch better than the brunch. Features range from a meatier jambalaya (shrimp, chicken, and andouille sausage) to Louisiana crawfish and shrimp étouffée to Cajun meatloaf. Kids' meals include grilled cheese, chicken tenders, pizza, burgers, turkey sandwiches, and more.

1490 Buena Vista Dr., at Disney's West Side, beneath water tower. ℂ 407/934-2583. www.hob.com. Kids' menu, highchairs, boosters. No Priority Seating (except brunch). Main courses $14–$26, pizza and sandwiches $9.50–$11, kids $5; brunch $30 adults, $15 kids 3–9. AE, DISC, MC, V. Daily 11am–2am; brunch 10:30am and 1pm. Free self-parking.

Wolfgang Puck Grand Café ✪ CALIFORNIA   The sushi bar at this restaurant is our favorite stop when our grandkids aren't in tow. It's an artistic copper-and-terrazzo masterpiece that delivers some of the best sushi in Orlando. You can also eat gourmet pizza, with thin crusts and exotic toppings, inside or on an outdoor patio. Upstairs, the main dining room is an adult affair that offers a changing, pricey menu that might feature rack of lamb with wasabi-infused mashed spuds, rare yellowfin tuna with tempura-style Bon Secour oysters, or smoked tropical duck with Boursin cheese, mango, and papaya between veggie wontons. The more kid-friendly lower level has pizzas, burgers, chicken tenders, ravioli, and mac and cheese for youngsters. Puck's also has a grab-and-go express restaurant that has sandwiches, pizzas, desserts, and more.

1482 Buena Vista Dr., at Disney's West Side. ℂ 407/938-9653. www.wolfgangpuck.com/myrestaurants. Highchairs. Reservations for dining room; Priority Seating in lower level. Main courses upstairs $26–$38, pizza and sushi $8–$25, kids $6–$7. AE, DC, DISC, MC, V. Daily 11am–1am. Free self-parking.

ELSEWHERE IN LAKE BUENA VISTA
MODERATE

Chili's Grill & Bar SOUTHWESTERN   This Texas-based chain has always been a good choice for family dining; the price is right and the portions are filling. The kids' menu offers ribs, chicken nuggets, grilled cheese, burgers, hot dogs, and mac and cheese. Adult specialties include a half-pound chili cheeseburger served with home fries. Other possibilities include ginger-and-citrus-glazed salmon, margarita-grilled tuna, wonderful steak- or chicken-fajitas, grilled baby back ribs, and salads. Save room for the Chocolate Chip Paradise Pie: a chocolate brownie topped with vanilla ice cream and hot fudge.

12172 Apopka–Vineland Rd. (just north of Hwy. 535/Palm Pkwy.). ℂ 407/239-6688. www.chilis.com. Kids' menu w/activities, highchairs, boosters. Reservations not accepted. Main courses $7.25–$21, kids $3.60–$6. AE, DC, DISC, MC, V. Sun–Thurs 11am–midnight; Fri–Sat 11am–1am. Take I-4 Exit 68, Hwy. 535/Apopka–Vineland Rd. north and continue straight when Hwy. 535 goes to the right.

Pebbles ⭐⭐ *Finds* CALIFORNIA   If you want to dine like a gourmet without paying a heavy price, and want a good selection of food for your kids without having to sacrifice your own taste buds in the process here's your meal ticket. Pebbles is a local chain that has earned a reputation for great food, a sexy though small wine list (which should appeal to the adults in your party), and creative appetizers. Its Ybor Gold twin filets are seared, then bathed in the namesake lager and delivered with caramelized onions and three-cheese spuds. The pesto linguine is served with pea pods and plum tomatoes. And the roast duck arrives in a glaze of strawberries, pistachios, and Triple Sec. There's also a small selection of sandwiches ($7–$10). **Choices for the younger set** include PBJs, pizzas, grilled cheese, pasta, and chicken fingers. Pebbles is popular among a crowd ranging from young yuppies to aging baby boomers.

Note: Pebbles also has locations downtown: 17 W. Church St. (ℂ **407/839-0892**), and in Winter Park, 2516 Aloma Ave. (ℂ **407/678-7001**).

12551 Apopka–Vineland Rd., in the Crossroads Shopping Center. ℂ 407/827-1111. www.pebblesworld wide.com. Kids' menu w/activities, highchairs, boosters. Reservations not accepted. Main courses $7–$18, kids $2.25–$4.25. AE, DC, DISC, MC, V. Sun–Thurs noon–11pm; Fri–Sat 11am–11pm; *sometimes closed Sun.* Free self-parking. Take I-4 Exit 68, Hwy. 535/Apopka–Vineland Rd., north to the Crossroads Shopping Center on the right.

INEXPENSIVE

Romano's Macaroni Grill ⭐ *Value* NORTHERN ITALIAN   Though it's part of a multi-state chain, Romano's has the down-to-earth cheerfulness of a mom and pop joint. The laid-back atmosphere makes it a good place for families looking for a casual dinner at a good price. The menu offers thin-crust pizzas made in a wood-burning oven and topped with such items as barbecued chicken. The grilled chicken portobello (simmering between smoked mozzarella and spinach orzo pasta) is worth the visit. Equally good is an entree of grilled salmon with a teriyaki glaze, also with spinach orzo pasta. Kids' options include pizza, lasagna, spaghetti, grilled chicken, and corn dogs, and all of them come with a dessert and a drink with free refills!. They serve premium wine by the glass.

12148 Apopka–Vineland Rd. (just north of County Rd. 535/Palm Pkwy.). © 407/239-6676. www.macaroni grill.com. Kids' menu w/activities, highchairs, boosters. Main courses $6–$15 lunch, kids $4; $7–$17 dinner (most under $12), kids $4. AE, DC, DISC, MC, V. Sun–Thurs 11am–10pm; Fri–Sat 11am–11pm. Free self-parking. Take I-4 Exit 68, Hwy. 535/Apopka–Vineland Rd. north and continue straight when Hwy. 535 goes to the right. Romano's is about 2 blocks on the left.

4 Places to Dine in Universal Orlando

Universal Orlando stormed onto the restaurant scene with the mid-1999 opening of its dining and entertainment venue, CityWalk, which is between and in front of its two parks, Universal Studios Florida and Islands of Adventure. But Universal's sudden entry onto the food front doesn't mean quality was lost in the rush. Two of its restaurants (Emeril's and Delfino Riviera at the Portofino Bay Hotel) make our all-star team, and several others offer cuisine ranging from respectable light bites to dependable dinners. And, of course, this is theme-park-ville, so family-friendliness is a given at most of the restaurants.

Note: Most of the restaurants below can be found on the "CityWalk" map on p. 295. All of the hotel restaurants listed can be found on the "International Drive Area Dining" map on p. 137.

VERY EXPENSIVE

Delfino Riviera ⭐ NORTHERN ITALIAN   The signature ristorante in Universal Orlando's Portofino Bay Hotel overlooks the Harbor Piazza and delivers a romantic mood reminiscent of the Italian Riviera—complete with strolling musicians and crooners. If you haven't guessed already, like Victoria & Albert's at Disney Grand Floridian (p. 72), the Delfino should be reserved for a special night out sans children (there's no kids' menu), though it isn't on the same level as the Disney restaurant. It has a chef's table for eight where you can watch the cooks at work (there's no extra charge, but you need to reserve at least 2–3 months in advance), in addition to lower-level and terrace dining. The menu changes quarterly, but on the pasta side it might feature whole wheat and egg noodles with green beans, potatoes, and pesto or Swiss chard ravioli with veal and meat sauce. Carnivores might find veal grilled with porcini mushrooms and garlic, while fish fans might reel in grouper roasted with mushrooms and garlic. The Delfino's service is snappy, and the dining areas are quiet enough to allow intimate conversation. Next to Emeril's, its wine list is one of the best in the I-Drive/Universal Orlando corridor.

5601 Universal Studios Blvd., in the Portofino Bay Hotel. © 407/503-3463 or 407/503-1000. Reservations recommended. Main courses $15–$42. AE, MC, V. Tues–Sat 5–10pm. Free 3-hr. validated self-parking, valet parking $10. From I-4, take Exit 75B, Kirkman Rd./Hwy. 435, and follow the signs to Universal.

Emeril's ⭐⭐ NEW ORLEANS   It's hard to get short-term reservations for dinner (less than 3–4 weeks in advance) at Emeril's unless your stars are aligned or you come at the opening bell and take your chances with no-shows. If you do get in, you'll find the dynamic, Creole-inspired cuisine is worth the struggle. Best bets include the andouille-crusted redfish (an extremely moist white fish with roasted pecan-vegetable relish and meunière sauce) and a quacker trilogy that includes pan-seared duck breast, confit leg, and Hudson Valley foie gras with dirty rice and crispy parsnip strips. If you want some vino with your meal, no problem; the back half of the building is a glass-walled 12,000-bottle above-ground wine cellar. Prices at Emeril's are high enough that the restaurant can afford tons of legroom between tables and an assortment of pricey abstract paintings on the walls.

Emeril Lagasse originally had few offerings penciled in for kids (in keeping with the adult atmosphere of his restaurants outside of Florida), but quickly adjusted his menu to suit Orlando's family atmosphere and now your children can feast on a mini filet, fried shrimp, cheese tortellini, chicken tenders, or a wood-oven pizza. He's also gone on record that parents introducing their kids to fine dining shouldn't make it a chore, but rather emphasize the special nature of the occasion. And that's exactly what this meal should be for your kids—a special treat.

> **Tips   No Reservation?**
>
> If you must have dinner at Emeril's and can't get a reservation, try dropping by around 3:15pm. Those who make a date have to confirm by 3pm on the day of their reservations, and there always are a few who don't show. If you're lucky, you may be able to pick up their slack.

Note: Lunch costs about two-thirds what you'll spend on dinner, and the menu has many of the same entrees. It's also easier to get a reservation, and the dress code is more casual—jackets are recommended for gents at dinner, although that goes against the grain after a long day in the parks.

6000 Universal Studios Blvd., in CityWalk. ☎ 407/224-2424. www.emerils.com/restaurants/index_orlando. htm. Kids' menu w/activities, highchairs, boosters. Reservations necessary. Main courses $18–$28 lunch, $18–$45 dinner, kids $7.50–$16.50. Daily 11:30am–2:30pm; Sun–Thurs 5:30–10pm; Fri–Sat 5:30–11pm. AE, DISC, MC, V. Parking $8 (free after 6pm). From I-4, take Exit 75B, Kirkman Rd./Hwy. 435, and follow the signs to Universal.

The Palm STEAKS/SEAFOOD   This upscale restaurant in the Hard Rock Hotel is the 23rd member of a chain started more than 75 years ago in New York. The food is good, though, as is the case with most Disney and Universal restaurants, somewhat overpriced for the value received. Beef and seafood rule a menu headlined by a 36-ounce New York strip steak for two ($62). Smaller appetites and budgets can feast on broiled crab cakes, veal piccata, and lamb chops. The kids' menu (steak, chicken, pasta, and burgers) is pricey though not quite as much as Emeril's. The decor leans toward the upscale supper club of the '30s and '40s, and the walls are lined with caricatures of celebrities and other famous people. Older kids will likely be impressed with the atmosphere, but this isn't the place to bring little ones.

5800 Universal Blvd., in the Hard Rock Hotel. ☎ 407/503-7256. www.thepalm.com. Reservations recommended. Main courses $16–$35, kids $8–$12. AE, DC, DISC, MC, V. Mon–Sat 5–11pm; Sun 5–10pm. Free 3-hr. validated self-parking, valet $10. From I-4, take Exit 75B, Kirkman Rd./Hwy. 435, and follow the signs to Universal.

EXPENSIVE

Mama Della's *(Overrated* NORTHERN ITALIAN   This trattoria is an alternative to Delfino Riviera (above) if you're at the Portofino Bay Hotel and don't want to move (and if you want to bring your kids to dinner). Alas, it's not in the same league as some of central Florida's better Italian restaurants, including Pacino's Italian Ristorante (p. 143) or the Portobello Yacht Club (p. 128). Expect marginal comfort food. The beef can be stringy and the *frutti di mare* is somewhat meager (two shrimp, four scallops, and a small hunk of red snapper when we visited), especially for this price group. The veal Marsala is a safe bet.

Chicken fingers, mac and cheese, pasta, and burgers round out the kids' menu. Appointments include family portraits, waiters who promise to get mama if you're not happy, tacky ceramics, wood floors, and an accordion player who plays "Amore" a little too often. The wine list, like the menu, could stand some improvement.

5601 Universal Blvd., in Portofino Bay Hotel. © **407/503-1432**. Kids' menu w/activities, highchairs, boosters. Reservations recommended. Main courses $17–$29, kids $5–$8. AE, MC, V. Daily 6–10pm. Free 3-hr. validated self-parking, valet $10. From I-4, take Exit 75B, Kirkman Rd./Hwy. 435, and follow the signs to Universal.

Tchoup Chop ★★ PACIFIC RIM Pronounced "chop chop," the Royal Pacific Hotel's headline restaurant and Emeril Lagasse's second in Orlando is named for the location of his original restaurant—Tchoupitoulous Street in New Orleans. It's a nice place for a special night out for the family and a good spot to introduce your kids to the pleasures of fine dining; they'll likely be very taken in with the atmosphere. The interior blends colorful flowers, sculpted gardens, and mini waterfalls with Batik fabrics, carved wood grilles, and glass chandeliers. The exhibition kitchen offers a look at the chefs making your meal in woks or on wood-burning grills. Tchoup Chop's January 2003 coming out introduced a Polynesian and Asian influenced menu with temptations such as macadamia nut–crusted Atlantic salmon with ginger soy butter sauce, braised Kobe beef short ribs with ham-hock red beans, and smoked oyster–stuffed quail with crispy spinach.

The chefs solicited opinions from both parents and kids when formulating the kids' menu and your offspring will find treats such as tempura chicken nuggets, stir-fried shrimp with noodles, chicken spring rolls, and burgers.

6300 Hollywood Way, in Universal's Royal Pacific Hotel. © **407/503-2467**. www.emerils.com/restaurants/index_orlando.htm. Kids' menu w/activities, highchairs, boosters. Reservations strongly recommended. Main courses $13–$20 lunch, $18–$32 dinner, kids $8–$12. AE, DISC, MC, V. Daily 11:30am–2pm; Sun–Thurs 5:30–10pm; Fri-Sat 5:30–11pm. Valet parking $5. From I-4, take Exit 75B, Kirkman Rd./Hwy. 435, and follow the signs to Universal.

Tips **More Kid Cuisine II . . .**

Here are a few additional places for your smaller fry to grab a bite in the Universal resorts and parks. You can find additional information on the Internet at **www.universalorlando.com**.

- **Confisco Grille,** Islands of Adventure, mac and cheese, cheese pizza, chicken tenders, burgers, and ravioli ($6–$7).
- **Finnegan's Bar & Grill,** Universal Studios Florida, grilled cheese, chicken fingers, burgers, mac and cheese, and PBJs ($5–$7).
- **Lombard's Landing,** Universal Studios Florida, chicken fingers, fried fish, burgers, and linguine with marinara sauce ($6.75–$7).
- **Motown Café,** CityWalk, chicken fingers, mac and cheese, burgers, and hot dogs ($6).
- **Mythos Restaurant,** Islands of Adventure, chicken fingers, cheese pizza, ravioli, ham and cheddar wrap, and burgers ($6–$7).
- **NASCAR Cafe,** CityWalk, chicken fingers, cheese pizza, spaghetti, burgers, and corn dogs ($5).

MODERATE

Hard Rock Cafe *Overrated* AMERICAN   Cut from the same cloth as Planet Hollywood (see earlier in this chapter), this is rock 'n' roll's entry in the too-much-noise, plenty-of-memorabilia sweepstakes. Kids adore it and will face the usual suspects (burgers, hot dogs, chicken nuggets, and such), but don't even think about having a conversation here. Adults can expect the same chain-style bar food (burgers, chicken, marginal steaks, and fried this-and-that), slow serv-ice, and souvenir shop as at the Planet. *Note:* The adjacent Hard Rock Live! is a huge venue for concerts.

6000 Universal Studios Blvd., near Universal CityWalk. © 407/351-7625. www.hardrock.com. Kids' menu w/activities, highchairs, boosters. Reservations not accepted. Main courses $9–$23, kids $7. AE, MC, V. Daily 11am–11pm. Parking $8 (free after 6pm). From I-4, take Exit 75B, Kirkman Rd./Hwy. 435, and follow the signs to Universal.

Jimmy Buffett's Margaritaville CARIBBEAN   As soon as the parrotheads have enough to drink (no later than 4pm on weekends, 4:05pm the rest of the week), the noise makes it futile to try to talk with your table mates, but most folks come to Margaritaville to sing and get stupid, not to gab in one of several bars here (we'll tell you about them on p. 294). Given that introduction, it should come as no surprise that we recommend you bring kids here for lunch only, before the hard partying starts. Despite the cheeseburgers in paradise (yes, they're on the menu at $7.95 and are some of the best in town), Jimmy's vittles have Caribbean leanings. And, while it's not contending for a critic's choice award, it's fairly tasty grub. But watch the tab. At $6 to $8 a pop for margaritas, the bill can climb to $50 or more per person for a routine meal that includes jerk chicken, jambalaya, or a Cuban meatloaf survival sandwich that's a cheese-burger of another kind. Kids' choices include a small cheeseburger in paradise, mac and cheese, chicken fingers, spaghetti and meatballs, and PBJs. If you don't thirst for margaritas, there's a long list of domestic and imported beer.

1000 Universal Studios Plaza, in CityWalk. © 407/224-2155. www.universalorlando.com. Kids' menu w/activities, highchairs, boosters. Reservations not accepted. Main courses $8–$22 (most under $15), kids $6. AE, DISC, MC, V. Daily 11am–midnight. Parking $8 (free after 6pm). From I-4, take Exit 75B, Kirkman Rd./Hwy. 435, and follow the signs to Universal.

Pastamore Ristorante ★ SOUTHERN ITALIAN   This family-style restau-rant greets you with display cases brimming with mozzarella and other goodies lurking on the menu. Speaking of menus, Pastamore's may have the longest kids' menu in O-Town: chicken parmigiana, chicken fingers, grilled shrimp, filet mignon, fettuccine alfredo, fried cheese ravioli, spaghetti and tomato sauce, pizza, and burgers. We highly recommend it for families with kids of all ages. On the adult side, the antipasto primo is a meal unto itself. The mound includes bruschetta, eggplant caponata, melon con prosciutto, grilled portobello mush-rooms, olives, a medley of Italian cold cuts, plum tomatoes, fresh mozzarella, and more. The menu also features such traditional offerings as veal Marsala, chicken piccata, shrimp scampi, fettuccine Alfredo, lasagna, and pizza. The food is actually pretty interesting, and the presentation isn't bad either. There's an open kitchen allowing a view of the chefs. Pastamore has a basic beer and wine menu. You can also eat in a cafe where a lighter menu—breakfast fare and sand-wiches—is served from 8am to 2am.

1000 Universal Studios Plaza, in CityWalk. © 407/363-8000. www.universalorlando.com. Kids' menu w/activities, highchairs, boosters. Reservations accepted. Main courses $7–$18, kids $5–$12. AE, DISC, MC, V. Daily 5pm–midnight. Parking $8 (free after 6pm). From I-4, take Exit 75B, Kirkman Rd./Hwy. 435, and fol-low the signs to Universal.

5 Places to Dine in the International Drive Area

International Drive has one of the area's larger collections of fast-food joints, but the midsection and southern third also have some of this region's better restaurants. South I-Drive is 10 minutes by auto from the Walt Disney World parks. Most of the restaurants listed here are located on the "International Drive Area Dining" map on p. 137.

VERY EXPENSIVE

Atlantis ⚜ SUNDAY BRUNCH   The signature restaurant at the Renaissance Orlando Resort at SeaWorld has a respectable evening menu (steaks, chops, and seafood), but our family favorite here is Sunday's champagne brunch, which is served in the resort's huge atrium. Themes change monthly, but the 100-item menu often has treats such as quail, duck, lamb chops, Cornish hen, clams, mussels, sea bass, sushi, and more. Although there isn't a kid-specific menu, with that many choices—including pastries!—young diners are sure to find some things they like.

6677 Sea Harbour Dr., in the Renaissance Orlando Resort. © 407/351-5555. www.renaissancehotels.com. No kids' menu; highchairs, boosters. Reservations recommended. Sunday brunch $32 adults, $16 children. AE, DC, DISC, MC, V. Sun 10:30am–2pm. Free self-parking, valet parking $9. From I-4, take Exit 71/Central Florida Pkwy. east and follow the signs to SeaWorld.

Charlie's Lobster House SEAFOOD   This 17-year-old, good-time eatery cranks out a menu bursting with treats from the Gulf of Mexico, Pacific, and Atlantic in a setting straight out of New England. Fish and shellfish specialties include pan-roasted Maine lobster, grilled or blackened yellowfin tuna, Alaskan king crab legs, Maryland-style crab cakes, and broiled shrimp with lump crab stuffing. Landlubbers can choose from a handful of steaks, including filets and strips. Although Charlie's is kid-friendly, there are only a few menu options specifically for small fry (shrimp, chicken fingers, and burgers).

8845 International Dr., in the Mercado Shopping Plaza. © 407/352-6929. www.charlieslobsterhouse.com. Kids' menu, highchairs, boosters. Reservations suggested. Main courses $19–$46, kids $7. AE, DC, DISC, MC, V. Daily 5–10pm. Free self-parking. From I-4, take Exit 74A, Sand Lake Rd./Hwy. 528, east to International Dr., then south.

Dux ⚜⚜ *Finds* INTERNATIONAL   The name is a tribute to the Peabody Orlando's resident ducks, which parade ceremoniously in and out of the lobby every day (p. 261), while the food is a tribute to chefs who create a menu that changes quarterly (ducks are one thing you *won't* see on it). Kids will enjoy the ducks in the lobby, but there's little to interest most of them in the dining room and, for that reason, this is another eatery we recommend for a special night without them. The changing menu might include succulent oven-roasted grouper with bok choy, mushrooms, and ginger sauce. At other times, hope for a tender veal chop marinated in apple cider and honey and served medium rare; steamed red snapper in tomato fricassee and fennel; or sautéed salmon on a bed of couscous with black olives, tomatoes, and chives. The wine list is fabulous.

Note: Because the convention trade slows in August, it's one of the best times to try Dux. Early birds sometimes have the dining room to themselves.

9801 International Dr., in the Peabody Orlando. © 407/345-4550. www.peabodyorlando.com. No kids' menu. Reservations recommended. Main courses $26–$45. AE, DC, DISC, MC, V. Mon–Sat 6–10pm. Free self- and validated valet parking. From I-4, take Exit 74A, Sand Lake Rd./Hwy. 528, east to International Dr., then south. Hotel is on the left across from the Convention Center.

EXPENSIVE

Ran-Getsu of Tokyo JAPANESE   Authentic cuisine, including a sushi bar, has made Ran-Getsu a popular haunt for moneyed Asian tourists, though some families may find the prices too high for its menu. *Tekka-don,* tender slices of tuna that are mild enough for first-timers, is a refreshing choice on the sushi side; so are platters, such as sashimi, maki rolls, and thinly sliced *chirashi* (rice topped with assorted seafood). *Yosenabe* is a bouillabaisse with an unconventional though savory twist—duck and chicken are added to the seafood mix; lobster is available at an added cost. Speaking of seafood, *una-ju* delights eel lovers; the filets are grilled in kabayaki sauce. Less adventurous palates may prefer shrimp tempura or a steak served in teriyaki sauce. Even kids get into the act here, with choices that include beef or chicken teriyaki, shrimp tempura, pork dumplings, and, for brave hearts, sushi. It's a good intro for kids to Japanese cuisine. Ran-Getsu serves sake and plum wine, among others.

8400 International Dr., near Orlando Convention Center. ☎ 407/345-0044. www.rangetsu.com. Kids' menu, highchairs, boosters. Reservations recommended. Main courses $14–$35 (most under $25), sushi entrees $14–$41 (most under $25), kids $6–$8. AE, DC, DISC, MC, V. Daily 5–11pm. From I-4, take Exit 74A, Sand Lake Rd./Hwy. 528, east to International Dr., then south. Restaurant is on right.

MODERATE

Bahama Breeze CARIBBEAN   This chain with spunk uses traditional Caribbean food as a base for creative items, such as moist and tasty "fish in a bag" (strips of tilapia in a parchment pillow flavored with sweet peppers, mushrooms, celery, and spices) and a B+ *paella* (rice with shrimp, fish, mussels, chicken, and sausage). There also are wood-fired pizzas and sandwiches. The tropical atmosphere should appeal to kids, who can dine on chicken fingers, cheese pizza, mac and cheese, and grilled cheese. It's loud and always crowded here, so arrive early and bring patience (the restaurant doesn't accept reservations, and during prime time, 6–8pm, the wait can be up to 2 hr.—probably too long for most young kids to wait). You can pass the time watching chefs working in the open kitchen, but the tropical drinks and 50 brands of beer make the time move faster (and there are shakes for the kids).

8849 International Dr. ☎ 407/248-2499. www.bahamabreeze.com. Kids' menu w/activities, highchairs, boosters. Reservations not accepted. Main courses $9–$25, kids $6–$8. AE, MC, V. Sun–Thurs 4pm–1am, Fri–Sat 4pm–1:30am. Free self-parking. From I-4, take Exit 74A, Sand Lake Rd./Hwy. 528, east to International Dr., then south.

B-Line Diner AMERICAN   You and your kids can sink into upholstered booths or belly up to the counter on a stool in this '50s-style diner with a fabulous dessert case (the cakes are a major hit with all ages, as are the yummy sundaes and shakes).

⟨Value⟩ Self-Service Suppers

If you're on a tight budget and your room has a kitchen or a spot to sit and grab a bite, consider dining in a night or 2 and saving a few bucks. Area grocers, many with delis that turn out ready-to-eat treats, include **Albertson's** near I-Drive (7524 Dr. Phillips Blvd.; ☎ 407/352-1552; www.albertsons.com) and **Gooding's** in Lake Buena Vista (Crossroads Shopping Plaza, 12521 Hwy. 535/Apopka–Vineland Ave.; ☎ 407/827-1200; www.goodings.com). You can find more locations and options in the Orlando Yellow Pages under "Grocers."

International Drive Area Dining

Atlantis (in the Renaissance
  Orlando Resort) **10**
B-Line Diner (in the
  Peabody Orlando) **9**
Bahama Breeze **6**
Cafe Tu Tu Tango **5**
Charlie's Lobster House **7**
Delfino Riviera (in the
  Portofino Bay Hotel) **1**
Dux (in the Peabody
  Orlando) **9**
Mama Della's (in the
  Portofino Bay Hotel) **1**
The Palm (in the Hard Rock
  Hotel) **3**
Ran-Getsu of Tokyo **8**
Tchoup Chop **2**
Wild Jacks **4**

*For restaurants in Universal
Orlando's CityWalk, please
see the "CityWalk" map
in Chapter 10.*

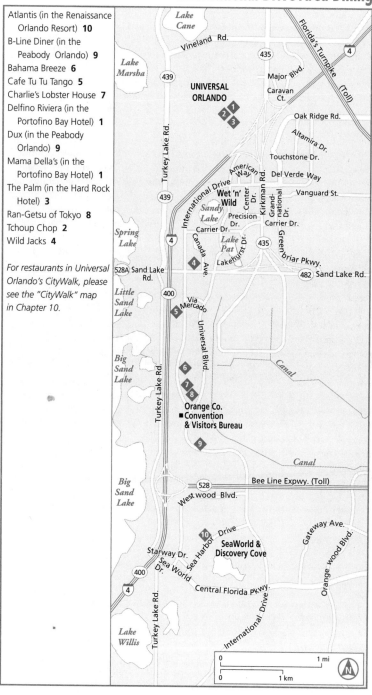

The round-the-clock menu features comfort foods such as a chicken potpie that's up to what mom made; a ham and cheese sandwich on a baguette; and roast pork with grilled apples, sun-dried cherry stuffing, and brandy-honey sauce. The kids' menu offers chicken fingers, spaghetti, grilled cheese, and burgers. Portions are hearty, but so are the prices for diner fare.

9801 International Dr., in the Peabody Orlando. © 407/345-4460. www.peabodyorlando.com. Kids' menu w/activities, highchairs, boosters. Reservations not accepted. Main courses $4–$14 breakfast, $7–$17 lunch, $9–$26 (most under $17) dinner, kids $5. AE, DC, DISC, MC, V. Daily 24 hr. Free self- and validated valet parking. From I-4, take Exit 74A, Sand Lake Rd./Hwy. 528, east to International Dr., then south. Hotel is on the left across from the Convention Center.

Cafe Tu Tu Tango 🎨 INTERNATIONAL/TAPAS   Designed like a Spanish artist's loft, this eclectic eatery offers performance or art experiences while you munch on appetizer-size mini-meals. The atmosphere—there's frequently an artist bringing a canvas to life—should keep your children reasonably entertained. Some of our favorites include Cajun egg rolls filled with blackened chicken, corn, and cheddar and goat cheeses, served with chunky tomato salsa and Creole mustard; cracked black pepper-crusted, seared tuna sashimi with rice noodles and cold spinach in a sesame-soy vinaigrette; and alligator bites in pepper sauce. Sampling can be quite expensive, but the larger your party, the more dishes you can sample without going bust (usually two or three per person does the trick). The kids' menu has grilled cheese, spaghetti, pizza (they can exercise their creativity by designing their own personal pie), chicken fingers, and corn dogs. Wine is available by the glass or bottle.

8625 International Dr., just west of the Mercado. © 407/248-2222. www.cafetututango.com. Kids' menu w/activities, highchairs, boosters. Reservations not required. Tapas (small plates) $4–$11, kids $5–$7. AE, DC, DISC, MC, V. Sun–Thurs 11:30am–11pm; Fri–Sat 11:30am–midnight. Free self-parking. From I-4, take Exit 74A, Sand Lake Rd./Hwy. 528, east to International Dr., then south. It's on the left.

Wild Jacks BARBECUE/STEAKS   Your family should come hankering red meat or not come at all to this chuck wagon–style eatery. Jacks serves Texas-size (and sometimes Texas tough) hunks of cow grilled on an open pit and served with jalapeño smashed potatoes and corn on the cob. It's a family-friendly spot that's a good place to bring the kids; the interior, filled with mounted buffalo heads, long-stuffed jack-a-lopes, and more dying-calf-in-a-hailstorm, twitch-and-twang country-western music than a city slicker can endure in a lifetime, should prove diverting for the young set. The ribs are generally moist and tender, but at crowded times, when the kitchen gets backed up, they may be dry and chewy. The menu also has chicken, salmon, and pork, but it's not a good idea to experiment in a beef house, even a marginal one. Kids have a range of choices, from pint-size steaks, ribs, and burgers to pasta and chicken tenders. Wash the meal down with an icy longneck (there is a wine list, but it's very basic).

7364 International Dr. (between Sand Lake Rd. and Carrier Dr.). © 407/352-4407. Kids' menu w/activities, highchairs, boosters. Reservations accepted. AE, DC, DISC, MC, V. Main courses $11–$21, kids $6.50. Daily 4–10pm. Free self-parking. From I-4, take Exit 74A, Sand Lake Rd./Hwy. 528, east to International Dr., then go south. It's on the right.

6 Places to Dine Elsewhere in Orlando

There's life in other areas, as locals and enterprising visitors discover, though many of them aren't as child-friendly as those near the theme parks and may not have a kids' menu. We list the family-friendly establishments off the beaten track below, as well as a few options that are best reserved for nights out on your own or for special forays with older kids and teens.

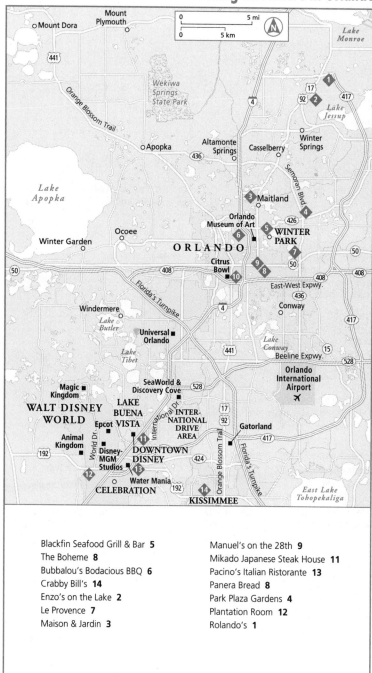

Blackfin Seafood Grill & Bar **5**
The Boheme **8**
Bubbalou's Bodacious BBQ **6**
Crabby Bill's **14**
Enzo's on the Lake **2**
Le Provence **7**
Maison & Jardin **3**

Manuel's on the 28th **9**
Mikado Japanese Steak House **11**
Pacino's Italian Ristorante **13**
Panera Bread **8**
Park Plaza Gardens **4**
Plantation Room **12**
Rolando's **1**

Note: The restaurants in this part of the chapter are located on the "Dining Elsewhere in Orlando" map on p. 139.

VERY EXPENSIVE

The Boheme ✦ INTERNATIONAL   This stylish 2001 arrival has wonderful abstract artwork, as well as an enterprising menu that's a cut above many hotel restaurants. Although it caters to a business crowd (the main reason we don't list it in our hotel chapter), it offers an upscale experience for vacationers looking for a meal while spending time north of the main tourist meccas. The menu changes with the wind, but it might feature peppercorn-seared breast of duck with grilled polenta, roasted Chilean sea bass with sweet corn custard and tomato ceviche, or venison chops with root vegetables and baked yams. The Boheme has a 2,000-bottle wine cellar with vintages from all over the world. The restaurant also has a Sunday jazz brunch (smoked salmon and other seafood, sushi, game, and chicken). **Kids can expect** many of the usual suspects: PBJs, grilled cheese, chicken fingers, burgers, pizza, and fish sticks.

325 S. Orange Ave., across from City Hall in Westin Grand Bohemian Hotel. ℂ 888/472-6312, 800/937-8461, or 407/313-9000. www.grandbohemianhotel.com. Kids' menu, highchairs, boosters. Reservations recommended. Main courses $7–$15 breakfast, $10–$17 lunch, $23–$35 dinner, chef's 6-course tasting menu $60 ($90 with paired wines), kids $7–$8; Sun brunch $35. AE, DC, DISC, MC, V. Sun–Thurs 6am–10:30pm; Fri–Sat 6am–11:30pm. Validated valet parking. Take I-4 Exit 83A, West Robinson/Hwy. 526, then south on Orange. The garage is 2 blocks west on Jackson.

Enzo's on the Lake ✦✦ *Finds* SOUTHERN ITALIAN   If you can afford a night out without kids (at least younger ones or those with fast-food palates), you'll love the lakefront view and the mood inside this restaurant, which evokes the atmosphere of a Mediterranean villa. But the kitchen creations are what pack people in. Enzo Perlini offers a menu from and beyond his native Rome. For the pasta course, try penne soaked in tomato sauce and cream (then given a kick with vodka-injected peppers) or fettuccine with lobster and shrimp in a light saffron salsa. We also recommend *sogliola al limone* (Dover sole sautéed in olive oil and lemon) and *abbacchio del ducca* (rack of lamb baked with shiitake mushrooms and herbs in a lightly spicy sauce). Enzo's dining room has a view of sculpted gardens and sunsets on Lake Fairy. In addition to the main dining room, there are a limited number of seats on a patio overlooking the lake. The menu is complemented by a good wine list, and the bar stocks most of the grappas on planet Earth.

1130 S. U.S. 17/92, Longwood. ℂ 407/834-9872. www.enzos.com. No kids' menu. Reservations recommended. Main courses $19–$46. AE, DC, DISC, MC, V. Mon–Sat 6–11pm; Fri 11:30am–2pm. Free self-parking. Take I-4 north to Exit 94/Hwy. 434, go east to U.S. 17/92, then right. Enzo's is on the right.

Manuel's on the 28th ✦✦✦ *Moments* INTERNATIONAL   Leave your heirs with a sitter or in a kids' center while you venture to the 28th floor of a downtown bank that provides part of this eatery's name and all of its view, which can be no less than beautiful after dark. You can see the city and the distant theme parks (fireworks, too) while fueling your tanks in a restaurant where the food matches the visuals. Despite a smallish kitchen, the chefs work wonders with a changing menu. When available, we can't resist the miso-marinated Chilean sea bass with seaweed salad. Seafood lovers also might encounter asparagus-seared ahi tuna with rice risotto and lump crab hollandaise. And the five peppercorn Angus filet with smoked gouda potatoes wows the red-meat crowd. To make sure you don't miss out on the view, the dining room has floor-to-ceiling windows. Expect very professional service and a far-above-par wine cellar.

390 N. Orange Ave., in the NationsBank Building. ℂ 407/246-6580. www.manuelsonthe28th.com. No kids' menu. Reservations required. Jackets suggested for men. Main courses $26–$45. AE, DC, DISC, MC, V. Tues–Sat 6–9:45pm. Free self-parking. From I-4 take Exit 82C/Anderson St. east to Orange Ave., then left/north to NationsBank Building.

EXPENSIVE

Blackfin Seafood Grill & Bar ✦ SEAFOOD   One of Orlando's better marine cuisineries (along with Crabby Bill's, which is listed a little later in this chapter), Blackfin is a classy and casual eatery for those flexible enough to get to the region's north end. Menu headliners include oak-grilled pompano or orange swordfish in lemon butter, delicately blackened wahoo with pan-seared sesame mayonnaise, and red snapper with a Parmesan crust. Landlubbers find an oak-grilled veal chop with a shiraz demi-glacé and herb-roasted chicken breasts delivered with wild rice. On the kiddie side, the limited options include corn dogs, chicken nuggets, spaghetti, and rock shrimp.

460 N. Orlando Ave., Winter Park. ℂ 407/691-4653. Kids' menu, highchairs, boosters. Reservations recommended. Main courses $25–$40 (most under $30), kids $3–$6. AE, DC, DISC, MC, V. Sun–Wed 5–10pm; Thurs–Sat 5–11pm. Free self-parking. From I-4 Exit 88, go east on Lee Rd.; turn south on US 17-92/N. Orlando Ave. It's located on the east side.

Le Provence ✦ MODERN FRENCH   As with many downtown eateries, this upscale local favorite is best reserved for adults or families with older children, because there is no kids' menu. This eatery serves dishes that feature duck, veal, lobster, scallops, and tuna. If you're in the mood for creative seafood, try the snapper stuffed with shrimp mousse, then wrapped in phyllo with smoked tomato compote and braised cabbage. Wow! Duck lovers can drool over a combo plate: breast meat grilled in a subtle citrus marinade and a leg with natural juices and pineapple salsa. Few restaurants in town offer rabbit, and none do it better than Le Provence, where the loin is stuffed with pâté and vegetables and served in cognac sauce. There are eight fixed-price menus that range from three to six courses. You can enjoy a martini or an after-dinner drink and a cigar next door at Monaco's, which also serves lunch.

Note: In addition to the valet parking noted below, early birds have a shot at a small amount of metered street parking.

50 E. Pine St., in downtown Orlando. ℂ 407/843-1320. www.cenfla.com/res/leprovence. No kids' menu. Reservations recommended. Main courses $8–$15 lunch, $18–$36 dinner (most under $25), $28–$62 prix fixe. AE, DC, MC, V. Mon–Fri 11:30am–2pm and 5:30–9:30pm; Sat 5:30–10:30pm. Valet parking $6. From I-4 take Exit 82C/Anderson St. east to Church St., then left/north on Court Ave. It's near the corner of Court and Pine.

Maison & Jardin ✦ TRADITIONAL FRENCH   This restaurant is a great choice for a romantic evening without the kids, even though the atmosphere is a trifle stuffy. If you're game (sorry!), try the venison chops (but they're small and usually chewy) or the seared quail and ostrich combo (ditto). For slightly tamer palates, there's veal tenderloin with Maine lobster meat and morel sauce, rack of lamb in an awakening mustard tarragon sauce, and shrimp and scallops sautéed with spicy tomato cream and served over pasta. The menu has fixed-price options (five or six courses). Maison & Jardin has one of the best wine cellars around; it's been honored by *Wine Spectator* magazine for an outstanding selection (1,200 varieties).

430 S. Wymore Rd., Altamonte Springs. ℂ 407/862-4410. www.maison-jardin.com. No kids' menu. Reservations recommended. Main courses $20–$30 dinner, $44.50–$59.50 prix fixe, $63.75–$82.25 with wine. AE, DC, DISC, MC, V. Tue–Sat 6–10pm. Free self-parking. Take I-4 Exit 92, Hwy. 436/Semoran Blvd., make a left at top of exit ramp, go to 2nd light, and turn left onto Wymore. It's ½ mile on the right.

Mikado Japanese Steak House ✸ JAPANESE   If you're hungry for sushi, consider an evening at the Mikado, which has one of the area's better menus in that department. Ditto for its teppanyaki, where chefs slice, dice, and hurl chicken, seafood, and beef from their grill to your plate. The latter is certainly better than the Teppanyaki Dining Room at Epcot (p. 113). So is the mood. Shoji screens lend intimacy to a dining area where windows overlook rock gardens, reflecting pools, and a palm-fringed pond. Sake, from the restaurant lounge, is the recommended mood enhancer for adults. Your children will likely find the atmosphere exotic and cool, but be aware that the kids' menu is very limited: grilled cheese, pizza, and burgers.

8701 World Center Dr. (off Hwy. 536), in Marriott's Orlando World Center. ✆ 407/239-4200. Kids' menu, highchairs, boosters. Reservations recommended. Main courses $16–$35 adults, $8–$10 children. AE, DC, DISC, MC, V. Daily 6–10pm. Free self- and validated valet parking. Take I-4 Exit 67/Hwy. 536 east to the Marriott World Center.

Park Plaza Gardens INTERNATIONAL   The decor of this Winter Park restaurant can best be described as EuroFloridian (imagine Art Deco colliding with black and white), and that description matches the cuisine as well. The inventive menu offers such treats as pan-seared ahi tuna with baby bok choy and shiitake mushrooms; spice-crusted double lamb chops in a pine-nut-ginger-carrot sauce; and Maryland crab cakes with mashed potatoes, asparagus, and spicy mayonnaise. Alas, as is the case throughout the non-tourist areas, the kids' menu isn't so inventive, but younger diners should be happy with the chicken strips, burgers, pizza, and pasta The house has an extensive selection of domestic, French, and Italian wines, and its staff is one of the best north of Orlando.

319 Park Ave. S., Winter Park. ✆ 407/645-2475. www.parkplazagardens.com. Kids' menu, highchairs, boosters. Reservations recommended. Main courses $8–$19 lunch (sandwiches $8–$9), $21–$29 dinner, kids $7. AE, DC, DISC, MC, V. Tue–Sat 11:30am–2:30pm and 6–9:30pm; Sun 11am–3pm and 6–9:30pm. Free self-parking. Take I-4 Exit 87, Fairbanks Ave./Hwy. 426, east past U.S. 17/92, and, as you pass Rollins College, turn left on Park. It's on the left.

Plantation Room SEAFOOD/STEAKS   New to the dinner scene, this restaurant in the Celebration hotel delivers a nice menu for a rookie. The seafood selections include sea bass with sweet potato grits and fried leeks as well as a medley of scallops, shrimp, and salmon seared, then comforted with grilled polenta and lobster reduction. Meat-lovers can dig into a New York strip that comes with roasted red potatoes and orange-glazed carrots, while vegetarians might consider the grilled portobello mushroom with roasted red-pepper coulis over wild mushroom risotto. The kids' menu has chicken fingers, burgers, mac and cheese, PBJs, and more. Sunday's champagne brunch features smoked salmon, omelets, breakfast meats, pancakes, Belgian waffles, and fresh fruit. The plantation-style dining room is cheerful, and there's also alfresco seating on a brick patio.

700 Bloom St., Celebration. ✆ 407/566-6000. www.celebrationhotel.com. Kids' menu, highchairs, boosters. Reservations recommended. Main courses $15–$36, kids $7–$10; brunch $29, kids $15. AE, DC, DISC, MC, V. Tue–Sat 5:30–10pm; Sun 11am–2pm. Free self-parking, valet parking $5 for dinner. Take I-4 Exit 64A/U.S. 192, go east to 2nd light, then right on Celebration Ave. and follow the signs.

MODERATE

Crabby Bill's ✸ SEAFOOD   This fun, friendly member of a small central Florida chain was launched by "Crabby Bill" Loder in 1975 and continues to deliver quality seafood to diners who dig in from family-style tables. In season, the grouper is fresh and fabulous. (We recommend trying it broiled, which keeps it juicy, but you also can order it blackened or fried, including in a sandwich.) If the oysters on the half-shell are farm-raised in Texas (ask), they're small but very sweet. The house specialties—no surprise here—include stone crab claws (Oct–May) as well as king, snow, and blue crabs. The menu also has a variety of fried, grilled, broiled, or blackened fish. Beer, wine, and other intoxicants are served. Kids will find burgers, chicken fingers, fried shrimp or fish, mac and cheese, and spaghetti and meatballs (all dishes are served with Oreos—sure to please your kids' palate).

5030 E. Irlo Bronson Memorial Hwy./U.S. 192, Kissimmee (between Poinciana Blvd. and Vineland Rd.). © 321/677-0303. www.crabbybills.com. Reservations not necessary. Main courses $9–$25 (most under $14), sandwiches $4.50–$7, kids $3–$4. AE, DC, DISC, MC, V. Daily 11:30am–10pm.

Pacino's Italian Ristorante ★ NORTHERN ITALIAN   The house spe-
cialty at this family-friendly spot, veal osso buco, is a delicious collision of veal shank, mushrooms, Barolo wine, herbs, and mushrooms. At 32 ounces, the porterhouse steak is a belly-buster, and the house's *frutti di mare* has shrimp, calamari, clams, and scallops sautéed with white wine and herbs and heaped onto a mound of linguine. Pasta-loving kids get their choice of spaghetti, lasagna, and pizza, while those craving something from the animal food group can dig into chicken tenders. The ceiling's fiber optics help create an illusion of dining under the stars; there's a patio if you want the real thing. Some servers can be a little aloof, but the price and taste make up for it.

5795 W. Irlo Bronson Memorial Hwy./U.S. 192, Kissimmee. © 407/396-8022. www.pacinos.com. Kids' menu w/activities, highchairs, boosters. Reservations accepted. Main courses $13–$27 (most under $20), pizza $9–$11, kids $4–$5. AE, MC, V. Daily 4–10pm. Free self-parking. From I-4, take Exit 64A/U.S. 192 exit east 1 mile.

Panera Bread ★ AMERICAN   This trendy cafe/bakery is a great place for a
light meal, and its quick growth in the area (there are several locations) attests to its popularity among locals and visitors alike. The cafe menu offers a variety of delicious soups (broccoli cheddar, black bean, vegetable sirloin, and others) and salads (Asian sesame chicken, Caesar, and more). But the real main events are sandwiches such as turkey with chipotle mayonnaise, roast beef with creamy horseradish sauce, portobello and mozzarella panini, and a dozen others. While there isn't a kid-specific menu, most young appetites would be happy to dive into the bakery menu (caramel pecan or very chocolate brownies, bear claws, and cherry Danish) or a PBJ on French bread from the cafe menu. There are other locations, including one at Mall of Millenia (© 407/248-0811).

296 E. Michigan St., Orlando. © 407/481-9880. www.panerabread.com. Reservations not accepted. Main courses $7–$14, baked goods $1–$5. AE, DISC, MC, V. Mon–Sat 6:30am–9:30pm; Sun 7am–8:30pm. Free self-parking. From I-4, take Exit 80B, U.S. 17/92, and go north to Michigan, then right 1½ miles.

Rolando's ★ *Finds* CUBAN   If you like neighborhood-style Cuban cuisine,
you won't be disappointed here. This mom-and-pop restaurant serves large portions of traditional Cuban fare, such as *arroz con pollo* (chicken with yellow rice), *ropa vieja* (shredded beef), and, if you call a few hours or a day in advance, *paella* (fish and shellfish served on a bed of rice). We also recommend Rolando's roast chicken, which is brushed with crushed garlic, white-wine vinegar, cumin, and oregano, then briefly deep-fried. Entrees are served with yucca (a chewy root) or plantains (a cooked banana-like fruit). Kids' options include mac and cheese, a ham-and-cheese sandwich, and chicken fingers. The plain dining room has Formica tables, old photographs of Cuba, and potted philodendrons suspended from the ceiling. Soft lighting adds a smidgen of ambience, and there's a very limited beer and wine list.

Value Bargain Buffets

We won't list them all, but if you spend time on International Drive or U.S. 192/Irlo Bronson Memorial Highway between Kissimmee and Disney, you'll see billboards peddling all-you-can-eat breakfast buffets for $3.99 to $5.99. All of these spots welcome kids and are a good way to fill your family's tanks early and skip or at least go easy on lunch, especially if your day is in the theme parks, where lunches are overpriced. Breakfast buffets are served by **Golden Corral,** 8033 International Dr. (© **407/352-6606**); **Ponderosa Steak House,** 6362 International Dr. (© **407/352-9343**) and 7598 U.S. 192 W. (© **407/396-7721**); and **Sizzler Restaurant,** 9142 International Dr. (© **407/351-5369**) and 7602 U.S. 192 W. (© **407/397-0997**).

870 E. Hwy. 436/Semoran Blvd., Casselberry. © **407/767-9677.** Kids' menu, highchairs, boosters. Reservations accepted. Main courses $4–$6 lunch, $8–$18 dinner, kids $4–$5. AE, DC, DISC, MC, V. Mon–Fri 11am–9:30pm; Sat noon–10pm; Sun noon–8:30pm. Free self-parking. From I-4, take Exit 82A, Hwy. 408/East–West Expwy., head east, and make a left on Hwy. 436.

INEXPENSIVE

Bubbalou's Bodacious BBQ ⭐ Value BARBECUE   You can smell the hickory smoke emerging from this family-friendly restaurant for blocks, the tangy scent cutting through the humid Florida air. This is, hands down, some of the best barbecue you'll find anywhere. And, if nothing else, you have to love the name. There are other things on the menu. If you can eat the night or day away, go for "The Big-Big Pig" platter (beef, sliced pork, and turkey with fixin's). There also are several barbecue baskets, combos, dinners, and sandwiches, as well as side orders ranging from fried pickles and okra to collard greens and black-eyed peas. The uninitiated should stay away from the "Killer" sauce, which produces a tongue buzz that's likely to last for hours; you might even taste-test the mild before moving up to the hot. The beans are the perfect side dish (if you don't mind producing methane hours later). Your kids have a choice of barbecued chicken or chicken strips, grilled cheese, burgers, or corn dogs. And there's takeout (including special family packs) available if you want to head back with something to snack on in your hotel room.

1471 Lee Rd., Winter Park (about 5 min. from downtown Orlando). © **407/628-1212.** www.bubbalous.com. Kids' menu, highchairs, boosters. Reservations not accepted. Main courses $4–$13, kids $3.50–$4. AE, MC, V. Mon–Thurs 10am–9pm; Fri–Sat 10am–10pm. Free self-parking. Take I-4 Exit 88, Lee Rd./Hwy. 423, and follow your nose; Bubbalou's is on the left next to a dry cleaner.

7 Only in Orlando: Dining with Disney Characters

Dining with costumed characters is a treat for many Disney fans, but it's a special occasion for those under 10. Some of their favorite cartoon characters show up to greet them, sign autographs, pose for family photos, and interact. These aren't low-turnout events—it's not uncommon for Chef Mickey's, listed below, to have *1,600 or more guests on a weekend morning*—so make reservations as far in advance as possible (up to 90 days in advance) and don't expect a lot of one-on-one. The crowds can dampen the event.

The prices for character meals are much the same, no matter where you're dining. At press time, breakfast (most serve it) ran $17 to $20 for adults and $9 to $10 for children 3 to 11; those that serve dinner charge $21 to $24 for adults and $10 to $11 for kids. The prices vary a bit, though, from location to location.

To make reservations for WDW character meals call ☏ **407/939-3463.** American Express, Diners Club, Discover, MasterCard, and Visa are accepted at all character meals.

You'll find all of the restaurants mentioned in this section on the map "Walt Disney World & Lake Buena Vista Dining," earlier in this chapter. For Internet information, go to **www.disneyworld.com**.

Note: Character appearances below were accurate when this book went to press, but *line-ups, prices, and menus change frequently.* We *strongly recommend* against promising children they will meet a specific character at a meal. If you have your heart set on meeting a certain character, call to confirm his or her appearance when making your Priority Seating arrangement. Kids' activities, highchairs, and boosters are available at all of these character meals.

Cape May Café   The Cape May Café, a delightful New England–themed dining room, serves lavish buffet breakfasts (eggs, pancakes, bacon, pastries) hosted by **Admiral Goofy** and his crew—**Chip 'n' Dale** and **Pluto** (characters may vary).

1800 Epcot Resorts Blvd., at Disney's Beach Club Resort. $16.99 adults, $8.99 kids. Daily 7:30–11am.

Chef Mickey's 🎭🎭   The whimsical Chef Mickey's offers buffet breakfasts (eggs, bacon, sausage, pancakes, fruit) and dinners (rotating hot entrees; salad bar, soups, vegetables, ice cream with toppings). **Mickey and various pals** are there to meet and mingle.

4600 N. World Dr., at Disney's Contemporary Resort. Breakfast $16.99 adults, $8.99 kids; dinner $23.99 adults, $10.99 kids. Daily 7:30–11:30am and 5–9:30pm.

Cinderella's Royal Table 🎭   Cinderella Castle—the focal point of the park—serves character breakfast buffets daily (eggs, bacon, Danish). Hosts vary, but **Cinderella** always puts in an appearance. This is one of the most popular character meals in the park and the hardest to get into, so **reserve far, far in advance** (reservations are taken 90 days in advance, and you must make them with a guaranteed credit card payment that will *cost you $10 for adults and $5 for kids if you cancel them*). To have the best shot at getting in, be flexible about your seating arrangements and dining times, and call Disney exactly at 7am EST on your first date of reservations eligibility (if you aren't sure what date that is, call Disney and they'll help you figure it out). If you get through on your first try (lucky you!), tell the reservations clerk you want Cinderella's Table for whatever date you picked. Don't even think about requesting a specific time—take whatever you can get (most reservations will be gone by 7:15am).

In Cinderella Castle, at the Magic Kingdom. $19.99 adults, $9.99 kids. Daily 8–10am. Theme park admission required.

Crystal Palace Buffet 🎭   **Winnie the Pooh** and pals hold court throughout the day. The restaurant serves breakfast (eggs, French toast, pancakes, bacon), lunch, and dinner (hot and cold entrees, peel-and-eat shrimp, and more).

At Crystal Palace, in the Magic Kingdom. Breakfast $16.99 adults, $8.99 kids; lunch $17.99 adults, $9.99 kids; dinner $21.99 adults, $9.99 kids. Daily 8–10:30am, 11:30am–2:45pm, 4pm–park closing. Theme park admission required.

Donald's Prehistoric Breakfastosaurus   **Donald, Goofy,** and **Pluto** host a buffet breakfast (eggs, bacon, French toast) in DinoLand U.S.A.'s Restaurantosaurus.

In DinoLand U.S.A., at Disney's Animal Kingdom. $16.99 adults, $8.99 kids. Daily park opening–10:30am. Theme park admission required.

Garden Grill ✎ There's a "Momma's-in-the-kitchen" theme at this revolving restaurant, where hearty, family-style meals are hosted by **Mickey** and **Chip 'n' Dale.** (Mickey sure gets around, eh?) Lunch and dinner (chicken, fish, steak, vegetables, potatoes) are served.

In The Land Pavilion at Epcot. Lunch $19.99 adults, $9.99 kids; dinner $21.99 adults, $9.99 kids. Daily noon–3:30pm, 5–8pm. Theme park admission required.

Liberty Tree Tavern ✎ This Colonial-style 18th-century pub offers character dinners hosted by **Minnie, Goofy, Pluto,** and **Chip 'n' Dale.** The family-style meals include salad, roast turkey, ham, flank steak, corn bread, and apple crisp with vanilla ice cream.

In Liberty Square, in the Magic Kingdom. $21.99 adults, $9.99 kids. Daily 4pm–park closing. Theme park admission required.

1900 Park Fare ✎ The elegant Grand Floridian offers breakfast (eggs, French toast, bacon, pancakes) and dinner buffets (steak, pork, fish) at the exposition-themed 1900 Park Fare. Big Bertha—a French band organ that plays pipes, drums, bells, cymbals, castanets, and xylophone—provides music. **Mary Poppins, Alice in Wonderland,** and friends appear at breakfasts; **Cinderella** and friends show up for Cinderella's Gala Feast at dinner.

4401 Floridian Way, at Disney's Grand Floridian Resort & Spa. Breakfast $16.99 adults, $9.99 kids; dinner $23.99 adults, $10.99 kids. Daily 7:30–11am and 5–9pm.

'Ohana Character Breakfast Traditional breakfasts (eggs, pancakes, bacon) are prepared on an 18-foot fire pit and served family style. **Mickey** and friends appear, and children are given the chance to parade around with Polynesian musical instruments.

1600 Seven Seas Dr., in 'Ohana at Disney's Polynesian Resort. $16.99 adults, $8.99 kids. Daily 7:30–11am.

Princess Storybook Breakfast **Snow White, Mary Poppins, Princess Aurora, Pocahontas,** *or* **Belle** might show up at this character meal buffet (scrambled eggs, French toast, sausage, bacon, and potatoes).

At Akershus Castle in Epcot's Norway Pavilion. $19.99 adults, $9.99 kids. Daily 8:30–10:30 am. Theme park admission required.

6

What Kids Like to See & Do in Walt Disney World

The Walt Disney World stable has resorts, restaurants, nightclub venues, smaller attractions, cruise ships, and four theme parks: the Magic Kingdom, Epcot, Disney–MGM Studios, and Animal Kingdom. Even in a sour economy, they attract some 38 million paying customers annually, according to estimates by *Amusement Business* magazine. All four make the country's top five in attendance (the other is Disneyland in California).

It's no wonder. They offer a star-spangled, self-sufficient vacation where wonderment, human progress, and old-fashioned family fun are the key themes. They strut their stuff with spectacular parades and fireworks displays, 3-D and CircleVision films, nerve-racking thrill rides, and adventurous journeys through time and space. All of the theme parks have at least a couple of rides and attractions geared to every age group, so no matter how old your children are, they will find something to their liking. Though the parks are expensive, you'll seldom hear people complain (too much) about failing to get their money's worth. Most leave saying Disney delivers.

One reason Disney stays in favor with the family set is that rides and shows are periodically updated. And if something doesn't quite work, Disney usually fixes it. As part of this process, the company interviews some of its park-goers to decide how well, or poorly, things are working.

There have been changes and additions as the Magic Kingdom—the park that started it all in 1971, and still the most popular in North America—has matured, although not as many as in the other parks. The oldest of its "lands," Tomorrowland, was more than a bit weary when it underwent a late 1990s upgrade. The redecorating slowed after 1999's torrid pace, which brought new thrill rides to Epcot and Disney–MGM Studios, a new "land" (Asia) in Animal Kingdom, the addition of Fantasmic! at Disney–MGM Studios, and the opening of Cirque du Soleil in Downtown Disney West Side. But they heated up a little in 2002 with the debut of **Primeval Whirl,** the twin, carnival-style roller coaster at Animal Kingdom, and in 2003 with the opening of Epcot's new **Mission: Space,** a NASA-caliber motion simulator, and the 3-D show **Mickey's PhilharMagic.**

But before we dive into the action, giving you details of these and other fun generators, let's take care of some basic business.

1 Essentials

GETTING INFORMATION IN ADVANCE

Before leaving home, call or write to the Walt Disney World Co., Box 10000, Lake Buena Vista, FL 32830-1000 (© **407/934-7639**), for a vacation video and the *Walt Disney World Vacations* brochure; both are valuable planning aids. When you call, also ask about special events that will be going on during your visit. While we list big-time events under "When to Go" in chapter 2, there are many other events that may be of interest to you.

Once you've arrived in town, Guest Services and the concierge desks in hotels (especially Disney properties and "official" hotels) have up-to-the-minute information about happenings in the parks. Stop by to ask questions and get literature, including a schedule of park hours and events. If you have questions your hotel's personnel can't answer, call Disney at ✆ **407/824-4321.**

There also are information areas at City Hall in the Magic Kingdom and Guest Relations at Epcot, Disney–MGM Studios, and Animal Kingdom.

If you're hooked into the Internet or have a local library with Internet access, try **www.disneyworld.com**, which features entertaining and regularly updated information on the parks.

You can also consult the Orlando/Orange County Convention & Visitors Bureau site (**www.orlandoinfo.com**). Another good site, **www.floridakiss.com**, is sponsored by the Kissimmee–St. Cloud Convention & Visitors Bureau. It, too, has an attractions link.

GETTING TO WDW BY CAR

The interstate exits to all Disney parks and resorts are well marked. Once you're off I-4, there are signs directing you to individual destinations. If you miss your exit, *don't panic.* Simply get off at the next one and turn around. It may take a little more time, but it's safer than cutting across five lanes of traffic to make the off-ramp, or worse—to risk a fender bender. Drive with extra caution in the attractions area. Disney drivers are divided into two categories: workers in a hurry to make their shift and tourists in a hurry to get to the fun (and trying to drive while looking at a map). Both kinds pull some really stupid moves.

Upon entering WDW grounds, you can tune your radio to **1030 AM** when you're approaching the Magic Kingdom, or **850 AM** when approaching Epcot, for park information. Tune to **1200 AM** when departing the Magic Kingdom, or **910 AM** when departing Epcot. TVs in all Disney resorts and "official" hotels also have park information channels.

PARKING

All WDW lots are tightly controlled; the Disney folks have parking down to a science. You park where they tell you to park—or here comes security. *Remember to write your parking place (lot and row number) on something so you can find your vehicle later.* Parking attendants won't be there to direct you to it when you leave the park, and, at the end of the day, you'd be surprised at how many autos look alike through tired eyes. The last thing you and your kids will want to do is play a game of "let's guess where we left the car."

Tips Tighter Security

Guards at the gates at all Disney parks check a variety of carry-ins, including backpacks and large purses. They also have been known to check guests' IDs, so be sure to bring a government-issued photo identification card. All this, of course, means it takes a little longer to get to the action.

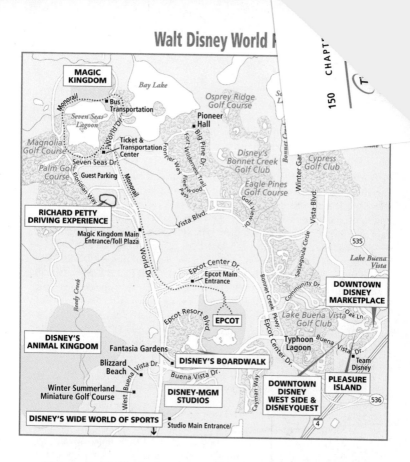

Walt Disney World

Visitors should ride the free trams in the massive Magic Kingdom lots, but some folks decide to skip them and walk to the gates at Epcot, Disney–MGM Studios, and Animal Kingdom. *Some also don't have a choice. Disney has cut service to some parking areas near the entrances to its parks.* Guests who can't make the hike have to park in handicapped areas or have a driver drop them at special unloading areas outside the entrances. If your kids are young and the tram is available, we recommend you use it—your children will be doing a lot of sustained walking in the parks, and it's best to preserve their energy for the fun stuff. If you end up walking from your car, be careful! These lots aren't designed for pedestrians, and you don't want your family to become road kill.

At press time, parking cost $7 at the four major WDW attractions ($8 for RVs). We expect the fees eventually will go up to $8 and $9, respectively, to match Universal Orlando's. There are special lots for travelers with disabilities (© **407/824-4321** for details). Disney resort guests do not have to pay for parking.

TICKETS & PASSES

There are several options, from single- to multiday tickets. Most people find the best bargains to be 4- and 5-day passes. All offer unlimited use of the WDW transportation system. *Note:* Children ages 2 and under enter all Disney parks for free when accompanied by a paying adult.

Price Alert

Single-day and multiday admission prices listed in this chapter don't include Florida's 6% sales tax and are subject to change. Annual price increases are normal, so when you visit, prices may be higher than those listed on these pages.

The **4-Day Park Hopper Passes** provide unlimited admission to the Magic Kingdom, Epcot, Animal Kingdom, and Disney–MGM Studios. The cost is just a few dollars a day less than the cost of single-park tickets, but you also get the option of returning to the parks as many times as you want and your unused days don't expire, so you can use them on a later visit. For a 4-day pass, adults pay $208; kids 3 to 9 pay $167. A **5-Day Park Hopper Plus Pass** also includes your choice of two 1-day admissions to Typhoon Lagoon, Blizzard Beach, Pleasure Island, or Disney's Wide World of Sports. The 5-day pass is $269 for adults and $216 for kids. Park Hopper Plus Passes for 6 and 7 days are available; call ℂ 407/824-4321 or on the Internet go to **www.disneyworld.com** for details. (*Note:* You can save a few dollars on multiday tickets if you buy them online at the WDW website.) Disney also offers length-of-stay passes, called **Ultimate Park Hopper Passes,** for WDW resort and "official" hotel guests.

A **1-day, 1-park ticket** for Magic Kingdom, Epcot, Animal Kingdom, or Disney–MGM Studios is $52 for adults, $42 for children 3 to 9.

A **1-day ticket to Typhoon Lagoon or Blizzard Beach** is $31 for adults, $25 for children.

A **1-day ticket** to **Pleasure Island** is $19.95. Because this is primarily an 18-and-over entertainment complex, there's no child's ticket.

If you're planning to stay at any WDW resort or "official" hotel (see chapter 4, "Family-Friendly Accommodations"), you're also eligible for money-saving Disney room-and-ticket packages priced according to the length of your stay.

If your stay is long enough or you're going to return within the year, annual passes ($369–$489 adults, $314–$416 children) can be a cheaper way to go than the longer Park Hopper Plus or Unlimited Magic tickets.

OPERATING HOURS

All of Disney's theme parks are open 365 days a year. Hours of operation vary throughout the year and can be influenced by special events, so it's a good idea to call to check opening/closing times. The **Magic Kingdom** and **Disney–MGM Studios** are generally open from 9am to 6 or 7pm, with hours often extended to 9pm and sometimes as late as midnight during major holidays and summer. **Animal Kingdom** usually is open from 8 or 9am to 5 or 6pm, but sometimes closes as late as 7pm.

Epcot's Future World is generally open from 9 or 10am to 6 or 7pm and occasionally later. **Epcot's World Showcase** usually opens at 11am or noon and closes at 9pm. Once again, there are extended holiday and summer hours.

Typhoon Lagoon and **Blizzard Beach** are open from 10am to 5pm most of the year (with extended hours during summer and some holidays). Note that during the summer and holiday periods, the water parks can fill up early and close to new visitors, so if you plan on visiting one of them at a busy time of year, do it early or pretty late in the day. Both parks are closed on a rotating basis during the winter for maintenance.

2 Making Your Visit More Enjoyable

HOW WE'VE MADE THIS CHAPTER USEFUL TO PARENTS

Before every listing in the major parks, you'll note the **"Recommended Ages"** entry that tells which ages will most appreciate that ride or show. Though most families want to do everything, this guideline is helpful in planning your daily itinerary. In our ride ratings, we also indicate whether a ride will be more enjoyable for kids than for adults or vice versa. Many, even a couple in the Magic Kingdom, are too intense for young kids, and one bad experience can spook them for a long time. You'll also find any *height and health restrictions* noted in the listings.

We're also going to give you two other yardsticks that will be helpful to you in evaluating some rides for your kids: **Jake (age 12) and Andy (age 6) ratings.** These two are our grandsons and they're theme-park veterans, having been hauled into the trenches by their parents and us early and often. (Now they do the hauling!) On select rides, we'll give you their reviews.

BEST TIME OF YEAR TO VISIT

Because of the large number of international visitors, there's really no "off season" at Disney, but during the winter months, usually mid-January through March, crowds are smaller (except weekends), and the weather can be mild. The crowds also thin from mid-September until the week before Thanksgiving, and in May, before Memorial Day weekend. (Again, weekends tend to get clogged with locals.) *Summer is the worst time.* The masses throng to the parks. It's also humid and hot, *Hot,* **HOT.** If you can skip a summer visit, you also have to worry less about the possibility of a hurricane (admittedly rare) or an electrical storm (an almost daily occurrence here). *Tip:* Summer in the parks is bad, but periods around major holidays also attract throngs and the absolute worst crowds show up mid-December through the first weekend in January. Admittedly, the festive atmosphere and holiday decor make Disney World that much more fun for the family, but if the thought of standing in long lines and dealing with massive crowds doesn't make you merry, don't even think of coming here for the holidays.

BEST DAYS TO VISIT

The busiest days at all parks are generally Saturday and Sunday. Seven-day guests usually arrive and depart on one of these days, so fewer of them turn the turnstiles; but weekends are when locals and Florida commuters invade. Beyond

---

Tips **New Kid on the Block**

Disney has introduced a new kind of tour guide. **Pal Mickey** is a 10½-inch-tall digital toy stuffed with all sorts of gizmos that turn him into a sometimes-funny guide that tells guests about parades, show times, and character greeting places. Pal Mickey is designed for 5 to 10 year olds (who find him a ton of fun). His computer chips pick up wireless signals throughout the park and dispense fun and facts. He's available for rent ($8 a day) or purchase ($60, including sales tax). He also provides games to keep kids entertained in those long theme park lines and offers tips, including ride height restrictions. Pal Mickey operates on three AA batteries and recites hundreds of lines of text. Pal Mickey also speaks Spanish.

that: Monday, Thursday, and Saturday are pretty frantic in the Magic Kingdom; Tuesday and Friday are hectic at Epcot; Sunday and Wednesday are crazy at Disney–MGM Studios; and Monday, Tuesday, and Wednesday are a zoo at Animal Kingdom. Crowds tend to thin later in the day, so if you're going to visit during the busy season and have the luxury of the Park Hopper or Park Hopper Plus passes, you'll bump into fewer guests the later you visit. This also applies to the water parks.

The big attractions at Animal Kingdom are, clearly, the animals, and the best time to see them is at the opening bell or late in the day, when things are cooler. You'll also get a decent midday glimpse of some of them during the cooler months.

PLAN YOUR VISIT

How you plan your time at Walt Disney World will depend on a number of factors. These include the ages of any children in your party, what, if anything, you've seen on previous visits, your interests, and whether you're traveling at peak time or off season. Preplanning is always essential. So is choosing age-appropriate activities.

Nothing can spoil a day in the parks more than a child devastated because he or she can't do something that was promised. Before you get to the park, review this book and the suggested ages for children, including **_height restrictions._** The WDW staff won't bend the rules despite the pitiful wails of your little ones. **_Note:_** Many rides that have minimum heights also have enough turbulence to make them unsuitable for folks with neck, back, or heart problems, those prone to motion sickness, or pregnant women.

Unless you're staying for more than a week, you can't experience all of the rides, shows, or attractions included in this chapter. A ride may last only 5 minutes, but you may have to wait an hour or so, even if you use FASTPASS (detailed shortly). You'll wear you and your kids to a frazzle trying to hit everything. It's better to follow a relaxed itinerary, including leisurely meals and some recreational activities, than to make a demanding job out of trying to see everything.

CREATE AN ITINERARY FOR EACH DAY

Read the previously mentioned _Walt Disney World Vacations_ brochure and the detailed descriptions in this book, and then plan your trip to include those shows and attractions that pique your family's interest and excitement.

Consider your loyalties. Winnie the Pooh doesn't move us the same way he moved our grandsons when they were younger. Put the ride featuring your favorite character, or your kids, at the top of your list. It's a good idea to make a daily itinerary, putting your choices in some kind of sensible geographical sequence, so you're not zigzagging all over the place. Consult the maps in this

---

Tips **Parental Touring Tip**

Many of the attractions at Walt Disney World offer a **Ride-Share program** for parents traveling with small children. One parent can ride an attraction while the other stays with the kids; then the adults can switch places without the second one having to stand in line again. Notify a cast member if you wish to participate when you get in line. Many other Orlando theme parks offer this option, too.

Tips FASTPASS

Don't want to stand in line as long as the other guests, yet not flush enough to hire a stand-in? Disney parks use a reservation system where you go to the primo rides, feed your theme-park ticket into a small ticket taker, and get an assigned 1-hour period in which to return. When you do, you get into a short line and climb aboard. The system *is totally free*, so there's no reason not to use it. Here's the drill:

Hang onto your ticket stub when you enter and head to the hottest ride on your list. If it's a FASTPASS attraction (they're noted in the guide map you get when you enter), feed your stub into the waist-level ticket taker (if you don't see it, ask a Disney employee at the ride's entrance to point it out). Retrieve your ticket stub and the FAST-PASS stub that comes with it. Look at the two times stamped on the latter. You can return during that window, usually 1 hour, and enter the ride with almost no wait. In the meantime, you can do something else until the appointed time.

Note: Early in the day, your window may begin 40 minutes after you feed the FASTPASS machine, but later in the day it may be hours later. Initially, Disney only allowed you to do this on one ride at a time. Now, your FASTPASS ticket has a time when you can get a second FASTPASS, usually 2 hours later, even if you haven't yet used the first pass.

Note II: Don't try to feed your ticket stub in multiple times, figuring you can hit the jackpot for multiple rides or help others in your group who lost their tickets. These "smart" stubs will reject your pitiful attempt by spitting out a coupon that says "Not A Valid FASTPASS."

book and familiarize yourself in advance with the layout of each park. Also recognize that rides or exhibits nearest an entrance may be the busiest when the gates open. That's because a lot of people visit the first thing they see, even if the more popular attractions are deeper into the park.

We repeat this advice: Schedule sit-down shows, recreational activities (a boat ride or a refreshing swim late in the afternoon), and at least some unhurried meals if time permits. This will save you and your kids from exhaustion and aggravation. Breaks in the day will give your family the much-needed opportunity to recharge their batteries and rest weary feet. Our suggested itineraries that follow allow you to see a great deal of the parks as efficiently as possible. And if you have the luxury of a multiday pass, you can divide and conquer at a slower pace and even repeat some favorites.

SUGGESTED ITINERARIES

Our suggested itineraries will allow you to cover most of the ground in each park in as efficient a manner as possible. Do note, though, that using FASTPASS may require you to double back to a land you've already covered.

There are a ton of ways to see the parks, and we feel, time and budget permitting, it's often better to do it in limited doses—those where you spend 2 or more days in a park at a casual pace. We're offering suggested itineraries as options for those on a tighter schedule. The following itineraries are organized to get the most out of the least amount of time.

We break things into one game plan for families with younger kids and another for those with older kids and teenagers. With few exceptions (we'll note them later), Disney World doesn't have enough true stomach-turning thrill rides to warrant a special itinerary for take-no-prisoners teens and adults. Frankly, the only Orlando park in that class is Universal's Islands of Adventure, which we'll tackle in chapter 7, "What Kids Like to See & Do Beyond Disney."

A Day in the Magic Kingdom with Younger Kids

Consider making a Priority Seating dinner reservation at **Cinderella's Royal Table** (© 407/939-3463), located inside Cinderella Castle.

If you have very young kids (preschool to around age 7 is the perfect age), go right to the **Walt Disney World Railroad** station on Main Street and take the next train. Get off at **Mickey's Toontown Fair** to meet Mickey, Minnie, and the gang. Ride the **Barnstormer at Goofy's Wiseacre Farm,** a mini–roller coaster, and explore **Mickey's** and **Minnie's Country Houses.**

If your kids are 8 or older, start the day at **Tomorrowland** and brave **Buzz Lightyear's Space Ranger Spin,** and **Space Mountain.** (Little ones like the **Tomorrowland Indy Speedway,** but there's not much else for them here.)

Most preteens will find something that's fun in Fantasyland, including **Dumbo the Flying Elephant, Mickey's PhilharMagic, It's a Small World, The Many Adventures of Winnie the Pooh,** and **Cinderella's Golden Carousel.**

After lunch at Cosmic Ray's Starlight Café, head west to **Liberty Square.** Some preteens will like the Animatronic history lesson in the **Hall of Presidents** show. Before leaving, visit the **Haunted Mansion,** then move to **Frontierland. Splash Mountain** and **Big Thunder Mountain Railroad** are best suited for those 8 and older, while **Goofy's Country Dancin' Jamboree** and **Tom Sawyer Island** are fun for the younger set and parents looking for a sit-down.

Go to **Adventureland** next. Ride **The Magic Carpets of Aladdin, Pirates of the Caribbean,** and **Jungle Cruise,** then let the kids burn some energy in the **Swiss Family Treehouse.**

Consult the guide map available as you enter the park, and if the **Wishes** fireworks display and **SpectroMagic** are scheduled, be sure to watch them.

A Day in the Magic Kingdom with Older Kids & Teenagers

As we mentioned earlier, consider making a Priority Seating reservation at **Cinderella's Royal Table** (© 407/939-3463) if you want a sit-down dinner.

From Main Street, cut through the center of the park to Frontierland and challenge **Splash Mountain,** then ride **Big Thunder Mountain Railroad.**

Next, go to Liberty Square and visit the **Haunted Mansion** and **Hall of Presidents.**

After lunch at Liberty Tree Tavern, cut diagonally through the park, past Cinderella Castle, and into Tomorrowland to ride **Space Mountain,** and **Buzz Lightyear's Space Ranger Spin.**

If it's scheduled, end the day with the **Wishes** fireworks display.

A Day in Epcot with Younger Kids

Remember to get a **Priority Seating** reservation if you want to eat in the park (call © 407/939-3463 before you arrive). For dinner, we suggest the **San Angel Inn** in the World Showcase's Mexico exhibit or the **Coral Reef** restaurant in the Living Seas. The **Sunshine Season Food Fair** in The Land is a good choice for lunch because of its diversity. See other options in chapter 5, "Family-Friendly Dining."

This is the least desirable of the parks for young kids, but there are a number of things that should entertain them.

Future World, near the front of the park, is the first of Epcot's two areas to open, so start there. Begin your day at Imagination! and its two great shows: **Journey into Imagination with Figment** and *Honey, I Shrunk the Audience.*

Next, visit **Innoventions.** On its East Side, all but the smallest kids will like seeing some of today's and tomorrow's high-tech gadgets at the **House of Innoventions.** Over on the West Side, kids and adults find it hard to leave **Video Games of Tomorrow.**

Unless you're eager for the **Spaceship Earth** snoozer, go to the **World Showcase** after a late lunch. To us, this is the best part of Epcot—the pavilions of 11 nations surround a big lagoon that you can cross by boat. But, again, young kids, especially wee ones, may get bored.

Norway delivers a history lesson and boat ride called *Maelstrom,* **China** and **Canada** offer fabulous 360-degree movies (China also has the engaging **Dragon Legend Acrobats**), and Germany's **Biergarten** is filled with oompah music. Also, take in the show and concerts at **U.S.A.—The American Adventure** before ending your day with **IllumiNations.**

A Day in Epcot with Older Kids & Teenagers

If you want to eat in the park, make a Priority Seating reservation before you arrive, if possible (call © 407/939-3463). For dinner, we suggest the **San Angel Inn** in the World Showcase's Mexico exhibit or the **Coral Reef** restaurant in the Living Seas. The **Sunshine Season Food Fair** in The Land is a good family choice for lunch because of its diversity. See other options in chapter 5, "Family-Friendly Dining."

Future World, near the front of the park, is the first of Epcot's two areas to open, so start there. Skip **Spaceship Earth,** at least for now. It's nearest the entrance, and that big golf ball and its boring show attract most guests as they enter. Go straight to **Body Wars,** which is in the **Wonders of Life** pavilion to the left of Spaceship Earth. Next is **Mission: Space** where you can train as the astronauts do. Follow up with next-door-neighbor **Test Track.** Then cut to the west to **Imagination** for *Honey, I Shrunk the Audience.*

After a late lunch, visit **Innoventions.** On its East Side, check out the high-tech gadgets at the **House of Innoventions,** then head to the West Side, for **Video Games of Tomorrow.**

Next, head to the **World Showcase,** where the pavilions of 11 nations surround a big lagoon that you can cross by boat.

Norway delivers a history lesson and boat ride called *Maelstrom,* **China** and **Canada** have fabulous 360-degree movies (China also has the engaging **Dragon Legend Acrobats**), and Germany's **Biergarten** is filled with oompah music (little kids usually love the model train set up right outside Germany). Also, take in the show and concerts at **U.S.A.—The American Adventure,** before ending your day by watching **IllumiNations.**

A Day at Disney–MGM Studios with Younger Kids

The layout and size of this park make it easier to backtrack from one area to another.

If you want to eat dinner in the park, make Priority Seating

(📞 407/939-3463) reservations in advance. The **Hollywood Brown Derby** is a decent sit-down option but one that's overpriced (see chapter 5, "Family-Friendly Dining," for more information on dining options). For lunch, we recommend **Toluca Legs Turkey Co.,** where the smoked turkey legs are one of the best grab-and-go meals in any park (you can also get hot dogs).

Voyage of the Little Mermaid is a must for the young (in years or yearnings); the same goes for **Jim Henson's Muppet*Vision 3-D,** a truly fun show for all ages.

Sounds Dangerous–Starring Drew Carey is a good chance to rest weary feet, though part of the show takes place in total darkness and could upset little ones. Ditto for the explosions and other noise in the **Indiana Jones Epic Stunt Spectacular,** but most kids ages 6 or older will love the action.

Visit the **Honey, I Shrunk the Kids Movie Set,** then check your show schedule for favorites such as **Playhouse Disney—Live on Stage!** (which is great for little kids) and **Beauty and the Beast.** At night, *don't miss* **Fantasmic!**

A Day at Disney–MGM Studios with Older Kids & Teenagers

Remember our advice on making Priority Seating (📞 407/939-3463) reservations in advance if you want to eat in the park. The **Hollywood Brown Derby** is a decent sit-down option but one that's overpriced (see chapter 5, "Family-Friendly Dining," for more restaurant options). For lunch, consider **Toluca Legs Turkey Co.,** where the smoked turkey legs are one of the best grab-and-go meals in any park (you can also get hot dogs).

Head directly to the **Twilight Zone Tower of Terror.** It's a high-voltage ride that's not for the young

or faint of heart, but adrenaline-crazed kids and teens adore it. The same goes for the new **Rock 'n' Roller Coaster,** which blends incredible take-off speed with three inversions.

The park is small, so backtracking isn't as much of a concern here. Consider passing up attractions that have long lines, or use FAST-PASS where you can. Lines can be long at **Star Tours** and the **Indiana Jones Epic Stunt Spectacular.**

Jim Henson's Muppet*Vision 3-D is a truly fun show for all ages.

Afterward, watch (and maybe win at) **Who Wants to Be a Millionaire—Play It!** and go on the ton-of-fun **Backlot Tour.**

At night, *don't miss* **Fantasmic!**

A Day at Animal Kingdom for Kids of All Ages

We're not breaking this park into separate itineraries for older and younger age groups because there are few things here that can't be done by most kids, no matter how old they are. Instead, we'll suggest age appeal for those attractions that warrant it.

Be here when the gates open, usually around 8 or 9am. (Call Disney information at 📞 **407/824-4321** to check the time.) This will give you the best chance of seeing animals, because they're most active in the morning air (the next best time is late in the afternoon, although some can be seen throughout the day if you come here during cooler months). If you want to eat at the **Rainforest Cafe,** make Priority Seating reservations by calling 📞 **407/939-3463.**

Flame Tree Barbecue, Pizzafari, and **Tusker House Restaurant** are fair lunch stops.

The size of the park (500 acres) means a lot of travel once you pass through the gates. Don't linger in the **Oasis** area or around the **Tree of Life;** instead, head directly to the back of the park to be first in line for **Kilimanjaro Safaris.** This will allow your family to see animals before it gets hot and the lines become monstrous. Work your way back through Africa, visiting **Pangani Forest Exploration Trail** and its lowland gorillas (this may be too long and lifeless for younger kids). Then head to the **Tree of Life** on Discovery Island for **It's Tough to Be a Bug!** Older kids, teens, and adults should ride **Dinosaur** and **Primeval Whirl** in Dinoland U.S.A., a good choice if you get there before lines form or if you use FASTPASS. Younger kids deserve

some time at the **Boneyard** and on **TriceraTop Spin** in Dinoland as well as a trip to **Camp Minnie-Mickey,** on the other side of the park.

Make sure to see the park's two best shows, **Tarzan Rocks!** in Dinoland and **Festival of the Lion King** in Camp Minnie-Mickey. If your time allows only one, Lion King is the best choice—it's one of the best in WDW.

If you want a bird-show fix, see **Flights of Wonder,** then go on the **Maharajah Jungle Trek,** both in Asia. Older kids and teens will love tackling **Kali River Rapids,** a great way to cool off at the end of the day (and they will get soaked).

SERVICES & FACILITIES IN THE PARKS

ATMs   Money machines are available near the entrances to all parks and usually at least one other place inside (see the handout guide map as you enter the park). They honor cards from banks using the Cirrus, Honor, and PLUS systems.

Baby Care   All parks have a Baby Care Center that's equipped with private rooms designated for breast-feeding and that sell baby-care basics, which are also available at Guest Relations. All women's restrooms, and some men's, are equipped with changing tables.

Cameras & Film   Film and Kodak disposable cameras are sold at various locations in all parks (at much higher prices than those in the free world).

Car Assistance   If you need a battery jump or other assistance, raise the hood of your vehicle and wait for security to arrive.

First Aid   All parks have stations marked on the handout guide maps.

> **Tips   Smoking Alert**
>
> WDW parks do not sell cigarettes and Disney prohibits smoking in shops, attractions, restaurants, and ride lines. Smokers are allowed to light up only in designated outdoor areas. We aren't making any predictions, but could WDW go smoke-free?

Internet Access   Walt Disney World has installed phones with large touch-screens and Internet access capabilities at several places in the theme parks, resorts, and other locations. You can use them to find a variety of information or make dining reservations and, for 25¢ a minute with a 4-minute minimum, you can access the Internet or check your e-mail.

Lost Children   Every park has a designated spot for lost children to be reunited with their families. In the Magic Kingdom, it's City Hall or the Baby Care Center; in Epcot, the Earth Center or the Baby Care Center; in Disney–MGM Studios, Guest Relations; and in Animal Kingdom, Discovery Island. Children under 7 should wear name-tags; older children and adults

Moments **Hidden Treasure**

If you're looking for something to do with your kids on Disney property that's out of the mainstream, consider becoming a **monorail pilot** (basically, you get to ride up front with the *real* monorail pilot). It requires a little patience, because no more than four or five people can do it per ride, so ask a cast member at the monorail stations at the Grand Floridian, Polynesian, or Contemporary resorts if there's room for you in the cockpit. You won't have much luck during peak seasons or times of day (such as when the parks open and close), during foul weather, or if there's a pilot trainee on board. But at other times, especially if you're patient enough to wait for the next train, it may be your lucky day. And you may be doubly rewarded with a monorail co-pilot's license. Best of all: It's free.

should have a prearranged meeting place in case your group gets separated. If that happens, tell the first park employee you see—many wear the same type of clothing and all have special name-tags. For more on lost children, see "Traveling Safely With Your Child," in chapter 2.

Package Pickup Clerks at nearly all WDW stores can arrange for large packages to be sent to the front of the park. Allow at least 3 hours for delivery. If you're staying at a Disney resort, you also can have them sent to your hotel room.

Parking At press time, Disney charged $7 for car, light truck, and van parking, and $8 for RVs.

Pets Don't leave yours in a parked car, even with a window cracked open. Cars become oven-like death traps in Florida's sun. Only service animals are permitted in the parks, but there are five kennels at WDW (© **407/824-6568;** $6 per day, $9 overnight for resort guests; $11 overnight for those staying elsewhere). The ones at the Transportation and Ticket Center in the Magic Kingdom and near the entrance to Fort Wilderness board animals overnight. Day accommodations are offered at kennels just outside the Entrance Plaza at Epcot and at the entrances to Disney–MGM Studios and Animal Kingdom. *Proof of vaccination is required.*

Shops In addition to the ones listed in the following pages, many of Disney's primo rides have small gift shops featuring souvenirs based on that ride's theme.

Stroller Rental Strollers are available near all of the park entrances. The cost is $8 for a single and $15 for a double, including a $1 Disney dollar refund on return.

Tips Boards Each park has a tip board that tells visitors the approximate waiting time at all of the major rides and attractions. In Magic Kingdom it's at the end of Main Street on the left as you face the castle; in Epcot, the digital board is in Innoventions Plaza; at MGM it's at the intersection of Hollywood and Sunset boulevards; inside Animal Kingdom, you'll find it just over the bridge to Discovery Island.

Wheelchair Rental A wheelchair is $8 per day, including a $1 deposit. Electric wheelchairs rent for $40, including a $10 deposit.

3 The Magic Kingdom

This is America's most popular theme park, and it's second in the world to Tokyo Disneyland, according to *Amusement Business,* a trade magazine that estimates annual attendance. The Magic Kingdom offers 40 attractions, plus shops and restaurants, in a 107-acre package. Its centerpiece and symbol, Cinderella Castle, forms the hub of a wheel whose spokes reach to **seven themed lands.**

ARRIVING   From the parking lot, you have to walk to a tram that will take you to the ticket windows, then wait for a ferry or monorail to take you to the entrance, where you meet post-September 11, 2001, security. Most of the year *it takes at least 35 to 45 minutes* and usually longer to get from your auto to the fun (unless you arrive late), and that doesn't count time spent in lines if you have to stop at Guest Relations or rent a stroller. You'll face the same agony minus security on the way out, so relax. Note that while actual ride times are short here, the wait times spent in line aren't during peak times. This is the worst park for crowds, so plan to arrive an hour before the opening bell or an hour or 2 later. Parking-lot sectors are named for Disney characters (Goofy, Pluto, Minnie, and so on) and aisles are numbered. *Be sure to write down the lot and row where you left your sedan.*

Upon entering the park, get a Magic Kingdom guide map (if you can't find one at the turnstiles, go to the nearest shop). It details restaurants and attractions. Also consult the entertainment schedule to see what's cooking during your visit. There are parades, musical performances, fireworks, character appearances, and more, but the days they're available are sometimes staggered.

If you have questions, all park employees are very knowledgeable, and City Hall, on your left as you enter, is an information center—and, like Mickey's Toontown Fair, a great place to meet costumed characters. Character greeting places are also featured on the map, and you should note these if you have young kids.

HOURS   The park is open from at least 9am to 6 or 7pm, sometimes later—as late as midnight during major holidays and summer.

TICKET PRICES   Tickets are $52 for adults, $42 for children 3 to 9. Kids under 3 get in free. See "Tickets & Passes," on p. 149, for information on multiday passes.

SERVICES & FACILITIES IN THE MAGIC KINGDOM
Most of the following are noted on the handout guide maps in the park:

ATMs   Machines inside the park honor cards from banks using the Cirrus, Honor, and PLUS systems. They're near the main entrance, in Adventureland, and in Tomorrowland.

Baby Care   Located next to the Crystal Palace at the end of Main Street, the Baby Care Center is furnished with a nursing room with rocking chairs and toddler-size toilets. Disposable diapers, formula, baby food, and pacifiers are sold at a premium (read: Bring your own or pay the price). There are changing tables here as well as in all women's restrooms and some men's.

Cameras & Film   Film and Kodak disposable cameras are available throughout the park.

First Aid   It's located beside the Crystal Palace next to Baby Care and staffed by registered nurses.

Lockers   Lockers are located in the arcade below the Main Street Railroad Station. The cost is $7, including a $2 refundable deposit.

The Magic Kingdom

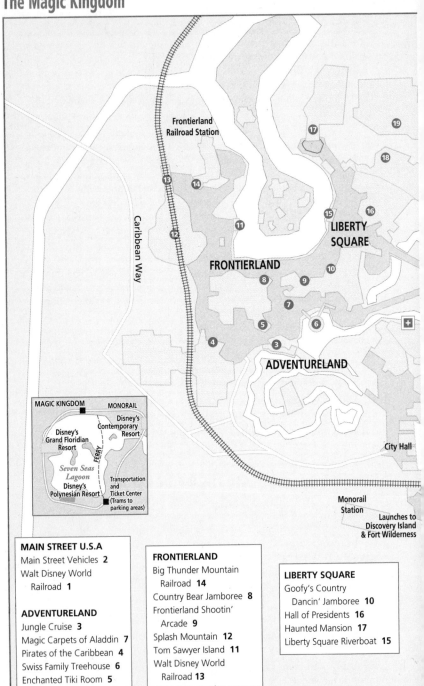

MAIN STREET U.S.A
Main Street Vehicles **2**
Walt Disney World
  Railroad **1**

ADVENTURELAND
Jungle Cruise **3**
Magic Carpets of Aladdin **7**
Pirates of the Caribbean **4**
Swiss Family Treehouse **6**
Enchanted Tiki Room **5**

FRONTIERLAND
Big Thunder Mountain
  Railroad **14**
Country Bear Jamboree **8**
Frontierland Shootin'
  Arcade **9**
Splash Mountain **12**
Tom Sawyer Island **11**
Walt Disney World
  Railroad **13**

LIBERTY SQUARE
Goofy's Country
  Dancin' Jamboree **10**
Hall of Presidents **16**
Haunted Mansion **17**
Liberty Square Riverboat **15**

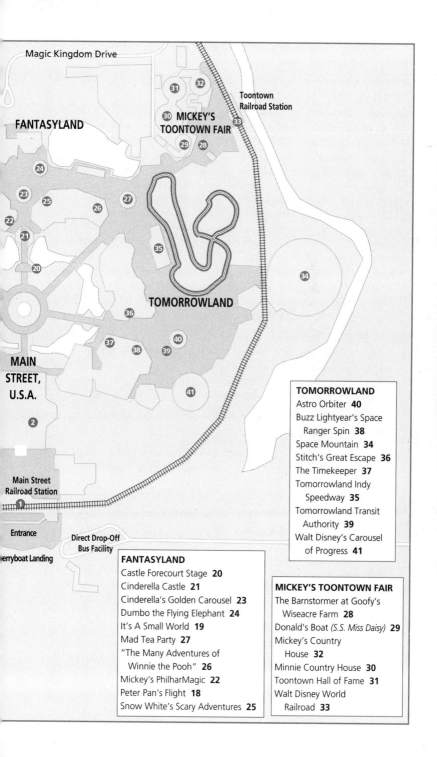

Magic Kingdom Drive

Toontown
Railroad Station

FANTASYLAND

③① ③②
③⓪ **MICKEY'S**
TOONTOWN FAIR
②⑨ ②⑧

㉔

㉓ ㉕ ㉖ ㉗

㉒

㉑

⑳

㉟

TOMORROWLAND

㉞

㊱

㊵
㊲ ㊳ ㊴

MAIN
STREET,
U.S.A.

❷

Main Street
Railroad Station

❶

Entrance

Direct Drop-Off
Bus Facility

erryboat Landing

TOMORROWLAND
Astro Orbiter **40**
Buzz Lightyear's Space
 Ranger Spin **38**
Space Mountain **34**
Stitch's Great Escape **36**
The Timekeeper **37**
Tomorrowland Indy
 Speedway **35**
Tomorrowland Transit
 Authority **39**
Walt Disney's Carousel
 of Progress **41**

FANTASYLAND
Castle Forecourt Stage **20**
Cinderella Castle **21**
Cinderella's Golden Carousel **23**
Dumbo the Flying Elephant **24**
It's A Small World **19**
Mad Tea Party **27**
"The Many Adventures of
 Winnie the Pooh" **26**
Mickey's PhilharMagic **22**
Peter Pan's Flight **18**
Snow White's Scary Adventures **25**

MICKEY'S TOONTOWN FAIR
The Barnstormer at Goofy's
 Wiseacre Farm **28**
Donald's Boat (*S.S. Miss Daisy*) **29**
Mickey's Country
 House **32**
Minnie Country House **30**
Toontown Hall of Fame **31**
Walt Disney World
 Railroad **33**

Lost Children   Lost children in the Magic Kingdom are usually taken to City Hall or the Baby Care Center. *Children under 7 should wear name-tags.*

Package Pickup   Any large package can be sent by a shop clerk to Guest Relations in the Entrance Plaza. Allow 3 hours for delivery.

Pet Care   Day boarding is available at the Transportation and Ticket Center for $6 (© **407/824-6568**). The center also boards animals overnight ($9 for Disney or official hotel guests, $11 for others). Proof of vaccination is required.

Strollers   They can be rented at the Stroller Shop near the entrance to the Magic Kingdom. The cost is $8 for a single and $15 for a double, including a $1 deposit. *Tip:* Because strollers often have to be parked outside of attractions (along with dozens of other identical strollers), it's easy to get confused about whose stroller is whose. Attach a brightly colored piece of cloth or some other identifier, so that someone doesn't accidentally walk off with your stroller. If it does go astray (and many will), just bring your receipt to the stroller rental location and you can get a replacement.

Wheelchair Rental   For wheelchairs, go to the gift shop to the left of the ticket booths at the Transportation and Ticket Center, or to the Stroller and Wheelchair Shop inside the main entrance to your right. The cost is $8, including a $1 deposit; $40, including a $10 deposit, for electric ones.

MAIN STREET, U.S.A

Designed to model a turn-of-the-20th-century American street (though it ends in a 13th-c. European castle), this is the gateway to the Kingdom and is filled with shops and some fast-food joints. Don't dawdle on Main Street when you enter; leave it for the end of the day when you're heading back to your hotel.

Main Street Vehicles
Frommer's Rating: C
Recommended Ages: Mainly nostalgic adults

Ride a horse-drawn trolley, jitney, vintage fire engine, or horseless carriage *only* if you don't mind waiting around. Otherwise, there are far, far better things to see and do throughout the realm.

Frommer's Rates the Rides

Because there's so much to do, we're shifting from the star-rating system used for rooms and restaurants to one that has a little more range. You'll notice most of the grades below are *A*s, *B*s, and *C*s. That's because Disney designers have done a reasonably good job on the attractions front. But occasionally our ratings show *D*s for Duds.

Here's what **Frommer's Ratings** mean:

A+	=	Your trip wouldn't be complete without it.
A	=	Put it at the top of your "to-do" list.
B+	=	Make a real effort to see or do it.
B	=	It's fun but not a "must see."
C+	=	A nice diversion; see it if you have time.
C	=	Go if there's no wait and you can walk right in.
D	=	Don't waste your time.

> **(Tips** **Mickey's Favorite Barber**
>
> The Harmony Barber Shop on Main Street is a real scissor shop where you can get your hair cut from 9am to 5pm daily. Adult haircuts are $15; kids' are $12. If it's your child's first haircut, Disney barbers will cut his or her hair free and throw in a certificate and set of mouse ears. The shop is on Main Street near the firehouse. For more on the shop, see "Haircuts," in chapter 9.

Walt Disney World Railroad
Frommer's Rating: B
Recommended Ages: All ages
You can board an authentic 1928 steam-powered train for a 15-minute trip clockwise around the perimeter of the park. This is a good way to save wear and tear on your feet *if* you're headed to one of its three stations—the park entrance, Frontierland, and Mickey's Toontown Fair—in that order.
Andy Rating: "Can't this train go faster?" (It does test a little one's patience.)

ADVENTURELAND
Cross a bridge and stroll through an exotic jungle of lush foliage, thatched roofs, and totems. Amid dense vines and stands of palm and bamboo, drums are beating and swashbuckling adventures await you and the kids.

The Enchanted Tiki Room
Frommer's Rating: C+
Recommended Ages: 2–10 and older adults
Once called the Tropical Serenade, this attraction's newer hosts include Iago of *Aladdin* fame. It's still in a large, hexagonal, Polynesian-style building with a thatched roof, bamboo beams, and tapa-bark murals. It's also still home to 250 tropical birds, chanting totem poles, and singing flowers that whistle, warble, and tweet. It's cute but corny.

Jungle Cruise
Frommer's Rating: C (B for the foot-weary)
Recommended Ages: 4–adult
This is a yawner for many older kids and teens, as well as some adults, but it's a nice break from the madness if the line isn't long or you use FASTPASS. In the course of 10 minutes, your boat sails through an African veldt and an Amazon rainforest, among other sets. There are dozens of Animatronic birds, elephants, zebras, lions, giraffes, crocodiles, and tigers in the scenery, which includes tropical foliage (most of it real). You'll pass a Cambodian temple guarded by snakes, a rhino chasing terrified African beaters, and a jungle camp taken over by apes. Most boat captains keep up an amusing-if-corny banter. This is one of the park's original attractions and the low-tech, not-so-special effects show their age.

Magic Carpets of Aladdin
Frommer's Rating: B+ for tykes and parents
Recommended Ages: 2–7
The first major ride added to Adventureland since 1971 delights wee ones and some older kids. Its 16 four-passenger carpets circle a giant genie's bottle while camels spit water at riders (in much the same way riders are spritzed at One Fish, Two Fish at Universal Orlando's Islands of Adventure; see p. 241). The fiberglass carpets spin and move up, down, forward, and back. Riders in the front seat

Tips A (Baker's) Dozen Suggestions
for Fewer Headaches

1. **Go Where the Crowds Aren't:** If you have time and aren't a slave to the compressed itinerary of a 1-day visit, go to the left when the masses go to the right. Try to get to one major attraction early, but save the others for later in the day or go the FASTPASS route. Eat a little earlier or later than others. That means 11am or 2pm for lunch and 4 or 7pm for dinner. A few minutes can make a big difference in restaurant lines and will make your kids less cranky.

2. **Note Your Car's Location:** That purple minivan in the next space may not be there when you get out. Write your lot and row number on something with ink that won't run if it gets wet.

3. **Avoid Rush Hour:** I-4 is woefully over capacity, so be ready for bumper-to-bumper traffic from 7 to 9am and 4 to 6pm, and often in between. This happens in both directions, 7 days a week.

4. **Don't Overplan:** You aren't going to be able to do everything in every park. As a group, list three or four "must-do" things each day. If your group is large enough, consider splitting up, with each adult taking one or more kids. You can compare notes later, and, if you're on a multiday pass, you can go where the others went the day before.

5. **Pace Yourself:** It's common to see people running across the parking lot to the trams, then to and through the turnstiles. Relax—the park isn't going anywhere, and they're just rushing to lines and exhaustion. Once inside, stagger those lines with indoor shows or breaks on a shady bench.

6. **Make Dining Reservations:** If a sit-down dinner is important, make sure to get Priority Seating reservations (© **407/939-3463**) either before your visit or at the restaurants after you enter the park.

7. **Set a Spending Limit:** Kids should know they have a set amount to spend on take-home trinkets. You should, too. But build in a small contingency "fun" fund.

control some of the action. If there's a downside here, it's that you may find yourself wishing for smaller lines—waiting times can get pretty long.

Pirates of the Caribbean
Frommer's Rating: B
Recommended Ages: 6–adult

Although the Disneyland version of this ride has been sanitized in the name of political correctness, the pirates in Florida still chase "wenches." You'll proceed through a long grotto to board a boat in a dark cave, which may frighten small kids. Therein, hundreds of audio-Animatronic figures (including lifelike dogs, cats, chickens, pigs, and donkeys) populate a faux Caribbean town. The painstaking detail work (right down to the "hair" on some of the pirate's legs) still stands out today. To a background of yo-ho-ho music, passengers pass into the line of fire as some fierce-looking pirates swig rum while they loot and plunder. Though it hasn't changed much since 1973, this sentimental favorite

8. **Take a Break:** If you're staying at a WDW property, spend the mid-afternoon napping or unwinding in the pool. It'll give you and your kids a chance to recharge your batteries. Return to the parks for a few more attractions and the closing shows. (Get your hand stamped when you leave, and you'll be readmitted without charge.)

9. **Dress Comfortably:** This may seem like a no-brainer, but judging by the limping, blistered crowds, some people don't understand they'll be walking—a lot! This isn't the place to break in clogs. Comfortable walking shoes and good socks are a must.

10. **Sunscreen, Sunscreen, Sunscreen:** Locals spot tourists by their bright-red glow. The Florida sun can bake you, even in the shade and in the cooler months, and a bad 1st-day burn can ruin your trip. Bring hats for toddlers and infants, even if they'll stay in a covered stroller. Also, drink plenty of water in summer to avoid dehydration. This is especially important for children. Bringing a pair of sunglasses is a smart move, too.

11. **Travel Light:** Don't carry large amounts of cash. The Pirates of the Caribbean aren't the only thieves in WDW. There are ATMs in the parks if you run short.

12. **Get a Little Goofy:** Relax, put on those mouse ears, eat that extra piece of fudge, and sing along at the shows. Your kids may think you've lost your mind, but don't worry about what the staff thinks; they've seen it all.

13. **Measure Your Kids' Heights Before You Arrive—and Don't Cheat:** This guide, park maps, and signs outside the more adventurous rides list minimum heights. If you know the restrictions early, you can avoid disappointment and sobbing children in the parks. Trust us—WDW plays hardball on this one.

(the director of Disney's archives told us this ride is his favorite) is a good spot to cool off during the heat of the day.

Andy Rating: "Where's Johnny Depp?" (Sorry, matey. These pirates are nothing like the ones in the 2003 Disney movie or those in the Pirates of the Caribbean virtual-reality ride at DisneyQuest, though a few scenes from the ride were appropriated by the film—notably the one with the prisoners and the dog.)

Swiss Family Treehouse

Frommer's Rating: C+

Recommended Ages: 4–12

This attraction, based on the 1960 Disney movie version of *Swiss Family Robinson*, was renovated in 1998, but die-hard fans needn't worry—it's still a life-size house in a sprawling banyan tree. Visitors can walk a rope-suspended bridge and ascend the 50-foot tree for a close-up look into the rooms. The "tree," designed by Disney Imagineers, has 330,000 polyethylene leaves sprouting from a 90-foot span of branches; although it isn't real, it's draped with actual Spanish moss. It's a good place for kids to work off some excess energy. ***Note:*** People with limited mobility beware—this attraction requires a lot of climbing.

FRONTIERLAND

From Adventureland, step into the wild and woolly past of the American frontier, where Disney employees (they're called "cast members") are clad in denim and calico, sidewalks are wooden, rough-and-tumble architecture runs to log cabins and rustic saloons, and the landscape is Southwestern scrubby with mesquite, cactus, yucca, and prickly pear.

Big Thunder Mountain Railroad
Frommer's Rating: A
Recommended Ages: 6–adult
This roller coaster earns high marks for what it is—a ride designed for those not quite up to the lunch-losing thrills of Rock 'n' Roller Coaster at Disney–MGM Studios (p. 200) or Dueling Dragons and Incredible Hulk Coaster at Islands of Adventure, listed in chapter 7. Think of Big Thunder as *Roller Coasters 101.* (Survive and graduate to the next level.) It sports fun hairpin turns and dark descents rather than sudden, steep drops and near collisions. Your runaway train covers 2,780 feet of track and careens through the ribs of a dinosaur, under a thundering waterfall, past spewing geysers, and over a bottomless volcanic pool. Animatronic characters (such as a long johns–clad fellow in a bathtub) and critters (goats, chickens, donkeys) enhance the scenic backdrop, along with several hundred thousand dollars' worth of authentic antique mining equipment. ***Note:*** You must be at least 40 inches tall to ride, and Disney discourages expectant mothers and people prone to motion sickness or those with heart, neck, or back problems from riding. It also may be too intense for some kids under 8.
Andy Rating: *"Hoo-ahh!!"* (He rode it at night, arms up like a real trooper, and kept going back until everyone else in the family begged for a change of scenery.)
Jake Rating: "Y'know, for a kids' ride that's cool." (Fact is, it's more than a kids' ride. It thrills a lot of adults, too!)

Country Bear Jamboree
Frommer's Rating: A
Recommended Ages: 4–adult
This is a foot-stomping hoot! (Middle and older teens, though, may hate it.) Like many of the shows and rides in the Magic Kingdom, it doesn't have a companion in the other parks because it opened when the park did (in 1971!) and dates to a time when entertainment was more low-tech but still fun. But it still has the power to bridge the generations. The 15-minute show stars a troupe of fiddlin', strummin', harmonica-playin' bears (audio-Animatronic, of course) belting out lively tunes and woeful love songs. The chubby Trixie, decked out in a satiny skirt, laments lost love as she sings "Tears Will Be the Chaser for Your Wine." Teddi Barra descends from the ceiling in a swing to perform "Heart, We Did All That We Could." In the finale, the cast joins in a rousing singalong.

Frontierland Shootin' Arcade
Frommer's Rating: C
Recommended Ages: 8–adult
Combining state-of-the-art electronics with a traditional shooting-gallery format, this arcade presents an array of targets (slow-moving ore cars, buzzards, and gravediggers) in an 1850s boomtown scenario. Fog creeps across the graveyard, and the setting changes as a calm, starlit night turns stormy with flashes of

---

Tips **Keep Your Wits About You**

Any theme or amusement park with moving rides has accidents and injuries. In 2003, Disney initiated a "Wild About Safety" campaign mainly to teach kids about ride safety through pins, illustrated books, and cartoon stickers. Ask about it at the theme park entrances. Stars Timon and Pumbaa from The Lion King warn visitors to keep everything from arms to hooves and tails inside the vehicles.

---

lightning and claps of thunder. Coyotes howl, bridges creak, and skeletal arms reach out from the grave. If you hit a tombstone, it might spin around and mysteriously change its epitaph. To keep things authentic, newfangled electronic firing mechanisms loaded with infrared bullets are concealed in vintage buffalo rifles. Fifty cents buys you 25 shots. It's good for a few minutes of fun for older kids.

Goofy's Country Dancin' Jamboree *Finds*
Frommer's Rating: B+
Recommended Ages: 3–7 and some adults

This interactive character show replaced the old Diamond Horseshoe Saloon Revue. Except for a short and sweet appearance by Chip 'n' Dale upstairs, all of the action happens downstairs and if you don't get to park it on one of the lower level benches at the back of the first floor, you will be standing for the 18-minute, song-and-dance show. Goofy stars, with backup from the chipmunks, Woody from *Toy Story*, and others who croon tunes and lead the way through country dance classics, including "Boot Scootin' Boogie," "Electric Slide," and the (yet-to-be classic) "Goofy Two-Step."

Andy Rating: "That was, uh, OK." (We think he's near the end of the character-greeting age and was just happy to be out of the sun.)

Splash Mountain
Frommer's Rating: A+
Recommended Ages: 8–adult

If you need a quick cooling off, this is the place to go—because you and your kids will get wet! Some kids may find it a little intimidating upon inspection, but most have a blast while riding it. Based on Disney's 1946 film *Song of the South*, Splash Mountain takes you flume-style down a flooded mountain, past 26 colorful scenes that include backwoods swamps, bayous, spooky caves, and waterfalls. Riders are caught in the bumbling schemes of Brer Fox and Brer Bear as they chase the ever-wily Brer Rabbit, who, against the advice of Mr. Bluebird, leaves his briar-patch home in search of fortune and the "laughing place." The music from the film forms a delightful audio backdrop. Your hollow-log vehicle twists, turns, and splashes, sometimes plummeting in darkness as the ride leads to a 52-foot, 45-degree, 40-mph splashdown in a briar-filled pond. *Note:* You must be at least 40 inches tall to ride. Also, expectant mothers and people prone to motion sickness or those with heart, neck, or back problems shouldn't climb aboard.

Jake Rating: "Man, that's steep!" (Yes, our butts came out of the seat, too!)

Tom Sawyer Island
Frommer's Rating: C for most, B+ for kids who need an energy burner
Recommended Ages: 4–12

Board Huck Finn's raft for a 2-minute crowded float across a river to the densely forested Tom Sawyer Island, where kids can explore the narrow passages of Injun

Joe's cave (complete with scary sound effects such as whistling wind that might intimidate very young children), a walk-through windmill, a serpentine abandoned mine, and Fort Sam Clemens, where an audio-Animatronic drunk is snoring off a bender. Maintaining one's balance while crossing rickety swing and barrel bridges is part of the fun for some, but not for those with mobility impairments. Narrow, winding dirt paths lined with oaks, pines, and sycamores create an authentic backwoods atmosphere. It's easy to get briefly lost and stumble upon some unexpected adventure. You can combine this attraction with lunch at Aunt Polly's Dockside Inn, which serves sandwiches and such, and has outdoor tables on a porch overlooking the river. Adults can rest while the kids explore.

LIBERTY SQUARE

This transition zone between Frontierland and Fantasyland has an 18th-century-America feel, complete with Federal and Georgian architecture, Colonial Williamsburg–type shops, and flower beds bordering manicured lawns. Thirteen lanterns, symbolizing the first colonies, are suspended from the Liberty Tree, an immense live oak. You might encounter a fife-and-drum corps marching along the cobblestone streets. The Liberty Tree Tavern (p. 117) is one of the better Magic Kingdom restaurants.

Hall of Presidents

Frommer's Rating: B+

Recommended Ages: 8–adult

American presidents from George Washington to George W. Bush are represented by lifelike audio-Animatronic figures. If you look closely, you'll see them fidget and whisper during the performance. The show begins with a film projected on a 180-degree, 70mm screen. It talks about the importance of the Constitution, then the curtain rises on America's leaders, and, as each comes into the spotlight, he nods or waves with presidential dignity. Lincoln then rises and speaks, occasionally referring to his notes. In a tribute to Disney thoroughness, painstaking research was done in creating the figures and scenery, with each president's costume reflecting period fashion, fabrics, and tailoring techniques.

Haunted Mansion

Frommer's Rating: B, A+ for faithful followers

Recommended Ages: 6–adult

What better way to show off Disney's special effects than through a decades-old ride in which ghostly attendants harry groups of visitors. They escort you past a graveyard (be sure to look at the epitaphs on the tombstones), then turn you over to a ghost host, who encloses you in a windowless portrait gallery (Are those eyes following you?) where the floor seems to descend (in actuality, it's the

---

Fun Fact **It's a Dirty Job . . .**

The Disney parks are usually fairly clean, but there's one notable spot in the Magic Kingdom that takes pride in its dreary image. In order to maintain the Haunted Mansion's worn appearance, employees spread large amounts of dust over the home's interior and also string up plenty of real-looking cobwebs. It takes a lot of effort to keep the place looking bedraggled, which may explain why your haunted hosts are only a handful of Disney cast members without smiles plastered on their faces.

ceiling that's rising). Darkness, spooky music, and mysterious screams and rappings enhance its ambience. Your vehicle, err . . . Doom Buggy, takes you past bizarre scenes and objects: a ghostly banquet and ball, a graveyard band, a suit of armor that comes alive, cobweb-draped chandeliers, luminous spiders, a talking head in a crystal ball, weird flying objects, and more. At the end of the ride, a ghost hitches a ride with you in your car. The experience is more amusing than terrifying, so you can take most children 6 and older inside. This ride has changed little over the years, but it continues to draw long lines and a cult following. It also bears more similarities to its recent namesake movie than Pirates of the Caribbean (p. 164).

Andy Rating: "I liked that. But how did that funny looking ghost get in our car?" (We don't know. Maybe that's why they call it the Magic Kingdom.)

Liberty Square Riverboat *Overrated*
Frommer's Rating: C
Recommended Ages: All ages

A steam-powered stern-wheeler called the *Liberty Belle* departs for cruises along the Rivers of America. The landscape sort of looks like the Wild West. It makes a restful interlude for foot-weary park-stompers but your kids will probably be bored.

FANTASYLAND

The attractions in this happy land are themed along Disney classics such as *Snow White, Peter Pan,* and *Dumbo.* They're especially popular with young visitors. If your kids are under 8, then this and Mickey's Toontown Fair (details later in this section) should be your first stops in the Magic Kingdom.

Cinderella Castle *Moments*
Frommer's Rating: A (for visuals)
Recommended Ages: All ages

There's not a lot to do here, but its status as the Magic Kingdom's icon makes it a must. It's at the end of Main Street, in the center of the park, a fairyland castle with Gothic spires 185 feet high. Inside, there's a restaurant, Cinderella's Royal Table (p. 145), and shops. Mosaic murals depict the Cinderella story, and Disney family coats of arms are displayed over a fireplace. An actress portraying Cinderella, dressed for the ball, often makes appearances in the lobby.

You can see live shows on the Castle Forecourt Stage; check the guide-map schedule for **Cinderella's Surprise Celebration,** a character show starring Cinderella and several other cartoon heroes (from Prince Charming to Donald and Goofy) and villains (including Captain Hook). After the show, several of the characters come down from the stage to greet guests.

Cinderella's Golden Carousel *Moments*
Frommer's Rating: B+, A for carousel fans
Recommended Ages: All ages

This beauty was built by the Philadelphia Toboggan Co. in 1917 and served tours of duty at amusement parks in Michigan and Illinois before Walt Disney bought it and brought it to Orlando 5 years before the Magic Kingdom opened. Disney artisans refurbished it and added 18 hand-painted scenes from Cinderella on a wooden canopy above the horses. Its organ plays Disney classics such as "When You Wish Upon a Star." Small children and their parents adore riding it, and older adults like reminiscing about past carousel rides. But here they often have to wait in long lines.

Fun Fact **Behind the Scenes**

Ever wonder why you never catch a glimpse of, say, Mickey relaxing with his head off, or Pluto taking a candy bar break? The people inside the characters, and other cast members, take breaks as well as travel around the park through an intricate system of underground tunnels that are off-limits to the public, unless you pay a premium for a behind-the-scenes tour that we'll tell you about on p. 182.

Dumbo the Flying Elephant
Frommer's Rating: B+ for young kids and parents
Recommended Ages: 2–7
This kiddie ride is very much like Magic Carpets of Aladdin (p. 163) except it features Dumbo cars that go around in a circle, gently rising and dipping. If you can stand the brutal lines, it's a favorite of the preschool set, although older children will probably want to run the other way.

It's a Small World
Frommer's Rating: B+ for youngsters and first-timers
Recommended Ages: 2–8
It rates a B+ (rather than a lower grade) because the very young are mesmerized by it, and adults ought to have to endure it at least once. If you don't know the song, you will by the end of the ride, which has you sailing around a world built for the 1964 New York World's Fair and later bought by Disney. In each country, appropriately costumed audio-Animatronic dolls greet you by singing "It's a Small World" in Munchkin-like voices (if you've ever talked after sucking on a helium balloon, you know the pitch). The cast of thousands includes Chinese acrobats, Russian kazatsky dancers, Indian snake charmers, French cancan girls, and, well, you get the picture.
Jake Rating: "That's the dumbest ride here." (The song isn't fun, either. It crawls into your mind like a brain-eating mite, but pay your dues and *ride* the ride.)

Mad Tea Party
Frommer's Rating: C+
Recommended Ages: 4–adult
This is a traditional amusement park ride a la Disney, with an Alice in Wonderland theme. Riders sit in big pastel-hued teacups on saucers that career around a circular platform while tilting and spinning. A woozy mouse pops out of a big teapot in the center of the platform. Believe it or not, this can be a pretty active or nauseating ride, depending on how much you spin your teacup's wheel. Adolescents seem to consider it a badge of honor if they can turn the unsuspecting adults in their cup green—you have been warned!
Jake and Andy Ratings: (In chorus) "Faster, Pop, faster, faster!" (Ugh!)

The Many Adventures of Winnie the Pooh
Frommer's Rating: B
Recommended Ages: 2–8 and their parents
This fun ride features the cute and cuddly little fellow along with Eeyore, Piglet, and Tigger. You board a golden honey pot and ride through a storybook version of the Hundred-Acre Wood, keeping an eye out for Heffulumps, Woozles, Blustery Days, and the Floody Place. Kids, especially those 3 to 5, love it, but prepare yourself for *very* long lines if you don't use FASTPASS.

Mickey's PhilharMagic
Frommer's Rating: A
Recommended Ages: All ages

This late 2003 arrival brings Mickey, Donald Duck (who gets the starring role in this production), Ariel, Aladdin, Jasmine, Simba, and other Disney favorites to 3-D life on a 150-foot screen (the largest wraparound screen on the planet). It's the first time the classic Disney characters have ever been rendered in 3-D. Like **Jim Henson's Muppet*Vision 3D** (p. 199) at Disney–MGM Studios, the show combines music, animated film, puppetry, and special effects that tickle several of your senses. The kids will love the animation and effects and parents will enjoy the nostalgia factor. *Note:* Donald Duck takes a classic comedic fall at the end of the show, and most kids will laugh as intended, but when we saw the show a 4-year-old burst into tears thinking that poor Donald was dying behind the curtains. A Disney employee quickly reassured the child that Donald was fine, but be advised that very young kids may take such things to heart—and they may not like the near-dark conditions in the theater either.

Peter Pan's Flight
Frommer's Rating: B+ for kids and parents
Recommended Ages: 3–8

Riding in airborne versions of Captain Hook's ship, passengers glide through dark passages while experiencing the story of Peter Pan. The adventure begins in the Darlings' nursery and includes a flight over nighttime London (one of the ride's saving graces) to Never-Never Land. There, you encounter mermaids, Indians, Tick Tock the Croc, the Lost Boys, Princess Tiger Lilly, Tinker Bell, Hook, and Smee, all while listening to the theme, "You Can Fly, You Can Fly, You Can Fly." It's *very* tame fun for the young. The technology is also very past its prime.
Andy Rating: "Zzzzzzzzz." (Too tame, it appears. After 4 hr. of heat and legwork, this lullaby of a ride rocked him to sleep. We almost joined him!)

Snow White's Scary Adventures
Frommer's Rating: B for young kids and parents
Recommended Ages: 4–8

Disney had to change the original incarnation of this ride to actually include Snow White and eliminate the way-too-scary-for-youngsters encounter with the wicked witch. The attraction once focused only on the more sinister elements of Grimm's fairy tale, most notably the evil queen and the cackling, toothless witch, leaving some small children terrorized. It's been toned down, with Snow White appearing in a number of pleasant scenes, such as at the wishing well and riding away with the prince to live happily ever after. There are new audio-Animatronic dwarfs, and the colors have been brightened and made less menacing. Even so, this ride could be scary for kids under 4.

Tips Not So Fast

If you're tackling rides with preshows, such as Mickey's PhilharMagic, don't try to be the first one inside. Hang back in the crowd a little and you may land in the center of the theater where the seats are better. Folks who rush in are shooed to the theater's far side.

MICKEY'S TOONTOWN FAIR

Head off those cries of "Where's Mickey?" by taking young kids to this 2-acre site. Toontown provides a chance to meet their favorite Disney characters, including Mickey, Minnie, Donald, Goofy, and Pluto. The Kingdom's smallest land is set in a whimsical collection of cottages and the candy-striped **Judge's** and **Toontown Hall of Fame tents,** home to several characters.

The Barnstormer at Goofy's Wiseacre Farm (Finds)

Frommer's Rating: A+ for kids and parents, B+ for others, except coaster crazies, who may find it a D

Recommended Ages: 4 and up

This mini–roller coaster is the twin of Woody Woodpecker's Nuthouse Coaster (which it likely inspired) at Universal Studios Florida (p. 233). It's designed to look and feel like a crop duster that flies slightly off course and right through the Goofmeister's barn. The ride has very little in the dip-and-drop department, but a little zip on the spin-and-spiral front. *Note:* The 60-second ride has a 35-inch height minimum and expectant mothers are warned not to ride it.

Andy Rating: "Two thumbs up! That's almost as cool as Big Thunder Mountain." (It even gets squeals from some adults.)

Donald's Boat (S.S. *Miss Daisy*)

Frommer's Rating: B+ for kids

Recommended Ages: 2–12

The good ship offers a lot of interactive fun, and the "waters" around it feature fountains of water snakes and other wet things that earn squeals of joy (and relief on hot days).

Mickey's & Minnie's Country Houses

Frommer's Rating: B+ for kids and parents

Recommended Ages: 2–8

These separate cottages offer a lot of visual fun and some marginal interactive areas for youngsters, but they're usually crowded and the lines flow like molasses. Mickey's place features garden and garage playgrounds. Minnie's lets kids play in her kitchen, where popcorn goes wild in a microwave and the utensils strike up a symphony of their own.

Tips It Ain't Fair, But . . .

Disney rides sometimes break down or need routine maintenance (called ride rehab) that can take them out of commission for a few hours, a day, a week, or a lot longer. Test Track at Epcot, for example, frequently had mechanical problems that shut it down during its first year, and occasionally it still experiences technical difficulties. The Hall of Presidents, at Magic Kingdom, was shut down for several months in 2001 for maintenance and the addition of the audio-Animatronic likeness of President George W. Bush.

Some, but not all, of the ride rehabs get listed on the Disney website (**www.disneyworld.com**; click "Parks & More," then "Parks & More FAQ" and go to "What Attractions Are Currently Closed?"). The moral of the story: Don't promise kids a particular ride just in case something happens. By the way, don't expect Disney—or Universal—to discount tickets when rehabs occur. You still get hit with the full price.

> ### *Value* Touring Tip
>
> The Magic Kingdom's **E-Ride Nights** are a bargain for Disney hotel and offi-
> cial hotel guests persistent enough to track them down. They're only sold
> to guests with multiday passes, and only are offered a few times a month
> with little advance notice. E-Ride tickets cost $12 for adults and $10 for
> kids 3 to 9. They give guests 3 hours to ride the nine most popular rides—
> Big Thunder Mountain Railroad, Space Mountain, and ExtraTERRORestrial
> Alien Encounter, to name three—as many times as they can. Better still,
> Disney only lets 5,000 guests into the park on these nights. They're a mar-
> velous option for families with kids old enough to tackle the big rides and
> the late hours. Tickets are sold on a first-come, first-served basis at the
> **Guest Services** desks in the Disney hotels and at the **Magic Kingdom** ticket
> window (you will be required to show a Disney Resort Guest ID and a valid
> multiday admission pass). Call ✆ **407/824-4321** for details.

TOMORROWLAND

This land attempts to focus on the future, but in 1994, the WDW folks decided
Tomorrowland (originally designed in the 1970s) was beginning to look a lot
like "Yesteryear." So it was revamped to show the future as a galactic, science
fiction–inspired community inhabited by humans, aliens, and robots. A video-
game arcade also was added.

Note: In 2003, the scary **ExtraTERRORestrial Alien Encounter** was closed
permanently to make way for a new attraction, **Stitch's Great Escape!** Envi-
sioned as a prequel to the Disney hit film *Lilo & Stitch,* the kid-friendly attraction will showcase the mayhem caused by the mischievous Stitch as he moves
through the Galactic Federation and will feature state-of-the-art audio-Animatronics. It's set to open sometime in 2004.

Astro Orbiter *(Overrated*

Frommer's Rating: B for the younger set
Recommended Ages: 3–8
This tame ride is like the ones you might have ridden when you were a child and
the carnivals came to town. Its "rockets" are on arms attached to "the center of
the galaxy," and they move up and down while orbiting planets, which are on
top of a tower. (Think of an elevated version of Magic Carpets of Aladdin,
which is reviewed on p. 163.) *Note:* The line tends to move at a snail's pace.

Buzz Lightyear's Space Ranger Spin

Frommer's Rating: B+
Recommended Ages: 5 and up
Join Buzz and try to save the universe, flying your cruiser through a world you'll
recognize from the original *Toy Story* movie. Kids enjoy using the dashboard-
mounted laser cannons as they spin through the sky (filled with gigantic toys
instead of stars). If they're good shots (and they'll have to be—the trigger mechanisms are hard to use), they can set off sight and sound gags with their lasers.
A display in the car keeps score, so take multiple cars if you have more than one
child. This is one of the newer additions to Tomorrowland. It uses the same
technology as Universal Studios Florida's Men in Black Alien Attack (p. 231),
but it's aimed at a younger audience, and, therefore, it's lamer and tamer.

Andy Rating: "That was like bumper cars with bullets." (Well, pretend bullets, anyway, but it's certainly a new spin on an old ride.)

Space Mountain
Frommer's Rating: B+
Recommended Ages: 10–adult
This cosmic roller coaster usually has *long* lines (but it has FASTPASS), and most guests find only marginal entertainment value in the pre-ride space-age music and exhibits (meteorites, shooting stars, and space debris whizzing past overhead). Once aboard your rocket, you'll climb and dive through the inky, starlit blackness of outer space. The hairpin turns and plunges make it seem as if you're going at breakneck speed, but your car doesn't go any faster than 28 mph. The front seat of the train offers the best bang, but Space Mountain is one of the first generation of modern, dark-side coasters, and, therefore, somewhat outdated. If you like dark or semidark thrill rides, you'll be much happier with Rock 'n' Roller Coaster at Disney–MGM Studios. *Note:* Riders must be at least 44 inches tall. Also, expectant moms and people prone to motion sickness or those with heart, neck, or back problems shouldn't climb aboard.
Jake Rating: "That was double awesome!" (In other words, it's a good coming-of-age test for thrill-ride junkies of the near future.)

The Timekeeper
Frommer's Rating: C
Recommended Ages: 8–adult
This Jules Verne/H. G. Wells–inspired multimedia show combines CircleVision and IMAX footage with audio-Animatronics. It's hosted by a robot/mad scientist (Robin Williams) and his assistant, 9-EYE, a flying, camera-headed 'droid that moonlights as a time-machine test pilot. In this escapade, the audience hears Mozart as a young prodigy playing for French royalty, visits medieval battlefields in Scotland, watches da Vinci work, and floats in a hot-air balloon over Moscow's Red Square. Voices include Jeremy Irons and Rhea Perlman. Older kids will like the robot, but younger ones will get bored and restless. *Note:* You have to stand during the show, which is only open seasonally.

Tomorrowland Indy Speedway
Frommer's Rating: B+ for kids, D for most teens and adults
Recommended Ages: 4–10
Younger kids love this ride, especially if their adult companion lets them drive (there's a 52-in. height minimum to take a lap without a big person), but teens and other fast starters hate it. The cars are *incredibly* slow (think of pine sap), the steering is atrocious, and the vehicles are on a loose track even though they're actual gas-powered, mini sports cars. Warp speed on this 4-minute spin around the track is 7 mph. The long lines for this ride move even slower than that. *Note:* It carries Disney's warning that expectant mothers and people with heart, neck, or back problems shouldn't climb aboard, likely because of the potential for getting bumped as you try to board or disembark.

Tips **Best Protein Snack in the Parks**

For our money, you can't beat the smoked turkey drumsticks sold for about $5 in WDW parks, including at The Lunching Pad in Tomorrowland. Apparently a lot of folks agree. Disney sells 1.6 million of them a year.

Tomorrowland Transit Authority
Frommer's Rating: C, B+ for tired adults or toddlers
Recommended Ages: All ages

A futuristic means of transportation, these small five-car trains are engineless. They work by electromagnets, belch no pollution, and use little power. Narrated by a computer guide named Horack I, TTA offers an overhead view of Tomorrowland, including an interior look at Space Mountain (kids not old enough to ride it usually like the peek inside). Lines are often nonexistent. If you're in the Magic Kingdom for only 1 day, skip this. If you're looking for a little snooze cruise or a chance to rest your feet, it's a must.

Walt Disney's Carousel of Progress (Overrated
Frommer's Rating: D
Recommended Ages: Only the comatose

Here's another attraction that's open seasonally. It debuted at the 1964 World's Fair and was "updated" a few years ago, but it still comes up short. We apologize to the few park veterans who like it, but it's a waste of 22 minutes unless: (a) you need the break from the insanity rampant through the rest of the park, (b) you have no clue what's happened technologically since the 1930s, or (c) you are a sentimentalist looking for any attraction that Uncle Walt actually designed. Even your children will be bored stiff.

PARADES, FIREWORKS & MORE

You can pick up a guide map when you enter the park. It should include an **entertainment schedule** that lists all kinds of special goings-on for the day. These include concerts, encounters with characters, holiday events, and the major happenings listed next.

Share a Dream Come True Parade
Frommer's Rating: B
Recommended Ages: All ages

Replacing Magical Moments, this is the Magic Kingdom's parade honoring the 100th anniversary of Uncle Walt's birth. Giant gloves and loads of Disney characters march up Main Street and into Frontierland daily.

SpectroMagic (Moments
Frommer's Rating: A
Recommended Ages: All ages

This 20-minute after-dark production combines fiber optics, holographic images, clouds of liquid nitrogen, old-fashioned twinkling lights, and a soundtrack featuring classic Disney tunes. Mickey, dressed in an amber and purple grand magician's cape, makes an appearance in a confetti of light. You'll also see the SpectroMen atop the title float, and Chernabog, *Fantasia*'s monstrous demon, who unfolds his 38-foot wingspan. It takes the electrical equivalent of seven lightning bolts (enough to power a fleet of 2,000 over-the-road trucks) to bring the show to life.

SpectroMagic is held only on a limited number of nights. See your entertainment schedule for availability. When it is held, there are usually two showings: one earlier in the evening and the next one near closing time. If you have little kids, go to the early showing. If you have older kids and teens, the later showing is usually less crowded (and you face shorter ride lines while the 1st production is going on). No matter which showing you attend, this one is worth having the kids stay up for—it's a memorable experience for the entire family.

Moments **Where to Find Characters**

Mickey's Toontown Fair was designed as a place where kids can meet and mingle with their favorite characters all day at the Judge's Tent and Toontown Hall of Fame Tent. Mickey and others are stars in residence. In **Fantasyland,** look for Ariel's Grotto and Fantasyland Character Festival for daily greetings. **Main Street** (Town Square) and **Adventureland** (at Pirates of the Caribbean and near Magic Carpets of Aladdin) are other hot spots. If your child has an autograph book for characters to sign, have it out and ready with a pen for Goofy to plop down his signature. And have your camera ready and waiting if you want to capture a picture of your kids with Pluto. And bring lots of patience—you won't be the only parent waiting for the Kodak moment.

Wishes *Moments*
Frommer's Rating: A+
Recommended Ages: All ages

It feels like the Fourth of July when you attend the 12-minute **Wishes** fireworks display, which replaced the old **Fantasy in the Sky** fireworks in October 2003. The new show, narrated by Jiminy Cricket and with background music from several Disney classics, is the story of a wish coming true, and it borrows one element from the old one—Tinker Bell still flies overhead. The fireworks go off nightly during summer and holidays and on selected nights (usually Mon and Wed–Sat) the rest of the year. See your entertainment schedule for details. Suggested viewing areas are Liberty Square, Frontierland, and Mickey's Toontown Fair. Disney hotels close to the park (Grand Floridian, Polynesian, Contemporary, and Wilderness Lodge) also offer excellent views.

Jake Rating: "That was better than the Fourth of July!" (It's true. Disney *really* has pyrotechnics down to an art form.)

4 Epcot

Epcot is an acronym for *Experimental Prototype Community of Tomorrow,* and it was Walt Disney's dream for a planned city. (For an idea of what he wanted, visit **www.waltopia.com** on the Internet.) Alas, after his death, it became a theme park—central Florida's second major one, which opened in 1982. Its aims are described in a dedication plaque: "May Epcot entertain, inform, and inspire. And, above all . . . instill a new sense of belief and pride in man's ability to shape a world that offers hope to people everywhere."

Ever growing and changing, Epcot occupies 300 vibrantly landscaped acres. If you can spare it, take a little time to stop and smell the roses on your way to and through the two major sections: Future World and World Showcase.

Epcot is so big that hiking the World Showcase end to end (1⅓ miles from the Canada pavilion on one side to Mexico on the other) can be exhausting (that goes double for your kids). That's why some folks are certain Epcot stands for "Every Person Comes Out Tired." Depending on how long you intend to linger at each country in World Showcase, this part of the park can be experienced in 1 day. One way to conserve energy is to take the launches across the lagoon from the edge of Future World to Germany or Morocco. But most visitors simply make a leisurely loop, working clockwise or counterclockwise from one side of the Showcase to the other.

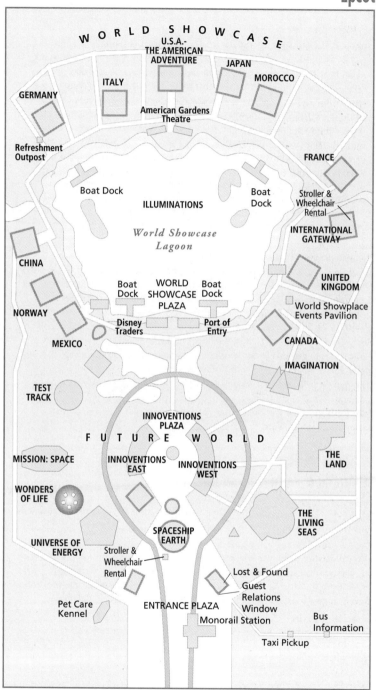

WORLD SHOWCASE

U.S.A.- THE AMERICAN ADVENTURE

ITALY

JAPAN

MOROCCO

GERMANY

American Gardens Theatre

Refreshment Outpost

FRANCE

Boat Dock

Boat Dock

ILLUMINATIONS

Stroller & Wheelchair Rental

World Showcase Lagoon

INTERNATIONAL GATEWAY

CHINA

Boat Dock

WORLD SHOWCASE PLAZA

Boat Dock

UNITED KINGDOM

NORWAY

Disney Traders

Port of Entry

World Showplace Events Pavilion

MEXICO

CANADA

IMAGINATION

TEST TRACK

INNOVENTIONS PLAZA

FUTURE WORLD

MISSION: SPACE

INNOVENTIONS EAST

INNOVENTIONS WEST

THE LAND

WONDERS OF LIFE

THE LIVING SEAS

UNIVERSE OF ENERGY

Stroller & Wheelchair Rental

SPACESHIP EARTH

Lost & Found

Guest Relations Window

Pet Care Kennel

ENTRANCE PLAZA

Monorail Station

Bus Information

Taxi Pickup

Tips **Fun for Kids at Epcot**

Epcot is the least kid-friendly of the Disney parks (especially for the pre-school and toddler set), but there are plenty of things for your kids to do.

Be sure to pick up a guide map and entertainment schedule as you enter the park. Folks with children can and should grab a copy of the *Epcot Kids' Guide*, which uses a yellow K in a red square to note **"Kidcot"** stops inside the World Showcase. These play and learning stations are for the younger set and allow them to stop at various World Showcase countries, do crafts, get autographs, have their Kidcot passports stamped (these are available for purchase in most Epcot stores and make a great souvenir), and chat with cast members native to those countries. Your kids will get the chance to learn about different countries, and make a souvenir to bring home. For more information, stop in at Guest Services when you get into the park. The stations open at 1pm daily.

Unlike Magic Kingdom, much of Epcot's parking lot is close to the gate. Parking sections are named for themes (Harvest, Energy, and so forth) and the aisles are numbered. While some guests are happy to walk to the gate from nearer areas, trams are available, but these days mainly to and from the outer areas.

If you plan to eat lunch or dinner here and haven't already made reservations (© **407/939-3463**), you can make them at the restaurants, many of which are described in chapter 5, "Family-Friendly Dining."

Before you get underway, check the map's schedule and incorporate any shows you want to see into your itinerary.

HOURS   Future World is usually open from 9 or 10am to 6 or 7pm but sometimes later during major holidays and the summer. World Showcase doesn't open until 11am or noon, and it usually closes at 9pm but sometimes later.

TICKET PRICES   Ticket are $52 for adults, $42 for children 3 to 9, free for children under 3. See "Tickets & Passes," earlier in this chapter, for information on multiday passes.

SERVICES & FACILITIES IN EPCOT

ATMs   The machines here accept cards issued by banks using the Cirrus, Honor, and PLUS systems and are located at the front of the park, in Italy, and near the bridge between World Showcase and Future World.

Baby Care   Epcot's Baby Care Center is by the First Aid station near the Odyssey Center in Future World. It's furnished with a nursing room with rocking chairs; disposable diapers, formula, baby food, and pacifiers are for sale. There are also changing tables in all women's restrooms, as well as in some of the men's restrooms. Disposable diapers are also available at Guest Relations.

Cameras & Film   Kodak disposable cameras are available throughout the park, including at the Kodak Camera Center at the Entrance Plaza.

First Aid   The First Aid Center, staffed by registered nurses, is located near the Odyssey Center in Future World.

Lockers   Lockers are to the west of Spaceship Earth, outside the Entrance Plaza, and in the Bus Information Center by the bus parking lot. The cost is $7 a day, including a $2 deposit.

Lost Children   Lost children in Epcot are usually taken to Earth Center or the Baby Care Center, where lost children logbooks are kept. *Children under 7 should wear name-tags.*

Package Pickup   Any large package you purchase can be sent by the shop clerk to Guest Relations in the Entrance Plaza. Allow 3 hours for delivery. There's also a package pickup location at the International Gateway entrance in the World Showcase.

Parking   It's $7 for cars, pickups, and vans; $8 for RVs.

Pet Care   Day accommodations are offered at kennels just outside the Entrance Plaza at Epcot for $6 (© **407/824-6568**). Proof of vaccination is required. There are also four other kennels in the WDW complex.

Strollers   These can be rented from special stands on the east side of the Entrance Plaza and at World Showcase's International Gateway. The cost is $8 for a single and $15 for a double, including a $1 refundable deposit. See "Strollers," in the "Magic Kingdom" section for tips on using a stroller at WDW.

Wheelchair Rental   Rent wheelchairs inside the Entrance Plaza to your left, to the right of ticket booths at the Gift Shop, and at World Showcase's International Gateway. The cost for regular chairs is $7, including a $1 refundable deposit. Electric wheelchairs cost $40 a day, including a $10 refundable deposit.

FUTURE WORLD

Future World is in the northern section of Epcot, the first area mainstream guests see after entering the park. Its icon is a huge geosphere known as Spaceship Earth—aka, that thing that looks like a giant golf ball. Major corporations sponsor Future World's 10 themed areas (that means they're making pricey investments, such as the $60 million that GM dropped on the Test Track ride you'll read about a little later in this chapter). The focus here is on discovery, scientific achievements, and tomorrow's technologies in areas running from energy to undersea exploration. This zone offers two thrill rides that will get the adrenaline pumping in your teens, and several attractions that will appeal to the small fry in your party.

Imagination
Frommer's Rating: B+
Recommended Ages: 6–adult
In this pavilion, even the fountains are magical. "Water snakes" arc in the air, offering kids a chance to dare them to "bite." (Little kids love them and it's a good place for them to work off a little energy and you to get a great photo.) This pavilion was upgraded in 2001 to include more high-tech gadgets, and a year later Figment, the pavilion's much-loved mascot, returned (see below).

The 3-D **Honey, I Shrunk the Audience** show is one of the big attractions here, deserving an **"A" rating** by itself. Based on the Disney hit *Honey, I Shrunk the Kids* film, you're terrorized by mice and, once you're shrunk, by a large cat; then you're given a good shaking by a gigantic 5-year-old. Vibrating seats and creepy tactile effects enhance dramatic 3-D action. Finally, everyone returns to proper size—except the family dog.
Jake Rating: "I liked that part where the dog sniffed us and acted like he was going to . . . " (Uh, Jake, this is a family book. Let's save the surprise.)

Figment, the crazy-but-lovable dragon, was resurrected in a new **Journey into Your Imagination** ride in June 2002. Things begin with an open house at the Imagination Institute, with Dr. Nigel Channing taking you on a tour of labs that

(Moments) Top 10 Orlando Family Attractions

For Very Young Kids:

1. **Caro-Seuss-El** Cowfish, elephant birds, and other wacky critters inhabit this Islands of Adventure merry-go-round, p. 240.

2. **A Day in the Park with Barney** The purple dinosaur drives some adults batty, but little Universal Studios guests love him, p. 230.

3. **Jim Henson's Muppet*Vision 3D** Don't miss Kermit, Miss Piggy, and the rest of the crew at Disney–MGM Studios, p. 199.

4. **Voyage of the Little Mermaid** Puppets, film, and special effects make for a lively show, also at Disney–MGM Studios, p. 203.

5. **If I Ran the Zoo** Let the little ones play with Seussian creatures at this 19-station, interactive play land at Islands of Adventure, p. 240.

6. **Ketchakiddie Creek** Disney's Typhoon Lagoon has lots of wet fun for the younger set (and older guests, too), p. 214.

7. **Magic Carpets of Aladdin** Watch out for spitting camels on this wheel-and-spoke kids' ride at Disney's Magic Kingdom, p. 163.

8. **Cinderella's Golden Carousel** Originally built in 1917, this grand old Magic Kingdom carousel delights plenty of adults, too, p. 169.

9. **Mickey's & Minnie's Country Houses** The utensils and furniture create some surprises inside these houses at Mickey's Toontown Fair in the Magic Kingdom, p. 172.

10. **One Fish, Two Fish, Red Fish, Blue Fish** Your little ones can fly their funky fish up and down as they spin above ground level at Islands of Adventure's Seuss Landing, p. 241.

For Kids 6–12 & Older:

1. **Big Thunder Mountain Railroad** Hold onto your skivvies as this runaway train at Disney's Magic Kingdom provides its share of thrills and chills, p. 166.

2. **Popeye & Bluto's Bilge-Rat Barges** Arguably, this Islands of Adventure entry is the best faux whitewater ride in Florida, p. 243.

3. **Indiana Jones Epic Stunt Spectacular** Indy and his stunt friends keep you on the edge of your seat at Disney–MGM Studios, p. 199.

4. **Dudley Do-Right's Ripsaw Falls** Expect to get wet on this Islands of Adventure log ride that reaches 50 mph, p. 243.

5. **The Barnstormer at Goofy's Wiseacre Farm** The Magic Kingdom's mini roller coaster is the fairest of this genre, p. 172.

6. **Woody Woodpecker's Nuthouse Coaster** But Islands' mini-coaster is just half a click behind Goofy's in the fun factor, p. 233.

demonstrate how the five senses capture and control one's imagination, except you never get to touch and taste once Figment arrives to prove it's far, far better to set your imagination free. He invites you to his upside-down house, where a new perspective enhances your imagination. "One Little Spark," an upbeat ditty that debuted when the attraction opened in 1983, has also been brought back.

7. **Jimmy Neutron's Nicktoon Blast**   Help Jimmy battle Yokians and meet SpongeBob and other 'toons at one of Universal Studios Florida's newest attractions, p. 231.

8. **Splash Mountain**   The Magic Kingdom's wettest ride will launch you at 40 mph down a 52-foot, 45-degree slope, p. 167.

9. **Jurassic Park River Adventure**   Made from the same mold as Splash Mountain, this Islands of Adventures wild ride adds hissing dinosaurs to the special effects, p. 244.

10. **Kali River Rapids**   Animal Kingdom's raft ride isn't quite up to Popeye & Bluto's at Islands, but it's still a ton of wet fun, p. 213.

For Thrill-Seeking Teens & Parents:

1. **Incredible Hulk Coaster**   In Florida, it doesn't get any scarier than this Islands of Adventure rocket ride, which offers seven rollovers and two deep drops, p. 242.

2. **Rock 'n' Roller Coaster**   You won't find a faster giddy-up-and-go than this 0 to 60 mph, Aerosmith-supported stretch limo at Disney–MGM Studios, p. 200.

3. **Dueling Dragons**   Test your courage on one of two coasters that hit speeds of 60 mph and come within 12 inches of each other at Islands of Adventure, p. 245.

4. **Summit Plummet**   Hang onto your swimsuit as you fall 120 feet at 60 mph—sans vehicle!—at this Blizzard Beach water slide, p. 217.

5. **The Twilight Zone Tower of Terror**   If you want to see what it's like to fall in an elevator, yo-yo style, tackle this Disney–MGM test of your nerve, p. 202.

6. **The Amazing Adventures of Spider-Man**   Bar none, this Islands of Adventure entry is the best 3-D simulator and action ride east of the Mississippi River, p. 241.

7. **Mission: Space**   Get ready to launch (maybe your lunch) if you climb aboard Epcot's new motion simulator, which NASA astronauts helped design and test, p. 185.

8. **Kraken**   Speaking of launching, SeaWorld's signature thrill ride is a floorless, open-sided roller coaster that hits 65 mph while making seven loops, p. 254.

9. **Doctor Doom's Fearfall**   While it's not quite as chilling as Twilight Zone Tower of Terror, this Islands of Adventure ride will make you glad to hit firm ground again, p. 241.

10. **Test Track**   Run your six-passenger convertible through a host of tests at this GM-sponsored attraction, which features a 65-mph speed burst on an elevated straightaway, p. 186.

Once you disembark from the ride, head for the **"What If"** labs, where your kids can burn lots of energy while exercising their imaginations at a number of interactive stations that allow them to conduct music, and experiment with video.

Moments Behind the Scenes: Special Tours in Walt Disney World

In addition to the greenhouse tour in Epcot's The Land pavilion (p. 184), the Disney parks offer a number of walking tours and learning programs, some of which are suitable for kids. The tours are subject to change. These tours represent the most recent ones available at press time. Times, days, and prices also change. It's best to call ahead to Disney's tour line, *©* **407/939-8687,** to make reservations or get additional information.

- Epcot's **Aqua Seas Tour** lends you a wetsuit, and then takes you on a 2½-hour journey that includes a 30-minute swim in the 5.7-million-gallon Living Seas Aquarium, home to some 65 marine species. The tour includes a souvenir T-shirt and group photo. The cost is $100, plus park admission, and it's open to guests 8 and older (those under 18 must be accompanied by an adult). It's offered daily at 12:30pm.
- The **Family Magic Tour** explores the nooks and crannies of the Magic Kingdom in the form of a 2-hour scavenger hunt. You meet and greet characters at the end. Children and adults are $25 per person. You must also buy admission tickets to the park and book in advance. If you have young kids and want to do a special tour, this is the one to take. It begins daily at 11:30am outside City Hall. It's sometimes held at 9:30am, too.
- The **Magic Behind Our Steam Trains** tour (ages 10 and up) is a fun one for locomotive buffs. A pair of inveterate conductors give you insight other guests don't get into the history and present operations of the little engines that could. Monday, Tuesday, Thursday, and Saturday at 7:30am, $40 per person, plus park admission.

Several tours are offered only to those age 16 and older. Most of these are aimed at adults (photos are not permitted on these backstage tours and photo ID is a must). A couple that might appeal to teens include:

- The 3-hour **Hidden Treasures of World Showcase** explores the architectural and entertainment offerings of Epcot's 11 "nations." The $59 tours (plus admission) are at 9:45am on Tuesday and Thursday.

Innoventions East and West
Frommer's Rating: A for hungry minds and game junkies
Recommended Ages: 8–adult
Innoventions East, behind Spaceship Earth and to the left as you enter the park, features the **House of Innoventions.** It's a preview of tomorrow's smart house, but many of its products are already on the market (at astronomical prices). Its refrigerator has an Internet-savvy computer that can make your grocery list and place the order. A smart picture frame can store and send photos to other smart frames. And its toilet has a seat warmer, automatic lid opener and closer, and a sprayer and blow dryer that eliminate the need for toilet paper if you're worldly. **Internet Zone** profiles tomorrow's online games for kids, including laser tag

If you're interested in your teen getting both an educational and entertaining tour, this is a good choice.

- The 4½-hour **Keys to the Kingdom** tour provides an orientation to the Magic Kingdom and a glimpse into the high-tech systems behind the magic. It's $58 (lunch is included, but mandatory park admission isn't) and is held daily at 8:30, 9:30, and 10am. It's got some interesting insights into the park, and you will get treated to a ride or two, so if your teen is wild about Disney, it's not a bad bet.

- At the top of the price chain ($199 per person) is **Backstage Magic,** a 7-hour, self-propelled bus tour through areas of Epcot, the Magic Kingdom, and Disney–MGM Studios that aren't seen by mainstream guests. The 10am weekday tour is limited to 20 people age 16 or older, and you might have trouble getting a date unless you book early. Some will find this one isn't worth the price, but if you or your teen has a brain that must know how things work or simply want to know more than your family or friends, you might find it's worth the cost. You'll see WDW mechanics and engineers repairing and building Animatronic beings from attractions such as "It's a Small World." You'll peek over the shoulders of cast members who watch close-circuit TVs to make sure other visitors are surviving the har-rowing rides. And at the Magic Kingdom, you'll venture into the tunnels used for work areas as well as corridors for the cast to get from one area to the others without fighting tourist crowds. It's not unusual for tour takers to see Snow White enjoying a Snickers bar, find Cinderella having her locks touched up at an underground salon, or view woodworkers as they restore the hard maple muscles of the carousel horses. Park admission *isn't* required.

- **Backstage Safari** at Animal Kingdom ($65 per person plus park admission) offers a 3-hour look at the park's veterinary hospital as well as lessons in conservation, animal nutrition, and medicine (Mon, Wed, and Fri). If your teen dreams of veterinary school, this is a good bet, otherwise, it may be a bit boring for them. *Note:* You won't see many animals.

with Disney characters. Across the plaza at **Innoventions West,** crowds flock to **Video Games of Tomorrow,** which has nearly three-dozen game stations.

Note: A new Underwriters Laboratories exhibit at Innoventions East, the **Test the Limits Lab,** has six kiosks that let kids and fun-loving adults try out a variety of products. In one, you can pull a rope attached to a hammer that crashes into a TV screen to see if it's shatter resistant. In another, you can push a button that releases a magnet that falls onto a firefighter's helmet (sans fire-fighter, of course).

Jake and Andy Ratings: "Free games—we don't want to leave!" (After a few miles around the park, adults don't either if there's space to park their keisters.)

The Land
Frommer's Rating: B+ for environmentalists, gardeners; B for others
Recommended Ages: 8–adult
The largest of Future World's pavilions highlights food and nature.

Living with the Land is a 13-minute boat ride through three ecological environments (a rainforest, an African desert, and the windswept American plains), each populated by appropriate audio-Animatronic denizens. New farming methods and experiments ranging from hydroponics to plants growing in simulated Martian soil are showcased in real gardens. If you'd like a more serious overview, take the 45-minute **Behind the Seeds** guided walking tour of the growing areas, offered daily. Sign up at the Green Thumb Emporium shop near the entrance to Food Rocks. The cost is $8 for adults, $6 for children 3 to 9. *Note:* It's really geared to children.

Circle of Life combines spectacular live-action footage with animation in a 15-minute motion picture based on *The Lion King.* In this cautionary environmental tale, Timon and Pumbaa are building a monument to the good life called Hakuna Matata Lakeside Village, but their project, as Simba points out, is damaging the savanna for other animals. The message: Everything is connected in the great circle of life.

Note: Longtime pavilion favorite **Food Rocks,** an entertaining audio-Animatronic rock performance on nutrition closed in January 2004 to make way for a new attraction. **Soarin' over California,** a copy of a popular attraction at Disney's California Adventure theme park, will be an IMAX theater adventure in which viewers are seat-belted into benches with their legs dangling. The benches rise and rock to and fro as guests are given a dozen aerial views of the state. Soaring Over California carries a 40-inch height minimum. It's set to open sometime in early 2005.

The Living Seas
Frommer's Rating: B
Recommended Ages: 8–adult
This pavilion contains a 5.7-million-gallon saltwater aquarium including coral reefs inhabited by some 4,000 sharks, barracudas, parrotfish, rays, dolphins, and other critters. While waiting in line, visitors pass exhibits tracing the history of undersea exploration, including a diving barrel used by Alexander the Great in 332 B.C. and Sir Edmund Halley's first diving bell (1697).

A 2½-minute multimedia preshow about today's ocean technology is followed by a 7-minute film demonstrating the formation of the earth and seas as a means to support life.

⎛*Moments* Kids in the Kitchen

Future cooks can take advantage of a free **Junior Chefs program** at The Land, which lets kids ages 3 to 10 assist real-life chefs in baking Nestle Tollhouse cookies. Your children will get their own chef's hat and a couple of cookies to take home (though most can't resist eating them right away). It usually runs about every hour or so (check when you get to the pavilion). There's no need to reserve a spot for your child. Just show up for the Junior Chef storefront in the Sunshine Food Fair on the first floor about 10 minutes before the program is set to begin. Your kids will have a great time and you'll get lots of opportunities to take pictures.

After the films, you enter "hydolators" for a hokey "descent" to the simulated ocean floor. Upon arrival, you can journey through a tunnel for close-up views through acrylic windows of the denizens, including manatees in all-too-tight quarters. Most young children will get bored after a few minutes of fish-watching, but older ones should enjoy exploring the various exhibits. ***Note:*** A program called **Epcot DiveQuest** enables certified divers 10 and older to participate in a 2½-hour program that includes a 30-minute dive in the Living Seas aquarium. The program costs $140. Call © **407/939-8687** for more information. It's not for kids, but your young ones might enjoy watching mom or dad brave the tank.

Mission: Space
Frommer's Rating: A+
Recommended Ages: 10–adult
This brand new, $100 million attraction seats up to four riders at a time in a simulated flight to the Red Planet. You'll assume the role of commander, pilot, navigator, or engineer, depending on where you sit, and must complete related jobs vital to the mission (don't worry if you miss your cue, you won't crash). The ride uses a combination of visuals, sound and centrifugal force to create the illusion of a launch and trip to Mars. Even veteran roller-coaster riders who tried the simulator said the sensation mimics a liftoff, as riders are pressed into their seats and the roar and vibration tricks the brain during the launch portion of the 4-minute adventure. NASA helped design and tweak this attraction. ***Note:*** Riders must be at least 44 inches tall. Mission: Space also carries a warning that people who are claustrophobic or have a low tolerance for loud noises should avoid the ride. If spinning causes you to get dizzy or motion sick, this isn't the ride for you, though you can reduce the effects by focusing straight ahead.
Jake Rating: "That was the coolest ride here—even better than Test Track (see below). Can we go again?" (Not until we stop spinning!)

Spaceship Earth *(Overrated)*
Frommer's Rating: C
Recommended Ages: All ages
This massive, silvery geosphere symbolizes Epcot. That makes it a must-do for many, though it's something of a yawner—another slow-track journey back in time to trace the progress of communications. Long lines can be avoided by saving it until late in the day when you might be able to just walk in. The 15-minute show/ride takes visitors to the distant past where an audio-Animatronic Cro-Magnon shaman recounts the story of a hunt while others record it on cave walls. You advance thousands of years to ancient Egypt, where hieroglyphics adorn temple walls and writing is recorded on papyrus scrolls. You'll progress through the Phoenician and Greek alphabets, the Gutenberg printing press, and the Renaissance, trying not to notice that several of these guys look an awful lot like Barbie's dream date, Ken. Technologies develop at a rapid pace, through the telegraph, telephone, radio, movies, and TV. It's but a short step to the age of electronic communications. You're catapulted into outer space to see Spaceship Earth from a new perspective, returning for a finale that places the audience amid interactive global networks. ***Note:***

> **Tips Stay Tuned**
>
> Local media scuttlebutt says Spaceship Earth will be shut down in 2005 so a new moving ride can be built in time for Epcot's 25th anniversary in 2007. At publication time, Disney wasn't commenting.

Tips Visual & Audio Assistance

Complimentary guided-tour audiocassette tapes and players are available at Guest Relations to assist visually impaired guests, and personal translator units are available to amplify the audio at some Epcot Attractions (inquire at Earth Station). For more information on services available to those with disabilities at Disney World, see p. 30.

Sharp-eyed or just plain bored riders may notice at least two green "exit" lights peeking through the heavens, one near the very end of the ride.
Andy Rating: "Zzzzzzzz." (Amen, Andy, it's a *real* snoozer.)

Test Track
Frommer's Rating: A
Recommended Ages: 8–adult

Test Track combines GM engineering and Disney Imagineering. It might leave some of you believing GM is making too much profit if it blew $60 million to build a ride, but most of you will have a blast. The line can be more than an hour long in peak periods, so consider the FASTPASS option. The last part of the line snakes through displays about corrosion, crash tests, and other things from the GM proving grounds (you can linger long enough to see them even with FASTPASS). The 5-minute ride follows what looks to be an actual highway. It includes braking tests, a hill climb, and tight S-curves in a six-passenger convertible. The left front seat offers the most thrills as the vehicle moves through the curves. There's also a 12-second burst of speed that reaches 65 mph on the straightaway. *Note:* Riders must be at least 40 inches tall. Also, expectant mothers and people prone to motion sickness or those with heart, neck, or back problems shouldn't test the track.

Note II: This is the only attraction in Epcot that has a single-rider line, which allows singles to fill in vacant spots in select cars. If you're part of a party of teens or older kids that doesn't mind splitting up and riding in singles, you can shave off some major waiting time by taking advantage of this option. But FASTPASS offers the same time savings without the break up.

Jake Rating: "That was *way* fast!" (Indeed, the last burst provides quite a rush.)

Universe of Energy
Frommer's Rating: B
Recommended Ages: 8–adult

Sponsored by Exxon, this pavilion has a roof full of solar panels and a goal of bettering your understanding of America's energy problems and potential solutions. Its headline ride, **Ellen's Energy Adventure,** features comedian Ellen DeGeneres being tutored (by Bill Nye the Science Guy) to be a *Jeopardy!* contestant. On a massive screen in Theater I, an animated motion picture depicts the Earth's molten beginnings, its cooling process, and the formation of fossil fuels. You move back in time 275 million years into an eerie, storm-wracked landscape of the Mesozoic Era, a time of violent geological activity. Here, giant audio-Animatronic dragonflies, earthquakes, and streams of molten lava threaten you before you enter a steam-filled tunnel deep in the bowels of a volcano. When you emerge, you're in Theater II and the present. In this new setting, which looks like a NASA Mission Control room, a 70mm film projected on a massive 210-foot wraparound screen depicts the challenges of the world's increasing energy demands and the emerging technologies that will help meet them. Your moving seats now return to Theater I, where swirling special effects herald a film about how energy impacts our lives. It ends on an upbeat note, with a vision of an energy-abundant future, and Ellen as a new *Jeopardy!* champion.

Note: Most kids enjoy the ride, though younger children may find the dinosaur scenes somewhat frightening and a little too intense.

Wonders of Life
Frommer's Rating: A
Recommended Ages: 10–adult
Housed in a vast geodesic dome fronted by a 75-foot replica of a DNA strand, this pavilion offers some of Future World's most engaging shows and attractions for older kids.

The *Making of Me,* starring Martin Short, is a captivating 15-minute motion picture combining live action with animation and spectacular *in utero* photography to create a sweet introduction to the facts of life. Don't miss it, although the presentation may prompt some questions from young children; therefore, we recommend it for ages 10 and up. Short travels back in time to witness his parents as children, their meeting at a college dance, their wedding, and their decision to have a baby. Along with him, we view his development inside his mother's womb and witness his birth.

During the very popular **Body Wars** ride, you're reduced to the size of a cell for a medical rescue mission inside the immune system of a human body. Your objective: Save a miniaturized immunologist who has been accidentally swept into the bloodstream. This motion-simulator ride takes you on a wild journey through gale-force winds in the lungs and pounding heart chambers. Engineers designed this ride from the last row of a car, so that's where to sit to get the most bang for your buck. Although you know they're part of the Disney show, it's a little eerie passing through derma topic purification stations in order to undergo miniaturization. It's not as good as the similarly built **Star Tours** at Disney–MGM studios (p. 202), but it definitely has its moments and is popular with teens. This one isn't a smart choice for those prone to motion sickness or who generally prefer to be stirred rather than shaken. *Note:* Riders must be at least 40 inches tall. Also, steer clear if you're an expectant mother, or have heart, neck, or back problems.

Jake Rating (upon seeing his 1st white blood cell): "That's disgusting" then, near the end, "Mayday, Mayday." (He was luckier than one of his adult copilots. At the 1st shake, she giggled. At the 1st rattle, it became a nervous laugh. At the 1st roll, she began frantically fanning herself. And at the 1st sign of daylight again, she was an odd shade of green.)

In the hilarious, multimedia **Cranium Command,** Buzzy, an audio-Animatronic brain-pilot-in-training, is charged with the seemingly impossible task of controlling the brain of an average 12-year-old boy. Charles Grodin, Jon Lovitz, Bob Goldthwait, George Wendt, and Kevin Nealon and Dana Carvey (as Hans and Franz) play the boy's body parts. It's another must-see attraction (recommended for ages 8 and up—it's not frightening, but younger kids may have trouble grasping some of the content) and has a loyal following among Disney veterans. The audience is seemingly seated inside Bobby's head as Buzzy guides him through a day of typical preadolescent traumas such as running for the school bus, meeting a girl, fighting bullies, and a run-in with the school principal.

The pavilion also has **Fitness Fairgrounds,** large areas filled with fitness-related shows, exhibits, and participatory activities, including a film called *Goofy About Health.* It's a good place for young children to expend some energy while learning valuable concepts about nutrition and physical fitness.

WORLD SHOWCASE

This community of 11 miniaturized nations surrounds the 40-acre World Showcase Lagoon on the park's southern side. All of the showcase's countries have authentically indigenous architecture, landscaping, background music, restaurants, and shops. The nations' cultural facets are explored in art exhibits, song and dance performances, and innovative rides, films, and attractions. And all of the employees in each pavilion are natives of the country represented.

All pavilions offer some kind of live entertainment throughout the day. Times and performances change, but they're listed in the guide map. World Showcase opens between 11am and noon daily, so there's time for a Future World excursion if you arrive earlier.

Note: With the exception of those with an appreciation of world geography and cultures, most young kids will find little of interest here other than a few tame rides and some activities as Kidcot stations (p. 178). There are, however, **regular appearances by characters** at Showcase Plaza (consult the daily schedule for times).

Canada
Frommer's Rating: A
Recommended Ages: 8–adult
Our neighbors to the north are represented by architecture ranging from a mansard-roofed replica of Ottawa's 19th-century French-style Château Laurier (here called Hôtel du Canada) to a British-influenced stone building modeled after a famous landmark near Niagara Falls.

An Indian village complete with a rough-hewn log trading post and 30-foot replicas of Ojibwa totem poles signifies the culture of the Northwest. The Canadian wilderness is reflected by a rocky mountain, a waterfall cascading into a whitewater stream, and a mini-forest of evergreens, stately cedars, maples, and birch trees. Don't miss the stunning floral displays of azaleas, roses, zinnias, chrysanthemums, petunias, and patches of wildflowers inspired by the Butchart Gardens in Victoria, British Columbia.

The pavilion's highlight attraction is *O Canada!*—a dazzling 18-minute, 360-degree CircleVision film that shows Canada's scenic splendor, from a dogsled race to the thundering flight of thousands of snow geese departing an autumn stopover near the St. Lawrence River. If you're looking for foot-tapping live entertainment, **Off Kilter** raises the roof with New Age Celtic music as well as some get-down country music. Days and times vary.

Northwest Mercantile carries sandstone and soapstone carvings, fringed leather vests, duck decoys, moccasins, an array of stuffed animals, Native American dolls, Native American spirit stones, rabbit-skin caps, heavy knitted sweaters, and, of course, maple syrup.

China
Frommer's Rating: A
Recommended Ages: 10–adult
Bounded by a serpentine wall that snakes around its perimeter, the China pavilion is entered via a triple-arched ceremonial gate inspired by the Temple of Heaven in Beijing, a summer retreat for Chinese emperors. Passing through the

gate, you'll see a half-size replica of this ornately embellished red-and-gold circular temple, built in 1420 during the Ming dynasty. Gardens simulate those in Suzhou, with miniature waterfalls, fragrant lotus ponds, and groves of bamboo, corkscrew willows, and weeping mulberry trees.

Reflections of China 👧👧 is a 20-minute movie that explores the culture and landscapes in and around seven Chinese cities. Shot over a 2-month period in 2002, it visits Beijing, Shanghai, and the Great Wall (begun 24 c. ago!), among other places. **Land of Many Faces** is an exhibit that introduces China's ethnic peoples, and entertainment is provided daily by the amazing and child-pleasing **Dragon Legend Acrobats** 👧★.

Jake Rating: "Whoa! Those kids are incredible. How do they do that stuff?" (The Dragon Legend Acrobats practice *a lot.* They are showstoppers, as evidenced by the crowds they draw to their performances.)

The **Yong Feng Shangdian Shopping Gallery** features silk robes, lacquer and inlaid mother-of-pearl furniture, jade figures, cloisonné vases, brocade pajamas, silk rugs and embroideries, wind chimes, and Chinese clothing. Artisans occasionally demonstrate calligraphy.

France
Frommer's Rating: B
Recommended Ages: 8–adult

This pavilion focuses on La Belle Epoque, a period from 1870 to 1910 in which French art, literature, and architecture flourished. It's entered via a replica of the beautiful cast-iron Pont des Arts footbridge over the Seine. It leads to a park with bleached sycamores, Bradford pear trees, flowering crape myrtle, and sculptured parterre flower gardens inspired by Seurat's painting *A Sunday Afternoon on the Island of La Grande Jatte.* A one-tenth-scale replica of the Eiffel Tower constructed from Gustave Eiffel's original blueprints looms overhead.

The highlight is **Impressions de France,** which is definitely more for the older set than for young kids. Shown in a palatial sit-down theater a la Fontainebleau, this 18-minute film is a scenic journey through diverse French landscapes projected on a vast 200-degree wraparound screen and enhanced by the music of French composers. The antics of **Serveur Amusant,** a comedic waiter; and the visual comedy of **Le Mime Roland** delights both children and adults, as do the yummy pastries at *Boulangerie Patisserie.*

The covered arcade has shops selling French prints and original art, cookbooks, wines (there's a tasting counter), French food, Babar books, perfumes,

---

Moments Water Fountain Conversations

Many an ordinary item at Disney World has hidden entertainment value for you and your kids. Take a drink at the water fountain in Innoventions Plaza (the one right next to Mouse Gear) and it may beg you not to drink it dry. No, you haven't gotten too much sun—the fountain actually talks (much to the delight of kids and the surprise of unsuspecting adults). A few more talking fountains are scattered around Epcot. The fountains aren't the only items at WDW that will chat you up. We've kibitzed with a walking and talking garbage can (named PUSH) in Magic Kingdom, and a personable palm tree (who goes by Wes Palm) at Animal Kingdom. Ask a Disney employee to direct you if you and your kids want to meet one of these conversational contraptions.

Finds **Great Things to Buy at Epcot**

Sure, *you* want to be educated about the cultures of the world, but for most of us the two big attractions at the World Showcase for families are eating and shopping. Dining options are explained in chapter 5. This list gives you an idea of additional items available for purchase.

If you'd like to check out the amazing scope of Disney merchandise at home, everything from furniture to bath toys, you can order a catalog by calling ℂ 800/237-5751 or surfing the Web to **www.disney store.com**.

- The toys and piñatas draw folks to the Mexico pavilion and the silver jewelry is beautiful. Choose from a range of merchandise that goes from a simple flowered hair clip to a kidney-shaped stone and silver bracelet.
- There are lots of great sweaters available in the shops of Norway, and it's really tough to resist the Scandinavian trolls. They're ugly, but you have to love them. Your kids will love the Lego that's for sale.
- Discover Disney trading pins and Coca-Cola memorabilia in the shops of U.S.A.—The American Adventure.
- Your funky teenager might like the Taquia knit cap, a colorful fez-like chapeau, that's available in Morocco. There's also a variety of celestial-patterned pottery available in vases and platters, and, for the little princesses, a Jasmine character costume.
- Toy soldiers, British games, candy, and music tapes are popular in the United Kingdom. Tennis fans may be interested in the Wimbledon shirts, shorts, and skirts. There's also a nice assortment of rose-patterned tea accessories, Shetland sweaters, tartans, pub accessories, and loads of other stuff from the U.K.

and original letters of famous Frenchmen ranging from Jean Cocteau to Napoleon. Another marketplace/tourism center revives the defunct Les Halles, where Parisians used to sip onion soup in the wee hours.

Germany
Frommer's Rating: C+
Recommended Ages: 8–adult
Enclosed by castle walls and towers, this festive pavilion is centered on a cobblestone *platz* (square) with pots of colorful flowers girding a fountain statue of St. George and the Dragon. An adjacent clock tower is embellished with whimsical glockenspiel figures that herald each hour with quaint melodies. The pavilion's **Biergarten** (p. 113) was inspired by medieval Rothenberg and features a year-round Oktoberfest and its music. And 16th-century facades replicate a merchant's hall in the Black Forest and the town hall in Römerberg Square.

The shops here carry Hummel figurines, crystal, glassware, cookware, Anton Schneider cuckoos, cowbells, Alpine hats, German wines (there's a tasting counter), and specialty foods, toys (German Disneyana, teddy bears, dolls, and puppets), and books. An artisan demonstrates molding and painting Hummel figures; another paints detailed scenes on eggs. Background music runs from oompah bands to Mozart symphonies.

Tip: Model train enthusiasts and kids enjoy the exquisitely detailed miniature version of a small Bavarian town, complete with working train station. Even the littlest members of your party will be fascinated as they watch the trains dart in and out of tunnels and stations.

Italy

Frommer's Rating: C+
Recommended Ages: 10–adult

One of the prettiest World Showcase pavilions, Italy lures visitors over an arched stone footbridge to a replica of Venice's intricately ornamented pink-and-white Doge's Palace. Other architectural highlights include the 83-foot Campanile (bell tower) of St. Mark's Square, Venetian bridges, and a piazza enclosing a version of Bernini's Neptune Fountain. A garden wall suggests a backdrop of provincial countryside, and citrus, cypress, pine, and olive trees frame a formal garden. Gondolas are moored on the lagoon.

Shops carry cameo and filigree jewelry, Armani figurines, kitchenware, Italian wines and foods, Murano and other Venetian glass, alabaster figurines, and inlaid wooden music boxes.

In the street entertainment department, the seemingly lifeless forms of **Imaginum, A Statue Act,** fascinate visitors young and old daily, and the **Character Masquerade** featuring traditional Carnevale masks and costumes will generate enthusiasm as well.

Japan

Frommer's Rating: A
Recommended Ages: 8–adult

A flaming red *torii* (gate of honor) on the banks of the lagoon and the graceful blue-roofed Goju No To pagoda, inspired by a shrine built at Nara in A.D. 700, welcome you to this pavilion, which focuses on Japan's ancient culture. In a traditional Japanese garden, cedars, yews, bamboo, "cloud-pruned" evergreens, willows, and flowering shrubs frame a contemplative setting of pebbled footpaths, rustic bridges, waterfalls, exquisite rock landscaping, and a pond of golden koi. It's a haven of tranquillity in a park that's anything but.

The **Yakitori House** is based on the renowned 16th-century Katsura Imperial Villa in Kyoto, designed as a royal summer residence and considered by many to be the crowning achievement of Japanese architecture. Exhibits ranging from 18th-century Bunraki puppets to samurai armor take place in the moated **White Heron Castle,** a replica of the Shirasagi-Jo, a 17th-century fortress overlooking the city of Himeji. There's also a gallery exhibit on **Japanese baseball** that young fans may enjoy.

The drums of **Matsuriza**—one of the best performances in the World Showcase—entertain guests daily (it's loud but kids love it). The **Mitsukoshi Department Store** (Japan's answer to Macy's) is housed in a replica of the Shishinden (Hall of Ceremonies) of the Gosho Imperial Palace, built in Kyoto in A.D. 794 and is popular with kids of all ages. It sells lacquerware, kimonos, kites, fans, dolls in traditional costumes (children love them), Pokémon and Hello Kitty items (ditto), origami books, samurai swords, Japanese Disneyana, bonsai trees, Japanese foods, Netsuke carvings, pottery, and modern electronics.

Mexico

Frommer's Rating: B+
Recommended Ages: 8–adult

You'll hear the music of marimbas and mariachi bands as you approach Mexico, fronted by a Mayan pyramid modeled on the Aztec temple of Quetzalcoatl (God of Life) and surrounded by dense Yucatán jungle landscaping. Upon entering the pavilion, you'll be in a museum of pre-Columbian art and artifacts.

Down a ramp, a small lagoon is the setting for **El Rio del Tiempo** (River of Time), where visitors board boats for an 8-minute cruise (reasonably entertaining for the young set) through Mexico's past and present. Passengers get a close-up look at the Mayan pyramid. **Mariachi Cobre,** a 12-piece band, plays Tuesday to Saturday.

Shops in and around the **Plaza de Los Amigos** (a "moonlit" Mexican *mercado* with a tiered fountain and street lamps) display an array of leather goods, baskets, sombreros, piñatas, pottery, embroidered dresses and blouses, maracas, jewelry, serapes, colorful papier-mâché birds, and blown-glass objects (an artisan occasionally gives demonstrations). The Mexican Tourist Office also provides travel information.

Morocco
Frommer's Rating: A
Recommended Ages: 10–adult

This exotic pavilion has architecture embellished with geometrically patterned tile work, minarets, hand-painted wood ceilings, and brass lighting fixtures. (The King of Morocco took a personal interest in the project and sent royal artisans to help out in its construction, and the result is one of the most authentic atmospheres at the World Showcase.) It's headlined by a replica of the Koutoubia Minaret, the prayer tower of a 12th-century mosque in Marrakech. The Medina (old city), entered via a replica of an arched gateway in Fez, leads to **Fez House** (a traditional Moroccan home) and the narrow, winding streets of the souk, a bustling marketplace where all manner of authentic handcrafted merchandise is on display. Here, you can browse or purchase pottery, brassware, hand-knotted Berber or colorful Rabat carpets, ornate silver and camel-bone boxes, straw baskets, and prayer rugs. There are weaving demonstrations in the souk periodically during the day. The Medina's rectangular courtyard centers on a replica of the ornately tiled Najjarine Fountain in Fez, the setting for musical entertainment.

Treasures of Morocco is a three-times-per-day 35-minute guided tour (1–5pm) that highlights this country's culture, architecture, and history (older kids will find it enjoyable and educational, but this is not for the young set). The pavilion's **Gallery of Arts and History** contains an ever-changing exhibit of Moroccan art, and the Center of Tourism offers a continuous three-screen slide show. Morocco's landscaping includes a formal garden, citrus and olive trees, date palms, and banana plants. On the entertainment side, **Mo'Rockin'** plays Arabian rock music on traditional instruments on Tuesday through Saturday.

Norway
Frommer's Rating: B+
Recommended Ages: 10–adult

This pavilion is centered on a picturesque cobblestone courtyard. A *stavekirke* (stave church), styled after the 13th-century Gol Church of Hallingdal, has changing exhibits. A replica of Oslo's 14th-century **Akershus Castle,** next to a cascading woodland waterfall, is the setting for the featured restaurant (p. 113). Other buildings simulate the red-roofed cottages of Bergen and the timber-sided farm buildings of the Nordic woodlands.

Maelstrom, a boat ride in a dragon-headed Viking vessel, traverses Norway's fjords and mythical forests to the music of Peer Gynt. Along the way, you'll see images of polar bears prowling the shore, then trolls cast a spell on the boat. The

> ### ⓘ Tips   Stay Tuned
>
> Disney hasn't added a new "nation" to World Showcase since Norway became the 11th country in 1988. But the latest buzz has Spain possibly becoming the 12th, with a pavilion that would blend the city of Toledo with some architectural highlights of Madrid and Barcelona. Call it another (potential) cash cow: Disney didn't pay to build the other countries (it charged the sponsoring companies and countries $50 million and up). Disney also doesn't pay any of the operating costs. But the Magic Mick collects rent and a share of all merchandise sales.

watercraft crashes through a narrow gorge and spins into the North Sea, where a storm is in progress. (This is a relatively calm ride that's fine for all but the littlest kids, though it's not recommended for expectant mothers or folks with heart, neck, or back problems.) The storm abates, and passengers disembark safely to a 10th-century Viking village to view the 5-minute 70mm film *Norway*, which documents 1,000 years of history. **Spelmanns Gledje** entertains with Norwegian folk music.

Shops sell hand-knit wool hats and sweaters, troll dolls, toys (there's a Lego table where kids can play), woodcarvings, Scandinavian foods, and jewelry.

United Kingdom
Frommer's Rating: B
Recommended Ages: 8–adult

The U.K. pavilion takes you to Merry Olde England through **Britannia Square,** a London-style park with a copper-roof gazebo bandstand, a stereotypical red phone booth, and a statue of the Bard. Four centuries of architecture are represented along quaint cobblestone streets; there's a traditional British pub; and a formal garden with low box hedges in geometric patterns, flagstone paths, and a stone fountain replicates the landscaping of 16th- and 17th-century palaces. Of special interest for the kids is a small, traditional hedge maze that features topiaries shaped like Disney characters at the back of the pavilion. **Note:** Characters, especially from British stories, such as *Winnie the Pooh* and *Alice in Wonderland,* tend to show up here quite often.

The **British Invasion,** a group that impersonates the Beatles daily except Sunday; pub pianist **Pam Brody** (Tues, Thurs, Fri, and Sun); and the comedic acting troupe, the **World Showcase Players** (daily), provide entertainment. High Street and Tudor Lane shops display a broad sampling of British merchandise, including toy soldiers, Paddington bears, personalized coats of arms, Scottish clothing (cashmere and Shetland sweaters, golf wear, tams, and tartans), English china, Waterford crystal, and pub items such as tankards, dartboards, and the like. A tea shop occupies a replica of Anne Hathaway's thatched-roof 16th-century cottage in Stratford-on-Avon. Other emporia represent the Georgian, Victorian, Queen Anne, and Tudor periods. Background music ranges from "Greensleeves" to the Beatles.

U.S.A.—The American Adventure
Frommer's Rating: A
Recommended Ages: 8–adult

Housed in a vast Georgian-style structure, **The American Adventure** is a 29-minute dramatization of U.S. history, utilizing a 72-foot rear-projection screen, rousing music, and a large cast of lifelike audio-Animatronic figures, including narrators Mark Twain and Ben Franklin. The adventure begins with the voyage of the *Mayflower* and encompasses major historic events. You'll view Jefferson writing the Declaration of Independence, Matthew Brady photographing a family about to be divided by the Civil War, the stock market crash of 1929, Pearl Harbor, and the *Eagle* heading toward the moon. Teddy Roosevelt discusses the need for national parks. Susan B. Anthony speaks out on women's rights; Frederick Douglass, on slavery; and Chief Joseph, on the plight of Native Americans. It's one of Disney's best historical productions and offers great entertainment for the entire family. Entertainment includes the **Spirit of America Fife & Drum Corps** and **Voices of Liberty,** an a cappella group that sings patriotic songs.

Formal gardens shaded by live oaks, sycamores, elms, and holly complement the 18th-century architecture. **Heritage Manor Gifts** sells autographed presidential photographs, needlepoint samplers, quilts, pottery, candles, Davy Crockett hats, American history books, historically costumed dolls, classic political campaign buttons, and vintage newspapers with banner headlines such as "Nixon Resigns!"

A NIGHTTIME SPECTACLE

IllumiNations *Moments*
Frommer's Rating: A+
Recommended Ages: 3–adult
Little has changed since Epcot's millennium version of IllumiNations ended on January 1, 2001. This 13-minute grand nightcap continues to be a blend of fireworks, lasers, and fountains in a display that's signature Disney. The show is worth the crowds that flock to the parking lot when it's over (just be sure to keep a firm grip on young kids). *Tip:* Stake your claim to your favorite viewing area a half-hour before show time (listed in your entertainment schedule). The ones near Showcase Plaza have a head start for the exits. Another good place for viewing the show is the terrace at the Rose & Crown Pub in the United Kingdom (p. 114). **Jake Rating:** "That was almost as cool as the Magic Kingdom's fireworks." (With the added dimensions—lasers and fountains—we'd have to say it rivals the Wishes fireworks display [p. 176]!)

5 Disney–MGM Studios

You'll probably see the Tower of Terror and the Earrfel Tower, a water tank with mouse ears, before you enter this park, which Disney bills as "the Hollywood that never was and always will be." Once inside, you'll find pulse-quickening rides such as **Rock 'n' Roller Coaster,** movie- and TV-themed shows such as **Jim Henson's Muppet*Vision 3D,** and a spectacular laser-light show called **Fantasmic!** The main streets include Hollywood and Sunset boulevards, where movie sets remember the golden age of Hollywood. New York Street is lined

---

Tips **Cruise Control**

There are two cruise-style options for watching Epcot's IllumiNations fireworks display (below) from World Showcase Lagoon. You can charter the 1930s vintage speedboat *Breathless* ($180, up to seven people) or catch the show aboard a less romantic but cheaper pontoon boat ($120, up to 10 people). Both last 45 to 50 minutes and you must rent the entire boat for your family or find your own boat mates. For information or to reserve a boat, call © 407/939-7529.

Disney–MGM Studios Theme Park

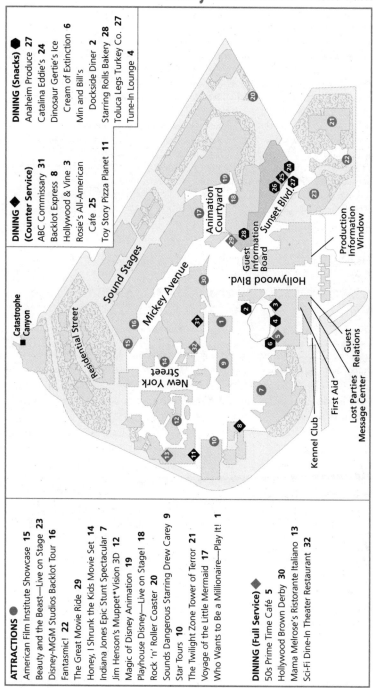

ATTRACTIONS ●

American Film Institute Showcase **15**
Beauty and the Beast—Live on Stage **23**
Disney-MGM Studios Backlot Tour **16**
Fantasmic! **22**
The Great Movie Ride **29**
Honey, I Shrunk the Kids Movie Set **14**
Indiana Jones Epic Stunt Spectacular **7**
Jim Henson's Muppet*Vision 3D **12**
Magic of Disney Animation **19**
Playhouse Disney—Live on Stage! **18**
Rock 'n' Roller Coaster **20**
Sounds Dangerous Starring Drew Carey **9**
Star Tours **10**
The Twilight Zone Tower of Terror **21**
Voyage of the Little Mermaid **17**
Who Wants to Be a Millionaire—Play It! **1**

DINING (Full Service) ◆

50s Prime Time Café **5**
Hollywood Brown Derby **30**
Mama Melrose's Ristorante Italiano **13**
Sci-Fi Dine-In Theater Restaurant **32**

DINING (Counter Service) ◆

ABC Commissary **31**
Backlot Express **8**
Hollywood & Vine **3**
Rosie's All-American Cafe **25**
Toy Story Pizza Planet **11**

DINING (Snacks) ⬡

Anaheim Produce **27**
Catalina Eddie's **24**
Dinosaur Gertie's Ice Cream of Extinction **6**
Min and Bill's Dockside Diner **2**
Starring Rolls Bakery **28**
Toluca Legs Turkey Co. **27**
Tune-In Lounge **4**

195

with miniature renditions of Gotham's landmarks (the Empire State, Flatiron, and Chrysler buildings) and characters peddling knock-off watches. You'll find some of the best street performing in the Disney parks here. More importantly, it's a working movie and TV studio where shows are occasionally in production.

Arrive early. Unlike Epcot, MGM's 154 acres of attractions are easier to see in 1 day. The parking lot reaches to the gate, but trams serve most areas. Pay attention to your parking location; this lot isn't as well marked as the Magic Kingdom's. Again, write your lot and row number on something you can find at day's end.

If you don't get a *Disney–MGM Studios Guide Map* and entertainment schedule as you enter the park, you can pick one up at Guest Relations or most shops. Straight off, check show times and work out an entertainment schedule based on highlight attractions and geographical proximity. Our favorite MGM restaurants are described in chapter 5, "Family-Friendly Dining."

There's a Tip Board listing the day's shows, ride closings, and other information at the corner of Hollywood and Sunset boulevards.

HOURS   The park is usually open from 9am to at least 6 or 7pm, with extended hours sometimes as late as midnight during holidays and summer.

TICKET PRICES   A 1-day park ticket is $52 for adults, $42 for children 3 to 9. Kids under 3 get in free.

SERVICES & FACILITIES IN DISNEY–MGM STUDIOS

ATMs   ATMs accepting cards from banks using the Cirrus, Honor, and PLUS systems are to the right of the entrance and near Toy Story Pizza Planet.

Baby Care   MGM has a small Baby Care Center to the left of the entrance where you'll find facilities for nursing and changing. Disposable diapers, formula, baby food, and pacifiers are for sale. Changing tables are also in all women's restrooms and some men's restrooms.

Cameras & Film   Film and Kodak disposable cameras are available throughout the park.

First Aid   The First Aid Center, staffed by registered nurses, is in the Entrance Plaza adjoining Guest Relations and the Baby Care Center.

Lockers   Lockers are located alongside Oscar's Classic Car Souvenirs, to the right of the Entrance Plaza after you pass through the turnstiles. The cost is $7, including a $2 deposit.

Lost Children   Lost children at Disney–MGM Studios are taken to Guest Relations, where lost children logbooks are kept. *Children under 7 should wear name-tags.*

Package Pickup   Any large purchase can be sent by the shop clerk to Guest Relations in the Entrance Plaza. Allow 3 hours for delivery.

Parking   It's $7 a day for cars, light trucks, and vans; $8 for RVs.

Pet Care   Day accommodations for $6 are offered at kennels to the left and just outside the entrance (© **407/824-6568**). There are also four other kennels in the WDW complex. Proof of vaccinations is required.

Strollers   Strollers can be rented at Oscar's Super Service, inside the main entrance, for $8 for a single and $15 for a double, including a $1 deposit.

Wheelchair Rental   Wheelchairs are rented at Oscar's Super Service inside the main entrance. The cost for regular chairs is $7 a day, including a $1 deposit. Electric wheelchairs rent for $40 including a $10 refundable deposit.

MAJOR ATTRACTIONS & SHOWS

American Film Institute Showcase
Frommer's Rating: C
Recommended Ages: 10–adult

This shop and exhibit area is the final stop on the Backlot Tour (see below) and looks at the efforts of the editors, cinematographers, producers, and directors whose names roll by in the blur of credits. It also showcases the work of the American Film Institute's Lifetime Achievement Award winners, including Bette Davis, Jack Nicholson, and Elizabeth Taylor. A special exhibit here, **"Villains: Movie Characters You Love to Hate,"** features the costumes and props of several notable bad guys, including Darth Vader.

Beauty and the Beast—Live on Stage
Frommer's Rating: B+
Recommended Ages: All ages

A 1,500-seat covered amphitheater is the home of this 30-minute live Broadway-style production of *Beauty and the Beast* that's adapted from the movie. Musical highlights from the show include the rousing "Be Our Guest" opening number and the poignant title song featured in the romantic waltz scene finale. The sets and costumes are lavish, and the production numbers are pretty spectacular. It's a treat for the whole family and a great place to rest your feet. There are usually four or five shows a day.

Disney–MGM Studios Backlot Tour
Frommer's Rating: B+
Recommended Ages: 6–adult

This 35-minute tram tour takes you behind the scenes for a close-up look at the vehicles, props, costumes, sets, and special effects used in movies and TV shows. On many days, you'll see costume makers at work in the wardrobe department (Disney has around two million garments here). But the real fun begins when the tram heads for **Catastrophe Canyon,** where an earthquake in the heart of oil country causes canyon walls to rumble. A raging oil fire, massive explosions, torrents of rain, and flash floods threaten you and other riders before you're taken behind the scenes to see how filmmakers use special effects to make such disasters (little kids may get a little intimidated if they aren't warned in advance). The preshow is almost as interesting. While waiting in line, you can watch entertaining videos hosted by several TV and movie stars. The Backlot Tour is a solid ride that's of the same type as Universal Studios Florida's Earthquake—The Big One (p. 230).

Andy Rating: "Holy cow! Do they really feel like that?" (In our lifetimes in Florida, the Richter scale hasn't gotten into whole numbers, and *we don't* want to know what it's like in California . . . or beyond.)

Fantasmic! *(Moments*
Frommer's Rating: A+
Recommended Ages: All ages

Disney mixes heroes, villains, stunt performers, choreography, laser lights, and fireworks into a spectacular end-of-the-day extravaganza. This is a 25-minute visual feast where the Magic Mickey comes to life in a show featuring shooting comets, great balls of fire (our apologies to Jerry Lee), and animated fountains that really charge the audience. The cast includes 50 performers, a giant dragon, a king cobra, and one million gallons of water, just about all of which are orchestrated by a sorcerer mouse that looks more than remotely familiar. You'll probably

> **Tips Dinner & a Show**
>
> At press time, Disney was offering preferred seating at the end-of-the-day spectacular, **Fantasmic!**, along with a fixed-price dinner at one of Disney–MGM's sit-down restaurants. All you need to do is make Priority Seating arrangements (© **407/939-3463**) and request the Fantasmic! package for the Hollywood Brown Derby ($36.99 adults, $9.99 kids 3–11), Mama Melrose's Ristorante Italiano ($28.99 adults, $9.99 kids), or Hollywood & Vine ($21.99 adults, $9.99 kids). You'll get your line pass at the restaurant and instructions on getting to the special entrance to the preferred seating area of the show.
>
> **Note:** The prices above are for a fixed-price meal and do not include sales tax, tip, or alcoholic beverages; if you order off the menu, you'll pay more. The prices also don't include a reserved seat at Fantasmic!, only a pass that will get you into the preferred seating area (you must arrive at least 30 min. in advance—a much shorter wait than usual, and a boon if you have restless kids).

recognize other characters as well as musical scores from Disney movie classics such as *Fantasia, Pinocchio, Snow White and the Seven Dwarfs, The Little Mermaid,* and *The Lion King.* You'll also shudder at the animated villainy of Jafar, Cruella De Vil, and Maleficent in the battle of good versus evil, part of which is projected onto huge, water-mist screens. The amphitheater holds 9,000 souls, and during holidays and summers it's often standing-room-only, so arrive early. (There is sometimes an additional show earlier in the evening.) **Note:** The show's loud pyrotechnics may frighten younger children.

Andy Rating: (He was wide-eyed and smiling, but silent. This isn't a good show for anyone with sensitive ears, including adults. If someone in your family has that problem, bring earplugs or cotton balls to deaden the sound effects.)

The Great Movie Ride
Frommer's Rating: C for most, B for adults who love classics
Recommended Ages: 8–adult
Film footage and 50 audio-Animatronic replicas of movie stars are used to re-create some of the most famous scenes in filmdom on this 22-minute ride through movie history. You'll relive magic moments from the 1930s through the present, starring Gene Kelly, Jimmy Cagney, John Wayne, Julie Andrews, Brando, and arguably the best Tarzan, Johnny Weissmuller, giving his trademark yell while swinging across the jungle. The action is enhanced by special effects, and outlaws hijack your tram en route. So pay attention when the conductor warns, "Fasten your seat belts. It's going to be a bumpy night." The setting is a full-scale reproduction of Hollywood's famous Mann's Chinese Theatre, complete with handprints of the stars out front. **Tip:** Some of the movie scenes, especially the ones from *Alien,* can frighten young kids.

Honey, I Shrunk the Kids Movie Set
Frommer's Rating: B+
Recommended Ages: 3–10
Let the kids catch up to you in the exhaustion category as they ride talking ants, slide through a film canister, get slimed by a giant dog's sinuses, crawl through LEGO-ville, and get chilled by a sneaky hose. It's a fabulous larger-than-life playground that young kids will love.

Indiana Jones Epic Stunt Spectacular
Frommer's Rating: A+
Recommended Ages: 6–adult
Visitors get a peek into the world of movie stunts in this dramatic 30-minute show, which re-creates major scenes from the Indiana Jones series. The show opens on an elaborate Mayan temple backdrop. Indy crashes onto the set via a rope, and, as he searches with a torch for the golden idol, he runs into booby traps. Then a boulder straight out of *Raiders of the Lost Ark* chases him! The set is dismantled to reveal a colorful Cairo marketplace where a sword fight ensues, and the action includes virtuoso bullwhip maneuvers, gunfire, and a truck bursting into flames. An explosive finale takes place in a desert scenario. Music and a narrative enhance the action. Throughout this, guests get to see how elaborate stunts are pulled off. Arrive early and sit near the stage if you want a shot at being picked as an audience participant. Alas, it's *a job for adults only.*
Jake Rating: "That guy kicks you know what!" (This show definitely is an adrenaline booster.)

Jim Henson's Muppet*Vision 3D
Frommer's Rating: A+
Recommended Ages: All ages
This must-see film stars Kermit and Miss Piggy in a delightful marriage of Jim Henson's puppets and Disney audio-Animatronics, special-effects wizardry, 70mm film, and cutting-edge 3-D technology. The action includes flying Muppets, cream pies, and cannonballs, plus high winds, fiber-optic fireworks, bubble showers, even an actual spray of water. Kermit is the host; Miss Piggy sings "Dream a Little Dream of Me"; Statler and Waldorf critique the action (which includes numerous mishaps and disasters); and Nicki Napoleon and his Emperor Penguins (a full Muppet orchestra) provide music from the pit. In the preshow area, guests view an entertaining video on overhead monitors. Note the Muppet fountain out front and the Muppet version of a Rousseau painting inside. The 25-minute show (including the 12-min. video preshow) runs continuously.
Andy Rating: "I almost touched Kermit." (That's how realistic the in-your-face, 3-D action is!) If your child won't mind a little live interaction, Sweetums, the giant but friendly Muppet monster, usually interacts with a few kids sitting in the front rows during the show.

Magic of Disney Animation
Frommer's Rating: B
Recommended Ages: 8–adult
At press time, Disney was revamping this attraction, ditching the old but beloved tour hosted by Walter Cronkite and Robin Williams in favor of more interactive options. Final details were not available, but the new attraction is set to feature characters from Disney's *Mulan* interacting with a live actor and a video on the making of that film. Visitors will also get a chance to watch real animators at work and ask questions about the animation process before attempting their own Disney character drawings while under the supervision of a working animator.

In the Words of Walt Disney
A family picture is one the kids can take their parents to see and not be embarrassed.

(Finds Find the Hidden Mickeys

Hidden Mickeys (HM, for short) started as an inside joke among early Disney Imagineers and soon became a park tradition. Today, dozens of subtle Mickey images—usually silhouettes of his world-famous ears, profile, or full figure—are hidden (more or less) in attractions and resorts throughout the Walt Disney empire. No one knows how many, because sometimes they exist only in the eye of the beholder. See how many Hidden Mickeys you can locate during your visit (keeping track of them is a cool game for kids and will keep them entertained throughout their visit). And be sharp-eyed about it. Those bubbles on your souvenir mug might be forming one. Here are a few to get you started:

In the Magic Kingdom
- In the Haunted Mansion banquet scene, check out the arrangement of the plate and adjoining saucers on the table.
- In the Africa scene of It's a Small World, note the purple flowers on a vine on the elephant's left side.
- While riding Splash Mountain, look for Mickey lying on his back in the pink clouds to the right of the *Zip-A-Dee Lady* paddle-wheeler.

At Epcot
- In Imagination, check out the little girl's dress in the lobby film of *Honey, I Shrunk the Audience,* one of five HMs in this pavilion.
- In The Land pavilion, don't miss the small stones in front of the Native American man on a horse and the baseball cap of the man driving a harvester in the *Circle of Life* film.
- As you cruise through the Mexico pavilion on El Rio del Tiempo, notice the arrangement of three clay pots in the marketplace scene.
- In Maelstrom in the Norway pavilion, a Viking wears Mickey ears in the wall mural facing the loading dock.

Playhouse Disney—Live on Stage!
Frommer's Rating: B
Recommended Ages: 2–5
Younger audiences love this 20-minute show where they meet characters from Bear in the Big Blue House, The Book of Pooh, and other stories. The show encourages preschoolers to dance, sing, and play along with the cast. If your kids are the right age, don't miss it. The action happens several times a day. Check your show schedule.

Rock 'n' Roller Coaster (Moments
Frommer's Rating: A+
Recommended Ages: 10–adult
Some say this is one of Disney's attempts to go head to head with Universal Orlando's Islands of Adventure. True or not, this inverted roller coaster, The Twilight Zone Tower of Terror (see below), and Epcot's Mission: Space (p. 185) are the best thrill rides WDW has to offer. Kids looking for an adrenaline rush

- There are four HMs inside Spaceship Earth, one of them in the Renaissance scene, on the page of a book behind the sleeping monk. Try to find the other three.

At Disney–MGM Studios

- On the Great Movie Ride, there's an HM on the window above the bank in the gangster scene.
- At Jim Henson's Muppet*Vision 3D, take a good look at the top of the sign listing five reasons for turning in your 3-D glasses, and note the balloons in the film's final scene.
- In the Twilight Zone Tower of Terror, note the bell for the elevator behind Rod Serling in the film. There are at least five other HMs in this attraction.
- Outside Rock 'n' Roller Coaster, look for two in the rotunda's tile floor.
- By the way, the park's least Hidden Mickey is what's called the Earr-fel Tower, Disney–MGM Studios' tall water tower, which is fitted with a huge pair of Mouseket-EARS.

In Animal Kingdom

- Look at The Boneyard in DinoLand U.S.A., where a fan and two hard hats form an HM.
- There are 25 Hidden Mickeys at Rafiki's Planet Watch, where Mickey lurks in the murals, tree trunks, and paintings of animals.

In the Resort Areas

- HMs are on the weather vane atop the Grand Floridian Resort & Spa's convention center, in the interactive fountains at the entrance to Downtown Disney Marketplace, and one forms a giant sand trap next to the green at the Magnolia Golf Course's sixth hole.

If you're Internet savvy, learn more at **www.hiddenmickeys.org**.

will demand to ride it. It's a fast-and-furious indoor ride in semidarkness. You sit in a 24-passenger "stretch limo" outfitted with 120 speakers that blare Aerosmith at 32,000 watts! Flashing lights deliver a variety of messages and warnings, including "prepare to merge as you've never merged before." Then, faster than you can scream "I want to live!" (2.8 sec., actually), you shoot from 0 to 60 mph and into the first gut-tightening inversion at 5Gs. It's a real launch (sometimes of lunch) followed by a wild ride through a make-believe California freeway system. One of three inversions cuts through an "O" in the Hollywood sign. The ride lasts 3 minutes, 12 seconds, the running time of Aerosmith's hit, "Sweet Emotion." ***Note:*** Riders must be at least 48 inches tall, and expectant moms and people prone to motion sickness or those with heart, neck, or back problems shouldn't try this ride.

Jake Rating: "So that's what an F-14 feels like?" (Well, it's something of a stretch of another kind, but the Disney hype says riding this coaster is similar to sitting atop an F-14 Tomcat.)

Sounds Dangerous Starring Drew Carey
Frommer's Rating: C+
Recommended Ages: All ages

Drew Carey provides laughs while dual audio technology provides some hair-raising effects during this 12-minute show at ABC Sound Studios. You'll feel like you're right in the middle of the action of a TV pilot featuring undercover police work and plenty of mishaps. Even when the picture disappears and the theater is plunged into darkness, you continue on Detective Charlie Foster's chase via headphones that show off "3-D" sound effects. Most of this attraction takes place in total darkness, which may disturb young kids.

Tip: After the show is over, check out **Sound Works,** which offers interactive activities that allows you and your kids to experiment with different sound effects.

Star Tours
Frommer's Rating: B
Recommended Ages: 8–adult

Cutting edge when it opened, this galactic journey based on the original *Star Wars* trilogy (George Lucas collaborated on the ride) is now a couple of rungs below the latest technology, but it's still fun. The preshow, which should eventually be updated with characters from *Episode II: Attack of the Clones,* now has R2-D2 and C-3PO running an intergalactic travel agency (it offers some of the best detailing of any preshow at Disney World). Once inside, you board a 40-seat spacecraft for a journey that greets you with sudden drops, crashes, and oncoming laser blasts as it careens out of control. This is another of those virtual-simulator rides where you go nowhere, but feel like you do. If you or your kids have sensitive stomachs, try to ride up front, where you won't get tossed around as much. *Note:* Riders must be at least 40 inches tall. Also, expectant mothers and people with neck, back, and heart problems or those prone to motion sickness shouldn't ride.

The Twilight Zone Tower of Terror *Moments*
Frommer's Rating: A+
Recommended Ages: 10–adult

This is a truly stomach-lifting (and dropping) ride, and Disney continues to fine-tune it to make it even better: A January 2003 upgrade added random drop sequences with individual features, meaning you might get a different fright from ride to ride. The legend says that during a violent storm on Halloween night 1939, lightning struck the Hollywood Tower Hotel, causing an entire wing and an elevator full of people to disappear. And you're about to meet them as you become the star in a special episode of . . . *The Twilight Zone.* En route to this formerly grand hotel, guests walk past overgrown landscaping and faded signs that once pointed the way to stables and tennis courts; the vines over the entrance trellis are dead; and the hotel is a crumbling ruin. Eerie corridors lead

---

Tips **Tune Time**

Weekdays from noon to 4pm, you can watch B. B. Good broadcast his Radio Disney show live from a studio next to Sounds Dangerous Starring Drew Carey. You can tune into the show and others on Radio Disney at 990 on your AM dial.

Tips **Coming Soon**

At press time, Disney–MGM Studios announced it would be adding a show very similar to the **Moteurs . . . Action! Stunt Show Spectacular** at Disneyland Paris. The attraction uses 20 cars and 40 stunt performers in a story line that involves a lot of high speed chases, crashes, walls of fire, and assorted other mayhem. The show will be staged in a revamped section of Disney's Backlot beginning sometime in 2005.

to a dimly lit library, where you can hear a storm raging outside. After various spooky adventures, the ride ends in a dramatic climax: a 13-story free fall in stages. Some believe this rivals Rock 'n' Roller Coaster in the thrill department (one of the major designers of the tower admitted to us that he's too scared to ride his own creation). At 199 feet, it's the tallest ride in the World, and it's a grade above Doctor Doom's Fearfall at Islands of Adventure. *Note:* You must be at least 40 inches tall to ride, and expectant moms and people prone to motion sickness or those with heart, neck, or back problems shouldn't try to tackle it. If you're scared of heights or darkness, this one isn't for you either.

Voyage of the Little Mermaid
Frommer's Rating: B+
Recommended Ages: 4–adult

Hazy lighting creates an underwater effect in a reef-walled theater and helps set the mood for this charming musical based on the Disney feature film, which charms even older kids and adults. The show combines live performers with more than 100 puppets, movie clips, and innovative special effects. Sebastian sings the movie's Academy Award–winning song, "Under the Sea"; the ethereal Ariel shares her dream of becoming human in a live performance of "Part of Your World"; and the evil Ursula, 12 feet tall and 10 feet wide, belts out "Poor Unfortunate Soul." It has a happy ending, as most of the young audience knows it will; they've seen the movie. This 17-minute show is a great place to rest your feet on a hot day, and you get misted inside the theater to further cool you off.

Who Wants to Be a Millionaire—Play It!
Frommer's Rating: B+
Recommended Ages: 8–adult

Contestants can't win $1 million, but they can win points used to buy prizes ranging from collectible pins to a leather jacket or a 3-night cruise on one of Disney–owned ABC TV's game show, the theme-park version features lifelines (such as asking the audience or calling a stranger on two phones set up in the park). Contestants get a shot at up to 15 multiple-choice questions in the climb to the top. Games run continuously in the 600-seat studio. Audience members play along on keypads. And unlike the TV show, the entire audience competes to get in the hot seat; the fastest to answer qualifying questions become contestants.

PARADES, PLAYGROUNDS & MORE
Disney Stars and Motor Cars is a motorcade filled with a procession of Disney characters in their chariots. The parade is popular enough that if you decide to skip it, you'll find shorter lines at the park's primo rides (check the parade schedule in your park map).

Moments **You Want Characters?**

Characters and hot spots change, but as of this writing, the best bets at Disney–MGM Studios are:

Toy Story Friends   Near Mama Melrose's Ristorante Italiano. See the handout Times Guide for the schedule.

Mickey & Friends   Mickey Avenue between Backlot Tour and Who Wants to Be a Millionaire. See the handout Times Guide.

6 Animal Kingdom

Disney's fourth major park combines animals, elaborate landscapes, and a handful of rides to create yet another reason that many WDW resort-goers don't venture outside this World. The bulk of the $800 million park opened in 1998. Its most recent "land," Asia, opened in 1999. Speaking of Asia, it will be the home of Animal Kingdom's long-awaited first true thrill ride. Expected to debut in 2006, **Expedition Everest** will be a high-speed, coaster-like train ride that moves forward and backward through glaciers, waterfalls, and canyons, climaxing with an encounter with a yeti. Even with that announcement, some visitors (and we're among them!) believe there isn't enough here to justify this being in the same league as other theme parks that charge $52 per adult.

But don't tell Disney CEO Michael Eisner. He says Animal Kingdom is the next best thing to going to Africa. Even those straddling the fence on this issue might suggest King Mike's losing touch with the real world. Sure, Animal Kingdom is different as Orlando theme parks go because it has exotic wildlife. There are also a couple of great shows—including Festival of the Lion King. And if the animals are cooperative, you can have an up-close encounter that you aren't likely to find in another theme park.

Animal Kingdom surely ranks as one of the top two critter parks in Florida when it comes to volume and diversity of things to do. Busch Gardens in Tampa (a $51.95 per-adult, $42.95 per-child entry) is the other. While that park will be discussed in depth in chapter 11, "Side Trips from Orlando," we're going to talk about it briefly here for the sake of drawing a few comparisons.

Animal Kingdom is more a park for animals, a conservation venue as much as an attraction. The short of it is that it's not as easy to see the critters here (and let's face it, that's what many of your kids will expect to see). They've been given a lot more cover than at Busch Gardens, so when they want to, they can escape your probing eyes and the heat. The best bet for animal viewing here is to arrive in time for the park's opening, usually 8 or 9am but sometimes earlier, or try to see them near closing. More animals are likely to be on the prowl then than at midday, especially in the heat of summer. *Note:* Both parks offer some shade for the animals, but the amount of cover given to tourists waiting in line is decidedly unimpressive. Arriving early at both parks, especially in summer, will save your family the *very* unpleasant experience of languishing under a blistering sun.

Animal Kingdom wins the battle of shows, with child-pleasing humdingers such as **Tarzan Rocks!** and **Festival of the Lion King.** But Busch Gardens clearly wins the battle of thrill rides. Whereas Animal Kingdom has three (and we're being kind to call two of them "thrill" rides), Busch Gardens has five adult-size roller coasters alone—including Gwazi, a dual wooden coaster.

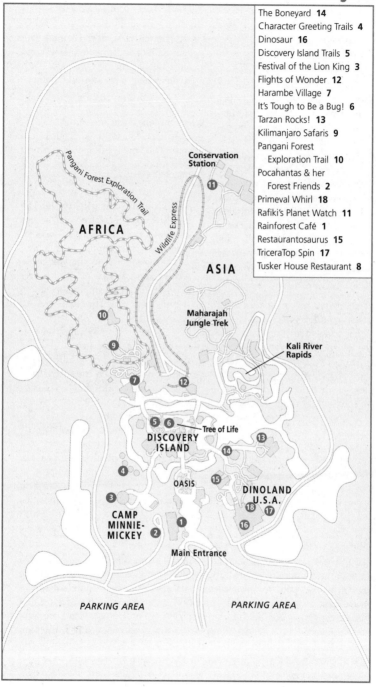

The Boneyard **14**
Character Greeting Trails **4**
Dinosaur **16**
Discovery Island Trails **5**
Festival of the Lion King **3**
Flights of Wonder **12**
Harambe Village **7**
It's Tough to Be a Bug! **6**
Tarzan Rocks! **13**
Kilimanjaro Safaris **9**
Pangani Forest
   Exploration Trail **10**
Pocahantas & her
   Forest Friends **2**
Primeval Whirl **18**
Rafiki's Planet Watch **11**
Rainforest Café **1**
Restaurantosaurus **15**
TriceraTop Spin **17**
Tusker House Restaurant **8**

Pangani Forest Exploration Trail

Conservation Station

⑪

AFRICA

Wildlife Express

ASIA

⑩

Maharajah
Jungle Trek

⑨

Kali River
Rapids

⑦   ⑫

⑤ ⑥ —Tree of Life

**DISCOVERY
ISLAND**

⑬

⑭

④

OASIS

⑮

**DINOLAND
U.S.A.**

③

⑱ ⑰

**CAMP
MINNIE-
MICKEY**

❶

⑯

❷

Main Entrance

PARKING AREA   *PARKING AREA*

Animal Kingdom is more centrally located. Busch Gardens is a 90-minute drive from Orlando, and there isn't as much to see and do elsewhere in Tampa. But even if that city is out of the picture geographically, those of you coming with younger kids and limited time will find more fun at other WDW parks, such as the Magic Kingdom and Disney–MGM, than at Animal Kingdom. Critter lovers, on the other hand, should put this one at the top of their list.

Animal Kingdom is divided into areas: The **Oasis,** a shopping area near the entrance that has limited animal viewing; **Discovery Island,** home of the Tree of Life, which is the park's icon; **Camp Minnie-Mickey,** the Animal Kingdom equivalent of Mickey's Toontown Fair in the Magic Kingdom; **Africa,** the main animal-viewing area, which is dedicated to the wildlife in Africa today; **Asia,** which has a river raft ride, animal exhibits (including Bengal tigers and giant fruit bats), and a bird show; and **Dinoland U.S.A.,** which has rides, games, and the show, Tarzan Rocks!

> **Tips Heat Alert!**
>
> Orlando is one place where you don't want to go for the burn. The scalding Florida sun can get you in many directions. Slather sunscreen on any exposed skin, including your back, shoulders, the backs of your legs, and anywhere else you leave exposed. Make sure infants and toddlers are protected by a hat or a stroller shade. And don't think winter is a safe time—you can get a burn on a chilly day, too.

The park covers more than 500 acres (Busch Gardens has 335), and your feet will tell you that you've covered the territory at the end of the day.

Most of the rides are accessible to guests with disabilities, but the hilly terrain, large crowds, narrow passages, and long hikes can make for a strenuous day if there's a wheelchair-bound person in your party or your schlepping lots of baby stuff. Anyone with neck or back problems as well as pregnant women may not be able to enjoy rides like **Kali River Rapids** and **Dinosaur.**

The 145-foot-tall **Tree of Life** is in the center of the park. It's an intricately carved free-form representation of animals, handcrafted by a team of artists over the period of a year. It's not nearly as tall or imposing as the silver golf ball–like dome, also known as Spaceship Earth, which has come to symbolize Epcot, or Cinderella Castle in the Magic Kingdom. The tree is impressive, though, with 8,000 limbs, 103,000 leaves and 325 mammals, reptiles, bugs, birds, dinosaurs, and Mickeys carved in its trunk, limbs, and roots. (One cool game to play with your young kids is to see how many animals they can find represented in the trunk.) For more on the tree, see "Discovery Island," below.

ARRIVING   From the parking lot, walk or (where available) ride one of the trams to the entrance. If you do walk, watch out for the trams and autos, because the lot isn't designed for pedestrians. Also, make certain to note where you parked (section and row). Lot signs aren't as prominent as in the Magic Kingdom, and the rows look alike when you come back out. Upon entering the park, consult the handout guide map for special events or entertainment. If you have questions, ask park staffers.

HOURS   Animal Kingdom is open at least from 8 or 9am to 5pm, but it sometimes stays open an hour or so later.

TICKET PRICES   The ticket prices are $52 for adults, $42 for children 3 to 9. See "Tickets & Passes," earlier in this chapter, for information on multiday options.

SERVICES & FACILITIES IN ANIMAL KINGDOM

ATMs Animal Kingdom has an ATM near Garden Gate Gifts to the right of the entrance. It accepts cards from banks using the Cirrus, Honor, and PLUS systems.

Baby Care The Baby Care Center is located near Creature Comforts gift shop on the west side of the Tree of Life, but as in the other Disney parks, you'll find changing tables in both restrooms, and you can buy disposable diapers at Guest Relations.

Cameras & Film You can drop film off for same-day developing at the Kodak Kiosk in Africa and Garden Gate Gifts near the park entrances. Cameras and film are available in Disney Outfitters in Safari Village; at the Kodak Kiosk in Africa, near the entrance to the Kilimanjaro Safari; and in Garden Gate Gifts.

First Aid The First Aid Center, which is staffed by registered nurses, is located near Creature Comforts gift shop on the west side of the Tree of Life.

Lockers Lockers ($7, including a $2 deposit) are located in Garden Gate Gifts to your right as you enter the park. They're also located to the left, near Rainforest Cafe.

Lost Children A center for lost children is near Creature Comforts at the Baby Care Center on the west side of the Tree of Life. At the risk of rehash, *make your younger kids wear name-tags.*

Package Pickup Any large packages can be sent to the front of the park at Garden Gate Gifts. Allow 3 hours for delivery.

Parking The cost is $7 a day for cars, light trucks, and vans; $8 for RVs.

Pet Care Pet facilities are located outside the park entrance ($6 per day; ✆ **407/824-6568**). There are four other kennels located in the WDW complex. Proof of vaccinations is required.

Strollers Stroller rentals are available at Garden Gate Gifts to the right as you enter the park ($8 for a single, $15 for a double, including a $1 refundable deposit). There are also satellite locations deeper into the park. Ask a Disney employee to steer you.

Wheelchair Rental You can rent wheelchairs at Garden Gate Gifts to the right as you enter the park. Rentals are $7, including a $1 deposit for a standard

Tips **Animal Kingdom Tip Sheet**

1. Arrive at the park's opening or stay until near closing for the best view of the animals.
2. **Kilimanjaro Safaris** is one of the most popular rides and the best place to see a lot of animals in one sitting. But in summer, the animals can be scarce except near park opening and closing times. If you can hoof it there first thing, do it. If not, try late in the day. The same applies to viewing the gorillas on the **Pangani Forest Exploration Trail**.
3. The **Festival of the Lion King** show is a must.
4. Looking for Disney characters? Go to the Character Greeting Trails in **Camp Minnie-Mickey**.

wheelchair; $40 for an electric wheelchair including a $10 deposit (both deposits are refundable). Ask Disney employees for other locations throughout the park.

THE OASIS
This painstakingly designed landscape of streams, grottoes, and mini-waterfalls sets the tone for the rest of the park. This is a good place to see wallabies, tiny deer, giant anteaters, sloths, iguanas, tree kangaroos, otters, and macaws (*if,* we remind *ad nauseum,* you get here early or stay late). But thick cover provides a jungle tone and makes seeing the animals sometimes difficult. There are no rides in this area, and, aside from the animals, it's mainly a pass-through zone. Those guests traveling with eager children will probably have more time to enjoy these exhibits on the way out—if everyone isn't too pooped.

DISCOVERY ISLAND
Like Cinderella Castle in the Magic Kingdom and Spaceship Earth in Epcot, the 14-story **Tree of Life** located here has been designed to be the park's central landmark. The man-made tree and its carved animals are the work of Disney artists. Teams of them worked for a full year creating the various sculptures, and it's worth a stroll on the walks around its roots, but most folks are smart to save it for the end of the day. (Much of it can be seen while you're in line for **It's Tough to Be a Bug!** or on **the Discovery Island Trails.**) The intricate design makes it seem as if a different animal appears from every angle. One of the creators says he expects it to become one of the most photographed works of art in the world. (He's probably a Disney shareholder.) There's a wading pond directly in front of the tree that often features flamingos.

Discovery Island Trails
Frommer's Rating: B
Recommended Ages: All ages
The old, pre-FASTPASS queue for It's Tough to Be a Bug! provides a leisurely path through the root system of the Tree of Life and a chance to see real, not-so-rare critters, such as axis deer, red kangaroos, otters, flamingos, lemurs, Galapagos tortoises, ducks, storks, and cockatoos. Again, the best viewing times are early or late in the day.

It's Tough to Be a Bug!
Frommer's Rating: A
Recommended Ages: 5–adult
This show's cuteness quotient is enough to earn it a B+. But it goes a rung higher thanks to the preshow: To get to the theater, you have to wind around the Tree of Life's 50-foot base, giving you a front-row look at this man-made marvel. After you've passed that, grab your 3-D glasses and settle into a sometimes creepy-crawly seat. Based on the film *A Bug's Life,* the special effects in this multimedia show

---

Tips Dehydration Alert!

Animal Kingdom can get very hot, especially during summer. Bring bottled water (unless you want to pay 2½ times the free-world price) and get refills at fountains inside the park. Remember to bring sunscreen and wide-brimmed hats *for the whole family,* and plan to ride Kali River Rapids during the hottest part of the day (bring a change of clothes as well, because you will get soaked).

are pretty impressive. It's *not a good one for very young kids* (it's dark and loud, and we've seen 4-year-olds reduced to hysteria by the effects) or bug haters, but for others it's a fun, sometimes poignant look at life from a smaller perspective. Flick, Hopper, and the rest of the cast—ants, beetles, and spiders—literally deliver some in-your-face action. And the show's finale always leaves the crowd buzzing.

Andy Rating (upon the appearance of a stink bug): "Oh, that's awful!" (We promise: Unless your sinuses are impacted, it will awaken your sense of smell.)

DINOLAND U.S.A

Enter by passing under Olden Gate Bridge, a 40-foot brachiosaurus reassembled from excavated fossils. Speaking of which, until late summer 1999, this land had three paleontologists working on the very real skeleton of Sue, a monstrously big *Tyrannosaurus rex* unearthed 9 years earlier in the Black Hills of South Dakota. They patched and assembled the bones here because Disney helped pay for the work. Alas, Sue's permanent home is at Chicago's Field Museum, but Dinoland U.S.A. has a replica cast from her 67-million-year-old bones. It's marked as **Dino-Sue** on park guide maps.

The Boneyard
Frommer's Rating: B+ for children, B for parents who need to rest their feet
Recommended Ages: 3–12

Kids love the chance to slip, slither, slide, and slink through this giant playground and dig site where they can discover the real-looking remains of triceratops, T-rex, and other vanished giants. They can even play music on a "xylobone." Contained within a latticework of metal bars and netting, this area is popular, but not as inviting as the *Honey, I Shrunk the Kids* play area in Disney–MGM Studios (p. 198).

Dinosaur
Frommer's Rating: B
Recommended Ages: 8–adult

This ride hurls you through darkness in CTX Rover "time machines" that pass an array of snarling (though sometimes hokey) dinosaurs. Young children may be frightened by the large lizards and the darkness. For now this is as close as Animal Kingdom gets to a thrill ride. Although we know people who like it better than we do, exceptional it isn't—and some find it jarring. As with most things in this Kingdom, there's a message about the frailty of all life forms, including big carnivores. At the end of the journey, a dinosaur, "hitches" a ride back with you. *Note:* You must be 40 inches or taller to climb aboard. Also, expectant mothers and people with neck, back, and heart problems or those prone to motion sickness shouldn't ride.

Jake Rating: "That was pretty cool, but we look goofy in that photo." (If you have the presence of mind to smile when you hear the T-rex roar, your souvenir photo will look a lot better. The cost of one: Ouch! $17 for an 8×10.)

Primeval Whirl
Frommer's Rating: B+
Recommended Ages: 8–adult

Disney introduced this spinning, free-style twin roller coaster in 2002 in an effort to broaden the park's appeal to young kids (odd, as this ride has a pretty tall height minimum). You control the action through its wacky maze of curves, peaks, and dippity-do-dahs, encountering faux asteroids and hokey cutouts of dinosaurs. This is a cross between those old carnival coasters of the '50s and '60s

---

(Fun Fact It Costs to Recycle

The animals here deposit more than 1,600 tons of dung a year. Disney pays a company to haul it away, then buys some of it back as compost for landscaping.

---

and a more daring version of the Barnstormer at Goofy's Wiseacre Farm (p. 172). *Note:* The ride carries a 48-inch height minimum, and expectant moms as well as those with neck, back, or heart problems and folks prone to motion sickness should stay planted on firm ground.

Tarzan Rocks!
Frommer's Rating: A
Recommended Ages: All ages
This 28-minute show pulses with music and occasional aerial theatrics. Phil Collins's movie soundtrack supports a cast of 27, including tumblers, dancers, and in-line skating daredevils who really get the audience into the act. Costumes and music are pretty spectacular, second in Animal Kingdom only to Festival of the Lion King in Camp Minnie-Mickey (see below). On the whole, this is a great outing for the whole family. Our only criticism: When Tarzan does appear, it's clear by his face, physique, and acting ability that he's there more for eye candy than anything. The show is held in the 1,500-seat Theater in the Wild.

TriceraTop Spin
Frommer's Rating: B+ for tykes and parents
Recommended Ages: 2–7
Cut from the same cloth as the Magic Carpets of Aladdin (p. 163), this is another mini-thrill for youngsters (and another ride with long lines). In this case, cars that look like cartoon dinosaurs are attached to arms that circle a hub while moving up and down and all around. This ride, Primeval Whirl, and an arcade-game area make up a Dinoland U.S.A. mini-land called Chester & Hester's Dino-Rama. It's a great spot to take little ones.

CAMP MINNIE-MICKEY
Disney characters are the main attraction in this land designed in the same vein as an Adirondack resort. Aside from those characters, however, this zone for the younger set *isn't as kid-friendly as* rivals Mickey's Toontown Fair in the Magic Kingdom (reviewed earlier in this chapter) or Woody Woodpecker's KidZone in Universal Studios Florida (see "Universal Studios Florida," in chapter 7).

Character Greeting Trails *(Moments*
Frommer's Rating: A for younger kids, parents, and Disney softies
Recommended Ages: 2–8
This is a must-do for people traveling with young children. A variety of Disney characters, from Winnie the Pooh and Pocahontas to Timon and Baloo, have separate trails where you can meet and mingle. Mickey, Minnie, Goofy, and Pluto also make appearances.

Festival of the Lion King *(Finds*
Frommer's Rating: A+
Recommended Ages: All ages
Almost everyone in the audience comes alive when the music starts in this rousing 28-minute show in the Lion King Theater. It's one of the top three theme-park

shows in central Florida and it thrills young and old alike. The production celebrates nature's diversity with a talented, colorfully attired cast of singers, dancers, and life-size critters leading the way to an inspiring singalong that gets the entire audience caught up in the fun. Based loosely on the animated film, this stage show blends the pageantry of a parade with a tribal celebration. The action is on stage as well as moving around the audience. Even though the pavilion has 1,000 seats, it's best to arrive at least 20 minutes early.

Pocahontas and Her Forest Friends

Frommer's Rating: C

Recommended Ages: All ages

The wait can be nightmarish, and the 15-minute show isn't close to the caliber of Festival of the Lion King and Tarzan Rocks! In this one, Pocahontas, Grandmother Willow, and some forest creatures (a raccoon, turkey, porcupine, snake, and some rats) hammer home the importance of treating nature with respect. If you must, go early. The theater only has 350 seats, but they allow standing-room crowds.

AFRICA

Enter through the town of Harambe, a run-down representation of an African coastal village poised on the edge of the 21st century. Costumed employees will greet you as you enter the buildings. The whitewashed structures, built of coral stone and thatched with reed by African craftspeople, surround a central marketplace rich with local wares and colors.

Kilimanjaro Safaris

Frommer's Rating: A+ early or late, B+ other times

Recommended Ages: All ages

Animal Kingdom doesn't have many rides, so calling this the best may sound like a qualified endorsement. But the animals make it a winner as long as your timing is right. They're scarce at midday during most times of the year (cooler months are the exception), so we recommend you ride it as close to the park's opening or closing as possible. Also, if you don't make it in time for one of the first or last journeys, the lines can be incredibly long, so consider using FASTPASS.

Your ride vehicle is a very large truck that takes you through what pretends to be an African landscape (just a few years ago it was a cow pasture). The animals usually seen along the way include black rhinos, hippos, antelopes, Nile crocodiles, zebras, cheetahs, and a pair of lions that may offer half-hearted roars toward some gazelles that are safely out of reach. Again, the theme is heavy on conservation. Early on, a shifting bridge gives riders a cheap thrill; later, there's some drama as you help catch some poachers. While everyone has a good view, photographers may get a few more shots when sitting on the left side of their row (let your kids sit there for a good view).

Tips Pin Mania

Pin buying, collecting, and trading can reach frenzied proportions among Disney fans, including many cast members. All of the theme parks have special locations set aside for the fun, which are marked on the handout guide maps. You can learn more about the madness on the Internet at **www.dizpins.com** and **www.officialdisneypintrading.com**.

Andy Rating: "What is that? It's the ugliest thing I ever saw." (Well, it did have a face only a mother wildebeest could love. Speaking of faces, Andy was wide-eyed during the trip. He'd only seen most of these animals in books before his first Animal Kingdom trip.)

Pangani Forest Exploration Trail *(Finds)*
Frommer's Rating: B+, A if you're lucky enough to see the gorillas
Recommended Ages: All ages

The hippos put on quite a display (and draw a riotous crowd reaction) when they do what comes naturally and use their tails to scatter it over everything above and below the surface. There are other animals here, including ever-active mole rats, but the **lowland gorillas** are the main event. The trail has two gorilla-viewing areas: One sports a family, including a 500-pound silverback, his ladies, and his children; the other has bachelors. Guests who are unaware of the treasures that lie herein often skip or rush through it, missing a chance to see some magnificent creatures. That said, they're not always cooperative, especially in hot weather, when they spend most of the day in shady areas out of view. There's also a new **Endangered Animal Rehabilitation Centre** with Colobus and Mona monkeys. Most children are usually delighted if they catch a glimpse of the playful meerkats, who young kids will recognize as the model for Timon in *The Lion King*. **Note:** The walk and frequent dearth of animal sightings can make this the wrong choice for families with restless little ones.

> **Fun Fact   Did You Know?**
>
> Tobacco products aren't the only things unavailable in the theme parks. You can't buy chewing or bubble gum either. It seems too many guests stuck it under tables, benches, and chairs—or tossed it on sidewalks, where it often hitched a ride on the soles of the unsuspecting.

Rafiki's Planet Watch *(Overrated)*
Frommer's Rating: C
Recommended Ages: All ages

Board an open-sided train (the Wildlife Express) near Pangani Forest Exploration Trail for a trip to the back edge of the park, which has three attractions. **Conservation Station** offers a behind-the-scenes look at how Disney cares for animals (and the entrance mural is loaded with Hidden Mickeys). You'll pass nurseries and veterinarian stations. But these facilities need to be staffed to be interesting, and that's not always the case. **Habitat Habit!** is a trail with small animals such as cotton-top tamarins. The **Affection Section**'s petting zoo has rare goats and potbelly pigs.

ASIA

Disney's Imagineers have outdone themselves in creating the kingdom of **Anandapur.** The intricately painted artwork at the front is appealing, and it also seems to make the lines move a tad faster.

Flights of Wonder
Frommer's Rating: B
Recommended Ages: All ages

This live-animal action show has undergone several transformations since the park opened. It's a low-key break from the madness and has a few laughs, including Groucho the African yellow-nape, who entertains the audience with his

---

Fun Fact **Cool Trivia**

Two things you might hear during your day in the park: Bugs make up 80% of the real animal kingdom, and cheetahs are the only great cats that purr. Both are true.

---

op-*parrot*-ic a cappella solos, and the just-above-your-head soaring of a Harris hawk and a Eurasian eagle owl. Young kids will especially enjoy it.

Kali River Rapids
Frommer's Rating: B+
Recommended Ages: 6–adult
Here's a pretty darn good raft ride—slightly better, we think, than Congo River Rapids at Busch Gardens in Tampa (p. 300), though not quite as good as Popeye & Bluto's Bilge-Rat Barges at Islands of Adventure (p. 243). Its churning water mimics real rapids, and optical illusions have you wondering if you're about to go over the falls. The ride begins with a peaceful tour of lush foliage, but soon you're dipping and dripping as your tiny craft is tossed and turned. You *will* get wet. (Bring a plastic garbage bag for your valuables or store them in a locker before riding. The rafts' center storage areas alone likely won't keep them dry.) The lines can be long, but keep your head up and enjoy the marvelous art overhead and on beautiful murals. *Note:* There's a 38-inch height minimum, and expectant moms and people with neck, back, and heart problems or those prone to motion sickness shouldn't ride it.
Jake Rating: "Wow, the water is *c-c-c-cold!* But the ride is a blast." (Made better, post ride, when he and his brother, Andy, manned the water cannons near the exit and fired at other raft riders.)

Maharajah Jungle Trek
Frommer's Rating: B
Recommended Ages: 6–adults
Disney keeps its promise to provide up-close views of animals with this exhibit. If you don't show up in the midday heat, you may see Bengal tigers through a wall of thick glass, while nothing but air separates you from dozens of giant fruit bats hanging in what appears to be a courtyard. Some have wingspans of 6 feet. (If you or your kids have a phobia, you can bypass this, though the bats are harmless.) There are lots of spots for your kids to get good views of the animals. Guides are on hand to answer questions, and you can also check a brochure that lists the animals you may spot; it's available on your right as you enter. You'll be asked to "recycle" it as you exit.

PARADES
Mickey's Jammin' Jungle Parade at Animal Kingdom is an interactive street party featuring characters and animals on expedition.

7 Disney Water Parks

Walt Disney World has two renowned water parks in which guests can cool off: **Typhoon Lagoon** and **Blizzard Beach.** The parks have attracted more than 50 million people since they opened, and both offer a slate of cool rides, and good swimming areas, including great spots to take young kids. *Note:* All of the attractions mentioned in this section can be found on the "Walt Disney World Parks & Attractions" map on p. 149.

TYPHOON LAGOON

Ahoy swimmers, floaters, run-aground boaters!

A furious storm once roared 'cross the sea

Catching ships in its path, helpless to flee . . .

Instead of a certain and watery doom

The winds swept them here to TYPHOON LAGOON.

Such is the Disney legend relating to **Typhoon Lagoon** ★★★, which you'll see posted on consecutive signs as you enter the park. Located off Buena Vista Drive between the Downtown Disney Marketplace and Disney–MGM Studios, this is the ultimate in water-theme parks. Its fantasy setting is a palm-fringed island village of ramshackle, tin-roofed structures, strewn with cargo, surfboards, and other marine wreckage left by the "great typhoon." A storm-stranded fishing boat (the *Miss Tilly*) dangles precariously atop 95-foot Mount Mayday, the steep setting for several attractions. Every half hour, the boat's smokestack erupts, shooting a 50-foot geyser of water into the air.

ESSENTIALS

HOURS   The park is open from at least 10am to 5pm, with extended hours during some holiday periods and summer (© **407/560-4141;** www.disneyworld.com).

ENTRANCE FEES   A 1-day ticket (without 6% tax) to Typhoon Lagoon is $31 for adults, $25 for kids 3 to 9.

HELPFUL HINTS   In summer, arrive no later than 9am to avoid long lines. The park is often filled to capacity by 10am and is then closed to later arrivals. Beach towels ($2) and lockers ($5 and $8) can be rented, and beachwear can be purchased at **Singapore Sal's.** Light fare is available at two eateries, **Leaning Palms** and **Typhoon Tillie's.** A beach bar called **Let's Go Slurpin'** sells beer and soft drinks. There are picnic tables (consider bringing picnic fare; you can keep it in your locker until lunch). Guests aren't permitted to bring their own flotation devices, and glass bottles are prohibited.

ATTRACTIONS IN THE PARK

Castaway Creek

Hop onto a raft or an inner tube and meander along this 2,100-foot lazy river that circles most of the park. It tumbles through a misty rainforest, then by caves and secluded grottoes. It has a theme area called **Water Works,** where jets of water spew from shipwrecked boats, and a Rube Goldberg assemblage of broken bamboo pipes and buckets wet you. Tubes are included in the admission price.

Ketchakiddie Creek

Many of the park's other attractions require guests to be older children, teens, or adults, but this section is a *kiddie area exclusively for 2- to 5-year-olds.* An

---

Tips **Closed for the Winter**

Both Disney water parks are refurbished on a rotating basis for a month or more each winter. So if a water park is on your itinerary, ask in advance about closings.

innovative water playground, it has bubbling fountains to frolic in, mini–water slides, a pint-size "white-water" tubing run, spouting whales and squirting seals, rubbery crocodiles to climb on, grottoes to explore, and waterfalls to loll under. It's also small enough for you to take good home videos or photographs.

Shark Reef
Guests are given free equipment (and instruction) for a 15-minute swim through this very small snorkeling area that includes a simulated coral reef populated by about 4,000 parrotfish, angelfish, yellowtail damselfish, and other cuties including small rays and sharks. If you don't want to get in, you can observe the fish via portholes in a walk-through viewing area.

Typhoon Lagoon Surf Pool
This large (2.75 million gal.) and lovely lagoon is the size of two football fields and is surrounded by a white sandy beach. It's the park's main swimming area. The chlorinated water has a turquoise hue much like the Caribbean. **Large waves** (about 6 ft.) roll through the deeper areas every 90 seconds. A foghorn sounds to warn you when one is coming. Young children can wade in the lagoon's more peaceful tidal pools—**Blustery Bay** or **Whitecap Cove**—but don't let little ones near the main pool without direct supervision, as a wave can easily knock a child over. The lagoon also is home to a **special weekly surfing program** (p. 268).

Andy (our resident water rat) **Rating:** "I'm not getting out!" (Well, he did, but not without a fuss. If your kids love the water, you may have the same problem.)

Water Slides
Humunga Kowabunga consists of three 214-foot Mount Mayday slides that propel you down the mountain on a serpentine route through waterfalls and bat caves and past nautical wreckage before depositing you into a bubbling catch pool; each offers slightly different views and 30-mph thrills. There's seating for non-Kowabunga folks whose braver kids have commissioned them to "watch me." *Note:* You must be 48 inches or taller to ride this. **Storm Slides** offer a tamer course through the park's man-made caves.

Jake Rating: "Tell them they better hang onto their skivvies." (Or the name of this ride will be Moon Over Orlando and you'll provide the lunar display. And girls should avoid two-piece bathing suits for the same reason.)

White-Water Rides
Mount Mayday is the setting for three white-water rafting adventures—**Keelhaul Falls, Mayday Falls,** and **Gangplank Falls**—all offering steep drops coursing through caves and passing lush scenery. Keelhaul Falls has the most winding route, Mayday Falls has the steepest drops and fastest water, and the slightly tamer Gangplank Falls uses large tubes so that the whole family can pile on.

BLIZZARD BEACH

Blizzard Beach ✩✩✩, the most popular water park in North America, is the younger of Disney's water parks, a 66-acre "ski resort" in the midst of a tropical lagoon centering on the 90-foot, uh-oh, Mount Gushmore. There's a legend for this one as well. Apparently a freak snowstorm dumped tons of snow on Walt Disney World, leading to the creation of Florida's first—and, so far, only—mountain ski resort (complete with Ice Gator, the park's mascot). Naturally, when temperatures returned to their normal broiling range, the snow bunnies prepared to close up shop, when they realized—this is Disney, happy endings are a must—that what remained of their snow resort could be turned into a water park featuring the fastest and tallest waterlogged "ski" runs in the country. The base of Mount Gushmore has a sand beach with several other attractions, including a wave pool and a smaller version of the mount for younger children. The park is located off World Drive, just north of the All-Star Movie, Music, and Sports resorts.

ESSENTIALS

HOURS It's open from at least 10am to 5pm, with extended hours during holiday periods and summer (© **407/560-3400;** www.disneyworld.com).

ENTRANCE FEES A 1-day ticket to Blizzard Beach is $31 (without 6% tax) for adults, $25 for children 3 to 9.

HELPFUL HINTS Arrive at or before opening to avoid long lines and to be sure you get in. Beach towels ($2) and lockers ($5 and $8) are available, and you can buy the beachwear you forgot to bring at the **Beach Haus.** You can grab something to eat at **Avalunch** and **Lottawatta Lodge** (burgers, hot dogs, nachos, pizza, and sandwiches).

MAJOR ATTRACTIONS IN THE PARK

Cross Country Creek

Inner-tubers can float lazily along this park-circling 2,900-foot creek, but beware of the mysterious cave where you'll get splashed with melting ice. It's a good ride for the entire family.

Melt-Away Bay

Waterfalls of melting "snow" feed this 1-acre bobbing wave pool and it features relatively calm waves.

Tips **Water Park Dos & Don'ts**

1. Go in the afternoons, about 2pm, even in summer, if you can stand the heat that long and want to avoid crowds. The early birds usually are gone by then.
2. Go early in the week when most of the weeklong guests are filling the lines at the theme parks.
3. Kids can get lost just as easily at a water park as at the other parks, and the consequences can be tragic. All Disney parks have lifeguards, usually wearing bright red suits, but, to be safe, make yourself the first line of safety for the kids in your crew (children 10 and under must be accompanied by an adult to get into the parks).
4. Women should wear a securely attached one-piece bathing suit unless they want to put on a show for the rest of the crowd. And all bathers should remember the **"wedgie" rule** on the more extreme rides, such as Summit Plummet (at Blizzard Beach, below). *What's the "wedgie" rule?* It's a principle of physics that says you may start out wearing baggies and end up in a thong.
5. Use a waterproof sunscreen with an SPF of at least 30 and drink plenty of fluids. Despite all that water, it's easy to get dehydrated in summer.

> **Fun Fact** **Did You Know?**
>
> • Walt Disney World sprawls across 47 square miles, which makes it the size of San Francisco or twice that of Manhattan. Less than a quarter of it is developed and another quarter is a preserve.
> • Mickey Mouse has more than 80 outfits, ranging from scuba gear to formal wear. Minnie has a mere 50.
> • There are enough Mouse ears sold yearly to cover the head of every man, woman, and child living in Pittsburgh.
> • The Liberty Oak, the big tree in Liberty Square, has produced more than 500 offspring, all of which began as acorns.
> • Spaceship Earth, the golf ball–like focal point of Epcot, weighs 16 million pounds.
> • On an average day, 100 pairs of sunglasses are turned in to the Lost and Found at the Magic Kingdom. That's more than 1.1 million since the opening bell in 1971.
> • In that same span, the WDW monorail has logged enough miles to travel 25 times to the moon.
> • Walt Disney World gift shops sell about 500,000 character watches annually. Not surprisingly, most of them are Mickeys.
> • Both Disneyland in California and Walt Disney World were built on former citrus groves in counties named Orange.

Runoff Rapids

Another tube job, this one lets you careen down any of three twisting-turning runs, one of which sends you through darkness.

Ski-Patrol Training Camp

Designed for preteens, it features a rope swing, a T-bar drop over water, slides like the wet and slippery **Mogul Mania** from the Mount, and a challenging ice-floe walk along slippery floating icebergs. It's a good spot for kids not up to the more adrenaline-pumping slides in the park.

Slush Gusher

This super-speed slide travels along a snow-banked gully. ***Note:*** It has a 48-inch height minimum.

Snow Stormers

These three flumes descend from the top of Mount Gushmore and follow a switchback course through ski-type slalom gates.

Summit Plummet *(Moments*

Read *every* speed, motion, vertical-dip, wedgie, and hold-onto-your-breast-plate warning in this guide. Then, test your bravado in a bullring, a space shuttle, or dozens of other death-defying hobbies as a warm-up. This puppy starts pretty slow, with a lift ride to the 120-foot summit. Then . . . well . . . kiss any kids or religious medal you may be carrying. Because, if you board, you *will enter* the World's fastest body slide, a test of your courage and swimsuit that virtually goes straight down and has you moving *sans* vehicle at 60 mph by the catch pool (aka, stop zone). ***Note:*** It has a 48-inch height minimum. Also, expectant mothers and people with neck, back, and heart problems shouldn't ride.

Jake Rating: "Uh, do you know what water at that speed would do to your sinuses? I think I'm going to skip it." (We don't blame him. Even the hardiest rider may find this one hard to handle; a veteran thrill-seeker we know described the experience as "15 sec. of paralyzing fear.")

Teamboat Springs
On the World's longest white-water raft ride, your six-passenger raft twists down a 1,200-foot series of rushing waterfalls.

Tike's Peak
This kid-size version of Mount Gushmore offers short water slides, rideable animals, a snow castle, a squirting ice pond, and a fountain play area for young guests. If you have kids under 48 inches in height, this is the place to take them.

Toboggan Racers
Here's an eight-lane slide that sends you racing head first over exhilarating dips into a snowy slope.
Andy Rating: "That was a blast! I want to go two out of three." (If you've ever been on one of those tall super slides at amusement parks, imagine doing it headfirst, on your belly, on a raft. This baby can pack a lot of zippity by the end.)

8 Other WDW Attractions

Note: All of the attractions mentioned in this section can be found on the "Walt Disney World Parks & Attractions" map on p. 149.

FANTASIA GARDENS & WINTER SUMMERLAND
Fantasia Gardens Miniature Golf ★★, located off Buena Vista Drive across from Disney–MGM Studios, offers two 18-hole miniature courses drawing inspiration from the Walt Disney classic cartoon of the same name. You'll find hippos, ostriches, and alligators on the **Fantasia Gardens** course, where the Sorcerer's Apprentice presides over the final hole. It's a good bet for beginners and kids. Seasoned mini-golfers probably will prefer **Fantasia Fairways,** which is a scaled-down golf course complete with sand traps, water hazards, tricky putting greens, and holes ranging from 40 to 75 feet.

Santa Claus and his elves provide the theme for **Winter Summerland** ★★ (Disney reports that Santa built it as a vacation resort for his off-duty elves), which has two 18-hole miniature golf courses across from Blizzard Beach on Buena Vista Drive. The **Winter** course takes you from an ice castle to a snowman to the North Pole (it's reportedly the easier of the two courses and the best one for young kids and beginners). The **Summer** course is pure Florida, from sandcastles to surfboards to a visit with Santa on the "Winternet."

Tickets at both venues are $10.40 for adults and $8.29 for children 3 to 9. Both are open from 10am to 10 or 11pm daily. For information about Fantasia Gardens, call ℂ **407/560-4582.** For information about Winter Summerland, call ℂ **407/560-3000.** You can find both on the Internet at **www.disneyworld. com.**

⌐Tips River Runs Dry

As this book goes to press, Disney's River Country water park remains closed for another season, and its future is uncertain. To check on its current status, call ℂ **407/824-4321** or visit **www.disneyworld.com.**

DISNEY'S WIDE WORLD OF SPORTS

This 200-acre complex has a 7,500-seat professional baseball stadium, 10 other baseball and softball fields, six basketball courts, 12 lighted tennis courts, a track-and-field complex, a golf driving range, and six sand volleyball courts. It's a haven for sports fans and wannabe athletes.

It's open daily from 10am to 5pm; the cost is $9.34 adults, $7.01 kids 3 to 9. Organized programs and events include:

- The **Multi-Sports Experience,** which challenges guests with a variety of activities, covering many sports: football, baseball, basketball, hockey, soccer, and volleyball. Run a football pass pattern in football, test your fastball's speed, or try and kick a game-winning field goal. There's a special play area for young kids. It's open on select days. *Note:* This replaced the NFL Experience in 2002.
- The **Atlanta Braves** play 16 spring-training games during a 1-month season that begins in early March. Tickets cost $12 to $19.75. For tickets call Ticketmaster (✆ 407/839-3900).
- The **NFL, NBA, NCAA, PGA,** and **Harlem Globetrotters** also host events, sometimes annually and sometimes more frequently, at the complex. Admission varies by event.

Disney's Wide World of Sports is located on Victory Way, just north of U.S. 192 (west of I-4; ✆ **407/939-1500;** www.disneyworld.com).

7

What Kids Like to See & Do Beyond Disney

Younger members of your party may not draw battle lines in so many words, but older kids may boldly declare they like one ride, show, or theme park better than another.

Veteran vacationers call it the Great Theme-Park War—the ongoing, "anything-you-can-do-we-can-do-better," knock-down-drag-out battle between the Magic Mickey and top-ranked challenger Universal Orlando, which each year since 1999 has chipped away at what was once Walt Disney World's virtual monopoly. Still, make no mistake: Disney is king, leading in theme parks (4–2) and smaller attractions (9–1). It has a 2-to-1 edge in nightclub venues, a huge lead in restaurants, and, when it comes to hotel rooms, its lead is probably insurmountable.

Nevertheless, Universal is trying. It had a substantial growth spurt in 1999, bolstering its original theme park, **Universal Studios Florida (USF),** with a second one, **Islands of Adventure,** that's the top park in town for teens and offers the city's largest collection of thrill rides. Universal also added a nightclub and restaurant complex, **CityWalk;** and three resorts: **Portofino Bay,** the **Hard Rock Hotel,** and the **Royal Pacific Resort.**

USF opened two new kid-friendly rides in 2003—**Jimmy Neutron's Nicktoon Blast** and **Shrek 4-D**—and it has plans to replace the old Kongfrontation ride in 2004 with a new one tentatively called **Revenge of the Mummy.** Furthermore, Universal Orlando has more than 2,000 adjoining acres on which to expand, and, while the company's lips are sealed, it's known there are plans for at least two more hotels, a golf course, and possibly 300 acres of additional rides and attractions.

A few miles south, **SeaWorld** and its sister park, **Discovery Cove,** also grab a share of the Orlando action (especially with the kid set). In 2003, SeaWorld opened a new Cirque du Soleil–style show called **Odyssea.**

Aside from greater variety, these players mean more multiday packages and special deals for you. To compete with Disney, SeaWorld and Universal Orlando teamed up on multiday pass options a few years back. They offer a **FlexTicket** that also includes admission to **Wet 'n Wild** (a Universal-owned water park) and **Busch Gardens** in Tampa. (Unfortunately for you, Universal, SeaWorld, and Busch Gardens also rival Disney with single-day tickets that, without tax, cost $51.95 for adults and $42.95 for children 3–9.)

While the wars rage on in the traditional tourist areas, it has finally dawned on the rest of Orlando that central Florida is one of the world's favorite vacation destinations.

Since the early 1990s, downtown Orlando has gotten a makeover that woos hundreds of thousands to its attractions, nightclubs, and restaurants. Recent expansions at the

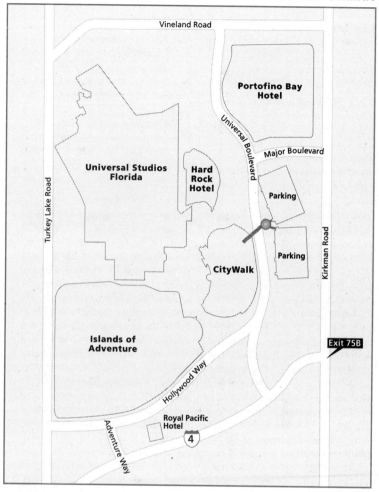

Orlando Museum of Art and the **Orlando Science Center** show the city is trying to grab its share of the tourist pie. This expansion means visitors can enjoy the spoils: more variety, greater opportunities, and a world beyond the theme parks.

THE FLEXTICKET The most economical way to see the various "other-than-Disney" parks is with these passes, which counter Disney's Park Hopper tickets. With the **FlexTicket,** you pay one price to visit any of the participating parks as many times as you want during a 14-day period. At press time, a four-park pass to Universal Studios Florida, Islands of Adventure, Wet 'n Wild, and SeaWorld was $175.95 for adults and $142.95 for children 3 to 9. A five-park pass, which adds Busch Gardens in Tampa, was $209.95 for adults and $175.95 for kids. The **FlexTicket** can be ordered through **Universal** (© 800/711-0080 or 407/363-8000; www.universalorlando.com); **SeaWorld** (© 800/327-2424 or 407/351-3600; www.seaworld.com); or **Wet 'n Wild**

(© **800/992-9453** or 407/351-9453; www.wetnwild.com).

Note: There's a round-trip shuttle available to Busch Gardens (p. 300) that's free for FlexTicket buyers (it's $5 for other guests; © **800/221-1339**).

UNIVERSAL EXPRESS This is Universal's answer to Disney's FAST-PASS. Universal Express has two tiers. Guests of the Portofino Bay, Hard Rock, and Royal Pacific hotels (see chapter 4, "Family-Friendly Accommodations") only need to show their room keys to get at or near the front of the line for most rides. Single-day and multiday ticket buyers who don't stay at a Universal resort can make one reservation at a time. Waits are usually 15 minutes or less. Guests can return for more when their reservations are used or expire (and like Disney, get a 2nd ticket 2 hr. after the 1st is issued). The system is available throughout the day. Call © **800/711-0080,** 800/837-2273, or 407/363-8000, or go to **www.universalorlando.com** for more information.

1 Universal Studios Florida

Even with fast-paced grown-up rides based on blockbusters such as *Twister, Terminator,* and *Men in Black,* Universal Studios Florida is a ton of fun for kids. And, as an added plus, it's a working motion picture and TV production studio, so occasionally there's some live filming done at Nickelodeon's sound stages or elsewhere in the park. Even if there isn't a film or show in production, you can see reel history displayed in the form of some 40 actual sets exhibited along Hollywood Boulevard and Rodeo Drive. And there are plenty of action shows and rides including **Twister . . . Ride It Out, Earthquake—The Big One, Back to the Future . . . The Ride, Jaws,** and **Terminator 2: 3-D Battle Across Time.**

While 2001 and 2002 were quiet on the expansion front, 2003 saw Universal open two new attractions: **Jimmy Neutron's Nicktoon Blast** replaced the old Funtastic World of Hanna-Barbera and **Shrek 4-D** opened where Alfred Hitchcock—the Art of Making Movies used to be. Additionally, Kongfrontation, one of the park's original rides, was mothballed to make way for a new one, tentatively called **Revenge of the Mummy,** which is scheduled to open in mid-2004. Universal also replaced some stale shows and characters with fresh ones (see "Universal Has New Characters & Shows," on p. 227). As a result, the park is better than it's ever been as a place to bring the kids.

ESSENTIALS
GETTING TO UNIVERSAL BY CAR Universal Orlando is a half-mile north of I-4 Exit 75B, Kirkman Road/Highway 435. There may be construction in the area, so follow the signs directing you to the parks.

PARKING If you park in the multilevel garages, remember the theme and row in your area to help you find your car later. Or, do it the old-fashioned way: Write it down. Parking costs $8 for cars, light trucks, and vans. Valet parking is $16. Universal's garages are connected to its parks and have moving sidewalks, but it's still a long walk.

TICKETS, PASSES & TOURS At press time, a **1-day ticket** cost $51.95 (plus 6% sales tax) for adults, $42.95 for children 3 to 9. A 2-day 2-park Unlimited-Access Escape Pass was $96.95 for adults, $83.95 for children 3 to 9; a 3-day 2-park pass was $111.95 for adults, $96.95 for children 3 to 9. (*Note:* Universal also sells a **2-Park Annual Power Pass** that's good for an entire year except for about 30 or so blackout dates, mainly during summer and around the Dec holidays. It costs $109.95 regardless of age.)

All multiday passes let you move between Universal Studios Florida and Islands of Adventure. *Multiday passes also give you free access to the CityWalk clubs at night.* See the beginning of this chapter for information on the **FlexTicket,** which provides multiple-day admission to Universal Studios Florida, Islands of Adventure, Sea-World, and Wet 'n Wild.

Because both Universal parks are within walking distance of each other, you won't lose much time jockeying back and forth, which is not the case at Disney. Nevertheless, it's a long walk for tykes and people with limited mobility, so consider a stroller or wheelchair.

There are also 5-hour **VIP tours** to Universal Studios Florida, Islands of Adventure, or both, that include line-cutting privileges for $100 to $125 per person including admission. The passes provide a guided tour with priority entrance to at least eight attractions. For more information on the VIP tour, call ✆ **800/711-0080** or 407/363-8295. Tours start at 10am and noon daily. If you plan on visiting during peak season, money isn't an issue, and you aren't staying at one of the Universal resorts, this is a good way to experience the best of the parks without having to spend most of your day in lines.

> **Tips Shorter Days**
>
> Like Disney, Universal juggles park hours to combat the soft economy. The hours listed in this chapter are generally accurate, but sometimes the parks close earlier, or some rides or shows open later. To avoid disappointment, check the park's website at **www.universalorlando.com** or call ✆ **800/711-0080** or 407/363-8000 for up-to-the-minute schedules.

HOURS   The park is open 365 days a year, usually at least from 9am to 6pm, though it's open later in summer and around holidays. The best bet is to call before you go so that you're not caught by surprise.

MAKING YOUR VISIT MORE ENJOYABLE
PLANNING YOUR VISIT
You can get information before you leave home by calling **Universal Orlando Guest Services** at ✆ **800/711-0080,** 800/837-2273, or 407/363-8000. Ask about travel packages as well as theme-park information. Universal sometimes offers a promotion that adds an extra day free on multiday passes, or at a deeply discounted price on single day passes. You can also write to Guest Services, 1000 Universal Studios Plaza, Orlando, FL 32819-7601.

ONLINE   Find information about Universal Orlando at **www.universal orlando.com**. Orlando's daily newspaper, the *Orlando Sentinel,* also produces Orlando Sentinel Online at **www.orlandosentinel.com**. Additionally, there's a lot of information about the parks, hotels, restaurants, and more at the Orlando/Orange County Convention and Visitors Bureau site: **www.orlandoinfo.com**.

INFORMATION FOR VISITORS WITH SPECIAL NEEDS
Guests with disabilities should go to **Guest Services,** located just inside the main entrance, for a *Disabled Guest Guidebook,* a Telecommunications Device for the Deaf (TDD), or other special assistance. You can rent a standard wheelchair for $10 or an electric one for $40 (both require a credit-card imprint, a driver's license, or $50 as a deposit). You can reserve them 24 hours or more in advance by calling ✆ **407/363-8000.** You can arrange for sign language

Universal Studios Florida

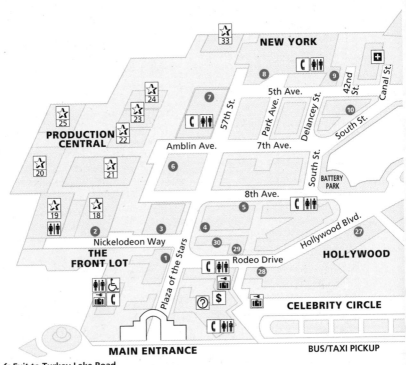

NEW YORK

5th Ave.

57th St.

Park Ave.

Delancey St.

42nd St.

Canal St.

PRODUCTION CENTRAL

Amblin Ave.

7th Ave.

South St.

South St.

BATTERY PARK

8th Ave.

Nickelodeon Way

Hollywood Blvd.

THE FRONT LOT

Plaza of the Stars

Rodeo Drive

HOLLYWOOD

CELEBRITY CIRCLE

MAIN ENTRANCE

BUS/TAXI PICKUP

← Exit to Turkey Lake Road

CityWalk *See CityWalk Map in Chapter 10*

PRODUCTION CENTRAL
The Bates Motel Gift Shop **5**
The Boneyard **6**
Jimmy Neutron's
    Nicktoon Blast **3**
Nickelodeon Studios **2**
Shrek 4-D **4**

NEW YORK
Blues Brothers **10**
Second Hand Rose **9**
Revenge of the Mummy **8**
Twister...Ride it Out **8**

THE FRONT LOT
Universal Studios Store **1**

HOLLYWOOD
Lucy, A Tribute **29**
Silver Screen Collectibles **30**
Terminator 2: 3-D Battle
    Across Time **28**
Universal Horror
    Make-Up Show **27**

WORLD EXPO
Back to the Future–The Store **20**
Back to the Future...The Ride **17**
Men in Black Alien Attack **16**

SAN FRANCISCO/AMITY

The Embarcadero

Amity Avenue

The Lagoon

CENTRAL PARK

Sunset Blvd.

WORLD EXPO

WOODY
WOODPECKER'S
KIDZONE

| Film & TV Production Stage |
| $ Banking |
| First Aid |
| Lockers |
| Restrooms |
| C Telephones |
| Guest Services |
| Wheelchair & Stroller Rental |

Exit to Vineland Rd. →

WOODY WOODPECKER'S KIDZONE
Animal Planet Live! **21**
The Barney Store **19**
Curious George Goes to Town **26**
A Day in the Park with Barney **18**
E.T. Adventure **24**
E.T.'s Toy Closet **25**
Fievel's Playland **22**
Woody Woodpecker's
  Nuthouse Coaster **23**

SAN FRANCISCO/AMITY
Beetlejuice's Rock 'n Roll
  Graveyard Revue **11**
Earthquake—The Big One **12**
Jaws **15**
Lombard's Seafood Grille **13**
Quint's Surf Shack **14**

interpreting services at no charge by calling ℂ **888/519-4899** (toll-free TDD), 407/224-4414 (local TDD), or 407/224-5929 (voice). Make arrangements for an appointment with an interpreter 1 to 2 weeks in advance. For more information on services available to those with disabilities, see p. 31.

PETS   You can board your small animals at the shelter located inside the parking garages for $10 a day (no overnight stays). Ask the attendant when you pay for parking to direct you to the kennel. Note that Universal's resorts all allow small pets to stay with you in your room.

HOW WE'VE MADE THIS CHAPTER USEFUL TO PARENTS

As in chapter 6, before every listing in the major parks, you'll note the **"Recommended Ages"** entry that tells which ages will most appreciate that ride or show. This guideline is helpful in planning your daily itinerary. In our ride ratings, we've indicated whether a ride will be more enjoyable for kids than for adults. Fewer of Universal Orlando's rides and shows appeal to very young kids than at some of the Disney parks, and one bad experience can spook your small fry for a long time. You'll also find any **height and health restrictions** noted in the ride and show listings that follow.

For the Universal and SeaWorld parks, we're also going to return to our **Jake (age 12) and Andy (age 6) ratings.** Our two grandsons are theme-park veterans who have enthusiastically tackled the parks often, as they drag us kicking and screaming along. On select rides, we'll give you their views and reviews.

BEST TIME OF YEAR TO VISIT

As with Walt Disney World, there's really no off-season for Universal, but the week after Labor Day until mid-December (excluding Thanksgiving week) and January to mid-May (excluding spring break) are known for smaller crowds, cooler weather, and less humid air. The summer months, when the masses throng to the parks, are the worst time for crowds and hot, sticky, humid days. During cooler months, you also won't have to worry much about daily thunderstorms. If you're planning a trip from mid-February to mid-April, keep in mind that a raucous Mardi Gras celebration goes on in the evenings (weekends only at first, but daily during the last 2 weeks). It's a very grown-up event with lots of alcohol flowing and a separate ticket price. It's really not suitable for younger children. The park is still open for all during the day, but it closes earlier than usual. (The same is true in Oct at Universal's other park, Islands of Adventure, which hosts the very grown-up, not to mention frightening, Halloween Horror Nights.)

Some of the park's best rides are action-based thrill rides, which means your options are limited if you're pregnant, are prone to motion sickness, or have heart, neck, or back problems. The same applies to smaller children. Review the rides and restrictions on the following pages or when you enter the park so

---

Moments **Universal Has a Few 'Toons, Too**

While the options pale in comparison to Disney, Universal has character meet-and-greets on a rotating basis. At **Universal Studios Florida,** you may run into Woody Woodpecker, SpongeBob SquarePants, Scooby Doo, Jimmy Neutron, and others. At **Islands of Adventure,** the cast may include Spider-Man, Popeye and Olive Oyl, Beetle Bailey, the Cat in the Hat, Betty Boop, or Boris and Natasha.

> **Tips   Universal Has New Characters & Shows**
>
> Universal Studios Florida has replaced some of its old (read—stale, if you've been there a few times) street characters and shows in favor of new ones. The occasionally changing lineup includes: **Lucy and Ricky Ricardo, Fred and Wilma Flintstone, Betty and Barney Rubble, Popeye and Olive Oyl, Doc Emmit Brown, Shaggy, Fiona,** and **Men in Black** agents. *Note:* Characters rotate or appear seasonally.

that you don't stand in line for something you're unable to enjoy. (There are stationary areas available at some moving rides. Check your park guide under "expectant mothers," as well as the boards in front of each ride, then ask the attendants for help as you enter.)

THE BEST DAYS TO VISIT
Go near the end of the week, on a Thursday or Friday. The pace is somewhat fast Monday through Wednesday, with the heaviest crowds on weekends and during summers and holidays.

CREATE AN ITINERARY
Pick three or four things that you must see or do and plan your day along a rough geographical guide. Universal Studios Florida is relatively small, so walking from one end of the park to the other isn't as daunting as it is in some of the Disney parks.

CHOOSE AGE-APPROPRIATE RIDES/SHOWS
Here, as in Walt Disney World, height and age restrictions aren't bent to accommodate a screaming child. Even where restrictions don't exist, some shows have loud music and pyrotechnics that can frighten kids. And, in a few cases, Universal employs a PG-13 rating, which suggests that ride or show may not be suitable for preteens. Check the attraction descriptions that follow to make sure your child won't be unduly disappointed or frightened.

SUGGESTED ITINERARIES

A Suggested Itinerary for Families with Young Children
Waste no time: Hoof it to Woody Woodpecker's KidZone, where you and your heirs can spend most of the day. If they're 36 inches or taller, don't miss multiple rides on **Woody Woodpecker's Nuthouse Coaster.** Try to make an early pit stop at **Fievel's Playland** (especially its water slide, which is slow-moving and has longer lines after 10:30am). Then take a leisurely pace to see **E.T. Adventure, A Day in the Park with Barney,** and **Animal Planet Live!**

Take a lunch break and don't leave before visiting the wet-and-wild **Curious George Goes to Town.** Round out the day with stops at the **Shrek 4-D** and **Nickelodeon Studios.**

A Suggested Itinerary for Older Children, Teens & Adults
A single day is usually sufficient to see the park if you arrive early and keep a fairly brisk pace. Skip the city sidewalks of the main gate and **Terminator 2: 3-D Battle Across Time** until later. Go to the right and tackle **Men in Black Alien**

Attack and Back to the Future . . . The Ride. Then make a counter-clockwise loop, visiting Jaws, Earthquake—The Big One, and Twister . . . Ride It Out. Break for lunch somewhere in that trio, then tackle the 'toons in the new Jimmy Neutron's Nicktoon Blast and the Shrek 4-D adventure, then catch the fun in Terminator 2: 3-D Battle Across Time. If your kids are young enough to appreciate the TV channel, catch the 45-minute Nickelodeon Studios tour and show (4- to 14-year-olds love it).

A second day lets you revisit some of your favorites or see those you missed. With the pressure to hit all the major rides lessened, you can delay your Nickelodeon Studios visit until day 2 (the 1st tour usually isn't until 10:30am or so). You can also visit the Universal Horror Makeup Show and Beetlejuice's Rock 'n Roll Graveyard Revue.

SERVICES & FACILITIES IN UNIVERSAL STUDIOS FLORIDA

ATMs Machines accepting cards from banks using the Cirrus, Honor, and PLUS systems are to the right of the main entrance (outside and inside the park) and in San Francisco/Amity near Lombard's Landing restaurant.

Baby Care Changing tables are in men's and women's restrooms; there are nursing facilities at Family Services, just inside the main entrance and to the right. Diapers aren't sold on the premises.

Cameras & Film Film and disposable cameras are available at the On Location shop in the Front Lot, just inside the main entrance. One-hour photo developing is available, though we don't recommend paying park prices.

Car Assistance Battery jumps are provided. If you need assistance with your car, raise the hood and use the call boxes located throughout the garage to call for security.

First Aid The First Aid Center is located between New York and San Francisco, next to Louie's Italian Restaurant on Canal Street. There's also one just inside the main entrance next to Guest Services.

Lockers Lockers are across from Guest Services near the main entrance and cost $7 and $10 a day, including a $2 refundable deposit.

Lost Children If you lose a child, go to Guest Services near the main entrance or contact any park employee for assistance. *Children under 7 should wear name-tags.*

Pet Care A kennel is available ($10 a day) near the newest parking lot. Ask the parking attendant for directions upon entering the toll plaza. Overnight boarding is not permitted. Remember to bring proof of vaccinations.

Stroller Rental Strollers can be rented in Amity and at Guest Services just inside the entrance to the right. The cost is $10 for a single, $16 for a double.

(*Value* **Money Saver**

You can save 10% off your purchase at many Universal Orlando gift shops or eateries by showing your AAA (American Automobile Association) card. This discount isn't available at food and merchandise carts or on tobacco, candy, film, collectibles, and sundry items.

Frommer's Rates the Rides

As we do for the Disney parks in chapter 6, "What Kids Like to See &
Do in Walt Disney World," we're using a grading system to score the
Universal Orlando and SeaWorld rides in this chapter. (We'll return to
the star-rating system toward the end of the chapter, when we explore
some of Orlando's smaller attractions.) Most of the grades below are
As, Bs, and Cs. That's because the major parks' designers have done a
pretty good job on the attractions. But you'll also find a few Ds for
Duds. Here's what the Frommer's ratings mean:

A+	=	Your trip wouldn't be complete without it.
A	=	Put it at the top of your "to-do" list.
B+	=	Make a real effort to see or do it.
B	=	It's fun but not a "must see."
C+	=	A nice diversion; see it if you have time.
C	=	Go if it appeals to you but not if there's a wait.
D	=	Don't waste your time.

Wheelchair Rental   Regular wheelchairs can be rented for $10 in Amity and
at Guest Services just inside the main gate. Electric wheelchairs are $40. Both
require a credit-card imprint, driver's license, or $50 as a deposit.

MAJOR ATTRACTIONS AT UNIVERSAL STUDIOS FLORIDA

Rides and attractions at this park have cutting-edge technology such as OMNI-
MAX 70mm film projected on seven-story screens to create terrific special effects.
While waiting in line, you'll be entertained by excellent preshows—better than
those at the Disney parks. Universal, as a whole, takes itself less seriously than
the Mouse That Roared, and the atmosphere is peppered by subtle reminders
that in the competitive theme-park industry, it's not a small world after all.

Animal Planet Live!
Frommer's Rating: B
Recommended Ages: All ages
Get a behind-the-scenes look at the Animal Planet television network through a
multimedia show that combines video with live actors. The stars can include pri-
mates, a fox, a raccoon, and a dog. Members of the audience occasionally get to
participate in the fun. If your kids love animals, it's a must.

Back to the Future . . . The Ride
Frommer's Rating: A
Recommended Ages: 8–adult
Blast through the space-time continuum in 1 of 24 flight simulators built to
look like the movie's famous DeLorean. Along the way, you'll dive into blazing
volcanic tunnels, collide with Ice Age glaciers, thunder through caves and
canyons, and briefly get swallowed by a dinosaur in an eye-crossing multi-sen-
sory adventure. You twist and turn, you dip and dive—all the while feeling as if
you're really flying. Sit in one of the car's back seats to avoid ruining the illusion
(in the front seat you can lean forward and see your neighbors careening hydrauli-
cally in the next bay). It's bumpy and might not be a good idea if you're prone
to dizziness or motion sickness. ***Note:*** Heed the health warnings displayed at the

---

Tips   Goodbye Kong, Hello Mummy

Kongfrontation was part of Universal Studios Florida when it opened in 1990, but the ride closed in September 2002 and will be replaced in spring 2004 with **Revenge of the Mummy.** The new $40-million indoor roller coaster will rely on speed, pyrotechnics, and robotics for its thrill factors as riders hurtle through Egyptian sets, passageways, and tombs in cars that move forward and in reverse. The 5-minute journey includes encounters with overhead flames and a skeletal warrior that hops aboard your coaster. Your teens should be delighted.

---

ride, which has a 40-inch height minimum. Also, Universal recommends that expectant mothers skip this ride.

Jake Rating: "Wow! That was pretty intense." (He's on target. It's similar to, but with more shake and bake than, Body Wars at Epcot, p. 187.)

Beetlejuice's Rock 'n Roll Graveyard Revue

Frommer's Rating: B for classic rock fans, C for others

Recommended Ages: 10–adult

Universal, in 2002, added some new steps and tunes to this rock musical that stars Dracula, Wolfman, the Phantom of the Opera, Frankenstein and his bride, and Beetlejuice. The fun includes pyrotechnic special effects, some adult jokes, and MTV-style choreography. It's loud and lively enough to scare some small children and frazzle some older adults. *Note:* It carries Universal's PG-13 rating, meaning it may not be suitable for preteens.

A Day in the Park with Barney

Frommer's Rating: A+ for tiny tots and their parents, D for everyone else

Recommended Ages: 2–6

Set in a parklike theater-in-the-round, this 25-minute musical stars the Purple One, Baby Bop, and BJ. It uses song, dance, and interactive play to deliver an environmental message. This could be the highlight of the day for preschoolers (parents can console themselves with their kids' happiness). The playground adjacent to the theater has chimes to ring, tree houses to explore, and lots to intrigue wee ones.

Andy Rating: "That was a real gagger." (From an adult perspective, we couldn't have said it better. The theater is air-conditioned, but, even in the hottest months, that's not enough to entice us to spend another nanosecond around Barney.)

Earthquake—The Big One

Frommer's Rating: B+

Recommended Ages: 6–adult

You climb on a BART train in San Francisco for a peaceful subway ride, but just as you pull into the Embarcadero Station, there's an earthquake—a big one, 8.3 on the Richter scale! As you sit helplessly trapped, slabs of concrete collapse around you, a propane truck bursts into flames, a runaway train hurtles your way, and the station floods (65,000 gal. of water cascade down the steps). *Note:* Universal says expectant moms should skip this one.

Andy Rating: "That was way cool." (A year earlier, we believe, the noise, flames, and other special effects might have been a bit too intense for him.)

E.T. Adventure
Frommer's Rating: B+ for preteens and their families
Recommended Ages: All ages

You'll soar with E.T. on a mission to save his ailing planet, through the forest and into space aboard an intergalactic bicycle. You'll also meet some characters created by Steven Spielberg for the ride, including Botanicus, Tickli Moot Moot, Horn Flowers, and Tympani Tremblies. This family favorite (young kids especially adore it) is definitely a charmer. If there is a knock, it's that there are two waiting areas—inside and outside. And wait you will.

Jaws
Frommer's Rating: B+
Recommended Ages: 6–adult

As your boat heads into the 7-acre, 5-million-gallon lagoon, a dorsal fin appears on the surface. Then, what goes with the fin—a 3-ton, 32-foot, mechanical great white shark—tries to sink its urethane teeth into your hide (or at least your boat's). A 30-foot wall of flame that surrounds the vessel truly causes you to feel the heat in this $45 million attraction. We won't tell you exactly how it ends, but in spite of a captain who can't hit the broad side of a dock with his grenade launcher, some lucky Orlando restaurant will be serving blackened shark tonight. (*Tip:* The effects of this ride are far more spectacular after dark.) *Note:* While it lacks a height requirement, the shark may be too intense for kids younger than 6, and Universal recommends that expectant mothers avoid it.
Jake Rating: "Gimme the gun! I can shoot better than that." (He's really enjoyed this ride the last several times he rode it, but when he climbed aboard years ago as a preschooler he got a stiff neck—we call it post-traumatic shark.)

Jimmy Neutron's Nicktoon Blast
Frommer's Rating: A
Recommended Ages: 6–adult

Buckle up for one of the park's two new rides. In this one, you climb aboard Jimmy's Rocket Pod, which hurtles you through hyperspace thanks to a motion simulator, sophisticated computer graphics, state-of-the-art ride technology, animation, and programmable motion-based seats. Your task: Defeat the evil Yokians—egg-shaped aliens that have stolen Jimmy's latest invention, the Mark IV rocket, and are threatening to take over Universal Orlando and the rest of the world. The attraction also features Jimmy's robot dog, Goddard, his nemesis, Cindy Vortex, and popular characters from several other cartoons, including SpongeBob SquarePants, Rugrats, Wild Thornberrys, and Fairly Odd Parents. *Note:* You must be 40 inches or taller to join Jimmy's Air Force.
Andy Rating: "That's the best ride here!" (Arguably, it is, though the fact that it's new and this was his 1st time on it may have influenced his vote just a little.)

Men in Black Alien Attack
Frommer's Rating: A+
Recommended Ages: 8–adult

Armageddon may be upon us unless you and your mates fly to the rescue and destroy the alien menace. Once aboard your six-passenger cruiser, you'll buzz the streets of New York, using your "zapper" to splatter up to 120 bug-eyed targets. You have to contend with return fire and distractions such as light, noise, and clouds of liquid nitrogen (aka fog), any of which can spin you out of control. Your laser tag–style gun fires infrared bullets. Earn a bonus by hitting Frank the Pug (to the right, just past the alien shipwreck). The 4-minute ride relies on

360-degree spins rather than speed for its thrill factor. At the conclusion, you're swallowed by a giant roach (it's 30 ft. tall with 8-ft. fangs and 20-ft. claws) that explodes, dousing you with bug guts as you blast your way to safety and into the pest-control hall of fame—maybe. When you exit, Will Smith rates you anywhere from galaxy defender to bug bait. (There are 38 possible scores; those assigned to less than full cars suffer the scoring consequences.) **Note:** Guests must be at least 42 inches tall to climb aboard this $70 million ride.

Note II: Men in Black often has a *much* shorter line for single riders. Even if you're not alone but have older kids and are willing to be split up, get in this line and hop right on a vehicle that has less than six passengers.

Jake Rating: "I *really* liked that! But those roach guts? Yucko." (Well, it's just warm water, but at the moment of impact we thought it was pretty disgusting, too.)

Nickelodeon Studios
Frommer's Rating: A for Nick fans, C+ for others
Recommended Ages: 4–14
You'll tour the sound stages where Nick shows are produced, view concept pilots, visit the kitchen where Gak and green slime are made, and try new Sega video games. This 45-minute behind-the-scenes walking tour is aimed at the young set and is a fun escape from the hustle of the midway. There's lots of audience participation. A child volunteer gets slimed during the show and the entire tour might get to meet one or more of their favorite characters, including SpongeBob SquarePants.
Andy Rating: "I didn't know slime tasted like apple sauce." (Most tour guides explain that the green stuff is made from leftover desserts.)

Shrek 4-D
Frommer's Rating: B+
Recommended Ages: All ages
Universal Studios' second new ride is a 20-minute show that can be seen, heard, felt, and smelled thanks to film, motion simulators, OgreVision glasses, and other special effects, such as water spritzers. The attraction picks up where the movie left off—allowing you to join Shrek and Princess Fiona on their honeymoon (at least the G-rated portions of it). Once settled in specially designed seats in the main auditorium, you're transported to the fairy-tale realm of Duloc, as the screen comes alive as you help Shrek and Donkey rescue Fiona from her kidnappers, Lord Farquaad and his knights. Along the way, spiders will try to crawl on you and you'll ride a dragon that spritzes you when she clears her sinuses. The theater's seats are pneumatic air propulsion nodules that are capable of turning and tilting.

Terminator 2: 3-D Battle Across Time
Frommer's Rating: A+
Recommended Ages: 10–adult
This is billed as "the quintessential sight and sound experience for the 21st century!" The same director who made the movie, Jim Cameron, supervised this $60 million production. After a slow start, it builds into an impressive experience featuring the *Ah-nud* (on film), along with other original cast members. It combines 70mm 3-D film (utilizing three 23-ft.-×-50-ft. screens) with thrilling technical effects and live stage action that includes a custom-built Harley Davidson "Fat Boy." **Note:** The crisp 3-D effects are among the best in any Orlando park, but Universal has given this show a PG-13 rating, meaning the violence

and loud noise may be too intense for preteens. That may be a little too cautious, but some kids under 10 may be frightened. The rest may proclaim they want to go back.

Jake Rating: "Those 'bots were huge. I bet they cost a bundle." (We don't know the cost, but the six gleaming cyberbots that are part of the show are a towering 8 ft. each.)

Twister . . . Ride It Out
Frommer's Rating: A
Recommended Ages: 8–adult
Visitors from the twister-prone Midwest may find this re-creation a little too close to the real thing. An ominous funnel cloud, five stories tall, is created by swirling 2 million cubic feet of air per minute (that's enough to fill four full-size blimps), and the sound of a freight train fills the theater at rock-concert level as cars, trucks, and a cow fly about while the audience stands just 20 feet away. It's the windy version of *Earthquake* and packs quite a wallop. Crowds have been known to applaud when it's over. *Note:* This show, too, comes with a PG-13 rating. Its loudness and intensity certainly can be too much for children under 8. Also, readers who have visited Universal Studios Hollywood in California will find Twister similar in theme to that park's Backdraft attraction, although (sacrilege!) we think the one in California offers a better overall experience.

Woody Woodpecker's Nuthouse Coaster
Frommer's Rating: A+ for kids and parents, B+ for others
Recommended Ages: 4–adult
This is the top attraction in Woody Woodpecker's KidZone, an 8-acre concession Universal Studios made several years ago after being criticized for having too little for young visitors. This ride is a kiddie coaster that will thrill some moms and dads, too. While only 30 feet at its peak, it offers quick, spiraling turns while you sit in a miniature steam train. The ride lasts only 55 seconds and waits can be 30 minutes or more, but few kids will want to miss it. It's very much like the Barnstormer at Goofy's Wiseacre Farm in the Magic Kingdom (p. 172). *Note:* Its height minimum is 36 inches.

Andy Rating: " . . . more, More, MORE!" (He finally quit after six trips. We didn't think he would ever run out of gas.)

ADDITIONAL ATTRACTIONS
The **Boneyard** is an oft-changing area where you can see props used in a number of Universal movies.

The somewhat corny **Universal Horror Makeup Show** gives behind-the-scene looks at what goes into (and oozes out of) some of Hollywood's most frightening monsters. It has a PG-13 rating and may frighten young kids. **Lucy, A Tribute** is a remembrance of America's queen of comedy that will bore most kids after a few minutes, and the **Blues Brothers** launch their foot-stomping revue several times a day on Delancy Street (most kids will find it entertaining).

Tips Another Bye-Bye

In summer 2003, as part of a continuing out-with-the-old, in-with-the-new campaign, Universal Studios closed its **Wild, Wild, Wild West Stunt Show,** which had been part of the park since 1991. At press time, there was no word on what, if anything, would replace the show.

Back at Woody Woodpecker's KidZone, **Fievel's Playland** is a wet, western-themed playground with a house to climb and a water slide for small fry (the ride lines can get long, but most little kids love it). **Curious George Goes to Town** has water- and ball-shooting cannons (you and your kids will get wet).

SHOPPING AT UNIVERSAL STUDIOS FLORIDA

Every major attraction has a theme store attached. Although the prices are high when you consider you're just buying a souvenir, the **Hard Rock Cafe** shop in adjacent CityWalk is extremely popular with teens and preteens and has a small but diverse selection of Hard Rock everything (including memorabilia with astronomical sticker prices). If you've often longed for your own *Psycho* shower curtain (or you have a teen with a perverse sense of humor), step right up to the counter at **The Bates Motel Gift Shop.**

More than two dozen other shops in the park sell collectibles. Be warned, though, that unlike Walt Disney World, where Mickey is everywhere, Universal's shops are specific to individual attractions. If you see something you like, buy it. You probably won't find it in another store, although those at Orlando International Airport carry some items.

Note: Universal has a service similar to Disney's in which you can have your purchases delivered to the front of the park. Allow 3 hours.

GREAT BUYS AT UNIVERSAL STUDIOS FLORIDA

Here's a sampling of the more unusual gifts available at some of the Universal stores. Of course, in addition to these options, you can find the standard tourist

---

Universal Cuisine

The best restaurants in the theme park are just outside the main gates at CityWalk, Universal's restaurant and nightclub venue. But there are more than a dozen places to eat inside the park. Here are our favorites:

Best Sit-Down Meal: Lombard's Seafood Grille has a hearty fried clam basket, as well as lobster, fish, steak, pasta, and burgers ($11–$30). It's located across from Earthquake.

Best Counter Service: Universal Studios' Classic Monsters Cafe is one of the newer park eateries. It serves salads, pizza, pasta, and rotisserie chicken ($6–$12). It's off 7th Avenue near the Boneyard.

Best Place for Hungry Families: Similar to a mall food court, the **International Food and Film Festival** offers a variety of food in one location. With options ranging from stir-fry to fajitas, it's a place where a family can split up and still eat under one roof. There are kid's meals for under $4 at most locations. The food is far from gourmet but a cut above regular fast food. Main courses run from $5.50 to $11. It's located near the back of Animal Planet Live! and the entrance to Back to the Future.

Best Snack: The floats ($3–$5) at **Brody's Ice Cream Shop** are just the thing to refresh you on a hot summer afternoon. Brody's is located near Jaws.

fare with a staggering array of mugs, key chains, T-shirts, and the like. We've tried to include things you wouldn't find (or consider buying) anywhere else.

- **Back to the Future—The Store**   Real fans of the movie series will find lots of intriguing stuff here, but one of the more interesting items is a miniature version of a DeLorean.
- **Second Hand Rose**   There's a wide range of Coca-Cola memorabilia and a ton of sweet gifts inside this shop in the park's New York section.
- **E.T.'s Toy Closet and Photo Spot**   This is the place for plush stuffed animals, including a replica of the alien namesake.
- **Quint's Surf Shack**   This is the place to go for a different kind of T-shirt. Tropical colors, with subtle Universal logos, are the thing here.
- **Silver Screen Collectibles**   For an interesting, practical, and inexpensive little something to take home, check out the Woody Woodpecker backscratcher.
- **Universal Studios Store**   This store, near the entrance, sells just about everything when it comes to Universal apparel.

2 Islands of Adventure

Universal's second theme park opened in 1999 with a colorful and cleverly themed collection of fast and sometimes furious rides. At 110 acres, it's the same size as its big brother, Universal Studios Florida, but it seems larger and it's definitely *the* Orlando destination for thrill-ride junkies. Roller coasters roar above pedestrian walkways, and water rides slice through the park. The trade-off: There are few shows. This *is not the best choice for families with small children*—we'll tell you why below under "Some Practical Advice for Island Adventurers"—but this is the primo park if you have teens.

Expect total immersion in the park's various "islands." From the wobbly angles and Day-Glo colors in **Seuss Landing** to the lush foliage of **Jurassic Park,** Universal has done a good job of differentiating various sections of this $1 billion park (unlike Universal Studios Florida, where it's hard to tell if you're in San Francisco or New York). It's also done an outstanding job of differentiating Islands from Disney or any other Orlando park. The closest competitor in Florida is Busch Gardens in Tampa, but this attraction clearly has the edge on the ride front—at least when it comes to diversity (one of the reasons it's gained in attendance figures even as other parks have suffered drops).

The adventure is spread across six islands: the **Port of Entry,** a pass-through zone that has a collection of shops and restaurants, and five themed areas—**Seuss Landing, The Lost Continent, Jurassic Park, Toon Lagoon,** and **Marvel Super Hero Island.** The park offers a concentration of thrill rides and coasters, plus it has generous play areas for kids.

ESSENTIALS

GETTING TO ISLANDS OF ADVENTURE BY CAR   Universal Orlando is a half-mile north of I-4 Exit 75B, Kirkman Road/Highway 435. There may be construction in the area, so follow the signs directing you to the park.

PARKING   If you park in the multilevel garage, make a note of the row and theme in your area to help you find your car later. Parking costs $8 for cars, light trucks, and vans. Valet parking is available for $16.

TICKET PRICES   At press time, a **1-day ticket** cost $51.95 (plus 6% sales tax) for adults, $42.95 for children 3 to 9. A 2-day 2-park unlimited-access

Tips   **Some Practical Advice for Island Adventurers**

1. **The Shorter They Are . . .**   *Nine of the 14 major rides at Islands of Adventure have height restrictions.* Dueling Dragons and the Incredible Hulk Coaster, for instance, deny access to anyone under 54 inches. For those who want to ride but come with little kids, there's a baby or child swap at all of the major attractions, allowing one parent to ride while the other watches the tykes. But sitting in a waiting room isn't much fun for the little ones. So take your child's height into consideration before coming to the park or at least some of the islands.

2. **Cruising the Islands**   If you hauled your stroller with you on your vacation, bring it with you to the park. It's a very long walk from your car, through the massive parking garage and the nighttime entertainment district, CityWalk, before you get to the fun. Carrying a young child and the accompanying paraphernalia, even with a series of moving sidewalks, can make the long trek seem even longer—especially at the end of the day.

3. **The Faint of Heart**   Even adults riding without children need to heed all of the ride restrictions. Expectant mothers, guests prone to motion sickness, and those with heart, neck, or back trouble will be discouraged—with good reason—from riding most primo attractions. There's still plenty to see and do, but without the roller coasters, Islands of Adventure isn't so special.

4. **Beat the Heat**   Several rides require that you wait outside without any cover to protect you from the sizzling Florida sun, so bring some bottled water with you for the long waits (a 99¢ free-world bottle costs $2.50 if you buy it here) or take a sip or two from the fountains placed in the waiting areas. Makes sure your kids wear hats, sunscreen, and get enough to drink as well. Also, beer, wine, and liquor are more available at the Universal parks than the Disney ones, but booze, roller coasters, and hot weather can make for a messy mix.

5. **Cash in on Your Card**   You can save 10% on your purchases at any gift shop or on a meal at Islands of Adventure by showing your AAA (American Automobile Association) card. This discount isn't available at food or merchandise carts. And tobacco, candy, film, collectibles, and sundry items aren't included.

escape pass was $96.95 for adults, $83.95 for children 3 to 9; a 3-day 2-park pass was $111.95 for adults, $96.95 for children 3 to 9.

For more information on multiday pass options and VIP tours, see "Tickets, Passes & Tours," in the Universal Studios Florida section earlier in this chapter.

HOURS   The park is open 365 days a year, generally from 9am to 6pm, though often later, especially in summer and around holidays, when it's sometimes open until 9pm. Also, during Halloween Horror Nights, the park closes around 5pm, reopens at 7pm (with a new admission), and remains open until at least midnight. The best bet is to call before you go so that you're not caught by surprise.

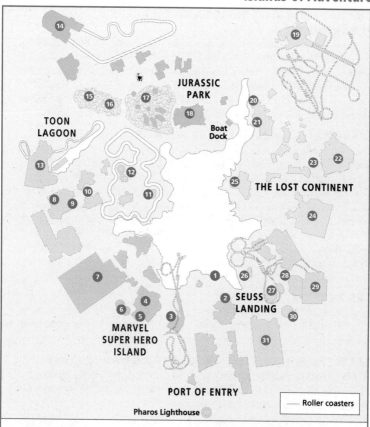

PORT OF ENTRY
Confisco Grille **2**
Island Skipper Tours **1**

MARVEL SUPER HERO ISLAND
The Amazing Adventures of Spider-Man **7**
Café 4 **4**
Doctor Doom's Fearfall **6**
Incredible Hulk Coaster **3**
Storm Force Accelatron **5**

TOON LAGOON
Comic Strip Café **8**
Comic Strip Lane **10**
Dudley Do-Right's Ripsaw Falls **13**
Me Ship, The Olive **11**
Popeye & Bluto's Bilge-Rat Barges **12**
Toon Trolley **9**

JURASSIC PARK
Camp Jurassic **15**
Jurassic Park Discovery Center **18**

Jurassic Park River Adventure **14**
Pteranodon Flyers **16**
Triceratops Discovery Trail **17**

THE LOST CONTINENT
Dueling Dragons **19**
Eighth Voyage of Sindbad **22**
Enchanted Oak Tavern
   (and Alchemy Bar) **21**
Flying Unicorn **20**
Mystic Fountain **23**
Mythos **25**
Poseidon's Fury **24**

SEUSS LANDING
Caro-Seuss-El **27**
The Cat in the Hat **31**
Circus McGurkus Cafe Stoo-pendous **29**
Green Eggs and Ham Cafe **26**
If I Ran the Zoo **28**
One Fish, Two Fish, Red Fish, Blue Fish **30**

MAKING YOUR VISIT MORE ENJOYABLE
PLANNING YOUR VISIT
You can get information before you leave by calling ℂ **800/711-0080,** 800/837-2273, or 407/363-8000. Ask for information about travel packages, as well as theme-park information. Universal sometimes offers a second day's ticket free or at a deeply discounted price. You can also write to Guest Services, 1000 Universal Studios Plaza, Orlando, FL 32819-7601. For online information, see "Planning Your Visit," for Universal Studios Florida earlier in this chapter.

INFORMATION FOR VISITORS WITH SPECIAL NEEDS
Guests with disabilities should go to **Guest Services,** located just inside the main entrance, for a *Disabled Guest Guidebook,* a Telecommunications Device for the Deaf (TDD), or other special assistance. You can rent a standard wheelchair for $10 or an electric one for $40 (both require a credit-card imprint, a driver's license, or $50 as a deposit). You can reserve them 24 hours or more in advance by calling ℂ **407/363-8000.** You can arrange for sign language interpreting services at no charge by calling ℂ **888/519-4899** (toll-free TDD), 407/224-4414 (local TDD), or 407/224-5929 (voice). Make arrangements for an appointment with an interpreter 1 to 2 weeks in advance. For more information on services available to those with disabilities, see p. 31.

THE BEST DAYS TO VISIT
Like Universal Studios Florida, it's best to visit Islands near the end of the week, on a Thursday or Friday. The pace is somewhat fast Monday to Wednesday, with the heaviest crowds on weekends and during summer and holidays.

SERVICES & FACILITIES AT ISLANDS OF ADVENTURE
ATMs   Machines accepting cards from banks using the Cirrus, Honor, and PLUS systems are located outside and to the right of the main entrance and in the Lost Continent near the bridge to Jurassic Park.

Baby Care   There are baby-swap stations at all of the major attractions. This allows one parent to wait while the other rides. Nursing facilities are located in the Guest Services building in the Port of Entry. Look for Family Services.

Cameras & Film   Film and disposable cameras are available at De Foto's Expedition Photography, to the right just inside the main entrance.

Car Assistance   Battery jumps are provided. If you need assistance with your car, raise the hood and use the call boxes located throughout the garage to call for security.

First Aid   There's one just inside and to the right of the main entrance and another in the Lost Continent, across from Oasis Coolers.

Lockers   Lockers are across from Guest Services near the main entrance and cost $7 and $10 a day, including a $2 refundable deposit. There are also lockers near the Incredible Hulk Coaster in Marvel Super Hero Island, the Jurassic Park River Adventure in Jurassic Park, and Dueling Dragons in the Lost Continent. The lockers at Dueling Dragons and the Incredible Hulk Coaster are free for the first 45 minutes. Thereafter or at the Jurassic Park River Adventure, they're $2 per hour to a maximum of $14 per day. You're not supposed to—and shouldn't—take things on these rides, so put them in a locker or give them to a nonrider for safekeeping.

Lost Children   If you lose a child, go to Guest Services near the main entrance or go to the first park employee you see. Children under 7 should wear name-tags.

Pets   You can board your small animals at the shelter in the parking garages for $10 a day (no overnight stays). Ask the attendant where you pay for parking to direct you to the kennel.

Ride Restrictions   Many of the park's attractions have minimum height requirements (see the listings that follow). Universal also recommends that expectant mothers steer clear of some rides (also noted in the listings).

Stroller Rental   Look to the left as you enter through the turnstiles. The cost is $10 for a single, $16 for a double.

Wheelchair Rental   Regular wheelchairs can be rented for $10 in the center concourse of the parking garage or to your left as you enter the turnstiles of the main entrance. Electric wheelchairs are $40. Both require a credit-card imprint, driver's license, or $50 as a deposit.

SUGGESTED ITINERARIES
For Families with Young Kids

If you have kids under 10, enter and go to the right to **Seuss Landing,** an island where everything is geared to the young and young at heart. You'll easily spend the morning or longer exploring real-life interpretations of the wacky, colorful world of Dr. Seuss. (The wild colors make for some good photographs.) Be sure to ride **The Cat in the Hat; One Fish, Two Fish, Red Fish, Blue Fish;** and **Caro-Seuss-El.** After all that waiting in line, let the little ones burn some energy playing in **If I Ran the Zoo.**

Grab lunch at the **Green Eggs and Ham Cafe** (yes, they really are green). Next, head to the **Lost Continent** to ride the **Flying Unicorn** (36-in. height minimum) and talk to the **Mystic Fountain,** then let them play in **Camp Jurassic** or watch a "hatching" at the **Discovery Center** in **Jurassic Park.** They can have some more interactive fun in **Toon Lagoon** aboard **Me Ship, The Olive** and meet characters on the **Toon Trolley** and Comic Strip Lane. Those 40 inches or taller can

end the day in **Marvel Super Hero Island** by riding the **Amazing Adventures of Spider-Man.**

For Families with Older Kids & Teens

Head left from Port of Entry to **Marvel Super Hero Island** and ride the **Incredible Hulk Coaster, The Amazing Adventures of Spider-Man,** and **Doctor Doom's Fearfall.** (If you arrive early, the line will be short for your 1st choice, but you'll have to wait or use Universal Express for the others.) There should be time to squeeze in **Dudley Do-Right's Ripsaw Falls** in **Toon Lagoon** before you break for lunch at **Comic Strip Café** or **Blondie's: Home of the Dagwood.**

Now that you're fully refueled, ride **Popeye & Bluto's Bilge-Rat Barges,** then move to **Jurassic Park,** where you can ride **Jurassic Park River Adventure** and visit the **Discovery Center.** End your day in the **Lost Continent,** where you can catch the show in **Poseidon's Fury,** then test your courage aboard **Dueling Dragons.**

PORT OF ENTRY
This "greeting card" to the park has five shops, four places to grab a bite, and **Island Skipper Tours,** which ferries passengers from the port to **Jurassic Park.** If you plan to save shopping for the end of the day, return to **Islands of**

Tips **Finding Your Way**

Other-than-English park maps are available at Guest Services in the Port of Entry in French, German, Japanese, Portuguese, and Spanish.

Adventure Trading Company, which offers a variety of merchandise linked to attractions throughout the park—from Jurassic T-shirts to stuffed Cat in the Hat dolls.

SEUSS LANDING

This 10-acre island, inspired by the works of the late Theodore Seuss Geisel, is awash in Day-Glo colors, whimsical architecture, and curved trees (the latter were downed and bent by Hurricane Andrew before the park acquired them). Needless to say, the main attractions here are aimed at the younger set, though anyone who loved the good Doctor as a child will enjoy some nostalgic fun on these rides. And those who aren't familiar with his work will enjoy the visuals— Seussian art is like Dalí for kids.

Caro-Seuss-El
Frommer's Rating: A+ for young kids, parents, and carousel lovers
Recommended Ages: All ages
Forget tradition. This not-so-average carousel gives you a chance to ride seven whimsical characters of Dr. Seuss (a total of 54 mounts), including cowfish, elephant birds, and mulligatawnies. They move up and down as well as in and out. Their eyes blink and heads bob as you twirl through the riot of color surrounding the ride. *Note:* A special ride platform lets guests in wheelchairs experience the up-and-down motion of the ride, making this a great stop for visitors with disabilities.

The Cat in the Hat
Frommer's Rating: A for preteens, C+ for teens and adults
Recommended Ages: All ages
Any Seuss fan will recognize the giant candy-striped hat looming over the entrance to this ride and probably the chaotic journey. Comparable to, but spunkier than, It's a Small World at Magic Kingdom (p. 170), The Cat in the Hat is among the signature children's experiences at Islands of Adventure. Love or hate the idea, *do it* and earn your stripes. Your couch travels through 18 scenes retelling *The Cat in the Hat*'s tale of a day gone very much awry. You, meanwhile, spin about and meet Thing 1 and Thing 2 in addition to other characters. *Note:* Pop-up characters may be scary for riders under 5, and expectant moms are discouraged from riding The Cat.
Andy Rating: "That felt weird. My eyes are still spinning." (The highlight is a revolving 24-ft. tunnel that alters your perceptions and leaves your head with a feeling oddly reminiscent of a hangover.)

If I Ran the Zoo
Frommer's Rating: A for the very young
Recommended Ages: 2–7
This 19-station interactive play land features flying water snakes and a chance to tickle the toes of a Seussian animal. Kids also can spin wheels, explore caves, fire water cannons, climb, slide, and otherwise burn off some excited energy. It's perfect for the preschool set.

One Fish, Two Fish, Red Fish, Blue Fish

Frommer's Rating: B+ for kids and parents

Recommended Ages: 2–7

This kiddie charmer is similar to the Dumbo ride (p. 170) at Magic Kingdom (including the ridiculously long line), although this one has a few added features. Your controls allow you to move your funky fish up or down 15 feet as you spin around on an arm attached to a hub. All the while, a song belts out rhyming flight instructions. Watch out for "squirt posts," which spray unsuspecting riders who don't follow the rhyme. Actually, even the most careful driver is likely to get wet.

MARVEL SUPER HERO ISLAND

Thrill junkies love the twisting, turning, stomach-churning rides on this island filled with building-tall murals of Marvel Super Heroes. Fans can **Meet the Marvel Super Heroes** in front of The Amazing Adventures of Spider-Man (check your guide map, handed out when you enter, or grab a copy at Guest Services, for times). And the munch crowd can dig into sandwiches and burgers at **Captain America's Diner** (in the $6–$10 range) and **Café 4** for pizza, pasta, and sandwiches ($4–$11).

The Amazing Adventures of Spider-Man *(Finds)*

Frommer's Rating: A+

Recommended Ages: 8–adult

The original Web Master stars in this exceptional show/ride (arguably, the best in town), which features 3-D action and special effects. The story line: You're on a tour of the *Daily Bugle* when—yikes!—something goes horribly wrong. Peter Parker suddenly encounters evil villains and becomes Spider-Man. This high-tech ride isn't stationary like the Back to the Future ride at Universal Studios Florida. Cars twist and spin, plunge and soar through a comic-book universe. Passengers wearing 3-D glasses squeal as computer-generated objects fly at their 12-person cars. There's a simulated 400-foot drop that feels an awful lot like the real thing. After the September 11, 2001, terrorist attacks, Universal removed preshow video depicting lower Manhattan under attack by comic-book villains. *Note:* Expectant mothers or those with heart, neck, or back problems shouldn't ride. There's a 40-inch height minimum.

Tip: Waits can be 45 minutes even on an off-day (and sometimes a whole lot longer), so use Universal Express if necessary. The ride also offers a single-rider line that can drastically reduce waiting times. So if it's an option on the day you're here and you've got older kids or teens who won't mind splitting up, take advantage of it.

Jake Rating: "I think I left my stomach back there." (He isn't the only one. This ride is unsuitable for young children and squeamish adults. If you are neither, it's an absolute must.)

Doctor Doom's Fearfall

Frommer's Rating: A

Recommended Ages: 8–adult

Look! Up in the sky! It's a bird, it's a plane . . . uh, it's you falling 150 feet, if you're courageous enough to climb aboard this towering metal skeleton. The screams that can be heard at the ride's entrance add to the anticipation of a big plunge followed by smaller ones. The plot? You're touring a lab when—are you sensing a recurring theme here?—something goes wrong as Doctor Doom tries to cure you of fear. You're fired to the top, with feet dangling, and dropped in intervals, feet first, leaving your stomach at several levels. The experience isn't quite up to the Tower of Terror's at Disney–MGM Studios (most of the velocity moves in the "up" direction, not the down one), but it's still frightful (and you do get a neat view of the entire park). The waiting times can also be scary, but the teens that flock here don't seem to mind too much. ***Note:*** Expectant mothers or those with heart, neck, or back problems shouldn't ride. If you or your kids are scared of heights, don't even think about getting on this one. Minimum height is 52 inches.

Incredible Hulk Coaster *(Finds*
Frommer's Rating: A+
Recommended Ages: 10–adult
Bruce Banner is working in his lab when—yes, again—something goes wrong. But this rocking rocket of a ride makes everything oh, so right, except maybe your heartbeat and stomach. From a dark tunnel, you burst into the sunlight, while accelerating from 0 to 40 mph in 2 seconds. While that's only two-thirds the speed of Disney–MGM's Rock 'n' Roller Coaster, this is in broad daylight, there's a lot more motion still to come, and you can *see* the asphalt! From there you spin upside down 128 feet from the ground, feel weightless, and careen through the center of the park over the heads of other visitors. Coaster-lovers will be pleased to know that this ride, which lasts 2 minutes and 15 seconds, includes seven inversions and two deep drops. Sunglasses, change, and an occasional set of car keys lie in a mesh net beneath the ride—proof of its motion and the fact that most folks don't heed the warnings to stash their stuff in the nearby lockers. As a nice touch, the 32-passenger metal coaster glows green at night (riders who ignore all the warnings occasionally turn green as well). ***Note:*** Expectant mothers or those with heart, neck, or back problems shouldn't ride it. Riders must be at least 54 inches tall.
Jake Rating: "No, thanks. I'm too young to die." (Once was more than enough for us, at least without a pint or 2 of courage lager. Adrenaline-seeking teens not only love this ride, they often wait in an even longer line to get a front-row seat for all the action.)

Storm Force Accelatron
Frommer's Rating: C
Recommended Ages: 4–adult
Despite the exotic name, this ride is little more than a spin-off of the Magic Kingdom's Mad Tea Party—spinning teacups that, in this case, have a 22nd-century design. While aboard, you and the X-Men's super heroine, Storm, try to defeat the evil Magneto by converting human energy into electrical forces. To do

---

Tips Out of Sight . . .

If your kids are at the age where they are just starting to test the more intense thrill rides, they may over-reach once or twice. To be on the safe side, tell your kids that if they find a ride a little too intense, they should hang on and *close their eyes*. A lot of the thrills at many of the parks are visually driven and the intensity will come down a notch or two if you can't see what's coming. The only exception to this is **Mission: Space** at Epcot (p. 185), where shutting your eyes may actually cause even more disorientation.

that, you need to spin faster and faster. In addition to some upset stomachs (your kids will be happy to give you one), the spiraling creates a thunderstorm of sound and light that gives Storm all the power she needs to blast Magneto into the ever-after (or until the next riders arrive). This ride is sometimes closed during off-peak periods. *Note:* Expectant moms are advised not to ride this ride.

TOON LAGOON

More than 150 life-size sculpted cartoon images—characters range from Betty Boop and Flash Gordon to Bullwinkle and Cathy—let you know you've entered an island dedicated to your favorites from the Sunday funnies. Many of the selected characters will probably be more familiar to parents than to children, but Popeye is present and the cool rides mean your kids will be happy anyway.

Dudley Do-Right's Ripsaw Falls
Frommer's Rating: A
Recommended Ages: 7–adult
The setting and effects at WDW's Splash Mountain are better, but the adrenaline rush here is higher. The staid red hat of the heroic Dudley can be deceiving: The ride that lies under it has a lot more speed and drop than onlookers suspect. Six-passenger logs take you around a 400,000-gallon lagoon before launching you into a 75-foot drop at 50 mph. At one point, you're 15 feet below the surface. Though the water is contained on either side, you *will* get wet. Younger kids may be a bit intimidated by the whole experience, but most children who make the height requirements like it. *Note:* Once again, expectant mothers or folks with heart, neck, or back problems should do something else. Riders must be at least 44 inches tall.
Jake Rating: "It was a little crowded in there." (One of the ride's biggest knocks is that its passenger logs are pretty cramped, especially if you have long legs.)

Me Ship, The Olive
Frommer's Rating: B+
Recommended Ages: 4–adult
This three-story boat is a family-friendly play land with dozens of interactive activities from bow to stern. Kids can toot whistles, clang bells, or play the organ. Sweet Pea's Playpen is a favorite of younger guests. Kids 6 and up will love Cargo Crane (adults will like it, too), where they can drench riders on Popeye & Bluto's Bilge-Rat Barges (see below). *Note:* If you or your kids are shutterbugs, the second and third deck of the good ship offer *great views and photo ops* of the Incredible Hulk Coaster and some of the rest of Islands of Adventure.

Popeye & Bluto's Bilge-Rat Barges
Frommer's Rating: A
Recommended Ages: 6–adult
This is the same kind of ride with the same kind of raft as Kali River Rapids at Animal Kingdom (p. 213), but it's a bit faster and bouncier. You'll be squirted by mechanical devices as well as the water cannons fired by guests at Me Ship, The Olive (see above). The 12-passenger rafts bump, churn, and dip (14 ft. at one point) along a white-water course lined with Bluto, Sea Hag, and other villains. You will get soaked—and then drenched for good measure. Kids find this a whole lot less intimidating than some of the other rides at Islands. *Note:* Yes, once again, expectant mothers or people with heart, neck, or back problems shouldn't ride this one. Riders must be at least 42 inches tall.

Jake Rating: "I think they put ice water in there." (The water is *c-c-cold,* a blessing on hot summer days but less so in Jan.)

Toon Trolley
Frommer's Rating: C+
Recommended Ages: All ages

Beetle Bailey and other favorites from the Sunday comics show up for high fives and autographs at this popular Universal character meet and greet. It's one to skip if you're on a tight schedule, but it's a nice respite from the madness. Check your handout show schedule or ask an Islands employee.

JURASSIC PARK

All of the basics and some of the high-tech wizardry from Steven Spielberg's wildly successful films are incorporated in this lushly landscaped tropical locale that includes a replica of the visitor's center from the movie. There's something here for every child in your party, from teens to toddlers. Expect long lines at the River Adventure and pleasant surprises at the Discovery Center.

Camp Jurassic
Frommer's Rating: A for young children
Recommended Ages: 2–7

This play area, similar in theme to the Boneyard in WDW's Animal Kingdom, has everything from lava pits with dinosaur bones to a rainforest and amber mines. Watch out for the spitters that lurk in dark caves. The multilevel play area has plenty of places for kids to crawl, explore, and spend energy. Young kids need close supervision, though. It's easy to get turned around inside the caverns.

Jurassic Park Discovery Center
Frommer's Rating: B
Recommended Ages: All ages

Here's an amusing, educational pit stop that has life-size dinosaur replicas and some interactive games, including a sequencer that pretends to combine your DNA with a dinosaur's. The "Beasaur" exhibit allows you to see and hear as the huge reptiles did. You can play the game show You Bet Jurassic (grin) and scan the walls for fossils. The highlight is watching a velociraptor "hatch" in the lab. Because there are a limited number of interactive stations, this can consume a lot of time on busy days.

Jurassic Park River Adventure
Frommer's Rating: A
Recommended Ages: 7–adult

After a leisurely raft tour along a faux river, some raptors escape and could hop aboard your boat at any moment. The ride lets you literally come face-to-face with "breathing" inhabitants of Jurassic Park. At one point, a *Tyrannosaurus rex* decides you look like a tasty morsel, and at another point, spitters launch venomous lungers your way. The only way out: an 85-foot plunge in your log-style life raft that will leave you dripping. If your stomach can take only one flume ride, this one's a lot more comfortable than Dudley Do-Right (see earlier), and the atmosphere is better. ***Note:*** Expectant mothers or those with heart, neck, or back problems shouldn't ride. Guests must be at least 42 inches tall.

Jake Rating: "Y'know, for a minute there I didn't think we were ever gonna get to the bottom." (It's steep and quick enough to lift your fanny out of the seat. Fact is, when Spielberg rode it, he made them stop the ride and let him out before the plunge.)

> **Tips Up, Up & Away**
>
> Strength and fitness folks can get a little extra workout at the small rock-climbing venue ($5 per person) outside the Thunder Falls Terrace restaurant in Jurassic Park. If you or the kids are looking for a more economical and less strenuous option, try walking the elevated trails and climbing the net ladders beneath the Pteranodon Flyers attraction, also in Jurassic Park (see above and below).

Pteranodon Flyers
Frommer's Rating: B
Recommended Ages: All ages (sort of—see restrictions below)
The 10-foot metal frames and simple seats are flimsy, but this quick spin around Jurassic Park offers a great bird's-eye view. The landing is bumpy and you'll swing side to side throughout, which makes some riders queasy. Unlike the traditional gondolas in sky rides, on this one your feet hang free from the two-seat skeletal flyer, and there's little but a restraining belt between you and the ground. *Note:* That said, this is a child's ride—single passengers must be between 36 and 56 inches tall; adults can climb aboard *only* when accompanying someone that size. And, because this ride launches only two passengers every 30 to 40 seconds, it can consume an hour of your day, even in the off-season. So, although it is nice and your little ones will love it, pass it up if you're pressed for time.
Andy Rating: "That was cool. It was like flying." (And the swaying adds a little thrill to the equation, too.)

Triceratops Discovery Trail
Frommer's Rating: C+
Recommended Ages: All ages
Meet a "living" dinosaur and learn from its "trainers" about the care and feeding of a 24-foot-long, 10-foot-high triceratops. It responds to touch, and its movements include realistic blinks, breathing, and flinches. Children (preschoolers and young kids are the ones who really like it best) get a chance to touch this heavyweight dino as it turns its head and groans. *Note:* This is another exhibit that's often closed seasonally and worthy of a visit only if you're not in a hurry.

THE LOST CONTINENT
Although they've mixed their millennia—ancient Greece with a medieval forest—Universal has done a good job creating a foreboding mood in this section of the park, whose entrance is marked by menacing stone griffins. This is another section that offers at least one attraction that every child in your party will find to their liking.

Dueling Dragons *(Moments*
Frommer's Rating: A+
Recommended Ages: 10–adult
Maniacal minds created this thrill ride—sending two roller coasters right at each other at high speeds (when both are running, which isn't always the case). True coaster crazies will love the intertwined set of leg-dangling racers that climb to 125 feet, invert five times, and three times come within 12 inches of each other as the two dragons battle and you prove your bravery by tagging along. A couple

> **Fun Fact Coaster Tidbit**
>
> One Dueling Dragon coaster seems to have an obvious advantage over the other. The Fire Dragon can reach speeds up to 60 mph, while the Ice Dragon has a top end of only 55 mph.

of thrill junkies (after riding this one for the 3rd time in a day) revealed to us that this is where they head in Orlando when they want the ultimate adrenaline rush. For the best ride, try to get one of the two outside seats in each of the eight rows. If you want to get into the front seat, there's a special (yes, longer!) line near the loading dock so that daredevils can claim the first car. *Note:* Expectant mothers or those with heart, neck, or back problems shouldn't ride. (Why aren't you surprised?) Riders must be at least 54 inches tall.

Eighth Voyage of Sindbad (Overrated

Frommer's Rating: C

Recommended Ages: 6–adult

The mythical sailor is the star of a stunt demonstration that takes place in a 1,700-seat theater decorated with blue stalagmites and eerie, gloomy shipwrecks. The show has water explosions and dozens of pyrotechnic effects including a 10-foot circle of flames. But it doesn't come close to the quality of the Indiana Jones stunt show in Disney–MGM Studios. Young kids will probably like it, and you can take solace in the fact that you get to rest your feet. (This show is closed from time to time, including during the run of Halloween Horror Nights, p. 20.)

Flying Unicorn

Frommer's Rating: A+ for kids and parents, B+ for others, except coaster crazies, who may find it a D

Recommended Ages: 4–adult

The Flying Unicorn is a small roller coaster that travels through a mythical forest on the Lost Continent, next to Dueling Dragons. It's very much like Woody Woodpecker's Nuthouse Coaster at Universal Studios Florida (p. 233) and The Barnstormer at Goofy's Wiseacre Farm in the Magic Kingdom (p. 172). That means a fast corkscrew run that is sure to earn squeals, but probably not at the risk of someone losing their lunch. It's the perfect introductory coaster for the young set. *Note:* Here's another one expectant moms are warned not to ride. The Unicorn has a 36-inch height minimum.

Mystic Fountain

Frommer's Rating: B+ for kids

Recommended Ages: 3–8

Located just outside Sindbad's theater, this interactive "smart" fountain delights younger guests (and usually provides a cool photo op or two for parents). It can see and hear, leading to a lot of kibitzing with those who stand before it. But if you want to stay dry, don't get too close when it starts "spouting" its wet wisdom. On the other hand, if you need a quick cool-off—go for it.

Poseidon's Fury

Frommer's Rating: B+

Recommended Ages: 6–adult

Clearly, this is the park's best show—though with a lack of competition, that's something of a backhanded compliment. The story line has changed a couple of times, but it still revolves around a battle between the evil Poseidon, god of the sea, and Zeus, king of the gods. Speaking of revolving, you'll pass through a small room that has a 42-foot vortex where 17,500 gallons of water swirl around you, barrel-roll style. (If you wear glasses, note that they will fog up completely when passing through the vortex—take them off if you can.) In the battle royale, the gods hurl 25-foot fireballs at each other. It's more interesting than frightening, but it's not worth the long lines that often plague it, so if you're on a tight schedule, use Universal Express or skip it. *Note:* The fireballs, explosive sounds, and rushing water may be a little too intense for children under 6.

SHOPPING AT ISLANDS OF ADVENTURE

There are more than 20 shops within the park, offering a variety of theme merchandise. You may want to check out **Cats, Hats & Things** and **Dr. Seuss' All the Books You Can Read** for special Seussian material. **Jurassic Outfitters** and **Dinostore** feature a variety of stuffed and plastic dinosaurs, plus safari-themed clothing. Superhero fans should check out **The Marvel Alterniverse Store** and the **Spider-Man Shop,** and the **Betty Boop Store** in Toon Lagoon is fun for her legions. **Islands of Adventure Trading Company** is a good stop on the way out if you're still searching for something that will help you or the folks back home remember your visit. For more on shopping at the theme parks, see chapter 9.

Note: Universal has a service similar to Disney's in which you can have your purchases delivered to the front of the park. Allow 3 hours.

DINING AT ISLANDS OF ADVENTURE

There are a number of stands where you can get a quick bite to eat, and a handful of full-service restaurants. The park's creators have taken some extra care to tie in restaurant offerings with the theme. The **Green Eggs and Ham Cafe** may be one of the few places on earth where you'd be willing to eat tinted huevos. (They sell as an egg-and-ham sandwich for about $6.) There are dozens of sit-down restaurants, eateries, and snack carts. To save money, look for the kiddie menus, offering a children's meal and a small beverage for $5. Also consider combo meals, which usually offer a slight price break. **Thunder Falls Terrace** in Jurassic Park, for instance, offers a rib-and-chicken combo as well as other options in the $8 to $12 range.

Here are some of our other favorites at Islands:

- **Best Sit-Down Restaurant** At **Mythos** in the Lost Continent, choose from occasionally changing selections such as jerk grouper, lobster-stuffed potato, pepper-painted salmon with lemon couscous, or pan-fried crab cakes with lobster sauce and basil. The atmospheric cavelike setting is pleasant. This is a grown-up dining affair, best suited for older children and adults. Entrees cost $10 to $21 and Mythos is usually open from 11:30am to 3:30pm daily.
- **Best Atmosphere for Adults & Teens** The **Enchanted Oak Tavern (and Alchemy Bar),** also in the Lost Continent, also has a cavelike interior, which from the outside looks like a mammoth tree, and is brightened by an azure blue skylight with a celestial theme. The tables and chairs are thick planks,

---

(*Fun Fact* **Food for Thought**

The green eggs at the Green Eggs & Ham Cafe get their color from a variety of spices, not food dye.

> **Tips Great Things to Buy at Islands of Adventure**
>
> Here's a sampling of some of the more unusual wares available at Islands of Adventure. It represents a cross section of tastes.
>
> **Jurassic Outfitters** There are plenty of T-shirts with slogans like "I Survived (the whatever ride)."
>
> **Spider-Man Shop** This shop specializes in its namesake's paraphernalia, including red Spidey caps covered with black webs and denim jackets with logos.
>
> **Toon Extra** Where else can you buy a miniature stuffed Mr. Peanut beanbag, an Olive Oyl and Popeye frame, or a stuffed Beetle Bailey? Life doesn't get any better for some of us.
>
> **Treasures of Poseidon** Located in the Lost Continent, it carries an array of blue glassware including tumblers; stuffed animals; and toys.

and the servers are clad in "wench wear." Try the chicken/rib combo with waffle fries for about $13. Mom and dad can sample 1 of the 45 types of beer on the menu.

- **Best Atmosphere for Kids** The fun never stops under the big top at **Circus McGurkus Cafe Stoo-pendous** in Seuss Landing, where animated trapeze artists swing from the ceiling. Kids' meals, including a souvenir cup, are $6 to $7. The adult menu features fried chicken, lasagna, spaghetti, and pizza ($7–$11). Try the fried chicken platter or the lasagna.
- **Best Vegetarian Fare** **Fire-Eater's Grill,** located in the Lost Continent, is a fast-food stand that offers a tasty veggie falafel for about $6. You can also get a tossed salad for about $3.
- **Best Diversity** **Comic Strip Café,** located in Toon Lagoon, is a four-in-one counter service–style eatery offering burgers, Chinese food, Mexican food, and pizza and pasta ($6–$9).

There are also several restaurants (see chapter 5, "Family-Friendly Dining") that are just a short walk from the park in Universal's entertainment complex, CityWalk.

3 SeaWorld

This popular 200-acre marine park explores the mysteries of the deep in a format that combines wildlife conservation awareness with plain old fun. While that's what Disney is attempting with its latest park, Animal Kingdom, the message here is subtle and a more inherent part of the experience.

SeaWorld's beautifully landscaped grounds center on a 17-acre lagoon and include flamingo and pelican ponds and a lush tropical rainforest. Shamu, a killer whale, is the star of the park along with his expanding family, which includes baby whales. The pace is much more laid-back than at either Universal or Disney, and it's a good way to break up a long week trudging through the other parks. Close encounters at feeding pools are among the real attractions (so be sure to budget a few extra dollars to buy fishy handouts for the sea lions and dolphins, who've turned begging into an art form).

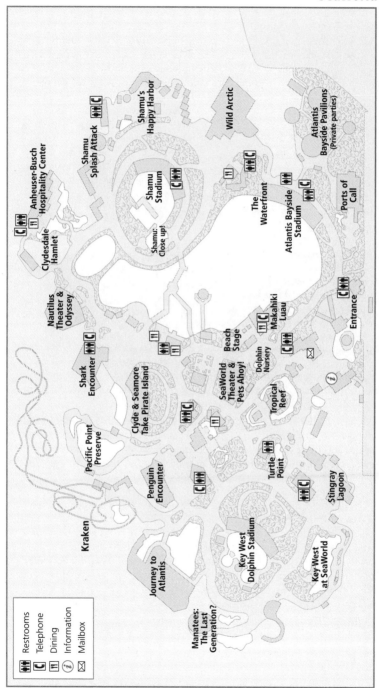

SeaWorld

Shamu's Happy Harbor

Wild Arctic

Shamu Splash Attack

Anheuser-Busch Hospitality Center

Atlantis Bayside Pavilions (Private parties)

Shamu Stadium

Clydesdale Hamlet

Shamu: Close up!

The Waterfront

Ports of Call

Nautilus Theater & Odyssey

Atlantis Bayside Stadium

Shark Encounter

Makahiki Luau

Entrance

Clyde & Seamore Take Pirate Island

Beach Stage

SeaWorld Theater & Pets Ahoy!

Dolphin Nursery

Pacific Point Preserve

Tropical Reef

Penguin Encounter

Turtle Point

Kraken

Stingray Lagoon

Journey to Atlantis

Key West Dolphin Stadium

Key West at SeaWorld

Manatees: The Last Generation?

Restrooms
Telephone
Dining
Information
Mailbox

249

SeaWorld manages a few thrills and chills. **Journey to Atlantis** is a high-tech water ride similar to Splash Mountain at Disney's Magic Kingdom and Jurassic Park River Adventure at Universal Orlando's Islands of Adventure. And **Kraken** is a floorless roller coaster that sports seven inversions, much like coasters such as Montu and Kumba at SeaWorld's sister, Busch Gardens in Tampa (p. 300). But this park doesn't try to compete with the wonders of WDW or Universal. Instead it lets you discover the crushed-velvet texture of a stingray or the song of the seals. And your children will enjoy that every bit as much as the techno wonders elsewhere.

In 2003, SeaWorld added a new waterfront area, featuring shows, music, and food; the park also replaced its Cirque de la Mer show with a new Cirque du Soleil–type show called **Odyssea.**

> *Tips* **Shuttle Service**
>
> SeaWorld and Busch Gardens in Tampa, both owned by Anheuser-Busch, have a shuttle service that offers $5 round-trip tickets to get you from Orlando to Tampa and back. The 1½- to 2-hour one-way shuttle runs daily and has five pick-up locations in Orlando, including at Universal and on I-Drive (*©* **800/221-1339**). The schedule allows about 7 hours at Busch Gardens. The service is free if you have a FlexTicket.

ESSENTIALS

GETTING TO SEAWORLD BY CAR The marine park is south of Orlando and Universal, north of Disney. From I-4, take Exit 72, Beeline Expressway/Highway 528, and follow the signs.

PARKING Parking costs $7 for cars, light trucks, and vans. The lots aren't huge, and most folks can walk to the entrance. Trams also run. Note the location of your car. SeaWorld characters such as Wally Walrus mark sections, but at the end of a long day it's easy to forget where you parked.

TICKET PRICES At press time, a **1-day ticket** cost $51.95 for ages 10 and over, $42.95 for children 3 to 9, plus 6% sales tax. (The price typically goes up $2 per year.) The park's new online ticketing allows you to go to its website, **www.seaworld.com**, buy your ticket over the Internet, then print it out and take the printout right to the turnstiles. *Note:* SeaWorld sometimes offers promotions that net you a second day free.

See p. 221 for information on the **FlexTicket**, multiday admission tickets for SeaWorld, Universal Orlando, Wet 'n Wild, and Busch Gardens.

SeaWorld's **Adventure Express Tour** ($80 adults, $75 kids plus park admission) is a 6-hour guided excursion that includes front-of-the-line access to Journey to Atlantis, Kraken, and Wild Arctic; reserved seating at two animal shows; lunch; and a chance to touch or feed penguins, dolphins, stingrays, and sea lions (*©* **800/406-2244** or 407/363-2380). It's the only way to dodge park lines, though these aren't as long as Disney's or Universal's.

HOURS The park is usually open from 9am to 6pm and sometimes later, 365 days a year. Call *©* **800/327-2424** for more information.

MAKING YOUR VISIT MORE ENJOYABLE
PLANNING YOUR VISIT

Get information before you leave by writing to **SeaWorld Guest Services** at 7007 SeaWorld Dr., Orlando, FL 32801, or call *©* **800/327-2424** or 407/351-3600.

ONLINE   SeaWorld information is available at **www.seaworld.com**. The *Orlando Sentinel* newspaper produces *Orlando Sentinel Online* at **www.orlando sentinel.com**. You can get a ton of information from the Orlando/Orange County Convention & Visitors Bureau website, **www.orlandoinfo.com**.

INFORMATION FOR VISITORS WITH SPECIAL NEEDS

The park publishes a guide for guests with disabilities, although most of its attractions are easily accessible to those in wheelchairs. SeaWorld also provides a Braille guide for the visually impaired. For the hearing impaired, there's a very brief synopsis of shows. For information, write to Guest Services at the address above or call ☎ **800/327-2424** or 407/351-3600. An accessibility guide is also available on SeaWorld's website (**www.seaworld.com**) in the "Park Information" section.

BEST TIME OF YEAR TO VISIT

Because this is a mostly outdoor, water-related park, you may want to keep in mind that even Florida gets a tad nippy during January and February. SeaWorld has smaller crowds from January through April, and from just after Labor Day until just before Thanksgiving.

BEST DAYS TO VISIT

Weekends, Thursday, and Friday are busy days at this park. Monday through Wednesday are usually better days to visit because tourists coming for a week go to the Disney and Universal parks early in their stays, saving SeaWorld for the end, if at all.

FAMILY-FUN ACTIVITIES

Because it has few thrill rides, SeaWorld has few restrictions, but you may want to check out the special tour programs offered through the education department. SeaWorld lives up to its reputation for making education fun and these wonderful experiences will entertain both you and your kids. They are well worth the extra expense. There are four 1-hour options: **Polar Expedition Tour** (touch a penguin), **Predators** (touch a shark), **Let's Talk Training** (sit in a training session), and **To the Rescue** (see manatees and sea turtles). All cost $15 for adults and $12 for children, plus park admission. Call ☎ **800/406-2244** or 407/351-3600 for information.

BUDGET YOUR TIME

SeaWorld has a leisurely pace because its biggest attractions are up-close encounters with the animals. Don't be in a rush. This park can easily be enjoyed in a day. Its layout and the many outdoor exhibits give it an open feel. Because of the large capacity and walk-through nature of many of the attractions, crowds generally aren't a concern except at Journey to Atlantis and Kraken. You also need to be in Shamu Stadium in plenty of time for the show. Wild Arctic also draws a sizable crowd. But the lines here don't reach Disney's proportions, so relax. Isn't that what a vacation is supposed to be about?

SERVICES & FACILITIES AT SEAWORLD

ATMs   An ATM is located at the front of the park. It accepts Cirrus-, Honor-, and PLUS-affiliated cards.

Baby Care   Changing tables are in or near most women's restrooms, and in the men's restroom at the front entrance near Shamu's Emporium. You can buy diapers in machines located near changing areas and at Shamu's Emporium.

> ### (Tips New Dining Programs
>
> SeaWorld is diving deeper into the restaurant game with **Dine with Shamu** (© **800/327-2424** or 407/351-3600 for information and reservations; www.seaworld.com), a reservations-only seafood buffet served poolside with Shamu as a special guest. While eating, guests can mingle and question SeaWorld trainers. The menu also includes chicken, beef, and salads. The cost is $32 for adults and $18 for kids 3 to 9, in addition to park admission. Reserving a spot 2 to 3 weeks in advance is usually more than enough unless you're coming in one of the crunch periods (summer, holidays), when you should reserve as soon as your travel plans are firm.
>
> **Sharks Underwater Grill** is an underwater venue with floor-to-ceiling windows where diners can dig into Florida and Caribbean treats while watching denizens swim by in the Shark Encounter exhibit. Menu prices are $16 to $24 for adults and $6 to $11 for kids 3 to 9 (pasta, hot dogs, chicken breast, steak, and popcorn shrimp) and theme-park admission is required. There also is the nightly **Makahiki Luau,** which blends Polynesian singers, musicians, and dancers with a menu that includes Hawaiian chicken, sweet and sour pork, and mahimahi in piña colada sauce ($37.95 adults, $27.95 kids 3–9). Theme park admission is not required. You can make a reservation for either dining option by calling © **800/327-2420;** for more information, head online to **www.seaworld.com**.
>
> Other dining options once you're inside the park include the **Seafire Inn** (stir-fry, burgers, coconut shrimp, chicken, and salads) and **Voyagers** (wood-fired pizza, grilled salmon, smoked chicken, and focaccia club sandwiches).

There's a special area for nursing mothers near the women's restroom at Friends of the Wild gift shop, near the center of the park.

Cameras & Film   Film and disposable cameras are available at stores throughout the park.

First Aid   First Aid Centers staffed with registered nurses are behind Stingray Lagoon and near Shamu's Happy Harbour.

Lockers   Lockers are located next to Shamu's Emporium, just inside the park entrance. The cost is $8 a day, plus a $2 deposit.

Lost Children   Lost children are taken to the Information Center. A parkwide paging system helps reunite guests. *Children under 7 should wear name-tags.*

Pet Care   A kennel is available between the parking lot and the main gate. The cost is $6 a day (no overnight stays).

Strollers   Dolphin-shaped strollers can be rented at the Information Center near the entrance. The cost is $10 for a single, $17 for a double.

Wheelchair Rental   Regular wheelchairs are available at the Information Center for $8; electric chairs are $32, with a $25 deposit.

MAJOR ATTRACTIONS

Clyde & Seamore Take Pirate Island
Frommer's Rating: B+
Recommended Ages: All ages

A lovable sea lion and otter, with a supporting cast of walruses and harbor seals, appear in this fish-breath comedy with a swashbuckling conservation theme. It's corny, but don't hold it against the animal stars. With all those high-tech rides at the other parks, you need a break, and this one delivers some laughs (as does a cute preshow).

Clydesdale Hitching Barn
Frommer's Rating: B (A for horse lovers)
Recommended Ages: All ages

You can get a gander at these Anheuser-Busch mascots (and equine beefcakes) throughout the day and, if you're timing is right, you might see them being groomed or exercised. In late winter and spring, you may get to see a mare and foal.

Journey to Atlantis
Frommer's Rating: A
Recommended Ages: 8–adult

Taking a cue from Disney Imagineers, SeaWorld has created a story line to go with this $30 million water ride. It has to do with a Greek fisherman and ancient Sirens in a battle between good and evil. But what really matters is the drop—a wild plunge from an altitude of 60 feet, in addition to lugelike curves and a shorter drop. Journey to Atlantis breaks from SeaWorld's edu-tainment formula and offers good old-fashioned fun. There's no hidden lesson, just a splashy thrill when you least expect it. And, yes, you will get wet. *Note:* Riders must be at least 42 inches tall. Expectant moms, as well as folks with heart, neck, or back problems, should find some other way to pass the time. **Jake Rating:** "I think I like that better than Splash Mountain." (We agree this

> **Tips Ski No More**
>
> In another sign of the economic cutbacks Central Florida attractions have made in the last few years, SeaWorld has closed its **Intensity Water Ski Show**, arguably the best ski show in the state.

ride has a slight edge over that Magic Kingdom ride, but we feel Jurassic Park River Adventure at Islands of Adventure, p. 244, wins the battle of Orlando's water coasters.)

Key West at SeaWorld
Frommer's Rating: B
Recommended Ages: All ages

This Caribbean-style village has island food, entertainers, and street vendors. But the big attractions are the hands-on encounters with harmless Southern diamond and cownose rays; Sea Turtle Point, the home of threatened and endangered species; and Dolphin Cove, where you can feed smelt to the namesakes. *Warning:* If you have a soft heart (and little kids are major softies for these animal encounters), it's easy to spend $20 feeding them.
Andy Rating: "That tickles!" (Indeed, those brave enough to feed the toothless rays likely will find one of their funny bones brushed.)

Key West Dolphin Fest
Frommer's Rating: B
Recommended Ages: All ages

At the partially covered, open-air Key West Dolphin Stadium, Atlantic bottlenose dolphins perform flips and high jumps, twirl, swim on their backs, and give rides to trainers. There's also an appearance by some false killer whales or *pseudocra crassidens* (see Whale Swim Adventure, below, for a special experience). The tricks are impressive, but it's like any other dolphin show (which will be just fine for your kids). If you go, see this before Shamu. He puts these little mammals to shame.

Kraken
Frommer's Rating: A+
Recommended Ages: 10–adult

SeaWorld's deepest venture onto the field of thrill-ride battle starts slow, like many coasters, but it ends with pure speed. Kraken is named for a massive, mythological, underwater beast kept caged by Poseidon. This 21st-century version offers floorless and open-sided 32-passenger trains (the better for you to see what awaits you) that plant you on a pedestal high above the track. When the monster breaks loose, you climb 151 feet, fall 144 feet, hit speeds of 65 mph, go underground three times (spraying bystanders with water), and make seven loops during a 4,177-foot course. It may be the longest 3 minutes, 39 seconds of your life. For adventurous teens, this is *the* top attraction in the park, and the lines can get very long. *Note:* Kraken carries a 54-inch height minimum. Expectant moms, as well as folks with heart, neck, or back problems, should skip this one.

Manatees: The Last Generation?
Frommer's Rating: B+
Recommended Ages: All ages

Today, the West Indian manatee is an endangered species. There are as few as 3,200 remaining in Florida's wild. Underwater viewing stations, innovative cinema techniques, and interactive displays combine here for a tribute to these gentle marine mammals. While this isn't as good as seeing them in the great outdoors, it's as close as most folks get, and it's a much roomier habitat than the tight quarters their kin have at the Living Seas in Epcot.

Odyssea
Frommer's Rating: B+
Recommended Ages: All ages

This 30-minute, Cirque du Soleil–style stage show opened at SeaWorld's Nautilus Theater in July 2003, replacing the Cirque de la Mer show that had a 5½-year run at the park. The new arrival combines acrobatics, music, comedy, and special effects on a set that transports guests into a faux underwater world. You and your kids will be entranced.

Penguin Encounter *(Overrated*
Frommer's Rating: C
Recommended Ages: All ages

Sadly, this is a very superficial encounter that transports you aboard a 120-foot moving sidewalk through Arctic and Antarctic displays. On the other side of the Plexiglas, you'll get a glimpse of 200 or so polar penguins as they preen, socialize, and swim at bullet speed in their 22°F (–6°C) habitat. You'll also see puffins and murres in a similar, separate area.

Pets Ahoy!
Frommer's Rating: B
Recommended Ages: All ages
Eighteen cats, 12 dogs, three pot-bellied pigs, and a horse are joined by birds and rats to perform comic relief in a 25-minute show held several times a day. Almost all of the stars were rescued from animal shelters. It's a charmer that appeals to young and old.

Shamu Adventure (Moments
Frommer's Rating: A+
Recommended Ages: All ages
Everyone comes to SeaWorld to see the big guy. The featured event is a well-choreographed show planned and carried out by very good trainers and very smart Orcas. The whales (reaching 25 ft. and 10,000 lb.) really dive into their work. The fun builds until the video monitor flashes an urgent Weather Watch and one of the trainers utters the fateful warning: "Uh-oh!" Hurricane Shamu is ready to make landfall. At this point, a lot of folks remember the warnings posted throughout the grandstand: *If you want to stay dry, don't sit in the first 14 rows.* Those who didn't pay attention get one last chance to flee. Then the Orcas race around the edge of the pool, creating huge waves of *icy* water and profoundly soaking anything in range. Veteran animal handler Jack Hanna also makes a video appearance on the huge overhead monitors, compliments of ShamuVision. ***Note:*** Arrive 30 minutes early for a good seat. The stadium is large, but it fills quickly.
Jake and Andy Rating, in unison: "That's *f-f-freezing!*" (We warned them about the splash zone.)

Shamu's Happy Harbor
Frommer's Rating: A for kids
Recommended Ages: 3–12
This 3-acre play area has a four-story net tower with a 35-foot crow's-nest lookout, water cannons, remote-controlled vehicles, nine slides, a submarine, tunnels, and a water maze. It's *one of the most extensive play areas* at any park and a great place for kids to unwind. Bring extra clothes for the kids (and maybe for yourself, too) because it's not designed to keep you dry.

Shark Encounter
Frommer's Rating: B
Recommended Ages: 3–adult
Remember Terrors of the Deep? Well, it's been renamed Shark Encounter, which also was the exhibit's original name. Pools out front have small sharks and rays (feeding isn't allowed here). The interior aquariums have big eels, beautiful but poisonous lionfish, hauntingly still barracudas, and bug-eyed pufferfish. This isn't a tour for the claustrophobic because you have to walk through an acrylic tube, beneath hundreds of millions of gallons of water. Also, small fry may find the swimming sharks a little too much to handle. ***Note:*** Part of this exhibit has given way to a new restaurant, **Sharks Underwater Grill** (p. 252).

Trainer for a Day
Frommer's Rating: A for trainer wannabes
Recommended Ages: 13–adult
Expect to invest a sizable chunk of your day and budget if you choose to do this 7-hour program. You work side-by-side with a trainer, meeting killer whales,

> *Fun Fact* **More Active Fun**
>
> SeaWorld offers three other hands-on programs. The 8-hour **Marine Mammal Keeper Experience** is similar to the Trainer for a Day program but lets you meet members of the veterinary staff and has encounters with dolphins, sea lions, beluga whales, and walruses ($389; minimum 13 years old and 52 in. tall; lunch, T-shirt and 7-day SeaWorld pass included).
>
> **Sharks Deep Dive** is a 2-hour experience that includes a 30-minute swim with sand tiger and nurse sharks, among other critters, in the Shark Encounter tank ($150 for certified divers, $125 for snorkelers, minimum age 10, T-shirt included).
>
> The 2-hour **Whale Swim Adventure** gives you a close encounter (about 30 min.) with false killer whales or pseudorcas, which are related to dolphins and killer whales ($200, minimum 13 years old and 52 in. tall, lunch and T-shirt included).
>
> The programs are not open to expectant mothers and park admission is required for the latter two. Call ✆ **407/370-1382** or visit **www.seaworld.com** for more information. *Note:* If you're willing to splurge on only one program, we'd opt for Discovery Cove (see below) over this one because it's much more hands-on.

dolphins, and sea lions, preparing meals, learning basic training techniques, and sharing lunch. It costs $389, which includes park admission for 7 consecutive days, plus lunch, a disposable camera, and T-shirt. If your teens are into this sort of thing, they'll have a great time. *Note:* You must be at least 13 years old, 52 inches tall, and able to climb, as well as able to lift and carry 15 pounds of critter cuisine. Expectant mothers are not allowed to participate. Call ✆ **407/370-1382** for reservations.

Wild Arctic
Frommer's Rating: B+
Recommended Ages: All ages for exhibit; 6–adult for ride
Enveloping guests in the beauty, exhilaration, and danger of a polar expedition, Wild Arctic combines a high-definition adventure film with flight-simulator technology to display breathtaking Arctic panoramas. After a hazardous faux flight over the frozen north, you emerge into an exhibit where you can see a playful polar bear or two, beautiful beluga whales, and walruses performing aquatic ballets (on different levels, you can see them both above and below the surface). Small kids and those prone to motion sickness may find the ride bumpy. There's a separate line if you want to skip the flight and just see the critters.

ADDITIONAL ATTRACTIONS
The park's other attractions include **Pacific Point Preserve,** a 2½-acre natural setting that duplicates the rocky home of California sea lions and harbor seals. It's another good opportunity for your kids to get up close and feed the animals. **Tropical Rain Forest,** a bamboo and banyan tree habitat, is the home of cockatoos and other birds. And the **Anheuser-Busch Hospitality Center** lets you indulge in free samples of Anheuser-Busch beers, after which the entire family

can stroll through the stables to watch the famous Budweiser Clydesdale horses being groomed.

SHOPPING AT SEAWORLD

SeaWorld doesn't have nearly as many shops as Walt Disney World and Universal Orlando, but there are lots of cuddly toys for sale around the park. Where else can you get a stuffed manatee but at **Manatee Cove?** The **Friends of the Wild** gift shop (it's near Penguin Encounter) is also nice, as is the shop attached to **Wild Arctic.**

DISCOVERY COVE: A DOLPHIN ENCOUNTER

Anheuser-Busch spent $100 million building this park, which debuted in 2000. That's one-tenth the price tag on Universal's Islands of Adventure. But Discovery Cove's gate price is substantially higher than its Universal and Disney rivals. At press time, visitors could choose from two options: $229 to $249 per person (depending on what season you visit the park) plus 6% sales tax—ages 6 and up—if you want to swim with a dolphin; $129 to $149 if you can skip that luxury. Both choices come with additional perks. We'll tell you more about those in a moment. First, let's dive into the main event.

If you've never gone for a dip with a dolphin, words hardly do it justice. But we'll try. It's exhilarating and exciting—exactly the kind of thing that can make for a most memorable occasion and vacation.

The actual dolphin encounter deserves an **"A+" rating.** It's open only to those ages 6 and older (younger guests or those who don't want to participate in the dolphin swim can take part in the other activities, although it's hard to imagine they will get $129 worth of benefit from them).

The park has a cast of more than two dozen dolphins, and each of them works from 2 to 4 hours a day. Many of them are mature critters that have spent their lives in captivity, around people. They love their bellies, flukes, and backs rubbed. They also have an impressive bag of tricks. Given the proper hand signals, they can make sounds much like a human passing gas, chatter in dolphin talk, and do seemingly effortless 1½ gainers in 12 feet of water. They take willing guests for rides in the piggyback or missionary position. They also wave "hello" and "goodbye" with their flippers and take great pleasure in roaring by guests at top speed, creating waves that drench them.

The dolphin experience lasts 90 minutes, about 35 to 40 minutes of which is spent in the lagoon with one of them. Trainers use the rest of the time to teach visitors about these remarkable mammals.

Tips New Arrival

SeaWorld's new 5-acre **Waterfront area,** which debuted in late spring 2003, added a seaport-themed village to the park's landscape. There are lots of entertainment options for the entire family here. On High Street, look for a blend of shops; "Kat 'n' Kaboodle," a purebred cat show; and the SeaFire Inn restaurant, where lunch includes a family-oriented musical revue called "Rico and Roza's Family Feast." The latter is heavily into audience participation. At Harbor Square, the funny Seaport Symphony orchestra has chefs making music with pots and pans. The park also is adding street performers, including a crusty old captain who tells fish tales and makes music with bottles and brandy glasses.

Unfortunately, the rest of the day isn't nearly as exciting. Discovery Cove doesn't deliver thrill rides, water slides, or acrobatic animal shows. But it has a number of other things to do if you're a member of the sun-and-surf set. Here's what you get even without the dolphin encounter:

- A limit of **no more than 1,000 other guests a day,** so you won't get that "crowded" feeling. (The average daily attendance at Disney's Magic Kingdom is 41,000.)
- Lunch, a towel, locker, sunscreen, snorkeling gear including a flotation vest, and free parking. Souvenir photos are about $20 a pop, but if you do the encounter, it's hard to resist one or more of you doing the tango with your dolphin.
- Other 9am-to-5:30pm activities include a chance to swim near (but on the other side of the Plexiglas from) **barracudas and black-tip sharks.** There are no barriers between you and the gentle rays and brightly colored tropical fish in a new 12,000-square-foot lagoon where some of the rays are 4 feet in diameter. The 3,300-foot Tropical River is a great place to swim or float in a mild current—it goes through a cave, two waterfalls, and a large aviary where you can also take a stroll, becoming a human perch for some of the 30 exotic bird species. There are also beach areas for catching a tan.
- **Seven consecutive days of unlimited admission** to either SeaWorld or Busch Gardens in Tampa (p. 300). Park admission normally costs $51.95 a day for adults and $42.95 for kids 3–9. *Note:* You can get 14 days of consecutive admission to *both* parks if you pay an extra $30 over the normal cost of admission to Discovery Cove.

One other option is Discovery Cove's trainer for a day ticket, which for $399 to $419 (depending on the season), allows guests 6 and older to also have a dolphin-training encounter, participate in guided snorkeling tours, feed fish, and interact with other critters, including rays. A paying adult must accompany guests ages 6 to 12.

You can drive to Discovery Cove by following the above directions to SeaWorld, then follow the signs. Unlike other parks, Discovery Cove doesn't have a parking charge. For up-to-the-minute information, call ✆ **877/434-7268,** or on the Internet go to **www.discoverycove.com**.

If you're headed for this adventure, we recommend making a reservation far in advance. There may be a lot of other deep-pocketed travelers landing when you do. *Note:* There is a chance of getting in as a walk-up customer. The park reserves a small number of tickets daily for folks whose earlier dolphin sessions were canceled due to bad weather. The best chance for last-minute guests comes during any extended period of good weather.

4 Other Area Attractions

There are—surprise!—a number of cool things in Orlando for families that don't revolve around Mickey, the Hulk, or Shamu. Now that we've covered the monster parks, we're going to explore some of central Florida's best smaller attractions.

IN KISSIMMEE

Kissimmee's tourist strip is on Walt Disney World's southern border and extends about 2 miles west and 8 to 10 miles east. Irlo Bronson Memorial Highway/U.S. 192, the highway linking the town to WDW and points west, is under perpetual road construction, and the development clutter can make it hard to see some

Orlando Area Attractions

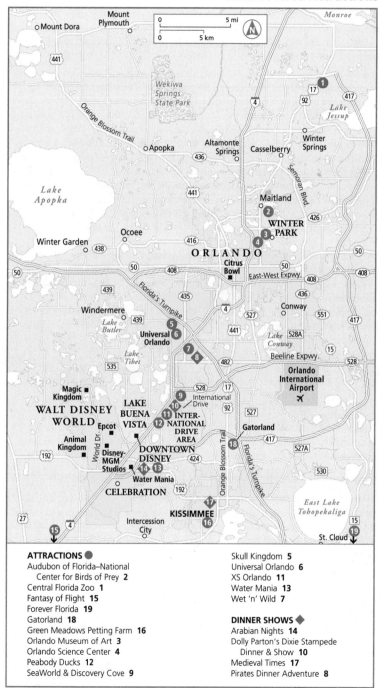

ATTRACTIONS ●
Audubon of Florida–National
  Center for Birds of Prey **2**
Central Florida Zoo **1**
Fantasy of Flight **15**
Forever Florida **19**
Gatorland **18**
Green Meadows Petting Farm **16**
Orlando Museum of Art **3**
Orlando Science Center **4**
Peabody Ducks **12**
SeaWorld & Discovery Cove **9**

Skull Kingdom **5**
Universal Orlando **6**
XS Orlando **11**
Water Mania **13**
Wet 'n' Wild **7**

DINNER SHOWS ◆
Arabian Nights **14**
Dolly Parton's Dixie Stampede
  Dinner & Show **10**
Medieval Times **17**
Pirates Dinner Adventure **8**

smaller destinations. Check with your hotel's front desk or the attractions for updates that might make finding them a little easier.

Note: The following prices don't include the 6% to 7% sales tax unless otherwise noted.

Gatorland *⚓ (Finds* **All ages** Founded in 1949 with only a handful of alligators living in huts and pens, Gatorland now houses thousands of alligators and crocodiles on its 70-acre spread. Breeding pens, nurseries, and rearing ponds are situated throughout the park, which also displays toads, insects, turtles, and a Galápagos tortoise. Its 2,000-foot boardwalk winds through a cypress swamp and breeding marsh. Your little ones will be thrilled with **Lily's Pad,** a pretty extensive water playground that's great for cooling off at the end of the day; and **Allie's Barnyard,** a petting zoo that's home to a llama.

There are three shows. **Gator Wrestlin'** uses the old "put-them-to-sleep" trick, but it's more of an environmental awareness program. The **Gator Jumparoo** is a crowd-pleaser for all ages in which the big reptiles lunge 4 or 5 feet out of the water to snatch a hunk of meat from a trainer's hand. And **Jungle Crocs of the World** showcases some of the world's toothiest carnivores. While you're here, try the smoked gator ribs or nuggets in the open-air restaurant (your kids will probably abstain), or grab a gator-skin souvenir in the gift shop. Allow 4 to 5 hours.

Note: Gatorland's new **Adventure Tours** program lets up to five guests become a Trainer for a Day. The $100, 2-hour experience (Gatorland admission included) puts you side by side with trainers and includes a chance to wrangle some alligators (minimum age 12). Other Adventure Tours include airboat rides ($55 adults, $45 kids), a nighttime airboat ride ($38 adults, $28 kids), and a spring alligator egg-collecting excursion ($49, minimum age 12).

14501 S. Orange Blossom Trail (U.S. 441; between Osceola Pkwy. and Hunter's Creek Blvd.). *©* **800/393-5297** or 407/855-5496. www.gatorland.com. Admission $19.95 adults, $9.95 children 3–12 including tax. Daily 9am–5 or 6pm usually, but closing times vary by season. Free parking. From I-4, take Exit 65/Osceola Pkwy. east to U.S. 17/92/441 and go left/north. Gatorland is 1½ miles on the right.

Green Meadows Petting Farm **All ages** Families can take a break from the razzle-dazzle and get a taste of country at this 300-critter farm that features pigs, chickens, ducks, geese, donkeys, and more. The 2-hour guided tour includes a chance to milk a cow and the farm also has pony, train, and hay rides. The emphasis is on teaching children and their tagalongs about life on a farm. Allow about 3 to 4 hours.

1368 S. Poinciana (5 miles south of U.S. 192). *©* **407/846-0770.** www.greenmeadowsfarm.com. Admission $17 3-adult. Daily 9:30am–4pm. From I-4, take Exit 64A/U.S. 192 east about 5 miles, then go south on Poinciana.

Water Mania **All ages** You'll find a variety of aquatic attractions in this 36-acre water park. You can boogie board or body surf in the wave pools, float lazily along an 850-foot river, enjoy a white-water tube run on **Riptide,** and spiral down the **Twin Tornadoes** water slide. If you dare, ride **The Screamer,** a 72-foot free-fall speed slide, or the **Abyss,** an enclosed tube slide that corkscrews through 380 feet of darkness, exiting into a splash pool. There's a rainforest-themed water playground and a miniature train ride for smaller kids, a miniature golf course, and a picnic area with arcade games, volleyball, and a beach. *Note:* This park has fewer thrill rides than Disney's Typhoon Lagoon (p. 214) and Blizzard Beach (p. 215) or Wet 'n Wild (listed a bit later), so it has fewer teens and young adults, making it more attractive to families with younger kids. Allow 4 to 5 hours.

Tips **The New Kid in Town**

The **Hard Rock Vault,** a $32 million collection of guitars, rock star costumes, photos, and other memorabilia owned by Hard Rock Cafe International, opened in late 2002. It's located in The Mercado, a shopping and entertainment plaza on International Drive (✆ **407/599-7625;** www. hardrock.com/Vault). Among the treasures: a pair of Jim Morrison's leather pants, Buddy Holly's signature specs, and an Elvis Presley electric guitar. Speaking of Elvis, he hasn't left this building. In fact, he has his own room—The King's Chamber. Admission costs $14.95 adults, $8.95 kids. If your kids have reached the rock- and pop-loving age, they'll likely enjoy it.

6073 W. Irlo Bronson Memorial Hwy./U.S. 192 (just east of I-4). ✆ 800/527-3092 or 407/396-2626. www. watermania-florida.com. Admission $19.95 adults, $16.95 kids 3–9. Mar–Sept daily 10am–5pm; Oct 10am–5pm Wed–Sat. Parking $6. From I-4, take Exit 64A/U.S. 192 east about ½ mile.

INTERNATIONAL DRIVE AREA

These attractions are a 10- to 15-minute drive from the Disney area and 5 to 10 minutes from Universal Orlando. Most appeal to special interests, but one is free (the Peabody Ducks' show) and another, Wet 'n Wild, is in the same class as Disney's water parks.

Peabody Ducks ★ *Moments* **All ages** One of the best shows in town is short but sweet, and, more importantly, *free.* And your children, especially young kids will love it. The Peabody Orlando's five mallards march into the lobby each morning, accompanied by John Philip Sousa's "King Cotton March" and their own red-coated duck master. They get to spend the day splashing in a marble fountain. Then, in the afternoon, they march back to the elevator and up to their fourth-floor "penthouse." Donald Duck never had it this good. And there are multiple crews, so every couple of months they get to rotate back to the farm for some extra R&R. Allow 1 hour.

9801 International Dr. (between the Bee Line Expwy. and Sand Lake Rd.). ✆ 800/732-2639 or 407/352-4000. Free admission. Daily at 11am and 5pm. Free self-parking, valet parking $8. From I-4, take Exit 74A, Sand Lake Rd./Hwy. 528, east to International Dr., then south. Hotel is on the left across from the Convention Center.

Skull Kingdom **Age 10 and up** As you wander the stone halls inside the Skull Castle, you'll be taunted and terrified by a cast of ghoulish characters second in central Florida only to the crew at Universal Orlando's Halloween Horror Nights, but this show runs year-round. It's not for children under 10. Allow about 30 minutes to walk through the castle.

5933 American Way (just off the intersection of International Dr. and Universal Blvd., 3 blocks east of Universal Orlando). ✆ 407/354-1564. www.skullkingdom.com. Admission $14.95 including tax per person. Free parking. Mon–Thurs 6–11pm; Fri–Sun noon–midnight. From I-4, take Exit 75A/Hwy. 435 South to American Way and look for the giant skull castle.

Wet 'n Wild ★★ **All ages** Who knew people came in so many shapes and sizes? Stacked or stubby, terribly tan or not, all kinds come here, so there's no reason to be bashful about squeezing into a bathing suit and going out in public. Wet 'n Wild is America's third most popular water park (behind Blizzard Beach and Typhoon Lagoon, respectively). It offers 25 acres of fun, including: **The Flyer,** a six-story four-passenger toboggan run through 450 feet of banked curves; the **Surge,** which is one of the longest (580 ft. of curves) and fastest multipassenger tube rides in the Southeast; and **Black Hole,** a two-person spaceship-style raft that makes a 500-foot twisting, turning voyage through darkness (all three rides have *a minimum height of 36 in.* and require that children 36 in.–48 in. be accompanied by an adult). You can also float for a mile on **Lazy River** and ride **Blue Niagara,** a 300-foot six-story loop-and-dipster that also has a plunge (48-in. height minimum); **Knee Ski,** a cable-operated half-mile knee-boarding course that's open in warm-weather months only (56-in. height minimum); **Der Stuka,** a six-story, free-fall speed slide (48-in. height minimum); and **Mach 5,** which has a trio of twisting, turning flumes. The park also has **a large kids' area** with mini-versions of the big rides. If you enjoy the water, plan on spending a full day here.

Note: In addition to the admission prices below, Wet 'n Wild is part of the multiday **FlexTicket package** (p. 221) that includes admission to Universal Orlando (which owns this attraction), SeaWorld, and Busch Gardens in Tampa (see the beginning of this chapter for more information).

6200 International Dr. (at Universal Blvd.). © **800/992-9453** or 407/351-1800. www.wetnwild.com. Admission $31.95 adults, $25.95 children 3–9. Hours vary seasonally, but the park usually is open at least 10am–5pm daily, weather permitting. You can rent tubes ($4), towels ($2), and lockers ($5); all require a $2 deposit. Parking is $6 for cars, light trucks, and vans. From I-4, take Exit 75A/Hwy. 435 South, and follow the signs.

XS Orlando   Age 6 and up

As the owners say, you can "dine, dance, and defend the world" inside this three-story building. The attraction's 110 simulators—featuring golf, thoroughbred racing, and NASCAR driving, among others—are the primary calling cards for some. You can win prizes (T-shirts and more) that also are sold in the gift shop. You can buy game cards by time ($20 an hour, $25 for 2 hr.) or dollar amount. If your children have reached the video game stage, they'll be in heaven. There's also a DJ and restaurant (serving seafood and steaks, with entrees running $17–$27). The later you arrive, the more adult the atmosphere.

9101 International Dr., in Pointe Orlando. © **407/226-8922.** www.xsorlando.com. Free admission. Sun–Thurs noon–midnight; Fri–Sat noon–2am. From I-4, take Exit 74A, Sand Lake Rd./Hwy. 528, east to International Dr.; turn south. Pointe Orlando is on the left.

ELSEWHERE IN CENTRAL FLORIDA

The listings that follow are out of the mainstream tourist areas, meaning you won't have to battle heavy crowds. The Central Florida Zoo, Orlando Museum of Art, and Orlando Science Center are close enough to incorporate a visit to Winter Park if you choose to make a day of it.

Central Florida Zoo *(Finds*   All ages

This community zoo has come a long way since it was born in 1923 when a circus came to town, leaving a monkey and a goat behind. The monkey rode the goat in the earliest show. Today, the animal collection includes beautiful clouded leopards, cheetahs, and black-footed cats, all of which are endangered. You'll also meet a ham of a hippo named Geraldine as well as black howler monkeys, siamangs, American crocodiles, a banded Egyptian cobra, a Gila monster, hyacinth macaws, barred owls, bald eagles, and dozens of other species. The zoo's website (see below) also has a fun and educational **"just for kids"** link. The zoo has half-price admission for everyone Thursdays from 9 to 10am and all day Tuesdays for seniors 60 and over. Allow 2 to 3 hours.

3755 NW U.S. 17/92, Sanford. © **407/323-4450.** www.centralfloridazoo.org. Admission $8 adults, $5 seniors, $4 children 3–12. Daily 9am–5pm. Free parking. Take I-4 Exit 104 right onto Orange Ave., turn left at the traffic light on Lake Monroe Rd., then right on U.S. 17/92. The zoo is on the right.

Forever Florida   All ages   The 4,700-acre Crescent J Ranch is a nature preserve that offers a chance to see native wildlife, Florida flora, and a working cat-
tle ranch by guided tour. Options include touring by horseback, bike, covered
wagon, and Cracker coach, a funky buggy that puts riders on a perch 10 feet
above ground level. Allow a half day or longer to get here, take the tour, and see
the grounds, which also include a pony riding ring (there are ponies set aside for
young kids to ride), hiking trails, and a petting zoo. Especially cool for kids is
the **Fossil Dig,** a sandpit that has real fossils (dinosaur bones,and so on) for
them to unearth.

4755 N. Kenansville Rd., St. Cloud (southeast of Kissimmee). ℭ **866/854-3837.** www.foreverflorida.com.
Tours and rides $28–$89.50. Mon–Thurs 8am–3pm; Fri–Sat 8am–6pm; first tours at 10am. Free parking. Take
I-4 Exit 64A/U.S. 192 east about 15 miles to U.S. 441, then go south 7½ miles to Forever Florida on the left.

Orlando Museum of Art ✿   **Age 6 and up**   This local heavyweight handles
some of the most prestigious traveling exhibits in the nation. The museum,
founded in 1924, hosts special exhibits throughout the year, but even if you miss
one, it's worth a stop to see its rotating permanent collection of 19th- and 20th-
century American art, pre-Columbian art dating from 1200 B.C to A.D. 1500,
and African art. The museum has interactive Discovery Centers and activity
bags that give kids (and their parents) hands-on activities that relate to the permanent exhibitions. It's still a little too sophisticated for very young children,
but older ones will enjoy some time here. Allow 2 to 3 hours.

2416 N. Mills Ave. (in Loch Haven Park). ℭ **407/896-4231.** www.omart.org. Admission $6 adults, $5 seniors and students, $3 children 4–11. Tues–Fri 10am–4pm; Sat-Sun noon–4pm. Free parking. Take I-4 Exit
85/Princeton St. east and follow signs to Loch Haven Park.

Orlando Science Center ✿✿ *Finds*   **All ages**   The four-story center, the
largest of its kind in the Southeast, provides 10 exhibit halls that allow visitors
to explore everything from Florida swamps to the arid plains of Mars to the
human body. There's also a **Weird Science** hall (hosted by Dr. Dare and his
creation, Frankenboy), featuring a number of interactive sound, graphics, animation, and video kiosks. One of the big attractions is the **Dr. Phillips Cine-
Dome,** a 310-seat theater that presents large-format films, planetarium shows,
and laser-light extravaganzas. In **KidsTown,** little folks wander in exhibits representing a miniature version of the big world around them. In one section,
there's a pint-size community that includes a construction site, park, and well-
ness center. **Science City,** located nearby, includes physics lessons and a power
plant, and **123 Math Avenue** uses puzzles and other things to make learning
math fun. Children of all ages will find at least one or two (and often more)
memorable experiences waiting for them. Allow 3 to 4 hours, more if your family has inquiring minds.

777 E. Princeton St. (between Orange and Mills aves., in Loch Haven Park). ℭ **888/672-4386** or 407/514-
2000. www.osc.org. All-in-one tickets $14.95 adults ($9.95 Fri–Sat after 6pm), $13.95 students and seniors
55 and older ($8.95 Fri–Sat after 6pm), and $9.95 children 3–11 ($4.95 Fri–Sat after 6pm). Tues–Thurs 9am–
5pm; Fri–Sat 9am–9pm; Sun noon–5pm. Parking available in a garage across the street for $3.50. Take I-4
Exit 85/Princeton St. east and cross Orange Ave.

5 Attractions Outside Orlando

Just outside Orlando, you'll find a couple more places to visit. **Fantasy of Flight**
offers a look at the yesterday, today, and tomorrow of aviation as well as a simulator. It's a good way for aviation buffs to spend a morning or an afternoon.
And a short drive from beautiful Winter Park, about 30 minutes from the

theme-park hubbub, the **Audubon of Florida—National Center for Birds of Prey** offers your kids the chance to get up close and personal with eagles, hawks, and other magnificent raptors.

Audubon of Florida—National Center for Birds of Prey 🐦 *(Finds)* **Age 8 and up**   In addition to being a rehabilitation center—one of the biggest and most successful in the Southeast—this is a great place to get to know winged wonders that roost here and earn their keep by entertaining the relatively few visitors who come. It's a wonderful chance for your kids to get an up-close look at these magnificent birds in a relaxed setting. You can get a close look at hams such as Elvis, the blue suede shoe–wearing American kestrel; Daisy, the polka dancing barn owl; and Trouble, a bald eagle born with a misaligned beak. *Note:* The nonprofit center reopened in spring 2002 after a $2 million, 4-year expansion. Allow 2 hours.

1101 Audubon Way, Maitland. © **407/644-0190.** www.adoptabird.org or www.audubonofflorida.org/conservation/cbop.htm. Recommended donation $5 adults, $4 children 3–12. Tues–Sun 10am–4pm. From Orlando, go north on I-4 Exit 88, Lee Rd./Hwy. 423, turn right/east, and at the first light (Wymore Rd.) go left, then right/east at the next light (Kennedy Blvd.). Continue a half-mile to East Ave., turn left, and go to the stop sign at Audubon Way. Turn left, and the center is on the right.

Fantasy of Flight   Age 8 and up   Wannabe flyboys and -girls can have all sorts of fantasies in this attraction, which takes guests to the days when earthlings, in this case pilots, went sky diving . . . because they had no other choice. The fun includes flying a fighter simulator outfitted with the sights, sounds, and (hang onto your lunch) motion of a World War II combat plane. Immersion experiences give you the feeling of flying through stratosphere clouds. Exhibits include a Douglas B-23 Dragon, an Fi-103 Flying Bomb, an F4U-4 Corsair, and a replica of the *Spirit of St. Louis*. You also can tour an airplane restoration shop. Allow 2 to 3 hours.

1400 Broadway Blvd., Polk City. © **863/984-3500.** www.fantasyofflight.com. Admission $24.95 adults, $22.95 seniors 60 and over, $13.95 children 5–12. Daily 9am–5pm. Free parking. Take I-4 south of Orlando to Exit 44/Hwy. 559, turn north to the attraction.

8

Orlando for Active Families

The majority of O-Town's visitors overlook the fact that there are plenty of things to do far, far away from the theme park razzle-dazzle (and at a much more laid-back pace and price). But Central Florida has a lengthy menu of outdoor and indoor recreation venues that cater to all members of the family, from championship golf courses and tennis centers to lakes for boating and fishing. (You can even grab a board and go surfing in a huge wave pool!) If you and your kids are looking for a little four-legged fun, you can giddy-up on horseback or stretch out and sing-along on an old-fashioned hayride.

Those of you who decide to become a POD (prisoner of Disney) will find plenty of greenery around Mickey's city-size property, but you won't be able to discover some of the real natural treasures—state and municipal parks—that offer relaxation and in many cases a chance to see wildlife. To get to most of these, you'll need a car (or you'll face a costly taxi or limo ride) because they're out of the mainstream tourist areas. *Note:* We'll tell you about a pair of pristine federal treasures, Canaveral National Seashore and Merritt Island National Wildlife Refuge, that are within driving distance of Walt Disney World in chapter 11.

1 Sports

Walt Disney World and the surrounding areas have plenty of recreational options for those who believe the theme parks aren't the be-all and end-all of Orlando's existence. Most of those that are listed below are open to everyone, no matter where you're staying. The prices listed don't include tax unless otherwise noted. For further information about WDW recreational facilities, call ☎ **407/939-7529,** or on the Internet go to **www.disneyworld.com** and click the "recreation" link.

AIRBOATING You can giddy-up-and-glide across the surface of local waters at **Boggy Creek Airboat Rides** in Kissimmee (☎ **407/344-9550;** www.bcairboats.com), where you'll pay $18 per adult and $13 per child for half-hour tours. Another choice is **Old Fashioned Airboat Rides** in Christmas, east of Orlando (☎ **407/568-4307;** www.airboatrides.com), which charges $35 per adult and $15 per child for 90 minutes.

BALLOONING There are several places in the area to experience an early-morning hot-air balloon flight, including **Orange Blossom Balloons** in Lake Buena Vista (☎ **407/239-7677;** www.orangeblossomballoons.com). Rates run about $165 per adult and $95 per child 10 to 15, and include a champagne toast (sorry, kids) at the conclusion of the flight and a breakfast buffet or picnic afterward. Children who make the age grade will probably be delighted with the view and the unique sensation, unless they (or you) don't see eye-to-eye with heights.

BICYCLING Bike rentals (single and multi-speed adult bikes, tandems, baby seats, and children's bikes—including those with training wheels) are available

Tips Hitting the Links

Walt Disney World operates five 18-hole, par-72 golf courses and one 9-hole, par-36 walking course, so if you want to work on your putting and need some time away from the kids (who will most likely prefer an outing on one of Disney's mini-golf courses—see p. 218), you'll have plenty of options. All of Disney's courses are open to the public and offer pro shops, equipment rentals, and instruction. The rates are $109 to $175 per 18-hole round for resort guests ($5 more if you're not staying at a WDW property). Twilight specials are available. For tee times and information, call ☏ 407/824-2270 up to 7 days in advance (up to 30 days for Disney resort and "official" property guests). Call ☏ 407/934-7639 for information about golf packages.

Beyond Mickey's shadow, try **Celebration Golf Club** (☏ 888/275-2918 or 407/566-4653; www.celebrationgolf.com), which has an 18-hole regulation course (greens fees $30–$115) that kids under 17 are eligible to play, and a 3-hole junior course for 5 to 9 year olds. Note that there is a dress code at the club, so be sure to ask ahead so that your kids are decked out in suitable attire. **Champions Gate** (☏ 888/554-9301 or 407/787-4653; www.championsgategolf.com) offers 36 holes designed by Greg Norman, where greens fees will set you back $82 to $125. **Orange County National** (☏ 407/656-2626; www.orangecounty nationalgolf.com) has 36 Phil Ritson–designed holes; greens fees run $50 to $135.

Golf magazine recognized the 45 holes designed by Jack Nicklaus at the **Villas of Grand Cypress** ✦✦✦ resort (p. 88) as among the best in the nation. Tee times begin at 8am daily. Special rates are available for children under 17 and the resort even runs a 5-day summer golf program for kids interested in the game. For information call ☏ 407/239-1909. The course is generally restricted to guests or guests of guests (an average of $175 per round), but there's limited play available to those not staying at the resort. Fees begin at $225.

Also consider **Golfpac** (☏ 888/848-8941 or 407/260-2288; www.golf pacinc.com), an organization that packages golf vacations with accommodations and other features and prearranges tee times at more than 40 Orlando-area courses. The earlier you call (months, if possible), the better your options. **Tee Times USA** (☏ 888/465-3356; www.teetimes usa.com) and **Florida Golfing** (☏ 877/263-4653; www.floridagolfing. com) are two other reservation services that offer packages and course information.

from the **Bike Barn** (☏ 407/824-2742) at Fort Wilderness Resort and Campground on Walt Disney World. Rates for each bike are $7.54 per hour, $20.75 per day, regardless of age. Fort Wilderness offers a lot of good bike trails. Many of the other Disney resorts also offer bicycle rentals at similar rates. Either call your hotel in advance or inquire upon check-in.

BOATING With a ton of man-made lakes and lagoons, WDW owns a navy of pleasure boats. **Capt. Jack's** at Downtown Disney rents Water Sprites and

canopy boats ($22–$37.50 per half-hour, including tax). For information call
© **407/828-2204.**

The **Bike Barn** at Fort Wilderness (© **407/824-2742**) rents canoes and paddleboats ($6.13 per half-hour, $10.38 per hour).

At both sites, kids must be at least 12 to rent a boat and those under 18 cannot rent without a signed parental waiver.

FISHING   There are several fishing excursions offered on Disney waterways, including Bay Lake and Seven Seas Lagoon. The lakes are stocked, so you may catch something, but true anglers probably won't find it much of a challenge. The excursions can be arranged 2 to 90 days in advance by calling © **407/824-2621.** A license isn't required. The fee is $185 to $210 for up to five people for 2 hours ($80 for each additional hour), including refreshments, gear, guide, bait, and tax. Children above the toddler stage are permitted on these tours when accompanied by an adult.

A less-expensive alternative: Rent fishing poles at the **Bike Barn** (© **407/824-2742**) to fish in the Fort Wilderness canals. Pole rentals cost $5.19 per hour, $8.96 per day (not including tax). Bait is $3.45 to $3.65. A license isn't necessary.

HAYRIDES   The hay wagon departs **Pioneer Hall** at Disney's Fort Wilderness nightly at 7 and 9:30pm for 45-minute old-fashioned hayrides with singing, jokes, and games. Most kids will find it enjoyable, though some teens may think it corny. The cost is $8 for adults, $4 for children ages 3 to 10; free for kids 2 and under. An adult must accompany children under 12. No reservations. Call © **407/824-2832** for more information.

HIKING   The **Nature Conservancy's Disney Wilderness Preserve** (© **407/682-3664;** www.nature.org/florida) is a 12,000-acre, little discovered getaway from the theme-park madness. It has 7 miles of trails at the headwaters of the Everglades ecosystem, just south of Orlando. Self-guided trails range from a half-mile interpretive trail good for younger kids, to a 4.5-mile hiking trail for adults and teens. Picnic facilities are available along the trails. Admission costs $2 adults, and $1 for kids ages 6 to 17. It's open Monday through Friday in summer from 9am to 5pm; it's open daily from 9am to 5pm the rest of the year.

HOOPS & MORE   Disney's **Multi-Sports Experience** at Disney's Wide World of Sports (p. 219) let's you and the kids try your hands at basketball, football, and soccer. Admission is $9.34 for adults and $7.01 for children 3 to 9. It's open on select days (© **407/939-1500**).

HORSEBACK RIDING   **Disney's Fort Wilderness Resort and Campground** offers 45-minute guided trail rides several times a day. The cost is $30.19 per person (tax not included). Children must be at least 9 years old. Maximum rider weight is 250 pounds. If you or your children have never ridden before, the tame horses and gentle terrain makes this ride a good intro experience. For information and reservations up to 30 days in advance, call © **407/824-2832.**

The **Villas of Grand Cypress** opens its equestrian center to outsiders and has programs and options for riders of all ages and all skill levels. You can go on a 45-minute walk-trot trail ride (offered four times daily) for $45, though your children must be at least 10 years of age to participate. A 30-minute private lesson is $55; an hour's lesson is $100. A private junior lesson (15 min.) is available for riders age 2 to 9 for $25. A host of other package options are offered. For more information, call © **800/835-7377** or 407/239-1938 or go online to **http://grandcypress.com.**

HORSE-DRAWN CARRIAGE RIDES   In 2002, Disney began offering evening carriage rides at two of its resort locations: **Fort Wilderness Resort and Campground** and the **Port Orleans Resort.** The 30-minute rides cost $30 for up to four people. Most kids will enjoy the ride and the sightseeing opportunity. For information, call ℂ **407/824-2832.**

JOGGING   Many of the Disney resorts have scenic jogging trails. For instance, the **Yacht** and **Beach Club** resorts share a 2-mile trail; the **Caribbean Beach Resort**'s 1.4-mile promenade circles a lake; **Port Orleans** has a 1.7-mile riverfront trail; and **Fort Wilderness**'s tree-shaded 2.3-mile jogging path has exercise stations about every quarter-mile. Pick up a jogging trail map at any Disney property's Guest Services desk.

PARASAILING   The **Sammy Duvall Watersports Centre** (ℂ **407/939-0754;** www.sammyduvall.com) at Disney's Contemporary Resort will take you up to 600 feet above Seven Seas Lagoon and Bay Lake on a flight that lasts 8 to 12 minutes. The cost ranges from $85 to $155. Kids over 2 are actually eligible if they fly in tandem with someone else (minimum weight of 115 lb.), though you'll have to judge whether your child is up to such an experience. Older kids and teens will probably be ok. Everyone who goes up has to sign a waiver and parents have to sign off on their kids' participation. You can reserve a spot up to 90 days in advance.

SURFING   It's true. The creative minds at Disney have added a way for you to learn how to catch a wave and "hang ten" at the Typhoon Lagoon water park (p. 214). Tuesdays and Fridays, instructors from **Carroll's Cocoa Beach Surfing School** show up for an early-bird session in the namesake lagoon, which has a wave machine capable of 8 footers. The 2½-hour sessions are held before the park opens to the general public and are limited to 14 people. Minimum age is 8 though you'll have to decide if your 8-year-old would enjoy the experience. The $135 per person cost (including tax) doesn't include park admission, which you'll have to pay if you want to hang around after the lesson (ℂ **407/939-7529**). You'll also need alternative transportation to get here if you're staying in Walt's World because the Disney transportation system doesn't service Typhoon Lagoon until official park opening time.

SWIMMING   Almost all of Orlando's resorts have their own pools (we discuss these in chapter 4), but if you're not satisfied with the one at your hotel, the **YMCA Aquatic Center,** 8422 International Dr. (ℂ **407/363-1911**), has a full fitness center, racquetball courts, an indoor Olympic-size pool, and a heated 25-meter pool for kids. All pools have lifeguards. Admission is $10 per person, $25 for families.

TENNIS   There are 22 lighted tennis courts scattered throughout the Disney properties. They're free and open to resort guests on a first-come, first-served basis. Call ℂ **407/939-7529** for more information. The Racquet Club at the Contemporary Resort has six clay courts, all lighted for evening play, and offers private lessons that range in price from $50 for a junior lesson (ages 10 and under) to $70 for a 1-hour adult lesson.

WATER-SKIING & WAKEBOARDING   Water-skiing trips (including boats, drivers, equipment, and instruction) can be arranged Tuesday through Saturday at **Walt Disney World** by calling the **Sammy Duvall Watersports Centre** at Disney's Contemporary Resort (ℂ **407/939-0754;** www.sammy duvall.com). Make reservations up to 14 days in advance. The cost for skiing is $140 per hour for up to five people. You also can arrange for wakeboarding for up to four people, also $140. There's no minimum age though we wouldn't recommend this for children under 7 or those not comfortable in the water.

Outside Disney, you can get some time behind a boat or at the end of an overhead cable at the **Orlando Watersports Complex,** which has lights for nighttime thrill seekers. Teens will likely think the nighttime option cool, but kids under 7 and those not completely comfortable in the water are not good candidates for this activity. The complex is located close to Orlando International Airport at 8615 Florida Rock Rd. Prices for skiing, including lessons, begin at about $45 an hour for a cable and $75 for a half-hour behind a boat. The complex offers a number of specials and discounts aimed at kids and families—call or check the website to see what's being offered during the time of your visit. For information call ✆ **407/251-3100** or on the Internet go to **www.orlando watersports.com**.

2 Spectator Sports

While Orlando isn't a sports town on par with New York, Los Angeles, or Miami, it does have a National Basketball Association franchise, and spring training and minor league baseball teams. So if you and your kids are sports nuts, you won't have to forgo your fix while in Orlando. (And if you're Atlanta Braves fans, you'll be in real luck if you touch down in Orlando in Mar.)

BASEBALL   The **Atlanta Braves** began spring training at Disney's Wide World of Sports (p. 219) in 1998. There are 18 games played during a 1-month season that begins in March. The smaller setting makes for a far more intimate experience for kids than a regular stadium game would and the atmosphere is usually a lot more relaxed. Tickets are $12 to $19.75. For information, call ✆ **407/828-3267.** You can get tickets through **Ticketmaster** (✆ **407/839-3900**).

From April to September, the **Orlando Rays** (www.orlandorays.com), the Tampa Bay Devil Rays' Class AA Southern League affiliate, play their 70 home games at Disney's Wide World of Sports (✆ **407/939-4263**). The team often sponsors family programs and its website has a great section designed for young kids that offers a coloring page and the story behind the team's mascot, Spike. You can get tickets through **Ticketmaster** (✆ **407/839-3900**). They sell for $5 to $8.

BASKETBALL   The 17,500-seat TD Waterhouse Centre—known in a prior life as the Orlando Arena—is the home court of the NBA's **Orlando Magic** (✆ **407/896-2442;** www.nba.com/magic), which plays 41 of its regular-season games here from October to April. To get there, take I-4 east to Exit 83B, Hwy. 50/U.S. 17/92 (Amelia St.), turn left at the traffic light at the bottom of the off-ramp, and follow the signs. Single-game tickets ($25–$175) can be hard to find. The team schedules special theme nights and promotions throughout the season, many of them family-related and mascot Stuff (that really is his name) the Dragon is a hit with kids. For up-to-the-minute parking information, turn your car radio to 1620 AM.

JAI ALAI

Orlando Jai Alai, 6405 S. U.S. 17/92, at Highway 436 in Fern Park (✆ **407/339-6221**), offers what's billed as the world's fastest game. It's like handball but with a much longer court (180 ft.), wicker "gloves" called cestas, and ball speeds that reach 150 mph. This is a pari-mutuel game, which means you can bet on the action.

The program/betting form offers information on how the game is played and how to wager (trust anyone who tells you how to gamble about as much as a chicken farmer would trust a fox).

Note: Live games are played late October to mid-March. The fronton also has simulcast wagering, which means you can bet on jai alai and other pari-mutuels such as greyhound and horse racing telecast from other locations. Kids 39 inches and taller are welcome, though we don't recommend you bring a child younger than age 6; the minimum betting age is 18. Admission is $1, reserved seats are $2 to $3, restaurant seating is $3 with a $7 minimum order, and box seats are $5. Parking is free; valet parking is $2. It's open year-round Wednesday to Sunday. Call for the evening and matinee schedule. From the Walt Disney World area, take I-4 east to Exit 90A, Maitland Blvd./Hwy. 414, turn right at U.S. 17/92, and look for the fronton 2 miles along on your right. It's about a 40-minute drive.

3 Playing on the Green: Orlando's Parks & Playgrounds

After several days of barnstorming through the theme parks and other tourist attractions, a day in the area's nature parks can be a refreshing break. Need we also mention that it will help you recover from sticker shock—digging deeply into your wallet day after day?

CITY PARKS

Big Tree Park   All ages   This north side park is named for the "Senator," a 500-year-old bald cypress tree that's a testament to the life-giving virtues of central Florida swamps. It's 17½ feet in diameter, 47 feet in circumference and 125 feet tall. The park also has picnic tables and a boardwalk through the adjoining cypress swamp (the intriguing but comfortable seats and tables here were carved by a local chain-saw artist).

930 N. Thornton Ave. (C) 407/246-2283. Free admission. Open 8am–sunset. Take I-4 to Anderson St. in downtown Orlando, go east past City Hall, cross Orange Ave., turn left at Rosalind, pass Lake Eola park and continue as Rosalind merges into Magnolia. Cross Hwy. 50, turn right on Marks St., turn right on Thornton, and go half a block to the park.

Lake Eola Park   All ages   More than a million people visit this 20-acre park each year. The .9-mile sidewalk that circles the downtown lake offers a good course for hikers and joggers. Visitors can feed the live birds that inhabit the park, catch a tan on the lawn, or burn some calories cruising the lake in swan-shaped paddleboats. There's a playground for kids and toddlers, and several concessions, picnic areas, and restrooms. This park is also the home of several annual events, including the Fourth of July fireworks blast.

195 N. Rosalind Ave. (C) 407/246-2827. Free admission. Open 8am–10pm. Take I-4 to Anderson St. in downtown Orlando, go east past City Hall, cross Orange and Magnolia aves., then turn left at Rosalind and into the park.

Turkey Lake Park   All ages   This 36-acre city park was originally a citrus grove and has one of the more natural settings of all of Orlando's parks. The park—last renovated in December 2002—has a swimming pool, large picnic pavilions, a lake stocked with fish, a large children's playground and two smaller ones, nature and jogging trails, an 18-hole disc golf course, a farm-animal petting zoo and a boardwalk running through a scrub-pine habitat. It also has an ecology center.

3401 S. Hiawassee Rd. (C) 407/299-5581. $4 per vehicle. Open 8am–5pm, sometimes later. Take I-4 to Kirkman Rd., go north to Conroy, then west/left to Hiawassee, then north to the park, which is just past the Florida Turnpike.

STATE PARKS & PRESERVES

Lake Louisa State Park   All ages   If you bring your own fishing gear (there are no concessionaires here) you and your kids can catch bass or bream. The beach has a bathhouse with showers and there's also a picnic area. White-tailed deer, wild turkeys, marsh rabbits, opossums and raccoons are seen on rare occasions along the nature trails.

12549 State Park Dr., Clermont. © 352/394-3969. $3.25 per vehicle. Open 8am–sundown. From Disney, take U.S. 192 west to U.S. 27 north about 15 miles to Lake Louisa Rd. and go left to the park.

Wekiwa Springs State Park   All ages   The namesake springs and river provide a fertile habitat for white-tailed deer, gray foxes, bobcats, raccoons, and (careful here) black bears. The waters here also offer some of the best paddling venues in central Florida. Canoe rentals are $14 for 2 hours, $2 per hour thereafter. There are bicycle and hiking trails and the park also has picnic, grilling, volleyball, and camping areas.

1800 Wekiva Springs Rd., Sanford. © 407/884-2008. www.floridaparks.com/stprks/centralstateparks.htm. $4 per vehicle. Open 8am to sundown. Take I-4 to Exit 94, then take SR 434 West to Wekiwa Springs Rd. or SR 436 to Wekiwa Springs Rd. near Apopka.

4 Kids' Camps & Classes

No attraction does kids' camps like **SeaWorld** does them and the camps that follow might be fodder for your heirs to get extra credit. (But don't take our word for it: If that's your objective ask before you come. And, because these are summer camps and your kids might be between teachers, it's best to ask a guidance counselor or an administrator where your child or children will be attending class after the summer break is over.)

SeaWorld (see chapter 7) offers three resident camps during the summer:

- **Florida Keys Adventure.** Also designed for grades 7 through 12, this program is similar to the Ultimate Florida Adventure, but it focuses more heavily on marine biology, including encounters with parrotfish, stingrays, barracuda, and maybe even a few small sharks. Duration: 5 days. Price: $925 per child.

- **Summer Splash.** Designed for grades 6 through 8, this program includes lessons about animal enrichment, rescue, and rehabilitation, as guests get familiar with polar bears, beluga whales, manatees, sea turtles, and Shamu. Your child will also get to have fun in the theme parks, including a day with the dolphins, sharks, stingrays and other critters at Discovery Cove (p. 257). Duration: 5 days. Price: $825 per child.

- **Ultimate Florida Adventure.** Appropriate for grades 7 through 12, this 10-day camp begins with a sleepover at SeaWorld, and then takes kids to the Florida Keys to discover marine sanctuaries, coral reefs, wetlands and creatures ranging from tropical fish to alligators. Then it's back to SeaWorld and Discovery Cove for lessons about preservation and rehabilitation programs and encounters with dolphins, stingrays, and more. Duration: 10 days. Price: $1,875 per child.

The cost of the camps includes meals, lodging, equipment, and more. For more information, call © 866/468-6226 or check out **www.seaworld.org**. Due to the camps' popularity, SeaWorld recommends making reservations between the preceding December and February.

9

Shopping for the Whole Family

Except for mouse ears and other tourist trinkets, Orlando has few products to call its own. Generally speaking, the merchandise and the malls won't be all that different than that which you have at home. Still, many of you need some kind of shopping fix, and goofy souvenirs often are among your priorities—especially for the kids. After all, what else says theme park better than a pair of Mickey Mouse ears? (Except perhaps, a Pluto leash, a Cinderella glass slipper, a Spider-Man outfit . . . you get the idea.)

But before putting your credit cards in high gear, consider these words to the wise: If you're going to ring registers in the theme parks, you're going to pay top dollar. Alas, most official Disney and Universal merchandise is only available in company stores. But when it comes to other goods, plan a day away from tourist central, and be as savvy here as you are at home. You can find a lot of what you want, and at the best possible prices, by knowing what is *and isn't* a bargain.

1 The Shopping Scene

SHOPPING HOURS & SALES TAXES

Generally speaking, neighborhood stores in Orlando open daily at around 9 or 10am and don't close before 5pm, at the very earliest. An exception would be some of the stores in Downtown Orlando, which are usually closed on Sundays. Malls and major shopping centers tend to open around 10am, often not closing before 9 or 10pm, except on Sundays, when they usually close around 5 or 6pm. Stores in all Orlando theme parks generally stay from the official park opening time until just after the official park closing time (giving you that last-minute opportunity to buy your child that stuffed Mickey or Cat in the Hat that she never knew she couldn't live without).

At all of the Disney resorts, you'll usually find at least one shop that's open by 8am and keeps going until 10 or 11pm. Stores in the Downtown Disney Marketplace are usually open daily from 9:30am until around 11pm; those in Downtown Disney West Side usually stay open from around 11am until 11pm (and later on weekends). The shops at Pleasure Island don't open until 7pm, but they also don't close until 1am.

The shops at Universal Orlando's CityWalk open at 11am and don't close until 2am.

You'll pay an extra 6% sales tax on every purchase you make in Orlando, except most edible grocery items and medicines.

GREAT SHOPPING AREAS

CELEBRATION   This isn't the place for power shopping, but it is a pleasant look at mid-20th-century mainstream America with a Disney spin (and 400%

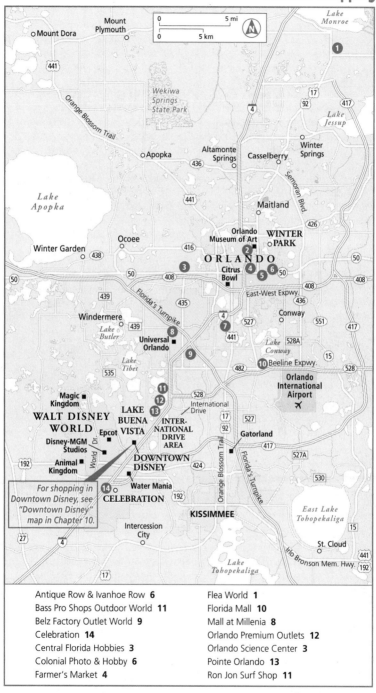

Antique Row & Ivanhoe Row **6**

Bass Pro Shops Outdoor World **11**

Belz Factory Outlet World **9**

Celebration **14**

Central Florida Hobbies **3**

Colonial Photo & Hobby **6**

Farmer's Market **4**

Flea World **1**

Florida Mall **10**

Mall at Millenia **8**

Orlando Premium Outlets **12**

Orlando Science Center **3**

Pointe Orlando **13**

Ron Jon Surf Shop **11**

Tips   Setting Limits

The theme parks are a giant hotbed of consumerism, and unless they've been properly prepared, your kids could catch a serious case of the "Buy me" flu. (You might also, but that's a whole different ball-game.) And nothing will sour a vacation faster than your kids whining at every minute that they want Mickey this and Mickey that.

Depending on your child's age, you'll need to set buying limits and make sure that your children know them in advance. Souvenirs aren't cheap in Disney, and if you give your kids' a set spending limit and stick to it, they may even learn a lesson or two about value shopping and getting their money's worth (we saw one 6-year-old have his first case of sticker shock while determining how to best spend his $30 allotment). Older kids might be persuaded to set aside portions of their allowance for use as souvenir money.

Another suggestion: Set specific shopping times, so your kids won't be continually bugging you every time you pass a souvenir shop. If junior knows he'll be getting his toy at the end of the day, he won't worry about passing up that store at the end of the ride. (It will also save you the trouble of carrying around a giant stuffed animal the whole day.) Just remember that outside of WDW, some stores at Universal and Sea-World carry ride-specific merchandise that may not be found elsewhere in the park. So if you promised a Spider-Man shirt to your budding web-slinger, or a Cat in the Hat doll to your young Seuss fan, you'll need to pay up after you ride or head back to the ride before you leave for the day.

markup). Celebration will eventually be home to about 20,000 people (it even has its own school district!). The downtown includes a dozen shops on or near Market Street, a couple of art galleries, some restaurants, and a three-screen theater. The storefronts, especially the galleries and gift shops, offer interesting but overpriced merchandise—including crystal, Disney collectibles, jewelry, and more. Not as much for small kids here, but there is a nice atmosphere. If Celebration reminds you of the movie *The Truman Show,* you won't be alone. The movie was filmed in Seaside, a Florida panhandle community that inspired the builders of this burg. © 407/566-2200.

DOWNTOWN DISNEY   There are three distinct areas that make up the complex of shops, restaurants, and entertainment venues known as Downtown Disney (**www.downtowndisney.com**): West Side, Pleasure Island, and Marketplace. Stars on the shopping front include the **LEGO Imagination Center** (© 407/828-0065), **Virgin Megastore** (© 407/828-0222), **Art of Disney** (© 407/824-4321), **Once Upon A Toy** (© 407/934-7775), and **Guitar Gallery** (© 407/827-0118).

INTERNATIONAL DRIVE AREA   This tourist mecca extends 7 to 10 miles northeast of the Disney parks between Highway 535 and the Florida Turnpike. From bungee jumping and ice-skating to dozens of themed restaurants and T-shirt shops, this is *the* tourist strip in central Florida. One of its main draws, **Pointe Orlando** (© 407/248-2838; www.pointeorlandofl.com), has restaurants and specialty shops such as **Abercrombie & Fitch** and the child-magnet **FAO Schwarz.** The other main draw on I-Drive, as the locals call it, is **Orlando Premium Outlets** (see "Factory Outlets," below).

KISSIMMEE   Kissimmee centers on U.S. 192/Irlo Bronson Memorial Highway—a somewhat tacky strip that runs east from Disney's southern border. U.S. 192 is lined with budget motels, smaller attractions, and every fast-food restaurant known to humankind. Kissimmee is still, in many ways, true to its cowboy roots, and there are some Western shops to prove it. The shopping here is notable for the quantity, not necessarily the quality, but it's a good place to pick up some knickknacks, cheap souvenirs for the kids, or white elephant gifts.

WINTER PARK   Just north of downtown Orlando, Winter Park (© **407/644-8281;** www.winterpark.org) is the place many of central Florida's old-money families call home. It began as a haven for Yankees trying to escape the cold. Today, its centerpiece is Park Avenue, which has quite a collection of upscale shops—Ann Taylor, Bari's, Bath & Body Works, and Restoration Hardware—along its cobblestone route. No matter which end of Park Avenue you start at, there are more shops than most can survive, but you're bound to find something here you'll not find anywhere else. Park Avenue also has restaurants and some art galleries. This is not the place to take young kids, but kids older than 10 should find something to their taste. To get here, take I-4 Exit 87, Fairbanks Avenue/Highway 426, east past U.S. 17/92 to Park Avenue and turn left.

SHOPPING AT DISNEY'S THEME PARKS

You'll find dozens of places to buy everything from trinkets to treasures at the WDW parks, many of which have shops bearing themes from specific rides. Most of the stores carry merchandise that will appeal to both kids and adults, so everyone can shop together without getting bored. And if you're staying at a Disney resort, the stores will ship your purchases straight to your room, so you won't have to carry everything around with you. (If you're not staying on Disney property, you can have shops send your merchandise to the package pick-up stations at each park, where you can get them before you leave, but you'll have to allot at least 3 hr. for them to get there.)

Here are our favorites in each of the parks.

MAGIC KINGDOM   The **Emporium** on Main Street has a huge collection of everything Mickey, including collectible Disneyana merchandise; the nearby **Main Street Gallery** sells original movie cels and more; and the **Toontown Hall of Fame Tent** in Mickey's Toontown Fair has an avalanche of things your pre-7-year-olds will beg you to buy for them.

EPCOT   *Careful:* With all of the cultural products (edible and otherwise), a stroll around the World Showcase can break your bank unless you keep your wits about you. The headliners include China's **Yong Feng Shangdian Shopping Gallery,** which features silk robes, lacquer and inlaid mother-of-pearl

---

Tips **Where Was That Piglet Doll?**

If you saw an eye-catching item when you were in the Disney theme parks and aren't sure where, call © **407/363-6200.** Tell the customer service rep the park you were in and describe the item; you'll likely be able to order it by phone.

furniture, jade figures, cloisonné vases, brocade pajamas, silk rugs and embroideries, wind chimes, and Chinese clothing. Artisans occasionally demonstrate calligraphy. **Mitsukoshi Department Store** (Japan's answer to Macy's) sells lacquerware, kimonos, kites, fans, dolls in traditional costumes, origami books, samurai swords, Japanese Disneyana, bonsai trees, Japanese foods, Netsuke carvings, pottery, modern electronics, and Pokémon cards (your kids will be thrilled). Shops in and around the **Plaza de Los Amigos** display an array of leather goods, baskets, sombreros, piñatas, pottery, embroidered dresses, maracas, serapes, colorful papier-mâché birds, and blown-glass objects (an artisan occasionally gives demonstrations). And Canada's **Northwest Mercantile** carries sandstone and soapstone carvings, fringed leather vests, duck decoys, moccasins, an array of stuffed animals, Native American dolls, Native American spirit stones, rabbit-skin caps, heavy knitted sweaters, and, of course, maple syrup. If you have little ones in tow, don't miss a stop at **MouseGear** in Future World's Innoventions East; it's loaded with toys and stuffed animals for the young set.

DISNEY–MGM STUDIOS   The best shopping at this park is aimed more at older kids and teens than very young kids. **Animation Courtyard Shops** carry collectible cels, costumes from Disney classic films, and pins. **Sid Cahuenga's One-of-a-Kind** sells autographed photos of the stars, original movie posters, and star-touched items such as canceled checks signed by Judy Garland and others. Star-crazed preteens and teens will be suitably impressed. **Celebrity 5 & 10,** modeled after a 1940s Woolworth's, has movie-related merchandise: *Gone With the Wind* memorabilia, MGM Studio T-shirts, movie posters, Elvis mugs, and more. If you're with little ones, your best bet is the **Stage One Company Store,** which carries Muppet-themed souvenirs.

ANIMAL KINGDOM   **Creature Comforts** on Discovery Island focuses on kids' things, including themed toys and clothing. **Mombasa Marketplace** in Africa has a nice selection of safari clothing and African-themed gifts. And if you or your kids are into yesterday, don't miss a look through **Chester & Hester's Dinosaur Treasures.** The store is themed after the Dinosaur ride (p. 209) and has plush dinosaurs, T-shirts, and ball-style caps.

SHOPPING AT UNIVERSAL'S THEME PARKS

At **Universal Studios Florida,** we're stuck on **Back to the Future—The Store** and its miniature version of a DeLorean (kids 6 and up will like browsing here); **Second Hand Rose,** which specializes in Coca-Cola memorabilia; **Silver Screen Collectibles,** which offers Lucy, Betty Boop, and Woody Woodpecker items (your younger children will be enthralled with the latter); and the **Universal Studios Store** near the park entrance, which appeals to all ages and sells just about everything when it comes to Universal apparel.

Next door at **Islands of Adventure,** there are more than 20 shops within the park, offering a variety of themed merchandise. You may want to check out **Cats, Hats & Things** and **Dr. Seuss' All the Books You Can Read** for special Seussian material, especially if you have little kids in tow. **Jurassic Outfitters** and **Dinostore** feature a variety of stuffed and plastic dinosaurs, plus safari-themed clothing. Superhero fans should check out the **Spider-Man Shop,** and if your kids are into comic books, then the **Comic Shop** offers a great selection of titles (Marvel comics only, of course). **Islands of Adventure Trading Company** is a good stop on the way out if you're still searching for something that will help you and your kids remember your visit. The store carries a wide variety of theme merchandise geared to visitors of all ages.

FACTORY OUTLETS

Sure you probably have one of these in your own hometown, and you won't get appreciatively better savings here. But if you're looking for theme-park souvenirs, the two outlet malls below house some of the few places on the planet where you can get official merchandise at discounted prices.

Belz Factory Outlet World   This is the largest of the Orlando factory outlet centers. It has 170 stores in two enclosed malls and four shopping annexes. It offers a wide range of merchandise, and in a few cases the savings can be 75% off retail prices, but, as is the case with most outlets, *most buys here are no better than what you'll find in discount houses in or near your town.* There are more than a dozen shoe stores (Bass, Nike, Rockport, and so on); nearly as many housewares shops (Fitz & Floyd, Oneida, and more); a **Universal Studios Outlet;** and 60-some clothing shops for men, women, and children (The Gap, Levi's, Van Heusen, Oshkosh B'gosh, Izod, Guess Jeans, and others). You can also shop for books, records, electronics, sporting goods, health and beauty aids, jewelry, toys, gifts, accessories, lingerie, hosiery, and parking spaces. 5401 W. Oak Ridge Rd. ℂ 407/ 354-0126. www.belz.com. From I-4, take Exit 74B and turn north on I-Drive, continuing to the mall.

Orlando Premium Outlets   Opened in June 2000, this 440,000-square-foot center is the new kid in town. It's billed as Orlando's only upscale outlet, which may be true, thanks to a dearth of true outlets, premium or otherwise. It has 110 tenants, including **Disney** and **Universal** outlets, K.B. Toys, Strasburg Children, Coach, DKNY, Giorgio Armani, Kenneth Cole, Nike, Polo/Ralph Lauren, Timberland, and Tommy Hilfiger. Some of the best buys are at Banana Republic (jeans usually are marked down 50% from retail). 8200 Vineland Ave. ℂ 407/238-7787. www.PremiumOutlets.com. From I-4, take Exit 68, Apopka-Vineland Rd./Hwy. 535 right/south to the first light, then go left at the first light to the outlet.

THE MALLS

Florida Mall   The exciting news at this popular shopping spot is the arrival of Nordstrom to combat the opening of Mall at Millenia (see below). Other anchors include Burdines, Dillard's, JCPenney, Sears, and Saks to go along with an Adam's Mark Hotel and more than 250 specialty stores, restaurants (Buca di Beppo, Le Jardin, and Ruby Tuesday), a food court, and entertainment venues. No less than 10 stores offer children's clothing, and there are three toy stores as well. Strollers can be rented at several locations inside the mall. If you have young children, this is definitely your best bet for a mall excursion. 8001 S. Orange Blossom Trail. ℂ 407/851-6255. www.shopsimon.com. Take I-4 Exit 74A, Sand Lake Rd./Hwy. 482, and look for it on the corner of Orange Blossom and Sand Lake.

(*Tips* **Homegrown Souvenirs**

Oranges, grapefruit, and other citrus products rank high on the list of local products. **Orange Blossom Indian River Citrus,** 5151 S. Orange Blossom Trail, Orlando (ℂ **800/624-8835** or 407/855-2837; www.orange-blossom.com), is one of the top sellers during the late-fall-to-late-spring season. If your kids are fruit-lovers, it's a great place to get a tasty souvenir. Alligator-skin leather goods are a specialty in the gift shop at **Gatorland Zoo,** 14501 S. Orange Blossom, Orlando (ℂ **407/855-5496;** www. gatorland.com).

Mall at Millenia   This 1.3-million-square-foot upscale center made quite a splash on the mall scene when it debuted in October 2002 with anchors that include Bloomingdale's, Macy's, and Neiman Marcus. The opening caused so much of a stir that former number-one Florida Mall (see above) went to work recruiting some new high-profile names. In addition to the heavyweight anchors, Millenia offers 200 specialty stores that include Cartier, Chanel, Crabtree & Evelyn, Giorgio's of Palm Beach, Gucci, Louis Vuitton, Swarovski, and Tiffany & Co. Your label-conscious teens will find the rarified air here to their liking, though you, like us, may find it nose-in-the-air snooty and overpriced. The mall is 5 miles from downtown Orlando and does offer shuttle service to some hotels. 4200 Conroy Rd. (at I-4 near Universal Orlando). ✆ 407/363-3555. www.mallat millenia.com. Take I-4 Exit 74A, Sand Lake Rd./Hwy. 482 east to the John Young Pkwy./Hwy. 423, and go north to Conroy, then west to mall.

Pointe Orlando   Although it's set up like a mall, this complex's two levels of stores, restaurants, and a 21-screen IMAX theater (p. 288) aren't under one roof, making it a mall with an open top. On the whole, the shopping is pretty mall bland, but what makes this a child-magnet is its 33,000-square-foot **FAO Schwarz,** whose exterior is adorned with a three-story Raggedy Ann and an equally tall stuffed bear. Inside this branch of the famous toy store, you can find a huge *Star Wars* area, including a 7-foot Darth Vader that retails for a cool $5,000, and an immense Barbie collection. On the first Friday of the month, Raggedy Ann, Mother Goose, and other characters usually offer good morning hugs to delighted preschoolers. 9101 International Dr. ✆ 407/248-2838. www.pointe orlandofl.com. Take I-4 to exit 74 (Sand Lake Rd.). Go right (east) on Sand Lake Rd. to International Dr. and turn right. The mall is 3 miles down International Dr. on your left.

2 Shopping A to Z

Most visitors to Orlando will spend their time—and money—shopping in the theme parks. That's what the city is renowned for, after all. But if you aren't happy confining your credit-card purchases to Disney, Universal, and SeaWorld, there are a few other shopping opportunities for family spending in the Orlando area.

ANTIQUES

If you can think of nothing better than a relaxing afternoon of bargain hunting or scouring thrift and antiques shops, check out **Antique Row** and **Ivanhoe Row** on North Orange Avenue (stretching from Colonial Dr./Hwy. 50 to Lake Ivanhoe) in downtown Orlando. This collection is a long way from the manufactured fun of Disney. The shops are an interesting assortment of the old, the new, and the unusual. **Flo's Attic,** 1800 N. Orange Ave. (✆ **407/895-1800**), and **A.J. Lillun,** 1913 N. Orange Ave. (✆ **407/895-6111**), sell traditional antiques. Kids who like perusing cool old stuff will enjoy the experience, but if your children aren't into that sort of an experience, they'll likely be bored stiff.

Most of these shops are open from 9 or 10am to 5pm, Monday through Saturday; the owners usually run them, so hours can vary. All are spread over 3 miles along Orange Avenue. The heaviest concentration of shops lies between Princeton Street and New Hampshire Avenue, although a few are scattered between New Hampshire and Virginia avenues. The upscale shops extend a few blocks beyond Virginia. To get there, take I-4 Exit 85/Princeton Street and turn right on Orange Avenue. Parking is limited, so stop wherever you find a space along the street.

BOOKS

All of the major bookstore chains have stores in the Orlando area, though there are one or two local shops as well. This is a city that caters to kids, so almost all bookstores have well-stocked children's sections.

Barnes & Noble   This branch of the nationwide chain offers a wide selection of books for all ages. It's open daily from 9am to 11pm. 8358 S. Orange Blossom Trail. ℭ 407/856-7200.

B. Dalton   This store has a large selection of children's books, as well as bestsellers and magazines. It's open 10am to 10pm Monday through Saturday, 11am to 9pm on Sunday. 9101 International Dr. ℭ 407/363-0500.

Borders   A cafe is a welcome addition to this store's collection of books appealing to all ages. It's open 9am to 10pm Monday through Thursday, until 11pm Friday, and 9am to 9pm Sunday. 1051 W. Sand Lake Rd. ℭ 407/826-8912.

Brandywine Books   This local bookstore specializes in rare, out-of-print, and used hardbacks. It's open 10:30am to 5pm Monday through Saturday. 114 S. Park Ave., Winter Park. ℭ 407/644-1711.

Long's Christian Book & Music Store   Families looking for Christian-oriented reading material, should head for this local shop. It sells cassettes, CDs, videos, church supplies, and cards in addition to a large selection of books and Bibles. Long's is open 9am to 9pm Monday through Saturday. 1610 Edgewater Dr. ℭ 407/422-6934.

Waldenbooks   This member of the popular chain features a nice selection of children's books as well as bestsellers and other books appealing to all ages. It's open 10:30am to 9pm Monday through Saturday, noon to 6pm Sunday. 8001 S. Orange Blossom Trail, in the Florida Mall. ℭ 407/859-8787.

COMICS

Coliseum of Comics   This regional chain has five locations spread across Central Florida, including this Orlando store. It's is a large purveyor of new and used comics (Wolverine, Cyclops, Superman, and more) as well as toys, games, videos, and collectible game cards. If your kids are comics-crazed, it's a sure bet they'll love this store. There's also a branch in Kissimmee at 1180 E. Vine St. (ℭ 407/870-5322). The stores usually are open from 9 or 10 am to 6 or 7 pm Monday through Saturday, noon to 6pm Sunday. 4722 S. Orange Blossom Trail. ℭ 407/240-7882. www.coliseumofcomics.com.

FARMERS MARKETS

You can shop for fresh produce, plants, baked goods, and crafts every Saturday from 8am to 2:30pm at the downtown Orlando **farmer's market.** It's located at the intersection of North Magnolia and East Central. Get more information at **www.downtownorlando.com**.

FLEA MARKETS

Flea World *Overrated*   Located in Sanford, about 45 minutes north of the attractions, this may be Florida's largest flea market. It's pretty much exactly what the name implies: a huge, tacky flea market with a twist. It has everything from dentists' and lawyers' offices to lingerie and lamp shops. Although many folks give it an assortment of derogatory names, it's fun for people-watchers as well as those in desperate need of tractor tires, leather chaps, ginsu knives, pocket fishing rods, and other uncommon merchandise.

It has some 2,000 booths. Among this babble of not-so-many bargains are many shops selling Florida T-shirts and souvenir-worthy knickknacks. Just in case the merchandise doesn't give you visual overload, sometimes there is entertainment as diverse as live lions and tigers, Elvis impersonators, and bingo. Other family-friendly activities include kiddie rides, miniature golf, and an arcade. If there are more than six people in your party, you can arrange a birthday party for your child, including food and entertainment (you'll need to call at least a week in advance). No matter what your children's ages, it's doubtful they'll get bored, though it might be overstimulating for young kids. It's open 10am to 6pm, Friday through Sunday. 4311 Orlando Ave., off U.S. 17/92. ℂ 407/330-1792. www.fleaworld.com.

GAMES & HOBBY SHOPS

Central Florida Hobbies   If your kids are into models (of the airplane variety, that is), here's a good option. This store specializes in radio-controlled boats, cars, helicopters, and more. It also stocks plastic models, modeling supplies, wooden ship models, and rockets. It's open 10:30am to 7pm Monday through Friday and 10:30am to 5pm Saturday. 5600 W. Colonial Dr./Hwy. 50. ℂ 407/295-9256. www.centralfloridahobbies.com.

Colonial Photo & Hobby   Here's another spot for kids who love miniatures that go vroom. In addition to its camera sales and repairs, this Downtown store has a large sales and service department for Lionel and HO trains. Colonial also sells radio-controlled airplanes, cars, trucks, and helicopters in addition to plastic models and rockets. It's open 9am to 7pm Monday through Thursday, 9am to 9pm Friday, and 9am to 6pm Saturday. 634 N. Mills Ave. ℂ 407/841-1485. www.colonialphotohobby.com.

HAIRCUTS

The **Harmony Barber Shop** on Main Street in Disney's Magic Kingdom is a real scissor shop (with a an atmospheric old-fashioned decor) where you can get your hair cut from 9am to 5pm daily. The barbers are incredibly friendly, give a good cut, and are an absolute marvel with kids. Adult haircuts are $15; kids' are $12. If it's your child's first haircut, Disney barbers will cut his or her hair free and throw in a certificate and set of mouse ears. The shop is on Main Street near the firehouse. If you're lucky, Disney's barbershop quartet, the Dapper Dans, will serenade you and your kids as your get your locks shorn.

MUSEUM STORES

Orlando Museum of Art   The museum not only has some exciting exhibits for kids and their caretakers (p. 263) but also a wonderful shop featuring jewelry, books, videos, posters, and Dale Chihuly glass art. You can access the store without having to pay admission to the museum. It's open 10am to 4pm Tuesday through Friday, noon to 4pm Saturday through Sunday. 2416 N. Mills Ave., in Loch Haven Park. ℂ 407/896-4231. www.omart.org.

MUSIC

Guitar Gallery in Downtown Disney West Side (ℂ **407/827-0118**) is a retail shop with more than 150 custom, collector, rare and unique guitars. (One ivory-and-rosewood number sports a $25,000 price tag!) There are hand-decorated guitars, including a "Wonderland" Washburn created by Sammy Hagar and his son, and an Ibanez model with a hand-carved Egyptian scene on its wooden face. Guitars are suspended from hand-brushed aluminum walls and encased in rotating display cases. There are a few things here that won't cost you a second mortgage. It's more of a collector's shop, but if you have a budding musician or your kids have a guitar-playing hero, they'll probably enjoy a quick stop here. The store is open daily 10:30am to 11pm, sometimes later.

Virgin Megastore, also in Downtown Disney West Side (© **407/828-0222**), stocks more than 150,000 titles on CDs and cassettes, has 2,000 CD-ROM and video game titles, and also sells books and magazines and graphic novels. If you have preteens and teens with you, they'll be in music heaven. The store also has CD listening stations, laser disc playing stations, video game demo stations, a cafe with indoor and outdoor seating, and an outdoor stage for concerts. It's open 11am to midnight Sunday through Thursday, until 1am Friday through Saturday.

SCIENCE STORES

Orlando Science Center   The center's (p. 263) store has a fun selection of mind-bending puzzles, interactive science games, theme clothing, and jewelry that will appeal to kids of all ages. You can access the shop without having to pay admission to the museum. It's open 9am to 5pm Tuesday through Thursday, 9am to 9pm Friday and Saturday, and noon to 5pm Sunday. 777 E. Princeton St., between Orange and Mills aves., in Loch Haven Park. © **407/514-2230.** www.osc.org.

SPORTS STUFF

Bass Pro Shops Outdoor World   This is the retail version of fishing and hunting (including archery) heaven. Located in Belz's Festival Bay shopping center, this store also features areas for watersports equipment, camping gear, and outdoor apparel as well as a golf pro shop and an aquarium. If your family interests trend towards the outdoors, this is a worthy shopping stop. The store is open daily, usually 9am to 6pm except Christmas. 5156 International Dr. © **407/563-5200.** www.basspro.com.

Ron Jon Surf Shop   Also located in Belz's Festival Bay, this is a clone of the wild and wacky Ron Jon's in Cocoa Beach. That means, if you're looking for legitimate surfboards and gear, T-shirts or bumper stickers that said you were here, or tacky trinkets (a 6-ft. foam palm tree anyone?), this is the place to find it. It's open 9am to 10pm Monday through Saturday and 10am to 7pm on Sunday. 5156 International Dr. © **407/481-2555.**

SWEETS

Downtown Disney West Side has our two favorite spots for sugar-loading in Orlando.

Candy Cauldron (© **407/828-1470**), will satisfy you and your kids' sweet tooth with 200 temptations, such as fudge, caramel apples, cotton candy, chocolate candies and fruit, and truffles. This candy-coated heaven is open 10:30am to 11pm daily.

On the candy side, **Ghirardelli Soda Fountain and Chocolate Shop** (© **407/934-8855**), a branch of the famous San Francisco institution, sells truffles, double-chocolate mocha bars, and more. But Ghirardelli's is famous for its ice cream concoctions and if you've promised your kids fountain drinks, this is the place to come. Ghirardelli's has a tantalizing selection of cones, floats, shakes, malts, and ice-cream sodas. The hot fudge sundae here is a classic, though we like the one at the Plaza Restaurant (p. 117) in Magic Kingdom just a tad better. Hours are 9:30am to 11pm daily.

TOYS

Need a way to keep the kids distracted while you shop for toys in peace? In the Downtown Disney Marketplace, the **LEGO Imagination Center** (© **407/828-0065**), has a nifty, 3,000-square-foot play area out back where kids can build monster robots, race cars, and other creations while you shop without hearing the "I-want-its" from your heirs. One parent told us her 4-year-old liked playing here more than touring the theme park (no lines!). There are large LEGO creations such as helicopters and dragons hanging from the ceiling and floor displays that will knock your eyes (as well as your bank account) out. There are LEGO pirate ships, cowboy towns, and high-rise dollhouses as well as the traditional LEGO buckets of building blocks. It's open 9:30am to 11pm daily.

Also in the Disney Marketplace, **Once Upon a Toy** (© **407/934-7775**), is a 16,000-square-foot store created by Disney and the Hasbro toy company. It's a toy-lover's nirvana. You can buy a Mr. Potato Head with Disney parts (or build your own on one of five touch-screens), a Clue board game based on WDW's *Haunted Mansion* attraction, a Disney theme park version of Monopoly, and a Play-Doh play set based on Disney's *It's a Small World* attraction. There also are Disney character dolls and miniature versions of Disney's monorail system. Other toys include Lincoln Logs (adults will marvel at the miniature replica of Disney's Wilderness Lodge displayed by the logs), Tinker Toys, and Star Wars memorabilia. The store is open 9:30am to 11pm daily. *Tip:* This is a great place for taking snapshots of the kids as the store is loaded with "backdrops" including a child-size version of the Walt Disney World Railroad, and a Peter Pan–themed castle.

Kids, especially those 12 and under, can browse for hours in the mammoth **World of Disney** (© **407/828-1451**), a Downtown Disney Marketplace store with a dozen themed rooms, featuring toys, dolls, and other trinkets in honor of Beauty and the Beast, Cinderella, Sleeping Beauty, Tinker Bell, and many others. You'll also find Disney art, clocks, and clothing in sizes ranging from infant to adult. Just keep an eye on the kids—the store is so big (about half a million sq. ft.), it's easy for the little shoppers in your party to wander off.

10

Entertainment for the Whole Family

After their 2-week annual assault on Disney and Universal Orlando, friends of ours from the United Kingdom need a week to recover (except the kids, who slept through the entire flight home and landed refreshed). That's true for a lot of adult visitors, especially first-timers, who burn it on both ends, wear themselves out, and then need a vacation after their vacation. (Your kids will probably bemoan the fact the vacation is over.)

Some of you know the feeling. You're hard-core partyers who aren't willing to give it up after a long day in the parks or have older kids and teens whose interest won't be flagging at the end of the day. You want after-hours adventure and, in the last decade, Orlando's tourism czars have built a bundle of entertainment to satisfy your family's cravings.

The success of central Florida's dinner shows, video arcades, cultural arts programs, and adult nightclub districts—including Universal's **City-Walk, Downtown Disney West Side,** and **Pleasure Island**—shows that many visitors have the pizzazz to withstand life after a day of schlepping around Mickeyville and Universal.

Check the "Calendar" section of Friday's *Orlando Sentinel* for up-to-the-minute details on local clubs, visiting performers, concerts, movies, and events. It has hundreds of listings, many of which are online at **www.orlandosentinel.com**. The *Orlando Weekly* is a free magazine found in red boxes throughout central Florida. It highlights the more offbeat and often more of-the-minute performances. You can see it online at **www.orlandoweekly.com**. Another good source on the Internet is **www.orlandoinfo.com**, operated by the Orlando/Orange County Convention & Visitors Bureau.

1 Dinner Shows

IN WALT DISNEY WORLD

The Magic Mickey offers tons of nighttime entertainment aimed at the whole family, including laser-light shows, fireworks, and IllumiNations (p. 194). There also are two dinner shows worthy of special note, the Hoop-Dee-Doo Musical Revue and the Spirit of Aloha Dinner Show, and a third show that's an occasional player.

Note: While they offer entertainment, don't expect haute cuisine. The food is edible—sometimes even good—but the emphasis is on the show, not the grub.

Hoop-Dee-Doo Musical Revue (Moments **All ages** This is Disney's most popular show, so make reservations *early*. The reward: You feast on a down-home, all-you-can-eat barbecue—fried chicken, smoked ribs, salad, corn on the cob, baked beans, bread, salad, strawberry shortcake, and your choice of coffee, tea, beer, wine, sangria, or soda. (There's no kids' menu, but your kids shouldn't have much of a problem finding something to their liking.) While you stuff yourself silly in Pioneer Hall, performers in 1890s garb lead you in a foot-stomping hand-clapping high-energy show that includes a lot of jokes you haven't heard since second grade. Kids of all ages love it (and some may be selected to participate in the proceedings). *Note:* Be prepared to join the fun or the singers and the rest of the crowd will humiliate you.

Reservations should be made 30 to 60 days in advance or earlier (you can make them up to 2 years in advance), especially during peak periods such as summer and holidays. Show times are 5, 7:15, and 9:30pm nightly. 3520 N. Fort Wilderness Trail (at Fort Wilderness Resort and Campground). © 407/939-3463. www.disneyworld. com. Reservations required. Adults $49.01, kids 3–11 $24.81, including tax and tip. Free parking.

Disney's Spirit of Aloha Dinner Show *Moments* **All ages** This slightly tweaked revue replaces the old Polynesian Luau Show. While not quite as much in demand as the Hoop-Dee-Doo, the Polynesian Resort's 2-hour show is like a big neighborhood party. Disney's Spirit of Aloha Dinner Show features Tahitian, Samoan, Hawaiian, and Polynesian singers, drummers, and dancers who entertain you while you feast on a menu that includes tropical appetizers, Lanai roasted chicken and pork ribs, Polynesian wild rice, South Seas vegetables, dessert, wine, beer, and other beverages. (There's no specific menu for the kids, though if you have picky eaters, ask your server if they can dig something up for you.) Some adults may find it lacks a certain authenticity, but most kids have a great time. It all takes place 5 nights a week in an open-air theater (dress accordingly, though it's canceled in bad weather) with candlelit tables, red-flame lanterns, and tapa-bark paintings on the walls.

Reservations should be made 30 to 60 days in advance or earlier (up to 2 years in advance!), especially during peak periods such as summer and holidays. Show times are 5:15 and 8pm Tuesday through Saturday. 1600 Seven Seas Dr. (at Disney's Polynesian Resort). © 407/939-3463. www.disneyworld.com. Reservations required. Adults $49.01, kids 3–11 $24.81, including tax and tip. Free parking.

ELSEWHERE IN ORLANDO

Outside the Disney zone, Orlando has an active dinner-theater scene, but its offerings are not on par with those in major cultural centers such as New York, London, or Paris. Most of the local dinner shows focus on pleasing the kids, so

---

Tips **If You're Lucky . . .**

Mickey's Backyard BBQ (© 407/939-3463; www.disneyworld.com) is a seasonal offering at Pioneer Hall at Fort Wilderness Resort & Campground, where Tom Sawyer and Huck Finn allow you onto their home turf to have a thigh-slapping time and a feast in a covered, outdoor pavilion. Expect Mickey and his pals to join you for a meal that includes barbecued pork ribs, baked chicken, hot dogs, corn on the cob, baked beans, macaroni and cheese, watermelon, beer, wine, lemonade, ice tea, and dessert. (There's no specific menu for kids, but there are plenty of options that will satisfy them on the regular menu.) The storytelling, games, and the character appearances make this a huge thrill for most young kids. Meals are at 6:30pm and cost $39.01 for adults, $25 for kids, including tax and tip. It only happens on Tuesdays and Thursdays . . . sometimes. So **call.**

if you're looking for fun, you and your family will find it; but if you want critically acclaimed entertainment, look elsewhere. You also won't find first-class food; dinner may remind you of your school lunch days, unless you consume enough alcohol to anesthetize your taste buds (in Dolly's case—see below—alcohol isn't served, so if this is your plan you'll need to numb your tongue before going). Still, attending a show is considered by many to be a quintessential Orlando experience, and if you arrive with the right attitude, you'll most likely have an enjoyable evening. Your children certainly will.

Note: Discount coupons to the dinner shows below can often be found inside the tourist magazines that are distributed in gas stations and tourist information centers; you'll also find them in many non-Disney hotels lobbies and sometimes on the listed websites.

Arabian Nights   Age 5 and up   If you're a horse fancier, this is *the* attraction to see in central Florida, and your kids will be impressed by the equestrian acrobatics even if you aren't hoof happy. Arabian Nights is one of the classier dinner-show experiences. It stars many of the most popular breeds, from chiseled Arabians to hard-driving Andalusians to beefcake Belgians. They giddy-up through performances that include Wild West trick riding, chariot races, slapstick comedy, and bareback bravado. Locals rate it No. 1 among Orlando dinner shows (maybe Dolly Parton's Dixie Stampede, below, will have a say about that). On most nights, the performance here opens with a ground trainer working one-on-one with a black stallion. The dinner, served during the 2-hour show, includes salad, prime rib (chicken fingers for the kids), vegetables, potatoes, dessert, wine, beer, and soft drinks. Special diets can be accommodated with advance notice. Show times vary, but there is at least one show nightly. 6225 W. Irlo Bronson Memorial Hwy. (U.S. 192), Kissimmee. ✆ 800/553-6116 or 407/239-9223. www.arabian-nights.com. Reservations recommended. $44 adults, $27 children 3–11. Free parking. Take I-4 Exit 64A/U.S. 192 and look for the white-light sign on the left.

Dolly Parton's Dixie Stampede Dinner & Show   Age 6 and up   Orlando's newest dinner show (it opened in mid-2003) is a hootin'-n-hollerin' good time. This $28 million venture is similar to the ones the actor and country singer has in other southern locations, although the venue is slightly larger. While horses have less of a role than at Arabian Nights (see above), the quarter horses, Appaloosas, Belgians, and others that perform here help put on a fun, "God Bless the U.S.A." show that opens with a herd of bison charging around the arena. Any weaknesses in the early themes and songs are forgotten when the fun and games begin, including a rivalry which pits half the audience (the North) against the other half (the South) in a who-can-cheer-and-stomp-the-loudest battle. There's also blue vs. gray competition in a number of offbeat events, including a chicken chase using four kids from the audience, pig races, a game of toilet-seat horseshoes, and more. Some may blink at the Civil War theme, but your kids will have a great time (provided they're around 6 and up, as the pyrotechnics can get a bit overwhelming). The vittles (plan to eat with your fingers—they don't give you utensils) include a small rotisserie chicken (whole), a slice of smoked pork tenderloin, a potato wedge, corn on the cob, soup, dessert, and unlimited coffee, tea, or Pepsi—*sorry,* there's no alcohol served in Dolly's place. There's no specific menu for kids and be advised that *children ages 3 and under are free only if they sit on a parent's lap.* Show times vary, but there is at least one show nightly. As Dolly said at the June 18 opening, "It's fun for families and I'm gettin' rich on it." 8251 Vineland Ave. (across from Orlando Premium

Tips **One More Fun Thing . . .**

While it may not appeal to some children (the 9-and-older squad should be okay), **SeaWorld's Makahiki Luau,** 7007 SeaWorld Dr. (© **800/327-2424** or 407/363-2559; www.seaworld.com), is another option during your Orlando visit. The show is a celebration of Hawaiian music and dance and the menu offers mahimahi in piña colada sauce, Hawaiian chicken, sweet and sour pork, rice, vegetables, fruit, dessert, and beverages. There isn't a kids' menu, per se, but you can order a hot dog or chicken tenders for those whose tastes refuse to accept menu fare. The price is $37.95 for adults, $27.95 for children 3 to 9. Park admission is not required.

Outlets), Orlando. © **866/443-4943** or 407/238-4455. www.dixiestampede.com. Reservations recommended. $43.99 adults, $18.99 children 4–11. Free parking. From I-4, take Exit 68, Apopka-Vineland Rd./Hwy. 535 right/south to the first light, then go left at the first light to the outlet.

Medieval Times   Age 5 and up   Orlando has one of the eight Medieval Times shows in the United States and Canada. Inside, guests gorge themselves on barbecued spare ribs, herb-roasted chicken, soup, appetizer, potatoes, dessert, and beverages including beer (there's no kids' menu). But since this is the 11th century, you eat with your fingers from metal plates while knights mounted on Andalusian horses run around the arena, jousting and clanging to please the fair ladies. Arrive 90 minutes early for good seats and to see the Medieval Village, a re-created Middle Ages settlement, and the Museum of Torture (think devices, such as The Rack, rather than blood and guts—it's good for kids 7 and older). Show times vary, but there is at least one show nightly. 4510 W. Irlo Bronson Memorial Hwy. (U.S. 192), Kissimmee. © **800/229-8300** or 407/396-1518. www.medievaltimes.com. Reservations recommended. $45.95 adults, $29.95 children 3–11. Free parking. Take I-4 Exit 64A/U.S. 192 5 miles until U.S. 192 makes a big sweeping curve to the right. It's on the right.

Pirates Dinner Adventure   Age 5 and up   The special-effects show at this theater includes a full-size ship in a 300,000-gallon lagoon, circus-style aerial acts, a lot of music, and a little drama. It's a big hit with pirate-happy kids. Dinner includes an appetizer buffet with the preshow, followed by roast chicken and beef, rice, vegetables, dessert, and coffee. The kids' menu has chicken fingers. After the show, you're invited to the Buccaneer Bash dance party where you can mingle with cast members. Show times vary, but there is at least one show nightly. 6400 Carrier Dr. © **800/866-2469** or 407/248-0590. www.orlandopirates.com. Reservations recommended. $44.95 adults, $27.50 children 3–11. Free parking. Take I-4 Exit 74A, Sand Lake Rd./Hwy. 482, north to Carrier, turn right.

2 Arcades & Fun Centers

DisneyQuest   Age 7 and up   The reaction to this five-level arcade is usually the same, whether it comes from children just reaching the video-game stage, firmly hooked teens, or adults who never outgrew Pong: "It's awesome!"

While you will find a few things for the younger set—such as video and pinball games—this high-tech arcade is geared more toward older children, teens, and adults. Options include **Aladdin's Magic Carpet,** a virtual-reality adventure that puts you astride a motorcycle-like seat for a journey into the 3D Cave of Wonders; **Invasion: An Extraterrestrial Alien Encounter,** where you and three others in your space module try to save colonists from intergalactic bad guys; **Pirates of the Caribbean: Battle for Buccaneer Gold,** another 3D VR adventure that has you and your ship mates fighting black hearts; the **Mighty Ducks Pinball Slam,** a life-size pinball game where body English and reflexes help you score; and **The Create Zone,** where you build, then ride, your own simulated roller coaster.

Warning: Heavy crowds after 1pm can significantly cut into your game time. Downtown Disney West Side. ℂ 407/828-4600. www.disneyquest.com. $31 adults, $25 kids 3–9. Open daily 11:30am–11pm, sometimes to midnight.

Fun Spot   Age 4 and up   This throwback amusement park on the north end of International Drive, near Universal Orlando, has something for just about everyone in the family (with the exception of your pets). There are bumper cars, bumper boats, a carousel, kiddie rides, spinning teacups, a Ferris wheel, several go-kart tracks, and a lift-and-drop ride that's a tame version of Universal's Doctor Doom's Fearfall (p. 241). General admission is free; you can pay as you play or ride. Tokens for the primo games (such as simulators, video games, and pinball) cost 25¢ each, 120 for $25, 400 for $75, or, if you're bringing an entourage, 1,000 for $175; most games take 2 to 4 tokens. There's also a $5.25-per-day arcade (older pinball, PlayStation2, and sports games). Rides range from $3 per to an array of multi-ride armbands ($3–$29.95, $9.95 kids 2–6) for go-kart and other rides. 5551 Del Verde Way. ℂ 407/363-3867. www.fun-spot.com. Mon–Fri 2–11pm (10am–midnight in summer); Sat–Sun 10am-midnight.

3 Movies

There are several theaters scattered through tourist and high-traffic areas in central Florida, many of them conveniently located to those staying near the theme park areas. Most theaters offer discounted ticket pricing for children under 12 and discounted matinees (though, really, who's going to sit in a movie theater instead of the theme parks?); some also offer discounts to students (bring ID). We definitely recommend that you head for those theaters that offer stadium seating (the ones we recommend below have it), so that even the shortest members of your party will get to see the picture.

AMC Theatres has a 24-screen complex at Pleasure Island in Downtown Disney (ℂ **407/298-4488**) that seats 6,000—the largest in the Southeast. It's got stadium seating and digital sound systems in most of its theaters. **Universal Cineplex** at CityWalk (ℂ **407/354-5998;** www.citywalk.com) has 20 screens, stadium seating, and a state-of-the-art projection system.

Tips Ghostly Experience

Orlando Ghost Tours (ℂ **407/423-5600;** www.hauntedorlando.com) puts a different spin on the city's nightlife with 2-hour walking tours that explore the downtown's spookier side. The tours include narratives (some funnier than others) on Florida history and folklore followed by a chance to use "ghost-finding" equipment in a haunted building. If your kids are over 6, aren't easily spooked, and are into the supernatural and ghost stories, it's good fun. The cost is $20 adults, $15 kids 6 to 12. Tours run Wednesday through Saturday at 8pm.

Muvico Pointe 21 houses 21 screens (surprise!) in the Pointe Orlando shopping center on International Drive (✆ **407/926-6843;** www.pointeorlandofl. com), including an IMAX screen that's nearly six and a half stories high. All of the theaters have stadium seating and top-of-the-line sound systems.

You can find other theaters, movies, and times in the Orlando Sentinel newspaper or at its website, **www.orlandosentinel.com/entertainment/movies**.

4 Theater

Orlando Youth Theatre   **Age 4 and up**   Here's a nifty way for families to keep the "kid" theme going outside the parks. This theater by the young includes 6 to 18 year olds presenting shows such as *James and the Giant Peach* and *Alice in Wonderland,* as well as drama and improv in fall and spring and during summer camps. 128 W. Church St. ✆ **407/254-4930.** www.orlandoyouththeatre.com. Tickets $8.

5 Concert Venues

Florida Citrus Bowl   With 70,000 seats, the bowl is the largest venue in the area for rock concerts, which in the past have featured such heavyweights as Elton John and the Rolling Stones. It's also home of the Capital One Florida Citrus Bowl (see chapter 2). 1610 W. Church St. (at Tampa St.). ✆ **407/849-2001** for event information, **407/849-2020** to get box office information, **877/803-7073** or 407/839-3900 to charge tickets via Ticketmaster. www.orlandocentroplex.com. Parking $5–$6.

TD Waterhouse Centre   Formerly the Orlando Arena, this 17,500-seat venue has a resume that includes the NBA's Orlando Magic (see "Spectator Sports," in chapter 8) as well as big-name concert performers such as Garth Brooks, Elton John, and Bruce Springsteen. It also features family-oriented entertainment including the Ringling Bros. Barnum & Bailey Circus in January and a slate of cultural offerings such as Broadway-style shows, ballets, plays, and symphony performances. 600 W. Amelia St. (between I-4 and Parramore Ave.). ✆ **407/ 849-2001** for event information, **407/849-2020** to get box office information, **877/803-7073** or 407/839-3900 for tickets through Ticketmaster. www.orlandocentroplex.com. Parking $5–$6.

6 Dance

Orlando Ballet   **Age 7 and up**   Formerly called the Southern Ballet Theatre, this troupe annually stages the holiday favorite *The Nutcracker* (on select days a child gets in free with a paying adult to this ballet) as well as a comedic version of the cherished classic, called the *Nutty Nutcracker.* Performances are usually held in the Bob Carr Performing Arts Centre during the 2 weeks preceding Christmas and feature the Orlando Philharmonic Orchestra. One cool program run during the holidays offers a "character" breakfast that lets families dine with characters from *The Nutcracker.* Call for details if you'll be visiting in December. 401 W. Livingston St. ✆ **407/426-1739** for information, **877/803-7073** or 407/839-3900 to get tickets via Ticketmaster. www.orlandoballet.org. Tickets $10–$60. Parking $5–$6.

7 Night Out for Mom & Dad

If you're so inclined, take advantage of the various babysitting services we tell you about in chapter 4 and step out for at least 1 night of fun sans the kids.

The places described here can be located on the map "Downtown Disney" on p. 291. For information about nighttime activities throughout Downtown Disney, call ✆ **407/939-2648.**

Tips **On the Boardwalk**

Disney's Boardwalk has a few options for folks searching for off-the-field nightlife. Street performers sing, dance, and do a little juggling and magic most evenings on the outdoor promenade.

Atlantic Dance (✆ 407/939-2444 for limited recorded information) features Top-40 and '80s dance hits Tuesday through Thursday, and live bands on Friday and Saturday nights. It's open to everyone 21 and over. Hours are from 9pm to 2am and admission is free.

The rustic saloon-style **Jellyrolls** (✆ 407/939-5100) offers dueling pianos and a boisterous crowd. Strictly for the over-21 set, it's popular with visiting business travelers. There's a $5 cover after 7pm.

If you're looking to hoist a pint, the **Big River Brewery and Grill** (✆ 407/560-0253) serves micro-brewed beer as well as steaks, ribs, chicken, fish, sandwiches, and salads. Prices range from $7 to $27, and there's no cover. It's open Monday through Thursday from 11:30am to 1am; Friday through Sunday from 11:30am to 2am. It's near Atlantic Dance.

If you're a sports nut, look no further than **ESPN Sports** (✆ 407/939-3463; www.disneyworld.com), where 90 monitors—there are even a few in the bathrooms—broadcast sporting events from around the world. Need we say more? There's a full-service bar, but there's also a restaurant and a small arcade, so if you're stuck for the night with the kids, you all will have something to do.

Disney's Boardwalk can be a cheap night out if you enjoy strolling and people-watching (and if you stay out of the restaurants and clubs). It has something of a midway atmosphere reminiscent of Atlantic City's heyday.

PLEASURE ISLAND

This rocking Walt Disney World launch pad is a 6-acre complex of nightclubs, restaurants, and shops, some of which can be visited during the day for free. At night, for a single admission price of $19.95, you can go club hopping and celebrate New Year's Eve into the wee hours every night of the week. Pay special attention to **Mannequins** (listed a little later). This club is the cream of Pleasure Island's crop and fills quickly, so late arrivals may be left at the door.

Pleasure Island is designed to look like an abandoned waterfront industrial district with clubs in its lofts and warehouses. But the streets are decorated with brightly colored lights and balloons. Dozens of searchlights play overhead and rock music emanates from the bushes. You'll be given a map and show schedule when you enter the park. Take a look at it and plan your evening around the shows that interest you. The mood is always festive, especially at midnight, which is celebrated with a high-energy street party, live entertainment, a barrage of fireworks, and showers of confetti.

Although this is Disney, it's essentially a bar district where liquor is served. *Kids under 18 must be accompanied by a parent or legal guardian* if they want to come here. If you do choose to bring older children (and they should be at least 10 or older), use the same rules you use at home. Your preteens and teens might think it cool to be allowed to hang out in most of the clubs, even if it is with mom and dad, but this is still an adult environment and you're better off leaving them to alternatives better suited to their age group. If you do let them tag along, bring 'em early (the later it is, the more adult the area becomes) and stick to the Comedy Warehouse, Rock 'n' Roll Beach Club, 8Trax, and Motion (all described below).

Pleasure Island has seven regular clubs, plus BET Soundstage, which is included in the ticket on nights it doesn't have a special concert going. There are also shops and eateries (with outdoor umbrella tables) on the island. **Planet Hollywood** (p. 128) is adjacent and doesn't require a Pleasure Island ticket.

For more information on Pleasure Island's clubs and events, call ✆ **407/934-7781** or surf over to **www.disneyworld.com**. Admission is free before 7pm and $19.95, plus tax, after 7pm. (It's $69 on New Year's Eve.) Admission is included in Disney's 5- to 7-day Park Hopper Plus and Ultimate Park Hopper passes. Clubs are open daily from 7pm to 2am; shops open at 11am and some are open till midnight or later. There's free self-parking; valet parking is $6.

Here's the club lineup:

Adventurers Club   The most unique of Pleasure Island's clubs occupies a multistory building that, according to legend, was designed to house the library and archaeological trophy collection of island founder and compulsive explorer, Merriweather Adam Pleasure, a figment of Disney's imagination. It's also the global headquarters for the Adventurers Club, which Pleasure headed until he vanished at sea in 1941. The plush club is chock-full of artifacts: early aviation photos, hunting trophies, shrunken heads, Buddhas, goddesses, and a mounted "yakoose," a half yak, half moose that occasionally speaks, whether you've been drinking or not. In the eerie Mask Room, more strange sounds are heard and the 100 or so masks move their eyes and make odd pronouncements. Also on hand are Pleasure's zany band of globetrotting friends and servants, played by skilled actors who interact with guests while staying in character. It's a hoot.

BET Soundstage   This club grooves—loudly—to the sounds of reggae, the smooth moves of traditional R&B and the rhyme of hip-hop. If you like the BET Cable Network, you'll love it. You can boogie on an expansive dance floor or kick back on an outdoor terrace. The club also serves Caribbean-style finger food and periodically has concerts for a separate charge (✆ **407/934-7666**). You must be 21 to enter (and they will check!).

Comedy Warehouse   Housed in the island's former power plant, the Comedy Warehouse has tiered seating. A troupe of comics—the Who, What and Warehouse Players—perform 45-minute improvisational comedy shows based on audience suggestions. This is Disney, so the shows are neither as risqué as those at other improv clubs nor candidates for anyone's top 10, but if you like your comedy clean, you're in luck. There are several shows nightly and drinks are served. Arrive early.

8Trax   Disco and bell bottoms rule in this 1970s-style club, where some 50 TV monitors air diverse shows and videos over the dance floor. A DJ plays everything from "YMCA" to "The Hustle" while the disco ball spins. All you need to bring is your polyester and patent leather. If you grew up during the Reagan years you can relive your musical past on Thursday nights, when the tunes fast-forward to the '80s.

Mannequins Dance Palace   Housed in a vast dance hall with a small-town movie-house facade, Mannequins is supposed to be a converted mannequin

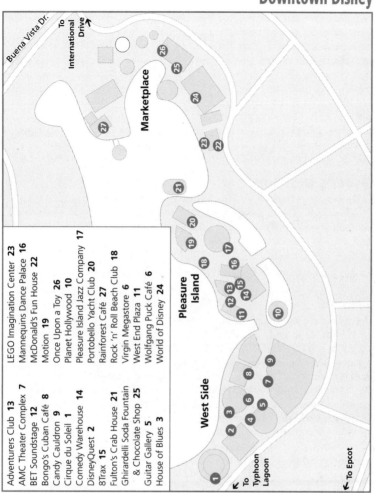

Marketplace

Pleasure Island

West Side

To International Drive

Buena Vista Dr.

To Typhoon Lagoon

To Epcot

Adventurers Club **13**
AMC Theater Complex **7**
BET Soundstage **12**
Bongo's Cuban Café **8**
Candy Cauldron **9**
Cirque du Soleil **1**
Comedy Warehouse **14**
DisneyQuest **2**
8Trax **15**
Fulton's Crab House **21**
Ghirardelli Soda Fountain
& Chocolate Shop **25**
Guitar Gallery **5**
House of Blues **3**

LEGO Imagination Center **23**
Mannequins Dance Palace **16**
McDonald's Fun House **22**
Motion **19**
Once Upon a Toy **26**
Planet Hollywood **10**
Pleasure Island Jazz Company **17**
Portobello Yacht Club **20**
Rainforest Café **27**
Rock 'n' Roll Beach Club **18**
Virgin Megastore **6**
West End Plaza **11**
Wolfgang Puck Café **6**
World of Disney **24**

warehouse (remember, you're still in Disney World). This high-energy club has a big rotating dance floor and it's a local favorite, so much so that it's one of the toughest clubs in Orlando to get into, so arrive early, especially on weekends. Those who get in will find three levels of bars and hangout spaces that are festooned with elaborately costumed mannequins and moving scenery suspended from the overhead rigging. A DJ plays contemporary tunes filtered through speakers powerful enough to wake Sleeping Beauty, and there are high-tech lighting effects. You must be 21 to get in, and they're very serious about it. Have your ID ready, even if you learned to dance to the Beatles.

Motion   Pleasure Island's newest dance club is a hyperactive joint that features Top-40 tunes and alternative rock, and appeals to younger or young-at-heart partyers. The club uses moody blue lighting to halfway convey the sensation that you're dancing the night away in space.

The Pleasure Island Jazz Company   This big barn-like club—purported to be an abandoned waterfront carousel factory—features contemporary and traditional live jazz, with funky coffees and, by club standards, a respectable domestic wine list. Performers are mostly locals, but sometimes there's a big name, such as Kenny Rankin, Lionel Hampton, Maynard Ferguson, the Rippingtons, or Billy Taylor.

Rock 'n' Roll Beach Club   Once the laboratory in which Pleasure developed a unique flying machine, this three-story structure today houses an always-crowded dance club where live bands play classic rock from the '60s through the '90s. There are bars on all three floors, including one that serves international brews. The first level contains the dance floor. The second and third levels offer air hockey, pool tables, basketball machines, pinball, video games, darts, and a pizza and beer stand.

DISNEY'S WEST SIDE
This area adjoins Pleasure Island and offers additional shops, restaurants, and a 24-screen AMC Theater (see "Movies," earlier in this chapter). Older kids and teens will find DisneyQuest (p. 286) an alluring if crowded enticement. The two most popular adult entries are:

Bongo's Cuban Café *(Overrated*   Created by Cuban-American singer Gloria Estefan and her husband, Emilio, the cafe is Downtown Disney's version of old Havana. There are leopard spotted chairs and mosaic bar stools shaped like

---

Finds Not Your Ordinary Circus

Lions and tigers and bears?

Oh, no. But neither you nor your kids will feel cheated.

This Disney partnership with the famed no-animals circus is located in Downtown Disney West Side. **Cirque du Soleil,** which translates to "circus of the sun" and flutters off the tongue as *"SAIRK doo so-LAY,"* is nonstop energy. At times it seems all 64 performers are on stage simultaneously, especially during the intricately choreographed trampoline routine. Trapeze artists, high-wire walkers, an airborne gymnast, a posing strongman, mimes, and two zany clowns cement a show called *La Nouba* (it means "live it up") into a five-star performance. You may not be able to explain it to your kids in advance, but most of them (especially those 8 and up) will come away impressed and amazed. And so will you.

Of all the Cirque du Soleil shows, we think this one may be second only to *O* at the Bellagio in Las Vegas. That said, though *La Nouba* is a ton of fun, it's also one of the priciest shows in town. If you're on a tight or even modest budget, it may be gut-check time: Can you blow your entertainment allowance for a day or 2 on 90 minutes of fun? There are two ticket categories: $82 for adults and $49 for kids 3 to 9 (plus tax) for center of the theater seats; $72 and $44, respectively, for seats to the right and left of the stage. Shows are at 6 and 9pm 5 nights a week, but times and nights rotate (the show was dark Sun and Mon at press time) and sometimes there's a matinee, so call ahead (© **407/939-7600**) or check the show's website (**www.cirquedusoleil. com**) for information and tickets.

bongo drums (and a Desi Arnaz impersonator every night). There's no dance floor to speak of, though you could cha-cha on the patio, an upstairs number that overlooks the rest of West Side. It's a great place to sit back and bask in the Latin rhythms. But, while the mood is good, we find the food a little lacking. Open daily 11am to 2am. © 407/828-0999. www.bongoscubancafe.com. No reservations or cover charge. Free self-parking.

House of Blues   Several well-known artists have performed here, including Jethro Tull, Blue Oyster Cult, Quiet Riot, Duran Duran, and others. The barn-like building, with three tiers, may be a little difficult for those with disabilities to maneuver, but there really isn't a bad seat in the house. The atmosphere is dark and boozy, perfect for the bluesy sounds that raise the rafters. The dance floor is big enough to boogie without doing the bump with a stranger. You can dine in the adjoining restaurant (p. 129). © 407/934-2583. www.hob.com. Cover charges vary by event/artist. Free self-parking.

CITYWALK

Located between the Islands of Adventure and Universal Studios Florida theme parks, this nightclub, restaurant, and shopping district had its coming-out party in 1999 and went nose-to-nose with Disney's Pleasure Island. It's open daily from 11am, but the hours of many clubs and restaurants vary, so call in advance if you're interested in a specific venue. Most clubs stay open until 2am and will not allow anyone under 21 to enter after a certain time (see listings below for details).

At 30 acres, CityWalk (© **407/363-8000** or 407/224-9255; www.citywalk. com or www.universalorlando.com) is five times larger than Pleasure Island. Alcohol is prominently featured here, and the nights can get pretty wild, so an adult should accompany all teens, young children, and party-hearty peers. Better yet—don't bring the kids at all, unless you're heading to the movies or one of the theme restaurants for dinner.

Unlike Pleasure Island, you can walk the district for free at night or visit individual clubs and pay an individual cover charge. CityWalk also offers two **party passes.** A pass to all clubs costs $8.95 plus tax. For $12 plus tax, you get a club pass and a movie at Universal Cineplex (© **407/354-3374**). Universal also offers free club access to those who buy multiday theme-park tickets (see chapter 7). If all you want on your night out is dinner and a movie, CityWalk's **Meal & Movie Deal** nets you dinner (an entree and a soft drink from a limited menu) at one of the district's restaurants and a movie ticket for $19.95, including tax and gratuity. Kids get no special price or meals—it's aimed at the moms and dads taking the night off. To get your tickets, ask at the CityWalk Guest Services Ticket Window or call © **407/224-CITY.**

Daytime parking in the Universal Orlando garages costs $8, but parking is free after 6pm. To get to CityWalk, take I-4 Exit 74B (westbound) or 75A (eastbound) and follow the signs to the parks.

Bob Marley—A Tribute to Freedom   This hybrid bar/restaurant has a party atmosphere that will make the food more appealing as the night wears on. The clapboard building is said to be a replica of Marley's home in Kingston. Jamaican vittles—such as meat patties, jerk snapper, and, the brew of champions, Red Stripe Beer—are served under patio umbrellas amid portraits of the original Rastamon. If you try an Extreme Measure, have a designated driver. Local and national reggae bands perform on a microdot stage. Open daily 4pm to 2am. © 407/224-2262. www.bobmarley.com. Cover charge $5 after 8pm, more for special acts. Must be 21 or over after 10pm.

> **Tips Chilling Out**
>
> You can grab a margarita to go and "chill" in the brightly colored wooden chairs (think of Adirondacks) outside Jimmy Buffet's Margaritaville. It's a perfect spot to watch the crowds scurrying to and from the theme parks.

CityJazz   The cover charge at this club includes the **Downbeat Jazz Hall of Fame** (with memorabilia from Louis Armstrong, Ella Fitzgerald, and other greats). The two-story, 10,500-square-foot building houses more than 500 pieces of memorabilia representing Dixieland, swing, bebop, and modern jazz. It also has a state-of-the-art sound system and stage. Graphic murals and over-size black-and-white photographs set the mood. Acts of national renown perform frequently. It's a real treat for true jazz fans, who can sip cocktails while browsing. Open Sunday through Thursday 8pm to 1am, and Friday and Saturday 7pm to 2am. ✆ **407/224-2189**. Cover charge $5 (more for special events). Must be 18 to get in.

the groove   This is Universal's answer to Mannequin's at Pleasure Island, though it's not as popular, and, therefore, has less of a waiting list. There's a high-tech sound system (read—*LOUD*) and a spacious dance floor in a room gleaming with chrome. Most nights, a DJ plays tunes featuring the latest in hip-hop, jazz-fusion, techno, and alternative rock. Bands occasionally play the house, too. The club features three themed lounges covering the '70s to alternative rock. Each spot has a decor, bar, and specialty drink to fit its ambience. It's open Sunday through Thursday 9pm to 2am, and Friday and Saturday 9pm to 3am. ✆ **407/363-8000**. Cover charge $5. Must be 21 to get in.

Hard Rock Cafe/Hard Rock Live   The first concert hall to bear the Hard Rock name is next door to the largest Hard Rock Cafe in the world (p. 134). This building, fashioned to look like an ancient coliseum, has a 2,500-seat concert venue. Call ahead to find out what acts will be featured during your visit. Tickets for big-name performers sell fast. A lot of bands only your teens will probably know play the venue, but oldies such as Crosby, Stills, and Nash, Bob Dylan, and the Moody Blues have performed here. Concerts generally begin about 8pm. The sound system is loud and the sightlines are pretty decent. The Cafe is open daily 11am to midnight. ✆ **407/351-5483**. www.hardrock.com. Tickets $6–$150, depending on concert.

Jimmy Buffett's Margaritaville   Flip-flops and flowered shirts are the proper apparel here. Music from the maestro is piped throughout the building, with live music performed on a small stage inside later in the evening. A Jimmy sound-alike strums on the spacious back porch. True parrot-heads know the lyrics at least as well as the singers. Bar-wise, there are three options. The Volcano erupts margarita mix; the Land Shark has fins hanging from the ceiling; and the 12 Volt, is, well, a little electrifying—we'll leave it at that. If you opt for dinner among the palm trees, go for the true Key West experience. Early in the day that means a cheeseburger (in paradise); later it's conch fritters, one of many kinds of fish (pompano, sea bass, dolphin), and key lime pie. Open daily 11am to 2am. (See p. 134 for more on the food here.) ✆ **407/224-2155**. Cover $5 after 10pm.

Latin Quarter   This two-level restaurant/club offers you a chance to absorb the salsa-and-samba culture and cuisine of 21 Latin nations. If you don't know how to move your hips, there's a dance studio to lend a hand. The club features

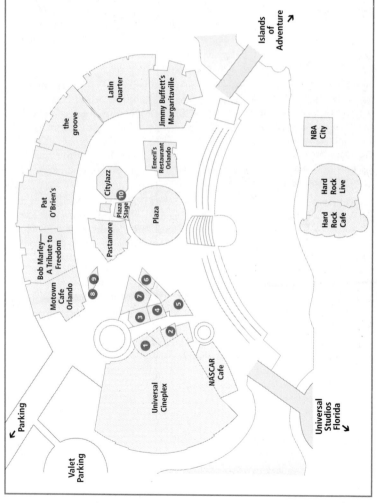

SPECIALTY SHOPS

All Star Collectibles **5**
Cigarz at Citywalk **1**
Dapy **3**
Elegant Illusions **2**
Endangered Species **9**
Fossil **6**
Glow! **4**
Quiet Flight **7**
Silver **8**
Universal Studios Store **10**

acts ranging from merengue to Latin rock. The sound system is loud enough to blow you into the next county, but before that happens you can leave on your own to see a Latin American art gallery. Open Monday through Friday 5pm to 2am, and Saturday and Sunday noon to 2am. © 407/363-8000. www.thelatin quarter.com. Cover $5–$10.

Motown Cafe Orlando   Refuel on finger food and sandwiches ($8–$16) or kick back to the music of Smokey Robinson, the Supremes, the Temptations, and Stevie Wonder (look for their statues, too). Spend time in the indoor/ outdoor Big Chill Lounge or browse through memorabilia that includes the light-blue skirts and blouses the Supremes wore in their 1965 Copacabana performance. A live band frequently plays, giving patrons plenty of incentive to shake their you-know-what's-its. Open Sunday through Thursday 11:30am to 11pm, Friday and Saturday 11am to 2am. © 407/363-8000. Cover charge $5 after 9pm.

NASCAR Café   This one-of-a-kind NASCAR-licensed eatery is a must for gearheads, though its basic vittles (so-so steaks, chicken, pork chops, shrimp, and sandwiches, most under $8) won't win culinary awards. The kids' menu has spaghetti, pizza, corn dogs, and more ($5.99). Race-related souvenirs abound. Open daily 11am to 11pm or later. © 407/224-7223.

NBA City   This typical theme restaurant and watering hole is an attempt to cash in on fans in a city that has a National Basketball Association team (the Orlando Magic). The mixed menu ($5–$20) ranges from steaks and chicken to fish, pasta, and sandwiches. The kids' menu ($5.95 including soda) has burgers, hot dogs, grilled cheese, chicken nuggets, and more. The eye candy includes videos and stills of the sport. Fans young and old will like it, but if you're looking for better-than-average food, look elsewhere. Daily 11am to midnight or later. © 407/363-5919.

Pat O'Brien's *(Overrated*   It doesn't take a genius to figure out the focus of a place that has a one-page food menu and a booklet filled with drinks. Just like the French Quarter, which is home to the original Patty O's, drinking, drinking, and more drinking are the highlights here. Enjoy the piano bar or the flame-throwing fountain while you suck down the drink of the Big Easy, a Hurricane. Although you can order a soft drink, Pat O'Brien's certainly promotes the hard stuff, and no one under 21 is permitted after 9pm (a kids' menu is available until then, but this is *not* the place to take them!). If your plans for the evening fall anything short of full intoxication (unless you're the designated driver for the aforementioned planners), this may not be the place for you. There's a limited menu of sandwiches and treats like jambalaya and shrimp Creole ($8–$10). Open daily 4pm to 2am. © 407/363-8000. Cover charge $5 after 9pm. You must be 21 to enter after 9pm.

11

Side Trips from Orlando

Although many visitors to Orlando never venture outside the city, an excursion away from the theme parks can allow you and your kids time to recharge your batteries, while still enjoying some of the best things Florida has to offer.

Many families who vacation in Orlando (especially those using the FlexTicket pass; see p. 221) eventually drive or hitch a ride an hour and a half west on I-4 to another major theme park, **Busch Gardens,** as well as some of Tampa's smaller attractions, including the **Museum of Science and**

Industry and some big-league spectator sports.

Others—especially those with space-crazed kids—head an hour east on Highway 528 to the Space Coast and its eye-popping fun, including rockets blasting off from **John F. Kennedy Space Center** at Cape Canaveral, which is also the home of **Canaveral National Seashore** and, nearby, some of Florida's finest surfing turf. Both of these spots offer a combination of entertainment and education (be it astronomy or the natural sciences) that the whole family will enjoy.

1 Tampa

84 miles W of Orlando

Children, animal lovers, or thrill-ride junkies may *demand* that you visit the Busch Gardens theme park in Tampa. While in town, you can also visit the much less frantic exhibits at the Lowry Park Zoo, educate your kids (and yourself) at the Florida Aquarium, and, in warmer months, take a refreshing plunge at the Adventure Island water park, which is next to Busch Gardens. You can do Tampa as a day trip out of Orlando or you can spend a day or 2 exploring the city with your kids (we provide accommodations and dining choices in this section if you choose to go that route); your choice will depend on your family's interests, your stamina after hitting all of the Orlando parks, and how much vacation time you have. Most people with only a week's vacation won't do more than travel to Busch Gardens before heading back to Mickeyville. If you've got more time, a day or 2 in Tampa is a fun and slightly less frenetic place than Orlando to wind down your vacation.

GETTING THERE

BY CAR From Orlando, take Interstate 4 west (it's really southwest), which can take you to the downtown or Interstate 275 North, which goes to Busch Gardens and other north-side attractions.

BY SHUTTLE **Busch Gardens** and **SeaWorld Orlando,** both owned by Anheuser-Busch, offer daily shuttle service between the parks for $5. The 1½- to 2-hour run (each way) has seven pick-up locations in Orlando, including SeaWorld, International Drive, and Universal Orlando (© **800/221-1339**). The

Tampa

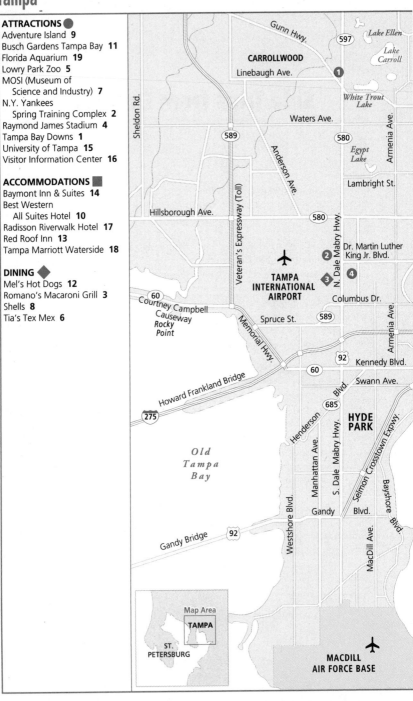

Gunn Hwy.
597
Lake Ellen
Lake Carroll
CARROLLWOOD
Linebaugh Ave.
❶
White Trout Lake
Waters Ave.
Armenia Ave.
580
Egypt Lake
Lambright St.
Sheldon Rd.
589
Anderson Ave.
580
N. Dale Mabry Hwy.
Hillsborough Ave.
580
Dr. Martin Luther King Jr. Blvd.
Veteran's Expressway (Toll)
❷
❸ ❹
TAMPA INTERNATIONAL AIRPORT
Columbus Dr.
60
Courtney Campbell Causeway
Rocky Point
Spruce St.
589
Memorial Hwy.
92
Kennedy Blvd.
60
Swann Ave.
Howard Frankland Bridge
Blvd.
685
HYDE PARK
275
Henderson
Manhattan Ave.
S. Dale Mabry Hwy.
Selmon Crosstown Expwy.
Bayshore Blvd.
Old Tampa Bay
Gandy Blvd.
MacDill Ave.
Gandy Bridge
92
Westshore Blvd.

Map Area
TAMPA
ST. PETERSBURG

MACDILL AIR FORCE BASE

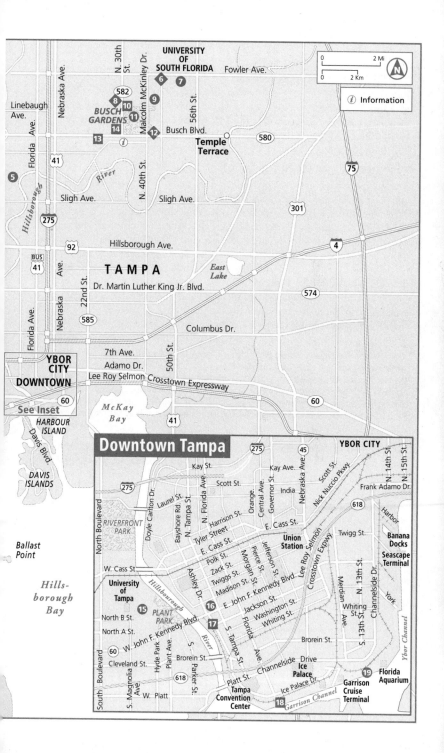

schedule allows about 5 to 7 hours at Busch Gardens and the service is free if you buy a FlexTicket (p. 221).

VISITOR INFORMATION Contact the **Tampa Bay Convention & Visitors Bureau,** 400 N. Tampa St., Tampa, FL 33602-4706 (© **800/448-2672,** 800/368-2672, or 813/223-2752; www.visittampabay.com), for advance information. Once you're downtown, head to the bureau's **visitor information center** at 400 N. Tampa St. (Channelside), Suite 2800 (© **813/223-1111**). It's open Monday through Saturday from 9:30am to 5:30pm.

EXPLORING THE PARKS & MORE

Adventure Island If the summer heat gets to you before one of Tampa's famous thunderstorms brings late-afternoon relief, your family can take a water-logged break at this 25-acre outdoor water park near Busch Gardens Tampa Bay (see below). You can also frolic here during the cooler days of spring and fall, when the water is heated. Adults and teens enjoy Key West Rapids, Tampa Typhoon, Gulf Scream, Wahoo Run, and other exciting water rides (there are height requirements on many of these thrill rides, usually starting at 48 in.). Young children can have a ton of fun in the miniature wave pool, water jets, bubbling springs, and aqua gym at Fabian's Funport. Lifeguards are there to supervise all of the attractions and activities. There are also places to picnic and sunbathe, a games arcade, a volleyball complex, and an outdoor cafe. If you forget to bring your own, a surf shop sells bathing suits, towels, and suntan lotion.

10001 Malcolm McKinley Dr. (between Busch Blvd. and Bougainvillea Ave.). © 813/987-5600. www. 4adventure.com. Admission $29.95 adults, $27.95 children 3–9, plus tax; free for children 2 and under. 2-day combination tickets with Busch Gardens Tampa Bay (1 day each) $64.95 adults, $54.95 children 3–9, free for children under 3. Website sometimes offers discounts. Parking $5. Mid-Mar to Labor Day daily 10am–5pm; Sept–Oct Fri–Sun 10am–5pm (extended hours in summer and on holidays). Closed Nov to mid-Mar. Take exit 50 off I-275 and go east on Busch Blvd. for 2 miles. Turn left onto McKinley Dr. (N. 40th St.) and entry is on right.

Busch Gardens Tampa Bay ✇✇✇ If you have time for a day trip, this venerable theme park is a don't-miss attraction for children and adults, who can see, in person, all those wild beasts you've watched on the *Animal Planet*—and you'll get better views of them here than at Disney's Animal Kingdom in Orlando (see "Animal Kingdom," in chapter 6). Busch Gardens has several thousand animals living in naturalistic environments that help carry out the park's overall African theme, including an 80-acre plain that's strongly reminiscent of the real Serengeti of Tanzania and Kenya, upon which zebras, giraffes, and other animals graze. Unlike the animals on the real Serengeti, however, the grazing animals have nothing to fear from lions, hyenas, crocodiles, and other predators, which are confined to enclosures—as are hippos and elephants. *Tip:* Before you leave home, spend some time with your kids on the park's website **(www.busch gardens.com),** which offers some wonderful educational information about the animals and environments in the park.

Timbuktu near the center of the park is a great place for smaller kids to enjoy miniature train and motorcycle rides as well as the whimsical **Carousel Caravan. Dumphrey's Special Day,** a show at the Dragon's Tale Theater at Stanleyville, is another high point for younger guests.

The entire family can enjoy the **Skyride cable cars** that glide high above the park; the Clydesdale barn, where these large horses are groomed several times daily; **Ubanga-Banga Bumper Cars;** and the arcade area, though the games here can significantly dent your budget. A baby animal nursery, petting zoo, and

Tips **Flexing Your Muscle**

Busch Gardens is part of the Orlando-Tampa **FlexTicket** that also includes Universal Studios Florida, Islands of Adventure, SeaWorld, and Wet 'n Wild. The ticket, which allows unlimited admission to the five parks for a 14-day period, costs $209.95 for adults and $175.95 for children 3 to 9.

elephant and hippo exhibits are other family favorites. Ditto for **Curiosity Caverns,** where bats, reptiles, and small mammals that are active in the dark are kept in cages. Note that the latter is housed in one of those faux tunnels made of concrete and stucco and the area is kept dark, so it could be frightening for some kids under 6.

Older thrill-ride fans find an enterprising mix of five roller coasters—**Montu, Kumba, Gwazi, Python, and Scorpion,** all with minimum height requirements of 42 to 54 inches. The park also has a pair of water rides: **Tanganyika Tidal Wave** (48-in. minimum height) and the **Stanley Falls Flume** (an aqua version of a roller coaster that's tame enough for most kids 6 and older). Near the back of the park, **Rhino Rally** puts you in a Land Rover for a bouncy ride through habitat that includes white rhinos, gazelles, Watusis, and wildebeests. When this ride is functioning properly, which isn't the case at all times, a "flash flood" turns the Rovers into rafts that float down a short, man-made river. This ride may not be suitable for those under 6.

Akbar's Adventure Tours, narrated by comedian Martin Short, is a wacky simulator that "transports" you across Egypt via camel, biplane, and mine car. It and the new **R. L. Stine's Haunted Lighthouse 4-D** offer fun and surprises for adults and older kids.

The park also offers exotic architecture, craft demonstrations, an alligator and turtle exhibit, a hospitality house with free beer for adults, and the **World Rhythms on Ice** and **Moroccan Roll** song-and-dance shows.

Note: You can get to Busch Gardens from Orlando via shuttle buses, which pick up at area hotels between 8:00 and 10:15am for the 1½- to 2-hour ride, with return trips starting at 5pm and continuing until the park closes. Round-trip fares are $5 per person. (It's free if you have a FlexTicket.) Call © **800/221-1339** for schedules, pickup locations, and reservations.

3000 E. Busch Blvd. (at McKinley Dr./N. 40th St.). © **888/800-5447** or 813/987-5283. www.buschgardens. com. Admission $51.95 adults, $42.95 children 3–9, plus tax; free for children 2 and under. Website offers discounts. Daily 10am–6pm (extended hours to 7 and 8pm in summer and on holidays). Parking $7. Take I-275 north of downtown to Busch Blvd. (exit 50) and go east 2 miles. From I-75, take Fowler Ave. (exit 54) and follow the signs west.

Florida Aquarium ✦✦   See more than 5,000 aquatic animals and plants that call Florida home at this entertaining and informative attraction, which appeals to all ages. The exhibits follow a drop of water from the pristine springs of the **Florida Wetlands Gallery,** through a mangrove forest in the **Bays and Beaches Gallery,** and out onto the **Coral Reefs,** where an impressive 43-foot-wide, 14-foot-tall panoramic window lets you look out to schools of fish and lots of sharks and stingrays. The **No Bone Zone** is an exhibit on invertebrate sea life that features a child-pleasing touch tank where kids can stroke sea stars and crabs, among others. Also worth visiting are the **"Explore a Shore"** playground to educate the kids, a deep-water exhibit, and a tank housing moray eels. You can

Moments   Special Meals & Tours at Busch Gardens

Busch Gardens offers a number of special options that are geared to families and kids.

If your kids are around Sesame Street age, then they'll be overjoyed by the opportunity to have breakfast, lunch, or dinner with Elmo, Ernie, Big Bird, and other Sesame Street characters. The food won't be gourmet but your kids won't care. **Breakfast** is an all-you-can-eat affair that starts at 9:30am and enables participants to get a jump on the park. It costs 12.95 adults; $9.95 children 3–9. **Lunch** ($14.95 for adults; $9.95 children 3–9) has a kids' buffet that features macaroni and cheese, chicken fingers, pizza and more. Adults get their own buffet with chicken Dijon, seafood, vegetable lasagna, and various salads and fruits. The dessert buffet will satisfy everyone's sugar cravings. Dinner ($19.95 for adults; $12.95 children 3–9) offerings are similar to though a bit more extensive than those at lunch. Children under 3 eat free though you'll have to reserve a space for them. Reservations can be made online at **www.buschgardens.com** or by calling ⓒ **888/800-5447.**

Although you and your kids will get close to Busch Garden's predators, hippos, and elephants in their glass-walled enclosures, the only way to mingle with the grazers is on a tour. The best is a **VIP Animal Adventure Tour,** on which you'll roam the plains in the company of a zoologist. These 1-hour excursions cost a pricey $75 per person (in addition to the park's entry fee) and usually leave about 1:30pm daily. The park provides bottled water on the tours but advises all participants to wear hats and lots of sunscreen. You can reserve spots on the tours (which fill up fast) by calling ⓒ **813/984-4043** or 813/984-4073. *Children under 5 are not permitted.*

Another (though less attractive) alternative is the 30-minute, zoologist-led **Serengeti Safari Special Tour,** in which you and 19 other people ride out among the grazers on the back of a flatbed truck. Five of these tours are offered daily and they are worth the extra $30 per person regardless of age. You can by buy tickets for the tours at the Edge of Africa and Outfitters gift shops inside the park, though you can reserve a space in advance on the 11:15am tour by calling ⓒ **813/984-4043** or 813/984-4073. *Children under 5 are not allowed on the tour.*

You can tack on a meal to the safari tour if you reserve the **Serengeti Dining Safari** option, which includes the 1pm Serengeti Safari Special Tour and a dining certificate good for a main course, a side dish, and a dessert at the park's Crown Colony Restaurant. The cost of this option is $49.99 adults; $39.99 children 5 to 9. Note that this option is available only if you book it online at **www.buschgardens.com.**

also go out on the bay to look for birds and sea life on 90-minute Dolphin Quest cruises in the *Bay Spirit,* a 64-foot diesel-powered catamaran.

Note: If your children are 8 and older, a cool "Behind the Scenes" program gives you an inside look at how the aquarium feeds and houses its marine residents, and also offers up-close encounters with some of the animals.

701 Channelside Dr. ℂ 813/273-4000. www.flaquarium.net. Admission $16 adults, $14 seniors, $11 children 3–11, free for children under 3. Dolphin Quest $19 adults, $18 seniors, $14 children 2–13, free for children under 2. Combination aquarium admission, Dolphin Quest, and Behind The Scenes Tour (children under 8 not permitted on tour) $37 adults, $34 seniors, $27 children 3–11, free for children under 3. Website sometimes offers discounts. Parking $4. Daily 9:30am–5pm. Dolphin Quest Mon–Fri 2pm; Sat–Sun 1 and 3pm. Closed Thanksgiving, Christmas.

Lowry Park Zoo ℱ The opportunity to view 3,000-pound manatees, Komodo dragons, Persian leopards, and rare red pandas makes this a worthwhile excursion. With lots of greenery, bubbling brooks, and cascading waterfalls, this 24-acre zoo displays animals in settings similar to their natural habitats. Other major exhibits include a Florida wildlife display, an Asian Domain, Primate World, an Aquatic Center, a free-flight aviary with a birds-of-prey show, a hands-on Discovery Center, and an endangered-species carousel ride that's a real hit for children as well as carousel lovers of all ages. **Wallaroo Station** has kids' rides, a small water park, a kangaroo walk-about, and a petting zoo. In 2004, a new African-themed habitat is scheduled to open. Lowry Park has one of Florida's three manatee hospitals and rehabilitation centers. It's also a sanctuary for Florida panthers and red wolves. The zoo also occasionally offers funs and educational classes and programs where kids can get an up-close encounter with some animals. Cost depends on the individual program. Call the zoo or consult its website (an excellent and entertaining resource for kids) for more information.

Tip: If you're a member at your local zoo, you may be eligible for discounted or free admission to the Lowry Zoo. Call ahead and ask.

1101 W. Sligh Ave. ℂ 813/935-8552 or 813/932-0245 for recorded information. www.lowryparkzoo.com. Admission $11.50 adults, $10.50 seniors, $7.95 children 3–11, free for children 2 and under. Daily 9:30am–5pm. Closed Thanksgiving, Christmas. Take I-275 to Sligh Ave. (exit 48) and follow the signs.

Museum of Science and Industry (MOSI) ℱℱ A great place to take the kids on a rainy day, MOSI is the largest science center in the Southeast and has more than 450 interactive exhibits. You can step into the **Gulf Hurricane** and experience 74 mile-per-hour winds, defy the laws of gravity in the unique *Challenger* space experience, and explore the human body in **The Amazing You.** If your heart is up to it, you can ride a bicycle across a 98-foot-long cable suspended 30 feet above the lobby (don't worry: You'll be harnessed to the bike). Your kids will likely find the dinosaurs in the lobby awe-inspiring. You can also watch stunning movies in Florida's first IMAX dome theater (free with admission) or take a 5-minute ride in a flight simulator ($3.50 additional charge). Outside, trails wind through a 47-acre nature preserve with a butterfly garden. The museum also has a planetarium.

4801 E. Fowler Ave. (at N. 50th St.). ℂ 813/987-6100. www.mosi.org. Admission $14.95 adults, $12.95 seniors, $10.95 children 2–12, free for children under 2. Admission includes IMAX movies. Daily 9am–5pm or later. From downtown, take I-275 north to the Fowler Ave. E. exit (exit 51). Take this 2 miles east to museum on right.

SPECTATOR SPORTS

National Football League fans can catch the **Tampa Bay Buccaneers** at the modern, 66,000-seat Raymond James Stadium, 4201 N. Dale Mabry Hwy., at Dr. Martin Luther King Jr. Boulevard (ℂ **813/879-2827;** www.buccaneers. com) August through December. Single-game tickets (starting at $30) are *very* hard to come by.

The National Hockey League's **Tampa Bay Lightning** play in the St. Pete Times Forum, beginning in October (ℂ **813/301-6500;** www.tampabay lightning.com). You can usually get single-game tickets ($8–$155) on game day.

New York Yankees fans can watch the Bronx Bombers during baseball spring training from mid-February to the end of March at Legends Field (© **813/879-2244** or 813/875-7753; www.yankees.mlb.com), opposite Raymond James Stadium. This scaled-down replica of Yankee Stadium is the largest spring-training facility in Florida, with a 10,000-seat capacity. Tickets are $10 to $16. The club's minor-league team, the **Tampa Yankees** (same phone and website), plays at Legends Field April through August.

WHERE TO STAY

If you're going to Busch Gardens, Adventure Island, Lowry Park Zoo, or MOSI, the motels we list in the "Near Busch Gardens" section are much more convenient than those downtown, about 7 miles to the south. Most of these are also geared to families, so you're more likely to find kid-friendly amenities in them. The Downtown Tampa hotels are geared to business travelers, but staying there will put you near the Florida Aquarium and reasonably close to the sports venues listed above (and may net you some weekend discounts when the business travelers fly the coop). For the latter, you can also check with your favorite chain, many of which have places in the Westshore area, a few miles west of downtown.

Room rates at most hotels in Tampa vary little from season to season. This is especially true downtown, where the hotels do a brisk convention business all year round. Hillsborough County adds 12% tax to your hotel room bill.

NEAR BUSCH GARDENS

Baymont Inn & Suites *Value*   Fake banana trees and a parrot cage welcome guests to the terra-cotta–floored lobby of this comfortable and convenient member of the small, cost-conscious chain. Rooms are spacious and have ceiling fans and desks. The two-room suites feature a king-size bed in the bedroom and a pullout couch in the sitting room; all suites have refrigerators and microwave ovens. It's designed for business travelers, but small families should do just fine and the free breakfast will help fuel you and the kids. Outside, a courtyard with an unheated swimming pool has plenty of space for sunning. There's no restaurant on the premises, but plenty are within walking distance.

9202 N. 30th St. (at Busch Blvd.), Tampa, FL 33612. © **866/999-1111** or 813/930-6900. Fax 813/930-0563. www.baymontinns.com. 146 units. Winter $99–$119 double; off-season $79–$99 double. Children under 18 stay free in parent's room. Rollaway beds (just 2) and cribs are available at no charge. Rates include breakfast and local phone calls. AE, DC, DISC, MC, V. **Amenities:** Outdoor pool; game room; coin-op washers and dryers. *In room:* A/C, TV w/Nintendo, dataport, coffeemaker, hair dryer, iron.

Best Western All Suites Hotel ★★ *Value*   This three-story all-suite hotel is the most beachlike vacation venue you'll find close to the park and its an attractive spot for families. Whimsical signs lead you around a lush tropical courtyard with a heated freshwater pool (popular with kids and adults alike), hot tub, and a lively, sports-oriented tiki bar. The bar can get noisy before closing at 9pm, and ground-level units are musty, so ask for an upstairs suite away from the action if you have little ones with early bedtimes. Suite living rooms are well equipped with fridges and microwaves, and separate bedrooms have narrow screened patios or balconies. Great for kids, the 11 "family suites" have bunk beds in

---

Value **Discount Packages**

Many Tampa hotels combine tickets to major attractions such as Busch Gardens in their packages, so always ask about special deals.

addition to a queen-size bed for parents and also sport VCRs. The hotel restaurant has a good kids' menu.

Behind Busch Gardens, 3001 University Center Dr. (faces N. 30th St. between Busch Blvd. and Fowler Ave.), Tampa, FL 33612. ☎ **800/786-7446** or 813/971-8930. Fax 813/971-8935. www.thatparrotplace.com. 150 units. Winter $99–$159 suite for 2; off-season $79–$99 suite for 2. Children under 17 stay free in parent's room. No rollaway beds, cribs available at no charge. Rates include hot and cold breakfast buffet. AE, DC, DISC, MC, V. **Amenities:** Restaurant (breakfast and dinner only); bar; heated outdoor pool; access to nearby health club; Jacuzzi; game room; limited room service; laundry service; coin-op washers and dryers. *In room:* A/C, TV, dataport, fridge, coffeemaker, hair dryer, iron, microwave.

Red Roof Inn Less than a mile west of Busch Gardens, this is the best low-budget choice for families that's close to the park. Most of the rooms in the pleasant two-story building are away from the busy boulevard, but make sure to request one toward the rear of the building to avoid the road noise. Although in-room amenities are scarce, the units are spacious for the price. And mom and dad can psyche themselves up for a day of touring with the free coffee in the lobby.

2307 E. Busch Blvd. (between 22nd and 26th sts.), Tampa, FL 33612. ☎ **800/733-7663** or 813/932-0073. Fax 813/933-5689. www.redroof.com. 108 units. Winter $60–$85 double; off-season $40–$76 double. Children 17 and under stay free in parent's room. Rollaway beds $8 a night, cribs free. Rates include local phone calls. AE, DC, DISC, MC, V. **Amenities:** Outdoor pool; Jacuzzi; sauna. *In room:* A/C, TV, dataport.

DOWNTOWN TAMPA

Radisson Riverwalk Hotel ⚘ Set on the east bank of the Hillsborough River, this six-story business hotel was completely remodeled in 1998. Half the comfortable rooms face west and have views from their balconies of the Arabesque minarets atop the University of Tampa campus across the river—quite a scene at sunset (your kids should be suitably impressed). They cost more but are more preferable to units on the east side of the building, which face downtown's skyscrapers and don't have balconies. There isn't much here that's especially aimed at the kid set, but children should find no fault with the pool that overlooks the riverfront. The Boulanger bakery and deli, open from 5am to midnight, purveys fresh pastries, soups, sandwiches, and snacks; it's your best bet for finicky eaters.

200 N. Ashley Dr. (at Jackson St.), Tampa, FL 33602. ☎ **800/333-3333** or 813/223-2222. Fax 813/221-5292. www.radisson.com/tampafl_riverwalk. 282 units. Winter $219–$239 double; off-season $129–$179 double. Children 17 and under stay free in parent's room. Rollaway beds $15, cribs $10. AE, DC, DISC, MC, V. Valet parking $10, self-parking $7. **Amenities:** 2 restaurants; bar; heated outdoor pool; exercise room; access to nearby health club; sauna; concierge; limited room service; laundry service; coin-op washers and dryers; concierge-level rooms. *In room:* A/C, TV w/Nintendo, dataport, coffeemaker, hair dryer, iron.

Tampa Marriott Waterside ⚘⚘ This luxurious 22-story hotel occupies downtown's most strategic location—beside the river and between the Tampa Convention Center and the St. Pete Times Forum—and was built for the business set, though it's not a bad choice for families. Opening onto a riverfront promenade, the towering, three-story lobby (look out for those palm trees) should suitably impress. The third floor has a fully equipped spa, modern exercise facility, and outdoor heated pool where kids and parents can relax. About half of the guest quarters have balconies overlooking the bay or city (choice views are high up on the south side). The regular rooms are spacious enough and can easily fit a family of four (you can ask for a refrigerator), though they're dwarfed by the 720-square-foot suites.

700 N. Florida Ave. (at St. Pete Times Forum Dr.), Tampa, FL 33602. ☎ **800/228-9290** or 813/221-4900. Fax 813/221-0923. www.marriott.com. 717 units. $215–$285 double. Children 17 and under stay free in parent's

room. Rollaway beds and cribs available at no charge. AE, DC, DISC, MC, V. Weekend rates available. Valet parking $12; no self-parking. **Amenities:** 3 restaurants (American); 3 bars; heated outdoor pool; health club; spa; Jacuzzi; concierge; activities desk; car-rental desk; business center; salon; limited room service; massage; laundry service; coin-op washers and dryers; concierge-level rooms. *In room:* A/C, TV, fax, dataport (with high-speed Internet), fridge (upon request), coffeemaker, hair dryer, iron.

WHERE TO DINE

As with the hotels, we have organized the restaurants that follow by geographic area: Near Busch Gardens and West of Downtown. You can find a number of fast food and chain eateries on Kennedy Boulevard, west of Dale Mabry.

IN & NEAR BUSCH GARDENS

You'll find several national chains and family restaurants east of I-275 on Busch Boulevard and Fowler Avenue.

Mel's Hot Dogs ★★ (*Value*) AMERICAN   Catering to everyone from business-people on a lunch break to hungry families craving inexpensive all-beef hot dogs, Mel Lohn's red-and-white cottage offers everything from "bagel-dogs" to bacon/cheddar Reuben-style hot dogs. All choices are served on a poppy-seed bun and can be ordered with french fries and a choice of coleslaw or baked beans. Even the decor is dedicated to wieners: The walls and windows are lined with hot-dog memorabilia, and there's usually a red wiener-mobile parked out front. Your kids will love it—and so will you. But just in case hot-dog mania hasn't won you over, there are a few alternative choices (chicken, beef and veggie burgers, and terrific onion rings). Children's meals include hot dogs, corn dogs, hamburgers, or chicken nuggets, all of which come with fries, dessert, and a toy.

4136 E. Busch Blvd., at 42nd St. © 813/985-8000. Kids' menu, highchairs, booster seats. Reservations not accepted. Most items $4–$12, kids $4–$4.50. No credit cards. Sun–Thurs 11am–8pm; Fri–Sat 11am–9pm.

Tia's Tex Mex (*Value*) SOUTHWEST   Create your own combination platter from a list that includes tamales, chicken flautas, chalupas, tacos, and enchiladas (all the taco shells here are made with vegetable oil). Or dig into one of the menu standards, such as mesquite-grilled shrimp with chipotle glaze or sizzling steak or chicken fajita skillets. The younger set's menu offers corn dogs, chicken fingers, tacos, and grilled cheese sandwiches. And your kids will also be kept busy by crayons and word games on their place mats.

2815 Fowler Ave. (between I-275 and Bruce B. Downs Blvd.). © 813/972-7737. www.tiastexmex.com. Kids' menu, highchairs, booster seats, placemats with crayons and word scramble game. Reservations recommended. Main courses $7–$15, kids $4–$5. AE, DC, DISC, MC, V. Daily 11am–10pm, except Thanksgiving and Christmas.

WEST OF DOWNTOWN

In addition to those listed below, you'll find the usual chain restaurants in town, including T.G.I. Friday's and Chili's, along North Dale Mabry, near Raymond James Stadium.

Romano's Macaroni Grill ★ (*Value*) ITALIAN   Romano's is a small chain with a nice family atmosphere (you can definitely hear the buzz of conversation) and, unlike most of Tampa's better restaurants, it's not oriented toward the business crowd. The staff will put jug wine on your table and deliver entrees such as veal piccata, chicken Marsala, shrimp scampi, and a meaty lasagna, which are reasonably priced and pretty tasty. Kids can feast on a grilled macaroni and cheese sandwich, a corn dog, pizza, or chicken fingers, among others, all of which come with refillable soft drinks and dessert. This place also offers stuff to keep the young ones busy while mom and dad eat their meals.

14904 N. Dale Mabry Hwy. Ⓒ 813/264-6676. www.macaronigrill.com. Kids' menu, highchairs, booster seats, placemats with crayons and word games. Reservations accepted. Main courses lunch $6–$15, kids $4; dinner $8–$19, kids $4. AE, MC, V. Daily 11am–10pm.

Shells ⭐ *Value* SEAFOOD   You'll see Shells restaurants in many parts of Florida, and with good reason, for this casual chain consistently provides excellent value for families. Each branch has virtually identical menus, prices, and hours. Particularly good for adults are the spicy Jack Daniel's buffalo shrimp and scallop appetizers. Main courses range from the usual fried seafood platters to pastas and charcoal-grilled shrimp, fish, steaks, and chicken. Kids can dig into fried chicken, shrimp, fish, or macaroni and cheese while they color on their placemats. At press time, on Friday and Saturday nights this Shells branch offers a kid-pleasing clown who makes balloon animals and does magic tricks.

14380 N. Dale Mabry (between Kennedy Blvd. and Hillsborough Ave.). Ⓒ 813/968-6686. www.shells seafood.com. Kids' menu, highchairs, booster seats, placemats with crayons. Reservations not accepted. Main courses $9–$20, kids $3–$5. AE, DISC, MC, V. Sun–Thurs 4–10pm; Fri–Sat 4–11pm.

2 Cocoa Beach, Cape Canaveral & Kennedy Space Center ⭐

46 miles SE of Orlando

Today, this once sleepy region produces and accommodates crowds attracted primarily by Kennedy Space Center, which is not only the launching pad for the U.S. space program but also a tourist attraction that thrills hundreds of thousands of visitors each year. A visit to the space center is usually an awe-inspiring experience for even the most jaded kids (and has launched many dreams about becoming an astronaut). If your kids' interests tend more towards natural life on earth, the area is also home to 72 miles of beaches (this is, after all, the closest beach to Orlando's mega-attractions) and the Brevard Zoo, which offers exhibits on par with Tampa's Lowry Park Zoo (earlier in this chapter).

GETTING THERE

BY CAR   From Orlando, take Highway 528, a toll road, exit on Highway 407 and go to Highway 405/NASA Parkway, then follow the signs east to the space center.

BY SHUTTLE   Mears Transportation (Ⓒ 407/423-5566; www.mears transportation.com) runs Kennedy Space Center shuttles Monday, Wednesday, and Friday from Lake Buena Vista and U.S. 192 (near Disney) and International Drive (near Universal). The cost is $20 per person round-trip (ages 3 and under free) and the trip allows for 7 hours at the center.

VISITOR INFORMATION   For information about the area, contact the **Florida Space Coast Office of Tourism/Brevard County Tourist Development Council,** 8810 Astronaut Blvd., Suite 102, Cape Canaveral, FL 32920 (Ⓒ **800/872-1969** or 321/868-1126; www.space-coast.com). The office is in the Sheldon Cove building, on Florida A1A a block north of Central Boulevard and is open Monday through Friday, 8am to 5pm.

The office also operates an information booth at the Kennedy Space Center Visitor Complex (see below).

EXPLORING THE ATTRACTIONS

Brevard Zoo   Howard and Max, a pair of white rhinos, are the newest additions at this delightful small-town zoo. The rhinos occupy a brand-new Expedition Africa exhibit that also features ostriches and giraffes (you and your kids can hand-feed the latter, whose 18-in. tongues usually startle when they snake out to grab a snack!). Other residents include dingoes, red kangaroos, wallabies, cotton-top tamarins, crocodiles, howler monkeys, bald eagles, red wolves, and river otters. There's a hands-on petting zoo featuring a miniature horse, miniature donkey, fallow deer, and goats. The zoo also offers a 10-minute train tour of the grounds ($3 for ages 2 and up), educational kayak trips ($3, kids must be at least 5), a tropical garden inhabited by flying fox bats and muntjac deer, a free-flight aviary, and alligator feedings usually 3 days a week (check the schedule or website below for days and times; they change, as do the gators' appetites over the year).

8225 N. Wickham Rd., Melbourne (just east of I-95 Exit 73/Wickham Rd.). © **321/254-9453.** www. brevardzoo.org. Admission $9 adults, $8 seniors, $6 children 2–12, free for kids under 2. Daily 10am–5pm. No admissions after 4:15pm. Closed Thanksgiving and Christmas.

Kennedy Space Center 🟀🟀🟀   Whether you and your kids are space buffs or not, you'll appreciate the sheer grandeur of the facilities and technological achievements displayed at NASA's primary space-launch facility, which is rich in history. (This is where Alan Shepard, America's 1st man in space, and Neil Armstrong, the 1st human on the moon, started their memorable journeys.)

Since all roads other than Highway 405 and Highway 3 are closed to the public in the space center, you must begin your visit at the **Kennedy Space Center Visitor Complex.** A bit like a themed amusement park, this privately run complex has had an ambitious $130 million renovation and expansion, and operators continue to tweak its offerings, so check the complex's website or call in advance to see if tours and exhibits have changed. Also check beforehand to see what's happening on the day you intend to be here, and arrive early to plan your visit. You'll need at least 2 hours to see the highlights on the bus tour through the center, up to 5 hours if you linger at the stops along the way (or if you've got small kids and end up making lots of stops), and a full day to see and do everything here.

Tips Out to Launch

If you'd like to see a launch at the **Kennedy Space Center,** first call © **321/867-5000,** 321/867-4636 for recorded information, or check NASA's official website (www.ksc.nasa.gov) for a schedule of upcoming takeoffs. You can buy launch tickets at the Kennedy Space Center Visitor Complex (© **321/449-4444**) or online at **www.ksctickets.com.** (*Note:* At press time, shuttle launches were still in a holding pattern due to the Feb 1, 2003, space shuttle *Columbia* disaster. Even when there is a regular schedule, launches are frequently delayed due to weather, equipment malfunctions, or other factors, so you might have to make multiple visits to see one. If you don't have that flexibility, the launch window may be delayed beyond your going-home date.)

If you can't get into the space center for launches, other good viewing spots are on the causeways leading to the islands and on U.S. 1 as it skirts the waterfront in Titusville. The **Holiday Inn Riverside–Kennedy Space Center,** on Washington Avenue (U.S. 1) in Titusville (© **800/465-4329** or 321/269-2121; www.holidayinnksc.com), also has a clear view of the launch pads across the Indian River, but area motels raise their rates and often book up during launch periods.

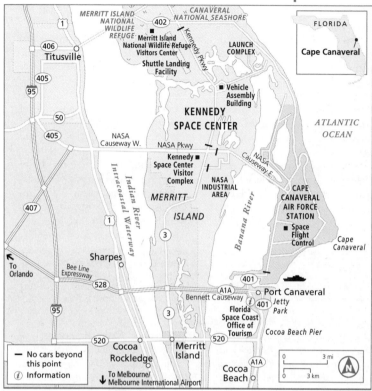

Cape Canaveral

MERRITT ISLAND NATIONAL WILDLIFE REFUGE

CANAVERAL NATIONAL SEASHORE

402

Kennedy Pkwy

LAUNCH COMPLEX

1

406

Titusville

Merritt Island National Wildlife Refuge Visitors Center

Shuttle Landing Facility

405

95

50

405

NASA Causeway W.

NASA Pkwy

Vehicle Assembly Building

KENNEDY SPACE CENTER

ATLANTIC OCEAN

NASA Causeway E.

Kennedy Space Center Visitor Complex

NASA INDUSTRIAL AREA

MERRITT

CAPE CANAVERAL AIR FORCE STATION

407

1

ISLAND

Banana River

Indian River Intracoastal Waterway

3

Space Flight Control

Cape Canaveral

Sharpes

To Orlando

Bee Line Expressway

528

95

3

401

A1A

Bennett Causeway

401

Port Canaveral

Jetty Park

Florida Space Coast Office of Tourism

Cocoa Beach Pier

520

Cocoa

Rockledge

Merritt Island

520

To Melbourne/ Melbourne International Airport

A1A

Cocoa Beach

FLORIDA

Cape Canaveral

0   3 mi
0   3 km

— No cars beyond this point

ⓘ Information

The visitor complex has real NASA rockets and the actual Mercury Mission Control Room from the 1960s. Exhibits look at early space exploration and where it's going in the new millennium. There's a rocket garden where kids of all ages can explore spacecraft including a shuttle, a daily "Encounter" with a real astronaut, several dining venues, and a shop selling a variety of space memorabilia and souvenirs. Two space-related IMAX movies (one in 3D) shown on five-and-a-half-story-high screens are informative and entertaining.

While you could spend your entire day at the visitor complex, you must take a **KSC Tour** to see the actual space center where rockets and shuttles are prepared and launched. Plan to take the bus tour early in your visit and be sure to hit the restrooms before boarding the bus—there's only one out on the tour. The buses depart every 10 minutes or so, and you can reboard as you wish. They stop at the **LC-39 Observation Gantry,** with a dramatic 360-degree view over launch pads where space shuttles blast off; the **International Space Station Center,** where scientists and engineers prepare additions to the space station now in orbit; and the impressive **Apollo/Saturn V Center,** which includes artifacts, photos, interactive exhibits, and the 363-foot **Saturn V,** the most powerful rocket ever launched by the United States.

Don't miss the **Astronaut Memorial,** a moving black-granite monument that has the names of the U.S. astronauts who have died on missions or while in training. (The names of those who perished in the 2003 *Columbia* tragedy should be up there by the time this book hits the stores.) The 60-ton structure rotates on a track that follows the movement of the sun (on clear days, of course), causing the names to stand out above a brilliant reflection of the sky.

The newest attraction (though it's actually located on S.R. 405 just west of the center) is the **U.S. Astronaut Hall of Fame,** which features displays, exhibits, and tributes to the heroes of the Mercury, Gemini, and Apollo space programs. There's also a collection of spacecraft, including a Mercury 7 capsule, a Gemini training capsule, and an Apollo 14 command module. And in "Simulator Station," guests can experience the pressure of four times the force of gravity, ride a rover across Mars, and land the Space Shuttle. Kids around 7 and up will think the experience out of this world. Adults will be suitably impressed as well.

Note: Pay an extra $20 per adult and $10 per child 3 to 11 over the cost of regular admission and you and your kids can **have lunch with a real-life astronaut.** It's usually a thrilling treat for kids old enough to appreciate it. The schedule of astronauts changes frequently and you'll need to book in advance (call the space center to check availability and book your lunch, or do it online at the center's website). Lunch is included in the price, though there's no kids' menu.

NASA Pkwy. (Fla. 405), 6 miles east of Titusville, ½ mile west of Fla. 3. ✆ 321/449-4444 for general information, 321/449-4444 for guided bus tours and launch reservations. www.kennedyspacecenter.com. Admission $34 adults, $24 children 3–11. Admission includes KSC tour, all exhibits, IMAX films, and admission to U.S. Astronaut Hall of Fame. Audio tours $5 per person. All tours and movies free for children under 3. Daily 9am–5:30pm. Shuttle-bus tours daily 9:45am–2:15pm. Closed Christmas and some launch days.

BEACHES & WILDLIFE REFUGES

To the north of the Kennedy Space Center, **Canaveral National Seashore** ✸✸ is a protected 13-mile barrier-island backed by cabbage palms, sea grapes, palmettos, marshes, and Mosquito Lagoon. This is a great area for watching herons, egrets, ibises, willets, terns, and other birds. You might also glimpse dolphins and manatees in the lagoon. It's a nice quiet spot for a family picnic. The beaches near parking lots 1 and 2 have lifeguards, in case you want to take a swim. Note that the park runs special Junior Ranger programs for children ages 6 to 12; ask at the visitor center or check the park's website.

The main **visitor center** is at 7611 S. Atlantic Ave., New Smyrna Beach, FL 32169 (✆ **321/867-4077** or 321/867-0677 for recorded information; www.nps.gov/cana), on Apollo Beach, at the north end of the island. The southern access gate to the island is 8 miles east of Titusville on Florida 402, just east of Highway 3.

Its neighbor to the south and west is the 140,000-acre **Merritt Island National Wildlife Refuge** ✸✸, home to hundreds of species of shorebirds, waterfowl, reptiles, alligators, and mammals, many of them endangered. Stop and pick up a map and other information at the visitor center, on Highway 402 about 4 miles east of Titusville. The center has a quarter-mile-long boardwalk along the edge of the marsh and has displays showing the animals you may see here. You can see them from the 7-mile-long Black Point Wildlife Drive or one of the nature trails through the hammocks and marshes. The visitor center is open Monday through Friday from 8am to 4:30pm, Saturday from 9am to 5pm (closed Sun Apr–Oct). Admission is free. For more information and a schedule of interpretive programs, contact the refuge at P.O. Box 6504, Titusville, FL 32782 (✆ **321/861-0667;** www.nbbd.com/godo/minwr).

Note: Those parts of the national seashore near the Kennedy Space Center and all of the refuge close 4 days before a shuttle launch and usually reopen the day after a launch.

OUTDOOR ACTIVITIES

FISHING   If you and your kids like to fish, head to Port Canaveral for catches such as snapper and grouper. **Jetty Park** (© 321/783-7111), at the south entry to the port, has a fishing pier equipped with a bait shop (see "Beaches & Wildlife Refuges," above). The south bank of the port is lined with charter boats, and you can go deep-sea fishing on the *Miss Cape Canaveral* (© **321/783-5274** or 321/648-2211 in Orlando; www.misscape.com), one of the party boats based here. All-day voyages (including all gear, bait, breakfast, lunch, and unlimited soft drinks) depart daily at 8am and cost $55 to $65 for adults, $45 to $60 for seniors, $40 to $55 for students 11 to 17, and $30 to $45 for kids 6 to 10. Be sure to bring hats, sunscreen, and shoes with good traction for you and the kids.

SURFING   Rip through some occasionally awesome waves (by Florida's standards, not California's or Hawaii's) at the **Cocoa Beach Pier** area or down south at **Sebastian Inlet.** Get outfitted at Ron Jon Surf Shop and learn how to hang five or ten with the store's **Cocoa Beach Surfing School** ⚡, 150 E. Columbia Lane (© **321/868-1980;** www.ronjons.com/surfschool). They offer equipment and lessons for beginners or pros at area beaches (kids should be at least 8 and able to swim in order to participate). Be sure to bring along a towel, flip-flops, sunscreen, and a lot of nerve. The school also offers 5-day surfing camps that cover water safety and surfing instruction for kids ages 8 to 16 from May to August. The cost is $250 per child and does not include lunch or snacks.

WHERE TO STAY

The hotels listed below are all in Cocoa Beach, the closest resort area to Kennedy Space Center, about a 30-minute drive to the north. You'll pay a 10% hotel tax here.

Though it's a comfortable and well-equipped business hotel not aimed at the family market (so it earns no listing below), one of the closest properties to the space center and Port Canaveral is the **Radisson Resort at the Port,** 8701 Astronaut Blvd. (Fla. A1A) in Cape Canaveral (© **800/333-3333** or 321/784-0000; www.radisson.com). It isn't on the beach, but your family can relax in a landscaped courtyard with a waterfall cascading over fake rocks into an outdoor heated pool (about a dozen parrots live in the trees overlooking the pool area). Suites here are the best family bet and offer a mini-kitchen with refrigerator, microwave, and utensils. Each two-room suite has tons of room and comes with one or two king-size beds in the bedroom and a queen pullout sofa in the living room. The layout of the room is inconvenient if parents want some private time: You have to walk though the bedroom to get to the bathroom, and the Jacuzzi tub is smack inside the bedroom (which your kids will doubtless find amusing).

DoubleTree Hotel Cocoa Beach Oceanfront ⚡   This six-story hotel is a good choice for families and was extensively remodeled and upgraded in 1998. Your kids should be suitably thrilled with the chain's signature chocolate chip cookie upon check-in. All rooms have balconies with ocean views and easy chairs, and 10 suites have living rooms with sleeper sofas and separate bedrooms. A charming dining room facing the beach serves decent Mediterranean fare (there's a kids' menu and highchairs are available) and opens to a bi-level brick patio with water cascading between two heated swimming pools. The beach is only a short walk away.

2080 N. Atlantic Ave., Cocoa Beach, FL 32931. © **800/552-3224** or 321/783-9222. Fax 321/799-3234. www. cocoabeachdoubletree.com. 148 units. $125–$179 double; $185–$275 suite. Children under 18 stay free in parent's or grandparent's room. Rollaway beds $15; cribs available at no charge. AE, DC, DISC, MC, V. **Amenities:** Restaurant; bar; 2 heated outdoor pools; exercise room; game room; limited room service; laundry service; coin-op washers and dryers; concierge-level rooms. *In room:* A/C, TV, dataport, coffeemaker, hair dryer, iron.

Hilton Cocoa Beach Oceanfront   Instead of balconies or patios from which you and the kids can enjoy the fresh air and view down the shore, the rooms at this seven-story Hilton have smallish, sealed-shut windows, and only 16 of them actually face the beach. That and other architectural features make it seem more like a downtown commercial hotel transplanted to a beachside location and like many other hotels of decent character in the area, this one caters more to business travelers than it does to families. Nevertheless, it's one of the few upscale oceanfront properties in the area and the heated pool, arcade, free breakfast, and nearby beach should keep your kids happy. Despite their lack of fresh air, the rooms are spacious and comfortable.

1550 N. Atlantic Ave., Cocoa Beach, FL 32931. © **800/774-1500** or 321/799-0003. Fax 321/799-0344. www. cocoabeachhilton.com. 296 units. $89–$199 double. Rollaway beds $15; cribs available at no charge. Rates include a free continental breakfast. AE, DC, DISC, MC, V. **Amenities:** Restaurant; 2 bars; heated outdoor pool; exercise room; game room; watersports equipment rentals; business center; limited room service; laundry service; coin-op washers and dryers; concierge-level rooms. *In room:* A/C, TV, dataport, coffeemaker, hair dryer, iron.

Holiday Inn Cocoa Beach Oceanfront Resort ⚐   Set on 30 beachside acres, this sprawling family-oriented complex, last renovated in 1999, offers a wide variety of spacious hotel rooms, efficiencies, and apartments and is the best bet in town for families with young kids. A few of the suites are themed Kid-suites with bunk beds, VCRs, and Sony Playstations for the kids; other suites feature sitting rooms with pullout couches. All suites come with refrigerators and microwaves. Most accommodations are in 1960s-style motel buildings flanking a long central courtyard with tropical foliage surrounding tennis courts. The pirate-themed kids' pool is popular with little ones, and adults can relax in the tropical-themed Olympic-size pool or the hot tub. Only those rooms directly facing the beach or pool have patios or balconies; the rest are entered from exterior corridors.

1300 N. Atlantic Ave. (Fla. A1A, at Holiday Lane), Cocoa Beach, FL 32931. © **800/206-2747** or 321/783-2271. www.holidayinnsofcentralflorida.com. Fax 321/783-8878. 500 units. $69–$220 double. Resort fee $4.95. Children under 18 stay free in parent's room. Rollaway beds $11; cribs available at no charge. AE, DC, DISC, MC, V. **Amenities:** 2 restaurants; 2 bars; heated outdoor pool; kiddie pool; 2 tennis courts; exercise room; Jacuzzi; watersports equipment rentals; game room; concierge; limited room service; laundry service; coin-op washers and dryers. *In room:* A/C, TV, dataport, coffeemaker, hair dryer, iron.

WHERE TO DINE

On the **Cocoa Beach Pier,** at the beach end of Meade Avenue, you'll get a fine view down the coast to accompany the seafood offerings at **Atlantic Ocean Grill** (© **321/783-7549**) and the fairly good pub fare at adjacent **Marlins Good Times Bar & Grill** (same phone).

Note: All of the restaurants we list below provide kids with crayons or other activities to keep them busy during mealtimes.

Bernard's Surf ⚐ SEAFOOD/STEAKS   Photos on the walls testify that many astronauts—and Russian cosmonauts, too—come to these adjoining establishments to celebrate their landings. It all started as Bernard's Surf, which has been serving standard steak-and-seafood fare in a nautically dressed setting since 1948. Bernard's offers house specials such as stone crab claws, Florida lobster tails stuffed with crab, char-grilled red snapper, and a belly-busting platter

of shrimp, scallops, grouper, crab cakes, lobster, and oysters. Little mates can choose from fried flounder, shrimp, chicken fingers, and clams, burgers or pasta marinara. All kids' meals include fries and ice cream.

2 S. Atlantic Ave. (at Minuteman Causeway Rd.), Cocoa Beach. (C) **321/783-2401.** Reservations recommended. Kids' menu, highchairs, booster seats, placemats with crayons. Main courses $14–$55, kids $5. AE, DC, DISC, MC, V. Mon–Thurs 4–10pm; Fri–Sat 4–11pm. Closed Christmas.

Fischer's Seafood Bar & Grill *(Value* SEAFOOD/STEAKS   The fresh seafood also finds its way into this adjoining bar and grill, a friendly, *Cheers*-like lounge popular with the locals. Fischer's menu features fried combo platters, shrimp and crab-claw meat sautéed in herb butter, and mussels with a wine sauce over pasta, to mention a few worthy selections. Fischer's also provides sandwiches, burgers, and other pub fare, and it has the same 25¢ happy-hour oysters and spicy wings as a branch of **Rusty's Seafood & Oyster Bar** (see below), which also has a branch in this complex. Fischer's kiddie menu has most of the same options at Bernard's (though cheaper) and a grilled cheese sandwich.

2 S. Atlantic Ave. (at Minuteman Causeway Rd.), Cocoa Beach. (C) **321/783-2401.** Reservations not accepted. Kids' menu, highchairs, booster seats, placemats with crayons. Main courses $9–$16, sandwiches and salads $4–$9, kids $3. AE, DC, DISC, MC, V. Mon–Thurs 11am–10pm; Fri–Sat 11am–11pm. Closed Christmas.

Rusty's Seafood & Oyster Bar *(Value* SEAFOOD   This lively sports bar beside Port Canaveral's man-made harbor offers inexpensive chow ranging from very spicy seafood gumbo to a pot of seafood that will give most families their fill of steamed oysters, clams, shrimp, crab legs, potatoes, and corn on the cob. Raw or steamed fresh oysters and clams from the raw bar are first-rate and a very good value, as is a lunch buffet on weekdays. Seating is available indoors or out, but the inside tables have the best view of fishing boats and cruise liners going in and out of the port (which should keep nautically minded children entertained). The kids' menu offers chicken nuggets, fried shrimp, burgers, grilled cheese sandwiches, and spaghetti.

Note: Daily happy hours from 3 to 6pm see beer drafted at 59¢ a mug, and tons of raw or steamed oysters and spicy Buffalo wings go for 25¢ each. As a result, lots of couples and adults will congregate here. It's a busy and sometimes-noisy joint, especially on weekend afternoons, but the clientele tends to be somewhat older and better behaved than at some other pubs along the banks of Port Canaveral. So it's unlikely you'll encounter a problem by bringing your kids here (and any noise they make will likely get lost in the din).

There's another **Rusty's** in the Bernard's Surf/Fischer's Seafood Bar & Grill restaurant complex in Cocoa Beach (see above). It has the same menu.

628 Glen Cheek Dr. (south side of the harbor), Port Canaveral. (C) **321/783-2033.** Kids' menu, highchairs, booster seats, placemats with crayons. Main courses $7–$25, sandwiches and salads $4–$7, lunch buffet $6, kids $3. AE, DC, DISC, MC, V. Sun–Thurs 11am–11:30pm; Fri–Sat 11am–12:30am (lunch buffet Mon–Fri 11am–2pm).

Appendix A:
For International Visitors

Whether it's your first visit or your tenth, a trip to the Orlando area may require additional planning. This chapter provides you with essential information, helpful tips, and advice for the more common problems that some visitors encounter.

1 Preparing for Your Trip

ENTRY REQUIREMENTS

Check at any U.S. embassy or consulate for current information and requirements. You can also obtain a visa application and other information online at the **U.S. State Department**'s website, at **www.travel.state.gov**.

VISAS The U.S. State Department has a **Visa Waiver Program** allowing citizens of certain countries to enter the United States without a visa for stays of up to 90 days. At press time these included Andorra, Australia, Austria, Belgium, Brunei, Denmark, Finland, France, Germany, Iceland, Ireland, Italy, Japan, Liechtenstein, Luxembourg, Monaco, the Netherlands, New Zealand, Norway, Portugal, San Marino, Singapore, Slovenia, Spain, Sweden, Switzerland, and the United Kingdom. Citizens of these countries need only a valid passport and a round-trip air or cruise ticket in their possession upon arrival. If they first enter the United States, they may also visit Mexico, Canada, Bermuda, and/or the Caribbean islands and return to the United States without a visa. Further information is available from any U.S. embassy or consulate. Canadian citizens may enter the United States without visas; they need only proof of residence.

Citizens of all other countries must have (1) a valid passport that expires at least 6 months later than the scheduled end of their visit to the United States, and (2) a tourist visa, which may be obtained without charge from any U.S. consulate.

To obtain a visa, the traveler must submit a completed application form (either in person or by mail) with a 1½-inch-square photo, and must demonstrate binding ties to a residence abroad. Usually you can obtain a visa at once or within 24 hours, but it may take longer during the summer rush from June through August. If you cannot go in person, contact the nearest U.S. embassy or consulate for directions on applying by mail. Your travel agent or airline office may also be able to provide you with visa applications and instructions. The U.S. consulate or embassy that issues your visa will determine whether you will be issued a multiple- or single-entry visa and any restrictions regarding the length of your stay.

British subjects can obtain up-to-date visa information by calling the **U.S. Embassy Visa Information Line** (© 0891/200-290) or by visiting the "Consular Services" section of the American Embassy London's website at www.usembassy. org.uk.

Irish citizens can obtain up-to-date visa information through the **Embassy of the USA Dublin,** 42 Elgin Rd., Dublin 4, Ireland (© 353/1-668-8777), or by checking the "Consular Services" section of the website at www.usembassy.ie.

Visitor Information Abroad

There are several **Orlando Tourism Offices** outside the United States. You can get information from the following sources:

- **Argentina**   ℂ **0800-999-1749**, www.orlandoinfo.com/argentina
- **Belgium**   ℂ **32-2/705-7897**, www.orlandoinfo.com
- **Brazil**   ℂ **0800/556652**, www.orlandoinfo.com/brasil
- **Canada**   ℂ **1-800-646-2079**, www.orlandokissimmee.com/canada
- **Germany**   ℂ **0800-100-7325**, www.orlandoinfo.com/de
- **Japan**   ℂ **3-3501-7245**, www.orlandoinfo.com/japan
- **Latin America**   ℂ **407/363-5872**, www.orlandoinfo.com/latinoamerica
- **Mexico**   ℂ **01-800/800-4636**, www.orlandoinfo.com/mexico
- **Spain**   ℂ **407/363-5872**, www.orlandoinfo.com/espana
- **United Kingdom**   ℂ **0800-018-6760**, www.orlandoinfo.com/uk

Australian citizens can obtain up-to-date visa information by contacting the **U.S. Embassy Canberra,** Moonah Place, Yarralumla, ACT 2600 (ℂ **02/ 6214-5600**), or by checking the U.S. Diplomatic Mission's website at http:// usembassy-australia.state.gov/consular.

Citizens of **New Zealand** can obtain up-to-date visa information by contacting the **U.S. Embassy New Zealand,** 29 Fitzherbert Terrace, Thorndon, Wellington (ℂ **644/472-2068**), or get the information directly from the "Services to New Zealanders" section of the website at http://usembassy.org.nz.

MEDICAL REQUIREMENTS   Unless you're arriving from an area known to be suffering from an epidemic (particularly cholera or yellow fever), inoculations or vaccinations are not required for entry into the United States. If you have a medical condition that requires **syringe-administered medications,** carry a valid signed prescription from your physician—the Federal Aviation Administration (FAA) no longer allows airline passengers to pack syringes in their carry-on baggage without documented proof of medical need. If you have a disease that requires treatment with **narcotics,** you should also carry documented proof with you—smuggling narcotics aboard a plane is a serious offense that carries severe penalties in the U.S.

For **HIV-positive visitors,** requirements for entering the United States are somewhat vague and change frequently. According to the latest publication of *HIV and Immigrants: A Manual for AIDS Service Providers,* the Immigration and Naturalization Service (INS) doesn't require a medical exam for entry into the United States, but INS officials may stop individuals because they look sick or because they are carrying AIDS/HIV medicine.

If an HIV-positive noncitizen applies for a non-immigrant visa, the question on the application regarding communicable diseases is tricky no matter which way it's answered. If the applicant checks "no," INS may deny the visa on the grounds that the applicant committed fraud. If the applicant checks "yes" or if INS suspects the person is HIV-positive, it will deny the visa unless the applicant asks for a special waiver for visitors. This waiver is for people visiting the United States for a short time, to attend a conference, for instance, to visit close relatives, or to receive medical treatment. It can be a confusing situation. For up-to-the-minute information, contact **AIDSinfo** (ℂ **800/448-0440** or 301/519-6616 outside the U.S.; www.aidsinfo.nih.gov) or the **Gay Men's Health Crisis** (*C* **212/ 367-1000;** www.gmhc.org).

DRIVER'S LICENSES   Foreign driver's licenses are mostly recognized in the U.S., although you may want to get an international driver's license if your home license is not written in English.

PASSPORT INFORMATION

Safeguard your passport in an inconspicuous, inaccessible place like a money belt. Make a copy of the critical pages, including the passport number, and store it in a safe place, separate from the passport itself. If you lose your passport, visit the nearest consulate of your native country as soon as possible for a replacement. Passport applications are downloadable from the websites listed below.

Note: The International Civil Aviation Organization has recommended a policy requiring that *every* individual who travels by air have a passport. In response, many countries are now requiring that children must be issued their own passport to travel internationally, where before those under 16 or so may have been allowed to travel on a parent or guardian's passport.

FOR RESIDENTS OF CANADA

You can pick up a passport application at 1 of 28 regional passport offices or most travel agencies. Canadian children who travel must have their own passport. However, if you hold a valid Canadian passport issued before December 11, 2001, that bears the name of your child, the passport remains valid for you and your child until it expires. Passports cost C$85 for those 16 years and older (valid 5 years), C$35 children 3 to 15 (valid 5 years), and C$20, children under 3 (valid 3 years). Applications, which must be accompanied by two identical passport-size photographs and proof of Canadian citizenship, are available at travel agencies throughout Canada or from the central **Passport Office,** Department of Foreign Affairs and International Trade, Ottawa, ON K1A 0G3 (*C* **800/ 567-6868;** www.dfait-maeci.gc.ca/passport). Processing takes 5 to 10 days if you apply in person, or about 3 weeks by mail.

FOR RESIDENTS OF THE UNITED KINGDOM

As a member of the European Union, you need only an identity card, not a passport, to travel to other EU countries. However, if you already possess a passport, it's always useful to carry it. To pick up an application for a standard 10-year passport (5-year passport for children under 16), visit the nearest Passport Office, major post office, or travel agency. You can also contact the **United Kingdom Passport Service** at *C* **0870/571-0410** or visit its website at **www.passport.gov.uk**. Passports are £33 for adults and £19 for children under 16, with another £30 fee if you apply in person at a Passport Office. Processing takes about 2 weeks (1 week if you apply at the Passport Office).

FOR RESIDENTS OF IRELAND

You can apply for a 10-year passport, costing €57, at the **Passport Office,** Setanta Centre, Molesworth Street, Dublin 2 (*C* **01/671-1633;** www.irlgov.ie/ iveagh). Those under age 18 and over 65 must apply for a €12 3-year passport. You can also apply at 1A South Mall, Cork (*C* **021/272-525**) or over the counter at most main post offices.

FOR RESIDENTS OF AUSTRALIA

You can get an application from your local post office or any branch of Passports Australia, but you must schedule an interview at the passport office to present your application materials. Call the **Australian Passport Information Service** at ℰ **131-232,** or visit the government website at **www.passports.gov.au.** Passports for adults are A$144 and for those under 18 are A$72.

FOR RESIDENTS OF NEW ZEALAND

You can pick up a passport application at any New Zealand Passports Office or download it from their website. Contact the **Passports Office** at ℰ **0800/225-050** in New Zealand or 04/474-8100, or log on to **www.passports.govt.nz.** Passports for adults are NZ$80 and for children under 16 NZ$40.

CUSTOMS
WHAT YOU CAN BRING IN

Every visitor more than 21 years of age may bring in, free of duty, the following: (1) 1 liter of wine or hard liquor; (2) 200 cigarettes, 100 cigars (but not from Cuba), or 3 pounds of smoking tobacco; and (3) $100 worth of gifts. These exemptions are offered to travelers who spend at least 72 hours in the United States and who have not claimed them within the preceding 6 months. It is altogether forbidden to bring into the country foodstuffs (particularly fruit, cooked meats, and canned goods) and plants (vegetables, seeds, tropical plants, and the like). Foreign tourists may bring in or take out up to $10,000 in U.S. or foreign currency with no formalities; larger sums must be declared to U.S. Customs on entering or leaving, which includes filing form CM 4790. For more specific information regarding U.S. Customs, contact your nearest U.S. embassy or consulate, or the **U.S. Customs** office (ℰ **202/927-1770** or www.customs. ustreas.gov).

WHAT YOU CAN TAKE HOME

U.K. citizens returning from a non-EU country have a customs allowance of: 200 cigarettes; 50 cigars; 250g of smoking tobacco; 2 liters of still table wine; 1 liter of spirits or strong liqueurs (over 22% volume); 2 liters of fortified wine, sparkling wine, or other liqueurs; 60cc (ml) perfume; 250cc (ml) of toilet water; and £145 worth of all other goods, including gifts and souvenirs. People under 17 cannot have the tobacco or alcohol allowance. For more information, contact HM Customs & Excise at ℰ **0845/010-9000** (020/8929-0152 from outside the U.K.), or consult their website at **www.hmce.gov.uk.**

For a clear summary of **Canadian** rules, request the booklet *I Declare,* issued by the **Canada Customs and Revenue Agency** (ℰ **800/461-9999** in Canada, or 204/983-3500; www.ccra-adrc.gc.ca). Canada allows its citizens a C$750 exemption, and you're allowed to bring back duty-free one carton of cigarettes, 1 can of tobacco, 40 imperial ounces of liquor, and 50 cigars. In addition, you're allowed to mail gifts to Canada valued at less than C$60 a day, provided they're unsolicited and don't contain alcohol or tobacco (write on the package "Unsolicited gift, under $60 value"). All valuables should be declared on the Y-38 form before departure from Canada, including serial numbers of valuables you already own, such as expensive foreign cameras. *Note:* The C$750 exemption can only be used once a year and only after an absence of 7 days.

The duty-free allowance in **Australia** is A$400 or, for those under 18, A$200. Citizens age 18 and over can bring in 250 cigarettes or 250 grams of loose tobacco, and 1,125 milliliters of alcohol. If you're returning with valuables you already own, such as foreign-made cameras, you should file form B263. A helpful brochure available from Australian consulates or Customs offices is *Know Before You Go.* For more information, call the **Australian Customs Service** at ℰ **1300/363-263,** or log on to **www.customs.gov.au.**

The duty-free allowance for **New Zealand** is NZ$700. Citizens over 17 can bring in 200 cigarettes, 50 cigars, or 250 grams of tobacco (or a mixture of all three if their combined weight doesn't exceed 250g); plus 4.5 liters of wine and beer, or 1.125 liters of liquor. New Zealand currency does not carry import or export restrictions. Fill out a certificate of export, listing the valuables you are taking out of the country; that way, you can bring them back without paying duty. Most questions are answered in a free pamphlet available at New Zealand consulates and Customs offices: *New Zealand Customs Guide for Travellers, Notice no. 4.* For more information, contact **New Zealand Customs,** The Customhouse, 17–21 Whitmore St., Box 2218, Wellington (℗ **0800/428-786** or 04/473-6099; www.customs.govt.nz).

HEALTH INSURANCE

Although it's not required of travelers, health insurance is highly recommended. Unlike many European countries, the United States does not usually offer free or low-cost medical care to its citizens or visitors. Doctors and hospitals are expensive, and in most cases will require advance payment or proof of coverage before they render their services. Policies can cover everything from the loss or theft of your baggage and trip cancellation to the guarantee of bail in case you're arrested. Good policies will also cover the costs of an accident, repatriation, or death. See "Insurance, Health & Safety," in chapter 2, for more information. Packages such as **Europ Assistance's "Worldwide Healthcare Plan"** are sold by European automobile clubs and travel agencies at attractive rates. **Worldwide Assistance Services, Inc.** (℗ **800/821-2828;** www.worldwideassistance.com) is the agent for Europ Assistance in the United States.

Though lack of health insurance may prevent you from being admitted to a hospital in nonemergencies, don't worry about being left on a street corner to die: The American way is to fix you now and bill the living daylights out of you later.

If you get sick or are injured, there are basic first-aid centers in all Orlando theme parks. Disney and many other resorts have in-room medical service 24 hours a day through **Centra Care** by calling ℗ **407/238-2000.**

Doctors on Call Service (℗ **407/399-3627**) is a group that makes house and room calls in most of the Orlando area. **Centra Care** has several walk-in clinics listed in the Yellow Pages, including ones on International Drive (℗ **407/370-4881**) and at Lake Buena Vista, near Disney (℗ **407/934-2273**). Prescriptions can be filled at pharmacies such as **Walgreen's** and **Eckerd Drugs,** which have some stores open 24 hours a day; all are listed in the Yellow Pages. Many discount stores, such as **Kmart** and **Target,** also have pharmacies.

INSURANCE FOR BRITISH TRAVELERS   Most big travel agents offer their own insurance and will probably try to sell you their package when you book a holiday. Think before you sign. **Britain's Consumers' Association** recommends that you insist on seeing the policy and reading the fine print before buying travel insurance. **The Association of British Insurers** (℗ **020/7600-3333;** www.abi.org.uk) gives advice by phone and publishes *Holiday Insurance,* a free guide to policy provisions and prices. You might also shop around for better deals: Try **Columbus Direct** (℗ **020/7375-0011;** www.columbusdirect.net).

INSURANCE FOR CANADIAN TRAVELERS   Canadians should check with their provincial health plan offices or call **Health Canada** (℗ **613/957-2991;** www.hc-sc.gc.ca) to find out the extent of their coverage and what documentation and receipts they must take home in case they are treated in the United States.

MONEY

CURRENCY   The U.S. monetary system is very simple: The most common **bills** are the $1 (colloquially, a "buck"), $5, $10, and $20 denominations. There are also $2 bills (seldom encountered), $50 bills, and $100 bills (the last two are usually not welcome as payment for small purchases). All the paper money was recently redesigned, making the famous faces adorning them disproportionately large. The old-style bills are still legal tender.

There are seven denominations of coins: 1¢ (1 cent, or a penny); 5¢ (5 cents, or a nickel); 10¢ (10 cents, or a dime); 25¢ (25 cents, or a quarter); 50¢ (50 cents, or a half dollar); the new gold "Sacagawea" coin worth $1; and, prized by collectors, the rare, older silver dollar.

Note: The "foreign-exchange bureaus" so common in Europe are rare even at airports in the United States, and nonexistent outside major cities. It's best not to change foreign money (or traveler's checks denominated in a currency other than U.S. dollars) at a small-town bank, or even a branch in a big city; in fact, leave any currency other than U.S. dollars at home—it may prove a greater nuisance to you than it's worth.

You can exchange foreign currency at **Guest Relations** windows at all four Disney parks, at **City Hall** in the Magic Kingdom, and **Earth Station** at Epcot. Currency can also be exchanged at Walt Disney World resorts and at the **Sun-Bank** across from Downtown Disney Marketplace. There are also currency exchanges at Guest Services at Universal Orlando and SeaWorld.

TRAVELER'S CHECKS   Though traveler's checks are widely accepted, make sure that they're denominated in U.S. dollars, as foreign-currency checks are often difficult to exchange. The three traveler's checks that are most widely recognized—and least likely to be denied—are **Visa, American Express,** and **Thomas Cook.** Be sure to record the numbers of the checks, and keep that information in a separate place in case they get lost or stolen. Most businesses are pretty good about taking traveler's checks, but you're better off cashing them in at a bank (in small amounts, of course) and paying in cash. Remember: You'll need identification, such as a driver's license or passport, to change a traveler's check.

CREDIT CARDS & ATMS   Credit cards are the most widely used form of payment in the United States: **Visa** (Barclaycard in Britain), **MasterCard** (Euro-Card in Europe, Access in Britain, Chargex in Canada), **American Express, Diners Club, Discover,** and **Carte Blanche.** There are, however, a handful of stores and restaurants that do not take credit cards, so be sure to ask in advance. Most businesses display a sticker near their entrance to let you know which cards they accept. (*Note:* Businesses may require a minimum purchase, usually around $10, to use a credit card.)

It is strongly recommended that you bring at least one major credit card. You must have a credit or charge card to rent a car. Hotels and airlines usually require a credit-card imprint as a deposit against expenses, and in an emergency a credit card can be priceless.

You'll find **automated teller machines (ATMs)** on just about every block—at least in almost every town—across the country. Some ATMs will allow you to draw U.S. currency against your bank and credit cards. Check with your bank before leaving home, and remember that you will need your personal identification number (PIN) to do so. Most accept Visa, MasterCard, and American Express, as well as ATM cards from other U.S. banks. Expect to be charged up to $3.60 per transaction, however, if you're not using your own bank's ATM.

See "Money," in chapter 2, for ATM locations.

Tips Walt Disney World Services for International Visitors

Disney welcomes millions of international guests every year and offers a phone service that provides information in many languages (© 407/824-2222). Here are other services in Disney theme parks and resorts:

- Personal translator units are available at Magic Kingdom, Epcot, Disney–MGM Studios, and Animal Kingdom in French, German, and Spanish to translate the narration at 25 shows and attractions.
- Detailed guidebooks and maps to the four major parks in Spanish, French, German, Portuguese, and Japanese are available at five International Information Centers (marked by an "i" on handout guide maps) in the theme parks and Downtown Disney.
- Most theme park restaurants that have table or counter service have menus written in Spanish, French, German, Portuguese, and Japanese.
- Theme park cast members who speak foreign languages wear a gold badge with the flag of that country on their name-tags.
- Resort phones are equipped with software that expedites international calls by allowing guests to dial direct to international destinations.
- There's also online help at **www.disneyworld.com**. Once you're on the website, go to the bottom of the screen and click "International Sites."

SAFETY

Walt Disney World and Orlando are safe in general, and the theme parks are even safer, but there are some general precautions you can take to minimize your chances of being the victim of a crime.

GENERAL SUGGESTIONS   Although tourist areas are generally safe, U.S. urban areas tend to be less safe than those in Europe or Japan. You should always stay alert. This is particularly true of large American cities. If you're in doubt about which neighborhoods are safe, don't hesitate to make inquiries with the hotel front desk staff or the local tourist office.

Avoid deserted areas, especially at night, and don't go into public parks after dark unless there's a concert or similar occasion that will attract a crowd.

Avoid carrying valuables with you on the street, and keep expensive cameras or electronic equipment bagged or covered when not in use. If you're using a map, try to consult it inconspicuously—or better yet, study it before leaving your room. Hold your pocketbook, and put your billfold in an inside pocket. In theaters, restaurants, and other public places, keep possessions in sight.

Always lock your room door—don't assume that once you're inside the hotel you are automatically safe and no longer need to be aware of your surroundings. Hotels are open to the public, and in a large hotel, security may not be able to screen everyone who enters.

DRIVING SAFETY   Driving safety is important too, and carjacking is not unprecedented. Question your rental agency about personal safety and ask for a traveler-safety brochure when you pick up your car. Obtain written directions—or a map with the route clearly marked—from the agency showing how to get to your destination. (Many agencies now offer the option of renting a cellphone for the duration of your car rental; check with the rental agent when you pick up the car. Otherwise, contact **InTouch USA** at © **800/872-7626** or www.intouchusa.com for short-term cellphone rental.) And, if possible, arrive and depart during daylight hours.

If you drive off a highway and end up in a dodgy-looking neighborhood, leave the area as quickly as possible. If you have an accident, even on the highway, stay in your car with the doors locked until you assess the situation or until the police arrive. If you're bumped from behind on the street or are involved in a minor accident with no injuries, and the situation appears to be suspicious, motion to the other driver to follow you. Never get out of your car in such situations. Go directly to the nearest police precinct, well-lit service station, or 24-hour store.

Park in well-lit and well-traveled areas whenever possible. Always keep your car doors locked, whether the vehicle is attended or unattended. Never leave any packages or valuables in sight. If someone attempts to rob you or steal your car, don't try to resist the thief/carjacker. Report the incident to the police department immediately by calling © **911**.

SIZE CONVERSION CHART

Women's Clothing							
American	4	6	8	10	12	14	16
French	34	36	38	40	42	44	46
British	6	8	10	12	14	16	18

Women's Shoes						
American	5	6	7	8	9	10
French	36	37	38	39	40	41
British	4	5	6	7	8	9

Men's Suits							
American	34	36	38	40	42	44	46	48
French	44	46	48	50	52	54	56	58
British	34	36	38	40	42	44	46	48

Men's Shirts							
American	14½	15	15½	16	16½	17	17½
French	37	38	39	41	42	43	44
British	14½	15	15½	16	16½	17	17½

Men's Shoes							
American	7	8	9	10	11	12	13
French	39½	41	42	43	44½	46	47
British	6	7	8	9	10	11	12

2 Getting to the U.S.

Twenty-two cities scattered throughout Europe, Central America, Mexico, and Canada, offer direct air service to **Orlando International Airport (www.state.fl.us/goaa).**

Major airlines offering service to and from Orlando out of international destinations include **Air Canada** (✆ **888/247-2262;** www.aircanada.ca); **AeroMexico** (✆ **800/237-6639;** www.aeromexico.com); **American** (✆ **800/433-7300;** www.americanair.com); **British Airways** (✆ **800/247-9297;** www.british-airways.com); **Continental** (✆ **800/525-0280;** www.continental.com); **Delta** (✆ **800/221-1212;** www.delta.com); **Iberia** (✆ **800/772-4642** in the U.S.; www.iberia.com); **Icelandair** (✆ **800/223-5500** in the U.S. or 020/7874-1000 in the U.K.; www.icelandair.com); **Northwest** (✆ **800/225-2525;** www.nwa.com); **United Airlines** (✆ **800/241-6522;** www.ual.com); **US Airways** (✆ **800/428-4322;** www.usairways.com); and **Virgin Atlantic** (✆ **800/862-8621;** www.virgin-atlantic.com).

AIRLINE DISCOUNTS   The smart traveler can find numerous ways to reduce the price of a plane ticket simply by taking time to shop around. For example, overseas visitors can take advantage of the APEX (Advance Purchase Excursion) reductions offered by all major U.S. and European carriers. For more money-saving airline advice, see "Getting There," in chapter 2. For the best rates, compare fares and be flexible with the dates and times of travel.

IMMIGRATION & CUSTOMS CLEARANCE   Visitors arriving by air, no matter what the port of entry, should cultivate patience and resignation before setting foot on U.S. soil. Getting through immigration control can take as long as 2 hours on some days, especially on summer weekends, so be sure to carry this guidebook or something else to read. This is especially true in the aftermath of the World Trade Center attacks, when security clearances were considerably beefed up at U.S. airports. According to Orlando International Airport's website, the average time between deplaning and leaving the airport for an international visitor is 46 minutes.

People traveling by air from Canada, Bermuda, and certain countries in the Caribbean can sometimes clear Customs and Immigration at the point of departure, which is much quicker.

3 Getting Around the U.S.

BY PLANE   Some large U.S. airlines (such as American, Northwest, US Airways, and Delta) offer travelers on their transatlantic or transpacific flights special discount tickets under the name **Visit USA,** allowing travel between U.S. destinations at minimum rates. They aren't on sale in the United States and must therefore be purchased before you leave your foreign point of departure. This system is the best, easiest, and fastest way to see the United States at low cost. You should obtain information well in advance from your travel agent or the airline's office, since conditions attached to these discounts can change without advance notice.

BY TRAIN   International visitors (excluding Canada) can buy a **USA Railpass,** good for 15 or 30 days of unlimited travel on Amtrak (✆ **800/USA-RAIL;** www.amtrak.com). Prices in 2003 for a 15-day pass were $295 off-peak, $440 peak; a 30-day pass costs $385 off-peak, $550 peak. The pass is available through many foreign travel agents. If you only plan on spending time on the East Coast of the U.S., prices in 2003 for a 15-day East Coast pass were $210 off-peak, $260 peak; a 30-day pass costs $265 off-peak, $320 peak. With a foreign passport, you can also buy passes at some Amtrak offices in the United States, including locations in San Francisco, Los Angeles, Chicago, New York, Miami, Boston, and Washington, D.C. Reservations are generally required and should be made as early as possible.

BY CAR   You're going to need a car to get around Orlando unless you're committed to staying at Disney, riding shuttles, or paying a premium for cabs. Relying on public transportation is futile, except in the downtown area.

To rent a car, you need a major credit card and a driver's license (sometimes a hefty cash deposit can be used instead of a credit card). You must also be at least 25 years old. Some companies rent to younger people but add a daily surcharge, which can run as high as $20 per day. There are two gas (petrol) options when renting a car: returning it with a full tank or bringing it back empty and paying the rental company's rate upfront. Refueling on your own is the more cost-effective option, but if you have an early flight home you may not want to waste the time to refuel on the way to the airport. All of the major car-rental companies are represented in Florida (see appendix B, "Useful Toll-Free Numbers & Websites," for the contact information for these companies).

FAST FACTS: For the International Traveler

Automobile Organizations   Auto clubs will supply maps, suggested routes, guidebooks, accident and bail-bond insurance, and emergency road service. The **American Automobile Association (AAA)** is the major auto club in the United States. If you belong to an auto club in your home country, inquire about AAA reciprocity before you leave. You may be able to join AAA even if you're not a member of a reciprocal club; to inquire, call AAA (© 800/222-4357). AAA is actually an organization of regional auto clubs; so look under "AAA Automobile Club" in the White Pages of the telephone directory. AAA has a nationwide emergency road service telephone number (© 800/AAA-HELP).

Business Hours   Offices are usually open weekdays from 9am to 5pm. Banks are open weekdays from 9am to 3pm or later and sometimes Saturday mornings. Stores typically open between 9 and 10am and close between 5 and 6pm from Monday through Saturday. Stores in shopping complexes or malls tend to stay open late: until about 9pm on weekdays and weekends, and many malls and larger department stores are open on Sundays.

Currency & Currency Exchange   See "Entry Requirements" and "Money" under "Preparing for Your Trip," above.

Drinking Laws   The legal age for purchase and consumption of alcoholic beverages is 21; proof of age is required and often requested at bars, nightclubs, and restaurants, so it's always a good idea to bring ID when you go out. Beer and wine often can be purchased in supermarkets, but liquor laws vary from state to state.

Do not carry open containers of alcohol in your car or any public area that isn't zoned for alcohol consumption. The police can fine you on the spot. And nothing will ruin your trip faster than getting a citation for DUI ("driving under the influence"), so don't even think about driving while intoxicated.

Electricity   Like Canada, the United States uses 110 to 120 volts AC (60 cycles), compared to 220 to 240 volts AC (50 cycles) in most of Europe, Australia, and New Zealand. If your small appliances use 220 to 240 volts, you'll need a 110-volt transformer and a plug adapter with two flat parallel pins to operate them here. Downward converters that change 220–240 volts to 110–120 volts are difficult to find in the United States, so bring one with you.

Embassies & Consulates All embassies are located in the nation's capital, Washington, D.C. Some consulates are located in major U.S. cities, and most nations have a mission to the United Nations in New York City. If your country isn't listed below, call for directory information in Washington, D.C. (📞 202/555-1212) or log on to **www.embassy.org/embassies**.

The embassy of **Australia** is at 1601 Massachusetts Ave. NW, Washington, DC 20036 (📞 202/797-3000; www.austemb.org). There are consulates in New York, Honolulu, Houston, Los Angeles, and San Francisco.

The embassy of **Canada** is at 501 Pennsylvania Ave. NW, Washington, DC 20001 (📞 202/682-1740; www.canadianembassy.org). The **Canadian consulate** closest to Orlando is at 200 S. Biscayne Blvd., Suite 1600, Miami (📞 305/579-1600).

The embassy of **Ireland** is at 2234 Massachusetts Ave. NW, Washington, DC 20008 (📞 202/462-3939; www.irelandemb.org). Irish consulates are in Boston, Chicago, New York, and San Francisco.

The embassy of **Japan** is at 2520 Massachusetts Ave. NW, Washington, DC 20008 (📞 202/238-6700; www.embjapan.org). Japanese consulates are located in many cities including Atlanta, Boston, Detroit, New York, San Francisco, and Seattle.

The embassy of **New Zealand** is at 37 Observatory Circle NW, Washington, DC 20008 (📞 202/328-4800; www.nzemb.org). New Zealand consulates are in Los Angeles, Salt Lake City, San Francisco, and Seattle.

The embassy of the **United Kingdom** is at 3100 Massachusetts Ave. NW, Washington, DC 20008 (📞 202/462-1340; www.britainusa.com). A **British consulate** is located at 200 S. Orange Ave., Orlando (📞 407/426-7855).

Emergencies Call 📞 911 to report a fire, call the police, or get an ambulance anywhere in the United States. This is a toll-free call. (No coins are required at public telephones.)

The Florida Tourism Industry Marketing Corporation, the state tourism promotions board, sponsors a help line (📞 800/647-9284). With operators **speaking over 100 languages,** it can provide general directions and can help with lost travel papers and credit cards, minor medical emergencies, accidents, money transfer, airline confirmation, and much more.

Gasoline (Petrol) Petrol is known as gasoline (or simply "gas") in the United States, and petrol stations are known as both gas stations and service stations. Gasoline costs about half as much here as it does in Europe (it was about $1.65 per gallon at press time, though major price swings are not uncommon), and taxes are already included in the printed price. One U.S. gallon equals 3.8 liters or .85 imperial gallons.

Holidays Banks, government offices, post offices, and many stores, restaurants, and museums are closed on the following legal national holidays: January 1 (New Year's Day), the third Monday in January (Martin Luther King Jr. Day), the third Monday in February (Presidents' Day, Washington's Birthday), the last Monday in May (Memorial Day), July 4 (Independence Day), the first Monday in September (Labor Day), the second Monday in

October (Columbus Day), November 11 (Veterans' Day/Armistice Day), the fourth Thursday in November (Thanksgiving Day), and December 25 (Christmas). Also, the Tuesday following the first Monday in November is Election Day and is a federal government holiday in presidential-election years (held every 4 years, and next in 2004).

Legal Aid As an international tourist, you'll probably never become involved with the American legal system. If you are stopped for a minor infraction, such as speeding or some other traffic violation, never attempt to pay the fine directly to a police officer; you may be arrested on the much more serious charge of attempted bribery. Pay fines to the clerk of the court (© **407/836-6000** in Orlando, or © **407/343-3530** in Kissimmee). If you're accused of a more serious offense, it's wise to say and do nothing before consulting a lawyer. Under U.S. law, an arrested person is allowed one telephone call to a party of his or her choice. Call your embassy or consulate.

Mail If you want to receive mail on your vacation and you aren't sure of your address, your mail can be sent to you, in your name, c/o General Delivery at the main post office of the city or region where you expect to be. The post office nearest Disney and Universal (© **800/275-8777**) is at 10450 Turkey Lake Rd., in Orlando. The zip code is 32819 You must pick up your mail in person and produce proof of identity (driver's license, passport, and so on).

Often found at intersections, mailboxes are blue with a red-and-white stripe and carry the inscription U.S. MAIL. Make sure you see this inscription; overnight delivery companies also often have drop-off boxes along the road. Don't forget to add the five-digit postal code, or ZIP code, after the two-letter abbreviation of the state to which the mail is addressed (FL for Florida, NY for New York, and so on).

At press time, domestic postage rates were 23¢ for a postcard and 37¢ for a letter. For international mail, a first-class letter of up to ½ ounce costs 80¢ (60¢ to Canada and Mexico); a first-class postcard costs 70¢ (50¢ to Canada and Mexico); and a preprinted postal aerogramme costs 70¢.

Measurements See the chart on the inside front cover of this book for details on converting metric measurements to U.S. equivalents.

Taxes The United States doesn't have a VAT (value-added tax) or other tax assessed on most things at a national level. In Florida, the state sales tax is 6%. Hotel tax in Orlando pushes the total to 11%; the total is 12% in Kissimmee.

Telephone, Telegraph, Telex & Fax The telephone system in the United States is run by private corporations, so rates, especially for long-distance service and operator-assisted calls, can vary widely. Generally, hotel surcharges on long-distance and local calls are astronomical, so you're usually better off using a **public pay telephone**, which you'll find clearly marked in most public buildings and private establishments as well as on the street. Convenience grocery stores and gas stations always have them. Many convenience groceries and packaging services sell **prepaid calling cards** in denominations up to $50; these can be the least expensive way to call home. Many public phones at airports now accept American Express, MasterCard, and Visa credit cards. **Local calls** made from public pay phones in most locales cost either 35¢ or 50¢. Pay phones do not accept pennies, and few will take anything larger than a quarter.

You may want to lease a cellphone for the duration of your trip.

Most long-distance and international calls can be dialed directly from any phone. **For calls within the United States and to Canada,** dial 1 followed by the area code and the seven-digit number. **For other international calls,** dial 011 followed by the country code, city code, and the telephone number of the person you are calling.

Calls to area codes **800, 888, 877,** and **866** are toll-free. However, calls to numbers in area codes **700** and **900** (chat lines, bulletin boards, "dating" services, and so on) can be very expensive—usually a charge of 95¢ to $3 or more per minute, and they sometimes have minimum charges that can run as high as $15 or more.

For **reversed-charge or collect calls,** and for person-to-person calls, dial 0 (zero, not the letter O) followed by the area code and number you want; an operator will then come on the line, and you should specify that you are calling collect, or person-to-person, or both. If your operator-assisted call is international, ask for the overseas operator.

For **local directory assistance** ("information"), dial 411; for long-distance information, dial 1, then the appropriate area code and 555-1212.

Most telegraph and telex services in the U.S. are provided by **Western Union.** You can dictate a telegram over the phone by calling ℂ **800/325-6000,** or use the number to check on the nearest location to wire money or have it sent to you.

Most hotels have **fax machines** available for guest use (be sure to ask about the charge to use it). If yours doesn't, small copy shops found in most neighborhoods provide fax service.

There are two kinds of telephone directories in the United States. The so-called **White Pages** list private households and business subscribers in alphabetical order. The inside front cover lists emergency numbers for police, fire, ambulance, the Coast Guard, poison-control center, crime-victims hot line, and so on. The first few pages will tell you how to make long-distance and international calls, complete with country codes and area codes. Government numbers are usually printed on blue paper within the White Pages. Printed on yellow paper, the so-called **Yellow Pages** list all local services, businesses, industries, and houses of worship according to activity with an index at the front or back. (Drugstores/pharmacies and restaurants are also listed by geographic location.) The Yellow Pages also include city plans or detailed area maps, postal ZIP codes, and public transportation routes.

Time The United States is divided into six time zones. From east to west, they are: Eastern Standard Time (EST), Central Standard Time (CST), Mountain Standard Time (MST), Pacific Standard Time (PST), Alaska Standard Time (AST), and Hawaii Standard Time (HST). **Orlando,** like most of Florida, is on **Eastern Standard Time.** When it's noon in Orlando, it's 7am in Honolulu, 8am in Anchorage, 9am in Vancouver and Los Angeles, 11am in Winnipeg and New Orleans, and 6pm in London.

Daylight savings time is in effect from 1am on the first Sunday in April through 1am on the last Sunday in October, except in Arizona, Hawaii, part of Indiana, and Puerto Rico. Daylight saving time moves the clock 1 hour ahead of standard time.

Tipping Tips are a very important part of certain workers' salaries, so it's necessary to leave appropriate gratuities. In hotels, tip **bellhops** at least $1 per bag ($2–$3 if you have a lot of luggage) and tip the **chamber staff** $1 to $2 per day (more if you've left a disaster area for him or her to clean up). Tip the **doorman** or **concierge** only if he or she has provided you with some specific service (for example, calling a cab for you or obtaining difficult-to-get theater tickets). Tip the **valet-parking attendant** $1 every time you get your car.

In restaurants, bars, and nightclubs, tip **service staff** 15% to 20% of the check, tip **bartenders** 10% to 15%, tip **checkroom attendants** $1 per garment, and tip **valet-parking attendants** $1 per vehicle.

As for other service personnel, tip **cab drivers** 15% of the fare; tip **skycaps** at airports at least $1 per bag ($2–$3 if you have a lot of luggage); and tip **hairdressers** and **barbers** 15% to 20%.

Toilets You won't find public toilets or "restrooms" on the streets in most U.S. cities, but they can be found in hotel lobbies, bars, restaurants, museums, department stores, railway and bus stations, and service stations. Large hotels and fast-food restaurants are probably the best bet for good, clean facilities. If possible, avoid the toilets at parks and beaches, which tend to be dirty; some may be unsafe. Restaurants and bars in resorts or heavily visited areas may reserve their restrooms for patrons. Some establishments display a notice indicating this. You can ignore this sign or, better yet, avoid arguments by paying for a cup of coffee or a soft drink, which will qualify you as a patron.

Appendix B:
Useful Toll-Free Numbers
& Websites

AIRLINES

Aer Lingus
℃ 800/474-7424 in the U.S.
℃ 01/886-8888 in Ireland
www.aerlingus.com

Aero Mexico
℃ 800/237-6639
www.aeromexico.com

Air Canada
℃ 888/247-2262
www.aircanada.ca

Air New Zealand
℃ 800/262-1234 or 800/262-2468
    in the U.S.
℃ 800/663-5494 in Canada
℃ 0800/737-767 in New Zealand
www.airnewzealand.com

Airtran Airlines
℃ 800/247-8726
www.airtran.com

Alaska Airlines
℃ 800/426-0333
www.alaskaair.com

American Airlines
℃ 800/433-7300
www.aa.com

American Trans Air
℃ 800/225-2995
www.ata.com

America West Airlines
℃ 800/235-9292
www.americawest.com

British Airways
℃ 800/247-9297
℃ 0345/222-111 or 0845/77-333-77
    in the U.K.
www.british-airways.com

Continental Airlines
℃ 800/525-0280
www.continental.com

Delta Air Lines
℃ 800/221-1212
www.delta.com

Frontier Airlines
℃ 800/432-1359
www.frontierairlines.com

JetBlue Airways
℃ 800/538-2583
www.jetblue.com

Midwest Express
℃ 800/452-2022
www.midwestexpress.com

Northwest Airlines
℃ 800/225-2525
www.nwa.com

Southwest Airlines
℃ 800/435-9792
www.southwest.com

Spirit Airlines
℃ 800/772-7117
www.spiritair.com

United Airlines
℃ 800/241-6522
www.united.com

US Airways
℃ 800/428-4322
www.usairways.com

Virgin Atlantic Airways
℃ 800/862-8621 in the continental
    U.S.
℃ 0293/747-747 in the U.K.
www.virgin-atlantic.com

CAR-RENTAL AGENCIES

Advantage
℡ 800/777-5500
www.advantagerentacar.com

Alamo
℡ 800/327-9633
www.goalamo.com

Avis
℡ 800/331-1212 in the continental U.S.
℡ 800/TRY-AVIS in Canada
www.avis.com

Budget
℡ 800/527-0700
https://rent.drivebudget.com/Home.jsp

Dollar
℡ 800/800-4000
www.dollar.com

Enterprise
℡ 800/325-8007
www.enterprise.com

Hertz
℡ 800/654-3131
www.hertz.com

National
℡ 800/CAR-RENT
www.nationalcar.com

Payless
℡ 800/PAYLESS
www.paylesscarrental.com

Rent-A-Wreck
℡ 800/535-1391
www.rentawreck.com

Thrifty
℡ 800/367-2277
www.thrifty.com

MAJOR HOTEL & MOTEL CHAINS

Baymont Inns & Suites
℡ 800/301-0200
www.baymontinns.com

Best Western International
℡ 800/528-1234
www.bestwestern.com

Clarion Hotels
℡ 800/CLARION
www.clarionhotel.com

Comfort Inns
℡ 800/228-5150
www.hotelchoice.com

Courtyard by Marriott
℡ 800/321-2211
www.courtyard.com

Days Inn
℡ 800/325-2525
www.daysinn.com

Doubletree Hotels
℡ 800/222-TREE
www.doubletree.com

Econo Lodges
℡ 800/55-ECONO
www.hotelchoice.com

Fairfield Inn by Marriott
℡ 800/228-2800
www.fairfieldinn.com

Hampton Inn
℡ 800/HAMPTON
www.hampton-inn.com

Hilton Hotels
℡ 800/HILTONS
www.hilton.com

Holiday Inn
℡ 800/HOLIDAY
www.basshotels.com

Howard Johnson
℡ 800/654-2000
www.hojo.com

Hyatt Hotels & Resorts
℡ 800/228-9000
www.hyatt.com

Inter-Continental Hotels & Resorts
℡ 888/567-8725
www.interconti.com

ITT Sheraton
℡ 800/325-3535
www.starwood.com

Knights Inn
© 800/843-5644
www.knightsinn.com

La Quinta Motor Inns
© 800/531-5900
www.laquinta.com

Marriott Hotels
© 800/228-9290
www.marriott.com

Motel 6
© 800/4-MOTEL6
www.motel6.com

Quality Inns
© 800/228-5151
www.hotelchoice.com

Radisson Hotels International
© 800/333-3333
www.radisson.com

Ramada Inns
© 800/2-RAMADA
www.ramada.com

Red Carpet Inns
© 800/251-1962
www.reservahost.com

Red Roof Inns
© 800/843-7663
www.redroof.com

Residence Inn by Marriott
© 800/331-3131
www.residenceinn.com

Rodeway Inns
© 800/228-2000
www.hotelchoice.com

Sheraton Hotels & Resorts
© 800/325-3535
www.sheraton.com

Sleep Inn
© 800/753-3746
www.sleepinn.com

Super 8 Motels
© 800/800-8000
www.super8.com

Travelodge
© 800/255-3050
www.travelodge.com

Westin Hotels & Resorts
© 800/937-8461
www.westin.com

Wyndham Hotels and Resorts
© 800/822-4200 in the continental
    U.S. and Canada
www.wyndham.com

Index

See also Accommodations and Restaurant indexes, below.

FROMMER'S® COMPLETE TRAVEL GUIDES

Alaska
Alaska Cruises & Ports of Call
Amsterdam
Argentina & Chile
Arizona
Atlanta
Australia
Austria
Bahamas
Barcelona, Madrid & Seville
Beijing
Belgium, Holland & Luxembourg
Bermuda
Boston
Brazil
British Columbia & the Canadian
  Rockies
Brussels & Bruges
Budapest & the Best of Hungary
California
Canada
Cancún, Cozumel & the Yucatán
Cape Cod, Nantucket & Martha's
  Vineyard
Caribbean
Caribbean Cruises & Ports of Call
Caribbean Ports of Call
Carolinas & Georgia
Chicago
China
Colorado
Costa Rica
Cuba
Denmark
Denver, Boulder & Colorado Springs
England
Europe
European Cruises & Ports of Call

Florida
France
Germany
Great Britain
Greece
Greek Islands
Hawaii
Hong Kong
Honolulu, Waikiki & Oahu
Ireland
Israel
Italy
Jamaica
Japan
Las Vegas
London
Los Angeles
Maryland & Delaware
Maui
Mexico
Montana & Wyoming
Montréal & Québec City
Munich & the Bavarian Alps
Nashville & Memphis
New England
New Mexico
New Orleans
New York City
New Zealand
Northern Italy
Norway
Nova Scotia, New Brunswick &
  Prince Edward Island
Oregon
Paris
Peru
Philadelphia & the Amish Country
Portugal

Prague & the Best of the Czech
  Republic
Provence & the Riviera
Puerto Rico
Rome
San Antonio & Austin
San Diego
San Francisco
Santa Fe, Taos & Albuquerque
Scandinavia
Scotland
Seattle & Portland
Shanghai
Sicily
Singapore & Malaysia
South Africa
South America
South Florida
South Pacific
Southeast Asia
Spain
Sweden
Switzerland
Texas
Thailand
Tokyo
Toronto
Tuscany & Umbria
USA
Utah
Vancouver & Victoria
Vermont, New Hampshire & Maine
Vienna & the Danube Valley
Virgin Islands
Virginia
Walt Disney World® & Orlando
Washington, D.C.
Washington State

FROMMER'S® DOLLAR-A-DAY GUIDES

Australia from $50 a Day
California from $70 a Day
England from $75 a Day
Europe from $70 a Day
Florida from $70 a Day
Hawaii from $80 a Day

Ireland from $60 a Day
Italy from $70 a Day
London from $85 a Day
New York from $90 a Day
Paris from $80 a Day

San Francisco from $70 a Day
Washington, D.C. from $80 a Day
Portable London from $85 a Day
Portable New York City from $90
  a Day

FROMMER'S® PORTABLE GUIDES

Acapulco, Ixtapa & Zihuatanejo
Amsterdam
Aruba
Australia's Great Barrier Reef
Bahamas
Berlin
Big Island of Hawaii
Boston
California Wine Country
Cancún
Cayman Islands
Charleston
Chicago
Disneyland®
Dublin
Florence

Frankfurt
Hong Kong
Houston
Las Vegas
Las Vegas for Non-Gamblers
London
Los Angeles
Los Cabos & Baja
Maine Coast
Maui
Miami
Nantucket & Martha's Vineyard
New Orleans
New York City
Paris
Phoenix & Scottsdale

Portland
Puerto Rico
Puerto Vallarta, Manzanillo &
  Guadalajara
Rio de Janeiro
San Diego
San Francisco
Savannah
Seattle
Sydney
Tampa & St. Petersburg
Vancouver
Venice
Virgin Islands
Washington, D.C.

FROMMER'S® NATIONAL PARK GUIDES

Banff & Jasper
Family Vacations in the National
  Parks

Grand Canyon
National Parks of the American West
Rocky Mountain

Yellowstone & Grand Teton
Yosemite & Sequoia/Kings Canyon
Zion & Bryce Canyon

Frommer's® Memorable Walks

Chicago
London

New York
Paris

San Francisco

Frommer's® With Kids Guides

Chicago
Las Vegas
New York City

Ottawa
San Francisco
Toronto

Vancouver
Washington, D.C.

Suzy Gershman's Born to Shop Guides

Born to Shop: France
Born to Shop: Hong Kong,
    Shanghai & Beijing

Born to Shop: Italy
Born to Shop: London

Born to Shop: New York
Born to Shop: Paris

Frommer's® Irreverent Guides

Amsterdam
Boston
Chicago
Las Vegas
London

Los Angeles
Manhattan
New Orleans
Paris
Rome

San Francisco
Seattle & Portland
Vancouver
Walt Disney World®
Washington, D.C.

Frommer's® Best-Loved Driving Tours

Britain
California
Florida
France

Germany
Ireland
Italy
New England

Northern Italy
Scotland
Spain
Tuscany & Umbria

Hanging Out™ Guides

Hanging Out in England
Hanging Out in Europe

Hanging Out in France
Hanging Out in Ireland

Hanging Out in Italy
Hanging Out in Spain

The Unofficial Guides®

Bed & Breakfasts and Country
    Inns in:
    California
    Great Lakes States
    Mid-Atlantic
    New England
    Northwest
    Rockies
    Southeast
    Southwest
Best RV & Tent Campgrounds in:
    California & the West
    Florida & the Southeast
    Great Lakes States
    Mid-Atlantic
    Northeast
    Northwest & Central Plains

Southwest & South Central
    Plains
    U.S.A.
Beyond Disney
Branson, Missouri
California with Kids
Central Italy
Chicago
Cruises
Disneyland®
Florida with Kids
Golf Vacations in the Eastern U.S.
Great Smoky & Blue Ridge Region
Inside Disney
Hawaii
Las Vegas
London
Maui

Mexio's Best Beach Resorts
Mid-Atlantic with Kids
Mini Las Vegas
Mini-Mickey
New England & New York with
    Kids
New Orleans
New York City
Paris
San Francisco
Skiing & Snowboarding in the West
Southeast with Kids
Walt Disney World®
Walt Disney World® for
    Grown-ups
Walt Disney World® with Kids
Washington, D.C.
World's Best Diving Vacations

Special-Interest Titles

Frommer's Adventure Guide to Australia &
    New Zealand
Frommer's Adventure Guide to Central America
Frommer's Adventure Guide to India & Pakistan
Frommer's Adventure Guide to South America
Frommer's Adventure Guide to Southeast Asia
Frommer's Adventure Guide to Southern Africa
Frommer's Britain's Best Bed & Breakfasts and
    Country Inns
Frommer's Caribbean Hideaways
Frommer's Exploring America by RV
Frommer's Fly Safe, Fly Smart

Frommer's France's Best Bed & Breakfasts and
    Country Inns
Frommer's Gay & Lesbian Europe
Frommer's Italy's Best Bed & Breakfasts and
    Country Inns
Frommer's Road Atlas Britain
Frommer's Road Atlas Europe
Frommer's Road Atlas France
The New York Times' Guide to Unforgettable
    Weekends
Places Rated Almanac
Retirement Places Rated
Rome Past & Present

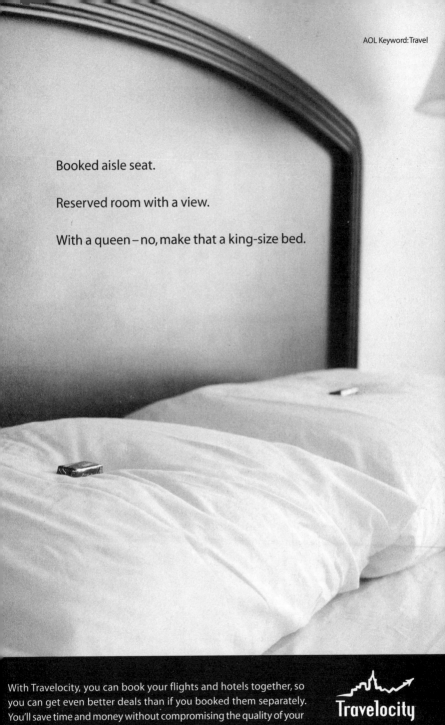